For David,
with best wishes,

Tim

Becoming a Revolutionary

Becoming a Revolutionary

THE DEPUTIES OF THE FRENCH NATIONAL ASSEMBLY AND THE EMERGENCE OF A REVOLUTIONARY CULTURE (1789–1790)

· *TIMOTHY TACKETT* ·

PRINCETON UNIVERSITY PRESS

PRINCETON, NEW JERSEY

Library of Congress Cataloging-in-Publication Data

Tackett, Timothy, 1945–
    Becoming a revolutionary : the deputies of the French National
Assembly and the emergence of a revolutionary culture (1789–1790) /
Timothy Tackett.
        p.   cm.
    Includes bibliographical references and index.
    ISBN 0-691-04384-1 (cl : alk. paper)
    1. France—History—Revolution, 1789–1799—Causes.   2. Political
culture—France—History—18th century.   3. France. Assemblée
nationale constituante (1789–1791)   4. Legislators—France—
Attitudes.   5. Enlightenment—France—Influence.   I. Title.
DC165.T33   1996
944.04—dc20   95-38122
                                                                          CIP

This book has been composed in Galliard

Princeton University Press books are printed on acid-free paper and meet the guidelines for
permanence and durability of the Committee on Production Guidelines for Book
Longevity of the Council on Library Resources

Printed in the United States of America by Princeton Academic Press

1   3   5   7   9   10   8   6   4   2

· C O N T E N T S ·

• ILLUSTRATIONS •

• A C K N O W L E D G M E N T S •

THE EARLIEST inspiration for the present work came from my studies many years ago with Philip Dawson, who so unsparingly shared his immense knowledge of the Constituent Assembly, the French Revolution, and French archival techniques. In assembling the body of deputy testimonies on which much of the study is based, I was greatly assisted by the research notes and card files compiled by Georges Lefebvre and a team of scholars during and immediately after World War II—materials more recently brought to light by Olga Ilovaïsky, and now preserved in the Institut de la Révolution française in Paris. Based on these indications and on my own correspondence with archivists, I pursued a tour de France in some fifty-seven public and private archives where deputy writings were thought to be preserved. I must also add a special word of thanks to Edna Hindie Lemay, who offered me much useful advice in the early stages of research, loaned me her notes and copies of manuscripts, and kindly allowed me to read the complete prepublished text of her dictionary of the Constituent deputies. Among other scholars and archivists who assisted me in locating documents or who shared their research notes with me, I would like to thank Claude Arabeyre, Michel Beauchet-Filleau, Jean Boutier, Françoise Brunel, Paul Cattin, Madeleine Chabrolin, Vital Chomel, Christiane Constant-Le Stum, Michèle Demarcy, Monique Dosdat, Alain Droguet, Yann Fauchois, Dr. Robert Favre, Christine Favre-Lejeune, Joël Félix, Jean-Louis Flandrin, Abbé Armand Freyne, the Comtesse de Gasquet, Jean Girardot, D. Grisel, Anne Goulet, Ran Halévi, Madame Herly-Chaunier, Madame Haselberger, Paul d'Hollander, Henri Hours, Olga Ilovaïsky, J. E. Jung, Yan Laborie, Marie-Christiane de La Conte, Catherine Marion, Vivienne Miguet, Françoise Missery, the Chanoine Noblat, Jean-Pierre Reynaud, Jean-Yves Roger, Armelle Sentilhes, Jacques-Yves de Sallier Dupin, and Dale Van Kley.

The research and writing would have been impossible without generous grants from the John Simon Guggenheim Memorial Foundation, the Camargo Foundation, the Woodrow Wilson Foundation, the National Endowment for the Humanities, and the School of Humanities at the University of California, Irvine. I received excellent assistance with research, compilation of data, illustrations, and copyediting from Carl Almer, Catherine Aubert-Tackett, Robert Blackman, Mindy Han, Bill Laznovsky, Morag Martin, Nicolas Tackett, Gregory Tackett, Katherine Turley, and Anna Watkins.

I am extremely grateful to Ann Blair, Jack Censer, Robert Forster, Claude Langlois, John Markoff, and Donald Sutherland who read the manuscript in its entirety. I also received helpful suggestions on portions of the text from Ted Barker, Elizabeth Eisenstein, Dominique Julia, Mark Poster, Paolo Viola, members of the Baltimore-Washington Old Regime Study Group, and the students in my French Seminar at U.C. Irvine. Various versions of various chapters were presented at the Society for French Historical Studies, the Scuola normale superiore in Pisa, the University of Rouen, Fudan University in Shanghai, the University of Paris-Sorbonne, the University of Maryland, the University of California, Irvine, the European University Institute in Florence, Stanford University, and the University of Haifa. In the winter of 1991 I was warmly welcomed by the history section of the Ecole des hautes études en sciences sociales in Paris, where I participated in the seminars of Ran Halévi, Patrice Gueniffey, and Edna Lemay, and had occasion to talk with François Furet and Mona Ozouf. Though there were many points on which we disagreed, the generous comments and critiques of these scholars were of immeasurable assistance in developing and refining the arguments of this book.

EXCEPT as otherwise indicated, all translations are my own. Many of the deputies used several versions and spellings of their names. I have standardized them on the basis of Armand Brette's *Recueil de documents relatifs à la convocation des Etats généraux*, corrected in some instances by Edna Lemay's *Dictionnaire des Constituants*. Insofar as possible, modern spelling has been used for all place names and in all French texts generally.

A.C.   Archives communales de

ACSS   *Actes du . . . Congrès national des sociétés savantes*

A.D.   Archives départementales de

A.E.   Archives de l'évêché de

AHR   *American Historical Review*

AHRF   *Annales historiques de la Révolution française*

A.M.   Archives municipales de

A.N.   Archives nationales

Annales.E.S.C.   *Annales. Economies. Sociétés. Civilisations*

AP   *Archives parlementaires de 1787 à 1860, recueil complet des débats législatifs et politiques des chambres françaises. Première série (1787–1799)*, eds. Jérôme Mavidal, Emile Laurent, et al., 82 vols. (Paris, 1867–1913)

AR   *Annales révolutionnaires*

B.M.   Bibliothèque municipale de

Brette, *Recueil*   Armand Brette, ed., *Recueil de documents relatifs à la convocation des Etats généraux de 1789*, 4 vols. (Paris, 1894–1915)

DC   *Dictionnaire des constituants, 1789–1791*, ed. Edna Hindie Lemay, 2 vols. (Paris, 1991)

Fichier Lefebvre   "bio-bibliographical" card file compiled by Georges Lefebvre and a team of researchers and presently held in the Institut de la Révolution française in the Sorbonne

FRCMPC   *The French Revolution and the Creation of Modern Political Culture*, eds. Keith Baker, et al., 4 vols. (Oxford, 1987–94)

JMH   *Journal of Modern History*

Lefebvre, *Recueil*   *Recueil de documents relatifs aux séances des Etats généraux. Tome premier. I. Les préliminaires. La séance du 5 mai*, eds. Georges Lefebvre and Anne Terroine (Paris, 1953); *Tome premier. II. La séance du 23 juin*, ed. Georges Lefebvre (Paris, 1962); *Tome II. Les séances de la Noblesse, 6 mai–16 juillet 1789. I. 6–27 mai*, ed. Olga Ilovaïsky (Paris, 1974)

Michaud	*Biographie universelle ancienne et moderne*, ed. M. Michaud, 45 vols. (Paris, 1854ff.)
Procédure	*Procédure criminelle instruite au Châtelet de Paris, sur la dénonciation des faits arrivés à Versailles dans la journée du 6 octobre 1789*, 3 vols. (Paris, 1790)
RF	*Révolution française*
RH	*Revue historique*
RHMC	*Revue d'histoire moderne et contemporaine*

Becoming a Revolutionary

ON A GLORIOUS spring morning in May 1789 close to a thousand men from every corner of France assembled in the royal capital of Versailles in the presence of their king. By every account it was an extraordinary spectacle, carefully crafted to represent the social and political nation as it was then conceived by the reigning elites. The royal architects and pageant masters had been at work for months to set up a hall for the occasion, constructed within the shell of the "Menus Plaisirs," the onetime depot of props and sets for the Versailles opera. It was a magnificent structure, with a large rectangular bay framed by colonnades and pilasters of fluted Doric columns, illuminated through three overhead windows, whose light was softened to a regal radiance by coverings of white silk. Dominating the hall at its far end was the great royal stage, backed with golden *fleurs de lis* on purple velvet and surmounted by a throne with a spectacular golden canopy. Here the reigning king, Louis XVI, dressed in the costume of the knights of Saint Louis, sat with his court arrayed hierarchically across the stage: the queen, the princes and princesses of the blood, peers and dukes of the realm, gentlemen and ladies in waiting, and on the floor below, the ministers and secretaries of the king's government. The remainder of the hall was adorned with three hundred Gobelin tapestries, a dozen marble bas-reliefs of famous events in French history, and the painted figures of thirteen centuries of French kings, from Clovis and Charlemagne to Louis XV, peering down on the proceedings from the surrounding walls. Perhaps two thousand spectators, the flower of French society, had come out from Paris to watch the events from the balconies, while tens of thousands more gathered outside, awaiting the results of the conclave and hoping to catch a glimpse of the various personalities. At the center of the room, the principal coplayers in the drama, the recently elected deputies of the Estates General, sat crowded together on padded benches: the First or Clerical Estate on the king's right, the Second or Noble Estate on his left, and the larger assemblage of commoners, the Third Estate, at the rear, separated from the two privileged orders by a small balustrade.[1]

Without a doubt it was one of the great moments in French history, both for what it represented and embodied of the past, and for what it portended for future generations. The culmination of months of rapidly expanding political awareness, it marked the beginning of an extraordinary series of events in which the deputies would unilaterally create a National or "Constituent" Assembly and seize power in the name of a new conception of

---

[1] Armand Brette, *Histoire des édifices où ont siégé les assemblées parlementaires de la Révolution* (Paris, 1902); Lefebvre, *Recueil. Tome I*, 1–42. Virtually all of the deputies who left accounts of their experiences commented on the opening ceremony.

national sovereignty and political legitimacy. In short order they would mobilize this power for the revolutionary transformation not only of the political and administrative structures of the country, but of fundamental components of the social system as well. In the longer term, the concatenation which they and their immediate successors helped set in motion, would lead to profound civil upheaval, to popular and state sponsored violence, and to attempts to uproot fundamental religious and cultural values which had held sway in France for centuries. It would lead to a quarter century of war with a sweeping impact on the whole of Europe. And it would lead also to generations of reflection and debate as to how such an amazing string of occurrences had come to pass.

The Enigma of the Revolution

From the earliest days of the Estates General, both participants and outside observers were intensely self-conscious of the historical significance of the times in which they were living. In diaries, in letters mailed home, in published brochures and books, many of the deputies who sat in the hall that May morning would seek to make sense of the swirl of events, to understand the links and breaks with France's long historical past. Indeed, the first "histories" of the Revolution were already in print before the end of 1789.[2] By the end of the decade, many of the basic explanatory models which would vie for prominence through the end of the twentieth century had already been elaborated by contemporaries. Debates raged and would continue to rage between those who extolled and those who castigated the achievements of the Revolution; between those who saw 1789 as the inevitable outcome of preexisting social and cultural transformations and those convinced that it was an aberration, instigated by subversive forces alien to France's true nature; between those who explained the origins of the Revolution through material injustice and those who appealed rather to political aspirations or to the power of ideas or to the abilities and charisma—or lack thereof—of specific personalities.

Throughout the first two-thirds of the present century, the dominant mode of explanation focused primarily on social and economic factors.[3] In-

---

[2] See, for example, the works of the deputies Antoine-François Delandine, *Mémorial historique des Etats généraux*, 5 vols. (n.p., 1789); and Jacques Dinochau, *Histoire philosophique et politique de l'Assemblée constituante*, 2 vols. (Paris, 1789).

[3] The details of the historiographical debates between Marxists and "revisionists" are endless and are only briefly summarized here. For good general overviews of the controversy, see William Doyle, *Origins of the French Revolution* (Oxford, 1980), 7–40; Lynn Hunt, *Politics, Culture, and Class in the French Revolution* (Berkeley, 1984), 3–10; and D.M.G. Sutherland, *France, 1789–1815: Revolution and Counterrevolution* (Oxford, 1985), 15–18; Michel Vovelle, "L'historiographie de la Révolution française à la veille du bicentenaire," *AHRF* 272 (1988), 113–26; Norman Hampson, "The French Revolution and Its Historians," in *The Permanent Revolution: The French Revolution and Its Legacy, 1789–1989*, ed. Geoffrey Best (London,

spired in large measure by Marxist perspectives and the Marxist adaptations of Jean Jaurès, historians such as Georges Lefebvre, Albert Soboul, and Michel Vovelle depicted a long-developing class struggle between the aristocracy and the bourgeoisie, a confrontation viewed as critical both for the initiation of events in 1789 and for the radicalization of the Revolution thereafter.[4] Since the late Middle Ages, so the argument went, commercial capitalism and economic growth throughout Europe and the world had progressively enriched the French bourgeois class. By the late eighteenth century the material situation of this class equaled or surpassed that of the landholding and still semifeudal aristocracy. Yet under the regime of the Bourbon monarchy the nobility continued to monopolize political power and status. The French Revolution marked the moment in time when the bourgeoisie rectified this unjust imbalance and seized power. In the ensuing years, the Revolution was driven forward, first, through the struggle of the bourgeois patriots to consolidate their control in the face of an intransigent aristocracy; second, through their efforts to come to terms with an emerging working class; and, third, through their attempts to preserve the Revolution against the military attacks of the European monarchies. In this view, the events of the Terror of 1793–94 had been compelled by circumstances and constituted a transient phase in the Revolution's struggle for survival.

Such an explanation was elegant, comprehensive, and persuasive and it energized three generations of exceptionally rich and creative historical scholarship, even among historians who would not otherwise have described themselves as "Marxists."[5] But the last third of the twentieth century witnessed a broad reaction to this interpretation. Led by scholars such as George Taylor, Elizabeth Eisenstein, William Doyle, François Furet, and Donald Sutherland, the "revisionist" historians put into question many of the basic assumptions and assertions of the Marxists.[6] The empirical evidence, it was argued, linking social antagonism to Revolutionary action was nonexistent or unconvincing. By the late eighteenth century, aristocracy and bourgeoisie were fundamentally similar both in their economic, "class" in-

---

1988), 211–34; and Robert Forster and Timothy Tackett, eds., "The Origins of the French Revolution: A Debate," *FHS* 16 (1990), 741–65.

[4] Jean Jaurès, *Histoire socialiste (1789–1900). Volume I. La Constituante (1789–91)* (Paris, 1901); Georges Lefebvre, *The Coming of the French Revolution* (Princeton, 1947); Albert Soboul, *Histoire de la Révolution française*, 2 vols. (Paris, 1962); and Michel Vovelle, *La chute de la monarchie* (Paris, 1972).

[5] Michel Vovelle prefers to call this explanatory model "Jacobin" rather than "Marxist," taking into account the many non-Marxists who have accepted it: "L'historiographie de la Révolution française," 115.

[6] George V. Taylor, "Noncapitalist Wealth and the Origins of the French Revolution," *AHR* 72 (1967), 469–96; Elizabeth L. Eisenstein, "Who Intervened? A Commentary on *The Coming of the French Revolution*," *AHR* 71 (1965), 77–103; Doyle, *Origins*; François Furet, *Interpreting the Revolution*, trans. Elborg Forster (Cambridge, 1981); and Sutherland, *France, 1789–1815*. See also Alfred Cobban, *The Social Interpretation of the French Revolution* (Cambridge, 1968).

terests—based primarily on the common ownership of land—and in their cultural adherence to Enlightened values. There was a veritable convergence of elites at the end of the Old Regime, a convergence solidified through the ample possibilities for social mobility from the upper middle class into the nobility.[7] For most revisionists, the Revolution ultimately arose not from social conflict, but from the internal collapse of the monarchy, instigated through the incompetence of the reigning king and the government's inability to resolve a major fiscal crisis.

But if the adherents to this interpretation generally concurred in their critique of the Marxists and in their assessment of the breakdown of the Old Regime, they had more difficulty agreeing on the causes of the actual outbreak of the Revolution. How was it that the two elements of a single elite, the Nobility and the Third Estate, fell into such bitter conflict in 1789? For Doyle the conflict seemed almost a political accident, arising from misunderstandings and a failure of imagination and leadership. Sutherland also perceived a failure of leadership on the part of the moderates, though he departed from most other revisionists in stressing a sharp difference in wealth and privilege between nobility and bourgeoisie. But perhaps the most influential explanation of the noble-bourgeois division has been ideological in nature. For Furet, Norman Hampson, and a number of others, the split represented, above all, the triumph of the radical Enlightenment and the ideas of Jean-Jacques Rousseau, mediated by a compelling new conception of public opinion which rapidly filled the power vacuum left by the collapsing monarchy.[8] It was the emergence of this victorious ideology that made revolution "conceivable" even before the events of May 1789.

For Hampson and Furet, moreover, the passion of the generation of 1789 for the ideas of the Enlightenment also helped explain the Revolution's later development. With little or no experience in practical politics, so it was argued, the patriots in the Assembly were increasingly dominated by the radical faction of the Jacobins, naively embracing Jean-Jacques Rousseau's conception of a unitary general will and rejecting the very idea of political pluralism. Reason dictated that in a given situation there could be only one rational and correct solution conducive to the overall welfare of a given society. Thus, all political opposition and disagreement could be viewed as intrinsically pernicious and "counterrevolutionary," undermining the public good through the workings of egotistical private motives. The

[7] Harriet Applewhite, *Political Alignment in the French National Assembly, 1789–1791* (Baton Rouge, La., 1993), 11. See also William Doyle, *The Ancien Régime* (Atlantic Highlands, N.J., 1986), 25–26; and David Bien, "La réaction aristocrate avant 1789: l'exemple de l'armée," *Annales E.S.C.* 29 (1974), 23–48, 505–34.

[8] Doyle, *Origins*; Sutherland, esp. 19–21; Furet, esp. 25–46; Norman Hampson, *Prelude to Terror: The Constituent Assembly and the Failure of Consensus* (Oxford, 1988), 5–7, 42. Cf. also the suggestions of Sarah Maza, for whom the split might be explained as the "unintended consequence" of a discursive strategy: i.e., the application to political rhetoric of the social imagery of the melodramatic theater: *Private Lives and Public Affairs: The Causes Célèbres of Prerevolutionary France* (Berkeley, 1993), esp. chap. 1.

Revolution was progressively democratized and radicalized as successive factions of patriots each claimed to be the authentic voice of popular sovereignty, the true mouthpiece of the general will. Political struggle became a battle of rhetoric and ideology, but with no class content. Thus, the state violence of 1794 was already inherent in the action and philosophy of 1789: the Estates General and the National Assembly were but the "prelude to Terror."[9]

Of course, it may be that the enigma of the Revolution is unresolvable, that historical interpretation will always be bound up in fundamental differences in historians' very personal understandings of the springs of human motivation; of why men and women do what they do in given situations; of whether ideas or power or material self-interest are the ultimate constituents of "human nature." Yet if we are ever to have the possibility of reaching a verdict, it is essential that we be in possession of all the relevant evidence, that we hear all the pertinent testimony. The fact remains that, despite the extraordinary quantity of writings about the Revolution over the past two hundred years, there is a great deal about the actions and options and aspirations of the participants of 1789 which remain uncertain or unknown. Indeed, it may be useful to shift the principal thrust of inquiry away from the broad analysis of the origins of the French Revolution in general, and to focus rather on the Revolutionary experience of the specific individuals who took part in and embodied that Revolution. How did men and women *become* Revolutionaries? How did they arrive at the stunning conclusion, so rare in the course of human affairs, that the political and institutional world they had always known should be overturned and reformed from top to bottom? What were their inner assumptions and rules of behavior, their political culture on the eve of the Revolution? What impact did the radical ideas of eighteenth-century intellectuals have on their day-to-day assumptions about state and society? Could they already be described as "Revolutionaries" in May 1789, or did the change emerge afterward, in the course of events? Was it a gradual process or did it occur more abruptly in the manner of a conversion experience?[10]

In an attempt to confront some of these questions and put to the test the

[9] Hampson, 1–5, 42, 61–62; and Furet, 55, 62–63. See also Keith Baker, *Inventing the French Revolution* (Cambridge, 1990), esp. the conclusion to the final chapter; Patrice Higonnet, *Class, Ideology, and the Rights of the Nobles during the French Revolution* (Oxford, 1981), esp. the "Introduction"; and Jack R. Censer, "The Coming of a New Interpretation of the French Revolution," *Journal of Social History* 21 (1987), 295–309. For critiques of revisionism, see, e.g., Bill Edmonds, "Successes and Excesses of Revisionist Writing about the French Revolution," *European Historical Quarterly* 17 (1987), 195–217; and Colin Jones, "Bourgeois Revolution Revivified, 1789 and Social Change," in Colin Lucas, ed., *Rewriting the French Revolution* (Oxford, 1991), 69–118.

[10] While there are many meanings to the word "revolution," the present study is particularly interested in this phenomenon in its cultural dimensions: as a psychological process, a mental restructuring, a transformation in the conceptions of the individual in relation to state and society.

diverse theories on the origins and nature of the Revolution, the present study proposes to examine the experiences of one particularly influential set of Revolutionaries: precisely that group of deputies who sat in the Menus Plaisirs on the morning of May 5 and who, as much as any single group, launched the Revolution. There is, to be sure, no shortage of general studies focusing on that Assembly—from those of Alexandre de Lameth and Alphonse de Lamartine in the nineteenth century to those of Frédéric Braesch in the early twentieth.[11] In recent years, the bicentennial of 1789 has excited a flurry of new works on the subject. In addition to Norman Hampson's general synthesis, studies by Edna Hindie Lemay, André Castaldo, Ran Halévi, Keith Baker, Michael Fitzsimmons, and Harriet Applewhite have all enriched our understanding of various aspects of the National Assembly and the deputies who sat there.[12] Yet no single work has attempted to integrate the history of the deputies both before and during the early stages of the Revolution and to follow systematically the emergence of a Revolutionary psychology and culture.

THE WITNESSES AND THEIR TESTIMONY

Obviously, if we are to approach the experiences and sentiments of the deputies of 1789, a wide array of evidence must be mobilized. We must utilize not only the formal minutes and reports produced by the National Assembly, but also newspaper accounts and reflections of outside observers. We must take note of the considerable biographical information on the deputies' careers and activities available from a variety of sources and studies.[13] Above all, we must turn to the accounts of the deputies themselves, in their contemporary diaries, letters, and memoirs. Though the writings of a few of the principal leaders—Mirabeau, Lafayette, Sieyès, Barnave—have been cited endlessly, almost no effort has been made to interrogate in a systematic fashion the great mass of the deputies, individuals without whose enthusiasm and political support the Revolution would have been quite incon-

[11] Alexandre de Lameth, *Histoire de l'Assemblée constituante*, 2 vols. (Paris, 1828–29); Alphonse de Lamartine, *Histoire des Constituants*, 4 vols. (Paris, 1855); Frédéric Braesch, *1789. L'année cruciale* (Paris, 1941).

[12] Hampson, *Prelude*; Edna Hindie Lemay, ed., *Dictionnaire des Constituants, 1789–1791*, 2 vols. (Paris, 1991); and "Les révélations d'un dictionnaire: du nouveau sur la composition de l'Assemblée nationale constituante (1789–1791)," *AHRF* no. 284 (1991), 159–89; André Castaldo, *Les méthodes de travail de la Constituante* (Paris, 1989); Ran Halévi, "L'idée et l'événement de la Révolution française," *Débat*, no. 38 (1986), 145–63; and "La république monarchique," in *Le siècle de l'avènement républicain*, eds. François Furet and Mona Ozouf (Paris, 1993), 165–196; Baker, *Inventing the French Revolution*, esp. the final chapter; Michael P. Fitzsimmons, *The Remaking of France: The National Assembly and the Constitution of 1791* (Cambridge, 1994); and Applewhite, *Political Alignment*.

[13] For present purposes such information has been systematically compiled in a database of some sixty variables. See below, chap. 1.

ceivable.[14] In fact, virtually all of the delegates probably left some written records of their experiences from day to day. In part, it was a question of reporting on events to family, friends, and colleagues back home. Particularly in the early days, before Revolutionary newspapers had been initiated and widely circulated, citizens in the hinterlands relied heavily on accounts mailed by their representatives. For many of the latter, these functions became virtually institutionalized, specifically requested in electoral mandates, and carried out by designated individuals within each regional delegation.[15] Such writings might also represent a self-conscious effort to preserve a record for posterity—a "memorial," as both Doctor Jean-François Campmas from Albi and Antoine-François Delandine from Lyon would call it.[16] In still other cases, deputies took careful personal notes in order to assist their memories and maintain some sense of continuity before the immense number of questions discussed by the Assembly from week to week. According to the Auvergne lawyer Jean-François Gaultier de Biauzat, numerous deputies of the Third Estate were busy taking notes throughout the hall during the early sessions of the Estates General.[17]

But whatever the quantity of testimony originally produced, only a relatively small portion has escaped the vicissitudes of war, fires, and family neglect, to be identified by the modern historian.[18] We will rely above all on the writings of some 129 "principal witnesses," about 10 percent of the deputies. We include in this category those whose memoirs have been preserved, or for whom at least ten letters or diary entries have been located.[19] Of this group, the Third Estate is clearly over-represented, with more than three-fifths of the total—the remainder being about equally split between members of the Nobility and the Clergy.[20] It was probably more likely for

[14] One exception is Edna Lemay, who has used portions of contemporary deputy testimonies in her *La vie quotidienne des députés aux Etats généraux, 1789* (Paris, 1987).

[15] See below, chap. 7.

[16] Jean-François Campmas to his brother, vicaire in Carmaux: B.M. Albi, Ms. 177, letter of June 6, 1789; Delandine, *Mémorial*. Jacque-Antoine Creuzé-Latouche took notes specifically for an eventual "histoire de notre nation": *Journal des Etats généraux et du début de l'Assemblée nationale, 18 mai-29 juillet 1789*, ed. Jean Marchand (Paris, 1946), 60 (letter of June 5, 1789).

[17] Jean-François Gaultier de Biauzat, *Gaultier de Biauzat, député du Tiers état aux Etats généraux de 1789. Sa vie et sa correspondance*, ed. Francisque Mège, 2 vols. (Clermont-Ferrand, 1890), 2:74 (letter of May 22, 1789).

[18] Some of the material has been lost or misplaced in relatively recent times. The letters of Marie-Jean-François Le Carlier of Laon were apparently lost from the municipal archives during World War II; the diary of Jean-Joseph Mougin de Roquefort, previously held in the chateau of Roquefort (Alpes-Maritimes) seems to have disappeared in the same war during the Italian occupation; the letters of Pierre-Joseph Meifrund were lost by the city archives of Toulon during the last twenty years.

[19] See the sources. I first located many of these testimonies, especially those in manuscript form, through a card file created by the team of scholars researching Georges Lefebvre's *Recueil* in the 1940s and 1950s. Today this card file is held by the Institut de la Révolution française in the Sorbonne as part of the "Fichier Lefebvre" (see above, "Abbreviations").

[20] I exclude here the collective correspondence written by delegations of deputies. Such series

the Commoners to send letters to official administrative bodies like the municipal or regional governments—to which many belonged—letters which then stood an excellent chance of being preserved in local archives. Most of the letters from nobles and clergymen were directed to friends and relatives, usually ending up in private hands where their preservation was far more problematic. Yet documents of this sort exist for almost every position on the political spectrum—for both leaders and backbenchers—and for virtually every sector of the kingdom: north and south, city and country, Paris and the provinces.[21]

Among the testimonies, twenty-three are preserved in the form of personal accounts written after the fact. In several cases, the composition of these memoirs or histories seems to have been almost contemporary with the deputies' Revolutionary experience. Delandine's unfinished *Mémorial historique* was conceived to appear in monthly installments as a kind of running commentary on the Revolution; and Rabaut Saint-Etienne's *Précis historique* was written immediately after the end of the Constituent Assembly, "as one might describe a battle the day after it took place."[22] But others were penned twenty or thirty years after the events described. Some of these, like the history of the Constituent by Alexandre de Lameth and the memoirs of the marquis de Ferrières are based on detailed personal notes and careful research. Others, by contrast, like the memoirs of the noble Nompère de Champagny or of the ex-priest Simon-Edme Monnel, are sketchy and unreliable. Few if any of the deputies writing in the early nineteenth century could detach themselves from the experience of the Terror, an event which invariably colored their memories of earlier Revolutionary events. All such works must be subjected to critical scrutiny and verification.[23]

Of the remaining testimonies of our principal witnesses, 19 are in the form of diaries and 87 are sets of contemporary correspondence.[24] We might also include here the regular newspaper accounts of that handful of deputy-journalists who sat in the Assembly—among whom the articles of Jacques-Samuel Dinochau and Dominique-Joseph Garat are undoubtedly

---

are, however, indicated in the bibliography and have been used when appropriate. Of the 129, 80 (62%) sat in the Third Estate; 27 (21%) sat with the Nobles; and 22 (17%) sat with the Clergy.

[21] The "principal witnesses" are somewhat younger and participated in debate more frequently than the average deputy: average age of witnesses: 43.2 years (cf. 46.5 for all deputies); average number of speeches: 42.8 per individual (cf. 17.4 for all deputies). The sample included nine of the top forty speakers: see below, chap. 7.

[22] *Précis historique de la Révolution française* (Paris, 1807), 377–78. Delandine's *Mémorial* was published monthly from May to Oct. 1789.

[23] Lameth, *Histoire de l'Assemblée constituante*; Charles-Elie de Ferrières, *Mémoires du marquis de Ferrières*, 3 vols. (Paris, 1825); Jean-Baptiste de Nompère de Champagny, *Souvenirs de M. de Champagny, duc de Cadore* (Paris, 1846); Simon-Edme Monnel, *Mémoires d'un prêtre régicide*, ed. Denis-Alexandre Martin, 2 vols. (Paris, 1829).

[24] Note that several deputies left testimonies in more than one form.

the most revealing.[25] The total correspondence amounts to over 5,600 letters, with individual sets ranging from 10 to 395 letters and averaging some 65 per deputy. In terms of their quality, interest, and reliability, the letters and diaries differ substantially, both between individual authors and by period of composition. With few exceptions, the most revealing of the documents were written toward the beginning of the Assembly. During those early weeks and months, while the experience retained its novelty and maximum shock value, many deputies penned long, probing, introspective notes of enormous interest both for their factual narrative of events and their revelations of individual psychological states. But as time went on, as the wonder of the moment paled before the oppressive routine of the task at hand, as newspapers with national circulations appeared in large numbers reducing the need for regular communication, as lack of sleep and the lassitude of factional struggles and the general burden of legislative work took their toll, the letters and diary entries grew progressively shorter. By 1790 many deputies confined themselves entirely to questions of local or personal interest, or to mechanical accounts of laws passed—sometimes merely verbatim transcriptions. And many of the letters and diaries ceased altogether: 23 before the end of 1789 and 12 more before the Revolution's first anniversary.[26]

Much also depended on the audience for whom the correspondence or diaries were intended. Many of those 47 sets of letters addressed to wives, family, or close friends were a good deal more frank and revealing than the 40 directed to administrators or correspondence committees.[27] In the first case deputies might readily share their private feelings and innermost fears with confidants of choice: the Le Mans magistrate François-René Ménard de La Groye, for example, with his wife of seventeen years; Doctor Campmas with his brother the vicaire of Carmaux; the Lyon printer Jean-André Périsse Du Luc with his closest friend and Masonic "brother"; or the aging archbishop Boisgelin with his aging mistress, the comtesse de Gramont. "I write as I think," wrote Ménard to his wife on the eve of the Revolution, "and I do not seek in any way to disguise my true feelings."[28]

Among those addressing groups of citizens and public bodies, however, it was not uncommon to assume a somewhat more cautious, "political" voice. The deputies knew that their letters might be read in public, circulated

---

[25] Jacques-Samuel Dinochau, *Courier* [sic] *de Madon à l'Assemblée nationale permanente*, 25 vols. (Paris, Nov. 2, 1789 through May 29, 1791); Dominique-Joseph Garat, *Journal de Paris* (Paris, 1789–91). Other deputy newspaper writers—Barère, Mirabeau, Gaultier de Biauzat, Michel-Louis-Etienne Regnaud—wrote only episodically or usually limited themselves to dry accounts of speeches and decrees.

[26] See the sources.

[27] Of the 87 sets of letters, 40 were addressed primarily to municipalities or to predetermined correspondence committees, 24 were to friends, 8 to wives, 8 to other family members (brothers, nephews, a brother-in-law, and a daughter), 1 to a mistress, and 6 to several different individuals—mostly friends and family members.

[28] A.D. Sarthe, 10 J 120, letter of Sept. 20, 1788.

among the towns of their electoral districts, and perhaps even published. They were, in effect, fulfilling the functions of public servants conveying public information, and they might well feel a responsibility not only to relay news, but also to allay fears, boost morale, or promote a particular political position. Especially after the first months, much of this "official" correspondence entailed straightforward accounts with little or no commentary—except insofar as new decrees related directly to local constituencies. Campmas specifically designated the parts of his letters that might be made public and those that were reserved for "family matters"; and the Quercy lawyer Jean-Félix Faydel confided that the letters he wrote to his close friend, Filsac, were altogether different in tone and content from those directed to the municipality of Cahors.[29] Here, as always, it is the historian's task to critically assess the reliability of testimonies on a case-by-case basis, and to situate each document in the context of the deputies' backgrounds, careers, and previous experience.

In any event, not all the "public" correspondence was so guarded and discreet in character. The Third Estate lawyers and legal men, in particular, were a garrulous lot, and the small world of urban notables to whom they directed their letters commonly included close friends and relatives. Thus, the writings of Gaultier de Biauzat from Clermont-Ferrand, of the lawyer Théodore Vernier from Lons-le-Saunier, and of the Draguignan magistrate Jacques-Athanase de Lombard-Taradeau could be strikingly forthright and personal. Both Gaultier and Vernier openly prided themselves in their complete honesty. "I open up my heart," wrote Vernier, "and convey all my thoughts as I feel them." On one occasion Gaultier was even taken to task by his constituency for being too loquacious and personal in his accounts. He tried for a time to confine himself to the "facts," but his irrepressible chattiness and penchant for openness soon reemerged.[30]

The majority of the letters, moreover, were not carefully polished and edited statements. Most deputies had numerous correspondents and few could afford personal secretaries. Attempting to stay abreast with constituent demands for information, they wrote on their laps during the sessions, or on café tables during brief recesses, or at night in their rooms until well past midnight. They were forever apologizing for the lack of care in their prose—"my scribbling and even the carelessness of my style," wrote Irland de Bazôges—and pleading that the endless burdens of their responsibilities prevented them from making final drafts or from rereading what they had

---

[29] Campmas, e.g., letter of Nov. 16, 1789; Faydel to Filsac, avocat in Cahors: A.N., W 368, no. 822, 4e partie, letter of Jan. 2, 1790. Cf. those which Faydel wrote to the municipality: A.M. Cahors, unclassed box of letters from Revolutionary deputies, held in B.M. Cahors. Faydel long concealed from his constituency the fact that he was voting with the "aristocrats" on the right.

[30] See, e.g., Théodore Vernier to the municipality of Lons-le-Saunier: A.C. Bletterans (non-classé), "Lettres de Vernier," letters of Dec. 13, 1789 and May 4, 1790; Gaultier de Biauzat, 2:88 (letter of May 29, 1789).

written. Many letters were filled with misspellings and grammatical errors.[31] But in the end, it is precisely this spontaneous, unpremeditated quality of much of the correspondence that makes it so valuable for the historian and useful for the study of Revolutionary becoming. Indeed, one can treat such testimony as a kind of "series" by systematically enumerating the attitudes expressed and the positions taken by the deputies at various moments during the first year of the Revolution.

PROSPECTUS

The goal of the present study, then, is to follow the itineraries of the deputies of 1789 and to explore the significance of their experience for our understanding of the origins and early development of the Revolution. Though much of the book is organized in chronological fashion, it should not be conceived as a political narrative in the traditional sense. It makes no pretense of covering all aspects of the Revolution, nor of providing a comprehensive treatment of events. It focuses rather on the collective psychology of one group of central participants. In this sense, it applies to the history of the political elites the approach taken by Georges Lefebvre and George Rudé in their studies of the collective psychology of the peasants and the urban masses.[32] But while Lefebvre and Rudé confine themselves primarily to a socioeconomic analysis, the present study also adopts the perspectives of cultural history. It follows, insofar as possible, the transformation of the deputies' values and mode of thinking, their manner of interpreting their changing relationship to state and society. In so doing, however, it makes the assumption that culture is "produced" not only through intellectual experience, but through social and political experience as well; and that it is impossible to understand how individuals "read" their world without a full delineation of the contours of their lives.

The first three chapters will focus on the deputies' careers before the convocation of the Estates General, examining successively their socioeconomic, their intellectual, and their political backgrounds. In order to assess the relative positions of the deputies in society, their professional activities, incomes, marriage dowries, educational patterns, political experiences, and pre-Revolutionary writings and brochures will all be scrutinized in turn. In the face of the "convergent elites" hypothesis of the revisionists, it will be

---

[31] Pierre-Marie Irland de Bazôges to Henri Filleau: A.D. Deux-Sèvres, Fonds Beauchet-Filleau, unclassed register of "lettres politiques, 1788–90," letter of Sept. 4, 1789; Joseph Delaville Le Roulx to the municipality of Lorient: A.C. Lorient, BB 12–13, letters of May 29 and Dec. 30, 1789; Jean-Pierre Boullé to the municipality of Pontivy: A.C. Pontivy, on microfilm in A.D. Morbihan, 1 Mi 140, letter of Dec. 15, 1789; Jean-Joseph Lucas de Bourgerel to municipal officials in Vannes: A.D Morbihan, 262 E(s), letter of April 16, 1790.

[32] See especially, Lefebvre, *Coming of the French Revolution*; and George Rudé, *The Crowd in the French Revolution* (Oxford, 1959).

argued that the principal contending groups within the Estates, the Nobility and the Third Estate, were separated by a considerable gulf, a gulf created not by class *per se*, but by a combination of wealth, status, and culture. Although the commoners in question were almost all successful men who had made their careers within the existing system, many had distinctly mixed feelings toward the aristocracy. Virtually all were familiar with some elements of the Enlightenment, yet little evidence can be found before the Revolution of an oppositional ideology or "discourse." Far from the inexperienced ideologues depicted in many revisionist accounts, most of the Third Estate deputies emerge as practical men, more attracted to law, history, and science, than to abstract philosophy. Insofar as they received advance instruction in the possibility of extensive reform, it came less from reading books than from an involvement in municipal and regional politics—a participation promoted at almost every step by the monarchy itself.

Chapters 4 through 6 will take up the train of events as experienced by the delegates from May to November 1789, from the opening of the Estates General in Versailles to the Assembly's move to Paris and the formation of the Jacobin club. The choice of emphasis will be based, in large measure, on those events which particularly impressed the deputies themselves and which seem most to have contributed to their political and psychological development. While the deputies arriving in Versailles clearly anticipated significant reforms, only a very few, it will be argued, envisioned changes that could be construed as "Revolutionary." Such a new vision would emerge relatively rapidly, however, in the process of the Assembly itself: through the group dynamics engendered by the meetings; through the intense social antagonism—an antagonism of status more than of class—that arose between commoners and nobles; through the psychological effects of violence and upheaval; through the deputies' agonizing reassessment of the position of the monarchy, stimulated by the continuing vacillation and indecision of the king. Moreover, the general breakdown of law and order throughout the realm would soon compel the deputies to assume powers far beyond those originally conceived. For the great majority of the deputies an intellectual buttressing for the Revolution was "discovered" only after the fact, as they sifted and chose among the diverse strands of the Enlightenment that best suited their purpose.

In chapter 7 the procedures for law-making within the National Assembly will be inspected more carefully. Special emphasis will be placed on the nature of constituency relations, on the development of the committee system, and on oratory and leadership. Despite the extraordinary difficulties of reconstructing the nation in the midst of anarchy and financial crisis, the deputies adapted rapidly to the process of democracy and representative government. Rather than the abstract philosophers portrayed by the revisionists, most revealed themselves as pragmatists, transforming themselves with some success into legislative professionals. Chapters 8 and 9 will pursue the political developments of the Assembly from the end of 1789

through the second summer of the Revolution and the Festival of the Federation of July 14, 1790. Stress will be placed on the often related problems of state finance, church reform, and the reorganization of the administration and the judiciary; and on how the deputies were driven by the imperious necessities of resolving these problems to accept laws that they would certainly have rejected only a few months earlier. But in addition, the period saw the rapid formation of well-organized political factions among a strong minority of the deputies. An examination of the policies and composition of the three major "parties" in contention—the Jacobins, the Capuchins, and the Society of 1789—will permit an assessment of the politicization of the Assembly after the October Days and of the effects of politics on the Revolutionary dynamic. Despite the contention of many historians, the period was not marked by the rapid triumph of the Jacobins. Indeed, at the end of a year of Revolution, leadership seemed firmly in the hands of the more moderate Society of 1789.

Though we might have pursued the study through the completion of the constitution and the disbanding of the Assembly, we have chosen rather to end this volume with the Federation and the first anniversary of the Bastille. The case will be made that for a great many deputies this date marked the end of the Assembly's "revolutionary" vocation. Thereafter, most of its energies were devoted to consolidating and institutionalizing gains already achieved. The final fifteen months of the Constituent Assembly, and the concerted effort to end a Revolution also pose an array of interesting problems. But these might more appropriately remain the subject of another volume.

PART ONE

Deputy Backgrounds

The Three Estates

A COLLECTIVE BIOGRAPHY

WHO were they, then, these men of the Estates General, who first took their seats in Versailles? Many of the representatives themselves would pose this question as they looked about the hall at their new colleagues and speculated on their qualifications for the task at hand. Over the next two centuries, historians intrigued by the links between Old Regime experience and Revolutionary action would continue to reflect on the pre-Revolutionary backgrounds of the deputies. Yet virtually all of the studies of the Assembly to date have been based on a few easily quantifiable variables like professional titles, age, and region represented.[1] If we are to grasp the full reality of the delegates' pre-Revolutionary experience, we must broaden the inquiry to include not only their social and geographical origins, their careers, and their economic situation, but also the far more difficult and complex problems of their values and political culture. Fortunately, in undertaking such a task, we can rely on several generations of individual biographies and collective biographical dictionaries.[2]

NUMBERS AND GENERAL PROFILE

In the earliest days of the Assembly, no one was even quite sure how many they were. The original royal ruling of December 1788 had projected 1,000: 250 from each of the privileged estates and 500 from the commoners.[3] But continual ministerial tinkering with the electoral guidelines for specific provinces increased that number substantially. By the time of the

---

[1] See especially Philippe Sagnac, "La composition des Etats généraux et de l'Assemblée nationale en 1789," *RH* 206 (1951), 8–28; Alfred Cobban, *Aspects of the French Revolution* (New York, 1968), 100–102, 109–11; Jean-Marie Murphy and Patrice Higonnet, "Notes sur la composition de l'Assemblée constituante," *AHRF* 46 (1974), 321–26; and Edna Hindie Lemay, "La composition de l'Assemblée nationale constituante: les hommes de la continuité," *RHMC* 24 (1977), 341–63.

[2] The present and the two following chapters rely heavily on the Fichier Lefebvre and on a wide variety of other biographies and biographic dictionaries. From these sources I have compiled a database of some 60 variables on the 1,315 individuals who sat as deputies during the entire period of the Estates General and the National Assembly. At a later stage in research, I was greatly aided by Edna Hindie Lemay's *Dictionnaire des constituants, 1789–1791*, 2 vols. (Paris, 1991).

[3] Brette, *Recueil*, 1:37.

official convocation, there should normally have been some 1,200 deputies on hand at Versailles. Yet for a variety of reasons, many of the deputies were slow in arriving, and witnesses estimated that only 800 participated in the procession on May 4, including about 500 of the predicted 600 members of the Third Estate.[4] Curé Barbotin and his fellow deputies from Le Quesnoy appeared in the Assembly only on May 11, Bailly and the other 39 delegates from Paris on May 24; while Escuret-Laborde rode in from the distant Pays de Soule only in late June; and deputies from France's far-flung colonies—two of whom had perished in a shipwreck en route—were still filtering in as late as February 1791.[5]

Moreover, since the problem of verifying credentials was at the heart of the initial political maneuvering between the Third Estate and the privileged orders, it was well into June before evaluation procedures were established for the Assembly as a whole, and it was mid-July before decisions were made on several of the more controversial elections.[6] By this time, some 1,177 deputies seem to have been certified to sit with the "National Assembly."[7] Of these, 604 were representatives of the Third Estate (51.3 percent of the total); 295 of the Clergy (25.1 percent); and 278 of the Nobles (23.6 percent). Over the entire life of the Assembly, taking into account replacements for deputy resignations and deaths, 1,315 men were officially accredited and seated—330 for the Clergy, 322 for the Nobles, and 663 for the Third Estate. While the royal guidelines had envisioned a balance between the number of Third deputies, on the one hand, and those from the two privileged orders, on the other, the quirks of the elections—and notably the boycott of the proceedings by the privileged deputies of Brittany—had actually given a slight majority to the Third Estate. Such a situation made the conservative leaders of the privileged orders all the more wary of uniting the estates.[8]

But whatever its precise numbers at a given point in time, the first French National Assembly was remarkably large, perhaps the largest such representative body in Western European history. It was almost three times as large as the previous Estates General of 1614 and it would have seemed a veritable sea of people beside the 55 men who assembled two years earlier to

---

[4] Adrien Duquesnoy, *Journal d'Adrien Duquesnoy*, ed. R. de Crèvecoeur, 2 vols. (Paris, 1894), 1:1 (entry of May 3); Emmanuel Barbotin, *Lettres de l'abbé Barbotin*, ed. A. Aulard (Paris, 1910), 3 (letter of May 10); Louis-Jean-Baptiste Leclerc de Lassigny de Juigné to his wife: family archives, Château de Saint-Martin (Taradeau, Var), letter of May 4.

[5] Barbotin, 3–4; Fichier Lefebvre; Armand Brette, "La vérification des pouvoirs à l'Assemblée constituante," *RF* 26 (1894), 39.

[6] Brette, "La vérification des pouvoirs" 25 (1893), 413–36.

[7] Estimates in this paragraph are based on an analysis of Brette, *Recueil*, vol. 2, complemented with information from a wide variety of biographic sources, including the Fichier Lefebvre and the *DC*. The nineteen deputies from the colonies, who were not actually elected by order, have been classified as Nobles or Commoners according to their legal status: ten as Nobles and nine as Commoners.

[8] Brette, *Recueil*, 2:343–44.

forge an American constitution or even the 558 members of the eighteenth-century House of Commons.[9] The very size of the Constituent inevitably helped fashion the particular personality of that body. To the end, the Assembly would maintain a distinctly impersonal character. A number of deputies commented on the difficulties of locating specific friends or associates in the great mass of men spread out around them, "although we spend seven to eight hours a day in the same hall." After eight months of daily sessions, Doctor Jean-Gabriel Gallot indicated his inability to learn the names of many of his colleagues, even among those who sat next to him on the same side of the room and whose faces he had grown to recognize.[10]

More important, the very size of the Assembly would measurably affect its operations. Virtually every action which it undertook was slowed by the sheer weight of numbers. Especially in the days before the committee system was perfected, a given debate might see thirty, fifty, eighty individuals sign up to speak. Roll calls could linger on interminably for three hours or more. "One has to consider," wrote the Flemish lawyer François-Joseph Bouchette, "what it is like to have 1,200 people in an assembly, and what would happen if everyone wanted to have his chance to speak. . . . We can only be patient."[11] Looking back after a year and a half of struggles, the comte de Mirabeau concluded that it was the "great size" of the Assembly, as much as anything else, which made it so unwieldy and difficult to organize. Frequently it took on a life of its own, veering off on any given day in quite unpredictable directions and rendering the exercise of leadership by specific factions or individuals extremely difficult to maintain—much to the chagrin of Mirabeau.[12] In addition, the considerable number of deputies would necessitate the use of very large assembly halls. Since both of the principal rooms used—the Menus Plaisirs in Versailles and the Manège des Tuileries in Paris—possessed deplorable acoustics, it was impossible to speak effectively without a particularly powerful voice. There was thus a physiological component to leadership, sharply limiting the proportion of members who could take active roles in debate.[13]

From the beginning, the ministers had sought to base representation on population and wealth as well as on territory. This no doubt explains the greater contingent of deputies from the electoral districts of northern

[9] J. Michael Hayden, *France and the Estates General of 1614* (Cambridge, 1974), 74; Gerrit P. Judd, *Members of Parliament, 1734–1832* (New Haven, 1955), 12; Clinton Rossiter, *1787: The Grand Convention* (New York, 1966), 139.

[10] Jean-François Campmas to his brother, vicaire in Carmaux: B.M. Albi, Ms. 177 (letter of July 25, 1789); Jean-Gabriel Gallot, *La vie et les oeuvres du Docteur Jean-Gabriel Gallot*, ed. Louis Merle (Poitiers, 1961), 132 (letter of Jan. 12, 1790).

[11] François-Joseph Bouchette, *Lettres*, ed. C. Looten (Lille, 1909), 276 (letter of Oct. 21 1789). See also Claude-Pierre Maillot to an unnamed municipal official of Toul, Aug. 1, 1789: A.C. Toul, JJ 7.

[12] Honoré-Gabriel Riqueti de Mirabeau, *Correspondance avec le comte de la Marck*, 3 vols., Adrien de Bacourt ed. (Paris, 1851), 2:420 (letter of ca. Dec. 23, 1790).

[13] See below, chap. 7.

France. Over 70 percent represented constituencies north of the line between La Rochelle and Geneva.[14] But not all milieus within those districts
were equally well represented. Thirty percent of the deputies resided in
towns of over 20,000 inhabitants and nearly two-thirds lived in "towns" of
any size—defined here as settlements with agglomerated populations of at
least 2,000 people. Indeed, if one excludes the deputy parish priests, overwhelmingly posted in rural parishes, the proportion of urban deputies rises
to almost 75 percent—compared to only 18 percent for the overall French
population.[15] A majority of the men of '89 probably envisioned themselves
more as the representatives of specific towns than as the representatives of
general rural districts. It is thus scarcely surprising that a great many deputies never really appreciated the problems of the countrypeople and would
seem altogether baffled by rural religious culture.[16]

Yet not all of the deputies lived in the districts they represented. There
were no residence requirements in the royal electoral regulations, and in the
end, at least 175 (13 percent) of the delegates were outsiders to their constituencies, linked at best through ties of landholding or family tradition.[17]
Many of the colonial representatives actually resided in France, some with
only the most tenuous connections to their electoral districts.[18] By far the
greatest number of nonresident deputies were from Paris. This was, as we
shall see, particularly the case among the deputies of the Nobility, over a
hundred of whom had left the capital in the spring of 1789 and scattered to
the four corners of the kingdom to seek election. In all, at least 211 deputies, better than one in six, resided in Paris.[19] Since most of these deputies
had substantial property holdings in the city, it is little wonder that they
would be particularly sensitive to events developing there.

On the whole, the men of the first National Assembly were mature and at
the peak of their powers, with an average age of about forty-six years at the
beginning of their tenures in office—a little over forty-five for the Nobles
and Commoners, and a little over fifty for the Clergy. In this, they were
about three years older than the representatives to the American Constitutional Convention, but probably somewhat younger than those sitting in

[14] Lemay, "La composition de l'Assemblée nationale," 349.

[15] Population estimates are based on René Le Mée, "Population agglomérée, population
éparse au début du XIXe siècle," *Annales de démographie historique, 1971* (Paris, 1972), 467–
93. By our calculations—excluding the 116 whose residence has not been determined—426
deputies (36%) resided in settlements of less than 2,000 inhabitants; 226 (19%) in those of 2–
8,000; 179 (15%) in those of 8–20,000; 94 (8%) in those of 20–50,000; 63 (5%) in those of
over 50,000; and 211 (18%) in Paris.

[16] See below, chap. 2.

[17] Figures estimated from my general database.

[18] See Jean Binoche, "Les députés d'Outre-Mer pendant la Révolution française (1789–99),"
AHRF 40 (1978), 45–80.

[19] *Almanach de Paris, Première partie, contenant les noms et qualités des personnes de condition
pour l'année 1789* (Paris, 1789). See also Jean-Pierre Boullé to municipality of Pontivy: A.C.
Pontivy, on microfilm in A.D. Morbihan, 1 Mi 140, letter of Nov. 20, 1789.

the House of Commons.[20] The statistical average concealed, however, an extraordinary range of ages: from young Mathieu de Montmorency, who had just turned twenty-two, through the aged bishop of Bazas, who was over eighty, and with at least one deputy at almost every age in between.[21] But neither the average age nor the range adequately describes the generational dynamic at work within the National Assembly. As we shall discover, positions of leadership—among both radicals and conservatives—were often dominated by the more youthful deputies. Perhaps this is one of the reasons why many of the deputies judged their colleagues to be younger than they really were. In describing the Third Estate, Creuzé-Latouche referred to "the fervor of the young men who constitute the majority," and he frequently attached the adjective "young" in describing leading Constituent speakers (Barnave, Robespierre, the comte de Virieu, the duc d'Aiguillon, and the abbé Grégoire). Adrien-Cyprien Duquesnoy—at the mature age of thirty—spoke disapprovingly of "legislators in bibs" (Montmorency and the comte de Castellane) and of "beardless young men" (Barnave and Alexandre de Lameth).[22]

As there were no age or residence requirements, neither were the deputies held to represent their "natural" orders. If all the clerical deputies were in fact clergymen—and apparently all but one were priests—at least eight of the Nobles were members of the clerical Order of Malta, and four deputies of the Third were full-fledged ecclesiastics (including one canon, two additional knights of Malta, and the vicar-general Sieyès). Indeed, the baron de Flachslanden, elected by the Third Estate of Haguenau, was both a clergyman and a member of the sword nobility. In addition to the 322 members of the Second Estate, all of whom were nobles, another 85 nobles sat with the Clergy and 58 with the Third Estate. Over a third of the entire membership of the National Assembly belonged to the nobility.[23]

Yet despite such overlaps, each of the three orders had its distinct character. Since social and cultural backgrounds were of no small importance in

[20] See Rossiter, 148; and Judd, 21. By our calculations, the mean age for all deputies was 46.4 years, the median 45. The Nobles averaged 45.6 years in 1789, the Third averaged 45.1, and the Clergy averaged 50.5.

[21] The ages were generally distributed in a classic bell curve. Every age between 24 and 77 was represented by at least one deputy.

[22] Jacques-Antoine Creuzé-Latouche, *Journal des Etats généraux et du début de l'Assemblée nationale, 18 mai–29 juillet 1789*, ed. Jean Marchand (Paris, 1946), 32 (entry of May 29, 1789); Duquesnoy, 2:20, 445 (entries of Nov. 5, 1789 and March 8, 1790).

[23] Among the Nobles associated with the Order of Malta were the chevalier de Boufflers, the marquis de Chambray, the vicomte de Desandrouin, the chevalier Masson d'Esclans, the marquis de Foucauld de Lardimalie, the chevalier Alexandre de Lameth, the marquis de Mesgrigny, and the vicomte de Mirabeau. In a speech of June 22, 1790, Boufflers specifically referred to himself as a member of the clergy: *AP*, 16:409. The three clergymen in the Third in addition to Sieyès were Du Plaquet (a knight of Malta), Texier (a canon in Chartres), and Flachslanden (baron and commander in the Order of Malta). Colaud de la Salcette, canon in Die, claimed that "je ne fus pas prêtre" in 1789: A.N. C 353. On the nobles in the Third, see below.

later political options, it is important to examine the three estates with some care.

THE CLERGY

The salient characteristic of the deputies of the First Estate, widely noted by contemporaries and by all historians since, was the extraordinary proportion of parish priests within that delegation.[24] Representing only about one in ten of the clergymen attending the Estates General of 1614, the "curés"—as the chief parish priests were called in France—now amounted to almost three-fourths of the total clerical contingent.[25] This curious turn of events can be directly attributed to the electoral rulings devised by the minister Jacques Necker in January 1789, rulings which gave one vote to every curé in the electoral assemblies and allowed proxy votes for those unable to attend. But it can also be ascribed to the intense politicization and active organization of the parish clergy which allowed the lower clergy to make maximum use of those procedures.[26] The remaining First Estate deputies represented a wide variety of clerical positions. Some 46 of the total were prelates—14 percent, compared to 41 percent in the Estates General of 1614—including 34 bishops, 10 archbishops, and 2 episcopal coadjutors. Closely associated with the episcopal contingent were the 27 other members of the upper clergy: vicars-general, for the most part, but also a retired bishop, an agent-general of the Clergy of France, 3 *conseillers clercs* attached to the sovereign courts, and an abbé *commendataire* linked to the royal ministry (the orator-academician, Maury). The clerical estate was rounded out with a group of 26 canons, ecclesiastical teachers or non-parish regulars.[27] Of all the elements of the Old Regime clergy, it was the last-mentioned category, the regulars, who were the most dramatically under-represented. Constituting close to half of the entire clerical corps—if one includes the women religious—the regulars held only about 3 percent of the clerical seats.[28] This state of affairs was related once again to Necker's electoral regulations, which allowed only one electoral delegate for each religious house, but it also reflected the low esteem in which such clergymen were held by the great bulk of the clerical electorate. In any case, the mere token presence of the regulars in

[24] See Jo Ann Browning Seeley, "The Parish Clergy in the French Constituent Assembly, 1789–1791," Ph.D. dissertation, the Catholic University of America, 1992, 34–48.

[25] Hayden, 93–94. The curés totaled 231 (70%) of the 330 who sat at any time during the National Assembly.

[26] Timothy Tackett, *Religion, Revolution, and Regional Culture in Eighteenth-Century France: The Ecclesiastical Oath of 1791* (Princeton, 1986), 141–46.

[27] There were 20 vicars general, 1 ex-vicar general, 1 ex-bishop, an agent-general of the clergy, 3 *conseillers clercs*, an abbé *commendataire*, 11 canons, 5 ecclesiastical teachers, and 10 regulars. There were also 11 regular curés among the deputies. Note that many of the vicars-general and several of the curés were also canons.

[28] Timothy Tackett and Claude Langlois, "Ecclesiastical Structures and Clerical Geography on the Eve of the French Revolution," *French Historical Studies* 11 (1980), 357.

the Assembly would render the defense of monastic orders much more difficult when the institution came under attack in the fall of 1789.

On the whole, the clerical deputies were a mature and highly respectable group of men. All had completed their secondary training and had spent from one to four years in a seminary. Over half are known to have held university diplomas in theology or canon law—the bachelor's degree or beyond—and the actual proportion might easily have been two-thirds or higher.[29] With an average age of over fifty years, the Clergy was also markedly older than the other two estates. Indeed, the bishops, who averaged almost fifty-five years, were the oldest of all the subgroups in the National Assembly. Only the vicars-general—most of whom were younger nobles waiting to assume posts as bishops—averaged substantially under fifty.[30] The age of the Clergy, however, was probably indicative less of an electoral preference for older men, than of the nature of the clerical electorate. The electoral regulations made no provisions for representation of the great mass of younger assistant parish priests or "vicaires." In fact, the average age of the curés deputies (about fifty years) was almost exactly the average of all curés in France at the time.[31]

Though they were clearly disadvantaged in terms of numbers, the deputy bishops were not without their strengths and assets. They were a distinguished group, representing ten of France's eighteen archbishoprics and many of the richest and most prestigious sees in the realm, including Paris, Bordeaux, Strasbourg, Toulouse, Rouen, Reims, Bourges, Aix, Poitiers, and Amiens. All, without exception, were nobles and most originated among the great aristocratic families of France. Nearly three-quarters could trace their nobility to the fourteenth century or earlier and only two were from families ennobled in the eighteenth century.[32] Many of the bishops, moreover, were related to one another. There were two Champion de Cicés, two Talleyrands, four La Rochefoucaulds, and almost certainly many other cousins with different surnames.[33] Similar ties of family and lineage bound them to most of the deputy vicars-general, who were also overwhelmingly noble. From the revenues of their bishoprics alone—not to mention additional benefices and personal family possessions—all were wealthy and some were immensely wealthy with yearly revenues well above

---

[29] All of the 72 upper clergymen are assumed to have held degrees. From incomplete information, which undoubtedly under-represents the reality, we have identified 48% of the curé deputies holding degrees: 71 with known degrees, 40 others holding posts (vicars-general, diocesan judges, or seminary or collège professors) for which degrees were virtually requisite: Fichier Lefebvre and *DC*.

[30] Curés: 50.3 years; bishops: 54.6; vicars-general: 44.9; canons: 49.8; regulars: 50.2.

[31] Tackett, *Religion, Revolution, and Regional Culture*, 80.

[32] Information on the bishops' families is available for 44 of the 46. For 32 (73%) of these, the male line can be traced back before 1400: Michel Peronnet, *Les évêques de l'ancienne France* (Lille, 1977), 1337–43.

[33] On the tight family networks among the bishops, see Peronnet, livre II, chap. 3.

100,000 *livres*.[34] All of the bishops and archbishops, moreover, and most of the vicars-general, had studied at the same seminary of Saint-Sulpice in Paris, and many had known each other well since school days. They sat together in the General Assembly of the Clergy which met every five years in Paris, and several—Boisgelin of Aix, Dulau of Arles, La Rochefoucauld of Rouen, Le Franc de Pompignan of Vienne—had played major leadership roles over the years within their order. Ignoring the canonical strictures on residence, over half of the bishops habitually resided in the capital, where they might meet at court or in Parisian salons or in the meetings of the General Assembly.[35] Their considerable experience with power and their long-developed habit of working with one another would greatly facilitate joint political action in the early weeks of the Revolution.[36]

The curé deputies were not undistinguished in their own right. Indeed, in their training, in their previous ecclesiastical experience, and even in their social origins, a great many were substantially superior to the French parish clergy as a whole. At least one in two held university degrees—compared to one in four or five among all curés—and at least forty-two were doctors or *licenciés* in the Sorbonne.[37] Twelve are known to have served as canons, while ten held high positions of diocesan responsibility as vicars-general, ecclesiastical magistrates, or personal secretaries to the bishops. Another five held posts conjointly as directors of local seminaries and at least six were former Jesuit fathers who had moved into the diocesan clergy after the expulsion of their order in the 1760s.[38] As a group they seem to have originated in families that were somewhat higher in the social scale than those of the typical French curés. Among those for whom information is available, 7 percent were members of the nobility and half came from "notable" families of either the Second or Third Estates—including families of "bourgeois," officeholders, and the liberal professions. Yet one should also not overlook the one-fourth to one-third of the curé-deputies originating in artisan or peasant families.[39] Henri Grégoire and Jacques Binot, for example, were sons of rural tailors; Jacques Jallet was the tenth child of a gardener in Poitou; Jacques Rangeard and Anne-Alexandre-Marie Thibault came from families of carpenters; and Simon-Edme Monnel, born in a peasant milieu,

[34] Norman Ravitch, *Sword and Mitre: Government and Episcopate in France and England in the Age of Aristocracy* (The Hague, 1966), Appendix II.

[35] Peronnet, 3–68; *Almanach de Paris*; and Eugène Lavaquery, *Le Cardinal de Boisgelin, 1732–1804*, 2 vols. (Paris, 1920), vol. I, chap. VII.

[36] See below, chap. 4.

[37] Seeley, 40–41; Tackett, *Religion, Revolution, and Regional Culture*, 104; and note 29, above.

[38] Fichier Lefebvre.

[39] Seeley, 36–39, gives information on social origins for 168 (73%) of the 231 curés. I have included in my calculations, in addition, 12 curé-deputies born of families in small rural villages whose fathers did not indicate their professions, but who were almost certainly cultivators. See also Timothy Tackett, "L'histoire sociale du clergé diocésain dans la France du XVIIIe siècle," *RHMC* 26 (1979), 227.

was too poor to attend school without the aid of a benefactor.[40] Men such as these had more humble beginnings than any other group in the National Assembly.

With little or no family resources on which to draw, most such curés could count on little income beyond their ecclesiastical benefices, benefices which might range from the meager 600 *livres* per year of curé Bigot in the Massif Central to the very ample 8,000 *livres* of Veytard, curé of Saint-Gervais in Paris, with the majority probably receiving something between 1,000 and 3,000 a year.[41] Based on the deputies' letters, no other group suffered more from the financial demands of living in Versailles and Paris. In correspondence with the friend watching over his parish in southern France, curé Gouttes continually referred to his economic difficulties, to the debts he had incurred to pay his travel and upkeep in Versailles, and to his difficulties in exploiting his benefice from so far away.[42] Likewise, both curés Barbotin and Rousselot complained of the challenge of making ends meet in the capital, and as late as 1790 the latter was still trying to pay back debts contracted for his trip to Versailles. Indeed, the precariousness of the curés' situation was one of the central rationales for instituting deputy salaries in the summer of 1789.[43]

Like parish priests everywhere in France in the late eighteenth century, the curé deputies experienced very mixed interests and emotions. Through their family origins and economic situation, many felt great sympathy for the Third Estate and hostility toward the upper clergy. A number of deputies—like Jallet from Poitou, Grégoire from Lorraine, Chatizel from Anjou, Bécherel from Normandy, or Forest de Masmoury from Limousin—had been among the most vigorous local leaders in the struggle for church reform and curé rights. Yet by their theological training, and by their tight links with the diocesan power structures they were also susceptible to the bonds of deference toward their hierarchical superiors. With little knowledge of one another prior to the Assembly, with little experience in the ways of high politics, without the family, the prestige, the aristocratic self-confidence of the upper clergy, the curé deputies would have great difficulty standing up to the bishops, whatever their numbers and the force of their convictions.[44]

[40] Fichier Lefebvre; D. Marié, ed., "Trois lettres de l'Abbé Jallet," *AHRF* 22 (1950), 326; and Simon-Edme Monnel, *Mémoires d'un prêtre régicide*, ed. Denis-Alexandre Martin, 2 vols. (Paris, 1829), 1:24–25.

[41] *DC*; and Timothy Tackett, "Les revenus des curés à la fin de l'Ancien régime: esquisse d'une géographie," in Alain Croix et al., eds., *La France d'Ancien régime, études réunies en l'honneur de Pierre Goubert* (Toulouse, 1984), 665–71.

[42] Jean-Louis Gouttes to Jean-Baptiste Cabanès, cadet, "bourgeois": A.C. Argelliers, S 12 A, letter of Feb. 5, 1791.

[43] Claude-Germain Rousselot to his nephew, Joseph Rousselot: Fonds Girardot, A.D. Hautes-Saônes, letter of Jan. 1, 1790; Barbotin, 3 (letter of May 10, 1789); Creuzé-Latouche, 247–48 (letter of July 18, 1789).

[44] See below, chap. 4.

THE NOBILITY

If the clerical delegation in Versailles was dominated by the lower ranks of the ecclesiastical hierarchy, the 322 deputies of the Second Estate came primarily from the highest and most distinguished elements of the traditional aristocracy.[45] One could pick out no less than 4 princes, 16 dukes—9 of whom were peers of the realm—83 marquis, 104 counts or viscounts, and 28 barons. In all, almost three-fourths of the Nobles held ranks of this kind, compared to a mere 2 to 6 percent of entitled nobles on the provincial tax rolls of the kingdom.[46] The list of the Estate read like a herald's roll of the great names of the realm: La Rochefoucauld, Orléans, Luynes, Aiguillon, Clermont-Tonnerre, Choiseul, Noailles, Mortemart, Montmorency, Liancourt, and many others. Indeed, some of the names appeared more than once, since 21 of the Nobles had at least one brother who had also been elected—a greater number than in the other two orders combined.[47] The very splendor of their costumes and ceremonial accoutrements left Garron de La Bévière—himself a mere chevalier—quite overwhelmed. "We have numerous great lords in our chamber," he wrote to his wife, "*cordons bleus, cordons rouges*, crosses of every color and shape."[48]

Only a lengthy genealogical study could determine the precise dates to which the various families could trace the origin of their noble lineage. Yet there is good evidence that more than eight out of ten had been ennobled before 1600, and that more than seven out of ten could claim proof of nobility dating back to the Middle Ages.[49] To be sure, there were no genealogical requirements for election and only those with nonhereditary, "personal" nobility were excluded from the electoral assemblies. A number of the "nobles of the second order"—as one deputy called them[50]—second-

---

[45] See esp. Jean-Marie Murphy and Patrice Higonnet, "Les députés de la noblesse aux Etats Généraux," *RHMC* 20 (1973), 230–47; and Alison Patrick, "The Second Estate in the Constituent Assembly, 1789–1791," *JMH* 62 (1990), 223–52. Also included here are the ten noble deputies representing the colonies.

[46] In noble *capitation* rolls drawn up between 1780 and 1789, titled nobles represented 3% of all nobles listed for the *généralité* of Bordeaux, 3% for Limoges, 6% for Grenoble, 5% for Châlons-sur-Marne, and 2% for Rouen, for an average of 3.5% overall: A.N., P 5170, 5298bis, 5392, 5417 and 5765. Compare also to the mere two-fifths of the Nobles in the Estates of 1614 who had been titled—half of whom had been simple barons: Hayden, 90. In all, 234 (73%) of the 322 noble deputies of 1789 are known to have had such titles.

[47] There were 41 deputies with brothers in the Assembly: 21 in the Nobility, 11 in the Clergy, and 9 in the Third Estate.

[48] Claude-Jean-Baptiste de Garron de La Bévière to his wife, letters of May 6 and 12, 1789: A.D. Ain, 1 Mi 1.

[49] Of the 281 for whom it has been possible to trace the noble lineage, 174 (62%) could trace their nobility to before 1400; 27 (10%) to between 1400 and 1500; 33 (12%) to between 1500 and 1600; 31 (11%) to between 1600 and 1700; and 16 (6%) to after 1700. I have used Henri Jougla de Morenas, *Grand armorial de France*, 6 vols. (Paris, 1934–49); and François Bluche, *Les honneurs de la cour* (Paris, 1957).

[50] Félix Faulcon, *Correspondance. Tome 2: 1789–91*, ed. G. Debien (Poitiers, 1953), 207 (letter to Presac-Desplanches, May 5, 1790).

generation nobles like Cazalès, Duval d'Eprémesnil, and Bureaux de Pusy, would play conspicuous leadership roles.[51] But in the final analysis, no more than 6 percent of the deputies sent by the nobility to Versailles seem to have been newly ennobled in the eighteenth century. When one considers that perhaps one-third of the nobles in the kingdom as a whole had been ennobled in the eighteenth century and two-thirds in the previous two centuries, the extraordinarily exclusive and aristocratic character of the Second Estate becomes all the more striking.[52]

A significant proportion of these aristocrats, moreover, were town dwellers and above all Parisians.[53] Half of the entire Second Estate had addresses in the capital—either their own residences or those of their families—where they lived all or much of the year.[54] We would search in vain for their names on the poll tax rolls of the provincial districts they represented.[55] Since nobles could participate in any of the bailliage assemblies in which they held fiefs,[56] numerous great aristocrats from Paris and Versailles scattered into the countryside seeking election from ancestral homelands. Thus, the marquis de Lafayette pursued a sentimental journey to family property in Auvergne which he had scarcely visited since boyhood; and Nompère de Champagny returned to his home district of Montbrison for the first time in twenty-five years.[57] In fact, only a handful of these Parisian noble deputies were "courtiers," with titles and responsibilities at the royal court in Versailles. Nine were so listed in the official almanac, not including the King's cousin the duc d'Orléans, and six other dukes and peers who had immediate access to the king's inner circle.[58] But a great many others undoubtedly attended court functions on occasion and knew and associated with one another in Paris.

In any case, almost without exception, the large contingent of aristocratic

[51] Brette, *Recueil*, 1:72–74. On noble leadership, see below chap. 7.

[52] Guy Chaussinand-Nogaret, *La noblesse au XVIIIe siècle. De la féodalité aux Lumières* (Paris, 1976), 48–49.

[53] Focusing on the bailliage the deputies represented rather than on their actual places of residence, some historians have mistakenly concluded the presence of a large group of rural nobles: e.g., J. M. Thompson, *The French Revolution* (Oxford, 1943), 9.

[54] Among the 244 (76% of the total 322) for whom residence is known, 127 (52%) had addresses in Paris; 63 (26%) lived in provincial capitals or other larger towns; 51 (21%) lived in rural areas, apparently in their châteaus; and 3 (1%) lived in foreign lands.

[55] The *capitation* was paid only in the tax district of principal residence. Examining the noble *capitation* rolls for 1788 and 1789 in the *généralités* of Bordeaux, Châlons-sur-Marne, Grenoble, and Orléans, we have located only 24 (49 %) of the 49 noble deputies representing those districts: A.N., P 5170, 5298bis, 5392, and 5591.

[56] Brette, *Recueil*, 1:74.

[57] Louis Gottschalk and Margaret Maddox, *Lafayette in the French Revolution through the October Days* (Chicago, 1969), 21; Jean-Baptiste de Nompère de Champagny, *Souvenirs de M. de Champagny, duc de Cadore* (Paris, 1846), 56–57.

[58] Deputies in the king's household: the duc de Liancourt, the prince de Poix, the comte d'Escars, and the duc Du Châtelet; in the households of the king's brothers: the comte de La Chastre, the marquis de Fumel, the marquis d'Avaray, the marquis de Montesquiou-Fezensac, and the comte de Lameth: *Almanach royal de 1789* (Paris, 1789).

deputies from Paris consisted of wealthy men, and in some cases, of colossally wealthy men. While a few of the younger deputies remained unmarried and lived with their families, the great majority were established and of independent means. It was scarcely possible for anyone to maintain the requisite status of a gentleman in Paris and Versailles with less than 50,000 *livres* per year.[59] The marquis de Vassé was said to have had an income of over 90,000 in 1778; Le Peletier de Saint-Fargeau declared about 117,000 the following year; the marquis de Lafayette possessed 108,000; the ducs de Luynes, de Liancourt, and de La Rochefoucauld probably had closer to 200,000; while the Aiguillon, Castellane, and Mortemart families held revenues that may have approached 500,000 *livres* per year. The Aguesseaus, Maillys, Luxembourgs, Sérents, Noailles, and Choiseuls were all among the great landholding families in the kingdom.[60] Furthermore, the wealth of the Parisian-based deputies was not only proprietary in nature, but also commercial. The Antraigues, the Clermont-Tonnerres, the Croÿs, the Montesquious, the Du Châtelets, and the Allardes, for example, were involved in substantial investments in mines. The baron de Batz had amassed a huge fortune through ownership of an insurance company. And a whole block of deputies—Charles de Lameth, Lemoyne de Bellisle, the marquis de Paroy, the marquis de Gouy d'Arsy, for example—had acquired fortunes, through inheritance or marriage, in Caribbean plantations and the slave trade.[61]

In addition to the large contingent of Parisian aristocrats, a fourth of the Second Estate deputies lived in the medium to large provincial towns of the kingdom. Some of these, no doubt, were military officers in residence with their regiments or serving as local commanders or governors. Appointed *commandant* of La Rochelle, the vicomte de Malartic had largely integrated himself into local society, married the daughter of a director of the *Compagnie des Indes*, joined the La Rochelle Academy, and served a stint as mayor.[62] Others were retired officers, who had returned to live among the prosperous regional nobility, dividing their time between rural estates and town houses in the provincial capitals. The comte de Marsane-Fontjuliane, for example, owned one of the most beautiful houses of Montélimar as well as a château and lands throughout rural Dauphiné.[63]

[59] Robert Forster, *The House of Saulx-Tavanes: Versailles and Burgundy, 1700–1830* (Baltimore, 1971), 57; Daniel L. Wick, *A Conspiracy of Well-Intentioned Men: The Society of Thirty and the French Revolution* (New York, 1987), 110.

[60] Wick, 110; Chaussinand-Nogaret, 78, 85–86; Gottschalk and Maddox, 19; Charles Girault, "La propriété foncière de la noblesse sarthoise au XVIIIe siècle," *Provence de Maine*, 2e série, 35 (1955), 202; and Fichier Lefebvre. Estimates for Le Peletier are based on A.N., 90 AP 50 (2).

[61] *DC*; Chaussinand-Nogaret, 82, 135–36, 148–50; Roselyne Tournebise, "Le baron de Batz," *La science historique*, n. sér., 67 (1988), 65–66.

[62] Gabriel Maurès de Malartic, *Le vicomte de Malartic* (La Rochelle, 1892), 7–17.

[63] Paul Messié, "Le comte de Marsane-Fontjuliane, député de Montélimar aux premières assemblées révolutionnaires," *Bulletin de la Société départementale d'archéologie et de statistique de*

In all, only a fifth to a fourth of the deputies were genuine country gentlemen, residing primarily in their rural manor houses.[64] Yet none of the provincial nobles among the deputies fit the image of the destitute "hobereau." Among those whose financial situations have been examined, even the least prosperous—the baron de Mercey with a "precarious" annual revenue of 10,000 *livres* per year or the marquis de Digoine whose "mediocrity of fortune" earned him a royal pension—even they possessed their own lands and were far from impoverished.[65] Garron de La Bévière, an ex-soldier who divided his time between his château in the Dombes and a house in Bourg-en-Bresse, often complained of the prices in Versailles and was unable to maintain his own carriage in the capital. Yet he was probably earning between 14,000 and 16,000 *livres* per year from his estates, and he had money enough to attend the Paris theater and opera and to have his portrait painted.[66] Reynaud de Montlosier was the twelfth child of a "modest" noble family near Clermont-Ferrand, but he married into a small estate and seemed to have ample resources to pursue scientific studies and later to finance his two-year stay in Paris.[67] Others seem to have possessed comfortable fortunes: the marquis de Ferrières, who corresponded regularly with his wife over the administration of their various lands in Poitou, or the rough-hewn marquis de Foucauld de Lardimalie—"this wild boar from Périgord," as Mirabeau called him—whose fortune amounted to 600,000 *livres*, yielding revenues of perhaps 30,000 per year.[68] In a sample of thirty provincial nobles located in the tax rolls, three-fourths ranked in the upper one-third of all nobles by income, and all of the remainder were in the middle one-third.[69] Though inferior in their fortunes to the Parisian nobles, the provincial deputies of the Second Estate all had comfortable revenues, and most were quite wealthy.

The precise functions and activities pursued by these nobles before the Revolution, the manner in which they actually spent their days, is not always simple to determine from the array of official and honorific titles which they listed after their names. Only a small number could be described

---

la Drôme 76 (1964), 74–75. On the prosperous provincial nobility, see Robert Forster, *The Nobility of Toulouse in the Eighteenth Century* (Baltimore, 1960).

[64] See above, note 54.

[65] F. Grandgérard, *Le bon vieux temps. Histoire d'un village franc-comtois* (Mercey-sur-Saône, 1911), 262–83; Paul Montarlot, "Les députés de Saône-et-Loire aux assemblées de la Révolution, 1789–99," *Mémoires de la société éduenne*, n. sér., 31 (1903), 347.

[66] La Bévière, esp. letters of Apr. 28, May 16, Nov. 9, 1789.

[67] François-Dominique de Reynaud de Montlosier, *Mémoires*, 2 vols. (Paris, 1830).

[68] Charles-Elie de Ferrières, *Correspondance inédite*, ed. Henri Carré (Paris, 1932); F. Bussière, "Le constituant Foucauld de Lardimalie," *RF* 22 (1892), 214.

[69] Nine had incomes higher than 90 to 99% of the nobles in their respective provinces; 7 were higher than 80 to 89%; 6 were higher than 70 to 79%; 5 were higher than 50 to 59%; 2 were higher than 40 to 49%; and 1 was higher than 30 to 39%: A.N., P 5170, 5298bis, 5557, 5765, 5105bis, 5269, 5392, 5591 (généralités of Bordeaux, Châlons-sur-Marne, Moulins, Rouen, Amiens, Caen, Grenoble, and Orléans).

as robe nobles: magistrates trained in the law and attached to the royal court system. In all, only thirty-eight—one-eighth of the total—exercised such professions, twenty-three in the various sovereign courts or parlements and fifteen others in lower royal courts, primarily at the bailliage level.[70] Several of the magistrates from the Parlement of Paris—especially Adrien Duport, Fréteau de Saint-Just, Le Peletier de Saint-Fargeau, and Duval d'Eprémesnil—were among the most active speakers in National Assembly debates.[71] Yet their reduced numbers left them little real influence as a corps—a dramatic turnabout from the power they had wielded in the last decades of the Old Regime. Equally noteworthy was the near absence of noble deputies attached to the royal ministries and the administrative hierarchy. The intendants and the influential *maîtres de requêtes* had been entirely shunned by the electorate of the Second Estate. The sole representative of the provincial administrative elite was the newly ennobled Rancourt de Villiers, subdelegate of Gien—who had in fact resigned his post shortly before the elections.[72] Otherwise, of those linked to the executive branch of the monarchy, there was only the baron de Wimpffen, onetime associate of the war minister Saint-Germain; the marquis d'Aguesseau, a titular "state counselor"; and four or five others who had been attached to foreign embassies in formal or informal capacities.[73]

The overwhelming majority of the Second Estate in 1789 were neither judges nor bureaucrats nor courtesans nor rural lords, but soldiers. At least four-fifths of the total had pursued careers as officers in the military.[74] In most cases, they were linked to the infantry or the cavalry. Only twenty-seven of the total had qualified, through competitive examinations, for the more elite forces of the navy, the artillery, or the corps of engineers. Though some would emerge as talented military figures, most had obtained their positions through the standard levers of influence and patronage. In fact, with an average age of about forty-six in 1789, the majority had already left active service, and had married and begun families. A certain number—and we shall examine them more carefully in the next chapter—passed all or much of their time in the pursuit of letters. Many of these—the comte d'Antraigues, the marquis de Ferrières, the marquis de Lézay-Marnésia, the vicomte de Toulongeon, for example—are known to have thoroughly detested military life and to have resigned as early as possible.[75]

[70] A few others had originated in robe families, but were pursuing careers in the military: e.g., Henri-Jean-Baptiste Bousmard de Chantraine and Gaspard-Claude-François de Chabrol.

[71] The small group of robe nobles spoke more frequently per individual than any other subgroup in the Assembly: see below, chap. 7.

[72] Brette, *Recueil*, 2:283.

[73] Fichier Lefebvre and *DC*.

[74] Of the total of 322, 259 (80%) are known to have held commissions in the armed forces. See also David Bien, "La réaction aristocratique avant 1789: l'exemple de l'armée," *Annales.E.S.C.* 29 (1974), 532.

[75] Fichier Lefebvre; L. Pingaud, *Un agent secret sous la Révolution et l'Empire* (Paris, 1893), 16; H. Carré, "Introduction," to Ferrières, *Correspondance*, 1–3; Michaud, 24:439.

Others, like the comte de Langhac, the marquis de Panat, or the comte de Clermont-Tonnerre, may have only gone through the motions of military service, spending most of their time on leave and returning to their troops only for ceremonial reviews and parades.[76]

Yet at least seventy-five of the Nobles—and probably more—had served during wartime, and many remained full-time soldiers in 1789.[77] The comte de Custine had entered the infantry at the age of eight and had fought in three wars, including service under the maréchal de Saxe. Both the marquis d'Ambly, another *aide* to de Saxe, and Wolter de Neuerbourg, had been in all wars since 1740. The comte de Gomer, who had participated in thirteen campaigns since the 1730s, was director of a school of artillery and author of several important works on the subject. The marquis de Toulongeon, the comte de Toulouse-Lautrec, the comte de La Marck, and the marquis d'Usson had all been seriously wounded in battle. Toulouse-Lautrec continued to limp in the Assembly, while Usson walked with an artificial leg.[78] Nompère de Champagny had never been wounded, but his life in the navy had strongly marked his personality: "After so many years spent at sea, I acquired a certain roughness of manners, the inevitable consequence of the life I had led."[79] Though there had been no French fighting in Europe during the quarter century prior to 1789, a number of the younger deputies had known action in Senegal or India, and no less than nineteen had fought in America or the surrounding waters during the Revolutionary War—fifteen in the army and four in the navy. The duc de Biron, the vicomte de Noailles, the comte de Custine, the comte de Lameth, and the marquis de Saint-Simon had all distinguished themselves in the Battle of Yorktown.[80]

Even among those who had never known the fire of battle, however, the military experience had left a deep impression on their lives. On several occasions in his letters, Garron de La Bévière recalled the years of his mili-

---

[76] Fichier Lefebvre; and Charles Du Bus, *Stanislas de Clermont-Tonnerre et l'échec de la Révolution monarchique, 1757–92* (Paris, 1931), 19–21.

[77] Figures on the noble war veterans are based primarily on the Fichier Lefebvre.

[78] Fichier Lefebvre; Brette, *Recueil*, 2:317; Stéphane Leroy, "Le Marquis d'Ambly, député aux Etats-généraux," *RF* 29 (1895), 437–39, and 445; Georges Lepreux, *Nos représentants pendant la Révolution (1789–99)* (Lille, 1898), 63.

[79] Cited in F. de Champagny, *Une famille d'autrefois* (Paris, 1874), 15.

[80] Among those known to have been in the Americas at the time of the Revolutionary War, are the vicomte de Beauharnais, the duc de Biron, the prince de Broglie, the duc de Castrie, the comte de Custine, the comte de Dillon, the marquis de Lafayette, the marquis de La Poype-Vertrieux (navy), the comte de La Touche (navy), the comte de Lameth, the chevalier de Lameth, Thibault de Ménonville, the vicomte de Mirabeau, the comte de Montmorency (following his father at age 15), the vicomte de Noailles, Nompère de Champagny (navy), the comte de Reynaud, Henri de Rochegude (navy), and the marquis de Rostaing. In addition, the commoner deputies Dabadie and Laborde de Méréville (navy), and the Noble suppléants, the comte de Ségur, the comte Boson de Talleyrand, and Chabannes de la Palice all participated. The list is taken from the Fichier Lefebvre and from Gilbert Bodinier, *Les officiers de l'armée royale combattants de la Guerre d'indépendance des Etats-Unis* (Vincennes, 1983), 383–87.

tary service in Metz and the strong sense of camaraderie which he felt for fellow soldiers and officers whom he met again in the Estates General.[81] Most of the deputies had entered service while still adolescents, after only the rudiments of secondary schooling. Indeed, by comparison with the deputies of the Clergy and the Third-Estate, those of the Nobility had certainly experienced fewer years of formal education. Among our deputy witnesses, Malartic had entered the army at eighteen, after having begun a career in the clergy; and Ferrières joined at seventeen on completion of the *collège* of La Flèche. Yet the comte de La Gallissonnière was already fighting in Canada in his mid-teens; Banyuls de Montferré embraced the military at fifteen; Antraigues, Virieux, Nompère, and Lafayette at fourteen; Gauville became a page at thirteen; and Biron, the comte de Lablache, and Lézay-Marnésia were enrolled at age twelve.[82]

We know little of the daily activities of such adolescent nobles living in the military. But with the exception of the handful joining the artillery or the corps of engineers, their instruction invariably placed a premium on martial skills over intellectual pursuits. Some would, of course, compensate for such deficiencies through tutors and private reading and a few would even go on to pursue literary careers. Yet the experience of Cazalès, who struggled for years reading in the barracks to remedy his dismal education, must not have been atypical. Another veteran, Achard de Bonvouloir, complained bitterly in early 1789 of his difficulties in defending the nobility against the attacks of the Third Estate: "My ideas are often sound and broadly conceived, but for lack of education, I have difficulty developing them."[83] Indeed, Lézay-Marnésia issued a general indictment against the inadequacies of noble education. Noble officers, "whose childhood formation is generally neglected, enter military service without education and leave without ever having acquired any."[84] Even if a minority of deputies had revolted against military values, the critical formative years spent in the armed forces, from the mid-teens to the early twenties, invariably had an impact. Training in swordplay and horsemanship, in military discipline, in the ideals of honor, hierarchical command, and devotion to the king, all left a stamp that would clearly distinguish the corps of the Second Estate from their colleagues in the Commons. It was an influence that would strongly affect many members of the Nobility in their fundamental assumptions about the nature of society and social relationships—despite the common

[81] La Bévière, letters of May 3 and 16, and Oct. 29, 1789.

[82] Fichier Lefebvre and the *DC*.

[83] Michaud, 7:284; Luc-René-Charles Achard de Bonvouloir to the marquis de Ségrie: A.D. Calvados, C 8582, letter of Jan. 11. Cf. also Henri Carré, *La noblesse de France et l'opinion publique au XVIII siècle* (Paris, 1920), 199–207; and Mark Motley, *Becoming an Aristocrat: The Education of the Court Nobility, 1580–1715* (Princeton, 1990), esp. 102–3.

[84] Claude-François-Adrien, comte de Lézay-Marnésia, *Le bonheur* (1785), 46–47. Cf. Chaussinand-Nogaret, 109.

veneer of eighteenth-century urban culture which touched both Nobles and Commoners.

Compared to the nobles in France as a whole in 1789, the deputies sent to the Estates General were in many respects remarkably homogeneous. As we have seen, the great majority were sword nobles of ancient lineage residing in Paris or the major provincial towns. To be sure, the order would rapidly split over political issues in the Estates General. A small minority—a minority that became even smaller in the course of the Constituent Assembly—would enthusiastically embrace a new value system and the political position of the Third Estate. But in our understanding and assessment of the great majority of the Nobility who would soon face off with the Third Estate, and in our understanding of the Third's image of that Nobility, it is essential to remember that they were, before all else, a corps of extremely wealthy, aristocratic soldiers.

THE THIRD ESTATE

If the Nobility was dominated by a military aristocracy, the Third Estate was marked above all by the legal profession.[85] The single largest occupational category in the Third Estate—and the third largest in the three estates after the military officers and the curés—was that of the 218 magistrates.[86] Of these, nine sat in the "sovereign courts" of the parlements or the *conseils supérieurs*, and forty-nine in the lower royal courts or other specialized or local jurisdictions.[87] All of the remaining judges—three-fourths of the total—held positions in the middle-level royal courts of the bailliages and sénéchaussées. The fact that these jurisdictions formed the basic organizational units for the elections of 1789 probably helped thrust their occupants into positions of prominence. Indeed, no less than fifty deputies were chosen from among the chief magistrates of these courts, the presiding officials at the electoral assemblies. Yet it is also true that judges such as these

[85] Among previous studies of the professions of Third Estate deputies, see above, note 1 and Harriet Applewhite, *Political Alignment in the French National Assembly, 1789–1791* (Baton Rouge, La., 1993), 42–43. The determination of deputies' occupations is complicated in that many deputies had multiple professions. I have attempted to use a variety of bibliographic notices to determine a "principal" occupation or activity on the eve of the Revolution for each deputy.

[86] I follow Philip Dawson in grouping the *procureurs du roi*, and *avocats du roi* with the judges per se (*lieutenants, conseillers*, etc.) as members of the magistry: *Baillage Magistrates and Revolutionary Politics* (Cambridge, Mass., 1972), 30. Within the Third Estate there was a total of 151 judges of various kinds, 45 *procureurs du roi*, and 22 *avocats du roi*.

[87] Sixteen were from *prévôté-viguerie-châtellenie* level courts; 22 from courts of the *eaux et forêts, greniers à sel, élections*, or *traites*; and 11 from municipal, seigneurial, or ecclesiastical courts. Including the 23 *parlementaires* who sat in the Nobles, and the 3 *conseillers clercs* in the Clergy, there was a total parlementary representation of 35—not quite 3% of the entire National Assembly.

were frequently the wealthiest and most prestigious commoners in the smaller provincial towns where the elections transpired.[88]

The second largest subgroup of Third deputies with legal training, 181 strong, consisted of those calling themselves "lawyers."[89] In fact, this designation covered an assortment of rather different social realities. For some of the "lawyers" in question, the title seems to have been little more than a status symbol, acquired primarily for its prestige value.[90] Thus Duquesnoy, Sieyès de La Baume, Laziroule, Ducellier, and a number of others were principally engaged in supervising the cultivation of their lands. Verdollin, Merle, and Mougins de Roquefort may have practiced in the past, but by 1789 they were entirely involved in municipal politics. Bergasse, Delandine, Démeunier, and Dominique-Joseph Garat were all essentially men of letters who rarely or never practiced law.[91] Many others, however, are known to have been full-time consulting or trial lawyers with substantial clienteles and important regional or national reputations. Jean-Guy-Baptiste Target, who had pleaded in several celebrated cases in Paris since the 1760s, was said to have been "the most sought-after lawyer of his age"; Dominique Garat— the elder brother of Dominique-Joseph—had much the same reputation in Bordeaux and was described as "one of the shining figures of the bar"; Armand-Gaston Camus and Pierre-Toussaint Durand de Maillane were specialists in canon law of national and even international stature. And a great many others—like Tronchet in Paris, Merlin in Douai, Reubell in Colmar, Gaultier de Biauzat in Clermont-Ferrand, Vernier in Lons-le-Saunier, Poncet-Delpech in Montauban, Regnier in Nancy, Jean-Denis Blanc in Besançon, or Pétion de Villeneuve in Chartres—were local lawyers of considerable repute.[92] As we shall see, many of these men were also among the most distinguished scholars and writers in the National Assembly.[93]

In all then, and including an additional thirty-nine minor royal officials— most of whom were notaries—at least two-thirds of the Commoner deputies had probably received training in the law.[94] The precise nature of this educational experience is difficult to determine and probably varied substantially, particularly since law studies in some of the universities were notoriously lax. Yet all of the deputies in question must have completed the full cycle of secondary education—unlike the great majority of the Nobles—and

[88] See Dawson, 186–89.

[89] I include here all those known to have used the title *avocats*, even those who never actually practiced law. See below.

[90] Lenard R. Berlanstein, *The Barristers of Toulouse in the Eighteenth Century, 1740–1793* (Baltimore, 1975), 11, 16; Michael Fitzsimmons, *The Parisian Order of Barristers and the French Revolution* (Cambridge, Mass., 1987), 9–10; and David A. Bell, *Lawyers and Citizens: The Making of a Political Elite in Old Regime France* (Oxford, 1994), 31–32.

[91] Information from a wide variety of sources, particularly the Fichier Lefebvre.

[92] Fichier Lefebvre; Michel Etcheverry, "Le rôle politique de Dominique Garat," *Bulletin de la Société des sciences, lettres, arts, et études régionales de Bayonne*, nouv. sér., no. 5 (1930), 72.

[93] See below, chap. 2.

[94] 438 (66%) of the 663 Third Estate deputies serving at any time during the Assembly.

most had undoubtedly pursued some form of university studies and professional apprenticeship related to the law.[95] A legal turn of mind would be
one of the most characteristic features of the culture of the Third Estate.

Training in the law was also the dominant form of preparation for the
twenty-two members of the Commons who were presently or who had
once been attached to the royal bureaucracy. No less than fifteen of these
were subdelegates to the provincial intendants—often combining the post
with continued activities as lawyer or judge.[96] Nine others had held much
higher positions, involving close contact with the royal ministers. Charles-
François Lebrun had been a key associate of the chancellor Maupeou.
Pierre-Victor Malouet and Charles-Claude Monneron—the oldest of three
brothers in the Assembly—had made careers in the colonies and had attained the title of "intendant." Pierre-Hubert Anson, Michel d'Ailly, Jean-
Baptiste Treilhard, and Pierre-Samuel Dupont de Nemours had all achieved
high positions in the finance ministry, the first as a protégé of the Ormesson
family, the last three as assistants to Turgot. Target and Louis-Simon Martineau had sat in chancellor Lamoignon's *Conseil de législation* in 1787 and
1788. Significantly, all nine were out of power at the time of their election
in 1789.[97] It was a measure of the general disrespect for the representatives
of "ministerial despotism," so widely decried on the eve of the Revolution,
that Malouet felt obliged to resign his intendancy of the navy in Toulon
before presenting his candidacy in his home town of Riom.[98] Yet all of these
men would bring an important store of administrative experience to the
Assembly and many would play significant roles in the formulation of legislation under the Constituent. Indeed, the argument can be made that the
deputies of the Third possessed as much, if not more, practical experience in
government and administration than the soldier-aristocrats who sat in the
Nobility.[99]

The remaining one-third of the Commoners represented widely diverse
sectors of society. Among the most highly educated were the twenty-one
medical doctors, the sixteen full-time or part-time professors, and the handful of professional men of letters.[100] Another one hundred or so represented
the various commercial classes.[101] The wealthy wholesale merchants or "négociants" proved only marginally successful in electoral competition with

[95] Fitzsimmons, 4–6; and David A. Bell, "Lawyers into Demagogues: Chancellor Maupeou
and the Transformation of Legal Practice in France, 1771–1789," *Past and Present* 130 (Feb.
1991), 112.

[96] Eleven of the 15 have been included above with the lawyers or office holders.

[97] Fichier Lefebvre and the *DC*; also Bell, *Lawyers and Citizens*, 181.

[98] Pierre-Victor Malouet, *Mémoires*, 2 vols., ed. Baron Malouet (Paris, 1868), 1:214–15.

[99] See also below, chap. 3.

[100] Among the professors, 10 taught or had taught law, 4 medicine or botany, 1 history, and
1 general secondary school. The only Noble known to have held such a post was the comte de
Gomer, who directed a school of artillery. On men of letters, see chap. 2.

[101] A total of 99. An additional 8 "merchants" or "*négociants*" residing in villages were almost
certainly grain or livestock merchants and have been included with the agricultural groups.

the lawyers and judges, despite their considerable political organization through the chambers of commerce. In the end, they succeeded in sending only sixty delegates, a mere seventeen of whom resided in the great port cities.[102] Also to be included in a potential commercial caucus were fourteen merchant-tradesmen, seven bankers or related professionals, and twenty-two individuals engaged in various aspects of manufacturing.[103] Though two of the latter, Pierre-Nicolas de Fontenay and Jean-Baptiste de Crétot from the bailliage of Rouen, were actively pursuing mechanized textile manufacturing in imitation of the English, the majority directed enterprises with traditional organizations and technologies, like iron forging, silk spinning, ship building, and glass manufacturing. On the other hand, the even more humble artisans and shopkeepers were altogether absent from the Assembly. The future sans-culottes of Paris and the provinces were conspicuously unrepresented. As "revisionist" historians have frequently noted, the representatives of commercial and industrial capitalism constituted scarcely a sixth of the Third Estate, a twelfth of the National Assembly as a whole.[104]

The final 10 or 11 percent of the deputies can be associated with various agriculturally related occupations. Some of these—particularly those calling themselves "bourgeois" or "property holders"—actually dwelled in the towns and lived off incomes from rural landholdings which they rarely if ever visited. Those genuinely residing in the countryside and pursuing agriculture as a full-time occupation amounted to only forty-three land-owning or lease-holding farmers, rural "merchants," and wine-growers.[105] In one of his early letters, Maximilien Robespierre noted the difficulties and prejudices which he and his friends had faced when they pushed the choice of four "farmers" in the electoral assemblies of Arras.[106] To judge from the election results, such prejudices may have been widespread. Among those who did win election, none seem to have been lower in society than those calling themselves "laboureurs," a designation generally indicating wealthy and largely independent farmers. As there were no true artisans or shopkeepers, neither were there any representatives of the great mass of the small and middling peasantry.

But while only a small minority of the deputies considered agriculture to be their principal profession, a large proportion undoubtedly owned land,

[102] J. Letaconnoux, "Le comité des députés extraordinaires des manufactures et du commerce de France et l'oeuvre économique de l'Assemblée constituante," *AR* 6 (1913), 151–53. Marseille sent 5; Bordeaux, Rouen, Lyon, and Nantes 2 each; Brest, Le Havre, Lorient, and Saint-Malo one each.

[103] I have classed as "merchant-tradesmen" the 3 booksellers/printers, 2 goldsmiths, 1 tanner, and 1 druggist.

[104] See, notably, Cobban, 100; and William Doyle, *The Origins of the French Revolution* (Oxford, 1980), 154–55.

[105] The terms *laboureur, cultivateur, propriétaire,* and even *marchand* and *négociant* were used almost interchangeably by certain of the rural deputies.

[106] Maximilien Robespierre, *Correspondance,* ed. Georges Michon (Paris, 1926), 40 (letter to Buissart, May 24, 1789).

with investments ranging from small plots and vineyards just outside the walls to country houses, entire farms, or even seigneurial estates. Land remained one of the central measures of status in Old Regime society, and a great many Third deputies, as we shall see, belonged to long-established provincial families who had accumulated land holdings over generations. The letters of several of our deputy witnesses to wives and family—those of Doctor Campmas, the lawyer Bouchette, or the judge Ménard de La Groye, for example—commonly interspersed descriptions of Revolutionary events with instructions concerning planting, harvesting, and relations with renters or sharecroppers.[107] The magistrates Creuzé-Latouche, Basquiat de Mugriet, and Gontier de Biran, and the lawyer Visme were all passionately interested in agriculture and pursued and wrote about the latest approaches to scientific agronomy.[108] It is in this sense, no doubt, that the vicomte de Mirabeau would declare "this Assembly is composed entirely of farmers, judges, and military men."[109] It is also in this sense, in the deputies' possession of proprietary wealth, in their tight relation to the agricultural mode of production, that some historians have closely linked the elites of the Third Estate to the Nobility, describing them as members of the same economic group or "class."[110]

Nevertheless, in the absolute *amount* of their wealth, as opposed to the *forms* of that wealth, the deputies of the Third Estate differed enormously from those of the Nobility. An indication of that difference is provided by the deputies' marriage contracts.[111] While sentiment was perhaps becoming more important in the choice of partners in the eighteenth century, marriage remained preeminently an economic arrangement entered into by two families. Thus, the nuptial market and the dowries which the two parties

---

[107] E.g., Campmas, letter of July 17–18, 1790; Bouchette, 247 (letter of Aug. 23, 1789); François-René-Pierre Ménard de La Groye to his wife: A.D. Sarthe: 10 J 122.

[108] Marcel Marion, "Un révolutionnaire très conservateur: Creuzé-Latouche," *Revue d'histoire moderne* 11 (1936), 102; Gabriel Cabannès, *Galérie des landais: Les parlementaires*, 2 vols. (Mont-de-Marsan, 1930), 1:20–21; Elie de Biran, *Notice sur G. Gontier de Biran, député de la Sénéchaussée du Périgord aux Etats-Généraux de 1789* (Périgueux, 1879), 7; and Fichier Lefebvre.

[109] *A.P.*, 8:497 (Aug. 27, 1789).

[110] See, George V. Taylor, "Non-capitalist Wealth and the Origins of the French Revolution," *AHR* 72 (1967), 469–96; and William Doyle, *The Ancien Régime* (Atlantic Highlands, N.J., 1986), 25–26.

[111] See Appendix I. Most marriage contracts have been located in the alphabetical tables of the *contrôle des actes*, using the marriage dates furnished by the *DC*. The sample is taken from A.D. Aube, Bouches-du-Rhône, Côte-d'Or, Loire-Atlantique, Lot, Maine-et-Loire, Haute-Marne, Rhône, Saône-et-Loire, Sarthe, Seine-Maritime, and Deux-Sèvres. In most cases, I have been able to determine only the bride's dowry, so that the analysis presented here must be based on this alone. Dowry values have been standardized for inflation using the curve of grain prices, where the price levels of 1787 are adopted as a base: Ernest Labrousse, *La crise de l'économie française à la fin de l'Ancien régime et au début de la Révolution* (Paris, 1944), 625. On the use of marriage contracts, see Adeline Daumard and François Furet, *Structures et relations sociales à Paris au XVIIIe siècle* (Paris, 1961); and Maurice Garden, *Lyon et les Lyonnais au XVIIIe siècle* (Paris, 1970), 213–23.

brought to their marriage contracts can be a sensitive indicator of the subtle variations in family wealth and status. The evidence of a sample of forty-three such documents suggests that a few of the Commoners ranked near the pinnacle of society in their levels of wealth. This was surely the case of Begouën-Demeaux, the great shipper and importer from Le Havre; of Le Couteulx de Canteleu, banker from Rouen; and of Charles-François Lebrun, landowner and former assistant to Maupeou—all of whom were recently ennobled, and all of whom made fabulous marriages, with several hundred thousand *livres* contributed by their future wives' families. The other dowries, however—representing over 90 percent of the sample—ranged from a few thousand *livres* for small provincial farmers or office-holders or lawyers to sixty or seventy thousand for certain of the merchants and magistrates. Excluding the three "outliers," our commoner deputies received an average of about 26,500 *livres*.[112] Unfortunately, the marriage contracts of the noble deputies are much more difficult to locate. Yet our sample of fourteen dowries includes a wide range of individuals, from modest provincial nobles to great court aristocrats living in Paris and Versailles. While there is some overlap with Third dowries, by and large the Nobles' marriages had been immensely more lucrative, averaging over 400,000 *livres*, some fifteen times larger than the average for the Third.[113]

Though yearly incomes themselves are notoriously difficult to determine under the Old Regime, the biographies of certain individual deputies provide us with an order of magnitude for a small sample of thirty-nine Constituents within the Second and Third Estates.[114] Not surprisingly, both estates contained a considerable spread of incomes, a spread that obviously overlapped between the wealthiest commoners and the more modest members of the Nobility. The commoner administrator of a great duchy in western France (Maupetit), the owner of a plantation in Saint-Domingue (Gérard), and the former assistant to a royal minister (Anson) could all claim incomes equal or superior to the wealthier—if not the wealthiest—members of the Second Estate. Yet clearly men such as these did not constitute the norm within the Third Estate. The median income within our sample was only about 7,000 *livres* per year.[115] By contrast, the revenues of a sample of the noble deputies ranged from about 10,000 *livres* for a modest rural seigneur to several hundred thousand for the great Parisian nobility, with a median over eight times that of the commoners, and a mean nearly fifteen

---

[112] Including the outliers, the average was 56,927 *livres*.

[113] The average Noble dowry was 406,712 *livres*, falling to 358,771 if we exclude the dowry of the Prince de Poix, valued at well over a million *livres*. A large proportion of the noble contracts were drawn up in Paris or Versailles. I have usually been unable to locate these.

[114] See appendix II. While most estimates seem to involve gross incomes, the nature of the calculations is not always clear.

[115] The median is 7,200 *livres*. The mean is 19,190, but excluding the "outliers" Maupetit, Gérard, and Anson, it is 8,570.

times greater.[116] Such revenues were enormous, by any measure, and would have permitted most noble deputies a strikingly superior standard of living, with elegant residences and clothing, coaches, and dozens of livried servants—all quite out of the reach of the typical Third Estate deputy. Whatever their theoretical relationship to the means of production, most of the commoner deputies lived in a substantially different economic universe than their colleagues of the Nobility.

Without a doubt, the most problematic category in the Third Estate was that of the lawyers. While the dowries obtained by the magistrates were very near the average for the order, and while those received by merchants and bankers were 10,000 *livres* higher, those for the lawyers among the deputies were 8,000 below the average.[117] Well-established individuals like Thouret, Merlin, or Reubell, and those with regular retainers from wealthy individuals or corporate bodies—such as Target, Treilhard, and Camus— lived very comfortable lives, with agreeable town houses and considerable land holdings. Merlin was said to have earned between 15,000 and 16,000 *livres* per year from cases alone and to have assembled enough capital to purchase a title of nobility.[118] Lesser-known provincial lawyers, like Boulouvard of Arles and Thibaudeau of Poitiers might take in a relatively decent four to six thousand *livres* per year.[119] Yet others, at the beginning of their careers or with a lack of family inheritance, were situated at a distinctly more modest position in the wealth hierarchy: Pierre-Louis Prieur, for example (said to have earned a mere 1,700 *livres* per year before the Revolution), or François-Nicolas Buzot (who, with a relatively meager dowry, had to borrow money to set up his household), or Robespierre (who had little or no property and had to live with relatives while he practiced law).[120] Jean de Turckheim, a noble by birth who sat with the Third Estate, spoke with scorn of "these lawyers . . . whose only possession is their talent for speaking."[121]

Though the latter deputies received revenues well above the average income for French citizens as a whole, they could probably be classed at the lower end of the economic scale among the Third Estate deputies, along

---

[116] The mean is 127,324 *livres*; the median, 60,000.

[117] The average dowry for the magistrates was 27,664 *livres*; that of the merchants and bankers, 36,770; and that of the lawyers, 18,635.

[118] Ernest Lebègue, *La vie et l'oeuvre d'un Constituant: Thouret* (Paris, 1910), 312–14; Gerlof D. Homan, *Jean-François Reubell: French Revolutionary, Patriot, and Director* (The Hague, 1971), 12–14; L. Gruffy, *La Vie et l'oeuvre juridique de Merlin de Douai* (Paris, 1934), 12–13; Fitzsimmons, 20.

[119] Pierre-Siffren Boulouvard to the municipality of Arles: A.C. Arles, AA 23: letter of Oct. 9, 1789; Antoine-Claire Thibaudeau, *Biographie, mémoires, 1765–92* (Paris, 1875), 63.

[120] Gustave Laurent, ed., *Notes et souvenirs inédits de Prieur de la Marne*, (Paris, 1912), 46– 48; Jacque Hérissay, *Un Girondin, François Buzot* (Paris, 1907), 22; J. M. Thompson, *Robespierre*, 2 vols. (Oxford, 1953), 1:17.

[121] Rodolphe Reuss, ed., *L'Alsace pendant la Révolution française*, 2 vols. (Paris, 1880–94), 1:259.

with many of the notaries, minor officeholders, and the rural *laboureurs*. The young deputy Jean-François Goupilleau was the newest of several notaries in Montaigu and was reputedly "almost penniless." The "farmer" and sometime tanner Jean François of the village of Marsac near the Garonne River worked on his uncle's lands and had a personal income of three to four thousand *livres* in *rentes*, but also extensive debts. In Versailles and Paris, he was able to live a simple if not disagreeable existence, and with careful budgeting he could save up enough to send souvenirs—a book and a pair of earrings—to his sixteen-year-old daughter.[122] The Flemish farmer Lepoutre was undoubtedly well-off by comparison with the peasantry of his home village. But the letters to his wife make it clear that his children were expected to labor in the fields with the hired hands, that his daughters were sent out as servants, and that the total expenses of his deputation to Versailles caused serious shortages of capital for the exploitation of his farm. He waited anxiously for the arrival of the salaries which the Constituent promised its members, and he even sought to supplement his income by bringing down a supply of linen cloth and a small herd of sheep for sale in Paris.[123] It is worth noting in passing that all of the more marginal Third deputies mentioned here—Robespierre, Prieur, Buzot, François, Goupilleau, and Lepoutre—would sit with the most radical section of the National Assembly.[124] Yet in economic terms they also constituted a minority within their estate.

There were a number of cases of spectacular social mobility among the Third deputies. Dupont de Nemours was the child prodigy son of a Protestant clockmaker who had risen by his wits and charm to become private secretary to Turgot and semiofficial adviser to Vergennes and Calonne. Perhaps even more meteoric was the career of Lebrun who rose from a modest landowning family in Normandy to become the chancellor's chief assistant. Philippe-Antoine Merlin, another son of a *cultivateur*, won fame and ennoblement as a brilliant lawyer and legal theorist. Jean-Nicolas Démeunier, a well-known author in Paris, was the son of an illiterate cloth merchant in rural Franche-Comté. While each of these four moved up primarily through his learning and brilliance, the wig-maker's son, Marc-Antoine Lavie, first made his fortune in Saint-Domingue—apparently bluffing his way into colonial society with dubious credentials as a "doctor," before returning to his native Alsace to become a large landowner.[125] In fact, Lavie was one of a number of Third Estate deputies—like Louis-Jean Pélerin de La Buxière,

[122] Charles Dugast-Matifeu, *Notice sur Goupilleau de Fontenay* (Nantes, 1845), 5–6; G. de Lagrange-Ferrègues, "Jean François, député de l'Assemblée nationale de 1789," *Revue de l'Agenais* 83 (1957), 229–33, 238, 251.

[123] Pierre-François Lepoutre to his wife: family archives of Adolphe Lepoutre-Dubreuil, Montignac-sur-Vezère, letters of Aug. 16 and Sept. 6, 1789, and Nov. 16, 1790.

[124] See below, chap. 8.

[125] Ambrose Saricks, *Pierre Samuel Du Pont de Nemours* (Lawrence, Kan., 1965), chap. 1; Michaud, 23:488–89; Edna Hindie Lemay, "Naissance de l'anthropologie sociale en France: Jean-Nicolas Démeunier et 'L'Esprit des usages et des coutumes' au XVIIIe siècle" (Thèse du 3e cycle, Paris, E.H.E.S.S., 1974), 8–37; Gruffy, 9–13; Fichier Lefebvre.

Jean Payen de Boisneuf, Samuel-Pierre-Isaac Garesché, and the three Monneron brothers—who had made their fortunes in the colonies before returning to landed estates or to new careers in the metropole.[126]

Without traveling half way around the world, other deputies had been able to advance their careers by moving away from their home towns and establishing themselves in larger French cities. In addition to Lebrun and Démeunier, mentioned above, Doctor Guillotin, the notary Dosfant, and the lawyers Hutteau, Martineau, Treilhard, and Lenoir de La Roche had all moved to Paris to make their fortunes. Pierre Roussillou had left his native Pyrenees to become a merchant in Toulouse; Bernard Gros found his way from a village in Burgundy to the coastal town of Boulogne; Joseph Delaville Le Roulx moved from central France by way of Amsterdam to become a merchant in Lorient; and Marie-André Merle, raised in Lons-le-Saunier, married into the power structure in Mâcon where he became a successful lawyer and eventually mayor.[127] In the context of Old Regime society, it was all the more remarkable that such "outsiders" were able to attain elections as representatives of their adopted towns.

But cases such as these were clearly exceptions. Perhaps a fifth of the Third deputies had precisely the same professions in precisely the same towns as their fathers and some three-fifths held positions that were more or less at the same level of status as that of their immediate families.[128] The two-fifths who may have moved upward in their own lifetimes had almost all done so by small, one-step increments, and they probably represented about the same proportion of upwardly mobile careers as one might have found in any group of provincial elite commoners.[129] Indeed, to judge by the scattering of deputies for which extended family histories are known, a substantial number must have come from family milieus which had remained stable over generations. Among our deputy witnesses, the Campmas family, residing in or near Albi, had produced medical doctors from father to son since the early seventeenth century. The family of Gontier de Biran had dominated Bergerac society for at least as long, filling spots as judges, mayors, subdelegates, and curés. And much the same could be said of

[126] Fichier Lefebvre.

[127] Fichier Lefebvre and the *DC*.

[128] Based on a sample study of 164 deputies. The sample consisted of all our "principal witnesses" among the Third deputies and all others whose names began with A, B, or L for whom family professions could be ascertained in the Fichier Lefebvre. For the sake of the comparison, I considered as "socially mobile" only those making obvious status jumps. A rough professional hierarchy was established with magistrates above lawyers above notaries; *négociants* above *marchands* above artisan/shopkeepers; and all but artisan/shopkeepers above *laboureurs/cultivateurs*. Ennoblement or a move from a village to a larger town were also considered factors relevant in upward mobility. By this method, 34 (21%) had precisely the same professions in the same towns, and 96 (59%) were more or less on the same level as their fathers.

[129] Upward social mobility was found in 61 of the 164 (37%) individuals in our sample. Cf. Dawson, 103–7; Berlanstein, 77.

the Basquiat de Mugriets in Saint-Sever, the Branches in Paulhaguet, the Turckheims in Strasbourg, the Roulhacs of Limoges, or the Couppés of Morlaix.[130]

Yet whether they represented upwardly mobile or relatively stable families, a substantial number of the individuals involved could be situated—by the standards and values of the Old Regime—on the very fringes of the nobility. In the electoral campaigns of 1789, some writers—including the future deputies Volney and Boislandry—had led efforts to prevent nobles from being chosen to seats in the Third Estate.[131] Many historians have assumed that, with a few notable exceptions such as Mirabeau, the Third was entirely composed of commoners.[132] In fact, a minimum of fifty-eight of the Third delegates could claim some degree of hereditary or personal nobility.[133] Though this was well below the 25 to 45 percent nobles in the Third Estate of 1614, it still represented close to one in twelve of the members of the Commons.[134] A handful of the deputies in question came from great and ancient families of the aristocracy: Mirabeau or the comte de Chambors or the marquis de Rostaing—who presided over the order of the Nobility in Montbrison before being elected by the Third of the same bailliage. All but seven of the Third nobles, however, were either recently ennobled, in the process of being ennobled, or in possession of various forms of "temporary" nobility. This list included men like the lawyers Merlin and Le Chapelier, the banker Le Couteulx de Canteleu, the paper manufacturer Riberolles, the colonial cotton merchant Begouën-Demeaux, the former intendant to the East Indies Monneron, and the chief judges Basquiat and Lasalle—whose

[130] Genealogical notes of Campmas family: B.M. Albi, ms. 177; B.M. Bergerac, dossier on genealogy of Gontier de Biran; Cabannès, 1:19–21; A. Fray-Fournier, *Notice biographique sur les députés de la Haute-Vienne aux assemblées législatives de la Révolution. I. L'Assemblée Constituante* (Limoges, 1893), 89–97; Xavier Lochmann, "Maurice Branche, de Paulhaguet, député à l'Assemblée constituante," *Almanach de Brioude* (1990) 199–238; Jules Keller, *Lili Schoenemann, baronne de Turckheim* (Bern, 1987), 36; René Kerviler, *Recherches et notices sur les députés de la Bretagne aux Etats-généraux*, 2 vols. (Rennes, 1889), entry for "Couppé."

[131] E.-B. Dubien, "Boislandry, député aux Etats-Généraux de 1789," *AHRF* 15 (1938), 349; Jean Gaulmier, *Un grand témoin de la Révolution et de l'Empire: Volney* (Paris, 1959), 74.

[132] E.g., A. Bouchard, *Le club Breton. Origine, composition, rôle à l'Assemblée constituante* (Paris, 1920), 17. Cf. Georges Lefebvre, *The Coming of the French Revolution* (Princeton, 1947), 67.

[133] Brette, *Recueil*, 2:616–19, supplemented by the Fichier Lefebvre and a wide variety of other biographies. As best I can determine, the following Third deputies held some form of nobility: Ailly, Alquier, Arraing, Basquiat, Begouën, Bernigaud, Bertrand de Montfort, the comte de Chambors, the comte Colonna de Césari-Roca, Cottin, Couppé, Darnaudat, Dubois-Crancé, Ducellier, Dufraisse, Dupont de Nemours, the baron de Flachslander, Fouquier, Gontier de Biran, Griffon de Romagné, Guilhermy, Guittard, Harmand, Hell, Hennet, Henry de Longuève, Henryot, Kérangon, Laborde, Lasalle, Laziroule, Charles-François Lebrun, Le Carlier, Le Chapelier, Le Couteulx, Le Deist, Lucas de Bourgerel, Merlin, the comte de Mirabeau, Charles-Claude Monneron, Mounier, Muguet, Naurissart, Pincipré de Buire, Raby de Saint-Médard, Raze, Repoux, Riberolles, Ricard de Séalt, Roederer, the marquis de Rostaing, Roulhac, Schwendt, Terrats, Tournyol-Duclos, Turckheim, Vaillant, and Vyau.

[134] Hayden, 96.

grandfather had been a wigmaker.[135] One deputy, Joseph-François-Simon Terrats of Perpignan obtained the final documents affirming his noble status only in the middle of May 1789, after the Estates General was already in progress.[136]

But even among the overwhelming majority who were not nobles, a significant number were closely linked to the nobility through their activities or lifestyles. At least sixteen had begun their careers with stints in the military—the profession *par excellence* of the aristocracy.[137] Many others had close ties to the nobles through family or marriage. The mothers of Barère, Dupont, and Barnave were nobles, and the latter's father possessed nonhereditary personal nobility. Barère, Redon, Regnaud de Saint-Jean d'Angély, Goupil de Préfelne, and at least a dozen others are known to have taken noble wives; while Quatrefages de Laroquete had married his daughter and Boulouvard his sister into noble families.[138] Though the lawyers Boissy d'Anglas and Thibaudeau were both of solid bourgeois stock, their occupations carried them into intimate contact with the nobility and Boissy even acquired the position of "maître d'hôtel" to the comte de Provence. Camus, who was the godson of the cardinal de Rohan, held retainers with the Clergy of France and the family of the prince de Salm-Salm; and Maupetit, who had known the duc de Liancourt as a schoolmate, was engaged as local agent for the duchy of Mayenne. Many others had open and unabashed pretensions of "living nobly" even if they could not claim full hereditary nobility.[139] The chief bailliage judge, Gontier de Biran, had established all four of his sons as officers in the elite *garde de corps du roi*. Ménard de La Groye and his family had "lived nobly" for generations, claimed distant links with the Norman aristocracy, and were widely accepted by local society as partaking of the nobility. Tailhardat de La Maisonneuve was born in a "château," married the sister of a nobleman, and owned a seigneurie, even

---

[135] Those nobles of older extraction in the Third Estate were the comte de Chambors, the comte de Colonna Roca, the baron de Flachslanden, Griffon de Romagné, the comte de Mirabeau, the marquis de Rostaing, and Turckheim. For sources, see above, note 49.

[136] Brette, *Recueil*, 2:312.

[137] Bizard, Branche, Dabadie, Dubois-Crancé, Frochot, Goupilleau, Guittard, Joüye Desroches, Laziroule, Le Bigot de Beauregard, Mortier, Paccard, Payan de Boisneuf, Pincipré de Buire, Vadier, and Vernier: Fichier Lefebvre, *DC*, and numerous other sources.

[138] E. D. Bradby, *The Life of Barnave*, 2 vols. (Oxford, 1915), 16–41; Leo Gershoy, *Bertrand Barère, the Reluctant Terrorist* (Princeton, 1962), 5, 32; François Rouvière, *Quatrefages de Laroquete* (Paris, 1886), 7–9; Octave Teissier, *Les députés de la Provence à l'Assemblée nationale de 1789* (Draguignan, 1898), 85; Fichier Lefebvre.

[139] Thibaudeau, 59–60; René Puaux, "Introduction" to François-Antoine Boissy d'Anglas, "Lettres inédites sur la Révolution française," *Bulletin de la Société de l'histoire du Protestantisme français* 75 (1926), 282–99; Michel-René Maupetit, "Lettres (1789–91)," ed. Quéruau-Lamérie, *Bulletin de la Commission historique et archéologique de la Mayenne*, 2ème sér., 18 (1902), 475 (letter of July 20, 1789); 19 (1903), 225 (letter of Aug. 8, 1789); 20 (1904), 118 (letter of Dec. 19, 1789); and Fichier Lefebvre.

though he had never attained the legal status of noble.[140] Indeed, at least thirty-two of the commoner deputies are known to have possessed seigneuries—and the number may have been substantially larger.[141]

With the exception of perhaps a hundred or so of the more modest younger lawyers, farmers, and small officeholders, the great majority of the Third Estate deputies were prosperous and successful men, men who had carved out comfortable niches for themselves within the confines of eighteenth-century society. Yet they were also clearly distinct and separate from the great aristocrats who dominated the Second Estate of 1789: distinct in their incomes and standard of living, distinct in their education and training in the law, distinct in their status within the value system of the Old Regime. A great many found themselves in a kind of "transitional category of indeterminate social mutants"—as Colin Lucas has termed it—somewhere between the nobility and the middle class, an intermediary group of newly ennobled or nearly ennobled, described by the Lyon deputy Périsse Du Luc as the "upper Third Estate."[142]

The very success of men such as these was a guarantee that most had learned to play by the rules of the game. Yet the condition of marginal men always involves a potential for frustration and tension, tension related as much to status as to economic position. For some individual deputies this ambiguous social standing had undoubtedly engendered a sense of humiliation and anger that remained close to the surface. Edmond-Louis Dubois-Crancé, whose father had been ennobled, would never forget being snubbed by courtiers in Versailles while serving as a musketeer, an experience which "had inspired in me an overwhelming aversion." The ambitious young Pierre-Louis Roederer encountered similar frustrations when his efforts to buy the office of *maître de requêtes* were thwarted for insufficient quarterings of nobility. The wealthy lawyer Target could scarcely conceal his bitterness when the comte d'Artois addressed him using his last name alone—without the word "Monsieur"—and the familiar "tu" form, as though he were a mere servant. And Barnave's musings in his notebook on the closing of careers to commoners has often been recounted: "All the roads to advancement are barred," he wrote. "Only petty and limited careers

---

[140] Elie de Biran, 6, 24; Montarlot, 355–59; Pierre Ballu, *François Ménard de La Groye (1742–1815). Magistrat manceau* (Le Mans, 1962), 7–8; Fichier Lefebvre.

[141] Bandy de Lachaud, Bignan de Coyrol, Brunet de Latuque, Cochon de Lapparent, Darnaudat, Despatys de Courteille, Girod de Pouzol, Goyard, Grand de Champrouet, Grenier, Huot de Goncourt, Laboreys de Châteaufavier, Le Clercq de Lannoy, Lescurier de La Vergne, Lombard-Taradeau, Malès, Marie de La Forge, Mathieu de Rondeville, Mauriet de Flory, Mayer (Pierre-François), Melon, Mestre, Mougins de Roquefort, Naurissart, Pélisson de Gennes, Picart de La Pointe, Pincepré de Buire, Poulain de Boutancourt, Rodat d'Olemps, Sentetz, Tailhardat de La Maisonneuve, Tournyol-Duclos: taken from a large number of sources, especially the notations in Brette, *Recueil*, vol. 2.

[142] Colin Lucas, "Nobles, Bourgeois, and the Origins of the French Revolution," *Past and Present*, no. 60 (August 1973), 90; Jean-André Périsse Du Luc to J. B. Willermoz: B.M. Lyon ms. 5430, letter of July 8, 1789, and elsewhere.

are left open." The dilemma and predicament of many Third deputies was epitomized by Charles-François Lebrun, who had been ennobled in 1768: "I no longer belong to the Third Estate," he wrote in early 1789, "but I am not yet accepted by the nobility."[143]

But how common and typical were such sentiments among the representatives of the Third Estate on the eve of the Revolution? To what extent did substantial numbers of the deputies view themselves as "social mutants"? In order to confront these questions, we must turn to the problem of the deputies' culture.

[143] Edmond-Louis-Alexis Dubois-Crancé, *Analyse de la Révolution française depuis l'ouverture des Etats généraux jusqu'au 6 Brumaire an IV de la République*, ed. Thomas Jung (Paris, 1885), 2–3; Michaud, 11:359; Kenneth Margerison, *Pierre-Louis Roederer, Political Thought and Practice during the French Revolution* (Philadelphia, 1983), 7–8; Paul-Louis Target, *Un avocat du XVIIIe siècle* (Paris, 1893), 53 (entry in Target's diary of Dec. 31, 1787); Jean-Jacques Chevallier, *Barnave ou les deux faces de la Révolution* (Grenoble, 1979), 33; Charles-François Lebrun, *La voix du citoyen* (n.p., 1789), 16.

A Revolution of the Mind?

FOR MANY commentators on the French Revolution, both contemporary observers and later historians, there could be little doubt that a revolution of the mind had preceded the revolution of state and society, and that the latter transformation would have been scarcely conceivable without the former. As early as July 1789 the deputy and scholar from Lyon, Delandine, argued that the extraordinary events of that summer were partly the product of "the philosophy and Enlightenment which spread among all ranks of society." Delandine's celebrated contemporaries, Edmund Burke and Thomas Paine, also shared this view, as did Alexis de Tocqueville and Hippolyte Taine in the nineteenth century. But for other writers and observers, ideas *per se* were only contributing factors at best in the origins of the Revolution and of a Revolutionary mentality. From the deputy and patriot leader Antoine Barnave through Karl Marx, Jean Jaurès, and Georges Lefebvre, a major strand of historiography has placed primary emphasis on the facts of political and economic injustice under the Old Regime.[1]

The last decades of the twentieth century witnessed a renewed intensity of this debate, as Marxist interpretations, in which ideas had usually been portrayed as mere "superstructure," came under increasing fire from historians who saw the ideas and beliefs of the patriots of 1789, and particularly the values of the Enlightenment, as fundamental to the inception of the Revolution. Following on an idea first substantially developed by Alexis de Tocqueville, a number of the revisionists argued for the pervasive influence of a homogeneous Enlightened elite whose cultural values cut across the boundaries of order and class.[2] More recently, Roger Chartier has attempted to reconceptualize the whole debate by focusing on the broader *cultural* context of the Enlightenment and on the critical issue of the reception—and

---

[1] Antoine-François Delandine, *Mémorial historique des Etats généraux*, 5 vols. (n.p., 1789), 3:271; Antoine-Pierre-Joseph-Marie Barnave, *Introduction à la Révolution française*, in *Oeuvres de Barnave. Vol I*, ed. Bérenger de la Drôme (Paris, 1843). See also William F. Church, *The Influence of the Enlightenment on the French Revolution* (Lexington, Mass., 1974), xi–xii; and Roger Chartier, *Les origines culturelles de la Révolution française* (Paris, 1990), 13–25.

[2] Alexis de Tocqueville, *L'Ancien régime et la Révolution* (Paris, 1856), esp. livre II, chap. VIII. See also, e.g., Elizabeth L. Eisenstein, "Who Intervened in 1790," *AHR* 71 (1965), 77–103; François Furet, *Interpreting the Revolution*, trans. Elborg Forster (Cambridge, 1981), 55, 62–63, 114–16; and Guy Chaussinand-Nogaret, *La noblesse au XVIIIe siècle. De la féodalité aux Lumières* (Paris, 1976), 108–11.

the possible transformation and reformulation—of Enlightenment ideas by the generation who made the Revolution.[3]

One of the principal difficulties in this long debate arises from the very complexity and multiplicity of the French Enlightenment. To be sure, the eighteenth-century writers themselves, both before and during the Revolution, commonly referred to "les lumières," as though they were dealing with an essentially homogeneous movement.[4] But, in retrospect, that movement appears to be anything but unified, cut by numerous conflicting traditions and contradictory strands of logic and methods of approach. The celebrated confrontation between Voltaire and Rousseau has frequently been described: a confrontation between an Enlightenment that emphasized reason and political elitism and an Enlightenment that placed a premium on emotion, instinct, and popular will. One would also need to distinguish a technocratic Enlightenment, centered on the efforts of the physiocrats and the minister Turgot to bring about major transformations in the economy and the government through administrative fiat from above; a scientific Enlightenment, heir to the great Scientific Revolution of the seventeenth century, and often only remotely and indirectly related to the movements of social reform; an "occult Enlightenment," in its various manifestations of Mesmerism, illuminism, and Freemasonry, whose enthusiasts often claimed full adhesion to the tenets of the philosophes, but whose rites and beliefs sometimes contradicted those very tenets; and finally, the so-called "Catholic Enlightenment"—which sought to reconcile the ideals of humanism and self-determination to the Christian message. Other scholars have taught us to appreciate the interplay of generations in the Enlightenment, stipulating the existence of a heroic phase earlier in the century whose adherents waged battle against much of the political and religious establishment, followed by a "High Enlightenment" after about 1770 in which the philosophes were increasingly accepted and even subsidized by the government. In this scenario, however, many of the most successful writers found themselves in confrontation with a swarm of impoverished individuals who were never able to break into the system and who frequently felt a visceral hatred for the establishment and all it represented.[5]

---

[3] Chartier, *Les origines culturelles*. Also, Thomas E. Kaiser, "This Strange Offspring of *Philosophie*: Recent Historiographical Problems in Relating the Enlightenment to the French Revolution," *FHS* 15 (1988), 549–62.

[4] E.g., Guy-Jean-Baptiste Target, *Les Etats généraux convoqués par Louis XVI* (Paris, ca. Dec. 1788), 1; Jacques-Guillaume Thouret, *Avis des bons normands à leurs frères, tous les bons français de toutes les provinces et de tous les ordres* (n.p., Feb. 1789), 4; and Bertrand Barère: *AP* 8:231 (speech of July 14, 1789).

[5] See, in particular, Keith Michael Baker, *Condorcet: From Natural Philosophy to Social Mathematics* (Chicago, 1975), 18; and *Inventing the French Revolution*, esp. chap. 1. On the Masons and Mesmerists, see Ran Halévi, *Les loges maçonniques dans la France d'Ancien régime. Aux origines de la sociabilité démocratique* (Paris, 1984); and Robert Darnton, *Mesmerism and the End of the Enlightenment in France* (Cambridge, Mass., 1968). On the Catholic Enlightenment, see Bernard Plongeron, "Recherches sur l'Aufklärung catholique en Europe occidentale (1770–

THE DEPUTIES AND THE ENLIGHTENMENT

If we turn to the membership of the Constituent Assembly, we are immediately struck by the rarity of professional men of letters directly linked to
the Enlightenment in any of its varieties. Even where such figures participated in the electoral assemblies, they were commonly shunted aside by the
voters. The marquis de Condorcet, protégé of d'Alembert and heir direct to
the mid-century generation of philosophes, failed in his candidacy for deputy of the Nobility in both Mantes and Paris.[6] Marmontel, Lacretelle,
Suard, Gaillard, and Panckouke were all overlooked by the electors of Paris.
Though the abbé Sieyès was chosen by the Third Estate on the final vote—
twentieth out of twenty deputies—other intellectuals from the capital obtained
election only by traveling deep into the provinces: Nicolas Bergasse to Lyon,
the comte de Mirabeau to Aix-en-Provence, and Dominique-Joseph Garat to
the Basque country on the Spanish border. Jean-Sylvain Bailly, who felt that
his own election in Paris had been extremely unusual, took note of the "general disfavor shown in the electoral assembly toward men of letters and academicians." He attributed this attitude to the dominant presence of merchants
and lawyers in the assemblies—the first group generally unfamiliar with the
intellectuals, the second traditionally their rivals.[7]

In all, perhaps ten deputies might have been designated "philosophes" in
the eighteenth-century sense of the term: men of letters, self-consciously
linked to one or another strand of the Enlightenment, and consecrating all
or a substantial portion of their professional life to writing. At the top of
the list, no doubt, was the comte de Mirabeau. Son of the celebrated physi-
ocrat, this restless and unpredictable polymath, was known to contemporaries for his wide-ranging essays, for his attacks on "despotism" and the
lettres de cachet, as well as for his success in another genre of eighteenth-
century "philosophy," the erotic novel. Nearly equal in prominence on the
eve of the Revolution was Constantin-François Chassebeuf, or "Volney" as
he called himself. Linked in his youth to Turgot, Holbach, d'Alembert, and
Franklin, among others, he had taught himself Arabic and traveled exten-
sively in the Middle East before publishing a travel description of Syria and
Egypt in the tradition of the critical works of the abbé Raynal. During the
Pre-Revolutionary period, Volney had traveled from Paris to Rennes, where
he wrote a series of influential pamphlets supporting the oppositional movement emerging in Brittany. There was also Nicolas Bergasse, hero of the

---

1830)," *RHMC* 16 (1969), 555–605. On generations, see Daniel Mornet, *Les origines intellectuelles de la Révolution française* (Paris, 1933); and Robert Darnton, "The High Enlightenment
and the Low Life of Literature," *Past and Present*, no. 51 (1971), 81–115.

[6] Baker, *Condorcet*, 266–67.

[7] Jean-Sylvain Bailly, *Mémoires d'un témoin de la Révolution*, ed. Berville and Barrière, 3 vols.
(Paris, 1821–22), 1:51. Cf. Jacques-Antoine Creuzé-Latouche, *Journal des Etats généraux et du
début de l'Assemblée nationale, 18 mai–29 juillet 1789*, ed. Jean Marchand (Paris, 1946), 32–33
(entry of May 29).

Kornmann affair, a widely followed marital scandal adroitly manipulated by Bergasse in a series of publications, interpreted by many readers as a broader indictment of the French regime. The ex-Oratorian and sometime lawyer had associated with the elderly Rousseau and self-consciously portrayed himself as the heir to Jean-Jacques.[8]

Perhaps a step lower in national notoriety were Bailly, Démeunier, Dupont de Nemours, and the chevalier de Boufflers. With a reputation as both an astronomer and a historian of science, Bailly had the unique distinction of belonging to all three of the Paris academies—the French Academy, the Literary Academy, and the Academy of Sciences. The close friend of Franklin and the long-standing correspondent of Voltaire, he had written numerous books and had been asked to participate in the *Encyclopedia*—though he had ultimately demurred. Démeunier, who had lived from his publications since he first arrived in Paris in the early 1770s, had acquired a considerable reputation as the collaborator of d'Alembert and Morellet and the author of a multivolume study of primitive customs and a three-volume treatise on America—duly read and approved by Jefferson. Dupont de Nemours, protégé and associate of Turgot, was the most prolific of all the future deputies, the author of an unending stream of books and tracts on commercial reform and political economy. Though many of his works were less accessible to the general public, he maintained his reputation as the most prominent living writer in the physiocratic tradition. The chevalier de Boufflers, whose love for letters was matched only by his passion for women and horses, had briefly collaborated in the *Encyclopedia*. But he made his reputation writing pale and somewhat flaccid poetry and imitations of the philosophical novels of Voltaire, with whom he had considerable contact during a trip to Switzerland.[9]

Distinctly less significant but tightly linked to the establishment of the "High Enlightenment" were three additional writer-philosophes: the younger of the Garat brothers, Dominique-Joseph, known for his poetry, plays, and newspaper articles; Delandine, poet and literary critic, director of the library of the Academy of Lyon; and Jean-Jacques Lenoir de La Roche, lawyer from Grenoble, who had come to Paris in 1777 to make his way as a minor writer.[10] It is not insignificant that all of the ten, with the exception of Boufflers, would be deputies of the Third Estate, and all but Delandine habitually resided in or near Paris.

---

[8] Georges Guibal, *Mirabeau et la Provence*, 2 vols. (Paris, 1901); Jean Gaulmier, *Un grand témoin de la Révolution et de l'Empire: Volney* (Paris, 1959); Etienne Lamy, *Un défenseur des principes traditionnels sous la Révolution: N. Bergasse* (Paris, 1910).

[9] Edna Hindie Lemay, "Naissance de l'anthropologie sociale en France: Jean-Nicolas Démeunier et 'L'Esprit des usages et des coutumes' au XVIIIe siècle," Thèse du 3e cycle, E.H.E.S.S., 1974; A. Berville, "Notice sur la vie de Bailly" in Bailly, *Mémoires*, 1:iii–xxxi; Ambrose Saricks, *Pierre Samuel Du Pont de Nemours* (Lawrence, Kan., 1965), chaps. 1–4; and Michaud, 5:194–200 (on Boufflers).

[10] Fichier Lefebvre.

If full-fledged philosophes were rare among the deputies, a number of others were associated with the Enlightenment through their occasional writings or their contacts and correspondence with the principal thinkers and intellectuals of their age. The marquis de Lézay-Marnésia was apparently the only other deputy "Encyclopédiste," having written an article on "theft." But the Douai lawyer Merlin, and the Limousin inspector of manufacturing, Pierre-Augustin Laboreys de Châteaufavier, had both contributed—along with Démeunier—to that second-generation version of Diderot's publication, the *Encyclopédie méthodique*. The comte de Lally-Tolendal and the Strasbourg patrician Turckheim pursued extended correspondence with Voltaire, while the comte Destutt de Tracy, the comte d'Antraigues, the vicomte de Toulongeon, the marquis de Mailly, and the lawyers Charles-Gabriel Christin and François-Antoine Boissy d'Anglas, had all made the trek to the Swiss border to confer with the sage of Ferney. Indeed, Mailly had served as Voltaire's private secretary, before assuming his post in the *cours des comptes* of Dole. The royal official Malouet had known numerous of the philosophes in Paris in the 1770s when he had resided in the home of abbé Raynal; the elder Garat, lawyer in Bordeaux, had met Montesquieu in his youth; and several of the deputies—Reynaud de Montlosier, bishop Boisgelin, the marquis de Panat, the lawyer Pierre-Louis Prieur, for example—had been linked to d'Alembert and Condorcet. The comte d'Antraigues and the young Robespierre, as well as Bergasse, Boufflers, and Garat the younger, are all known to have met Rousseau. D'Antraigues portrayed himself as Jean-Jacques' closest friend in the last days of his life and claimed to have received over two hundred letters and manuscripts from him. A number of other deputies—Lézay-Marnésia, the marquis de Ferrières, the comte d'Eymar, and the Angers "bourgeois" Jean-Baptiste Leclerc, for example—sought self-consciously to imitate Rousseau in both the subjects and style of their writings.[11]

Nearly sixty of the delegates of 1789, about 4 percent of the total, are known to have been members of at least one of the late eighteenth-century learned academies, principal organs of the "Enlightenment in the provinces," as Daniel Roche has described them.[12] Some, in fact, were associated with similar institutes throughout Europe: Delandine was said to have been a member of the Antiquarian Society of London, Dionis Du Séjour was linked to both London and Stockholm, de Loynes to Copenhagen, the duc de La Rochefoucauld to Sweden, the baron d'Aigalliers to Padua, and Delay d'Agier to Saint-Petersburg. And eight held chairs among the "forty Immortals" of the French Academy, the onetime bastion of intellectual traditionalism, which for a time was strongly influenced by a substantial con-

---

[11] Michaud; Fichier Lefebvre; the *DC*; Bourget-Besnier, *Une famille française sous la Révolution et l'Empire: la famille de Lézay-Marnésia* (Paris, 1985), 17; and Roger Barny, *Le comte d'Antraigues: un disciple aristocrate de Jean-Jacques Rousseau* (Oxford, 1991).

[12] In all, we have identified 4 clerical deputies, 22 noble deputies, and 32 deputies of the Third Estate sitting in at least one academy; but the list is almost certainly incomplete: based on the *DC* and the Fichier Lefebvre. See also Daniel Roche, *Le siècle des Lumières en province*, 2 vols. (Paris, 1978).

tingent of philosophes. In addition to Bailly and Boufflers, there was the humanist courtier-archbishop Boisgelin, the celebrated trial lawyer and reformer, Target; the marquis d'Aguesseau, a minor writer; the marquis de Montesquiou-Fezenzac, a sometime playwright; the abbé Maury, known for his sermons, essays, and funeral oratory; and the cardinal de Rohan, veteran of the Diamond Necklace affair—whose credentials for academic status were somewhat obscure. All but the final two clerical academicians would undoubtedly have identified themselves with various strands of the Enlightenment.[13]

If we cast our nets even further, we might also include those associated with the "occult Enlightenment," the Freemasons and Mesmerists. At least sixteen future deputies participated regularly in the mysteries of Mesmer, including such direct associates to the Austrian "doctor" as Bergasse and the young parlementary magistrate Adrien Duport, and such aristocratic luminaries as the duc d'Orléans, the marquis de Lafayette, the duc de Biron, and the vicomte de Noailles.[14] And some 20 percent of the Constituent membership were members of various Masonic lodges. The breakdown by order of the deputy-Masons was almost exactly the same as for the deputy-academicians: nearly three-fifths from the Third Estate, one-third from the nobility, and less than a tenth from the clergy. At least fifty-seven future deputies, moreover, had held high offices in the Masonic establishment. The duc de Luxembourg, had been the prime instigator in the creation of the French wing of the Grand Orient. Turckheim had served as *visiteur général* of the society for the province of Burgundy; and baron de Wimpffen had published an important Masonic text, the *Xéfolius*.[15]

Among deputies from the provinces the number belonging to lodges or academies was probably no more or less than what might have been expected from a random sample of late eighteenth-century notables. The over-

---

[13] Emile Gassier, *Les cinq cents immortels* (Paris, 1906), 478–82.

[14] Among the known deputy participants in Mesmerism were Bergasse, the duc de Biron, the duc de Coigny, the comte de Crillon, Delandine, Duport, Duval d'Eprémesnil, the marquis de Lafayette, the marquis de Mailly, Malouet, the comte de Marsane-Fontjuliane, the marquis de Montesquiou-Fezenzac, the vicomte de Noailles, the duc d'Orléans, Périsse Du Luc, and Reynaud de Montlosier. Sources: Darnton, *Mesmerism*, 68, 74, 78–79; Louis Gottschalk, *Lafayette between the American and the French Revolution (1783–1789)* (Chicago, 1950), 77–82; Paul Messié. "Le comte de Marsane-Fontjuliane, député de Montélimar aux premières assemblées révolutionnaires," *Bulletin de la Société départementale d'archéologie et de statistique de la Drôme* 76 (1964), 75; Jean-André Périsse Du Luc to J. B. Willermoz: B.M. Lyon ms. 5430, esp. letter of Dec. 27, 1789; G. Michon, *Essai sur l'histoire du parti Feuillant: Adrien Duport* (Paris, 1924), 4–5; Pierre-Victor Malouet, *Mémoires*, 2 vols., ed. Baron Malouet (Paris, 1868), 1:195; François-Dominique de Reynaud de Montlosier, *Mémoires* 2 vols. (Paris, 1830), 1:133 and 2:324–27; and the Fichier Lefebvre.

[15] I am particularly grateful to Ran Halévi for loaning me his manuscript card file on the deputy-Masons. Estimates of the total number of deputy-Masons are based primarily on this file and on P. Lamarque, *Les francs-maçons aux Etats-généraux et à l'Assemblée nationale* (Paris, 1981). Also Jules Keller, *Lili Schoenemann, baronne de Turckheim* (Bern, 1987), 40; the Fichier Lefebvre; and the *DC*. Of the 269 known deputy members, 155 were members of the Third Estate, 89 of the Nobility, and 25 of the Clergy.

whelming majority—and it is a fact worth noting—had no connection with these various overt manifestations of Enlightenment culture.[16] In Paris, by contrast, participation in such organizations created dense networks of association and friendship among some of the future deputies, especially among the aristocracy. About one-fifth of the academicians and one-fourth of all Masons resided in the capital. No less than eighteen sat in the same Masonic lodge of Sainte-Olympe, eleven were brothers in the Neuf Soeurs, eight in La Candeur.[17] An individual Parisian like the marquis de Lafayette might find himself linked to a whole array of future deputies through his membership in the Freemasons, his association with the Mesmerists, his affiliation in the abolitionist Friends of the Blacks, and his links to groups formed to promote religious toleration—not to mention his attendance at various of the Enlightened Parisian salons of the 1780s. Networks of Enlightened sociability such as these would form the matrix of the so-called "Committee of Thirty," the Parisian gathering organized to promote patriotic reform on the eve of the Revolution.[18]

DEPUTY PUBLICATIONS BEFORE THE REVOLUTION

Links of this kind, between some of the men of '89 and different manifestations of the Enlightenment—links identified from a wide variety of biographical and anecdotal sources—are not difficult to find. But how typical are such examples of the cultural orientations of the deputies as a whole? To what extent had Enlightened values been integrated into the deputies' working assumptions about the world in which they lived? Could ideas alone have bound together individuals from the sharply differing social milieus of the nobility and the Third Estate? In order to assess more systematically the range of interests and the possible differences in perspective among the estates, it is useful to focus on the deputies' published writings.[19] In fact at least 116 of the future Constituents had made their entry into the "Republic of Letters" prior to the Revolutionary era. Slightly under one-fifth sat with the Clergy, slightly over one-fourth sat with the Nobility, while some 53

[16] Cf. the 4% of deputies belonging to academies with Daniel Roche's estimate of 10% of all urban notables belonging to such organizations: Roche, 1:189.

[17] Ran Halévi's manuscript card file; also Louis Amiable, *Une loge maçonnique d'avant 1789: les Neufs soeurs* (Paris, 1897), 248–51, 389–93. Sixty-seven of 269 (25%) deputy-Masons and 11 of 58 (19%) deputy-academicians resided in Paris.

[18] Gottschalk, 310, 370–71, 380; Geoffrey Adams, *The Huguenots and French Opinion, 1685–1787: The Enlightenment Debate on Toleration* (Waterloo, Ontario, 1991), 267–77. On the Committee of Thirty, see below, chap. 3.

[19] I have included here all those deputies whose writings—whether books, brochures, or items in periodicals—are preserved in the published catalogue of the Bibliothèque nationale, or otherwise known—usually through individual biographies—to have been written for publication before the Revolution. Political works published during the Pre-Revolutionary period—from March 1787 through April 1789 will be considered in chap. 3.

percent were members of the Third Estate—roughly the breakdown one might have expected given the composition of the Estates General, and approximately the same proportions as the authors enumerated in the 1784 edition of *La France littéraire*.[20] Despite the dominance of Paris in the cultural framework of the period, only about thirty of the deputy authors resided habitually in the capital, with most of the remainder scattered in the principal towns and cities of the provinces.

The publications in question spread across the entire range of literary and scholarly genres. If the largest single category concerned the arts and letters, respectable numbers of works had also appeared on economics, law, science, politics and society, history and geography, and religion and theology.[21] But there were also some significant differences in the types of subjects treated by members of the different estates. Not surprisingly, over 90 percent of the works on religion and theology were produced by clergymen. Nobles were more likely to publish works of literature or poetry—over a third of their production—and wrote almost nothing on legal questions. As for the members of the Third Estate, they produced nothing at all on theological or religious subjects, while they were largely dominant in learned and scholarly publications dealing with law, economics, history, politics, and geography.[22]

In addition to the "professional" philosophes among the deputies—Démeunier, Volney, Mirabeau, etc.—several of the deputy writers made local or even national reputations for themselves in a variety of reforming causes that were squarely in the tradition of the great Enlightenment authors of the mid-century. Jean-Paul Rabaut Saint-Etienne had done battle for over a decade in favor of toleration for the Protestants. The lawyers Target, Charles-Jean-Marie Alquier, and Jean-Baptiste Poncet-Delpech had pub-

[20] Robert Darnton, "The Facts of Literary Life in Eighteenth-Century France," in *FRCMPC*, 1:261–91. Of the 116, 23 (20%) sat in the Clergy, 31 (27%) in the Nobility, and 62 (53%) in the Third Estate.

[21] Since some deputies wrote in more than one category, the following statistics consider the total number of subject-categories (153) treated by the corps of deputy-authors. Fourteen (9%) were in theology-religion; 42 (27%) in belles lettres; 24 (16%) in history; 17 (11%) on economics; 20 (13%) on law; 22 (14%) on political or social questions; 14 (9%) on science, mathematics or "pseudo-science"; and 2 (1%) in miscellaneous categories.

[22] The following chart summarizes the breakdown by order of the total 153 subjects treated by the 116 deputy authors (percentages are in parentheses):

CATEGORY	CLERGY	NOBLES	THIRD	TOTALS
Theology/religion	13 (93)	1 (7)	0 (0)	14 (100)
Letters	7 (17)	13 (31)	22 (52)	42 (100)
History/geography	2 (8)	6 (25)	16 (67)	24 (100)
Politics/society	2 (9)	5 (23)	15 (68)	22 (100)
Law	0 (0)	1 (5)	19 (95)	20 (100)
Economics	1 (6)	4 (24)	12 (71)	17 (100)
Science/Math	0 (0)	6 (50)	6 (50)	12 (100)
Miscellaneous		2 (100)		2 (100)

lished briefs or brochures on behalf of the same cause; while Curé Grégoire had penned a landmark tract in defense of the Jews.[23] Curé Clerget of Onans in Franche-Comté and the lawyer Christin of Saint-Claude—writing jointly with Voltaire—had leveled stinging attacks against the remnants of serfdom in eastern France.[24] Lally-Tolendal, Jérôme Pétion de Villeneuve, and Robespierre all advocated reforms of the criminal justice system—the latter writing for an essay contest organized by the academy of Metz. The noble army officer, Bousmard de Chantraine, had likewise won a prize with his essay on the plight of illegitimate children.[25] There were a variety of publications proposing economic reform in the physiocratic tradition. To the numerous works by Dupont de Nemours, one can add the writings of the Poitevin magistrate Jacques-Antoine Creuzé-Latouche on political economy; those of the Versailles merchant Boislandry on the relation of commerce and agriculture; and those of the noble Lemoyne de Bellisle, on free grain trade.[26]

And nevertheless, works such as these, directly linked to the critical propensities and reforming zeal of the Enlightenment, were clearly in the minority. A substantially larger group of deputy publications fell into the category of *belles lettres*. With a few minor exceptions, there was nothing radical in this literature, which was far less in the tradition of the philosophes than of Marivaux or Jean-Baptiste Rousseau or Saint-Lambert. There were the noblemen story writers Boufflers and Mirabeau, who specialized in the titillating and erotic; and Lézay-Marnésia and Ferrières who opted rather for the moralistic and melodramatic. Though several of their stories had been billed as *contes philosophiques*, they were mild indeed by comparison with the works of Voltaire or Diderot and went little beyond a stylish anti-clericalism

[23] Jean-Paul Rabaut Saint-Etienne, *Le vieux Cévenol, ou anecdotes de la vie d'Ambroise Borély* (1779) and *La justice et la nécessité d'assurer en France un état légal aux Protestants* (n.d.); E. Forestié, "Notes bibliographiques sur Jean-Baptiste Poncet-Delpech," *Recueil de l'Académie de Montauban* (1890), 240; Charles-Jean-Marie Alquier, *Réquisition . . . contre un mandement de l'évêque de La Rochelle* (La Rochelle, 1788), 20–21; Guy-Jean-Baptiste Target, *Consultation sur l'affaire de la dame Marquise d'Anglare* (1787); Henri Grégoire, *Essai sur la régénération physique, morale, et politique des Juifs* (Metz, 1789).

[24] Pierre-François Clerget, *Coup d'oeil philosophique et politique sur la main-morte* (1785); Charles-Gabriel-Frédéric Christin, *Collection des mémoires présentés au Conseil du roi par les habitants du Mont Jura et le chapitre de S.-Claude* (1772). Christin was said to have collaborated with Voltaire on the *Lettres du Père Polycarpe* (1772): Fichier Lefebvre.

[25] Trophème-Gérard, comte de Lally-Tolendal, *Essai sur quelques changements qu'on pourrait faire dans les loix criminelles* (1786); Jérôme Pétion de Villeneuve, *Les loix civiles et l'administration de la justice ramenées à un ordre simple et uniforme* (1788). Maximilien Robespierre, "Discours sur les peines infamantes," in *Oeuvres*, ed. Emile Lesueur (Paris, 1912), 1:5–47. See also J. M. Thompson, *Robespierre*, 2 vols. (Oxford, 1953), 1:17. Henri-Jean-Baptiste de Bousmard de Chantraine, *Mémoire sur les moyens compatibles avec les bonnes moeurs d'assurer la conservation des bâtards* (Metz, 1787).

[26] See Saricks, 34–58; Creuzé-Latouche, *Journal des Etats généraux*, "Introduction" by Marchand; François-Louis-Legrand Boislandry, *Mémoire sur les manufactures, le commerce, et leurs rapports avec l'agriculture* (1787); Jean-Baptiste Le Moyne de Bellisle, *Mémoire sur la liberté de l'exportation et de l'importation des grains* (1764).

and an occasional promotion of physiocratic doctrine.[27] There were the deputy playwrights: the royal financial administrator, Anson, and the Bourges magistrate, Jérôme Le Grand. Le Grand's tragedy, *Zarine, reine des scythes*, was largely in the style of Racine and was prefaced with a long, erudite discussion of the classical texts on which the story was based; and his comedy, *Le bon ami* contained none of the critical satire of Beaumarchais or even Molière.[28] And there was a whole array of deputy poets, largely taken with a Rococo esthetic of gallant light verse, sentimental pastorales, or pompous odes and epics in imitation of the classics. Poncet-Delpech, the judges Thomas Verny and Brevet de Beaujour, and the merchant Michel Roussier had all tried their hand at it. But it was the noble authors who seemed to have a particular predilection for poetry: the marquis de Bonnay, the comte de Clermont-Tonnerre, the marquis de Brulart de Sillery, Eymar du Bignosc, the marquis de Montesquiou, the vicomte de Malartic, the duc de Croÿ, the baron d'Aigalliers, as well as Boufflers, Lézay, Boisgelin, and Ferrières.[29]

Another group of deputies had received some measure of local acclaim through their published eulogies of great men: archbishop Boisgelin once again, as well as Garat, Delandine, Bertrand Barère, Jean-Denis Lanjuinais, and the chevalier Deschamps, had all written in this genre—sometimes in conjunction with academy essay contests.[30] Several of the same individuals had revealed a bent toward literary scholarship. Delandine had written on the novels of Madame de Lafayette, Lanjuinais on eloquence among the Romans, and Boisgelin had translated Ovid—a curious choice for a prelate of the church. Charles-François Lebrun's translation of the *Iliad*, is still considered a model of its kind. Other noteworthy translations had been published by the Paris canonist Camus (Aristotle); the Besançon lawyer Fran-

---

[27] E.g., Stanislas-Jean de Boufflers, *Aline, la reine de Golconde* (1763); Gabriel-Jean-Honoré de Riquetti, comte de Mirabeau, *Recueil de contes*, 2 vols. (1775) and *Erotika biblion* (1783); Charles-Elie marquis de Ferrières, *Saint-Flour et Justine*, 4 vols. (1791) [the first volumes were published in 1786 under the title *La femme dans l'ordre social et dans la nature*]. Claude-François-Adrien marquis de Lézay-Marnésia, *L'heureuse famille: conte moral* (1766). On the latter, see Bourget-Besnier, 18.

[28] Pierre-Hubert Anson and Marie-Louis-Thérèse Hérissant, *Les deux seigneurs ou l'alchimiste* (1783); Jérôme Le Grand, *Le bon ami* (Paris, 1781); and *Zarine, reine des Scythes* (Paris, 1782).

[29] In addition to the Fichier Lefebvre and Michaud, see Forestié, 236–40; Ange-Marie d'Eymar du Bignosc, *Amusements de ma solitude* (n.p., 1805); Lézay-Marnésia, *Essai sur la nature champêtre* (1787); Boufflers, *Le coeur* (1763); Edouard Bougler, *Mouvement provincial en 1789. Biographie des députés de l'Anjou*, 2 vols. (Paris, 1865), 225–30; Gabriel de Maurès de Malartic, *Le vicomte de Maurès de Malartic* (La Rochelle, 1892), 10–11; Charles Du Bus, *Stanislas de Clermont-Tonnerre et l'échec de la Révolution monarchique, 1757–92* (Paris, 1931), 29–35; Gabriel-François, baron d'Aigalliers, *Oeuvres choisies* (Nîmes, 1805); Eugène Lavaquery, *Le Cardinal de Boisgelin, 1732–1804*, 2 vols. (Paris, 1920), 1:285–305.

[30] E.g., Bertrand Barère, *Eloge de Louis XIII* (1783) and *Eloge du chancelier Séguier* (1784); Dominique-Joseph Garat, *Eloge de Fontenelle* (Paris, 1778); Pierre-Suzanne Deschamps, "Extrait de l'éloge de feu M. l'abbé Le Croix," *Journal de Lyon* (Oct. 11, 1786); Jean-Denis Lanjuinais, *L'éloge de Joseph II* (1774); Antoine-François Delandine, *Eloge du Duc d'Orléans* (1778).

çois Martin (Cornelius Nepos); the marquis de Bonnay (*Tristam Shandy*); and the comte de Clermont-Tonnerre (Ossian)—not to mention the numerous renderings of English histories and essays by Démeunier.[31]

Indeed, a major proportion of the deputies' pre-Revolutionary publications might more aptly be described as learned and scholarly than as critical or creative. It was in this domain, in particular, that the commoner deputies seemed to excel. There were historical studies by René-Antoine Thibaudeau, Charles-François Bouche, Boissy d'Anglas, Jean-Louis-Claude Emmery, as well as Bailly, Rabaut, Anson, and Delandine. There were medical treatises by doctors Gallot and Paul-Victor de Sèze; important astronomical research by Bailly and the parlementarian Dionis Du Séjour; natural history by the Orleans merchant François-Simon Defay-Boutheroue; and a moving account of ascents in hot-air balloons by the Metz magistrate Pierre-Louis Roederer.[32]

But in no single area did the deputies have a more distinguished publishing record than in law and legal theory. Camus, Merlin, Lanjuinais, Bouche, Target, Durand de Maillane, and Jean-François-Régis Mourot were all nationally known within the legal community and might well be ranked among the most eminent scholars in the National Assembly. Durand de Maillane's multivolume dictionary of French canon law, for example, is still considered the standard work on the subject; and Merlin's general *Répertoire* on civil jurisprudence went through several editions into the nineteenth century. Guillaume Bonnemant in Arles had produced a two-volume study of the *Institutes*; Creuzé-Latouche a discourse on legal ethics; Turckheim a treatise on Merovingian and Carolingian law; the Lannion lawyer Baudouin

---

[31] Delandine, *Observations sur Madame de La Fayette* (1786); Lanjuinais, *L'éloquence chez les Romains*, 2 vols. (1777); Charles-François Lebrun, trans., *L'Iliade* (1776); Boisgelin, *Les Héroïdes d'Ovide* (1786); Armand-Gaston Camus, trans., *Histoire des animaux d'Aristote* (1783); Marquis Charles-François de Bonnay, trans., *Tristam Shandy*, 2 vols. (1785); Stanislas-Marie de Clermont-Tonnerre, trans., *Traduction libre du premier chant de Fingal d'Ossian* (1784). On François Martin, see the *DC*.

[32] René-Antoine-Hyacinthe Thibaudeau, *Abrégé de l'Histoire du Poitou*, 6 vols. (1782–86), re-edited in 1840 and 1889; Charles-François Bouche, *Essai sur l'histoire de Provence*, 2 vols. (1785); Bailly, *Histoire de l'astronomie*, 5 vols. (Paris, 1775–85); and *Lettres sur l'origine des sciences adressées à M. de Voltaire* (1777); Delandine, *Dissertation sur des antiquités de Bresse et de Lyon* (1780); Jean-Paul Rabaut Saint-Etienne, *Lettre à M. Bailly sur l'histoire primitive de la Grèce* (1787); Anson, "Mémoire historique sur les villes de Milly et de Nemours" in *Nouvelles recherches sur la France* (1766); Jean-Louis-Claude Emmery, *Faits concernant la ville de Metz et le pays messin* (1788). On Boissy, see René Puaux, "Introduction" to François-Antoine Boissy d'Anglas, "Lettres inédites sur la Révolution française," *Bulletin de la Société de l'histoire du Protestantisme français* 75 (1926), 282–99. Meynier de Salinelles was also said to have written a work on the classical period: *DC*. Among the scientific and medical works: Bailly, *Essai sur les satellites de Jupiter* (1766); and Achille-Pierre Dionis Du Séjour, *Traité sur les mouvements apparents des corps célestes* (1786); Jean-Gabriel Gallot, *Mémoire historique sur la fièvre catarrhale bilieuse [de]* ... *1784* (1786); Paul-Victor de Sèze, *Recherches physiologiques et philosophiques sur la sensibilité ou la vie animale* (1786); François-Simon Defay-Boutheroue, *La nature considérée dans plusieurs de ses opérations* ... *avec la minéralogie de l'Orléanais* (1783); Pierre-Louis Roederer, *Eloge de Pilâtre de Rozier* (1786).

de Maisonblanche a two-volume work on the Breton *domaine congéable*; the Parisian lawyer Moreau de Saint-Méry a six-volume study on the laws and "constitution" of the French Caribbean. And Emmery, Jacques-Guillaume Thouret, Gaultier de Biauzat, François-Antoine-Joseph de Hell, François Martin, Mathieu de Rondeville, Adrien-Pierre-Barthélemy Cochelet, and Joseph Tuault de La Bouvrie had all edited works on various aspects of local legal traditions.[33]

To be sure, not all of the writings of our deputy men of law were so scholarly and erudite. The two Parisian lawyers Bergasse and Target made their reputations by mobilizing legal suits and *mémoires judiciaires* for broader reforming causes—exemplifying the new style of lawyer/author and Enlightened man of letters described by Sarah Maza.[34] We have previously taken note of Bergasse's writings on the Kornmann affair. Target utilized a whole series of widely followed briefs to do battle against Jesuit domination, ministerial despotism, arbitrary imprisonment, and religious repression. Though long a bachelor—he married only during the Revolution—he opened his town house in the Marais to the leading writers and philosophers of his age: Condorcet and d'Alembert, Franklin and Jefferson, Marmontel, Mirabeau, Laharpe, Grimm, Cabanis, and Beaumarchais all spent time in his salon on rue Sainte-Croix-de-La-Bretonnerie.[35] Yet Target and Bergasse were clearly exceptions among jurists elected to the Estates General. To judge by their writings, most of the deputy lawyers and magistrates subscribed *not* to the image of the Enlightened man of letters, but to what David Bell has described as the "traditionalist" image of the learned and sober "priests of justice," working in the service of society and the public interest, tenaciously defending the virtues of justice, equity, and consistency

[33] E.g., Pierre-Toussaint Durand de Maillane, *Dictionnaire de droit canonique et de pratique bénéficiale*, 4 vols. (1770) and *Histoire du droit canon* (1770); Philippe-Antoine Merlin, *Répertoire universel et raisonné de jurisprudence* (1775), re-edited in four later editions in the nineteenth century; and, with M. Guyot, *Traité des droits, fonctions, franchises, exemptions, prérogations et privilèges*, 4 vols. (1788); Guillaume Bonnemant, *Maximes du palais sur les titres les plus utiles des Institutes*, 2 vols. (1785); Jacques-Antoine Creuzé-Latouche, *De l'union de la vertu et de la science dans un jurisconsulte* (1784); Jean de Turckheim, *De jure legislatorio Merovaeorum et Carolingorum Galliae* (1772); Jean-Marie Baudouin de Maisonblanche, *Traité raisonné des domaines congéables*, 2 vols. (1776); Médérie-Louis-Elie Moreau de Saint-Méry, *Lois et constitutions des colonies françaises de l'Amérique sous le vent*, 6 vols. (Paris, 1784–90); Jean-Louis-Claude Emmery, *Recueil des édits . . . enregistrés au Parlement de Metz*, 5 vols. (1774–88); François-Antoine-Joseph de Hell, *Dissertatio inauguralis juridice de successione feodali* (1753); and Adrien-Pierre-Barthélémy Cochelet, *Etude du droit civil et coutumier français dans un ordre naturel* (Paris, 1789). Also Fichier Lefebvre; Francisque Mège, *Gaultier de Biauzat, député du Tiers état aux Etats généraux de 1789. Sa vie et sa correspondance*, 2 vols. (Clermont-Ferrand, 1890), 1:1–5; and G. Coeuret, *L'assemblée provinciale de la Haute-Normandie (1787–1789)* (Paris, 1927), 43.

[34] Sarah Maza, "Le tribunal de la nation: Les mémoires judiciaires et l'opinion publique à la fin de l'Ancien régime," *Annales.E.S.C.* 42 (1987), 73–90; and *Private Lives and Public Affairs: The Causes Célèbres of Prerevolutionary France* (Berkeley, 1993). Also, David A. Bell, *Lawyers and Citizens: The Making of a Political Elite in Old Regime France* (Oxford, 1994).

[35] Paul-Louis Target, *Un avocat du XVIIIe siècle* (Paris, 1893), 28–34.

over the more "philosophical" values of abstract reason and natural law. To be sure, under certain circumstances, their deep respect for the law could generate an impatience with arbitrary authority and a sympathy for legal and even constitutional reform. Yet the *mémoires judiciaires* of most were standard legal briefs in the time-honored fashion, filled with scholarly references to Roman law, to royal decrees of the medieval and Old Regime periods, and even to the Bible.[36] It is not surprising, in this sense, that Bailly had considered the lawyers to be the rivals, more than the allies of the literary men. The publication record of these legal theorists was all the more significant in that many would rank among the most active and influential speakers and committee workers in the entire National Assembly.[37]

One should also not overlook those deputies whose publications were squarely in opposition, even antithetical to the fundamental values of the Enlightenment tradition. Close to a sixth of the deputy authors—almost all of them clergymen—had published on theology or religion.[38] The Jansenist canon Charrier de La Roche was a coauthor of the six-volume *Institutiones theologicae*, widely known as the "Theology of Lyon," one of the major works of its kind in the eighteenth century. The abbés Eymar, Champion de Cicé, Maury, Beauvais, and Coster, were among the more celebrated practitioners of funeral oratory. Most of their sermons continued in the tradition of Bossuet and Bourdaloue, praising the deceased for their virtues and meditating on death's indiscriminate harvest of the highborn and the lowly. But both Maury and Beauvais took the occasion to attack the philosophes in general and Voltaire in particular.[39] Other future deputies excelled in defenses of Christianity that were direct challenges to the Enlightenment. The essays by Le Franc de Pompignan, bishop of Vienne, were among the most

[36] See Bell, *Lawyers and Citizens*, esp. 38 and 168; and "Safeguarding the Rights of the Accused: Lawyers and Political Trials in France, 1716–1789," in Dale Van Kley, ed., *The French Idea of Freedom* (Stanford, 1994), 234–64. I have read a sample of *mémoires judiciaires* written by future deputies as located in A. Corda and A. Trudon des Ormes, *Catalogue des factums et d'autres documents judiciaires antérieurs à 1790*, 10 vols. (Paris, 1890–1936). See, for example, the brief of Louis-Simon Martineau, who took up the rights of a Jew living in Paris, but argued in traditional judicial language, using precedents in the Justinian Code, various royal decrees, and the Bible, and who never appealed to Enlightenment values: *Mémoire pour les héritiers d'Abraham Vidal, juif portugais, négociant à Paris* (Paris, 1784). See also, Lenard R. Berlanstein, *The Barristers of Toulouse in the Eighteenth Century, 1740–1793* (Baltimore, 1975), 109; Michael P. Fitzsimmons, *The Parisian Order of Barristers and the French Revolution* (Cambridge, Mass., 1987), 28–32; Gerlof D. Homan, *Jean-François Reubell: French Revolutionary Patriot and Director* (The Hague, 1971), 12.

[37] See below, chap. 7.

[38] The one exception was the marquis de Ferrières's treatise on *Le théisme* (1785).

[39] Louis Charrier de La Roche, *Institutiones theologicae*, 6 vols. (1784); Jean-François-Ange d'Eymar, *Oraison funèbre . . . de Mgr. Louis, Dauphin* (1766); Jean-Baptiste-Marie Champion de Cicé, *Oraison funèbre . . . de Louis, Dauphin* (1766); Jean-Siffrein Maury, *Eloge funèbre du très haut, très puissant et excellent prince Monseigneur Louis, Dauphin de France* (1766); Jean-Baptiste-Charles-Marie de Beauvais, *Oraison funèbre . . . de Louis XV, le Bien-aimé* (1774); Sigisbert-Etienne Coster, *Oraison funèbre de . . . Marie, princesse de Pologne, reine de France* (1768).

popular pieces of the century on the "advantages of the Christian religion" and the "speciousness" and "naiveté" of the philosophes' conception of reason. Bishop La Luzerne of Langres and abbé Thiébault, seminary director in Metz, had also published numerous works of Christian apologetics directed in large measure at the philosophical writings of the century. Canon Louis de Bonnefoy collaborated in a defense of monks and the regular clergy. The Parisian canon, Charles-Jean-François Legros, had made his career ferreting out and lacerating the fundamental assumptions of Rousseau and several other philosophers, taking them to task not only for their positions on religion, but for their logical and epistemological contradictions and their perceived threats to civil stability.[40]

Certain of the deputies' secular writings might also be classed with a kind of "counter-Enlightenment." There was Hell's manifesto of antisemitism, for example, and Bergasse's early *Discours sur les préjugés*, which argued that tradition, authority, and God were the basis of all sound society. There was Malouet's *Mémoire sur l'esclavage des nègres*, which adamantly opposed emancipating black slaves and which urged intransigeance to the shortsighted appeals of "philosophy."[41] And there were the essays and novels of Lézay-Marnésia and Ferrières. Though they fancied themselves disciples of Rousseau, the two marquis wrote essays and novels describing an ideal rural society that was in many respects dominated by traditional hierarchical and religious values. Both made reference to the paternalistic relations which must exist between the "lord" and his "vassals," and between men and women. Though Ferrières had also written a two-volume treatise promoting "theism," he made it clear that in the real world he preferred "religion with all its faults to this demented philosophy, enemy of all that is good, . . . which is undermining the very foundation of social virtue."[42] In sum, an element of the deputies would arrive in Versailles with a solid intellectual basis for conservative opposition to social and ecclesiastical reform.

Little if anything in this corpus of deputy publications anticipated the revolutionary events of the spring and summer of 1789. The great majority

[40] Jean-Georges Le Franc de Pompignan, *La dévotion réconciliée avec l'esprit* (1754); *Les avantages de la religion chrétienne* (1775); and *La religion vengée de l'incrédulité par l'incrédulité elle-même* (1772); Louis de Bonnefoy and Abbé de Bernard, *De l'état religieux* (Paris, 1784); César-Guillaume de La Luzerne, *Instruction pastorale sur l'excellence de la religion* (Paris, 1786); Martin-François Thiébault, *Doctrine chrétienne en forme de prônes*, 6 vols. (1772); Charles-Jean-François Le Gros, *Examen des ouvrages de Jean-Jacques Rousseau* (Geneva, 1785); and *Analyse de l'antiquité dévoilée, du Despotisme oriental, et Du christianisme dévoilé* (Geneva, 1788). On Le Franc de Pompignan, Le Gros, and La Luzerne, see Robert R. Palmer, *Catholics and Unbelievers in Eighteenth-Century France* (Princeton, 1939), 14–15, 175–76, 182–83.

[41] François-Antoine-Joseph de Hell, *Observations sur les Juifs d'Alsace* (1779); Bergasse, *Discours sur les préjugés* (1775); Pierre-Victor Malouet, *Mémoire sur l'esclavage des nègres* (1788). On Bergasse, see Lamy, 16–19, 46. On Malouet's essay, see Carl Ludwig Lokke, *France and the Colonial Question* (New York, 1932), 83–85.

[42] Bourget-Besnier, 15–23; Lézay-Marnésia, *Le bonheur* (1785), 57–58; Ferrières, *La femme*, 2 vols. (1788), 1:5–7; and *Le théisme*, 2 vols. (1785).

of such works were essentially of a literary or scholarly bent. While many revealed a familiarity with elements of Enlightenment thought and vocabulary, very few indeed conveyed the fire and anger, the corrosive wit and sarcasm commonly associated with the best-known philosophes. Their plays and novels were infused with a mild and pleasing Rococo esthetic that might have been written in almost any decade in the eighteenth century; their poetry was characterized by "a gallantry that is always clever, a teasing wit that is always decent, an imagery that is always reasonable."[43] Their prose eulogies in praise of great men, placed a premium on "Enlightened" rule and concern for public welfare, but the general emphasis was on reforms engineered from above.[44] Their research and scholarship were characterized by an almost obsessive preoccupation with facts and detail. Defay-Boutheroue's treatise on "Nature" was in fact a long compendium of miscellaneous observations on the natural history of Orléanais. Thibaudeau's history, entirely secular in its conception, anticipated Ranke in its self-conscious search for "the truth" and its general eschewal of critical condemnations of the past.[45] In his immense compilation of details on customs from around the world, a precursor to nineteenth- and twentieth-century ethnography, Démeunier occasionally reflected on the tension between the way things were and the way they should be—on the general rarity of social equality in the world, for example, and the empirical prevalence of societies based on caste. But he resigned himself to a kind of fatalism: one could only "describe the evils of the world about which it is useless to complain." Apparently "nature has decided that strength should dominate weakness"; and that "distinctions of rank are necessary in a state"—even if, in the ideal case, the world should be a very different place.[46] Garat probably summed up the views of a great many future deputies on the prospects of radical change in the real world. "Perhaps," he wrote in 1778 in his essay on Fontenelle, "there once were countries and ages where the boldest truths directly presented to a sovereign people . . . could make a revolution as soon as they were known." But "for us," he argued, "it is only with time that truth can triumph over prejudice."[47]

In the end, the Constituents who had participated in the "Republic of Letters" prior to 1789 represented only a small minority, about one-twelfth of

---

[43] Description by Suard of the poetry of the marquis de Montesquiou: Anne-Pierre Montesquiou-Fezenzac, *Discours prononcé dans l'Académie française . . . à la réception de Monsieur le Marquis de Montesquiou* (Paris, 1784), 23.

[44] See the works by Lanjuinais, Delandine, and Barère cited above in note 30.

[45] See especially the "Introduction" of Thibaudeau's *Abrégé*. Unlike Voltaire, Thibaudeau never condemned the church nor spoke disparagingly of the Middle Ages. Bouche's *Essai* likewise prided itself on recounting the objective historical truth, though the author did sometimes insert anticlerical remarks.

[46] Jean-Nicolas Démeunier, *L'esprit des usages et coutumes des différents peuples*, 3 vols. (Paris, 1776), 2:74, 83, 95. See also Edna Lemay, "Hierarchy and the Search for Social Equality at the French Constituent Assembly, 1789–91," *History of European Ideas* 11 (1989), 21–26.

[47] Garat, *Eloge de Bernard de Fontenelle*, 82.

the Assembly's membership. The extent to which this sample was characteristic of the corps as a whole is extremely difficult to say. Yet the glimpses we catch of the culture of our deputy witnesses in their early letters and diaries would seem to confirm the complexity and ambiguity of their outlook and attitudes at the end of the Old Regime.

During two trips to Paris in the 1780s, the provincial magistrate Ménard de La Groye pursued a lengthy correspondence with his wife in Le Mans. But his detailed descriptions gave no indication whatsoever of interest in the Enlightened culture and ideas which he might surely have encountered in the capital. Much of his leisure time was spent sight-seeing among the "monuments" of the city and admiring from afar—or so he assured his wife—the ladies and ladies' fashions in Paris and the court at Versailles. He was enormously impressed by a mass and funeral oration which he witnessed at Notre Dame, commemorating the death of the empress Maria-Theresa. But without a doubt, the highlight of his second stay was more directly related to his profession as a jurist: attendance at the Parlement, where he delighted in the oratory of the most celebrated lawyers in Paris, an experience which he described with great zest to his wife.[48] Félix Faulcon, a generation younger than Ménard, also visited Paris on two occasions, and directed a stream of letters to a variety of male acquaintances. His epistolary style was strongly marked by imitations of the classics, a literature which he pursued with much enthusiasm. His comments about Paris focused almost exclusively on women, poetry, and law practice. Like Ménard, he was particularly fascinated by contemporary legal oratory. Though he once heard d'Alembert speak to the French Academy, his descriptions were exclusively concerned with the philosophe's form, diction, and rhetorical expression and made no comment whatsoever on his ideas. The one evident impact of the Enlightenment on Faulcon—as best as we can tell—was his confirmed skepticism and anticlericalism, his dislike of Rome and the church. His most critical observations on contemporary society before 1787 concerned the need for reform of "this absurd confusion of laws and customs" in France.[49]

Deputy letters from the Revolutionary period itself reveal considerable culture and relatively broad reading on the part of the authors—even when the testimonies in question had been written in haste and with no care for future publication. Yet the nature and extent of such readings invariably depended on the profession and stature in life of the individuals involved. In a letter discussing the education of his sixteen-year-old daughter, the Gascon farmer and ex-merchant from Bordeaux, Jean François, was somewhat unsteady in his memory of French literature. He specifically mentioned Madame de Sévigné, who greatly bored him and Rousseau, whom he may or may not actually have read. But he also admitted his inadequacy

[48] François-René-Pierre Ménard de La Groye to his wife: A.D. Sarthe, 10 J 120, letters of May and June 1781.

[49] Félix Faulcon, *Correspondance. Tome 1: 1770–89*, ed. G. Debien (Poitiers, 1939), esp. 217 (letter of Apr. 28, 1785) and the other letters of 1785 and 1787.

and looked forward to more tranquil times when he could "work again on my education." Nompère de Champagny, the stern and seasoned naval commander who had spent much of his adult life at sea, admitted that he seldom read and he gave no indication whatsoever of familiarity with the Enlightenment—though his impatience with the inefficiency of the royal government lead him to embrace a liberal position at the beginning of the Revolution.[50] The small-town Flemish lawyer François-Joseph Bouchette possessed a spectacular Enlightenment library, with multivolume sets not only of Montesquieu, Voltaire, Diderot, and Condillac, but of such radical authors as Helvétius, Holbach, Mably, and Rousseau. We will probably never know whether he had actually read his collection and, if so, whether he had accepted and internalized the ideas he encountered. Conceivably it was these readings which aroused in him an exceptionally intense dislike of the clergy and the nobility. But it seems much more likely that such animosities arose out of the struggles with local notables—and especially with the noble subdelegate and a powerful local monastery—which had so passionately engaged him for over a decade. In any case, in his long correspondence with his close friend Winoc-Antoine Moutton, there was no mention of any of the writers whose works he possessed, nor of any of the obvious Enlightenment phrases or concepts which the books contained. Indeed, based on Bouchette's letters alone, one would never imagine the works which sat on his bookshelves—perhaps unread and gathering dust.[51]

It would be impossible here to pursue a systematic content analysis of the language used by our deputy witnesses in all their diaries and correspondence. Yet a close reading of the testimonies of twenty-five Third Estate deputies during the first month of the Assembly reveals almost no references to the writings of the philosophes—though such references did begin to appear later, after the early months of the sessions.[52] While a third of the witnesses examined occasionally used the words "reason" or "natural rights," such usages generally appeared only at the end of May or the beginning of June and may well have been inspired by the speeches of a few of

[50] Jean François, "Jean François, député de l'Assemblée nationale de 1789," ed. G. de Lagrange-Ferrègues, *Revue de l'Agenais* 83 (1957), 240, 244, 248; Jean-Baptiste de Nompère de Champagny, *Souvenirs de M. de Champagny, duc de Cadore* (Paris, 1846).

[51] François-Joseph Bouchette, *Lettres de François-Joseph Bouchette (1735–1810)*, ed. Camille Looten (Lille, 1909), esp. Looten's introduction, 15–18 and 28–71.

[52] The diaries and correspondence of the following deputies have been read carefully for language usage during the period May 6 to June 6, 1789: Basquiat de Mugriet, Charles-François Bouche, Bouchette, Boullé, Campmas, Creuzé-Latouche, Delaville Le Roulx, Duquesnoy, Durand, Faulcon, Gallot, Gantheret, Gaultier de Biauzat, Goupilleau, Grellet de Beauregard, Lepoutre, Lofficial, Maillot, Maupetit, Meifrund, Ménard de La Groye, Pellerin, Périsse Du Luc, Poncet-Delpech, and Robespierre. None of the writers of the Enlightenment were mentioned during this period, though Creuzé cited the *Encyclopédie* as a source for the history of the previous Estates General, and Maillot used the terms "general will" and "social contract": Creuzé, 9 (letter of May 22); Claude-Pierre Maillot to an unnamed municipal official of Toul: A.C. Toul, JJ 7, letter of June 3.

their more intellectual colleagues.[53] As educated men of the late eighteenth century, nearly all of the deputies were familiar with at least some strands of Enlightenment discourse. But at least through the beginning of June, they seem rarely to have associated such ideas with the concrete problems facing them in the Assembly. Particularly during the early months of the Revolution, the deputies, in their diary entries and letters home, alluded more frequently to history and the classics, than to reason and the general will or to Rousseau and Voltaire.

THE RELIGIOUS CULTURE OF THE DEPUTIES

The deputies of the second and third estates largely avoided theology and religion in their published writings. Yet their attitudes toward these subjects are important elements in their worldview and frame of reference on the eve of the Revolution, and they need to be examined more carefully. The critique of revealed religion and the attack on the Catholic church were among the earliest and most persistent themes, the central common denominators in much of Enlightenment writings. Since the opening salvos of the movement in the 1720s and 1730s, numerous French philosophes had indulged in vigorous and enthusiastic anticlericalism. Such assaults were buttressed, moreover, by two powerful strands of self-criticism arising within the church itself, the Jansenist movement and a movement of protest and independence among French curés, both of which targeted violent attacks on elements of the ecclesiastical hierarchy and intensified the atmosphere of anticlericalism.[54]

In terms of their religious orientations, two small but influential groups of deputies stood out from the others: the Protestants and the Jansenists. The fact that at least twenty-four of the representatives were from Protestant backgrounds was a remarkable testimony to the spread of toleration among portions of the urban electorate.[55] All but one of these deputies—the

[53] One or the other of the two phrases appear in Basquiat (May 29); Campmas (May 30); Creuzé (May 22); Delaville (May 22); Duquesnoy (June 5); Goupilleau (June 1); Maillot (June 3); Ménard (June 5); and Robespierre (May 24). Most of these deputies specifically mention and were almost certainly paraphrasing recent reports by the deputies Rabaut, Mounier, and Target on their commission debates with the Nobles over the vote by head.

[54] Dale Van Kley, *The Jansenists and the Expulsion of the Jesuits from France, 1757–1765* (New Haven, Conn., 1975); and "Church, State, and the Ideological Origins of the French Revolution," *JMH* 51 (1979), 630–64; and the author's *Religion, Revolution, and Regional Culture* (Princeton, 1986), esp. chap. 10.

[55] The following deputies are known Protestants: Augier, Barnave, Blancard, Boissy d'Anglas, Chambon-Latour, Couderc, Cussy, Dupont de Nemours, Gallot, Garesché, Lamy, Lavie, Liquier, Mestre, Meynier de Salinelles, Missy, Nairac, Quatrefages de Laroquete, Rabaut Saint-Etienne, Rathsamhausen, Soustelle, Turckheim, Valete, and Visme. Though most were Calvinist, Lavie, Rathsamhausen, and Turckheim were Lutheran. The list has been constructed from a wide variety of sources; see, notably, Burdette Poland, *French Protestantism and the*

baron de Rathsamhausen—sat in the Third Estate, where they accounted for some 3.5 percent of the order, slightly more than their proportion in the French population as a whole.[56] If we also include those deputies whose families had recently converted to Catholicism, the number with Protestant forbearers appears even larger.[57] No less than eleven of the non-Catholics were wealthy merchants who resided in the largest provincial cities of the realm. Others represented diverse professions, from the Calvinist pastor Rabaut, to the country physician Gallot and the Strasbourg Lutheran patrician Turckheim. Most probably partook of the secularized perspective, strongly stamped by the Enlightenment, typical of the Calvinist elites at the end of the eighteenth century. Of the two most prominent Protestant political figures, Barnave was a self-proclaimed deist, while Rabaut had probably been more influenced by Condillac and Voltaire than by Calvin.[58] In any case, the great majority of the Protestant deputies would soon emerge as strong patriots.

Unfortunately, the Jansenists in the Assembly are substantially more difficult to identify. Best estimates would place some thirty to forty deputies in the Jansenist or Jansenist-leaning camp. Of these, most were probably clergymen, led by such curé radicals as Henri Grégoire, Jacques Jallet, and Louis Charrier de La Roche. But there was also a small core of jurists: the three canonists, Camus, Lanjuinais, and Durand de Maillane; the noble magistrate in the Parlement of Paris, Fréteau de Saint-Just; the Norman judge Guillaume-François Goupil de Préfelne; and the lawyers Martineau, Treilhard, and perhaps Charles-François Bouche.[59] All of these men took religion extremely seriously in their daily lives and were probably among the most pious individuals in the entire Assembly. Camus, who was said to have kept a life-sized crucifix in his office, wrote in 1793 that "nothing in the world is more precious to me than religion."[60] The fact that many of the Jansenist sympathizers were among the most active speakers and committee

---

French Revolution (Princeton, N.J., 1957), 291; Rolland Marx, *Recherches sur la vie politique de l'Alsace pré-révolutionnaire et révolutionnaire* (Strasbourg, 1966), 32; the Fichier Lefebvre; and the *DC*.

[56] Poland, p. 8, estimates a Protestant population of about 2% in 1789.

[57] There were at least five of recent Calvinist stock from Poitou and Saintonge: Alquier, Cochon de Lapparent, Creuzé-Latouche, Faulcon, and Thibaudeau: H. Perrin de Boussac, *Un témoin de la Révolution et de l'Empire: Charles-Jean-Marie Alquier* (Paris, 1983), 10–11; Debien, introduction to Faulcon's *Correspondance*, vii; Paul Boucher, *Charles Cochon de Lapparent. Conventionnel, ministre de la police, préfet de l'Empire* (Paris, 1969), 11–12.

[58] *Histoire des Protestants en France* (Toulouse, 1977), 233–36; E. D. Bradby, *The Life of Barnave*, 2 vols. (Oxford, 1915), 1:33.

[59] J. Du Breuil de Saint-Germain, "Les Jansénistes à la Constituante," *Revue des études historiques* 79 (1913), 163–76; and information kindly shared with me by Dale Van Kley. See also Yann Fauchois, "Les Jansénistes et la Constitution civile du clergé," in *Jansénisme et Révolution*, ed. Catherine Maire (Paris, 1990), 200–201.

[60] Pierre Préteux, *Armand-Gaston Camus, 1740–1804* (Paris, 1932), 15.

workers in the Assembly gave them an influence far beyond their numbers.[61] Like the Protestants, moreover, the great majority soon opted for political positions on the patriot left.

Beyond the small groups of Jansenists and Protestants, the religious views of the deputies in 1789 are often difficult to ascertain. The near totality had taken part in the signal experiences that marked a Catholic upbringing in eighteenth-century France: baptism, catechism, confirmation, and attendance at clerically directed schools. A large proportion of the older deputies had undoubtedly passed through the Jesuit *collèges*, while many of their younger colleagues had received their secondary formation with the Oratorians or the secular priests who had replaced the Jesuits.[62] Indeed, a small but significant number in both the Third and the Nobility had initially considered careers in the clergy and had even advanced through the orders and studied in seminaries.[63]

The extent to which the deputies actually practiced their religion and attended mass regularly—or even once a year, the canonical minimum—the extent to which they identified themselves as members of the Catholic Church, is far more uncertain. Among our deputy witnesses, only Bouchette, Lepoutre, Ménard de La Groye, and Garron de La Bévière ever mentioned attending religious service beyond the requisite ceremonial functions of the Assembly. Jean-Baptiste Grellet de Beauregard was probably more typical when he admitted that he was "scarcely scrupulous in following the precepts [of the religion of my fathers]."[64] Most of the deputies of the Third Estate preferred to distance themselves from the more conspicuous manifestations of orthodox Catholicism. In the early days of the National Assembly, the majority ostentatiously refused proposals to place a crucifix in the meeting hall or to set up an adjoining chapel or to cancel sessions on Sundays and feast days of the Virgin. When the king announced twenty-four places for deputies in the royal Corpus Christi processions, it was impossible to find enough interested individuals to fill out the invitation. And when on August 3, 1789, a curé deputy gave a speech laced with Latin, demanding that mass be celebrated every morning in the Assembly, the deputies broke out in laughter, and allowed him to finish his dis-

[61] See below, chap. 7.

[62] Of the 125 Second and Third Estate deputies for whom such information has been found, 33 (26%) had attended collèges with the Jesuits, 42 (34%) with the Oratorians, 34 (27%) with local secular clergy, and 16 (13%) with other regular orders.

[63] Thirteen commoners and 14 nobles are known to have taken orders or attended seminaries.

[64] Bouchette, 248 (letter of Aug. 21, 1789); Pierre-François Lepoutre to his wife: family archives of Adolphe Lepoutre-Dubreuil, Montignac-sur-Vezère, letter of Jan. 21, 1791; François-René-Pierre Ménard de La Groye, *Correspondance (1789–1791)* (Le Mans, 1989), 163 (letter of Dec. 25, 1789); Claude-Jean-Baptiste de Garron de La Bévière, ms. letters to his wife: A.D. Ain, 1 Mi 1, e.g., letters of May 3 and Oct. 11, 1789; Jean-Bernard Grellet de Beauregard, "Lettres de M. Grellet de Beauregard," ed. Abbé Dardy, *Mémoires de la Société des sciences naturelles et archéologiques de la Creuse*, 2e sér., 7 (1899), 81 (letter of May 29, 1790).

course—according to Laurent Visme—only because "we felt the need to rest our minds with a little recreation."[65]

Moreover, it is clear from their writings that a profound, resolute, and aggressive anticlericalism was integral to the thinking of a substantial number of deputies. Certain of the letters and diaries were peppered with derogatory epithets in reference to clergymen: "blacks," "crows," "les calotins," "la prêtraille."[66] Even in the earliest days of the Estates General, when the deputies were laboring to win clerical support for a vote by head, anticlerical rhetoric toward the upper clergy seemed irrepressible. A June 6 proposition by the episcopacy that each estate should meet separately to consider the plight of the poor brought an explosion of sarcasm and derision. "We all rushed forward," wrote Camusat de Belombre, "asking the right to speak out against . . . [the bishops'] absurd expenses, their ridiculous luxury, their useless residence in the voluptuous society of Paris." Others commented that the bishops would do better to sell their elegant carriages and golden dinnerware and generally redirect their ostentatious affluence toward charity.[67] But even the supposed affection for the humble parish clergy, foils to the aristocratic episcopacy, seemed superficial at best to some of the patriot deputies. When, at the beginning of June, the liberal clergy failed to convince a majority of their colleagues to join the Third Estate, Goupilleau accused them all of being "traitors" and "chameleons." And when a handful of parish clergymen unilaterally joined the Third several days later, the moderate deputy from Lorraine, Duquesnoy, confided to a friend, "You cannot imagine the ridiculous importance attached to the appearance of these new recruits. . . . I wish someone would tell me what good twenty-odd curés will do for the Commons."[68]

We can sample the range of sentiments toward religion at the beginning of the Revolution, first among the Third deputies and then among the Nobles, by focusing on those individuals for whom substantial testimonies are preserved during the early stages of the Assembly. Obviously, the inclusion or exclusion of religious references in a letter could depend on the parties to whom an individual was writing. It might also depend on the personality of the deputy and his willingness to share his personal beliefs—or lack

---

[65] Claude-Benjamin Vallet, "Souvenirs de l'abbé Vallet, député de Gien à l'Assemblée constituante," *Nouvelle revue rétrospective* 16 (1902), 315; *AP*, 8:335; Joseph-Michel Pellerin, ms. journal: B.M. Versailles, Ms. 823F, entry of June 17, 1789; Laurent de Visme, ms. "Journal des Etats généraux": B.N., Nouv. acq. fr. 12938, entry of Aug. 3, 1789.

[66] Bouchette, 337 (letter of Feb. 2, 1790); Périsse, letter of July 8, 1789; Jean-Gabriel Gallot, *La vie et les oeuvres du Docteur Jean-Gabriel Gallot*, ed. Louis Merle (Poitiers, 1961), 128 (letter of Sept. 16, 1789).

[67] Nicolas-Jean Camusat de Belombre, cited in Henri Diné, "Le journal de Camusat de Belombre, député du Tiers de la ville de Troyes (6 mai–8 août 1789)," *AHRF* 37 (1965), 267; Duquesnoy, 1:77 (entry of June 7, 1789); Creuzé-Latouche, 62–65; Visme, entry of June 6, 1789.

[68] Duquesnoy, 1:95 (entry of June 15); Jean-François-Marie Goupilleau to his cousin, sénéchal in Rochefervière: B.M. Nantes, Collection Dugast-Matifeux, no. 98, letter of June 1, 1789.

thereof—with others. Nevertheless, when used with care and as a series, the initial letters are often revealing of the attitudes and presuppositions which individuals brought with them on their arrival in Versailles.[69]

In fact, among the forty-five Third Estate witnesses sampled, only four seem to have identified with orthodox Catholicism. The Breton lawyer Joseph-Michel Pellerin felt sympathy for "our errant brothers" the Protestants, but he confessed that the idea of permitting them to worship in public was deeply disturbing to "real Catholics" like himself. Pierre-François Lepoutre, a modest farmer with a leasehold near Lille, closed almost all of his early letters to his wife with pious prayers for her health and protection. He took care to remind her to have special masses said in November for their deceased parents, and he asked both his family and his farmworkers to pray for him and for the National Assembly. The publisher from Lyon, Périsse Du Luc, apparently saw no difficulty in reconciling a distinctly Catholic worldview with his Masonic and Mesmerist convictions. On occasion he asked his friend Willermoz to pray for their Masonic brother, the comte de Virieu, who was becoming a full-fledged aristocrat. And speaking of two Swedish friends visiting him in Paris, he noted with some satisfaction that they were making great strides "in Catholicism." Gaultier de Biauzat, the former Jesuit who had become a lawyer after the expulsion of his order, also invoked a specific Christian and Catholic God. He began one of his letters to the municipal leaders of Clermont-Ferrand with a passage from the Bible and as he prepared to deliver his first speech, he asked them, "Please pray to the Holy Spirit that He might enlighten me for this occasion."[70]

Of the remaining deputies another eleven are found to make relatively frequent references to God or religion throughout their letters.[71] There were recurring allusions to God's providence in watching over the nation and the Revolution. This was especially the case in descriptions of the night of August 4. "It is fitting that we show our reverence to the Supreme Being for this great event," wrote Maupetit to his friend near Mayenne. For Théodore Vernier, addressing his fellow citizens in Lons-le-Saunier, "Everything that has happened thus far is clearly the work of Providence, a Providence who will undoubtedly determine our future."[72] Though such expressions might

[69] Note that there were two particular circumstances which led deputies to mention God or religion, when they might not have done so in normal correspondence: first, the early decision to restructure many of the fundamental institutions of the church; and second, the deeply unsettling, often traumatic events of the summer and autumn of 1789, which frequently provided the context for public affirmations of religious belief.

[70] Pellerin, entry of Aug. 23, 1789; Lepoutre, letters of June 5 and 16, July 16, Aug. 5, and Nov. 15, 1789; Périsse, letter of Dec. 27, 1789; Gaultier, 2:69 (letter of May 18, 1789).

[71] Boullé, Campmas, Dusers, François, Gontier de Biran, Goupilleau, Grellet, Lasalle, Maupetit, Ménard, and Vernier.

[72] Michel-René Maupetit, "Lettres de Maupetit (1789–91)," ed. Quéruau-Lamérie, *Bulletin de la Commission historique et archéologique de la Mayenne*, 2e sér., 19 (1901), 219 (letter of Aug. 5, 1789); Théodore Vernier to the municipality of Lons-le-Saunier: A.C. Bletterans (non-classé), "Lettres de Vernier," letter of Aug. 6, 1789.

have been taken from the deist or Masonic vocabulary, they were not simple allusions to a clock-maker God, but rather to an active deity who directly intervened in support of the Revolution. Grellet made reference to "the Guiding Spirit who watches over the destiny of our country"; "I will confide the ship of state," he added, "to that Providence whose immutable decrees are accomplished despite the efforts of feeble humanity." Vernier was very self-conscious on this score: "Don't be surprised to find my frequent homages and invocations [to God]. Who else can we thank, if it's not the Universal Agent." And he worked vigorously and successfully against "the philosophes" in order to have a reference to "the Supreme Being" inserted in the preamble to the Declaration of the Rights of Man and the Citizen: "A great many delegates support me, and many philosophes are opposed"[73]

Yet most of the deputies in this group indicated that theirs was a very particular reading of the Catholic religion, somewhere between that of the Catholic Enlightenment and the "theism" of Jean-Jacques Rousseau. Grellet, Campmas, Ménard, and Jean François all expressed their desire for a return to the religion of Jesus and the Gospels, as contrasted with a religion corrupted over time by the clergy—a common theme among the reformist parish clergy on the eve of the Revolution. Campmas, Ménard, and Goupilleau commented on the intrinsic link which they perceived between Christianity and equality. Christian morality, wrote Goupilleau, "condemns all prejudices and distinctions of birth."[74]

Of the remaining two-thirds of the commoner deputies for whom substantial testimonies are preserved, nineteen made only passing allusions to God or Providence, and eleven made no mention whatsoever.[75] The references that appear in their testimonies usually involve appeals to divine help in times of trial, such as "May God will that . . ." and "May it please God that . . ." Merle mentioned the deity only in the contexts of two oaths made to his constituency: "I swear before God and the nation. . . ."[76] Though such expressions were written with apparent sincerity—not only in letters to friends and family members but in those intended for public circulation—they were hardly indicative of profound religious faith. While the religious sentiments of this group are usually impossible to determine, it is

[73] Grellet, 65, 91–92 (letters of July 10, 1789 and July 31, 1790); and Vernier, letters of August 6, 8, and 13, 1789.

[74] Grellet, 92 (letter of July 31, 1790); Campmas, letter of Nov. 28, 1789; Ménard, 235, 333 (letters of June 22, 1790 and Jan. 22, 1791); François, 237 (letter of Dec. 5, 1789); Goupilleau, letter of May 11, 1789.

[75] Included in the group of nineteen: Basquiat de Mugriet, Begouën-Demeaux, Bonnemant, Bouchette, Boulouvard, Delandine, Dinochau, Durand, Duval de Grandpré, Gallot, Gantheret, Lofficial, Lombard, Meifrund, Merle, Poncet-Delpech, Quatrefage de Laroquete, Thibaudeau, and Verdollin. The eleven making no mention of religion or the deity were Boissy d'Anglas, Pierre-François-Balthazar Bouche, Creuzé-Latouche, Delaville Le Roulx, Duquesnoy, Faulcon, Maillot, Nairac, Rabaut Saint-Etienne, Robespierre, and Visme.

[76] André-Marie Merle to the municipality of Mâcon: A.C. Mâcon, letter of Jan. 7, 1790.

unlikely that any of the individuals in question shared the pervasive religious commitment of Gaultier or Lepoutre. Both Thibaudeau and Duquesnoy were confirmed deists. The former was described by his son as a "philosopher and deist" who "offered his prayers morning and night, his hat in his hand, while walking in his garden or his study." Duquesnoy referred to "the eternal and imprescriptible right of all men to worship . . . in their own way the One who makes the sun shine for all." Toward the end of the Assembly, Faulcon would write that he considered religion only an opinion and that he was strongly in favor of keeping all religious issues out of the new constitution: "Our constitution must last for centuries. . . . It would be absurd to include in it anything arising from a transient opinion." "It is not in our power to decree the beliefs of our successors."[77]

In sum, then, the deputies of the Third Estate arrived in the Revolution with a considerable range of positions on religion and the church. The overwhelming majority of our sample witnesses seem to have had very little attachment to the clergy, particularly the upper clergy. One would be hard pressed to find any of them expressing a word of affection for ecclesiastics, no matter what their rank or position. In their religious beliefs per se they spread out across the spectrum from those like Gaultier who seemed to profess a deep Catholic faith, to those like Faulcon who approached a position of agnosticism. The majority would seem to have situated themselves somewhere in the deist camp, a deism which varied substantially in its conception of God, however—from the actively intervening Supreme Being of Grellet or Vernier, to the abstract deity of Duquesnoy. They practiced only rarely and were generally detached from theology. Indeed, patriot deputies who took Catholic theology seriously were clearly considered a bit odd. Dubois-Crancé ridiculed Gaultier's religiosity, even though he respected the patriotism of the deputy from Clermont: "he would have made an excellent village curé." Visme commented on the canon lawyer, Durand de Maillane, whose frequent references in one of his speeches to the "Holy Trinity" were considered "tiresome" and "in very bad taste." Duquesnoy, for his part, could not but admire the Jansenist Fréteau de Saint-Just who had "the courage to express religious principles in an Assembly where such principles are considered a bit ridiculous."[78] But there was also a clear double standard on the part of many deputies—whatever their personal beliefs—in their utilitarian desire to promote traditional religion for the masses as a means of social cohesion. "Like nineteen-twentieths of the Assembly," wrote Campmas in early 1790, "I believe that religion is useful and that we must therefore allow public worship." "Religion," argued Dinochau, "is the first foundation of the social order; it is the cornerstone of the edifice. . . . It would

---

[77] Antoine-Claire Thibaudeau, *Biographie, mémoires, 1765–92* (Paris, 1875), 53; Duquesnoy, I:310 (entry of Aug. 23, 1789); Félix Faulcon, *Correspondance. Tome 2: 1789–91*, ed. G. Debien (Poitiers, 1953), 450 (journal entry of Aug. 5, 1791).

[78] Edmond-Louis-Alexis Dubois-Crancé, *Véritable portrait de nos législateurs* (Paris, 1792), 131; Visme, entry of Aug. 1, 1789; Duquesnoy, 1:435 (entry of Oct. 13, 1789).

be most unfortunate if the common people did not believe in God; if one's valets, one's business agents, one's tradesmen, and one's workers did not believe in God."[79]

The religious culture of the Nobility, like that of the Third Estate, was variegated and complex. The Nobles, no less than the Commoners, had their share of anticlerical scoffers. It would be a pair of young aristocrats, the marquis de La Coste and Alexandre de Lameth, who first proposed the confiscation of church property.[80] The anticlerical rhetoric of these two men probably reflected the position of many of the liberal nobles—like Duport or Mirabeau or Destutt de Tracy—all of whom had formerly been members of the Committee of Thirty. A few years before the Revolution, the marquis de Ferrières had written an intensely anticlerical essay, inspired by Rousseau, castigating the clergy for foisting the monstrous concoction of theology on the true religion of the Supreme Being. Reynaud de Montlosier had also passed through a period of skepticism and anticlericalism, after having been rather pious in his youth. Yet Montlosier had been converted away from "materialism" through his discovery of the mysteries of Mesmer; and his description of the clergy at the time of the Revolution was far from negative. And even Ferrières had ultimately concluded that he preferred the church with all its abuses to the reign of "philosophy."[81] Indeed, the letters and diaries of our Noble witnesses contrast markedly with those of the Third in the near absence of anticlerical themes—even in the earliest weeks before the Assembly began debating the issue of the church.

Regrettably, far fewer contemporary testimonies are preserved for Second Estate deputies than for those of the Third.[82] Among the fifteen individuals for whom sets of documents have been analyzed, only four—the duc de Biron, the comte de La Marck, the comte de Castellane, and the baron de Pinteville—made no references at all to God or religious belief. Six others by contrast—the comte de Crécy, the comte de Virieu, the Vicomte de Malartic, the comte de La Gallissonnière, Garron de La Bévière, and Le Clerc de Lassigny—made numerous such references. Once again, the most common expressions were "May God preserve us" or similar stock appeals

[79] Campmas, letter of Mar. 8, 1790; Jacques Dinochau, *Histoire philosophique et politique de l'Assemblée constituante*, 2 vols. (Paris, 1789), 1:108. See also Charles-François Bouche, *Charte contenant la constitution française dans ses objets fondamentaux* (Versailles, 1789), 7–17.

[80] Duquesnoy, 1:278–79 (entry of Aug. 9, 1789).

[81] "Introduction" by Henri Carré to Charles-Elie Ferrières, *Correspondance inédite* (Paris, 1932), 4–6; Reynaud de Montlosier, 22, 133–37.

[82] Included here are the duc de Biron, the marquis de Brulart de Sillery, the comte de Castellane, the comte de Crécy, the marquis de Ferrières, the baron de Gauville, the marquis de Guilhem-Clermont-Lodève, Garron de La Bévière, the comte de Lablache, the comte de La Gallissonnière, the comte de La Marck, Le Clerc de Lassigny, the vicomte de Malartic, the baron de Pinteville, and the comte de Virieu. They represent about 4.5% of all noble deputies, as opposed to the approximately 7% of Third deputies for which such series of letters or diary entries have been examined.

to the deity in times of difficulty. But several of the nobles were a good deal more expressive than any of the Third deputies. Le Clerc asked that "the good Lord might lend His blessed hand, for otherwise I cannot imagine how it will all end"; while Virieu was almost Baroque in his pleas: "May Heaven direct the angel of celestial vengeance to promptly end [this anarchy]." And two of the deputies sought divine solace for the specific plight of the Nobility in the summer of 1789. "The arm of the Almighty weighs heavily upon us," commented La Bévière to his wife, "and we have no choice but to humble ourselves and bless the hand that strikes us"; and elsewhere, "I beseech God that He might soon remove the cup of bitterness that I must drink each day." La Gallissonnière noted in his diary the depth of his disappointment over the king's lack of leadership: "We can only believe, with the humble resignation of faith, that when God in His eternal wisdom decided the fate of the nation, He struck down its leaders with blindness."[83]

An important segment of our Noble witnesses linked themselves to a traditional religious and specifically Catholic worldview. For the marquis de Guilhem-Clermont-Lodève, the Catholic religion guaranteed a meaning and a moral structure to existence. "Without religion, all the bonds of society are broken; without religion I could scarcely master my own life. Without religion, in a word . . . we would be the playthings of mere chance." Garron de La Bévière attended mass regularly throughout his stay in Versailles and Paris "every Sunday and holy day." He confided his consternation when some of the commoner deputies broke into applause in the middle of the sermon on the opening day of the Estates General, an act "which should never have been allowed in the sanctity of the church"; and he was profoundly upset by Chénier's anticlerical play, *Charles IX*, which he saw in December: "The Catholic religion and its ministers are depicted in the most horrible colors. . . . It was written to dishonor our religion." The vicomte de Malartic, who had started as a canon before entering the army and who had continued to take a keen interest in theological questions, was outraged when the deputies attempted to negate the solemn "religious oaths" of the electoral mandates with the simple fiat of the National Assembly. Le Clerc de Lassigny was soon disconsolate in letters to his wife that "good Catholics" in the Assembly were being outmaneuvered by "philosophical reasoning."[84]

---

[83] Denis-Ferdinand de Crécy to Hecquet de Bérenger, *trésorier de la guerre*: A.N., AB XIX 3562(1), letters of Oct. 7 and 24, 1789; François-Henri de Virieu to the marquis de Viennois: Archives of the Château d'Avauges, reproduced in A.D. Isère, 1 Mi 461, letter of August 4, 1789; Augustin-Félix-Elisabeth Barin de La Gallissonnière, ms. journal: Archives de la Guerre, A4 LVI, entry of June 21, 1789; La Bévière, letters of July 27 and August 12, 1789; Louis-Jean-Baptiste Leclerc de Lassigny de Juigné to his wife: Archives of the Château de Saint-Martin, letter of [July] 24, 1789. See also the letter of the marquis de Fumel-Monségur, to the correspondence bureau of Agen, Dec. 22, 1789: Desgraves, 91.

[84] Speech by Guilhem of August 22, 1789, cited by Octave Teissier, *Les députés de la Provence*

Thus, the testimony of the deputy witnesses suggests a certain continuity in religious values between the Nobility and the Third Estate. To judge by the letters preserved, both corps contained a considerable range of views and opinions on the subject. A segment of the worldly wise aristocrats, no less than the Third Estate, had apparently internalized the religious perspectives of the Enlightenment. Indeed, the argument might be made that in no other area had that movement exercised so profound an effect on the attitudes of the deputies as in the realm of religious culture. And yet the sample examined here also suggests that the spectrum of Noble religious attitudes, by comparison with that of the Commoners, was distinctly skewed in the direction of orthodox Catholicism. None of the noble writers exhibited the aggressive anticlericalism so common among the Third. And several seemed to link themselves with a distinctly Catholic worldview from the earliest stages of the Assembly. It was from a specifically orthodox religious perspective that many of these same Nobles would view the debates over the disposition of the clergy and the reorganization of the church.

IDEOLOGY AND REVOLUTION

Despite the inevitable similarities and the elements of a common culture, the deputies differed considerably in their opinions and perspectives. Virtually all strands of the Enlightenment tradition were represented among them. There were disciples of Voltaire and disciples of Rousseau; there were deputy physiocrats and deputy scientists; there were former associates of Enlightened bureaucracy and substantial numbers from both the Catholic Enlightenment and the "occult Enlightenment." There were respectable contingents from the provincial academies and the Masonic lodges, though neither could be said to represent a dominant presence, and most deputies did not belong to any such organizations.[85] There was also that large and powerful element of jurists, who, while not impervious to the language of the philosophes, were far more conversant with the venerable legacy of law, justice, and legal precedent. And there was a smaller but influential group, primarily among segments of the Clergy and the Nobility, whose writings were quite in contradiction with, even explicitly hostile to, the spirit and major tenets of the Enlightenment—particularly in their defense of religion and of a hierarchical and authoritarian view of society.

To a certain extent, the specific range of intellectual concerns differed between the three orders. This was particularly the case among the deputy

---

à l'Assemblée nationale de 1789 (Draguignan, 1898), 106–7; La Bévière, letters of May 5 and Dec. 4, 1789; Malartic, 8; Le Clerc, letter of April 14, 1790. See also, Louis-Henri-Charles de Gauville, Journal, ed. Edouard de Barthélémy (Paris, 1864), 42.

[85] Significantly, one strand that seems to have been entirely unrepresented among the membership of the Estates General was that of the grubstreet philosophes described by Robert Darnton.

clergymen. Not only were they proportionately underrepresented among the deputy authors, the deputy academicians, and the deputy Freemasons, but most of their pre-Revolutionary writings were on religious subjects, a domain almost entirely abandoned by the deputies of the other two estates. While the Nobles and the Third Estate were more closely linked in some respects, there were important differences between the deputies in these two orders as well. It is a mistake to judge the entire Second Estate by the activities of the relatively small group of young liberal nobles, most of whom resided in Paris and Versailles. The previous chapter underlined the considerable differences in educational patterns between the Nobles and the Third Estate. While some of the Nobles, in their published works, dabbled in virtually all categories of writing, they involved themselves more frequently in the various literary genres, and were substantially less interested in scholarship or legal studies. And an important segment of the Nobles revealed themselves as more traditionally Catholic than the bulk of the Third Estate deputies. Despite their use of the standard Enlightenment watchwords, nobles like Ferrières and Lézay-Marnésia developed elaborate schemes for the preservation of rural religion and the social status quo.

Yet the commoner deputies were by no means revolutionaries on the eve of the Estates General. Undoubtedly, their views on religion, the deism, theism, or various forms of modified Christianity which so many seemed to embrace, constituted a major departure from the positions of previous generations. But in most of their Old Regime writings their principal preoccupations were anything but radical. Particularly prominent within the Third Estate was that ample group of deputies for whom Enlightenment seemed to signify—if it signified anything at all—research, scholarly inquiry, and practical problem solving: in law, in history, in science, or in economic analysis. This was clearly Enlightenment in its most expansive definition, in the definition of Immanuel Kant, for whom the essence of the movement could be reduced to a general humanistic attitude of free inquiry under the motto of "Sapere aude"—dare to know.

Indeed, overt affiliation with the various cultural institutions or manifestations of the Old Regime predicted rather poorly the political options which individuals would follow at the beginning of the Revolution. Among those identified above as "professional" philosophes, Mirabeau, Démeunier, Bailly and Dupont de Nemours, soon emerged as important patriot leaders; Boufflers and Bergasse linked themselves with the "Monarchien" right; and Volney, Garat, Delandine, and Lenoir slipped rapidly into a silent obscurity. Among those adhering to Masonic lodges, there was a slight tendency for members of the Third Estate to opt for the left in the first year of the Revolution; but the Nobles were far more likely to sit on the right.[86] Or, to

---

[86] According to our database, 46 of 149 Third-masons (31%) joined the Jacobins, compared to the 167 of 656 (25%) of all Third deputies who were Jacobins. By contrast, 12 of 85 Noble-Masons (14%) were Jacobins, compared to 25 of 85 (29%) who sat on the right—

focus only on the most prominent enthusiasts and imitators of Rousseau, Robespierre and Leclerc became Jacobins; Bergasse and Boufflers, Monarchiens; Ferrières and Lézay, members of the aristocratic right; and d'Antraigues a prominent leader of the emigrant counterrevolution.[87]

It is the argument of the present and the following chapters that the ideological mix, the conceptual frameworks were present among the men of '89 for any number of political options, for any number of revolutions or reform movements or counterrevolutions. The ideological choices that emerged most dominant in the course of the Revolution developed, above all, as a function of specific political contingencies and social interactions within the Assembly and between the Assembly and the population as a whole.

---

defined here as those who supported Dom Gerle's motion of April 13, 1790. On the identification of the various factions, see below, chaps. 6 and 8. Cf. also Pierre Lamarque, *Les Francsmaçons aux Etats généraux et à l'Assemblée nationale* (Paris, 1981), 1–13.

[87] Fichier Lefebvre. See also Roger Barny, *Jean-Jacques Rousseau dans la Révolution française, 1789–1801* (Paris, 1977); and *Rousseau dans la Révolution: le personnage de Jean-Jacques et les débuts du culte révolutionnaire (1787–1791)* (Oxford, 1986).

The Political Apprenticeship

WRITING his memoirs in 1792, the Parisian scholar Bailly vividly recalled both his exhilaration during the electoral process of 1789 and his consternation when he was asked to preside in one of the meetings: "I was completely ignorant of the organization and rules in such assemblies." Up until that time, he wrote, his experience with politics had been confined to his readings and discussions in Parisian clubs. Only now, for the first time, had he become "*something* in the political order."[1] Bailly's image of the deputies of 1789 as political neophytes, more adept in political ideology than in political action, has been a persistent theme in much of French Revolutionary historiography. For Edmund Burke, as for Alexis de Tocqueville, the deputies were largely inexperienced in the realities of power and public affairs, and based their comprehension of politics primarily on abstract reasoning and philosophical tracts. In the late twentieth century, Norman Hampson and François Furet have argued much the same position, suggesting in addition that the Constituents' impractical understanding of power linked them directly to the mentality of the Terror.[2]

Yet without questioning the authenticity of Bailly's recollections, one may wonder if this Parisian intellectual and academician was typical of the deputies as a whole. Clearly a number of the delegates had been involved in Old Regime politics and political maneuvering at the highest levels. Among the privileged deputies, most of the bishops were veterans of the General Assembly of the Clergy, the national institution which determined the clergy's fiscal contributions to the king and which frequently used its financial leverage to lobby for policy changes. Several of the twenty-odd nobles who sat in the sovereign courts—Duval d'Eprémesnil and Fréteau de Saint-Just in Paris, Perreney de Grosbois in Besançon, Lambert de Frondeville in Rouen, for example—had played leadership roles in the parlementary opposition to the monarchy in the last decades of the Old Regime. Even among the Third Estate deputies, a small but significant number—including Dupont de Nemours, Lebrun, Anson, d'Ailly, Malouet, Treilhard, Le Couteulx de Canteleu, Target, and Martineau—had held positions which put

---

[1] Jean-Sylvain Bailly, *Mémoires d'un témoin de la Révolution*, ed. Berville and Barrière, 3 vols. (Paris, 1821–22), 1:9, 21 (entries of April 21 and 23, 1789).

[2] Norman Hampson, *Prelude to Terror: The Constituent Assembly and the Failure of Consensus* (Oxford, 1988), 1–5, 42, 61–62; François Furet, *Interpreting the French Revolution*, trans. Elborg Forster (Cambridge, 1981), 55, 62–63.

them close to the principal lines of power within the bureaucratic system, with substantial experience in national policy making.[3]

Participation in a whole array of Old-Regime institutions, moreover, had probably exposed the great majority of the future Constituents to the forms and procedures of collective political processes.[4] Most of the Third Estate deputies would have had experience in the meetings of corporate bodies— whether guilds, professional associations, chambers of commerce and industry, or corps of judges, lawyers, or university professors—bodies which retained a substantial vitality through the end of the Old Regime.[5] We have already noted those individuals—perhaps a fifth to a fourth of the Constituents—who had participated in learned academies and Masonic lodges. In their membership, such organizations were anything but democratic and were often extremely exclusive and elitist. Nevertheless, the lodges and academies may well have provided substantial experience in the techniques and ethos of quasi-political assemblies.[6]

Perhaps even more important was the deputies' experience in municipal government. Almost one in five of the Third deputies are known to have held municipal functions, including at least sixty-two who had served as mayors and at least seventy who had held other municipal positions.[7] Substantially more of the commoners, most of whom were "notables" in their local communities, were undoubtedly linked to municipal governments in a variety of contexts, from town councils to hospital administrations to municipal charity boards. Even if many of the mayors had been appointed by the monarchy, all would have been exposed to the lively and vigorous municipal politics which persisted in most towns throughout the eighteenth century—and which were notably invigorated after 1787.[8] In this respect, the deputies of the Third were substantially more experienced in day-to-day governmental activities than many of the military aristocrats who predominated in the Noble Estate.

Yet above and beyond the political initiation derived from professional experience and normal civic responsibilities, national events in the last years

[3] See above, chap. 1.

[4] André Castaldo, *Les méthodes de travail de la Constituante* (Paris, 1989), 53; Keith Michael Baker, *Inventing the French Revolution* (Cambridge, Mass., 1990), 20–23.

[5] David Bien, "Offices, Corps, and a System of State Credit: The Uses of Privilege under the Ancien Régime," in *FRCMPC*, 1:89–114.

[6] Castaldo, 69–70. Augustin Cochin, *Les sociétés de pensée et la démocratie moderne* (Paris, 1921); and Ran Halévi, *Les loges maçonniques dans la France d'Ancien régime* (Paris, 1984), esp. 9–16. On the nondemocratic nature of lodges, see Roger Chartier, *The Cultural Origins of the French Revolution* (Durham, N.C., 1991), 165–66.

[7] Based primarily on Fichier Lefebvre and the *DC*. We have found a total of 70 known mayors or ex-mayors among the deputies, 62 from the Third (89% of the total) and 8 from the nobility. Another 70 commoners and 1 noble are known to have held other municipal functions. These figures are almost certainly incomplete.

[8] On the lively politics in the town of Vannes—in which the commoners were particularly active—see T.G.A. Le Goff, *Vannes and Its Region: A Study of Town and Country in Eighteenth-Century France* (Oxford, 1981), chap. IV.

of the Old Regime would lead to a veritable political mobilization of the kingdom with profound effects on virtually all of the deputies. There can be no question here of fully recounting the political history of France in the two decades before the Revolution. Our objective is rather to explore the impact of these events on the political apprenticeship of the future representatives of the nation.

POLITICAL MOBILIZATION AFTER 1770

After generations of study, the direct political origins of the French Revolution, the impending bankruptcy of the state, and the progressive breakdown of the Bourbon government, are now fairly well understood. In the intensifying competition among the great powers of eighteenth-century Europe, an antiquated fiscal apparatus and a system of privilege, which drew inordinately on the least wealthy classes, left the French monarchy increasingly unable to mobilize sufficient revenues and credit to maintain its position and pay its debts.[9] The perpetual need for new taxes brought the king into confrontation with the French sovereign courts, who maintained a lofty image of their own authority and claimed the right to veto any royal decree. The situation was enormously exacerbated, moreover, by the weakness and inadequacies of the last of the Bourbon monarchs. That Louis XVI wished to act in the best interests of his people is probably not to be doubted. But a persistent lassitude, even lethargy before the duties of kingship, an insouciance that saw him drop off to sleep—and snore—in the midst of his most critical political functions, left him chronically dependent on the guidance of others. He was equally indecisive about his choice of counselors, so that royal policy in the final years of the reign revealed an erratic instability that left informed French observers at a loss for explanation. "The continual mixture," as Pétion described it, "of authority and weakness, of cruelty and clemency, of respect for and violation of the laws, the perpetual variations in policy" invariably helped undermine the government's credibility and authority.[10] As we follow the evolving psychology of our deputy witnesses, we shall discover a persistent longing for the patriarchal leadership of a good king that remained strong and remarkably forgiving long after the institutional structures of absolutism had been dismantled. Yet some of those witnesses were increasingly aware of the problems posed by the particular king with whom they had to deal. In January 1787 the lawyer Target, veteran observer of thirty years of royal policy struggles, penned in his diary: "Louis XVI: should act through his own volition, but only follows the will of others. Instability, increasing from day to day, in the exercise of power."

[9] On the nature of the fiscal crisis, see esp. J. F. Bosher, *French Government Finances, 1770–1795* (Cambridge, 1970); and Gail Bossenga, "Impôt," in *Dictionnaire critique de la Révolution française*, ed. François Furet and Mona Ozouf (Paris, 1988), 586–95.

[10] Jérôme Pétion de Villeneuve, *Avis aux Français sur le salut de la patrie* (n.p., 1789), 226.

The Lorraine landowner and amateur intellectual, Duquesnoy, came to much the same conclusion at the beginning of the Estates General: "The king is carried along endlessly from one policy to another, changing them, adopting them, rejecting them with an inconceivable capriciousness; exercising force, then weakly retreating. He has entirely lost his authority."[11]

For the older generations of the deputies of 1789, the experience of the so-called "Maupeou Revolution," at the end of the previous reign, had marked a watershed in political attitudes. The efforts of Louis XV's last chancellor to block opposition to royal policies through a sweeping reorganization of the judicial system had stimulated the expansion of a self-styled "patriot party," which defended the rights of the "nation" and called for a rule of law based on a "constitution" and a convocation of the Estates General.[12] Among the important opponents of the "Maupeou Parlements" in the capital at the time were several future deputies, including the young duke and peer, La Rochefoucauld; the parlementary magistrate, Fréteau de Saint-Just; the future *parlementaire*, Duval d'Eprémesnil; and six of the nine lawyers who would sit in the Paris delegation in 1789: Target, Treilhard, Tronchet, Hutteau, Camus, and Martineau. Indeed, Target wrote one of the more widely read pamphlets opposing the measures. With the exception of Eprémesnil all of these men would work closely together as "patriots" during the early months of the Constituent Assembly.[13] In the provinces, the Le Mans magistrate Ménard de La Groye, the Pau law professor Jean-François-Régis Mourot, the Nîmes chief magistrate Louis-Etienne Ricard, and the Poitevin lawyer Thibaudeau, all vigorously opposed Maupeou's judicial reorganization. Though many of the deputies would have been too young to hold positions of power in 1770, a number were undoubtedly influenced by the rhetoric and the pamphlet campaigns. Bertrand Barère remembered the impact of events on law students and lawyers in Toulouse at the time, sensitizing them to national issues, and introducing them to the concepts of "patriots" and "ministerial despotism."[14] In this respect, the Maupeou affair was a rehearsal for the crisis of the "Pre-Revolution."

[11] Paul-Louis Target, *Un avocat du XVIIIe siècle* (Paris, 1893), 47; Adrien Duquesnoy, *Journal d'Adrien Duquesnoy*, ed. R. de Crèvecoeur, 2 vols. (Paris, 1894), 1:29 (entry of May 22, 1789). Cf. Jean-Paul Rabaut Saint-Etienne, *A la nation française* (n.p., Nov. 1788), 14–15.

[12] Jules Flammermont, *Le chancelier Maupeou et les parlements* (Paris, 1885); Jean Egret, *Louis XV et l'opposition parlementaire* (Paris, 1970), 182–228; and Durand Echeverria, *The Maupeou Revolution* (Baton Rouge, La., 1985).

[13] Fichier Lefebvre; *DC*; Jean Egret, *La Pré-révolution française, 1787–1788* (Paris, 1962), 214; Target, 15; Pierre Préteux, *Armand-Gaston Camus, 1740–1804* (Paris, 1932), 19–22; and David A. Bell, "Lawyers into Demagogues: Chancellor Maupeou and the Transformation of Legal Practice in France, 1771–1789," *Past and Present*, no. 130 (Feb. 1991), 140–41.

[14] Fichier Lefebvre; Pierre Ballu, *François Ménard de La Groye (1742–1815). Magistrat manceau* (Le Mans, 1962), 17–22; René-Antoine-Hyacinthe Thibaudeau, *Abrégé de l'histoire du Poitou*, 6 vols. (Poitiers, 1782–86), "Préface"; Leo Gershoy, *Bertrand Barère, the Reluctant Terrorist* (Princeton, 1962), 13–14; Léopold Soublin, *Le premier vote des Normands, 1789* (Fécamp, 1981), 255–56.

While the early years of Louis XVI were relatively quiescent—favored with the popular ministers Turgot and Necker and a successful war against the English—the fiscal crisis of 1786 generated a political mobilization even more extensive than that of the Maupeou era. Some twenty-two future deputies sat on the Assembly of Notables of 1787.[15] After the notables had been dismissed and the finance minister Calonne had been replaced by Loménie de Brienne, the royal government and the various parlements entered into a period of almost continual confrontation. It was in November of 1787, during a rare personal appearance before the Parlement of Paris, that the king and his chancellor formally announced an eventual convocation of the Estates General, promised within the coming five years.[16]

For most of the future deputies, the skirmishes between the monarchy, the Notables, and the parlements could only be viewed from afar. From his home in Poitiers, Faulcon was now following and commenting on the national political scene more than ever before, and he dreamed that a substantial reform of the justice system might emerge from it all. But he was little optimistic: "all such ideas are merely illusions; these salutary reforms will never be accomplished. . . ."[17] The organization of the provincial assemblies of 1787–88, however, had a far more direct effect on the political education of the future Constituents. Conceived by Calonne and maintained largely intact by his successor, the assemblies were designed to elicit local support for tax increases. As the system ultimately evolved, it affected only about two-thirds of the kingdom (twenty-two of the thirty-four *généralités*). Nevertheless, the experience had an impact on the evolving political culture of the country. The initial decrees specified that the number of representatives of the Third Estate was to be equal to that of the other two orders combined and that all votes were to be counted by head—thus widely publicizing a principle soon to be invoked in the Estates General. Perhaps more important, the new system established a uniform national structure for town and village elections throughout much of the kingdom, elections in which virtually all of the future Third Estate and curé deputies probably took part. At least 217 deputies from all three orders also participated in the various regional assemblies, with no less than 50 serving on the permanent "intermediary commissions" and 23 appointed as *syndics*, the principal executive figures in the system.[18] In certain instances—such as the provincial estates of

---

[15] *Procès-verbal de l'Assemblée de notables tenue à Versailles en l'année 1787* (Paris, 1788), 3–29.

[16] *AP*, 1:264–69.

[17] Félix Faulcon, *Correspondance. Tome 1: 1770–89*, ed. G. Debien (Poitiers, 1939), 289–90 (letter to Texier, Oct. 3, 1787).

[18] From a wide variety of biographic sources, especially Fichier Lefebvre and the *DC*. Also included are those future deputies who sat in the provincial estates, including the 28 elected by the Estates of Dauphiné. Overall, 30 of the participants in the various levels of regional estates and assemblies would later be elected to the Clergy (14% of the total), 78 to the Nobility (36%), and 109 to the Third Estate (50%). All inhabitants paying over ten *livres* in taxes had the right to participate in municipal elections—thus almost certainly including all future Third-Estate deputies—and all curés sat in the first- and second-level assemblies: Pierre Renouvin, *Les*

Poitou or the intermediary commission of Lyon—half or more of the future Third Estate delegation to the Estates General sat in their order's provincial assembly. Thus, the assemblies served not only as additional training grounds in collective political procedures, but as the meeting places where future provincial leaders might come to know one another.[19]

THE MUNICIPAL MOBILIZATION OF 1788–1789

In May 1788 the continued inability of the monarchy to obtain parlementary endorsement for financial reforms and an increase in taxes produced what seemed like a veritable reprise of the Maupeou affair. With the sovereign courts abolished or entirely reformed and a new system of "grand bailliage" courts established to replace them, all of those future deputies attached to the royal judicial system as magistrates or lawyers—perhaps three hundred or more—found themselves forced to confront the crisis and take a political stand.[20] In Paris the fiery orator Eprémesnil, who had led the parlementary opposition the previous year and who had already become a hero for many Parisians, took the offensive against "ministerial despotism" and was forced into exile with his colleague Fréteau de Saint-Just. In the provinces, the future deputies Milscent of Angers, Creuzé-Latouche of Châtellerault, and Lambert de Frondeville of Rouen were at the forefront of local protest. Ménard de La Groye, the most vociferous opponent of the May Edicts in Le Mans found himself exiled to the province of Berry, "for my attachment to the law and to the true interests of the nation." In the process, these men—and several future deputies taking similar positions—made reputations that would greatly facilitate their elections to the Estates General a half year later.[21]

Through most of the kingdom, judicial opposition to the May Edicts largely followed the traditional modes of protest, with the courts striking and refusing to function, and with individual supporters publishing large numbers of pamphlets. But in Dauphiné events evolved rather differently, in a manner that was to exercise a significant influence on the country as a whole. Critical to these events was the inspired leadership of a twenty-nine-year-old Grenoble magistrate who was not even attached to the royal courts, Jean-Joseph Mounier. Son of a local cloth merchant, Mounier had

---

assemblées provinciales de 1787 (Paris, 1921), 100–102, 111–12, 157–59, 238, 242, 263, 270–76, 348–49; and Egret, *La Pré-révolution*, 111.

[19] E.g., of the 18 Third-Estate deputies from the bailliages of Poitiers and Châtellerault, 9 had served in the provincial assemblies; and 4 future deputies sat on the *Commission intermédiaire* of Lyon.

[20] In addition to the 38 noble and the 169 commoner deputies who sat on the parlementary or bailliage-level courts, a substantial number of the 181 "lawyers" were active in the courts. See above, chap. 1.

[21] Letter from Ménard to his wife, Aug. 9, 1788: A.D. Sarthe 10 J 121; Fichier Lefebvre; *DC*.

relied on his family fortune and precocious intelligence to make a substantial jump upward in social status, serving first as lawyer and then municipal judge—a position that imparted nonhereditary nobility. Like both Ménard and Faulcon and many others in the legal profession at the time, he was impatient with the abstract ideas of the philosophes and was inspired rather by a traditional conception of law and of justice.[22] Though sometimes described as distant and aloof in his personal relations, he was possessed of an intense self-confidence and a power and rigor of thought that brought him rapidly to the fore in the summer of 1788.

In mid-June, following a violent popular protest in the streets of Grenoble against the suppression of the local parlement, Mounier organized an ad hoc meeting of the three estates, demanding not only the return of the parlement, but the restoration of the provincial estates in Dauphiné—in which the Third Estate would be doubled and would vote by head—and a summoning of the Estates General to resolve the problems of the nation. With the complicity of local authorities and a systematic mobilization of other towns in the province, Mounier was able to convene a second organizational meeting in July leading to the revival of the provincial estates that September. He rapidly gathered around him an exceptionally talented coalition of collaborators, including the brilliant and even younger lawyer, Antoine Barnave, the eminent Catholic apologist and archbishop of Vienne, Le Franc de Pompignan, and a whole contingent of liberal nobles—like the comte de Virieu, the comte de Lablache, and the marquis de Viennois. Most of these men became close friends, referring to each other as "comrades" and even using the familiar "tu" form of address, and many would be elected by the provincial estates to sit in the Estates General. Brochures written by Mounier, Barnave, and Virieu were soon circulating throughout the country, describing and justifying their success and establishing the Dauphiné experience as a model for political organization everywhere.[23]

But if the provincial experience of Dauphiné played an important role in the political mobilization of 1788, a second powerful impulse came from the central government itself. Of critical importance was the royal decree of July 5, 1788, written by the "principal minister" Loménie de Brienne, announcing the convocation of the Estates General.[24] Though the body of the decree entailed a straightforward request for local documents verifying electoral procedures for the previous Estates General in 1614, the introductory remarks went a great deal further. The municipal governments, the primary recipients of the request, were encouraged not only to identify historical precedents for the elections but also to present their "wishes" on the sub-

[22] Jean Egret, *La révolution des notables: Mounier et les monarchiens* (Paris, 1950), 9–12.

[23] Egret, ibid., 20–21; and Paolo Viola, *Il crollo del'antico regime* (Rome, 1993), part II. Also, François-Henri de Virieu to the marquis de Viennois: Archives of the Château d' Avauges, reproduced in A.D. Isère, 1 Mi 461, letters of June 22 and July 28, 1789; Alexandre-Joseph de Lablache to marquis de Viennois: ibid, letter of Oct. 20, 1789.

[24] Egret, *La Pré-révolution*, 306–7.

ject. To ensure that the meeting would be a "truly national assembly"—the precise words used by Brienne—citizens were encouraged to reflect on how it might be "properly balanced" among the three orders: an open invitation to reconsider the number of delegates from each order and the manner of voting. Finally, the decree strongly reinforced what was to be a dominant motif in the image of relations between the king and the commoners for the next three years, describing the proposed meeting as the "assembly of a large family, with the common father as its leader."[25] Even after the replacement of Brienne by Necker, the decree of July 5 remained a central statement of policy: "The single goal, the essential goal towards which I directed my efforts was the convocation of an Estates General, organized rationally and convened peacefully."[26] Indeed, under Necker's ministry, the Keeper of the Seals seems to have systematically circulated the decree in the provinces, soliciting the opinion of local authorities everywhere.[27]

The history of the political mobilization of the fall of 1788 is still poorly known and remains to be written. It was a complex development, driven by the efforts of Necker, the example of Dauphiné, and the perceived desires of the king, but it evolved regionally in a myriad of manners, depending on local institutional contours and power alignments.[28] The most common locus for discussion was the municipality, sometimes through instituted governments, sometimes through ad hoc committees set up in opposition. But in certain areas the provincial estates might also serve as a rallying point. Such regional activities saw the emergence of numerous future deputies as local political leaders, organizing their colleagues, friends, and neighbors in response to changing events, and articulating for others and for themselves a first elucidation of their aspirations.

One of the earliest and most vigorous responses during this period arose in Brittany. Here, as in Dauphiné, the movement was initiated in the provincial capital by a group of young legal men: notably the Jansenist canonist Lanjuinais and the lawyer and gifted orator Isaac-René-Guy Le Chapelier. But unlike the Dauphinois, the Breton patriots found themselves in confrontation with the powerful provincial estates, dominated by an entrenched nobility who adamantly refused to share power with the commoners. Thus the lines of confrontation rapidly developed between nobles and commoners rather than between the combined three estates and the ministry in

---

[25] Brette, *Recueil*, 1:19–23.

[26] Egret, *La Pré-révolution*, 325.

[27] Ibid., 313, 324–25. See also F. Lorin, "Dourdan et la convocation des Etats généraux en 1789," *Mémoires de la Société archéologique de Rambouillet* 10 (1895), 114–15; and Jean-Pierre Donnadieu, *Les Etats-généraux de 1789: sénéchaussée de Béziers et Montpellier* (Montpellier, 1989), 22.

[28] Augustin Cochin and Charles Charpentier argued that a national Jacobin-like conspiracy incited towns all over France to vote the same resolutions: *La campagne électorale de 1789 en Bourgogne* (Paris, 1904), esp. 8, 13. In fact, the meetings in different regions were spaced over a period of several months, from September to January, and there were numerous variations in the demands made.

Versailles—as had been the case in Dauphiné. In August 1788 the political leadership was joined by the scholar and writer Volney. Through his newspaper, *La sentinelle du peuple*, Volney lent the struggle a philosophical voice and a trenchant antiaristocratic tone that differed substantially from the rhetoric of Mounier and his associates. As in Dauphiné, the Bretons rapidly established a correspondence network throughout the region, and soon letters and brochures of support were emanating from virtually every town in the province. Most of the future Breton deputies, many of whom had previously been active in municipal politics and the provincial estates, now emerged as local patriot leaders. Their angry and impassioned pamphlets circulated throughout France, so that the revolt in Brittany became a second model for protest, strikingly different from that in Dauphiné: impatient and antagonistic toward the nobility, increasingly inclined toward a more radical reform of society—including, in some cases, the total suppression of the nobility—anticipating in many respects the arguments in praise of the Third Estate later popularized by the abbé Sieyès.[29]

In both Franche-Comté and Provence, where intransigent nobilities also held power bases in both parlements and estates, the political configuration was similar in many respects to that in Brittany. Thus, in Aix-en-Provence, the second order proved uncompromising not only on the question of the internal organization of the estates but on the issue of equal taxation. When the estates claimed the right to choose Provence's delegation to the Estates General, liberals in Aix and throughout the province successfully petitioned the government for elections organized by judicial districts—as in the rest of the kingdom. After January, patriot leadership in Aix was increasingly assumed by the comte de Mirabeau, who had recently arrived from Paris. An inextricable mixture of demagoguery and idealism, equally committed to the reform program of the patriots and to the refurbishing of his personal reputation and "glory," the philosopher-count ostentatiously repudiated his own order and became the hero of the Third Estate. As in Brittany, the commoner deputies, chosen primarily from the Pre-Revolutionary leadership, arrived in Versailles with a deep-seated hatred for "aristocrats" and privilege in general.[30]

But through most of France during the fall of 1788, the example of Dauphiné was far more attractive than that of Brittany. In Normandy, where municipal meetings were already taking place in Caen by late September—

---

[29] See especially Barthélémy Pocquet, *Les origines de la Révolution en Bretagne*, 2 vols. (Paris, 1885), 2:60–82, 97, 100, 107–16; and Roger Dupuy, "La prérévolution en Bretagne (octobre 1788–janvier 1789), ou l'anti-Dauphiné, d'après *La sentinelle du peuple* de Volney" in *La Bretagne, une province à l'aube de la Révolution. Actes du Colloque de Brest, 25–30 septembre 1988* (Brest, 1989), 335–41. Also, Jean Gaulmier, *Un grand témoin de la Révolution et de l'Empire: Volney* (Paris, 1959), 65–74; and Viola, part III.

[30] Georges Guibal, *Mirabeau et la Provence. Première partie. Du 14 mai 1770 au 5 mai 1789*, 2d ed. (Paris, 1901), 52–59, 235–80, 360–72; and Monique Cubells, *Les horizons de la liberté: naissance de la Révolution en Provence, 1787–1789* (Aix, 1987). On Franche-Comté, see below.

and in other smaller towns from October to December—commoner elites militated for the resurrection of the Estates of Normandy, specifically evoking Dauphiné as their source of inspiration. Here the influential Rouen lawyer and future deputy Thouret played a moderating role similar to that of Mounier.[31] Dauphiné was likewise presented as a model in Le Mans, where a joint committee of the bishop, the mayor, the intermediary commission, and the principal nobles and commoner elites pushed for the creation of provincial estates.[32] So too in Lorraine, under the leadership of the chevalier-philosophe Boufflers, the privileged estates worked closely with a committee from Nancy, calling for equal taxation, a doubling of the Third, and a vote by head.[33]

With both a parlement and the traditionally powerful provincial estates, Languedoc might have developed a political configuration similar to that of Brittany and Franche-Comté. But here membership in the estates was far more narrow than in Brittany, excluding all but a handful of nobles. With a seigneurial system that was probably substantially less onerous than in northern France and with the common enemy of the exclusionist estates, nobles and commoners seem initially to have worked closely together.[34] One of the earliest emulations of the Grenoble movement arose in the Vivarais section of Languedoc, where the reform movement was led by a group of like-minded nobles and commoners, many of whom would soon be elected deputies to Versailles. At the forefront of the movement were the Protestant lawyer and writer Boissy d'Anglas and the talented but erratic follower of Rousseau, the comte d'Antraigues—both natives of Vivarais who had frequently lived in Paris. Working closely with a variety of local leaders, Boissy and d'Antraigues organized the entire region, village by village, in a campaign to deny the Estates of Languedoc the exclusive right of choosing deputies to the Estates General. Meeting first in Annonay (in October) and then in Privas (in November), they were able to agree on a recommendation to double the third and vote by head in the coming Estates General. As in Dauphiné, a sentiment of camaraderie seems to have bound together many of the leading figures of the three estates. Thus, Boissy, in a warm

---

[31] Félix Mourlot, *La fin de l'ancien régime et les débuts de la Révolution dans la généralité de Caen* (Paris, 1913), 160–67; Ernest Lebègue, *La vie et l'oeuvre d'un Constituant: Thouret* (Paris, 1910); Soublin, 257–59.

[32] Robert Triger, *L'année 1789 au Mans et dans le Haut-Maine* (Mamers, 1889), 122–27.

[33] Cardinal Mathieu, *L'Ancien régime en Lorraine et Barrois d'après des documents inédits*, 3d ed. (Paris, 1907), 422–44.

[34] See, e.g., Pierre-Henri Thore, "Le Tiers état de Toulouse à la veille des élections de 1789. Querelles intestines et requêtes partisanes, mai–décembre 1788," *Annales du Midi* 65 (1953); and "Le Tiers état de Toulouse à la veille des élections de 1789. L'union dans la lutte contre les états de Languedoc, janvier–février 1789," *Bulletin d'études scientifiques de l'Aude* 53 (1952), 225–42; and Jean-Pierre Donnadieu, "Rabaut Saint-Etienne et la rédaction des cahiers de doléances," in *Les Rabaut: du désert à la Révolution* (Nîmes, 1988), 86–87.

personal letter, could address the marquis de Satillieu as his "brave and faithful companion in arms."[35]

By the beginning of 1789, the political mobilization and the growing vision of national renewal were touching even the most isolated towns of Berry, Gascony, and the Massif Central.[36] Not infrequently, this politicization was closely related to preexisting municipal power alignments and political rivalries, as individuals soon to be elected deputies rose to prominence through the interplay of national and municipal politics. Thus, Pierre-Charles-François Dupont, first counsel of Saint-Jean-de-Luz, near the Spanish border, had been locked for years in a bitter battle with the local subdelegate. Eventually, the latter had engineered Dupont's humiliation and removal from office. When Dupont established himself as a leader of the local patriots in the late 1780s, he was motivated as much by a desire for revenge against a hated local rival as by a desire to end "ministerial despotism" in general.[37] So too the rise to prominence of the Flemish lawyer Bouchette grew directly out of his long confrontation with another subdelegate, a close ally to the municipal oligarchy of Bergues. Bouchette was able to use the ad hoc municipal assemblies to defeat his enemies in a way that would never have been possible under the institutional structures of the Old Regime, a victory which translated directly into a seat for Bouchette in the Estates General.[38]

The case of Bergues, in which reigning municipal authorities were outmaneuvered by patriots in a kind of first-generation municipal revolution, was by no means unique. In Toulouse, the future deputies Jean-Baptiste Viguier and Pierre Roussillou were among the leaders of an improvised "intermediary commission" set up in opposition to the municipal leaders— the *Capitouls*—when the latter refused to open up debate to a citywide assembly. All four of Lyon's future deputies played central roles in the movement of "principal citizens" opposing the pretensions of the Lyon Consulate to dominate the upcoming elections. Indeed, the Consulate's at-

[35] Charles Jolivet, *La Révolution dans l'Ardèche, 1788–1795* (Largentière, 1930), 51–78; and François-Antoine Boissy d'Anglas, "Correspondance de Boissy d'Anglas avec le marquis de Satillieu au début de la Révolution," ed. H. Hillaire, *Revue du Vivarais* 48 (1942), 213 (letter of ca. late Nov. 1788).

[36] Marcel Bruneau, *Les débuts de la Révolution en Berry (1789–1791)* (Paris, 1902), 5–10; G. Brégail, "Le Gers pendant la Révolution," *Bulletin de la Société d'histoire et d'archéologie du Gers* 30 (1929), 245–50; Pierre-Jean-Baptiste Delon, *Les élections de 1789 en Gévaudan* (Mende, 1922), 48.

[37] Vincent-Raymond Rivière-Chalan, *Dupont de Bigorre, le démocrate, 1740–1793* (Paris, 1989), 1–5. As a deputy, Dupont would take the first opportunity to denounce the subdelegate before the National Assembly: Jacques-Samuel Dinochau, *Courier de Madon*, issue of Dec. 28, 1789.

[38] Camille Looten, ed., *Lettres de François-Joseph Bouchette (1735–1810)*, (Lille, 1909), 48–71. Similar scenarios seem to have unrolled in the victory of the deputy Agier in Saint-Maixent: *DC* 3; and of the deputies Dumoustier and Bion in Loudun: Marquis Marie de Roux, *La Révolution à Poitiers et dans la Vienne* (Paris, 1911), 109–12.

tempt to invalidate the election of Périsse Du Luc as representative of the booksellers' guild may well have increased his visibility and general popularity. In Metz, the lawyer Emmery and the parlementary magistrate Roederer, who had collaborated in the 1770s against the Maupeou parlements, joined forces again in 1789 to battle the conservative establishment led by the mayor of Metz, Pierre Maujean.[39]

In most cases, the municipal conflicts over the organization of the Estates General primarily involved the local elites of the Third Estate—the "upper Third" as Périsse liked to call them—and various elements of the local nobility and clergy. But in a few instances, future deputies found themselves appealing to much more humble segments of the urban population. Though an outsider by birth Marie-André Merle had risen rapidly to prominence through a judicious marriage and the patronage of the aristocracy to become mayor of Mâcon. But in 1788, sensing the changing political situation and the disfavor and jealousy with which he was viewed by the town's indigenous notability, Merle rapidly developed a new power base among the city's lower middle class and artisan population. He was accused at the time of distributing wine and even fomenting a riot in order to ensure his popularity, and he was denounced by the intendant for "the complete dedication which he promised not only to the inhabitants' best interests but to their desires." Likewise, the magistrate and future terrorist Marc-Guillaume-Alexis Vadier, in his struggle for municipal influence in Pamiers, seems to have relied increasingly on popular favor, earning a reputation as voice of the poor and disinherited. In Arles, the influence of the lawyer Guillaume Bonnemant rested entirely on his position as representative of the guilds, which the town notability was attempting to exclude altogether from political influence.[40] Though cases such as Merle, Vadier, and Bonnemant were perhaps relatively unusual, their experiences should not be underestimated in the later development of an expanded definition of the National Assembly's constituency. Significantly, all three deputies would soon be associated with the most radical faction within that Assembly.

Compared to this flurry of assemblies and political organization in the provinces, independent municipal activity in Paris was at first relatively modest. In response to the decree of July 5, the city council had met briefly in late July to order archival research but had taken no stand of its own on

[39] Thore, "L'union dans la lutte," 229–33; Maurice Wahl, *Les premières années de la Révolution à Lyon (1788–1792)* (Paris, 1894), 34–35, 38–45, 59, 75–76; P. Lesprand, "Election du député direct et cahier du Tiers état de la ville de Metz en 1789," *Jahrbuch der Gesellschaft für lothringische Geschichte und Altertumskunde* 15 (1903), 159–92. Cf. the situation in Dijon: Cochin and Charpentier, 9, 12–20, 35–40; and in Strasbourg: Rolland Marx, *Recherches sur la vie politique de l'Alsace prérévolutionnaire et révolutionnaire* (Strasbourg, 1966), 38.

[40] Gilles Dussert, *Vadier, le grand inquisiteur* (Paris, 1989), 61–62, 71–72; Fichier Lefebvre; Paul Montarlot, *Les députés de Saône-et-Loire aux assemblées de la Révolution, 1789–99* (Autun, 1905), 215–21; and Fernand Evrard, "Les paysans du Mâconnais et les brigandages de juillet 1789," *Annales de Bourgogne* 19 (1947), 38–39.

the issue.[41] Yet on the whole, and with the notable exception of the Parlement of Paris, the political life of the city remained more closely controlled than in the provinces. Nevertheless, the city's citizens avidly followed events throughout the kingdom, and the cafés and printing offices and various informal societies and clubs were alive with discussion and debate.[42] Though the Masons never played the role of master conspirators and instigators of the Revolution which has sometimes been attributed to them, the lodges were important nevertheless as centers for discussion and the distribution of information. During his mission to Paris from Vivarais, Boissy d'Anglas seems to have used one such lodge to keep abreast of the latest news on the deputies elected to the Estates General.[43] Paris was also crowded with delegations and lobbyists from towns and provincial assemblies all over the country, arriving to seek audiences with Necker and the king. Boissy found so many other representatives from towns in his home province—like Viguier from Toulouse—that he set up a Club du Languedoc where they could all get together regularly and compare strategies.[44] A number of future deputies undoubtedly first met and began associating in the capital during the winter of 1788–1789.

The most important and influential of these informal societies in Paris was the group which began meeting in the home of the parlementary magistrate Adrien Duport in November 1788 and which is known to historians as the "Committee of Thirty." Only twenty-nine years old—the same age as Mounier—Duport was by all accounts a brilliant thinker and theorist, with a real measure of personal charisma: "a man with a precocious maturity in his ideas and his character, and a nobility of heart and mind," as the Constituent Toulongeon described him. "Systematic and self-assured, two centuries earlier he might have become the leader of a religious sect."[45] The core of the "Committee" was a small group of Duport's associates from the Parlement of Paris, particularly active in the recent struggles with the monarchy, including the future deputies Eprémesnil, Fréteau, and Le Peletier de Saint-Fargeau. But he also gathered together Parisian acquaintances known from a variety of Masonic, Mesmerist, and philanthropic associations to which he belonged. There was the marquis de Lafayette and his comrades from the American War, the duc de Biron, the vicomte de Noailles, and the three Lameth brothers; there were the intellectuals Condorcet, La Rochefoucauld, Dupont de Nemours, Destutt de Tracy, and—until he left for

---

[41] Charles-Louis Chassin, *Les élections et les cahiers de Paris en 1789*, 4 vols. (Paris, 1888–89), 1:14–16, 23–34.

[42] Bailly, 1:7, 9–10; Alexandre de Lameth, *Histoire de l'Assemblée constituante*, 2 vols. (Paris, 1828–29), 2:6–7; Augustin Challamel, *Les clubs contre-révolutionnaires* (Paris, 1895), 23–66.

[43] Boissy to Satillieu, 140 (letter of Apr. 4, 1789).

[44] Ibid.; comte Emmanuel-Henri-Louis-Alexandre d'Antraigues, "Correspondance du Marquis de Satillieu au début de la Révolution. Lettres du comte d'Antraigues," *Revue du Vivarais* 60 (1956), 104 (letter of Feb. 11, 1789).

[45] François-Emmanuel Toulongeon, *Histoire de la France depuis la Révolution*, 7 vols. (Paris, 1801), 1:108–9.

Aix—the comte de Mirabeau; and there was a whole coterie of young liberal courtiers from the greatest families of France, many of whom—through a variety of squabbles and intrigues—had been prevented from achieving expected honors in the court of Louis XVI: like the duc de Montmorency-Luxembourg or the duc de Liancourt or the duc d'Aiguillon. There was also a small sprinkling of commoners, among whom the ubiquitous Target and the abbé Sieyès were undoubtedly the most important.[46]

The Committee of "Thirty"—which actually included over fifty individuals—clearly did not initiate the political mobilization of the kingdom—as has sometimes been suggested.[47] At its inception, patriots had already been battling for many weeks in Dauphiné, in Brittany, in Provence, and in several other provinces. In the first political mobilization of the Revolutionary period, the lawyers and the other men of law had already taken the initiative over the Parisian intellectuals. Yet the "Thirty" represented a formidable collection of prestige, talent, and energy. After November 1788, it probably played a significant part in the dissemination of liberal pamphlets—notably those of Sieyès and Target—in the widespread call for the vote by head in the Estates, and in the generalization of the "war on privilege." The twenty-eight members of the group elected to the Estates General would form a major component of the liberal leadership in the National Assembly during the first year of its existence.[48]

BIRTH OF THE ARISTOCRATIC PARTY

With the notable exceptions of Brittany and a few other provinces, much of the initial political mobilization in the fall of 1788 was characterized by a spirit of cooperation between the three orders. The Estates of Dauphiné, the Vivarais meetings, the meetings in Lorraine, and many of the municipal assemblies had all involved the substantial participation of nobles and clergy. Though the liberal nobles involved included only a small minority of the Second Estate as a whole, their readiness to accept the call for general elections, the suppression of tax privileges, and the doubling of the Third Estate had greatly encouraged the commoners. But the winter and spring of 1789 would witness a substantial backlash against such policies from nobles throughout the kingdom.

The prelude to this reaction came from the much-heralded declarations against the doubling of the Third Estate issued by the Parlement of Paris and the second Assembly of Notables. In the Parisian milieu, at least, the Parlement's statement of September 25 seems to have shocked and catalyzed

---

[46] On the "Thirty," see esp. Daniel L. Wick, *A Conspiracy of Well-Intentioned Men: The Society of Thirty and the French Revolution* (New York, 1987), esp. Appendix I, Table 1.

[47] E.g., Georges Lefebvre, *The Coming of the French Revolution* (Princeton, 1947), 53; and William Doyle, *The Oxford History of the French Revolution* (Oxford, 1989), 95.

[48] Wick, Appendix I, Table 6. Wick inadvertently excluded Luxembourg from his list.

the patriot group "from one day to the next."[49] But the intransigent stance of the Notables in December—following their more liberal position in the spring of 1787—made an equally strong impression on contemporaries. The leaders of the Assembly made it clear that they were reacting in large measure to the explosion of brochures favoring the Third Estate: the "scandalous writings" as the prince de Conti described them, "which spread trouble and division throughout the kingdom." The prince took pains to persuade the monarch "how important it is, for the stability of his throne, for his authority, for the preservation of law and order, that all these new proposals be forever outlawed and that the time-honored arrangements of the Constitution be maintained in all their integrity."[50]

The most powerful conservative resistance arose in precisely those regions of the kingdom where nobles were already organized and experienced in collective action through existing estates or parlements. Since these were also the areas in which commoner opposition had been most aggressive, a political dialectic of action and reaction evolved rapidly. In Brittany, for example, a response to the patriot demands of October 1788 began mobilizing within days. By the end of the month petitions were circulating throughout the province, to be signed by 880 nobles, denouncing any modifications to the 1614 procedures for the Estates General, a position that was immediately supported by the Parlement of Rennes. The nobles also attacked on the pamphlet front, matching in energy, if not always in talent, the brochures of Volney and Lanjuinais. By late January, the standoff had became so bitter that fighting broke out in the streets of Rennes between groups of commoners—mostly students—and ranks of gentlemen organized to do battle. Maintaining their intransigence to the very end, the Breton nobles rejected Necker's decrees doubling the Third and removing the election of the Estates General from the provincial estates. Ultimately, in alliance with the upper clergy, they chose to boycott the elections and send no deputies to Versailles.[51]

Similar movements of noble opposition were associated with the provincial estates in Provence and Franche-Comté, where conservative gentlemen almost certainly commanded a strong majority within their order. In January the Comtois aristocracy issued a solemn protest against Necker's decrees, rejecting in advance any choice of deputies not carried out through the provincial estates. While most of the nobles finally acquiesced to elections by *bailliage*, they initially succeeded in invalidating the victory of three liberal nobles in Vesoul and replacing them with their own list of archconservatives. A strikingly similar scenario unrolled in Provence, where the

[49] Lefebvre, *Coming of the French Revolution*, 51–52.

[50] Cited in Egret, *La Pré-révolution*, 345. See also E. I. Lébédeva, "Die Notabelnversammlungen am Vorabend der grossen französischen Revolution und die Entwicklung der politischen Positionen des Adels," *Jahrbuch für Geschichte* 39 (1990), 163–77.

[51] Pocquet, 2:91–97, 133; also, by the same author, *Histoire de Bretagne*, 6 vols. (Rennes, 1914), 6:382–88.

Nobles responded to the organized protest of the Third with extensive organization of their own. Inflexible and disdainful toward the commoners,
the majority of conservative nobles—particularly among those possessing
fiefs—chose to boycott the regular elections and send an alternate protest
delegation to Versailles, a delegation eventually rejected by the National
Assembly.[52]

In Burgundy, where provincial estates existed but did not meet in 1788–
89, magistrates of the Parlement of Dijon joined with elements of the military nobility in confronting the liberal movement.[53] From early December
1788 a group of patriot notables, led by the future deputies Volfius and
Arnoult, had begun rallying the province to appeal for a greater Third Estate role in the upcoming elections. Within a week some sixty nobles had
launched an opposition campaign in Dijon. Unlike their intransigent Breton
and Provençal counterparts, the Burgundian nobility was often prepared to
follow the methods of the patriots. Under their leadership, a general meeting of the three estates of Dijon was convoked in late December, in which
the nobles offered a "compromise," supporting free elections and an end to
tax privileges, but rejecting the doubling of the Third and the vote by head.
When the local patriots refused these overtures, the nobility redirected its
efforts toward organizing the coming elections. The future deputy, the marquis de Digoine, spent much of the winter traveling from town to town
throughout the province, talking to small groups of nobles, promoting his
own candidacy, and arguing the necessity of maintaining the system of
1614 in the Estates General.[54]

Elsewhere in the kingdom, particularly in the areas where the nobles had
little previous practice in collective action, the aristocratic opposition was
less well organized. Given the paucity of political experience and the relatively meager education of much of the provincial nobility, pamphlet defenses of the conservative position were few and far between.[55] Yet the minority of patriots within the second estate was clearly aware of the broad
current of dissatisfaction toward liberal views. Etienne-François-Joseph
Schwendt, *syndic* of the nobles of Lower Alsace and a future deputy, encountered wide grassroots opposition to his circular letter urging an end to
tax privileges. So too in Poitou, the *cahiers de doléances* preserved for individual nobles reveal an overwhelmingly conservative mode of thought and a
general refusal to budge on any of the traditional prerogatives, including

[52] Jean Girardot, "Les trois députés de la noblesse du bailliage d'Amont," *Bulletin de la Société
d'agriculture, lettres, sciences et arts du département de la Haute-Saône* (1930), 37–84; and *Le
département de la Haute-Saône pendant la Révolution*, 3 vols. (Vesoul, 1973), 1:34–45; and
Jules Viguier, *Les débuts de la Révolution en Provence* (Paris, 1894), 12–24.

[53] They normally met every three years, and had last met in 1787: A. Kleinclausz, *Histoire de
Bourgogne* (Paris, 1909), 291.

[54] Cochin and Charpentier, 22, 26–32, 45–46; and E. Nolin, ed. "Correspondance de l'avocat C. B. Navier, 1789–1791," *La Révolution en Côte-d'Or*, n. sér., fasc. 6 (1930), 7–10, 24.

[55] See above, chap. 1; also, e.g., Roux, 127.

fiscal immunities.[56] By the eve of the elections for the Estates General, a number of local nobles, many of them future deputies, were stepping forward to rally their troops to the conservative cause. In Anjou Walsh de Serrant, a former participant in the provincial assemblies, entered into a pitched battle of words with the patriot party, and especially with Volney—who had now left Brittany to seek election in his native province. In Perpignan the aristocrat Noguer d'Albert described his efforts to ensure the election of "right-thinking men" who would not cede to the liberal agenda. He was particularly critical of those nobles who would abandon their natural alliance with the king, "who alone can uphold the privileges inevitably coveted by the commoners"; and he hoped that a renewed "spirit of chivalry" would engender a sense of unity between king and nobility.[57]

Even in Vivarais, where Boissy and his friends had initially engineered a Dauphiné-like compromise, many of the local nobles had second thoughts and began distancing themselves from the patriots. A key figure here was the future deputy the comte de Vogué, who had never accepted the conclusions of the assembly of Privas in November 1788 and who subsequently began organizing a conservative front to maintain the nobles' prerogatives. Vogué seems also to have played a role in the dramatic conversion of the comte d'Antraigues, Boissy's former associate. By the spring of 1789 the onetime liberal count had entirely reversed his position and linked himself to a group of Paris conservatives. In scarcely more than a year, d'Antraigues would emerge as one of the principal leaders of the armed counterrevolution.[58]

By d'Antraigues' own account, a second important influence on his change of heart came from a new "club" of conservative nobles recently organized in Paris. Duval d'Eprémesnil, devoutly Catholic and a generation older than most of the Young Turks of the Parlement of Paris, was probably never at ease with Adrien Duport and his youthful intellectual companions. Sometime toward the end of 1788 he seems to have come to much the same conclusion as Noguer d'Albert, that the threat from the radical patriots was far greater than that of the royal ministers, and that an alliance with the king was the only real buttress to the continued existence of the nobility. By December 20, Eprémesnil had definitively broken with the "Committee of Thirty"—taking with him two other future deputies, the duc de Luxembourg and the abbé de Barmond—and had gathered around him some one hundred like-minded followers. Although we know very little of their assemblies, they apparently met regularly and almost certainly entered into correspondence with provincial acquaintances in much the same manner as Duport's committee—reactivating the protest networks organized by

[56] Marx, 28–29; Roux, 128–29, 164–65.

[57] Jean-Louis Ormières, "Les députés du Maine et de l'Anjou aux Etats généraux," *Mayenne*, no. 12 (1989), 88–91; Pierre Vidal, *Histoire de la Révolution française dans le département des Pyrénées orientales*, 3 vols. (Perpignan, 1885), 1:lxii. See also Mourlot, 193–96.

[58] Jolivet, 72–77.

Eprémesnil in 1788 in the wake of the May edicts.[59] The group may also have made contact with the numerous nobles arriving in Paris to formally protest the political advances of the commoners in the provinces. At any rate, Boissy d'Anglas was amazed at the number of such deputations of "noblemen who complain against the recognition of the Third Estate's rights."[60] In the end, Eprémesnil's conservative "Committee of One Hundred" probably had a far greater influence on the nobility of France than the Committee of Thirty.

As nobles, clergy, and commoners began coming together all over the country to elect their deputies and draw up their grievances for the king, many of the future deputies had a keen sense of a political polarization over stakes that were extremely high. "The two parties," as Rabaut Saint-Etienne described it, "had already formed" before the opening of the Estates General.[61]

THE ELECTORAL ASSEMBLIES OF 1789

The number of future deputies who had involved themselves in political activities prior to 1789 is difficult to ascertain. Among our 129 principal witnesses, almost three-fifths are known to have participated in municipal or provincial assemblies, or to have written political pamphlets. Significantly, this entailed only a third of the future clerical deputies and slightly under half of the nobles, but over two-thirds of the commoners.[62] Yet ineluctably, as the machinery for the elections to the Estates General was set into motion, all of the deputies—as virtually all of educated France—were swept up in the tide of national politics. By February 1789 no one with a role of any significance in society could have ignored the central constitutional issues under debate in hundreds of pamphlets and "model cahiers," some of which had been written by the future deputies themselves.

Among the nobility, many future deputies eagerly sought election to the Estates General and organized veritable pre-electoral campaigns. This was perhaps particularly the case among the high aristocracy who normally lived in Paris and Versailles and who now returned to the electoral districts of their ancestral lands. When the prince de Salm-Salm decided to seek a mandate from Nancy, he first wrote to a local contact for advice on tactics. The contact urged the prince to travel to Lorraine early, since he was almost unknown there, and sent a list of local nobles "whom he must visit and

[59] D'Antraigues, 97 (letter of Dec. 20, 1788). See also Wick, 155–58.

[60] Boissy d'Anglas, "La Révolution vue de Paris et d'Annonay," *La revue universelle* 139 (1988), 50 (letter of Jan. 12, 1789).

[61] Jean-Paul Rabaut Saint-Etienne, *Précis historique de la Révolution française* (Paris, 1807), 92.

[62] Considered here are the 129 principal "witnesses" listed in the introduction. We have found 6 of 22 clerical deputies (29%), 14 of 27 nobles (52%), and 56 of 80 Third deputies (70%) involved in these kinds of Pre-Revolutionary activities.

approach for support." The marquis de Gouy d'Arsy sought election in several bailliages in succession before finally obtaining a seat as representative of the colony of Saint-Domingue—which he had never seen and knew only through his wife's family. The chevalier de Boufflers was said to have spent six thousand *livres* on "festivities" in Nancy to curry favor with local gentlemen; the prince de Condé organized an electoral "clique" in Dijon; the comte de Tessé, the marquis de Vassé, and the comte de Choiseul, all actively campaigned and held "open invitations to meals" in Le Mans; and the duc de Choiseul, who "intensely desired" to become a deputy, passed out slips with his name printed on them to all nobles present in the Angers assembly.[63] But even provincial nobles sometimes pursued pre-electoral campaigns. We have already noted the systematic electioneering of the marquis de Digoine in Burgundy. The chevalier de Cazalès attended three assemblies before securing a place from the tiny bailliage of Rivière-Verdun.[64]

Most of the affiliates of the Committee of Thirty also sought election as part of their general strategy of achieving a liberal constitution for the kingdom. Mirabeau was so anxious to be elected that, as he announced in a letter, "he would have accepted a deputation from the devil himself."[65] In the end, seventeen of the twenty-three military nobles from the Thirty attained such mandates. In many cases they returned to family lands which they had not visited for decades and set about reestablishing their positions within local patronage networks. Thus, the liberal marquis de La Tour-Maubourg, revived his family's ancient ties with Le Puy and organized proxy votes in his favor from gentlemen who could not attend the meeting themselves. He remained in close correspondence with the marquis de Satillieu, just to the south in Annonay, to whom he promised a proxy of his own for lands he possessed in Vivarais. Further north, in Lower Auvergne, Maubourg's friend the marquis de Lafayette engaged in similar politicking. All three liberals, however, soon found themselves facing formidable opposition from conservatives who were increasingly well organized in their own right. Satillieu almost failed in his bid, despite months of local leadership in the struggle against the Estates of Languedoc. When Lafayette arrived in Riom he discovered a reactionary "clique of princes"—perhaps a reference to Eprémesnil's club in Paris—already at work promoting conservative candidates and forewarning the local nobles of Lafayette's "radical" opinions. The young general managed to obtain a seat only after numerous compromises in which he promised to follow the district's conservative cahier.[66]

[63] Fichier Lefebvre; Brette, *Recueil*, 2:158–59; Nolin, 36; Triger, 129, 139; A.N., B(a) 13, liasse 9; Armand Brette, "Papiers et correspondance du Prince Emmanuel de Salm-Salm pendant la Révolution," *RH* 71 (1899), 71–74. Salm-Salm ultimately succeeded in the local election of Vézelise but was downgraded to the status of alternate in the regional election at Nancy.

[64] *Dictionnaire de biographie française*, entry "Cazalès"; Brette, *Recueil*, 2:283.

[65] Guibal, 236.

[66] Louis Gottschalk and Margaret Maddox, *Lafayette in the French Revolution through the*

Many of the prelates, like their noble cousins in the Second Estate, openly aspired to be chosen deputies. They carefully courted the votes of the parish clergy with patriotic pastoral letters and timely donations to charity. Several even presented their candidacy in more than one district to ensure success. It was only with tactics such as these that nonresident political prelates like Champion de Cicé of Bordeaux, or Boisgelin of Aix, or Talleyrand of Autun engineered their elections.[67] The curés, by contrast, were often far more reticent to assume the burdens of a deputy status. Among our curé witnesses, abbés Pous, Vallet, and Barbotin, all seemed sincerely unhappy at the prospect of leaving their parishes and traveling to Versailles.[68]

Within the Third Estate, Dupont de Nemours, Malouet, and Laborde de Méréville all took part in systematic electioneering. As early as October 1788, Dupont had written his son that "I will do all I can to become a member"; and Malouet had resigned his intendancy and courted the municipality of Riom with services rendered in Paris during the last months of 1788. But Dupont, Malouet, and Laborde were likewise trying to live down their previous associations with the royal administration.[69] In general, among the commoners, openly soliciting election was regarded as inappropriate behavior for the truly patriotic citizen. Boissy d'Anglas, who had performed many of the same kinds of services for Annonay as Malouet had for Riom, steadfastly maintained his indifference to becoming a deputy. Couderc in Lyon, Faulcon in Poitiers, and Maupetit in Le Mans took similar positions in their correspondence with close friends.[70]

October Days (Chicago, 1969), 21–22; H. Hillaire, ed., "Correspondance du Marquis de Satillieu au début de la Révolution," *Revue du Vivarais* 46 (1939), 124–27 (letters of Mar. 16 and Apr. 5, 1789); L. Nicod, "L'assemblée de la noblesse du Haut-Vivarais, tenues à Privas pour l'élection d'un député aux Etats généraux," *Revue du Vivarais* 47 (1940), 21; Keith Michael Baker, *Condorcet. From Natural Philosophy to Social Mathematics* (Chicago, 1975), 266–67.

[67] Nigel Aston, *The End of an Elite: The French Bishops and the Coming of the Revolution, 1786–1790* (Oxford, 1992), 134–51.

[68] Paul-Augustin Pous, "Correspondance inédite," *Revue de l'Anjou* 21 (1878), 291; Claude-Benjamin Vallet, "Souvenirs de l'abbé Vallet, député de Gien à l'Assemblée constituante," *Nouvelle revue rétrospective* 16 (1902), 224–26; Emmanuel Barbotin, *Lettres de l'abbé Barbotin*, ed. A. Aulard (Paris, 1910), 1 (letter of Apr. 13, 1789).

[69] Ambrose Saricks, *Pierre Samuel Du Pont de Nemours* (Lawrence, Kan., 1965), 139; Pierre-Victor Malouet, *Correspondance de Malouet avec les officiers municipaux de la ville de Riom, 1788–1789*, ed. F. Boyer (Riom, n.d.), 1:214–15; Jean-François Gaultier de Biauzat, *Gaultier de Biauzat, député du Tiers état aux Etats généraux de 1789. Sa vie et sa correspondance*, ed. Francisque Mège, 2 vols. (Clermont-Ferrand, 1890), 2:71 (letter of May 20, 1789, concerning Laborde).

[70] Boissy, *La nouvelle revue* 139 (1988), 57; Guillaume-Benoît Couderc, "Lettres de Guillaume-Benoît Couderc (1781–92)," ed. M. O. Monod, *Revue d'histoire de Lyon* 5 (1906), 415–16 (letters of Feb. 12 and Mar. 20, 1789); Faulcon, 2:18–19 (letter of Mar. 27, 1789); Michel-René Maupetit, "Lettres de Maupetit (1789–91)," ed. Quéruau-Lamérie, *Bulletin de la Commission historique et archéologique de la Mayenne*, 2e sér., 17 (1901), 315 (letter of Mar. 21, 1789).

The political dynamics of the electoral assemblies themselves are seldom revealed in the formalized minutes of the meetings, though they must commonly have entailed complicated negotiations and horse-trading among a diversity of personal, regional, and ideological factions.[71] The assemblies also differed substantially in character from region to region and between the three orders. While noble and clerical elections normally involved but a single meeting, those for the Third Estate unrolled in a series of three or even four stages, so that a victorious commoner deputy would have passed through several successive electoral assemblies. For the Third Estate in particular, the assemblies served as a series of workshops for practicing political procedures and developing and honing political programs for reform. This additional training garnered by the commoners—as compared to the experience of clergymen and nobles—may well have given the Third an advantage in its complex maneuvering with the privileged estates during the opening weeks of the Estates General. The lengthier electoral process may also have promoted more liberal positions on the part of the commoner deputies. At any rate, the Third-Estate's statements of grievances often became more radical and broader in scope from one stage to the next of that process.[72]

Among the three orders, the assemblies of the Clergy were almost certainly the most contentious and acrimonious. The electoral process represented the culmination of years—and in some cases decades—of struggles between French parish priests and the upper hierarchy of bishops, vicars-general, and canons. A combination of grievances concerning status and the distribution of wealth within the church were buttressed by the ideas of Richerism and Jansenism and by the class animosity of the curés toward the aristocratic power elites. Significant segments of the lower clergy had thus been mobilized to demand a more democratic organization of the church. The electoral assemblies were frequently marked by bitter denunciations and invectives exchanged between the two groups, and on occasion by open splits in which one of the contending parties walked out.[73]

For the most part, the assemblies of the Nobility seem to have been relatively more civil and sedate than those of the Clergy, yet here too there was a potential for rancor and divisiveness. To what extent the competing factions in Paris, Eprémesnil's "club" of conservatives and Duport's "committee" of liberals, had been able systematically to coordinate their influence on the different meetings is difficult to determine. Yet oppositional factions with positions similar to the two groups appeared in many bailliages and sénéchaussées around the kingdom. The situation was further complicated by the resentment of some rural nobles against Parisian aristocrats in gen-

[71] See esp. Brette, *Recueil*, vols. 3 and 4.

[72] Beatrice Hyslop, *A Guide to the General Cahiers* (New York, 1936), 3–31; George V. Taylor, "Revolutionary and Non-Revolutionary Content in the *Cahiers* of 1789: An Interim Report," *French Historical Studies* 7 (1971–72), 479–502.

[73] See the author's *Priest and Parish in Eighteenth-Century France* (Princeton, 1977), chaps. 9 and 10; and *Religion, Revolution, and Regional Culture* (Princeton, 1986), chap. 6.

eral, whatever their political persuasions. In Rouen, the nobles were sharply split over the basic issue of taxes and by a vote of 140 to 107 refused to cede their tax privileges. The majority concluded that "we have no need to abandon any of our rights or prerogatives." In Châtillon-sur-Seine, "there was a small-scale war," as Madame de Chastenay described it, pitting her father's liberal friends against the majority of conservatives who gathered around the marquis d'Argenteuil. Gouy d'Arsy confronted much the same phenomenon in Melun, opening the assembly with strongly liberal remarks, only to be taken to task by the majority of conservatives present, who ultimately rejected both his ideas and his candidacy.[74] On occasion, there were fears that the members of the different factions, many of whom arrived with swords at their sides, might fall into armed combat. In Villeneuve-de-Berg, the comte d'Antraigues was challenged to a duel by a local chevalier in the midst of the meetings. And several threatened to draw their swords against their opponents in Poitiers, "interpreting statements of disagreement as personal insults."[75]

Of the three orders, the meetings of the Third Estate seem generally to have been the most harmonious. After two or three successive electoral stages, the more humble elements of the population were largely filtered out. The assemblies of the "principal bailliages," the final step in the process before Versailles, were dominated by relatively homogeneous groups of wealthy urban commoners and a scattering of the newly ennobled who had not yet qualified or who had no desire to be included in the Second Estate. Perhaps the most contentious problem for the Third arose from the efforts of the various subregions within the electoral districts to ensure representation at Versailles. In Dijon, the lawyer Navier—bitter perhaps at his own failure to win election—was outraged by the "cabals" formed by certain groups of towns to promote their own men. In his opinion, this was the only reason that Hernoux of Saint-Jean-de-Losne and Gantheret of Beaune had been chosen, neither of whom "deserved the honor of election." It was also extraordinarily effective organization that ensured an equal number of deputies in the bailliage of Le Mans for both Upper and Lower Maine— much to the anger of the Manceaux and despite the fact that the latter had a much larger population and more delegates at the meeting.[76] But on the critical question of the *cahiers de doléances*, there is little evidence anywhere of major fights and divisions.

While a great many of the deputies in all three orders participated in drafting the cahiers, the final documents were usually collaborative efforts,

[74] Soublin, 170–71; Madame de Chastenay, *Mémoires de Madame de Chastenay*, 2 vols. (Paris, 1896–97), 1:77; Brette, *Recueil*, 3:393.

[75] Jolivet, 102; Roux, 167.

[76] Nolin, 36–37; Maupetit, 17 (1901), 319–20 (letter of Mar. 24, 1789); Triger, 145; Ferdinand Gaugain, *Histoire de la Révolution dans la Mayenne. I. Histoire politique et religieuse* (Laval, 1921), 127. Cf. Ran Halévi, "The Monarchy and the Elections of 1789," in *FRCMPC*, 1:394–99.

the result of numerous compromises in both cahier committees and bailliage assemblies.[77] All things considered, the cahiers produced by the assemblies of the Nobility were relatively moderate—though generally far more conservative than the cahiers of the Third Estate.[78] The majority of the nobles were convinced they must cede their tax privileges, and this in itself was a measure of a substantial evolution of opinion within the Second Estate. Yet only rarely did they accept the idea of a general vote by head on all issues in the Estates General—a position taken almost everywhere by the commoners. Their most frequent demands concerned questions of arbitrary central authority and the guarantee of civil liberties. They were almost unanimous in their criticisms of absolute monarchy. But the great majority were distinctly less progressive in their views on society and on the position of the nobility. They mentioned the seigneurial system relatively rarely, and when they did make such references, it was usually to ask that the institutions in question be maintained and preserved. They were particularly concerned with preserving their various honorific and status enhancing rights—like the right to hunt or receive special distinctions in church. In fact, throughout their cahiers, verbs such as "preserve" or "maintain" were much more common than verbs such as "abolish" or "suppress." While they clearly desired substantial change in the state and the government, their vision of society was fundamentally conservative.[79]

Like the Nobility, the commoners were also concerned in their cahiers with issues of civil rights and the constitution. But unlike the Second Estate, they leveled numerous demands against the seigneurial system. To be sure, there was not a cohesive cluster of antiseigneurial demands common to the Third cahiers everywhere, and frequently the commoners asked for modifications and reforms in the system rather than its outright suppression. In no way did they prefigure the wholesale onslaught against "feudalism" which transpired on the night of August 4. Yet overall they sought to abolish institutions far more frequently than to preserve them. Antinoble and antiseigneurial sentiments and a readiness for change—even when the specifics of those changes remained somewhat undefined—were much in the minds of the Third Estate, as measured by cahiers drawn up on the eve of the Estates General. In this they differed dramatically from the majority of the nobles.[80]

[77] There were some exceptions: Charles-François Lebrun, Pierre-Samuel Dupont de Nemours, and Pierre-Victor Malouet were said to have been sole authors of their cahiers (respectively of Dourdan, Nemours, and Riom).

[78] More recent studies put into question some of the conclusions on noble cahiers of Guy Chaussinand-Nogaret, *La noblesse au XVIIIe siècle* (Paris, 1976), 190, 208–16, 225.

[79] Ludmila Pimenova, "Analyse des cahiers de doléances: l'exemple des cahiers de la Noblesse," *Mélanges de l'Ecole de Rome* 103 (1991), 85–101; and John Markoff, *The Abolition of Feudalism: Peasants, Lords, and Legislators in the French Revolution* (University Park, Pa., 1996), in press.

[80] Markoff, *The Abolition of Feudalism*.

THIRD OPINION ON THE EVE OF THE ESTATES GENERAL

By the spring of 1789—Bailly's comments notwithstanding—a substantial and influential segment of the deputies had acquired practice in collective politics at the town, provincial, and even national levels. Above and beyond their participation in municipal and corporate activities under the Old Regime, their involvement in the provincial assemblies, in the protests against the May Edicts, in the municipal mobilization of 1788, and in the elections of 1789, had given them valuable experience with electoral procedures, the organization of meetings, constituent relations, factional formation, and negotiations with royal officials. Such experience would prove invaluable in their adaptation to the new kinds of politics evolving in Versailles after May 1789.

But if in many respects the deputies were already prepared for the *forms* of Revolutionary politics, to what extent had they also anticipated the *content* of Revolutionary thought? To what extent had their contact with eighteenth-century ideas and their experience of the "Pre-Revolution" led them to embrace a unified vision of a new society and political order, a vision that was generally missing in their writings prior to 1787?

That a few of the future deputies had already developed such coherent conceptions before the Revolution can scarcely be doubted. The exceptionally radical vision of certain of the Breton delegates—in their pamphlets and pronouncements—has already been noted. The same could be said of that former Breton resident and sometime philosophe, the abbé Sieyès. Sieyès's writings in 1788 and 1789, and above all his celebrated *What Is the Third Estate?*, now strike us as the articulate manifesto for a new understanding of popular sovereignty, a new formula for social relations in which virtually all the political prerogatives and privileges of the first two estates were to be eliminated, and in which commoners were to be invested with a position of parity in politics and society. In this sense, as one historian has phrased it, "the decisive conceptual break with the past that lay at the heart of the Revolutionary political culture had already occurred before the actual meeting of the Estates General."[81]

But was such a unified conception, anticipating the achievements of the early Revolution, widely shared by other newly elected representatives? The best sources for the opinions of individual deputies are the published brochures and pamphlets written in late 1788 and early 1789, in the final months before the meeting of the Estates General. The forty-four individuals—thirty commoners and fourteen nobles—whose writings have been

---

[81] Baker, *The Political Culture of the Old Regime*, xxi. Baker is summarizing and interpreting the ideas of Lynn Hunt. See also Ran Halévi, "La république monarchique," in *Le siècle de l'avènement républicain*, ed. François Furet and Mona Ozouf (Paris, 1993), 173–74; and William H. Sewell, Jr., *A Rhetoric of Bourgeois Revolution: The Abbé Sieyès and "What Is the Third Estate"* (Durham, 1994).

located in the French National Library hardly constitute a random sample of the future representatives.[82] The list includes not only three of our "deputy-philosophers" (Volney, Delandine, and Lenoir de la Roche) but also many of those who would soon emerge as principal leaders and participants in the National Assembly (Barnave, Bouche, Malouet, Mounier, Rabaut Saint-Etienne, Robespierre, Target, and Thouret) or in later assemblies (Boissy d'Anglas, La Revellière-Lépeaux, and Lebrun). Most of the commoner deputies involved were among that small minority who had already published prior to 1788.[83] Yet such an analysis can assist us in a preliminary assessment of the range and diversity of opinion of some of the most eminent future Revolutionaries.

The writings in question varied substantially in form and format. While a few were conceived as comprehensive programs for the coming Estates General, the majority concentrated on procedural issues, especially on the question of voting. The objectives of the Estates, as described by the authors, commonly remained vague and often went little beyond the agenda established by the monarchy itself in its official pronouncements. Most of the writers, however, were intensely aware of the significance of the events through which they were passing, and they were strikingly optimistic and self-confident that a positive outcome was in the offing, even when they were uncertain about the details of that outcome.

For purposes of comparison, we will focus on the writers' attitudes toward four themes which are particularly revealing of the degree to which individuals anticipated the Revolutionary events of the late spring and summer: the monarchy and the general question of sovereignty; the masses of the common people and their political role; the nobility and the feudal system; and the types of rationales mobilized to justify the need for action and change. We will initially concentrate our attention exclusively on the Third Estate: that group which would, after all, be largely responsible for the

---

[82] The sample is confined to those brochures preserved in the Bibliothèque nationale. I have usually accepted the attributions of authorship given by the B.N. *Catalogue des imprimés*, though in a few cases I have relied on deputy biographies. Cf. the study of Harriet Applewhite, *Political Alignment in the French National Assembly, 1789–1791* (Baton Rouge, La., 1993), esp. chap. 2. Applewhite has examined a greater number of deputy pamphlets, but has combined the Pre-Revolutionary pamphlets with those published during the first six weeks of the Estates General. Included in our sample are writings by the following deputies: Achard de Bonvouloir, the comte d'Antraigues, Barnave, Bergasse, Boislandry, Boissy d'Anglas, Charles-François Bouche, Bouchotte, Etienne Chevalier, Anne-Emmanuel-François-Georges de Crussol d'Uzès, the comte de Custine, Delandine, Duval d'Eprémesnil, the marquis d'Estourmel, Gaultier de Biauzat, Gauthier des Orcières, Gleises de Lablanque, le marquis de Gouy d'Arsy, Guillotin, Hell, Lanjuinais, La Revellière-Lépeaux, the comte de La Touche, Charles-François Lebrun, Jean-Baptiste Leclerc, Le Goazre de Kervélégan, Lenoir de La Roche, the baron de Luppé-Taybosc, the duc de Luynes, Malouet, the marquis de Monspey, Mounier, the marquis de Montesquiou-Fezenzac, Pellerin, Pétion de Villeneuve, Rabaut Saint-Etienne, Robespierre, Roederer, Sèze, Target, Thouret, the vicomte de Toulongeon, Vernier, and Volney.

[83] Of the 30 commoner writers, only 8 (Barnave, Bouchotte, Gauthier des Orcières, Guillotin, Le Goazre, Mounier, Pellerin, and Vernier) are not known to have published previously.

revolutionary actions of June, and for which the greatest number of published writings have been preserved. But we shall also consider more briefly the limited documentation for the positions of the Nobility.[84]

In most of the Third Estate brochures, as in most of the cahiers of 1789, one cannot but be impressed by the strong sentiments of respect and devotion toward the king, whatever the critiques of the current monarchical government. Though much has been made of the "desacralization" of the kingship in later eighteenth-century France, one can find only marginal evidence of such a trend among the future deputies on the eve of the Revolution.[85] To be sure, a great deal of the praise and adoration seemed to be directed toward the specific figure of Louis XVI for his actions in restoring the Estates General. We know that Necker and the other ministers were self-consciously doing all in their power to promote such an image.[86] Yet the brochures commonly contained a rhetoric of paternal sentiments and emotional attachment that went beyond mere gratitude for a particular act. The Parisian Doctor Guillotin spoke of Louis as a king who "is seeking his happiness ... in the happiness of the beloved children who adore their father. He is doing everything for them and they will do everything for him." The self-consciously radical Breton, Le Goazre de Kervélégan, maintained that "the king, as the true father of his country, admits his whole family into his counsel." Target spoke of "a single family deliberating with their father"; Robespierre of "the solemn and touching voice of our king who is offering us happiness and liberty"; Barnave of a "prince inspired by justice and guided by genius."[87] Some deputies went beyond the eighteenth-century "bourgeois" representation of the king as a good and kindly father, and embraced the older, medieval image of the king as a distant, exalted, and sacred figure. The future Monarchien Malouet wrote of the "august character of the royalty." The Protestant patriot Boissy d'Anglas used much the same language, referring directly to the king's "sacred authority" and arguing that all citizens should be "submissive to royal authority until death." So too, the lawyer and future Jacobin Vernier, who feared that the nobles were sowing suspicions of the government's "despotism," urged his French countryman to "have no fear of idolizing your kings. . . . Gather

---

[84] Only four brochures by clerical deputies were located in the original sample, a selection that seemed too small for meaningful comparisons.

[85] E.g., Jeffrey Merrick, *The Desacralization of the French Monarchy in the Eighteenth Century* (Baton Rouge, La., 1990); Chartier, chap. 6; and Lynn Hunt, *The Family Romance of the French Revolution* (Berkeley, 1992), chap. 2.

[86] Jacques Necker, *De la Révolution française*, 2 vols. (n.p., 1796), 1:104.

[87] Joseph-Ignace Guillotin, *Pétition des citoyens domiciliés à Paris* (Paris, Dec. 8, 1788), 1; Augustin-Bernard-François Le Goazre de Kervélégan, *Lettre ... à M. Balais, subdélégué de Nantes* (Quimper, Nov. 17, 1788), 32–33; Guy-Jean-Baptiste Target, *Les Etats généraux convoqués par Louis XVI* (Paris, ca. Dec. 1788), 2; Maximilien Robespierre, *A la nation artésienne, sur la nécessité de réformer les Etats d'Artois* (n.p., 1788), 82; Antoine-Pierre-Joseph Barnave, *Coup d'oeil sur la lettre de Monsieur de Calonne* ([Grenoble], Mar. 28, 1789), 28.

around the throne and . . . preserve the power of the monarchy." Even in the unlikely case that conniving ministers and courtiers succeeded in tricking the king into an unjust organization of the Estates General, good citizens must still submit and "through your submissiveness, be deserving of your king's good graces." Pellerin, who followed much the same reasoning, even counseled a return to "the principles of Bossuet."[88] Of all the writers, only Lanjuinais and Doctor Sèze felt compelled to develop rational justifications for the existence of a monarchy in France, with Sèze calling on the geographic and ecological arguments of his former Bordeaux compatriot, Montesquieu, and with Lanjuinais stressing the monarch's role in maintaining social stability: it was "the essential support of the people . . . the cornerstone of our social edifice."[89]

The deputies seemed much more divided and often uncertain, however, as to the future relationship between the king and the Estates General and the question of ultimate sovereignty. Only Volney and Pétion—by far the most radical on this question—specifically demanded that the king's power be confined to the executive authority to implement the "will of the people." Volney's longtime friends and schoolmates La Revellière-Lépeaux and Leclerc seemed to take a similar position, though they would have granted the Estates General only an episodic authority by specifying its convocation at five-year intervals. At the opposite extreme, Bergasse stipulated that the Estates General's prerogatives were limited to a "moral force" and that one must "leave all power to the prince and all opinion to the people"; while Lebrun, the former assistant to Turgot, indicated a clear preference for enlightened reform dictated from above, in the manner of Henri IV or of various contemporary European monarchs. Yet Lebrun also expressed doubts whether the current monarchy was capable of such leadership and ultimately left the relationship between king and estates unresolved. Thouret, normally a paragon of rigor and logic, seemed almost confused in his analysis of the issue: sovereign authority, he announced, resides wholly in the person of the king, but such sovereignty could not always be exercised without the consent of the nation, a proviso that would "regulate but not diminish the legitimate use of power."[90] Barnave proposed that the king be given full executive

---

[88] Pierre-Victor Malouet, "Discours prononcé par M. Malouet, 1789," in *Mémoires*, 2 vols., ed. Baron Malouet (Paris, 1868), 1:229; François-Antoine Boissy d'Anglas, *Adresse au peuple languedocien par un citoyen du Languedoc* (n.p., 1789), 15–16; Théodore Vernier, *Le cri de la vérité* (n.p, ca. Dec. 1788), 2, 6, 10; Joseph-Michel Pellerin, *Mémoire historique sur la constitution des Etats de Bretagne, adressée aux gentilhommes bretons* (n.p., 1788), 48–49.

[89] Jean-Denis Lanjuinais, *Le préservatif contre l'avis à mes compatriotes, avec des observations sur l'affaire présente* (n.p., n.d.), 14–15; Paul-Victor de Sèze, *Les voeux d'un citoyen* (Bordeaux, 1789), 21–22.

[90] Constantin-François de Volney, *Des conditions nécessaires à la légalité aux Etats généraux* ([Rennes, Nov. 1788]), 13; Jérôme Pétion de Villeneuve, *Avis aux français sur le salut de la patrie* (n.p., 1789), 81–82, 214; Louis-Marie de La Revellière-Lépeaux and Jean-Baptiste Leclerc, *Doléances, voeux et pétitions pour les représentants des paroisses . . .* (Angers, 1789), 5; Nicolas Bergasse, *Lettre de M. Bergasse à MM. les Officiers de la ville de Saint-Germain-Laval, en*

power and that king and Estates divide the legislative authority, though the precise contours of this division were somewhat obscure. The young lawyer from Grenoble advocated giving both the monarch and the assembly a veto, but then argued, in apparent contradiction, that the nation would never even consider diminishing the king's authority. Target and Boissy noted that the king had voluntarily offered to give up a part of his authority, but Target interpreted this to mean that the king would ask their "advice" on all legislation; and Boissy hastened to add that any actions taken by the Estates "will in no way undermine his sacred authority." Boissy's friend and fellow Protestant, Rabaut Saint-Etienne, also acknowledged that by calling the Estates General the king had inevitably diminished his own authority. Yet for Rabaut, this was a mere technicality, since the "nation" would invariably sanction all just laws that were submitted to it, and it seemed inconceivable that the king might propose anything but just laws. Indeed, by reducing the power of the Parlements and the ministries, the new arrangement would actually strengthen the monarchy overall.[91]

In the end, there was a curious reticence to push the analysis of sovereignty to its logical extreme, to consider the possibility that the will of the king and the will of the "nation" might ever be at variance. The king and the monarchy remained a fundamental element in the worldview of the deputies, a nexus of security and an object of considerable emotional and filial attachment that often quite transcended rational analysis and debate. Indeed, in the audacious perspectives for reform presenting themselves to the Third Estate in May and June of 1789, the presumed support of the king would be of enormous importance in fueling and sustaining the deputies' courage and self-confidence.[92]

Compared to their comments on the king, most of the deputies were far more parsimonious in their pronouncements concerning the masses of the common people—and the observations that did appear were sharply divergent and often ambiguous. Several of the writers were quite specific in their desire to limit popular political participation. For the Lyonais Delandine, the coming constitution would necessarily be the work of "all those who, by their understanding, their depth of vision, and their enlightened minds, distinguish themselves from the masses of ordinary men." The Alsatian judge Hell seemed altogether obsessed with the prospect that the ongoing political process might stir up the population. Everything possible must be done to ensure that the peasants remained in their places, did not waste their time

Forez (Paris, Feb. 12, 1789), 49; Charles-François Lebrun, *La voix du citoyen* (n.p., 1789), 11; Jacques-Guillaume Thouret, *Suite de l'avis des bons normands, dédiée aux Assemblées de bailliage, sur la rédaction des cahiers des pouvoirs et instructions* (n.p., Feb. 1789), 37.

[91] Barnave, 11–12; Target, *Les Etats généraux*, 4–5; Boissy, *Adresse*, 16; Jean-Paul Rabaut Saint-Etienne, *A la nation française* (n.p., Nov. 1788), 52–55.

[92] See chap. 4.

mulling over politics, and generally continued to accept their station in life. Lebrun specified that people without property could only be "partial citizens" at best. Even Rabaut, despite his demands that the "peuple" be consulted on the laws that were to govern them, was openly fearful that the state might collapse "in an immense democracy which will lead inevitably to anarchy or despotism"—a sentiment shared by the otherwise radical Lanjuinais, who rejected "with horror" the concept of democracy "where each citizen is a despot and a tyrant."[93]

At the opposite extreme, an impassioned group of deputies seemed to back precisely this kind of "immense democracy." The magistrate from Bar-sur-Seine, Bouchotte, lamented that "the men who, through their labor, fertilize the land and provide us with abundance" were denied a voice because of "Gothic and feudal laws"; and he argued that they should have the status of a "fourth estate" as in Sweden. Target, Lenoir de la Roche, Volney, Roederer, and Pétion, all promoted the inclusion of every element of the population in the political process, not just those with landed property. If the first two were somewhat vague as to what this would entail in practice, Volney was quite explicit that suffrage "must be as widespread as possible," incorporating all heads of household over the age of twenty-five—including peasants, sharecroppers, artisans, and widows, and excluding only those such as servants and soldiers whose votes could be controlled by others. Pétion and Roederer likewise specified that the right to vote or hold office should not be dependent on property qualifications and Roederer even proposed including women.[94] Gaultier de Biauzat, Robespierre, and the wealthy farmer Etienne Chevalier also revealed enormous sympathy for the economic and social plight of "the common people." Gaultier was outraged by the injustices done to them through the present tax system and strongly commiserated with their suffering and poverty; and Robespierre stormed against the aristocrats who seemed utterly callous to the fact that "the people are dying of hunger," that "the greater part of mankind . . . is debased by indigence." Chevalier wrote likewise of "these men so useful to society who suffer under the weight of oppression and poverty."[95]

Curiously, however, none of the latter three writers—all of whom would

[93] Antoine-François Delandine *Des Etats généraux, ou histoire des assemblées nationales en France* (Paris, 1788), iii; Malouet, "Discours," 227; François-Antoine-Joseph Hell, *Formes des élections [des députés aux Etats généraux]* ([Colmar], Feb. 1789); Lebrun, *La voix du citoyen*, 19; Jean-Paul Rabaut Saint-Etienne, "Considérations sur les intérêts du Tiers état," in *Oeuvres*, 2 vols. (Paris, 1826), 2:288; Lanjuinais, 19.

[94] Pierre-Paul-Alexandre Bouchotte, *Discours prononcé . . . à la cour des aides, le 8 octobre 1788* (n.p., 1788), 11; Target, *Les Etats généraux*, 26–27; Jean-Jacques Lenoir de La Roche, *Observations sur les principes de la constitution des Etats de Dauphiné* (n.p., 1788), 66–68; Volney, 18–19; Pierre-Louis Roederer, *De la députation aux Etats-généraux* (n.p., 3 Nov. 1788), 26, 35–40; Pétion, 105.

[95] Jean-François Gaultier de Biauzat, *Doléances sur les surcharges que les gens du peuple supportent en toute espèce d'impôts* (n.p., 1788); Robespierre, 25, 30–31; Etienne Chevalier, *Voeux d'un patriote et réflexions* (n.p., 1789), 3.

soon embrace the Jacobin cause—advocated political rights for the socially and economically downtrodden, and Chevalier clearly specified that "democracy" must be avoided.[96] While Target seemed to promote suffrage for the masses, he also found it inconceivable that they could ever be legislators or hold positions of power. Other future deputies who supported a greater measure of power for "the common people" seemed ambiguous or inconsistent in the meaning which they lent to that phrase. Both Vernier and Gauthier des Orcières made ample use of the term, but appeared at times to associate it with "the citizens of the towns" (Vernier) or "the most important property owners" (Gauthier). Barnave, who had aroused opposition through his use of the word "peuple" in his earlier writings, hastened to explain that he had only wanted to signify the "nation" as a whole and not the common people.[97] And indeed, the majority of the brochure writers—as nearly all of the early letter writers—simply ignored the question of the common people altogether.[98] A great many would seem to have become conscience of their potential political existence only in the first weeks of the Estates General itself. The deputies' efforts to come to grips with the unanticipated participation of the masses would rapidly become, as we shall see, an important element in the revolutionary dynamic of the Assembly.

On the question of the nobility, the future deputies of the Third Estate also appeared divided. Only two of the writers pressed to perpetuate the reigning system of social hierarchy. "Distinctions of rank," wrote Thouret, "are consecrated in society through the principles of constitutional monarchy," and the nobles' rights, as all other rights of property, could not and should not be touched. Malouet likewise spoke favorably of "the distinctions adhering to families of ancient lineage, a preeminence of rank and of function" which had been consecrated by time. Four others supported the institution of the nobility, as long as it was based on a value system of talent and merit rather than of birth. Lebrun, the commoner who had achieved noble status through his brilliance and good connections, endorsed such a concept as a means of attaching talented individuals to the state. Rabaut concurred: "Decorated men are absolutely necessary. The privileges offered to the illustrious are essential in a great state." "The philosopher must oppose the abuse of distinctions," added Boissy, "but deserved distinctions do exist," justified by intelligence, patriotism, and virtue. Delandine, alone among the writers, argued that such a situation already existed, and that an Enlightened elite cutting across the boundaries of orders could easily work together

[96] Chevalier, 3.

[97] Guy-Jean-Baptiste Target, *Suite de l'écrit intitulé "Les Etats généraux convoqués par Louis XVI* (n.p., ca. Dec. 1788), 35; Vernier, 3; Antoine-François Gauthier des Orcières, *Considérations sur l'état actuel de la province de Bresse* (Lyon, Aug. 20, 1788), 22, 38; Barnave, 2.

[98] In general, the letter writers began mentioning the spectators in their assembly and the "peuple" in the streets only at the end of May: see chap. 4.

to effect needed reforms: "The most enlightened citizens, who constitute a single useful and virtuous body," would cooperate in the common goal of "prosperity for France and glory for its monarchy."[99]

In most instances, however, where support for the nobility did exist, it seemed motivated primarily by pragmatic considerations. The writers could not have been unaware of the sharp aristocratic backlash by early 1789. Both Thouret and Lebrun expressed their fear of frightening the powerful, incurring their wrath and suspicion and thus vitiating any possibility of reform. Without attempting abstract justifications for the existence of a nobility, the Parisians Target and Lenoir and the Versailles merchant Boislandry all supported cooperation with the nobles and the promotion of unity as the most practical means of effecting needed transformations. Lenoir praised the actions of the elites in Dauphiné for promoting "this spirit of unity among the three orders" without which the coming Estates General would end in the same chaos and disarray that had marred the meetings of the previous estates. Boislandry hoped that by relinquishing their tax privileges, the nobles had "forever eliminated all hatred and discord."[100]

The obvious anxiety of these writers over commoner antagonism toward the Second Estate was not without justification. The majority of the future Third deputies was clearly impatient, if not openly hostile toward the nobility. Indeed, in no other area was their rhetoric so strident, in no other area did the majority reveal such passion and antipathy for Old Regime institutions as in their comments on the nobility. Fresh from his bitter confrontation in Brittany, Lanjuinais displayed a veritable fury against the aristocracy. The nobles were "a body of parasites living off the labors of the people," who would like nothing better than to "hunt us down like so many wild animals." If the people did not soon take steps to "throw off their chains," they would be transformed into a class of Helots. Alone among the authors, the Breton Jansenist suggested that the nobility might be abolished: "nobles are not a necessary evil." The Comtois Vernier also raged against the nobles whom he found, with few exceptions, utterly untrustworthy. "United by family relations and by economic self-interest," the first two estates were the enemies by definition of the nation. Robespierre seemed beside himself with anger against the "aristocrats" of his province of Artois, conspiring to dominate and maintain the people in "slavery" and "indigence," despising all commoners "as vile footboards." Doctor Sèze wrote of the "monstrous feudal aristocracy"; and Pétion demanded the suppression

---

[99] Jacques-Guillaume Thouret, *Avis des bons Normands à leurs frères tous les bons Français de toutes les provinces et de tous les ordres* (n.p., Feb. 1789), 12; Malouet, *Discours*, 229; Lebrun, *La voix du citoyen*, 20–22; Rabaut Saint-Etienne, "Considérations," 288; Boissy, *Adresse*, 21–22; Delandine, xxii. Cf. Chevalier, 10.

[100] Thouret, ibid.; Lebrun, *La voix du citoyen*, 82; François-Louis Boislandry, *Réponse aux auteurs d'un écrit intitulé ≪Avis aux citoyens du bailliage de Versailles≫* (n.p., [spring 1789]), 5–6; Target, *Les Etats généraux*, 3; Lenoir de La Roche, 85–86.

of all noble privileges without exception, since "all can be reduced to a few imaginary distinctions and to the desire for display."[101]

But even those deputies soon to emerge as conservatives within the National Assembly displayed considerable impatience toward the nobles. Malouet soundly reprimanded them for their intransigence and refusal to adapt to a changing reality, and he warned them that if they did not cede, they were in danger of losing everything. The *anobli* Lebrun described their monopoly on high office as "a crime." Mounier rejected the theories of Montesquieu, concluding that whenever the aristocrats were given too much power, they abused it. And Bergasse wrote at length of the constant humiliation suffered by commoners at the hands of the hereditary nobility. He was outraged that one could not even be presented to the king without giving proof of noble lineage dating to the fourteenth century. With "Gothic customs" of this kind, neither Descartes, Pascal, Corneille, nor Montesquieu would have qualified as "proper company for a king."[102] This indignation over questions of status, this theme of the nobles' scorn and haughtiness toward the commoners, of the commoners being treated as "vile footboards," is in evidence in numerous of the writings. Mounier spoke of "humiliating exclusions"; Gauthier des Orcières of the lords' "humiliating" domination of the countryside; and Doctor Guillotin, in his otherwise mild and measured brochure, called for an end to all the "demeaning distinctions" foisted on the Third Estate. Both Mounier and Lanjuinais were convinced, moreover, that the humiliation and exclusion of the Third had become progressively worse in the course of the eighteenth century. Because of such "innovations," "all the doors leading to honor and prestige . . . are closed to the Third Estate."[103]

The intensity of antinoble sentiments among deputies of such widely divergent views on other subjects is impressive and significant. To some extent, it is corroborated by the letters and diaries of our deputy witnesses penned during the earliest weeks of the Assembly. The notary Goupilleau, in his first letter to his cousin in Rochefervière, launched into an eloquent plea for "equality among men": "all prejudices and distinctions based on birth" are invalidated, he argued, by both "the order of nature" and "religious morality." The Poitevin chief judge, Creuzé-Latouche, argued that for pragmatic reasons the Third Estate should assure the Nobles that they would not destroy their order, no matter how "absurd" that order might be—though, in fact, the nation would probably be much better off without any nobles at all. And numerous testimonies took note of the overt "implacable hatred towards the nobility," of the deputies from Brittany and from

[101] Lanjuinais, 15, 22; Vernier, esp. 6; Robespierre, esp. 81; Sèze, 16; and Pétion, 247–48 and 262–63.

[102] Pierre-Victor Malouet, *Avis à la noblesse* (n.p., 1788); Jean-Joseph Mounier, *Nouvelles observations sur les Etats-généraux de France* (n.p., 1789), 211–13; Bergasse, *Lettre*, 3–5.

[103] Mounier, 202; Gauthier des Orcières, 22; Guillotin, 13; Lanjuinais, 9.

several other provinces.[104] Certain deputies, who had avoided the subject altogether in their earliest letters, could no longer suppress their joy and gloating delight in July and August as the nobles lost most of their political and social privileges. Campmas expressed his disappointment that he could not see the faces of the local aristocrats when they learned of the recent decrees, decrees which, as Gantheret put it, "ought to take the nobles down a peg." Gallot noted to his wife, "After their abominable behavior, all this noble scum, with all their coats of arms, deserves to be humiliated." "You've told me nothing of our local god," wrote Bouchette in reference to one of the nobles. "Does our Jupiter no longer make all Olympus shake each time he blinks his eyes? Is he no longer able to smile as he makes his inferiors tremble?"[105]

Quotations such as these take us well beyond the period of the Pre-Revolution. Yet they are revealing of the deep-seated antiaristocratic bitterness, the jealousy and sense of injustice present in the hearts of many Third Estate deputies as they assumed their seats in Versailles, a bitterness that was to be a central element, as we shall see, in the emergence of a revolutionary consensus within that Estate at the beginning of June 1789.[106] We have previously explored the very considerable social, economic, and cultural distinctions separating the deputies of the Third Estate from those of the Nobility, distinctions that were reinforced by a whole series of legal and symbolic privileges and prerogatives. By the spring of 1789 a significant number of commoner deputies had come to judge these distinctions and privileges as profoundly humiliating and degrading.

How and when individual Third Estate deputies first came consciously to formulate such antipathies, first began thinking in categories of "injustice" and "humiliation," is usually impossible to know. Whether they genuinely believed in the value system of a hierarchical nobility, or whether it did not occur to them that change could take place, many deputies probably never even articulated feelings such as these before the period of the Pre-Revolution. There is some evidence that for the Lyon publisher, Périsse Du Luc, this transformation occurred only after the aristocratic backlash of early 1789. In a letter to his closest friend, he described an altercation with one of his Masonic brothers, an aristocrat who sat with him on the intermediary commission. Like his Lyon compatriot Delandine, Périsse hoped that a

---

[104] Jean-François-Marie Goupilleau to his cousin: B.M. Nantes, Collection Dugast-Matifeux, no. 98, letter of May 11, 1789; Jacques-Antoine Creuzé-Latouche, *Journal des Etats généraux et du début de l'Assemblée nationale, 18 mai–29 juillet 1789*, ed. Jean Marchand (Paris, 1946), 13, 15 (letter of May 25, 1789); Laurent de Visme, ms. "Journal des Etats généraux": B.N., Nouv. acq. fr. 12938, entry of May 14, 1789.

[105] François Campmas to his brother, vicaire in Carmaux: B.M. Albi, Ms. 177, letter of Aug. 8, 1789; Claude Gantheret to Pierre Leflaive, his brother-in-law: private collection of Françoise Misserey, letter of July 3, 1789; François-Joseph Bouchette, in Looten, 243 (letter of Aug. 13, 1789); Jean-Gabriel Gallot, *La vie et les oeuvres du Docteur Jean-Gabriel Gallot*, ed. Louis Merle (Poitiers, 1961), 121 (letter of Aug. 2, 1789).

[106] See the following chapter.

common eighteenth-century culture had effectively swept aside all distinctions of birth among the elites. He was thus stunned to hear his colleague argue one day that nobles "were in fact members of another race, with a different blood" and that they alone constituted the nation. Despite the vows of brotherhood that bound the two together, Périsse felt compelled to reply that "I was as much a noble as he, and that he was as much a commoner as I" and that "hereditary nobility was a political monstrosity." The dispute soon led to an irrevocable break between the two, and within a year Périsse was sitting with the Jacobins and the noble was entrenched as a confirmed counterrevolutionary.[107]

But for other deputies, the very intensity and anger of their rhetoric—of Gaultier de Biauzat or Bouchette or Robespierre—suggests that such feelings were not of recent origin and had long festered inside them, engendered by the social and legal system in which they lived; and that the individuals involved did not feel they had merged with a common "elite." In an introduction to his pamphlet in favor of "the common people," Gaultier announced that he had always been indignant over the inequities of the Old Regime. If he had never previously spoken up, it was "out of trepidation for a group to be feared under the old regime of abuse and privilege." After all, he had a family to think about and his fear of the consequences at that time "did not allow me to confront such rich and selfish [aristocrats]." For the lawyer from Clermont-Ferrand, the turning point had come in July 1788 when the king himself asked all Frenchmen for their sentiments about the coming Estates General. Only then, at last, could he openly announce his long concealed feelings.[108]

As the Third Estate deputies often differed in their specific demands and visions of the future, so too in their rationales for change, their grounds for judgment, their justifications for choices, individual writers often found themselves substantially at variance. Most of the brochure writers were obviously conversant with the chief elements of the Enlightened vocabulary and modes of thought. Such *mots clefs* as "reason," "happiness," "philosophy," or the "Gothic and barbarian past," were commonly mobilized by individuals in their efforts to analyze present ills, prescribe future courses of action, and propose a new constitution. Both Sèze—who made specific references to Montesquieu and Rousseau—and Lenoir argued that it was the triumph of reason and enlightenment which distinguished the present situation in France from all other events in the past. What others had won only through blood and struggle, they would now obtain through the force of their arguments: "without weapons, without violence, through the power

---

[107] Jean-André Périsse Du Luc to J. B. Willermoz: B.M. Lyon ms. 5430, letter of Sept. 12, 1789.

[108] Gaultier, *Doléances*, iii–vi. Cf. the similar statement by Antoine Durand to the municipality of Cahors: A.M. Cahors, unclassed box of letters from Revolutionary deputies, held in B.M. Cahors, letter of Sept. 4, 1789.

of reason alone."[109] In their presentations of France's options Sèze, Delandine, Volney, Pétion, Target, and Rabaut were all self-consciously prepared to repudiate historical prescription. Delandine wrote nearly three hundred pages on the history of the previous Estates General, only to conclude that no fixed and consistent procedures were followed in the past and that a "constitution" would now have to be created from scratch, in a manner "worthy of a philosopher." Target determined that if any such constitution had ever existed historically in France it was a "masterpiece of chance and accident" and that a new constitution must be based on the "general will." Rabaut followed much the same line of argument, encouraging the French, in their creation of a constitution, to follow the example of the Americans, "this people of philosophers."[110]

Yet the number of deputies in our sample endorsing the use of reason and "philosophy" alone was ultimately rather small. The great majority seemed to subscribe to a pragmatic, multifaceted approach to the problems of determining a new constitution, an approach that might well include the abstract rational assessment of the philosophers, but that also relied on history, experience, even custom and religion. Several individuals, in their brochures or in their diaries, were quite explicit in this regard: "laws, customs, and reason" (the prescription of Guillotin); "reason, equity, and law" (Pellerin); "experience, history, reason, and general interest" (Lebrun); "nature and God" (Chevalier).[111] With the standard Enlightenment clichés, Barnave appealed to "the light of reason" which would cast aside "the barbarous institutions" of the present; but he also argued for a return to the past, to the constitution long forgotten now rediscovered in the history of the first centuries of the monarchy, a constitution that was not only enriched with "the gifts of philosophy" but was also "decorated with the fruits of experience." Even Target and Pétion were prepared to develop long historical justifications on occasion—since to do otherwise, as Target described it, "would be to subtract from the wisdom of our fathers."[112] For Gaultier de Biauzat, one must be attentive to "the voice of reason," yet one must also study the past, because "any new system would be dangerous"; and in point of fact, much of his brochure consisted of a series of historical developments. Vernier seemed to mix a logic drawn from "the immutable principles of reason and justice" with a very traditional argument for allegiance to the king based essentially on filial obedience and authority. Robespierre, too, resorted to a lengthy development on the institutional history of Artois to prove usurpations by the local aristocracy, even though he also appealed continually to an abstract conception of "sacred and imprescriptible rights"

---

[109] Sèze, 27; Lenoir, 1–2.

[110] Sèze, 57; Delandine, xx–xxi; Rabaut, *A la nation française*, 14, 29; Target, *Les Etats généraux*, 44; and *Deuxième suite de l'écrit intitulé "Etats généraux convoqués par Louis XVI"* (Paris, 1789), 30; Volney, 5; Pétion, 2–3, 11–12.

[111] Guillotine, 5; Pellerin, 48–49; Lebrun, *La voix du citoyen*, 18; Chevalier, 11.

[112] Barnave, 9, 16; Target, *Deuxième suite*, 21, 26; Pétion, 17ff.

in the face of the oppression exercised by that aristocracy.[113] Other deputies placed even greater stress on empirical and practical considerations in the determination of choices. Thus, the primary objective of both Thouret and Chevalier seemed to be the creation of a more efficient financial system and administration, an administration that worked effectively and with fewer abuses in carrying out its tasks.[114]

Lenoir, who made ample use of historical developments in justifying the actions of the Dauphinois and who also stressed that "one must begin with things as they are, not things as they could be," included the additional proviso that all actions would have to be ratified, as it were, by public opinion. But those deputies who did make mention of public opinion—only a small minority at best—had rather different conceptions of its meaning and determination. For some it implied nothing more than the whims and passions of the masses, which in Pétion's view were prejudiced, easily manipulated, and altogether unreliable: "public opinion can never serve as a bastion of liberty." For others, it seemed to represent a kind of common denominator of popular will, to be identified empirically and pragmatically in the course of the elections of the Estates General and the Estates' subsequent deliberations: "public opinion will be formed in the midst" of the various assemblies.[115] For others still, public opinion was treated as the abstraction of what the public *should* desire if it knew what was best for it, a concept closely approaching Rousseau's general will. Volney, Pétion, Target, Thouret, and Malouet all made references to the latter concept, though here too interpretations of its meaning differed considerably. For Volney and Pétion it was clearly a question of some kind of referendum or appeal to the people, which alone could legitimize the decisions of the Estates General. For Target, Thouret, and Malouet, however, the general will was apparently to be determined from above, by the assembly if not by the king himself. In Malouet's understanding, moreover, this general will, "the true sovereign," was closely related to custom and historical tradition, to "principles consecrated by time."[116]

In sum, within the Pre-Revolutionary texts of future Third Estate deputies there were numerous ambiguities, contradictions, and uncertainties, as diverse rationales and lines of logic found themselves mixed pell-mell. Without exception, all of the authors seemed prepared for significant changes and believed that such changes were possible. But in their writings there was at least as much potential for slow and cautious reform as for revolutionary mutation, and indeed, none of the writers anticipated the full extent of the decrees that would soon be promulgated. There was as much diver-

[113] Gaultier de Biauzat, *Doléances*, 242; Vernier, 4–6; Robespierre, 4.

[114] Thouret, *Avis des bons Normands*, 5; Chevalier, 22–23.

[115] Lenoir, 8–12, 61; Pétion, 4; Bergasse, 47–49; Lebrun, 90. Cf. Mona Ozouf, "L'opinion publique," in *FRCMPC*, 419–34.

[116] Volney, 13; Pétion, 9; Target, *Deuxième Suite*, 30; Thouret, *Avis des bons Normands*, 4; Malouet, "Discours," 228–29.

sity over how such transformations might be determined as over what specific transformations should be accomplished. Though a few seemed to believe that France could be remade from the ground up on the basis of reason and "philosophy," most assumed that all reforms must be linked in some way to the history and customs of the kingdom, and several cautioned specifically against any "esprit de système" that would cut France off from its past and its traditions.[117] There was a general lack of unified strands of argument, of a predictable "discourse," as though the individuals in question were still scrambling to make sense of their transforming world, to improvise new frameworks appropriate for the extraordinary series of events which they were compelled to confront.[118]

NOBLE OPINION ON THE EVE OF THE ESTATES GENERAL

Unfortunately, the Pre-Revolutionary attitudes and modes of thought of the future deputies of the Nobility are far more difficult to discern. Beyond the small but visible contingent of Parisian liberals, the great majority of future noble deputies of both Paris and the provinces have left us few documentary indications of their positions before traveling to Versailles. Contemporaries themselves took note of this paucity of writings, and some attributed it to the Nobles' general feelings of self-satisfaction and to their confidence that the status quo was safe and had no need of being defended. However, the Norman seigneur and future deputy, Achard de Bonvouloir, felt that it was above all a question of education and culture. Trained as a cavalry officer, Achard bitterly regretted that he and so many of his peers lacked the mastery of words necessary to compete with the commoners. Before the powerful logic and expression of a Target or a Thouret, the nobles remained all but silent—even though their cause was just. "These men are seducing others with their pens, and we write nothing at all. In everything that is printed, nary a word for the nobility."[119]

While only a handful of brochures written by future deputies of the Second Estate have been located, it is evident that the aristocracy, no less than the commoners, held a substantial range of opinions. The views of the "patriot" nobles of the Committee of Thirty are generally assumed to have closely matched the program of the patriot commoners: the doubling of the Third and the vote by head; the expansion and guarantee of basic civil liberties; the creation or re-creation of a French constitution; and the transformation of the Estates General from a simple consultative body to a legislature with the right to ratify taxes. Yet not all the Parisian liberals agreed on all elements of this program, even among the members of the Thirty.

[117] E.g, Lenoir, 85.
[118] Cf. Baker, *Inventing the French Revolution*, chap. 1: also Gail Bossenga, *The Politics of Privilege* (Cambridge, 1991), 88; and Halévi, "La république monarchique."
[119] Letter to the marquis de Ségrie, Jan. 11, 1789: A.D. Calvados, C 8582.

The duc de Luynes, for example, wrote a long historical account of the Estates General in France, strongly influenced by Boulainvilliers and in which Enlightenment language was almost totally absent. Like many of the noble cahiers, his focus was primarily on ministerial despotism, while he strongly defended the hereditary rights of nobles. He also carefully avoided taking any position at all on the issue of voting in the Estates General.[120] Outside the milieu of the Thirty, moreover, the range of noble opinion, by comparison with that of the Third, was distinctly shifted to the conservative end of the spectrum. An examination of the writings of three individual nobles—the marquis de Montesquiou, the baron de Luppé, and Achard de Bonvouloir—illustrates both the diversity and the general tendencies within the Second Estate.

A Freemason and member of the French Academy, the marquis de Montesquiou would undoubtedly have described himself as a moderate. Exuding the confidence and rhetoric of the Enlightenment, he embraced the position that the "progress of reason" and the "spirit of philosophy" had largely swept away the differences between the Nobles and commoners "in the eyes of society." All depended, or at least should depend, on merit and "personal qualities." As most of the Third authors, the marquis had little to say about the specific agenda for the Estates General. He embraced the liberal objectives of equal taxation and a doubling of the Third, though he was typically vague on the issue of ultimate authority, suggesting that basic decisions should be left to the king, who takes the interests of all to heart. However, he was also deeply concerned about the other, less enlightened members of his order, those who "superstitiously hold even the most absurd beliefs in highest regard, as long as those beliefs are deemed sufficiently ancient." Perhaps it was in the face of the reaction of so many of his peers, that he adopted the vote by head only on tax measures, while maintaining a vote by order for all other "legislation"—a proposal that seemed curiously out of step with the rest of his arguments. Such a proposition would certainly have been rejected by all of our Third Estate brochure writers without exception.[121]

The baron de Luppé, a retired musketeer living in the small provincial town of Auch, had been active in the Pre-Revolutionary period as a member of the intermediary commission for the local provincial assembly. In his brochure of early 1789 he also made ample references to Enlightenment texts, including both Rousseau's *Social Contract* and Montesquieu's *Spirit of the Laws*. In the end, however, he came down solidly for Montesquieu. The Estates General was portrayed as a necessary "intermediate body," preserv-

---

[120] Louis-Joseph-Charles-Amable, duc de Luynes, *L'histoire, le cérémonial, et les droits des Etats généraux du royaume de France* (n.p., Feb. 1789). Cf. the widely read tract by the comte d'Antraigues, *Mémoire sur les Etats-généraux* (1788). See also Wick, chap. 11.

[121] Anne-Pierre, marquis de Montesquiou-Fezensac, *Aux trois ordres de la nation* (n.p., [1789]). Cf. the similar positions of Adam-Philippe de Custine, *Plan à consulter, d'instructions et de pouvoirs à donner aux députés de la province de Lorraine* (Nancy, 1789).

ing liberty against the dangers of monarchical despotism, on the one hand, and democratic anarchy, on the other. Yet this body could maintain its independence, he argued, only if the three orders debated and voted separately on all questions. He seemed to have reached this position partly in reaction to the great flood of pamphlets pouring forth from the patriot press. He was outraged and frightened by their ever increasing boldness and by the "metaphysics" and "sophisms" with which they abounded: "this general agitation of public insanity." While he agreed with the commoners' initial request for equality of taxation, there now seemed to be no end to their pretensions, and they were even demanding "honors, positions and dignities" that were the traditional rights of the nobility alone. Demands such as these, in Luppé's view, must be resisted at all cost: "the mingling of classes has always led to the fall of empires."[122]

A growing anxiety over the Third's ambitions was also conveyed by Achard de Bonvouloir. But the Norman gentleman was even more adamant than Luppé in his resistance to change. Entirely rejecting Montesquieu, he castigated those nobles who would declare their independence against the monarchy and who had thus lost sight of the fact that "the throne is the nobility's only support" against the pretensions of the lower classes. Like the baron from Auch he trembled at the demands now being made by the commoners: "The whole universe seems in the throes of convulsions." He was particularly angered at their grasping for the nobles' symbolic privileges: "The Third is after our swords even more than our purses. . . . They want the right to hunt and fish, and even make claim to our honorific rights." For Achard, the only solution was complete and total intransigence. There should be no doubling, no vote by head, no equality of taxation. If one acquiesced to any of the commoners' demands, they would only want more and more: "Their pretensions are boundless."[123] Despite their differences on the eve of the Revolution, Achard and Luppé would soon sit side by side on the far right of the Constituent Assembly.

Which of our three witnesses was most typical of noble opinion on the eve of the Estates General—the relative moderation of Montesquiou or the reactive intransigence of Luppé and Achard—is not immediately clear from our small sample of Noble brochures. Yet to judge by the published speeches of several future deputies of the Second Estate, pronounced in the opening ceremonies of the bailliage electoral assemblies, the fears of the nobility and their growing spirit of resistance were increasingly widespread. One cannot but be impressed by the extent to which all of the noble orators either felt that their positions were directly threatened by the Third or sensed that many of their peers were experiencing such threats. The marquis d'Es-

[122] Jean-Phinée-Suzanne, baron de Luppé-Taybosc, *Réflexions d'un citoyen sur l'assemblée prochaine des Etats généraux* (n.p., 1789). I have relied on the analysis of this pamphlet in Brégail, 248–51.

[123] Luc-René-Charles Achard de Bonvouloir, *Tribut d'un gentilhomme normand à l'Assemblée des notables* (n.p., [Nov. 1788]); Mourlot, 194–95; and Achard's letter to Ségrie, cited above.

tourmel believed that the nobles' rights, both honorific and otherwise, were under attack and must be defended. The marquis de Monspey seemed to concur, and felt compelled to defend the organization of the Estates by orders and the existence of the nobility as integral to the very constitution of the realm. Neither the comte de La Touche nor the marquis de Gouy d'Arsy—both liberals who would soon cooperate closely with the patriots in the National Assembly—seemed to think such fears were justified, but they realized that they were widespread and they tried to counter them in their speeches. La Touche was hopeful that once the nobles agreed to abandon their tax privileges, the fundamental status of the nobility would no longer come under attack; while Gouy d'Arsy asked his colleagues rhetorically whether the commoners were likely "to abolish the very privileges which they hoped eventually to obtain?" Indeed, several of the Second Estate writers specifically urged the commoners to work through the system rather than trying to destroy it. "Let the first two orders maintain the splendor of their honors," counseled Gleises de Lablanque, "while you strive to make yourselves worthy of one day being raised to their level." And La Touche, who was convinced that the concept of nobility was inscribed "in the human heart," tried to calm his fellow nobles with an anticipation of the dictum of Guizot: "In a kingdom . . . where all citizens become rich in order to become noble, why should the nobility have anything to fear?"[124] Yet clearly a substantial number of nobles *were* fearful in 1789; and their defensiveness in the face of those fears would be a critical factor in the Revolutionary development after May, a development to which we must turn in the following chapter.

[124] Louis-Marie, marquis d'Estourmel, *Discours prononcé par M. le marquis d'Estourmel, grand-bailli du Cambrésis* (Paris, Apr. 1789), 1–3; Louis-Alexandre-Elisée, marquis de Monspey, *Discours . . . [à] l'ordre de la noblesse de Beaujolais* (n.p., Mar. 1789), 3–5, 7; Louis-Marthe, marquis de Gouy d'Arsy, *Discours . . . à l'ouverture des états de Melun en présence des trois ordres* (n.p., Mar. 1789), 10; Louis-René-Madeleine, comte de La Touche, *Discours prononcé le 16 mars 1789 à l'ouverture de l'assemblée des trois ordres réunis du bailliage de Montargis* (n.p., 1789), 9; Joseph-Gabriel Gleises de Lablanque, *Discours . . . pour l'ouverture de l'assemblée générale des trois ordres de la sénéchaussée de Béziers* (n.p., Mar. 1789), 9. Cf. Anne-Emmanuel-François-Georges de Crussol d'Uzès, *Discours . . . prononcé à l'assemblée des trois ordres de la province d'Angoumois* (n.p., Apr. 1789), 7. See also Kenneth Margerison, "The Movement for the Creation of a Union of Orders in the Estates General of 1789," *French History* 3 (1989), 48–70.

Origins of the Revolutionary Dynamic

The Creation of the National Assembly

REMINISCING many years later on his experience in the Revolution, the Constituent Pierre-Victor Malouet was still incredulous at what the Third Estate had managed to achieve in 1789: "We will never know how a group of men, without any plan, without any definite goal, divided in their intentions, their manners, their interests, managed nevertheless to follow the same road and arrive together at a total subversion [of the Old Regime]."[1] To be sure, anyone who had taken the trouble of reading all the decrees issued in the king's name over the previous year could assemble a royal "mandate" that seemed to offer some semblance of a program. Target made just such an enumeration, and he concluded that "all the principles of a national constitution are therein avowed, recognized, and consecrated by the king himself"—including the Estates' right to consent to all taxes and to be "associated" with all "legislation."[2] But the identification of such a mandate required one to pick and choose among a wide variety of often inconsistent and erratic royal statements, and in any case, the precise nature of the "association" mentioned by the king remained vague and uncertain.

In fact, on the eve of the Estates General, as Malouet suggested, the future Third Estate deputies remained widely at variance and at times confused as to the purpose and goals of the coming assembly. Those who took the time to elucidate their cause in letters and diary entries during the earliest days of the meeting generally persisted in their relatively moderate objectives. Their most aggressive demands arose from a burning desire for legal and fiscal equality: the end of all tax privileges, a single written constitution for all citizens, positions open to talent, a vote by head in the Estates General.[3] As we have seen, many harbored deep-seated resentment and animosity toward the aristocrats, their privileges, and their condescending attitude. Most, however, were cautious and practical men, whose successful careers had been achieved by working within the system. Even as late as the middle of May, after the Estates General had begun meeting, Duquesnoy

---

[1] Pierre-Victor Malouet, *Mémoires*, 2 vols., ed. Baron Malouet (Paris, 1868), 2:246.

[2] Guy-Jean-Baptiste Target, *Les Etats généraux convoqués par Louis XVI* (Paris, ca. Dec. 1788), 4–6. Cf. Ran Halévi, "La monarchie et les élections: position des problèmes," in *FRCMPC*, 1:389.

[3] See, e.g., Antoine Durand to Delcamp-Boytré in Gourdan: A.E. Cahors, carton 5–56, letter of May 13; Joseph Delaville Le Roulx to municipality of Lorient: A.C. Lorient, BB 12, letter of June 9. Such relatively limited objectives often continued even after the formation of the National Assembly: see Pierre-François Lepoutre to his wife: family archives of Adolphe Lepoutre-Dubreuil, Montignac-sur-Vezère, letter of July 30.

felt that a great many of his colleagues were prepared to renounce the vote by head—either for political reasons or because they feared it could lead to civil war—and Duquesnoy himself wondered if it might not be best to postpone the Estates for a time. Mainstream patriots like the Bordeaux merchant Paul Nairac, the estate manager from Mayenne Michel-René Maupetit, and the royal magistrate Ménard de La Groye believed that a compromise might have to be worked out, a compromise which could entail voting by order on certain issues or the creation of a bicameral legislature—like that in England—with a privileged house and a commoner house balancing one another.[4] And the overwhelming majority of the deputies were convinced that all reforms must be accomplished under the auspices of the monarchy, in close cooperation with a king for whom they continued to show strong filial devotion. They persisted in their vision of a return to an idealized past, of a reform process in which historical precedent remained of considerable importance. Significantly, the conciliatory commission elected by the Third in mid-May specifically designated one of its members (Mounier) to take charge of historical arguments for a vote by head, while another (Target) was to focus on natural law and reason.[5]

Yet somehow, in the space of six weeks of extraordinarily intense meetings, these same Third deputies would evolve a position that could only be described as revolutionary. In a series of celebrated debates and decrees in the week following June 10, they embraced a new concept of national sovereignty, fundamentally democratic in its implications, sweeping away the corporate political privileges of nobility and clergy alike. On June 17 they transformed themselves into a National Assembly, implicitly assuming sovereignty over and above the monarchy. That same day they unilaterally and unanimously declared all previous taxes to be illegal—though they would be maintained temporarily—granting themselves exclusive authority to create new ones. On June 20, all but one of the commoners swore the Tennis Court Oath, solemnly affirming their intention to write a constitution regardless of the actions of the king or the nobles. All such positions, moreover, were increasingly legitimized by reason, natural law, and the rights of man, justifications for which history and past precedent were deemed largely irrelevant. This remarkably rapid radicalization of the Third Estate is

---

[4] Adrien Duquesnoy, *Journal d'Adrien Duquesnoy*, ed. R. de Crèvecoeur, 2 vols. (Paris, 1894), 1:22 (entry of May 15); Pierre-Paul Nairac, ms. "Journal": A.D. Eure, 5 F 63, entry of May 19; Michel-René Maupetit, "Lettres de Maupetit (1789–91)," ed. Quéruau-Lamérie, *Bulletin de la Commission historique et archéologique de la Mayenne*, 2e sér., 17 (1901), 450 (letter of May 12); François-René-Pierre Ménard de La Groye, *François Ménard de La Groye, député du Maine aux Etats généraux. Correspondance, 1789–1791*, Florence Mirouse, ed. (Le Mans, 1989), 38 (letter of June 5); and the retrospective letter of Jean-Bernard Grellet de Beauregard, "Lettres de M. Grellet de Beauregard," ed. Abbé Dardy, *Mémoires de la Société des sciences naturelles et archéologiques de la Creuse*, 2e sér., 7 (1899), 65 (letter of July 10). See also Mirabeau's speech of May 18, assessing the situation: *AP*, 8:43.

[5] *AP*, 8:49 (Report by Rabaut Saint-Etienne).

one of the major interpretive problems in our assessment of the French Revolution and it will provide the central theme for the present chapter.[6]

FACTIONAL FORMATION IN THE EARLY THIRD ESTATE

It was in the last days of April 1789 that the newly elected deputies of the three estates, filled with excitement and anticipation, began filtering into Versailles from around the kingdom. Most of the deputy witnesses were enormously impressed by the three days of opening ceremonies. On Saturday May 2 they were led single file through the rooms of the palace of Versailles and presented one by one to the king and his court in the magnificent Hall of Hercules.[7] Monday the 4th was given over to the requisite religious rites, beseeching divine blessing and the wisdom of the Holy Spirit with a procession of the deputies across Versailles and a mass and a two-hour sermon by the bishop of Nancy. On May 5 the deputies assembled for the first time in the hall of the Menus Plaisirs, to hear a short discourse from Louis and four hours of speeches from the keeper of the seals Barentin and the finance minister Necker. It was an imposing pageant, and the deputy witnesses dwelt at length on the splendors of the scene: the royal heralds, accompanied by trumpets and drums, proclaiming events throughout the town; the king's arrival at Notre Dame in his coronation carriage pulled by eight magnificent horses; the hush of the crowds—estimated at several hundred thousand people—as the deputies walked in procession through the streets, two by two, each holding a large gilded candle; the first impression of splendor as they entered the Menus Plaisirs on the morning of the 5th.[8] But even in the midst of all this brilliance, a number of the Third Estate deputies were quick to seek symbolic representations of the equality which they sought to promote. While waiting for the opening day's procession to assemble, Gaultier de Biauzat passed the word through the crowd that they should march in random order rather than by bailliage, and by the time they reached the church of Saint-Louis, many had agreed to take seats "more or less pell-mell," rather than by order and bailliage as prescribed by the royal master of ceremonies. They chafed at the dress requirements which had been handed down to them, instructing the Third to appear all in black, and

---

[6] See esp. François Furet and Ran Halévi, eds., *Orateurs de la Révolution française. I. Les Constituants* (Paris, 1989), "Introduction."

[7] Lefebvre, *Recueil, Tome Premier*, 1:104–13.

[8] See, e.g., Jean-François Gaultier de Biauzat, *Gaultier de Biauzat, député du Tiers état aux Etats généraux de 1789. Sa vie et sa correspondance*, ed. Francisque Mège, 2 vols. (Clermont-Ferrand, 1890), 2:26 (letter of May 4); Jean-Baptiste Poncet-Delpech, "Documents sur les premiers mois de la Révolution," ed. Daniel Ligou, *AHRF* 38 (1966), 429 (letter of May 6); Charles-Alexis de Brulart de Sillery, ms. "Journal des Etats généraux," addressed to the correspondence committee of the Nobles of Champagne: A.N., KK 641, entries of May 2–5. See also Lefebvre, *Recueil, Tome Premier*, 1:117–208.

several, like La Revellière-Lépeaux, ostentatiously wore brightly colored clothes.[9]

But in some respects, even more stunning than the regal opening ceremonies was the Third Estates' experience on the morning of May 6: stunning, indeed, not for the royal presence but for the royal absence. Instructed to return to the central assembly hall, the commoner deputies found the throne and the great canopy dismantled and removed and the Clergy and the Nobility retired to separate rooms. Beyond the general suggestions of Necker the day before—hidden away in the three-hour oration which few had been able to digest—the Third was given no instructions, guidelines, or directions whatsoever as to how they were to organize or what they were to discuss. It was precisely this lack of direction that led many of the commoners to conclude that they had the full confidence of the royal government to proceed as they saw fit.[10]

The initial challenge for the Third Estate, however, was to organize a coherent political strategy among several hundred deputies from all over the kingdom, most of whom had never laid eyes on one another. To rely on the deputies' early reports, a sentiment of bewilderment at the large number of unknown faces in the meeting hall must have been widespread. Several revealed difficulty in recognizing the different speakers, and their notes were filled with garbled transcriptions of names they thought they had heard across the noisy hall, with faulty associations between names and faces, with uncertain references to "a very young man" or "a deputy from Provence" or "an eloquent speaker" who had impressed them in one of the debates.[11] Only a handful of the Third deputies seem to have possessed national name recognition. Gaultier de Biauzat suggested that among the delegates from outside his province of Auvergne, only Mounier and Mirabeau were known to him; while Claude Gantheret, the Burgundy wine merchant, appeared never to have heard of Mirabeau. When the Breton deputy Jean-Pierre Boullé wrote home about the newly elected members of the conciliation commission, he admitted that he knew very little about any of them, and that he had to base his judgment on hearsay or on the speeches they had given during the first weeks of the meetings.[12] "We are all here," confided

---

[9] Duquesnoy, 1:3–4 (entry of May 4); Alexis Basquiat de Mugriet and Pierre-Joseph Lamarque to municipality of Bayonne: A.C. Bayonne, AA 51, letter of May 8; Gaultier, 2:13 and 27 (letters of April 28 and May 4); Jean-Paul Rabaut Saint-Etienne, *Précis historique de la Révolution française* (Paris, 1807), 100.

[10] E.g., Grellet, 63 (letter of June 12).

[11] E.g., Gaultier's references to "M. Gazarve ou Bazarve"—undoubtedly Barnave: 2:58 (letter of May 15). Also Louis-Jean-Jacques Laurence, "Journal," ed. Charles de Beaumont, *Le Carnet historique et littéraire* 12 (1902), 70 (entry of May 11); and Jacques-Antoine Creuzé-Latouche, *Journal des Etats généraux et du début de l'Assemblée nationale, 18 mai–29 juillet 1789*, ed. Jean Marchand (Paris, 1946), xxxvii.

[12] Gaultier, 2:32–35 (letter of May 6); Claude Gantheret to Pierre Leflaive, his brother-in-law: private collection of Françoise Misserey, letter of May 13; Jean-Pierre Boullé, "Ouverture

Palasne de Champeaux, "as though dropped from the sky, in a country that is totally unknown to us."[13]

There were, to be sure, certain national associational networks which had linked some elements of the Third prior to the convocation. In the relatively closed society of Protestant notables, the twenty-odd Calvinist deputies almost certainly knew or had heard of one another. As early as May 3, Doctor Gallot had met with several of the other Protestants—Rabaut Saint-Etienne from Nîmes, Garesché from Sainte, Lamy from Caen—to discuss participation in the Catholic procession which was to open the Estates.[14] Similar ties probably united the small group of Jansenists and elements of the much larger contingent of Freemasons. Périsse Du Luc wrote regular updates to his Masonic soul mate, Willermoz, on "the news of our brothers in Versailles," many of whom he had known personally before the meeting.[15] There were also informal professional associations reactivated in Versailles, like the group of deputy-physicians convened over dinner by Gallot, or the numerous cohort of legal men, some of whom had attended school together or had met in professional capacities.[16] Other individual deputies had made contact during the Pre-Revolutionary period. Lebrun remembered having first encountered the abbé Sieyès in the provincial assembly of Chartres where they had both served as electors. While on a commission to the king from Vivarais, Boissy d'Anglas had met the marquis de Lafayette, the marquis de La Tour-Maubourg, Le Chapelier, and several of the future Breton deputies.[17]

But the tightest bonds linking Third deputies together at the beginning were not national but provincial in nature. The world of provincial notables in the eighteenth century was always a small one. Many of the families from individual regions had probably known one another for generations, and some were linked through marriage.[18] Such ties were reinforced in many cases by common schooling and professional association and by the experi-

---

des Etats généraux de 1789," ed. Albert Macé, *Revue de la Révolution. Documents inédits* 11 (1888), 16–17 (letter of May 22).

[13] Bertrand de Moleville, *Mémoires particuliers sur le règne de Louis XVI*, 2 vols. (Paris, 1816), 1:44.

[14] Jean-Gabriel Gallot, *La vie et les oeuvres du Docteur Jean-Gabriel Gallot*, ed. Louis Merle (Poitiers, 1961), 62 (letters of May 3 and 4).

[15] Jean-André Périsse Du Luc to J. B. Willermoz: B.M. Lyon ms. 5430, letters of July 8, Nov. 16, Dec. 27, 1789.

[16] Gallot, 104 (letter of May 21). The Le Mans magistrate Ménard de La Groye met regularly with "mes bons amis," Claude Redon from Riom, Jérôme Le Grand from Châteauroux, and Urbain-Adrien-Louis Gaultier from Tours—all magistrates or lawyers: Ménard, 24, 27, 31 (letters of May 8, 15, 26).

[17] Charles-François Lebrun, *Opinions, rapports, et choix d'écrits politiques* (Paris, 1829), 54; François-Antoine Boissy d'Anglas, "La Révolution vue de Paris et d'Annonay," *La revue universelle* 139 (1988), 51, 56 (letters of Jan. 12 and Feb. 14, 1789).

[18] Thus, Charles Cochon de Lapparent and Mathieu-Joseph Pervinquière from Fontenay in Poitou were cousins; Nicolas-Bernard Belzais de Courmenil was the son-in-law of Guillaume-François-Charles Goupil de Prefelne, both from Argentan in Normandy: Fichier Lefebvre.

ence of collaborating in the provincial assemblies and the municipal mobilization of 1787–88.[19] Groups of provincial deputies traveled to the capital together, took lodging in the same rooms or boarding houses, and sat together as a unit in the Assembly hall. The merchant Michel Roussier spoke affectionately of the bonds that tied him to the other deputies from Marseille "with whom I was linked through a unity of outlook, a similarity of feelings, and the fraternal sentiments of friendship."[20] Of course not all such relations were so amicable and some of the regional delegations were far from homogeneous.[21] Long-standing interurban rivalries were played out once again in the shadow of Versailles: like those that pitted Bergues and Dunkerque or Clermont-Ferrand and Riom or Gien and Montargis. In the case of Auvergne, the schism which first arose over questions of procedure and representation—dividing the Riom contingent centered on the deputy Malouet from the Clermont delegation led by Gaultier de Biauzat—rapidly took on all the ideological colorations of a break between conservatives and radicals.[22] Yet internal squabbles of this kind seem to have been unusual in the early weeks of the Third Estate meetings, and provincial delegations would frequently serve as prime building blocks for the creation of political organization within the Estates General.

Once in Versailles, some of the regional delegations created quasi-institutional structures to correspond with constituencies back home and coordinate joint responses for provincial problems.[23] The delegation from Poitou, for example, seems initially to have congregated every evening in the apartment of Pervinquière and Cochon de Lapparent to consider the day's debates and develop a common voting strategy.[24] The deputies from Provence began regular meetings toward the middle of May, largely at the urging of the intermediate commission of Aix, gathering first in Bouche's room and

[19] E.g., the Poitou deputies Alquier, Creuzé, and Cochon had attended the Oratorian *collège* of Niort at approximately the same time; and La Revellière-Lépeaux, Pilastre, Leclerc, and Volney had all been classmates in the Oratorians' *collège* of Angers: Robison, 26, 37–38, 59; Jean Gaulmier, *Un grand témoin de la Révolution et de l'Empire: Volney* (Paris, 1959), 74–78.

[20] A.C. Marseille, BB 361, undated letter of ca. early Aug. 1789.

[21] See, e.g., the split within the Maine delegation over positions taken on the May edicts: Ménard, 36 (letter of June 2); and in the Agen delegation for unknown reasons: L. Desgraves, "Correspondance des députés de la sénéchaussée d'Agen aux Etats-Généraux et à l'Assemblée nationale," *Recueil des travaux de la société académique d'Agen. Sciences, lettres, et arts*, 3e sér., I (1967), 27–28, 45 (letters of June 22 and Aug. 31).

[22] E.g., Gaultier. 2:9, 22–23 (letters of Apr. 25 and May 2); Claude-Benjamin Vallet, "Souvenirs de l'abbé Vallet, député de Gien à l'Assemblée constituante," *Nouvelle revue rétrospective* 17 (1902), 25–37.

[23] Provincial collaboration was strengthened by the Third Estate's decision to organize certain discussions and committees by province: e.g., *AP*, 8:35 (May 12).

[24] Gallot, 63–65, 68, 90, 106 (entries and letters of May 5, 6, 8, 13, 14, 21, and July 7); Laurence, 72–73 (letter of May 13); Jean-François-Marie Goupilleau to his cousin, sénéchal in Rochefervière: B.M. Nantes, Collection Dugast-Matifeux, no. 98, undated letter of late Sept. 1789.

then in Mirabeau's more spacious apartment.[25] There were also active and well-organized city caucuses, like those uniting the deputies of Lyon and Marseille.[26] But in most cases—in Maine, Burgundy, Lorraine, Ile-de-France, Quercy, and Paris, for example—the efforts to create institutional cooperation among provincial representatives seem to have been episodic and short lived. After the National Assembly moved toward breaking up provincial allegiances through the "bureau" system of discussion groups, and even later, when the deputies left Versailles and took up more dispersed lodgings in Paris, most such organizations disappeared entirely.[27]

Of all the provincial caucuses the most cohesive and influential were those of Dauphiné and Brittany. Not only had the delegations of these two provinces collaborated for relatively longer periods of time, but they had each developed plans of action and programs for reform which they sought to promote in the nation as a whole. By the beginning of the Estates General much of the Dauphinois delegation had worked closely in concert for over a year and many of the members were intimate friends. Soon after their arrival in Versailles, the deputies of all three orders held a strategy session in the apartment of the archbishop of Vienne, and by May 5 they had resolved to work within their respective orders for a union of the estates. The group also invited joint conferences with deputies from other provinces who embraced the "principles of Dauphiné," stressing compromise and conciliation between the three estates.[28] Though there is no way of knowing how many other deputies did so attend, the Dauphinois clearly exercised a major influence on the proceedings of the Third Estate during the first weeks.

As for the Bretons, many had taken the habit of working in concert during the last Estates of Brittany in 1788, gathering each night to develop a common position for the next day's meeting. Those chosen deputies in 1789 had continued their group consultations, first in the seats of their local electoral districts and then in Rennes, where the full provincial contingent met before departing as a group for Versailles. Several of the deputies, moreover, were specifically instructed by their constituencies to maintain provincial consultations throughout the Estates General. Acting on these mandates, the Bretons called their first meeting on April 30 in the rented back room of a Versailles café, and like the Dauphinois they immediately urged deputies from other provinces to join them. There would be two

[25] Charles-François Bouche to the *commissaire des communautés de Provence*: A.D. Bouches-du-Rhône, C 1046, letter of May 12; Jacques Verdollin to ibid.: A.D. Bouches-du-Rhône, C 1337, esp. letters of May 23, July 5, Aug. 16.

[26] B.M. Lyon, ms. 147; and A.C. Marseille, BB 358–61 and 4 D 43.

[27] E.g., Maupetit, 17 (1901), 324 (letter of Apr. 28); Ménard, 36, 82 (letters of June 2 and Aug. 11); Gantheret, letter of May 13; Jean Colson, "Notes d'un curé Saargovien, député aux Etats généraux de 1789," ed. Arthur Benoît, *Revue nouvelle d'Alsace-Lorraine et du Rhin* 8 (1888), 139; Laurent de Visme, ms. "Journal des Etats généraux": B.N., Nouv. acq. fr. 12938, entry of May 27; Durand, letters of July 24 and 27; Jean-Sylvain Bailly, *Mémoires d'un témoin de la Révolution*, ed. Berville and Barrière, 3 vols. (Paris, 1821–22), 1:260 (entry of June 29).

[28] Jean Egret, *La révolution des notables: Mounier et les monarchiens* (Paris, 1950), 52–53.

meetings each evening, one for problems exclusive to the province, and a second for general questions concerning the Estates. The "Breton Club," as it soon became known, resolved to decide each question by majority vote, and then support all decisions in the Estates as a bloc.[29] Since both the nobles and the episcopacy in Brittany had rejected the regular electoral process, the delegation consisted exclusively of the Third Estate and the lower clergy, a composition that invariably influenced the group's decisions. From the beginning contemporaries were impressed by their fervent and steadfast hatred of nobles and of privilege in general, and their unwillingness to compromise with the Second Estate in any way. They "harbored an implacable hatred against the nobility," "an uncontrollable passion" to see the aristocracy humiliated.[30]

In the earliest days of the Estates, portions of the Dauphiné and Brittany delegations seem to have attempted a joint meeting.[31] But given their divergent views on the privileged orders, such an alliance was short lived, and the two groups rapidly went their separate ways. In general, the Bretons proved substantially more successful in attracting the participation of other provincial delegations. The Third deputies of Provence, Artois, and Franche-Comté were soon taking part in the nightly "club"—three delegations who, like the Bretons, had known particularly acrimonious relations with the local nobilities before 1789. The representatives from Anjou—closely linked to Brittany through Volney—also participated, along with a number of individual deputies from various other provinces.[32] Antoine Durand, a lawyer from Quercy, came away from one such meeting enormously impressed by the "forthright tone and friendly atmosphere appropriate for a meeting of brothers."[33]

Even before the first session of the Third Estate, the Breton group had decided on the basic strategy which it would pursue over the next month. Under no circumstances, it was agreed, could decisions of the Estates be reached or votes taken in separate chambers. The Third should not even accept the verification of deputy credentials unless such an inspection were

---

[29] Boullé, 10 (1887), 163 (letter of May 1); Julien-François Palasne de Champeaux and Jean-François-Pierre Poulain de Corbion, "Correspondance des députés des Côtes-du-Nord aux Etats généraux et à l'Assemblée nationale constituante," ed. D. Tempier, *Bulletins et mémoires de la Société d'émulation des Côtes-du-Nord* 26 (1888), 218 (letter of May 1). See also A. Bouchard, *Le club Breton. Origine, composition, rôle à l'Assemblée constituante* (Paris, 1920), 21–22; and Gérard Walter, *Histoire des Jacobins* (Paris, 1946), 12–14.

[30] Visme, entry of May 14; Duquesnoy, 1:9 (entry of May 7). See also "Correspondance d'un député de la noblesse avec la Marquise de Créquy," ed. B. d'Agours, *Revue de la Révolution. Documents inédits* 2 (1883), 8 (letter of June 6).

[31] Boullé, 163 (letter of May 1); Gaultier, 2:118 (letter of June 16).

[32] Both Bouche and Duquesnoy mentioned the Comtois and the Provençaux: Duquesnoy, 1:13–14 (entry of May 10); Bouche, letter of June 27, 1789; also Maximilien Robespierre, *Correspondance*, 2 vols., ed. Georges Michon (Paris, 1926–41), 40 (letter May 24); and Gaulmier, 74–81.

[33] Durand, entry of May 2.

carried out by all three orders voting together by head. If the Nobility and the Clergy refused to merge with the Third, the latter should move unilaterally, as the Breton magistrate Boullé described it, "to set itself up as a national body without [the two other orders] and to form by itself the Estates General." Even in early May, before the first session of the Third, individual Bretons were using the terms "national chamber" and "national assembly." Through the initiative of the Breton Club, this "strategy of inertia" was early discussed in various of the other provincial caucuses. Already on May 5 Maupetit announced a portion of the plan to a close friend in his home province of Maine.[34]

Unfortunately, the earliest sessions of the Third Estate are poorly documented.[35] As best can be determined, virtually all of the deputies present announced their preference for a vote by head. But there was far more reticence to follow the rest of the Breton plan, and there was a sharp division over the immediate tactics to be adopted. In the first session, both Le Chapelier, the Bretons' principal spokesman, and the comte de Mirabeau argued for a policy of total inaction, in which the Third would remain "a collection of individuals who can confer with one another on a friendly basis, but who have no power to act [in an official capacity]," and in which the commoners would refuse all contact with the privileged orders until the latter agreed to their demands.[36] Mounier and Malouet, however, urged the deputies to establish contact with the Nobles and the Clergy. On May 7, in the earliest vote on the question, the deputies overwhelmingly supported Mounier's proposal to pursue unofficial discussions with the other two orders, "without the specific instructions of the Assembly."[37] But in the meantime, the very division and indecision on the part of the Third effectively sustained the policy of "inactivity." Over the following weeks, the commoners refused to accept formal rules of debate, the election of permanent officers, or the recording of official minutes—all of which might be construed as the activities of a functioning "estate."

Yet it is also clear that the great majority of the Third was prepared to support conciliation and perhaps even compromise. On May 13, responding in part to Mounier's "unofficial" appeal, the Clergy and the Nobility proposed the creation of a "conciliation commission" in which representatives from each of the three estates would participate. Faced with this proposal, the Third initiated its first great debate, a five-day affair in which virtually all of the deputies, called in the order of their electoral districts, were invited to present their opinions on what should be done. Elaborating a plan drawn up the night before in the Breton Club, Le Chapelier vigor-

[34] Boullé, 10 (1887), 169 (letter of May 8); Maupetit, 17 (1901), 442 (letter of May 5); Delaville, letter of May 3; Durand, entry of May 6.

[35] The *AP* is particularly incomplete for this period. Usually it lists only a handful of speakers, although we know from other sources that scores of deputies actually spoke.

[36] Durand, entry of May 6; *AP*, 8:28–29.

[37] Delaville, letter of May 8; Maupetit, 444–45 (letter of May 8); *AP*, 8:29–30.

ously opposed any "conciliatory gesture," including the creation of the proposed commission. He asked rather that the Third "invite and summon" the
other two orders to join with the commoners in the "national assembly"
which alone could represent the "public spirit" of the nation. Once again,
however, a major proposal from the Breton group was massively defeated,
this time by a vote of 320 to 66 in favor of a counter motion for reconciliation by Rabaut Saint-Etienne—with 44 of the 66 minority votes cast by the
Bretons. The sixteen Third deputies chosen on May 19 to represent their
order in the conferences consisted primarily of moderate men and included
only two associated with the Bretons.[38] As late as May 29 a similar majority
continued to oppose the Bretons, voting rather for a prolongation of the
conferences with the other two orders. "The proposal to formally empower
ourselves and call ourselves 'the nation,'" wrote Pierre-François Bouche, "is
much too extreme." "The assembly," noted Nairac, "is leaning more towards conciliation and concord than toward drastic measures."[39]

When deputies took the time to explain their opposition to the Breton
Club, they expressed hostility not only to the boldness and innovation of its
motions, but to the very style and vehemence of its approach. For Duquesnoy, Poncet-Delpech, and many of the other deputies, Le Chapelier
and his associates were "hot heads, without measure or moderation," "passionate men," who want to "overturn everything." The Alsatians Schwendt
and Turckheim deeply resented what they felt was their intolerance and
spirit of domination: "The Bretons are good citizens, but they remain bitter
. . . and they want to exert their authority over everyone else. They are
unjustly suspicious of anyone who favors a more conciliatory approach."
"You cannot imagine the vehemence and passion of the inhabitants of this
province," added Maupetit. "Whoever rejects their idea is a debased and
feeble human being who wants only to remain a slave."[40] Duquesnoy worried about the possible social consequences of the Breton "system," even
comparing them to the English Levellers "who would like to eliminate all
inequality of social condition."[41] There were also objections to their continual attacks on the nobility. Many had harbored high hopes of the possibilities of unity when they first arrived, and held great expectations for the

[38] The radicals were Le Chapelier and Volney. See also *AP*, 8:37–43; Maupetit, 18 (1902),
136 (letter of May 21); Nairac, entry of May 29; Duquesnoy, 1:19–20 (entry of May 15).
Unfortunately, there are very meager records of the major debate of May 14 to 18, which
included speeches, long or short, by several hundred deputies.

[39] Pierre-François-Balthazar Bouche to municipality of Forcalquier: A.C. Forcalquier, Series
D, "Correspondance 1789," letter of May 31; Nairac, entries of May 19 and 29; and Duquesnoy, 1:53 (entry of May 31).

[40] Duquesnoy, 1:2, 9 (entries of May 3, 7); Jean-Baptiste Poncet-Delpech, *La première année
de la Révolution vue par un témoin*, ed. Daniel Ligou (Paris, 1961), 21–22 (letter of May 9);
Etienne-François Schwendt and Jean de Turckheim, *L'Alsace pendant la Révolution française*, ed.
Rodolphe Reuss, 2 vols. (Paris, 1880–94), 1:108 (letter of June 17); Maupetit, 18 (1902),
151 (letter of May 30).

[41] Duquesnoy, 1:36 (entry of May 22).

"principles of Dauphiné." But the constant attacks of a small minority seemed to put all that in jeopardy. Charles-Claude Monneron, veteran of the Vivarais compromise, noted in his diary that "I cannot approve of these charges against [the nobility] of arrogance and insidious manipulations."[42] Whatever the deputies' feelings toward the nobility—a complex mixture of admiration, envy, and bitterness—it was hard to imagine winning concessions from the powerful aristocrats without cooperation and compromise.

If we are to understand how the ideas of the Breton group ultimately came to triumph, we must first examine the evolving positions of the two privileged estates, and then turn to the psychological dynamic within the Third in late May and June.

THE CLERICAL ESTATE AND THE DOMINANCE OF THE EPISCOPACY

Of the three estates assembling in Versailles in late April and early May, the Clergy was almost certainly the most sharply and bitterly divided. Despite the numerical predominance of the curés and the political consciousness which many of them had developed during their bouts with the upper clergy in the electoral assemblies, the contesting groups were relatively evenly divided. Not all the curés deputies were salaried and impoverished, smoldering with resentment against their aristocratic superiors. A significant minority held posts of diocesan responsibility which linked them to the hierarchy, and many were unusually well trained in theology and canon law. Though the new model of "citizen" curé—servant to the parish and tutor of Enlightened reform—had deeply effected the self-image of many, the older Tridentine model of the priest, tightly bound to the hierarchical lines of clerical authority, also maintained a powerful hold.[43] Even the most enthusiastic advocates of ecclesiastical regeneration, the most embittered opponents of the "tyranny" of the aristocratic upper clergy, could be susceptible to episcopal influence—especially when individual bishops chose to exercise that influence in a conciliatory and pastoral fashion.

At their very first meeting on May 6, the Clergy considered the proposal for a joint verification of credentials with the Third Estate. The patriot position for merging was vigorously argued by two archbishops, the Dauphinois Le Franc de Pompignan of Vienne, and the liberal prelate from Bordeaux, Champion de Cicé. But most of the prelates rejected the proposition, and they were able to influence enough of the curés and other nonparish clergymen to defeat the motion by a vote of 133 to 114.[44] Though it was a

---

[42] Charles-Claude-Ange Monneron, in Emmanuel Nicod, "Monneron aîné, député de la sénéchaussée d'Annonay," *Revue du Vivarais* 4 (1896), 482 (undated entry of mid-May). Cf. Visme, entry of June 12; and Poncet, *Documents*, 21–22 (letter of May 9).

[43] See the author's *Religion, Revolution, and Regional Culture in Eighteenth-Century France: The Ecclesiastical Oath of 1791* (Princeton, 1986), chap. 3.

[44] *AP*, 8:27.

considerable disappointment to the liberals in both the Clergy and the Third Estate, the patriot curés remained hopeful and began organizing politically within their order to maintain discipline and win over converts—particularly among those thirty-odd ecclesiastics who arrived late at the meeting.[45] Abbé Jacques Jallet and his four curé associates from Poitou seem to have taken the initiative, continuing the practice they had developed in the Poitiers electoral assembly of nightly meetings to discuss options and tactics. Soon some sixty curés and an assortment of other clerical deputies were convening regularly from five to eight in the evening in the Clergy's meeting hall at the Menus Plaisirs.[46] Without a doubt, class antagonisms played a major role in mobilizing many of the curés, and the debates sometimes attained an extraordinary level of bitterness and vituperation. Bishops referred to parish priests as "peasants' sons," and curés spoke out against the prelates "with unprecedented effrontery," calling them "mercenaries," refusing to use the standard address of "Monseigneur," and lecturing them to their faces on their nonresidence, excessive luxury, and laziness.[47] Other curés, who normally cultivated good relations with the bishops, opted for the patriot position out of sheer frustration with the delays and a conviction that the clergy's principal task was to serve the public welfare: "How would we dare return home," wrote Bigot de Vernières of Saint-Flour, "if we failed to bring back the relief which our people have every right to expect from us."[48]

For a time in mid-May, according to curé Barbotin, up to 120 curés were "strongly decided to go over to the common chamber" unilaterally, even without a majority of the order as a whole.[49] But by the end of the month, to the bitter disappointment of both the curé leadership and the Third Estate, this initial enthusiasm began to wane. Some curés may have been shocked and frightened by the very violence of the antiepiscopal rhetoric. Even curé Rousselot from Franche-Comté, who ultimately supported union with the Third, found such attacks "inappropriate" and generally frowned on by the majority of curé deputies.[50] Others claimed to be discouraged by

[45] The politics of the Clergy during the Estates General have been carefully treated by Maurice Hutt, "The Role of the Curés in the Estates General of 1789," *Journal of Ecclesiastical History* 6 (1955), 190–220; and Ruth F. Necheles, "The Curés in the Estates General of 1789," *Journal of Modern History* 46 (1974), 425–44.

[46] Jacques Jallet, *Journal inédit*, ed. J.-J. Brethé (Fontenay-le-Comte, 1871), 63–64, 69, 83 (entries of May 23 and 27, and June 11); and "Trois lettres de l'Abbé Jallet," *AHRF* 22 (1950), introduction by D. Marié, 332–37, and 342 (letter of May 22).

[47] Coster, 86, 95–96 (entries of May 9 and 19, and June 13); Emmanuel Barbotin, *Lettres de l'abbé Barbotin*, ed. A. Aulard (Paris, 1910), 9 (letter of May 30); Jallet, *Journal*, 91–92 (entry of June 19).

[48] Jean-Joseph Bigot de Vernières to his nephew, avocat in Saint-Flour: copies in A.D. Cantal, Fonds Delmas, letter of June 13.

[49] Barbotin, 5 (letter of May 23). Also the letter of Jallet of May 18, "Trois lettres," 39–42.

[50] Claude-Germain Rousselot to his nephew, Joseph Rousselot: Fonds Girardot, A.D. Haute-Saône, letter of May 21.

the dilatory pace with which the Third pursued its own negotiations with the Nobility. The magistrate Creuzé-Latouche described a chance meeting one evening between the Poitou caucus and the "committee of curés," in which the latter urged the commoners to take a position before liberal support in the First Estate melted away.[51]

But key to the failure of the clerical patriots were the actions and organization of the bishops themselves. We have already examined the strong social and political cohesion of the episcopal corps, this conclave of "cousins" from the oldest noble families with long experience working together in the General Assembly of the Clergy. Led primarily by archbishops Dulau of Arles and Boisgelin of Aix—each with considerable leadership experience in the General Assemblies—the prelates gathered for their own nighttime strategy sessions, sometimes in the church of Notre-Dame in Versailles, sometimes in the chapel of the Lazarists.[52] Soon they had organized a variety of delay tactics, using every kind of "chicanery," as Jallet described it, to prevent the curés from speaking and to put off all decisions as long as possible, hoping no doubt for the intervention of the king or a decisive victory of the Nobles in their struggle with the Third. At the same time, the bishops seem carefully to have courted individual curés, inviting them to dinner, introducing them to ecclesiastical dignitaries, and generally favoring them with a kind of personal attention which many could only have found flattering. Several members of the upper clergy—like Boisgelin, the abbé Maury, and the agent-general Montesquiou—predicted the impending danger to church privileges and property, and even to religion itself, if the Third Estate were allowed to take control.[53] Much was made of the Third's selection of Rabaut Saint-Etienne to the conciliation committee, as proof that the commoners were under the influence of the Protestants and might soon abandon Catholicism as the state religion.[54]

By the end of May, Barbotin complained that numerous curés had gone over to the "episcopal party," "seduced by promises, by threats, by appeals to their love of the monarchy and religion which would be abandoned to the whims of the Third Estate." In early June, both he and Bigot were themselves backing away from their earlier positions, announcing that they now planned to remain with their order until a majority could be obtained in favor of merging.[55] A critical moment came on May 27 when a delegation from the Third Estate appeared in the Clergy's chamber and directly appealed to its members "in the name of the God of Peace, to whom they were ministers, and in the name of the nation, to join with them in the hall

---

[51] Creuzé, 22.

[52] Jallet, *Journal*, 69 (letter of May 26); Bigot de Vernières, letter of July 6.

[53] Bigot, undated letter of mid-May and of June 13; Jallet, *Journal*, 60 and 68 (entries of May 19 and 27); and "Trois lettres," 339–46 (letters of May 18 and 22). Delaville viewed Boisgelin and Maury as the principal leaders of the upper clergy: letter of May 29.

[54] Duquesnoy, 50 and 77 (entries of May 30 and June 7).

[55] Barbotin, 7, 13 (letters of May 30 and June 11); Bigot, retrospective letter of July 6.

of the common assembly."[56] But to the commoners' immense disenchantment, the bishops were soon able to divert the debate, successfully arguing that the First Estate must postpone any such discussion until the royal arbitration commission had met. The situation remained little changed on June 12 when Jallet could find only twenty-two curés still prepared to act and begin sitting with the Third. Indeed, only two Poitou colleagues ultimately joined him and appeared the next day in the hall of the commoners. Even though most of the twenty-two eventually did go over to the commons, Jallet had promised far more to both the Third and to the liberals in the Second Estate, and he was deeply mortified.[57]

In retrospect, it is not clear whether the remainder of the "liberal" clergy would ever have joined the Third for the verification of credentials, if the commoners had not unilaterally created the National Assembly on June 17. In any case, by early June the Third Estate seemed generally convinced that the bishops' intransigent refusal to compromise had won the day and that no significant clerical support was in the offing. One of the bishops, noted Bailly, was said to have "swallowed another curé every day." The prelates, wrote Doctor Campmas, "depict us as planning to tamper with religion, an accusation which is merely a sham for most of them, but which the poor curés foolishly accept." "The curés," added Visme, "have so few advantages, and they must deal with men who have so many ... through their wit, through their practice in speaking, through their experience in large assemblies"; and less charitably, on June 6: "in truth, these curés are pathetic."[58]

THE NOBLE ESTATE AND THE CULTURE OF INTRANSIGENCE

Like the Clergy, the Second Estate was also deeply divided from the first day of its sessions. On the face of it, the most important divisions might have been social and cultural in nature, rooted in the differences in background between the court and Parisian nobles, on the one hand, and the provincial gentlemen, on the other. While most of the Nobles arriving from the provinces—three-fifths of the total—possessed titles and substantial revenues, many remained angry over the pensions, positions, and prestige monopolized by "the great" in Versailles. "The provincial nobles," wrote the marquis de Ferrières many years later, "absolutely rejected the great courtiers." And he recalled his own "secret joy" on coming to Versailles from his lands in Poitou: "long cut off from any position which might have allowed me to employ my talents and virtues in public service, ... I could at last be useful to my country." In early June Achard de Bonvouloir leveled a veritable tirade against the accumulation of offices and pensions in the hands of a

---

[56] The words were delivered by Target, on a proposal by Mirabeau: *AP*, 8:49.

[57] Jallet, *Journal*, 84–85 (entry of June 12).

[58] Bailly, 1:177 (entry of June 19); Jean-François Campmas to his brother, vicaire in Carmaux: B.M. Albi, Ms. 177, letter of May 30; Visme, entries of May 27 and June 6.

few.[59] But few of the provincial gentlemen had experience in politics or court intrigue. "Busily engaged in military service or in exploiting their ancestral lands near their châteaus," wrote the comte de Mathieu, "the nobility has until now little involved itself in political discussions." Or as the comte de Puisaye put it, they were "made more for military tactics than for the tactics of [political] deliberation."[60] In the end, the political choices of most nobles were determined less by inter-estate rivalries than by the ideological positions and cultural values shared by a great many nobles at all levels in society.

Like the patriot curés in the First Estate, an active and vociferous minority of liberal nobles hoped to bring a merger of the three estates as a prelude to writing a constitution and instituting major reforms throughout the kingdom. The liberals in question were substantially younger than their order in general, with an average age of about forty—compared to about forty-five for the Second Estate as a whole. They also tended to originate in urban areas and in Paris and to have had war experience—including a dozen or so who had fought in the American Revolution.[61] At the core of liberal leadership were seventeen Nobles who had been members of the Committee of Thirty, including such important future leaders of the National Assembly as the marquis de Lafayette, Alexandre and Charles de Lameth, Adrien Duport, the duc de La Rochefoucauld, Fréteau de Saint-Just, and the comte de Clermont-Tonnerre.[62] Others, however, like the veteran naval officer Nompère de Champagny, had few previous links with the patriot group, and claimed to support their position for purely pragmatic reasons, convinced that noble resistance to change could only lead to political upheaval and social turmoil.[63]

At the beginning of the Estates General, many of the Parisian liberals continued coming together to pursue the tactics of the Thirty, frequently meeting in the country house of the duc d'Aumont in Viroflay near Versailles, or at the home of the duchess d'Enville, mother of La Rochefoucauld. The "Viroflay club" invited the participation of nobles from other provinces and deputies from the First and Third Estates, including Barnave, the abbé Sieyès, and Rabaut Saint-Etienne.[64] Yet despite their extensive

[59] Charles-Elie de Ferrières, *Mémoires*, 3 vols. (Paris, 1825), 1:3–4; Sillery, entry of June 8.

[60] Marquis Marie de Roux, *La Révolution à Poitiers et dans la Vienne* (Paris, 1911), 167; Joseph-Geneviève Puisaye, *Mémoires du comte de Puisaye*, 6 vols. (London and Paris, 1803–25), 1:199.

[61] Jean-Marie Murphy and Patrice Higonnet, "Les députés de la noblesse aux Etats généraux," *RHMC* 20 (1973), 244–46. The average age of the liberal nobles was 40.5 years, compared to 45.3 for the nonliberals. Twenty-nine percent (26 of 90) are known to have had war experience, compared to 18% of the nonliberals.

[62] Daniel L. Wick, *A Conspiracy of Well-Intentioned Men: The Society of Thirty and the French Revolution* (New York, 1987), appendix I, tables 1, 2, and 6.

[63] Jean-Baptiste de Nompère de Champagny, *Souvenirs de M. de Champagny, duc de Cadore* (Paris, 1846), 58. Cf. Puisaye, 1:200–203.

[64] Alexandre de Lameth, *Histoire de l'Assemblée constituante*, (Paris, 1828–29), 1:34n-36n,

meetings and organization, and their considerable kingdomwide influence during the Pre-Revolutionary period, the liberals soon found that they were only a small minority within the Second Estate as a whole. In their first separate session, on May 6, the Nobles rejected the idea of a common verification of credentials by the overwhelming margin of 188 to 46. Though the vote took place without the participation of three "patriot" delegations—whose credentials were still being contested—and before the arrival of the distinctly liberal contingent from Paris, the liberal faction never amounted to more than about seventy deputies, a fourth of the Second Estate, at most.[65]

Provincial and Parisian, titled and untitled, robe and sword, young and old, the great majority of all Nobles were aggressively hostile to the liberals and the position they represented. Whatever their animosities toward the great courtiers, both Ferrières and Achard rapidly joined forces with the majority in all the key votes. For the marquis from Poitou, the liberals were simply "young colonels, creatures of the minister Necker, insanely anxious to achieve popular fame." The rural gentleman from Bresse, Garron de La Bévière, dismissed them summarily as a group of noisy "enthusiasts given over to theories."[66] Very early, moreover, the reactionary contingent also began organizing to maintain discipline in the various votes and elections. As the liberal leaders of the Second Estate were closely linked to the Committee of Thirty, so their opponents included several of those who had rallied around Duval d'Eprémesnil in late 1788 and early 1789 to organize a conservative reaction. The duc de Luxembourg, the comte d'Antraigues, and Eprémesnil (after his late arrival on May 14) were usually listed among the principal animators of the movement, along with the marquis de Bouthillier and the ex-liberal from Auvergne, the marquis de Laqueuille. Meeting at times in Luxembourg's residence, at times in the indoor Tennis Court where the Third Estate would later take its oath, the "club" seems to have carefully controlled the election of officers and committee members and to have orchestrated the principal policy decisions of the Second Estate— probably in alignment with the reactionary Polignac faction at the court.[67] The president, vice-president, and secretaries of the order, and all of the

420–21; Puisaye, 1:242–43; G. Michon, *Essai sur l'histoire du parti Feuillant: Adrien Duport* (Paris, 1924), 48.

[65] Lefebvre, *Recueil, Tome II.*, 1:226. Deputies whose credentials were still being contested were not allowed to vote—a ploy specifically designed to keep many liberals from participating. Otherwise, the liberals might have received 8 additional votes from the Dauphiné nobles, 4 from Artois, and 3 from Vesoul. The Paris nobles, 9 of whom were generally liberal, arrived later in May to fill out the contingent.

[66] Ferrières, 1:26; Claude-Jean-Baptiste de Garron de La Bévière to his wife: A.D. Ain, 1 Mi 1, letter of May 26.

[67] Sillery, entries of June 6 and 21; Edme-Louis-Alexis Dubois-Crancé, *Lettre de M. Dubois de Crancé . . . à ses commettants* (Paris, 1790), 5; Charles-Elie de Ferrières, *Correspondance inédite*, ed. Henri Carré (Paris, 1932), 60 (letter of June 5); and *Mémoires*, 1:37; Boullé, 12 (1888), 50 (letter of June 9).

members of the "conciliatory commission," without exception, were chosen from among the conservatives. The moderate Brulart de Sillery grew increasingly frustrated over the faction's control of deliberations. When four secretaries were chosen on June 6, he had no doubts that "their nomination had been determined the previous night in the club." When a reactionary amendment was appended to the king's mediation proposal, "the motion had been proposed and decided in the Tennis Court Club." Sillery was also convinced that the group was engaged in a veritable vendetta against liberal or potentially liberal deputies within the Nobility. The delegations from Franche-Comté and Dauphiné were long denied participation—the latter, in Sillery's view, on totally trumped-up charges—and the Parisian delegation was excluded for two days on a petty technicality. The liberal vicomte de Toulongeon recalled with anger the manner in which he and his associates had been treated by the majority: "instead of attempting to win them over through tact or at least through fairness, they embittered them through a conduct that was out of place and badly miscalculated."[68]

As the bishops courted the curés, so too the conservative Nobles were often successful in courting and flattering the provincial gentlemen. Despite his initial suspicions, Ferrières was soon dining with the archconservative Polignac faction, where he delighted in conversing with the comte d'Artois himself and with others of "the great."[69] But the group was equally successful through the power of their rhetoric. La Bévière specifically credited Eprémesnil—who spoke "with a force, a courage, a logic that were truly admirable"—with winning over several delegations.[70] D'Antraigues and Cazalès also emerged as talented orators, playing on both the inherent "justice" of their cause and on the dire dangers to noble rights and property if the Third Estate won the day. If the Nobles were to protect themselves from the commoners' "threats," they could never accept the vote by head or joint sessions of all three orders, nor even permit the Third's use of the word "commons," with its obvious English connotations. Though the Nobles did ultimately agree to cede their tax privileges, even this concession was to take effect only after a constitution had been completed.[71]

Moreover, the conservatives seemed even to strengthen and consolidate their position over time. Soon after his arrival in Versailles, the marquis de Guilhem-Clermont-Lodève became convinced that any semblance of joining the Third would compromise the sovereign rights of the monarch and place noble property in jeopardy. He announced that he was planning to ignore his cahier mandate calling for a vote by head; and he claimed that several others were likewise changing their positions. The baron de Pinteville, who

---

[68] Sillery, entries of June 6 and 21; François-Emmanuel Toulongeon, *Histoire de la France depuis la Révolution*, 7 vols. (Paris, 1801), 1:56; also Michon, 47–48.

[69] Ferrières, *Correspondance*, 55, 58 (letters of May 29 and ca. June 4). By mid-June, however, he began to grow wary of intrigue and kept a greater distance: 67 (letter of June 12).

[70] La Bévière, letter of May 30.

[71] Sillery, entry of May 23.

had originally linked himself to the patriots, was appalled by the Third's "insurrection that verged on frenzy" and was convinced by early June that the Nobles must "give up nothing."[72] In the critical vote of May 28, in which the Nobles now affected that a vote by order was integral to the "Constitution" and necessary for the preservation of the monarchy, the conservatives obtained an even larger majority than on May 6, winning 207 to 38.[73] By mid-June, even the comte de Lablache, one of the major architects of the liberal movement in Dauphiné, had concluded that a joint verification would be impossible. Though he still believed in the cause, he was now convinced that the overwhelming majority of the Nobles would always reject it, and he was obviously affected by a sentiment of esprit de corps and loyalty to his order. The Dauphinois could never act alone, he thought, without being seen by the rest of the French nobility as infamous and dishonorable.[74]

But the positions taken by the Second Estate in May and June were dependent not only on the political dynamics and ideology of the period, but also on the Nobles' underlying political culture and the military-aristocratic ethos which informed that culture. Madame de Staël, who was present at the time and knew many of the Nobles personally, was almost incredulous at the attitudes she encountered. "They had a certain aristocratic self-complacency," she wrote, "that can hardly be imagined, . . . a mixture of frivolity of manners and pedantry of opinion; and all this combined with an utter disdain for ideas and intelligence." The great majority remained deeply convinced of their innate superiority, of the fundamental justice of their rights and privileges: "It was enough to hear them speak of their rank as if such rank had existed before the creation of the world. . . . They considered their privileges, which were of no use to anyone but themselves, as the property rights which underlay the security of the entire society."[75] The Third magistrate Bertrand Barère remembered the baron de Gonnès, his codeputy from Tarbes, as the "ardent and imperturbable supporter of the feudal system, which he considered to be the perfection of the social order"; and curé Monnel described a conversation with a noble delegate from his bailliage who "spoke of serfs and vassals like a baron of the fourteenth century." Indeed, La Bévière commonly referred to "my vassals" when writing of the peasants of his village.[76]

---

[72] Charles-François de Guilhem-Clermont-Lodève to the municipality of Arles: A.C. Arles, AA 23, letter of May 21. Jean-Baptiste de Cernon de Pinteville to his brother: A.D. Marne, J 2286, letters of Apr. 24 and June 4. Cf. Ambroise-Eulalie de Maurès de Malartic, ms. "Journal de ma députation aux Etats généraux": B.M. La Rochelle, ms. 21, entry of June 25.

[73] Sillery, entry of May 28. The newly arrived Parisian delegation was prevented from voting on a technicality.

[74] Lablache, letter of June 12. On the Nobles' fears of the Third, cf. Ferrières, *Correspondance*, 74 (letter of June 22); and La Bévière, letter of June 20.

[75] Anne-Louise-Germaine de Staël, *Considérations sur les principaux événements de la Révolution française*, 3 vols. (London, 1818), 1:196–97.

[76] Bertrand Barère, *Mémoires*, ed. Hippolyte Carnot, 4 vols. (Paris, 1842–44), 1:241; Si-

The majority was strongly penetrated with a military, even feudal sense of honor and duty. There were frequent references in their writings and speeches to models of noble courage and chivalry from the past. Le Clerc de Lassigny would appeal to the mythical medieval knight Le Cid as a model for his own conduct; and one of his colleagues delighted in citing the celebrated chivalric phrases of the duc de Vendôme from the sixteenth century. As Puisaye remembered it, "There was no anecdote about the courage of the nobility, drawn from the whole history of the French monarchy, that was not emphatically cited and enthusiastically applauded. There was no heroic phrase, [pronounced by a noble] and consecrated by history, that was not quoted on every occasion. It was not in vain that the word honor was repeated profusely . . . among men who had more valor than logic."[77]

Throughout the period of the Estates General and the National Assembly the noble deputies were continually challenging one another to duels over political debates which they felt had touched their honor. The intense clash between conservatives and liberals in June led to at least two such duels—between the prince de Poix and the comte de Lambertye, and between Cazalès and Puisaye. La Gallissonnière was ready "to take up his sword to keep liberals from leaving the room," proposing to settle the whole issue at once "on the field of honor," between an equal number of swordsmen from the two sides. At one point, as Alexandre Lameth described it, the duc de Caylus leaped into the middle of the room with his hand on his sword and several of the liberals began reaching for their weapons. "A bloody scene" was averted only when the comte de Clermont-Tonnerre lead the patriot contingent out of the room.[78]

In the tense atmosphere of mid-June, the chivalric vocabulary of defending one's honor and proving one's loyalty to the king permeated the Nobles' letters and diary entries, and increasingly dominated over all other motives in the Nobles' appraisal of their situation. For La Gallissonnière, "the Nobles' duty made it a sacred law never to meet in the common chamber; . . . they were bound to remain faithful to their honor and their duty." The two gentlemen from Perpignan, Banyuls de Montferré and Coma Serra, announced their intention never to join the Third, "governed by that sense of honor which characterizes the French nobility." And both they and an unknown noble from Provence complained of the insults implicit in the Third's lack of respect. The Provençal in question vowed "to defend both the king's authority, which has been horribly compromised, and our own honor, which has been horribly insulted." The marquis de Ferrières, whose cahier would have permitted him to join the Third, rejected the idea in large

---

mon-Edme Monnel, *Mémoires d'un prêtre régicide*, ed. Denis-Alexandre Martin, 2 vols. (Paris, 1829), 1:37; La Bévière, e.g., letter of Aug. 4.

[77] Le Clerc, letter of Oct. 23; Sillery, entry of June 19; Puisaye, 1:215.

[78] La Bévière, letter of June 23; Gaultier, 2:133, 137 (letters of June 23 and 25); Augustin-Félix-Elisabeth Barin de La Gallissonnière, ms. journal: Arch. de la Guerre, A4 LVI, entry of June 24; Lameth, 1:412.

measure out of a sense of pride and honor and a refusal to be pressured by the plebs. La Bévière grew increasingly fatalistic that the Third would in fact triumph through the influence and violence of the crowds. Yet all were prepared, he explained to his wife, "as brave and loyal gentlemen," to "offer their swords and their lives to the king." "Whatever transpires, we must do our duty."[79]

The deputies of the Third were only too aware of the Nobles' sense of honor and of their appeal to that honor in their utter refusal to consider compromise. During the conferences between the orders in late May and early June, the magistrate and playwright Jérôme Le Grand pleaded that the question of honor should have no bearing on the decision to merge the three estates. But as one of the noble commissioners announced, "regardless of the arguments made, their honor would not allow them to reconsider a resolution previously taken."[80]

THE BRETON CLUB AND THE EMERGENCE OF A THIRD CONSENSUS

As the Clergy and the Nobility pursued their internal battles through late May and early June, the Third Estate found itself in a curious state of limbo. The vigorous debates of May 14–18 were followed by a long period of waiting, while the representatives of the three estates discussed their differences in the "conciliation commission." After three relatively fruitless conferences between May 23 and 27, the royal ministry at last stepped in as mediator and the meetings were prolonged episodically through June 9. But as the days and weeks dragged on, dramatic changes were transpiring in the perspectives and general psychology of the Third deputies, changes that would ultimately lead the majority to embrace the very positions of the Breton group which they had initially so overwhelmingly rejected. Based on the descriptions of our deputy witnesses, four factors were particularly important in this psychological transformation: the growing group consciousness of the deputies, the didactic effects of Assembly oratory, the impact of the crowds, and the attitudes and behavior of the Nobility.

There can be no doubt that the assembly process itself played a major role in fostering a new sentiment of group consciousness and self-confidence within the Third Estate. It is ironic that by refusing to meet with the commoners, by compelling them to congregate on their own—in meetings which took place, significantly and symbolically, in the "common" assembly hall where the entire Estates General had first met—the privileged orders

[79] La Gallissonnière, entry of June 24; Raymond-Antoine de Banyuls de Monferré and Michel de Coma Serra to the correspondence committee of Perpignan: A.D. Pyrénées-Orientales, C 2119, letter of July 6; "Correspondance d'un député de la noblesse," 7 (letter of May 31); Ferrières, *Correspondance*, 76 (letter to his sister of June 28); La Bévière, letters of June 20, 23, and 27.

[80] Creuzé, 19 and 77 (entries of May 26 and June 9); Coster, 103 (entry of May 25).

helped promote a sense of cohesion within the Third. Deputies commented on the exhilaration of the moment when they first came together in that hall in early May and held an informal roll call in which each member announced his position on the manner of voting; and all proclaimed their preference for a vote by head. After this experience, Ménard immediately wrote to his wife that the privileged orders "should expect us to offer an absolutely invincible resistance."[81] Without any form of truly national media, the provincial deputies had no way of knowing in advance the opinions of other Frenchmen throughout the kingdom. It was a revelation that could only boost their confidence when they discovered, as both Pellerin and Gantheret put it, that the "same public attitude" on the issue of the vote existed everywhere.[82] Many deputies observed the intense sense of camaraderie and brotherhood which rapidly arose among them. Despite numerous heated debates, Bailly was still convinced that "we were united then and shared feelings of intense fraternity"—an ambiance which he sadly compared with the bitter fratricidal wrangling of later stages in the Revolution.[83] Creuzé-Latouche thought that the Third's confidence had clearly augmented over time as the Nobles and upper Clergy increased their intransigent efforts to stop them at all cost: such extraordinary efforts, in and of themselves, revealed to the Third deputies how frightening they were to the First and Second orders.[84] The young Antoine-Claire Thibaudeau, the future conventional who assisted his constituent father in 1789, was aware of this emerging group psychology and self-confidence and its ultimate significance in effecting Third actions: "If the deputies in isolation were prone to fear, when they were assembled together they displayed great courage and were imperturbable."[85] For Creuzé-Latouche, it was the process and experience of the meetings themselves which "enabled us to develop virtues, strengths, and capabilities that no one imagined we possessed."[86]

A number of letter writers also noted their feelings of pride when they discovered how many first-rate orators could be found among their colleagues. Both Gaultier de Biauzat and Nairac took careful notes on the speakers as they stepped to the rostrum for the first time, grading each on his debating techniques and rhetorical talents as much as on his ideas. Nairac was convinced that there were at least a hundred "first-rate orators, born eloquent, speaking with ease." "Perhaps the greatest minds in the universe," was Lepoutre's even more enthusiastic assessment. Such feelings of pride were fortified when they saw the Nobles bested in the conference

---

[81] Ménard, 25 (letter of May 9); Joseph-Michel Pellerin, ms. journal: B.M. Versailles, Ms. 823F, entry of May 11.

[82] Joseph-Michel Pellerin, *Correspondance, 5 mai 1789–29 mai 1790*, ed. Gustave Bord (Paris, 1883), 7 (letter of May 5); Gantheret, letter of May 13.

[83] Bailly, 1:176–77 (entry of June 19).

[84] Creuzé, 133 (June 20).

[85] Antoine-Claire Thibaudeau, *Biographie, mémoires, 1765–92* (Paris, 1875), 82.

[86] Creuzé, 133 (June 20).

debates by the delegation of commoners.[87] But the Third deputies also listened to the content of the speeches, and they found themselves increasingly touched by the force and the logic of the proposals presented to them by the Breton deputies and their allies. Antoine Durand, who considered himself a "moderate man" intent on compromise, readily admitted the persuasive power of the radicals who "have such a force of imagination that they rush along like a flood, carrying along anyone who would try to stop them." Though many of the speeches were boring and repetitive, he was constantly discovering new "insights" and by mid-June he was clearly being won over by orators who "impressed [the deputies'] minds with an irresistible force, convinced them of the dangers of their previous opinions and brought them over to the correct way of thinking."[88] One could see the moderate and usually practically minded Gantheret pick up new ideas and new vocabulary from letter to letter during May and June. The metamorphosis culminated in a long epistle of June 17, in which he justified the creation of the National Assembly and announced that "we will destroy every form of aristocracy and all arbitrary power." He then went through much of his reasoning a second time for added insistence (and perhaps to convince himself), and ended quite dazzled by what he had just written: "I become dizzy by dint of writing!"[89]

Several of the deputies described the Assembly as an intense didactic experience, an experience which began with the earliest debates and continued through the summer and beyond: "a school of public law" (Boullé); "an academic lecture" (Gaultier). "For me our sessions are like a school," wrote Ménard some months later, "a school as agreeable as it is instructive. In it I see universal reason establishing its empire." In his memoirs Rabaut took much the same position. Initially "only a few of the boldest commoners" considered the deputies of the Third to be the "representatives of the nation." They were uncertain, however, whether "the nation was advanced enough to support them," and they were extremely nervous over the possible reaction of the ministers and courtiers if the Third tried to go too far. It was only after the lengthy debates of mid-June that "there emerged so much wisdom and so much energy among the deputies, that nearly all joined together in the same opinion."[90]

But there was an additional critical element in this "group therapy," this "school" of the Revolution: the actions of the Versailles and Parisian crowds. From the opening procession on May 4, several deputies had re-

---

[87] Nairac, entries of May 13–18; Gaultier, 2:74 (letter of May 22); Lepoutre, letter of July 24. See also Pierre-Joseph Meifrund, ms. journal, copy in l'Institut de la Révolution française, letter of May 20; and Campmas, letter of July 27.

[88] Durand, entries of May 8 and June 16.

[89] Gantheret, letter of June 17.

[90] Ménard, 161 (letter of Dec. 22); also pp. 38 and 95 (letters of June 5 and Sept. 1); Gaultier, 2:44 (letter of May 9); Boullé, 15 (1889), 116 (letter of Sept. 8, misdated Sept. 28 in publication); Rabaut, 116–17.

marked on the exhilarating effects of the spectators' enthusiasm and support for the Third—and their corresponding disapproval of the Nobles and Clergy. Duquesnoy was greeted by a soldier as he left the hall toward the beginning of May: "For God's sake, sir, hold steadfast!" Durand found the commoner deputies welcomed everywhere with "a joy verging on frenzy."[91] As events unfolded in late May and June, the crowds were constantly in evidence, following the deputies wherever they went, cheering, chanting, encouraging the Third at every step, dogging them like a Greek chorus when they walked from the locked hall to the tennis court or moved to the church of Saint-Louis or sent a delegation to the king. After the critical days of mid-June, the deputies found themselves continually feted, hugged in the streets and serenaded by fishwives, handed bouquets of flowers as they ate their meals.[92] Beyond boosting the deputies' confidence and sense of power, the spectators might also measurably influence the debates. The Third had early realized the value of opening up its sessions to the public, both to keep that public informed and to be in a position to seek its support. With no arms directly at their disposal, with no real force beyond the logic of their arguments, the deputies were soon self-consciously cultivating and encouraging popular attendance and support. "The deputies," noted Maillot, "had to draw their energy and their purity from the opinion and attention of the public." "Public opinion is our strength," reasoned Visme. Or as Poncet-Delpech observed, "The uprightness of our intentions and our actions makes us continually look to the nation as our audience."[93]

From the last days of May most of the deputies began commenting in their letters on the size and enthusiasm of the crowds present: cheering their approval for some speakers, hooting and deriding those whose ideas they rejected or whose speeches they felt were too long-winded or disorganized. On occasion, speakers even turned and specifically addressed the galleries for support, so that debate became a three-way dialogue between speaker, deputies, and audience.[94] Inevitably, many deputies came to view the crowds and spectators as the tangible embodiment of public opinion and the general will. When on May 28 Malouet urged that the audience—now perhaps two thousand strong—be kept away from the debates, Volney bolted to his feet and responded that the people were "your brothers and your fellow-citizens," and Charles-François Bouche added, "Let it be known, gentlemen, that we deliberate here in the presence of our masters and that we owe them an account of our positions."[95] Basquiat de Mugriet

---

[91] Duquesnoy, 1:12 (entry of May 8); Durand, entries of May 4 and June 17.

[92] Poncet, "Documents," 431–32 (letter of June 20); Durand, entry of June 20; Delaville, letter of June 21; Charles-François Bouche, letter of June 22; Gallot, 85 (entry of June 23); Boullé, 14 (1889), 30–31 (letter of June 28). Cf. Jallet, *Journal*, 93 (entry of June 19).

[93] Claude-Pierre Maillot to an unnamed municipal official of Toul: A.C. Toul, JJ 7, letter of May 7; Poncet, "Documents," 430 (letter of May 23); Visme, entry of June 23.

[94] Malouet, 2:10; Duquesnoy, 1:101 (entry of June 17); Creuzé, 123 (entry of June 16).

[95] *AP*, 8:55; Malouet, 2:10–11; Creuzé, 25–26 (entry of May 28); Monneron, 480–81.

and Lamarque even argued that the support and activities of the crowds were critical in bringing the Third Estate to create a "National Assembly": "public opinion made it absolutely requisite."[96] The very concept of "public opinion," which had previously appeared as a somewhat disembodied abstraction, associated more commonly with the opinion of literary and social elites, now took on a new and far more concrete meaning. And invariably, the experience had an enormous impact on the deputies' confidence and self-esteem.

To be sure, the potentials of this "group therapy" were partly vitiated in the early weeks of the Estates by the very tumultuous and unruly nature of the discussions. The Third remained wary of establishing discipline and rules of debate, for fear such rules might suggest the existence of a separate order. The character of the hall itself, with its cavernous acoustics where one could only make oneself heard by shouting, added to the tension. Nearly all of the deputies commented on the chaotic conditions of the May debates, and many of the more moderate were clearly disenchanted.[97] Eventually, however, the Assembly was forced to establish a rough organization and set of rules, with a "dean" and a dozen or so "assistants" to help organize the proceedings—avoiding the terms "president" and "secretary," out of fear of suggesting an established order.[98] Perhaps even more important in changing the atmosphere of the meetings was the increasingly common practice of gathering together in small nightly conclaves outside the large hall. In addition to the provincial caucuses already functioning, the Commons established in early June twenty smaller discussion groups or "bureaus," with membership determined at random.[99] Assembling in small rooms without the presence of spectators, the bureaus and the provincial meetings facilitated the participation of the more timid—and often more conservative—deputies. The bureaus, in particular, helped integrate many moderates into the parliamentary process and perhaps helped win them over to the more radical patriot proposals.

But while all of these elements of group psychology and growing self-confidence were undoubtedly important, the critical factor transforming the positions of the majority and forging the revolutionary consensus—to judge by the deputy letters and diaries—was the Nobility's resolute unwillingness to compromise. As we have seen, many of the Third deputies had originally been prepared for some kind of arrangement with the Nobles, accepting perhaps a vote by order on certain issues.[100] But it seemed increasingly ap-

[96] Basquiat and Lamarque, AA 51, letter of June 17.

[97] E.g., Duquesnoy, 1:10 (entry of May 7); Gallot, 73 (entry of May 25); Durand, entry of May 6.

[98] *AP*, 8:35, 49 (May 12 and 26). See also below, chap. 7.

[99] André Castaldo, *Les méthodes de travail de la Constituante* (Paris, 1989), 120–21. Also Nairac, entry of June 8.

[100] See above, note 4.

parent that intransigent nobles entirely dominated the Second Estate. For most of the moderates, the turning point came in late May or early June. More frustrated from day to day by the complete inactivity of the Estates, the commoners were particularly enraged when the Nobles issued a declaration on May 28, prior to the opening of the royal arbitration commission, rejecting in advance any possibility of a vote by head.[101] "The mask has been removed," wrote Creuzé-Latouche, "and now we can see how little the nobles ever deserved our confidence when they spoke of generosity, honor, justice and selflessness." "Never," wrote Duquesnoy, "has hatred and dissatisfaction with this order . . . been so clearly expressed." "The violence of the Nobles' declarations," concluded Maillot, "has more strengthened than weakened the strong determination of the Commons"—a statement echoed almost word for word by the usually cautious Nairac. The retired colonial official Monneron was incensed by the arrogant remarks made to him by one of the noble deputies: "What good is this resistance: where can it lead you? We will not change our position, and we have nothing to ask of you. We are fine as we are." And Gantheret now deeply regretted having rejected "the advice of the Bretons . . . because we wanted to be so cautious and prudent in our demands." Visme came to much the same conclusion. Under normal circumstance, as he confided to his diary, he would never have considered such proposals, but now he was inclined to do so: "The nobles' actions have justified it."[102]

There was also increasing concern that the aristocracy was doing everything in its power to influence and mislead the king. Most of the deputies remained confident in Louis XVI's fundamental justice and support of the Third's objectives. But it now appeared that the king was being screened and isolated by the reactionary courtiers, and that the commoners' actions were being twisted and misrepresented. There were wide suspicions that the royal arbitration commissioners were taking the side of the Second Estate. Fears were heightened when—following the death of the king's oldest son—Louis postponed a meeting with the Third delegation for several days, requiring all communication between the Commons and himself to pass through the intermediary of his ministers. The commoners were well aware that no such procedure was required for the leaders of the Clergy and the Nobility, and that even in the midst of the king's mourning, aristocrats and bishops were allowed direct access to the royal chambers. Several of the Third deputies felt a deep sense of humiliation at such a state of affairs:

---

[101] *AP*, 8:54 (May 28).

[102] Creuzé, 37 (entry of May 30); Duquesnoy, 1:48 (entry of May 28); Maillot, letter of June 3; Nairac, entry of June 9; Monneron, 482 (entry of May 27); Gantheret, letter of June 5; Visme, entry of June 10. See also Meifrund, entry of June 10; Durand, entry of May 30; Basquiat and Lamarque, letter of June 8; Bailly, 1:107 (entry of June 5); Périsse, letter of July 8.

"This is the proof," as one put it, "that the Nobility has the upper hand, and that the king now favors the Nobility."[103]

For some of the commoners, this growing hostility toward the Nobles was a wrenching experience, entailing an agonizing re-evaluation of a value system to which they had long acquiesced. Both Ménard, whose family had "lived nobly" in Le Mans for generations, and the Arles merchant Pierre-Siffren Boulouvard, whose brother-in-law was a noble, felt almost ashamed of their growing resentment against the Second Estate. The Nobles' actions, wrote Boulouvard, "may perhaps lead me, in spite of myself, to blame the conduct of certain individuals to whom we owe respect." Ménard concurred: "All my life I will fear having been unjust toward an order of our most distinguished citizens. But for the moment I cannot avoid accusing and reproaching the Nobility for a stubbornness that could expose France to the greatest danger." In a long letter to his friend the marquis de La Celle, the magistrate Grellet de Beauregard described his experience in the Estates. He was convinced that if the Nobility had displayed any flexibility whatsoever, a compromise might well have been acceptable—despite all the sound and fury emanating from the Breton contingent—with a vote by head on some issues and a vote by order on others, implicitly recognizing the existence of separate orders. But "those who led the Nobility have blocked off every road," so that the nation had come to "anathematize the very word 'order.'"[104]

For a great many others, however, the position of the nobles and the bishops aroused long-held sentiments of animosity and resentment, feelings which most had labored to suppress in the name of unity, in the pious hope that they might now be regarded as equals. It was not only the intransigence of the Nobles which incensed them, but the haughtiness, the disdain, the insolence with which they were treated: "the arrogance and pride of an order that refuses to yield an inch of ground" (Durand); their "supreme imperiousness" (Lepoutre); their "high degree of haughtiness" (Rabaut).[105] For a large number of deputies, a deep-seated revulsion for the years of condescension and scorn was released by the current confrontation. The struggle for status, the desire—in abbé Sieyès's phrase—to be recognized as "something" in the social order, became an all-consuming passion, pushing them toward a break.

By the end of the first week in June, members of the Commons could sense a perceptible shift in opinion within their chamber, an increasing

---

[103] Words overheard in the hall by Maupetit: 18 (1902), 154 (letter of June 5). Also Maillot, letter of June 1; and Duquesnoy, I, 65 (entry of June 3).

[104] Pierre-Siffren Boulouvard to municipality of Arles: A.C. Arles, AA 23, letter of June 25; Ménard, 40 (letter of June 9); Grellet, 65 (letter of July 10).

[105] Durand, entry of May 30; Lepoutre, letter of May 28; Rabaud, 120; Félix Faulcon, *Correspondance. Tome 2: 1789–91*, ed. G. Debien (Poitiers, 1953), 37 (letter to Desplanches, June 18). Also Goupilleau, letter of June 1.

readiness to see the Third go it alone. As the full assembly of the Third Estate remained on hold, awaiting the results of the arbitration commission, the focus of activity shifted for a time to the smaller evening meetings, the provincial caucuses and the newly created bureaus. But it was above all the Breton club which emerged as the dynamic center of leadership. "Over the last few days," wrote Boullé on June 9, "our meeting room has become the gathering place for all good citizens. . . . The best citizens from every province come together there."[106] It was here on the evening of June 8 that the abbé Sieyès, only recently arrived in Versailles after his election in Paris, first read a motion which he proposed to present to the Assembly. The motion differed little from Le Chapelier's proposal three weeks earlier, that the privileged deputies be summoned to join with "all the representatives of the nation" for a joint verification of credentials—though Sieyès now added specific provisions for a roll call to which Nobles and Clergy would be invited to appear. But by choosing the well-known clergymen to present their motion, the Breton group probably hoped to win over some of the still undecided deputies.[107]

In a tense but increasingly exhilarating series of meetings on June 9, first in the bureaus and then in the various provincial caucuses, small groups of deputies passed in review the frustrations of their month of inaction and the various options now open to them. The Breton club seems also to have sent out delegates to the bureaus to argue its case. In any case, two of the more radical patriots, Pétion and Populus, appeared that evening in Nairac's twentieth bureau and joined with Jean-Louis Prieur—the future "Prieur de la Marne"—to urge adoption of Sieyès's plan. Those still uncertain could console themselves that the privileged orders were not being excluded—as the earlier Breton plan had stipulated—but "invited" to participate; and that in its amended version the Third would send a message to the king to explain their purpose and proclaim their loyalty. Thus, "long prepared in individual meetings in order to have it adopted in advance," as Nairac described it, Sieyès's motion passed the next evening in its amended version before the full Assembly by a near unanimous vote.[108]

The roll call itself began only on June 12, after a one-day pause for Corpus Christi. The secretaries called out the deputies' districts one by one and those in attendance came forward to present their electoral credentials. Despite the expectations of many commoners, only the three curés from Poitou initially responded to the roll call from the two privileged orders.

[106] Boullé, 12 (1888), 40 and 49 (letters of June 9). Cf. Pellerin, ms., entries of June 7 and 8.

[107] Boullé, ibid.; Pellerin, ms., entry of June 8; *AP*, 8:84–85 (June 10).

[108] Nairac, entries of May 9 and 10; Durand, entry of June 10; Visme, entry of June 10; Grellet, 64 (letter of June 12); Creuzé, 94–95 (entry of June 10); Pellerin, ms., entry of June 10.

The deputies' papers were then divided up for consideration among the bureaus and the verification process began at long last.

THE REVOLUTIONARY MOMENT

After the weeks of indecision and hesitation, the Third Estate had made its break, had "cut the cables" as Sieyès described it, and claimed the right to go it alone. It is difficult to say how many of the deputies were fully aware of the significance of their action. Most of the debates through June 10 had focused almost entirely on the procedural issues. There had been precious little discussion of what the Third would do once it actually achieved a single assembly and a vote by head. But it was to precisely this question that the Assembly turned in the major debates of June 15 to 17, debates that represented in themselves an extraordinary expansion of the Revolutionary vision and psychology. Ostensibly at stake was the formal "constituting" of the Assembly and the choice of the name to be given to the newly formed body. But with the growing feeling of camaraderie as the deputies urged each other forward, with the huge crowds inside and outside cheering them on, with the mounting sense of urgency born of rumors that the Assembly might soon be dissolved, the "school" of the Revolution entered into full session. All of the greatest orators came forward to offer wide-ranging reflections on how the Assembly should be conceived, what its immediate goals ought to be, how it should handle taxation and the debt, and what should be its relations with the people and the king. Marked by "numerous argumentations—models of carefully articulated logic—penetrated with the most profound understanding and the most seductive eloquence," the sessions of mid-June were a trial run for the great constitutional debates of August and September.[109] As he listened with rapt attention, Nicolas-Jean Camusat de Belombre felt himself swayed first one way and then the other by successive speeches, each "supported with such a force of reasoning, that one's mind, confused and hesitant, was hard pressed to make a decision." During the night, alone in the silence of his room, he passed in review the various arguments, and in the process, there emerged a whole new vision of the assembly's purpose as a truly national and sovereign body, a vision which he had never clearly articulated before.[110]

In this way, the dynamic of the debates pushed the great majority of deputies progressively toward a more expansive conception of their situation. At first, the speakers proposed restricted and often convoluted titles for the new body, such as Sieyès's "assembly of the known and verified representatives of the French nation" or Mounier's "legitimate assembly of

[109] Basquiat and Lamarque, letter of June 15. Visme described the debate as "magnifique par l'éloquence": entry for June 16.
[110] Nicolas-Jean Camusat de Belombre, ms. notes for letters to unknown party in Troyes: A.N., W 306 (377), entry of June 18.

the representatives of the larger part of the nation, acting in the absence of the smaller part." But the term "National Assembly," initially avoided by Sieyès because he was convinced that his colleagues would never accept it, began to appear in several of the speeches. Finally, on the afternoon of June 16, the playwright-magistrate Jérôme Legrand directly proposed it, and the deputies responded with enthusiastic applause. That evening, after further discussions in the bureaus, Sieyès himself endorsed the term, and the Third officially adopted the name National Assembly on the morning of June 17 by a vote of 491 to 90.[111] Creuzé-Latouche described the final roll call vote that morning. Despite the presence of some four thousand spectators, there was silence throughout the hall, broken only by the sound of quills and the shuffling of pages as the secretaries went through the list of deputies. When the results were announced a great cheer rose up, with everyone, on the floor and in the stands, shouting "long live the king, long live the nation, long live the National Assembly."[112]

Much was made, among journalists at the time and among historians later, of the division in the vote and of the ninety who rejected the new designation.[113] The reputation of the Norman lawyer and orator Thouret, who had opposed the term, was still tarnished six weeks later when he was forced under pressure to renounce his election as president. Yet the overwhelming majority of the ninety were strong patriots who simply preferred one of the more cumbersome formulations for the new Assembly. Bailly went out of his way to make this clear in his memoirs, elucidating the outrage and mortification of those who found their names circulating on lists of "opponents of the National Assembly." Though a few of the individuals in question—like Malouet and Mounier—would rapidly move in a more conservative direction, most would continue to support the patriots. As soon as the vote was completed, virtually all took steps to affirm their solidarity with the majority.[114]

In any case, with the vote complete, the deputies quickly and unanimously moved to take a solemn oath, the first of many Revolutionary oaths—but for many of those present the most memorable of all. Bailly, now "president" of the Assembly, stood alone and pronounced the words of "a great and sacred commitment": "I hereby swear, in the name of God, the king, and the nation, to fulfill faithfully and zealously the functions with

---

[111] The term had frequently been used over the previous weeks and months. See, for example, Emmanuel-Joseph Sieyès, *Qu'est-ce que le Tiers état?* (Paris, 1982), 79; Maximilien Robespierre, *A la nation arlésienne* (n.p., 1788), 6; Guy-Jean-Baptiste Target, *Deuxième suite de l'écrit intitulé "Etats généraux convoqués par Louis XVI"* (Paris, 1789), 5.

[112] Creuzé, 125–26 (entry of June 17).

[113] E.g., Christophe-Félix-Louis de Montjoie, *Histoire de la Révolution de France*, 2 vols. (Paris, 1797), 2:542; Georges Lefebvre, *The Coming of the French Revolution* (Princeton, 1947), 72.

[114] See Nairac, entry of June 17; Maupetit, 19 (1903), 215 (letter of Aug. 3—relating to Thouret's election); and Bailly, 1:179–80 (entry of June 19); Montjoie, 2:542; and Creuzé, 124 (entry of June 16).

which I have been entrusted." Then all the deputies, without exception, stood with their right hands raised and affirmed the same oath.[115] Thereafter, Target (who had opposed the new name) and Le Chapelier (who had supported it) joined in a motion granting the body complete control over taxes and implicitly asserting that all taxes should cease to be paid if the government tried to dissolve the Assembly. This, the National Assembly's first decree, remarkably revolutionary and unthinkable for most deputies only a few weeks earlier, was passed without dissent. As the session adjourned and the deputies filed out of their hall, they were met by enormous crowds throughout Versailles, cheering and applauding, deferentially backing away and forming "a line of honor" on either side of their path to allow "the nation" to pass through their midst. "Joy and exhilaration," wrote Pierre-François Bouche, "were in every heart and on every face."[116]

The first two and a half weeks in June had produced a dramatic transformation in the thinking of a substantial number of the Third Estate deputies. It was a true revolutionary moment, born of a complex convergence of factors, some long developing and rooted in the social and cultural structures of the Old Regime and their consequent effects on noble-commoner relations, some related to the contingent lack of leadership and to the deputies' immediate experience in the Estates General and the actions and reactions of Third Estate and Nobility after May 5. To call it a "paradigm shift" is undoubtedly too strong. A great many of the deputies were now prepared for a break with the past, but they were far from certain where and how far they should go, and to what extent that past should be reformed or replaced. And the central dilemma of their relationship to the king had hardly been broached. The Revolutionary process would continue for many weeks and months to come. Yet the events of mid-June 1789 left an indelible mark, and the great majority of commoner deputies would never again think of themselves and their relationship to the king and the kingdom in quite the same way. The merchant Gantheret, only recently so cautious and fearful, was dazzled and thrilled by the sudden turn of events: "Through this coup d'état"—the word "revolution" not yet having entered his vocabulary—"we have obliterated all distinctions of privilege by order, every privilege of voting by order, and all semblance of a veto, except for that of the king." Laurent Visme, who *had* adopted the word, put it more simply: "There has now taken place, suddenly, a prodigious revolution of the mind."[117]

---

[115] Bailly, 1:163–64 (entry of June 17); Nairac, entry of June 17. See also, e.g., Pellerin, ms., entry of June 17; Meifrund, entry of June 17; Charles-François Bouche, letter of June 18.

[116] Pierre-François Bouche, letter of June 18.

[117] Gantheret, letter of June 17; Visme, entry of June 16.

The Experience of Revolution

IN THE EARLY DAYS of their stay in Versailles, the mood of the deputies as reflected in their letters and diaries had been generally optimistic and tranquil. Most of the commoners were undoubting in their conviction of the reason and justice of their demands, and they were convinced that the monarch was on their side. With the Third rejecting the possibility of substantive debates until credentials were verified in common, meetings tended to be relatively short, and the First and Second Estates sometimes went several days without any assemblies at all. The relaxed pace and the warm spring weather of that early May left the deputies free for walks and sightseeing in Versailles or visits to friends in Paris. They were given full access to the palace and its grounds and many availed themselves to take walks and rides through the forest, or visit the royal menagerie, or stroll through the great hallways and watch courtiers and dignitaries go about their business. Gantheret, the Burgundy wine merchant, delighted in observing the queen and the other great ladies of the realm on their afternoon outings. Bergasse and curé Rousselot were fascinated by the wildlife in the parks, where rabbits, doves, and pheasants were "more common than chickens" in the curé's parish; while Doctor Gallot spent evenings attending the public ceremony of the royal dinner.[1] A week after the opening, the king organized free dramatic productions for the deputies in the Versailles theater, and though a few radicals complained of the unnecessary expense incurred by such frivolities, the plays went on and were generally well attended through May.[2]

But by the month of June, as the Third Estate deputies found themselves swept up in the evolving political drama, as their sessions became increasingly long—continuing on occasion well into the night—the tone of their writings changed perceptibly. Though they revealed great courage and determination when meeting in assembly, once they had left the hall and retired alone to their rooms, their thoughts shared with colleagues and family

---

[1] Claude Gantheret to Pierre Leflaive, his brother-in-law: private collection of Françoise Misserey, letter of May 13; Etienne Lamy, *Un défenseur des principes traditionnels sous la Révolution: N. Bergasse* (Paris, 1910), 87; Claude-Germain Rousselot to his nephew, Joseph Rousselot: Fonds Girardot, A.D. Haute-Saône, letter of May 21; Jean-Gabriel Gallot, *La vie et les oeuvres du Docteur Jean-Gabriel Gallot*, ed. Louis Merle (Poitiers, 1961), 104–5 (letter of May 21). On the weather, Claude-Jean-Baptiste de Garron de La Bévière to his wife: A.D. Ain, 1 Mi 1, letters of May 16, and June 9 and 30.

[2] Joseph-Michel Pellerin, ms. "Journal": B.M. Versailles, Ms. 823F, entry of May 12; Claude-Pierre Maillot to an unnamed municipal official of Toul: A.C. Toul, JJ 7, entry of June 3; Jean-Pierre Boullé, "Ouverture des Etats généraux de 1789," ed. Albert Macé, *Revue de la Révolution. Documents inédits* 11 (1888), 20 and 46 (letters of May 22 and 25).

members were fraught with tension and anxiety. They were only too aware of the precariousness of their situation. Whatever the moral authority of their cause, whatever the power of their ideas and rhetoric, they could do little or nothing if the government turned against them and resorted to physical force. On the morning of June 9, as they contemplated summoning the two privileged orders to a roll call, tensions ran so high that the president could find no one at all who wanted to speak: an unprecedented event for the generally loquacious lawyers and magistrates. "We all found ourselves in a state of indecision," wrote Gaultier, "over the rumors of plots to dissolve the Estates General. The importance of the question and the uncertainty of the latest news left the patriots quite at a loss, and no one dared to speak." "You cannot imagine how tormented I am by doubts," commented Boullé. "I am consumed by anxiety." Gantheret, beside himself with fear over the possible reactions of the king and the ministers to the commoners' recent decisions, begged his friends in Beaune to write back immediately and tell him what to do: "We are all in a state of unbelievable agitation." A week later, more calm and a bit embarrassed, he tried to explain his previous state of mind: "We didn't know how the king would take our deliberation, more audacious than anything since the beginning of the monarchy."[3]

In fact, Gantheret's volatility, his inconsistency of mood from one letter to the next, was not untypical of many of the deputies from all three estates. Throughout the period of June, July, and August—and sometimes beyond—they were beset by variations of emotions and feelings. At the end of June, according to Gontier de Biran, all of the deputies were "continually alternating between fear and hope." So too in the crisis of mid-July, the "striking contrasts" as Durand described it, "between good and bad, fear and hope, joy and sadness, arrived in rapid succession." "We never know," wrote curé Barbotin, "whether to laugh or to cry."[4]

Fluctuations of this kind could be attributed in part to the very nature of the situation in which the deputies now found themselves: a kind of liminal state between the old and the new, in which much of the world they had previously known was collapsing or being torn down around them. They had never imagined or prepared for the sweep of the changes transpiring, and whatever their previous experience in public affairs, they were impressed and disconcerted by the awesome task of reconstruction which lay

---

[3] Jean-François Gaultier de Biauzat, *Gaultier de Biauzat, député du Tiers état aux Etats généraux de 1789. Sa vie et sa correspondance*, ed. Francisque Mège, 2 vols. (Clermont-Ferrand, 1890), 2:101 (letter of ca. June 10); Boullé, 12 (1888), 40 (letter of June 9); Gantheret, letters of June 26 and July 3.

[4] Guillaume Gontier de Biran to the municipality of Bergerac: A.C. Bergerac, Fonds Faugère, carton 1, letter of June 26; Antoine Durand to Delcamp-Boytré in Gourdan: A.E. Cahors, carton 5–56, entry of July 14; Emmanuel Barbotin, *Lettres de l'abbé Barbotin*, ed. A. Aulard (Paris, 1910), 39 (letter of July 16). See also Boullé, 12 (1888), 49 (letter of ca. June 9); and Alexis Basquiat de Mugriet and Pierre-Joseph de Lamarque to municipality of Bayonne: A.C. Bayonne, AA 51, letter of July 15.

before them.[5] The vacillation in mood could also be attributed to the inconstancy of royal policy. The weak and unstable character of the king and the ongoing power struggle among his ministers led to a series of oscillations between hard line and soft line, between repressive and conciliatory strategies. Such oscillations, which had begun with the calling of the Assembly of Notables in 1787, if not earlier, and which continued in accelerated fashion throughout 1789, left the deputies perpetually in doubt about the intentions of the government and the real position of the king. And soon there was another, quite unexpected element of instability, erupting violently onto the scene: the activities of the popular classes in Paris and the countryside. By the beginning of July the deputies found themselves forced to confront a group in society which they once thought they understood, but which now seemed increasingly "foreign" and uncontrollable.

In sum, we must avoid seeing the deputies' Revolutionary itinerary that summer as a series of calculated decisions based on careful deliberation and foresight. Although clusters of deputies, both liberal and conservative, might attempt to exercise leadership; although the Breton Club, for a time, seemed to direct the flow of events; for the most part, all of the deputies found themselves swept along by circumstances over which they had only limited control. There was an erratic, unpredictable, chaotic quality to political action, action born as much of passion, fear, and uncertainty as of reason and premeditation. We must keep these observations in mind as we follow the men of the National Assembly through the night of August 4, the single most revolutionary moment of the entire Constituent experience.

THE DEPUTIES AND THE KING

Throughout the spring of 1789, the Third Estate deputies had strongly supported the person of Louis XVI and deeply believed, hoped to believe that the king supported them as representatives of the nation. Their near unanimous praise of the monarch, expressed during the opening day's ceremonies, persisted through the month of May and beyond. "We have a great resource in the paternal feelings of the king," wrote Campmas, "and I cannot tell you how much love and respect he inspires in us." Immediately following the great decrees of June 10 and 17, the hall was swept by spontaneous cries of "long live the king." Most of the commoners convinced themselves that the monarch remained on their side, and that Louis's initial noncommittal response was a sign of endorsement: "It's the proof," confided Pellerin to his diary, "that His Majesty is not unhappy with us and that he gives us full freedom to formally constitute ourselves as an assembly."[6] But the period after June 17 would seriously test the deputies' relationship with their king.

---

[5] See below, chap. 6.

[6] Jean-François Campmas to his brother, vicaire in Carmaux: B.M. Albi, Ms. 177, letter of

On the morning of June 20, the representatives were shocked and disconcerted when they arrived to find their hall surrounded by soldiers and closed
by royal order. The day before, after a particularly uproarious session, the
liberal curés and a handful of liberal bishops had finally squeezed out a
victory for a unified vote on credentials, and the session of the 20th promised a first major merging of the First and Third Estates.[7] But the dissident
bishops and the conservative Nobles, shaken by the new turn of events, had
intensely lobbied the king to intervene and halt the deterioration of their
position. After six weeks of silence, Louis at last announced that he would
hold a royal session to present the delegates with instructions, and that the
halls of all three Estates would be locked in preparation. Thrown into turmoil by fear of an impending dissolution of the Assembly, and spurred
forward by the near panic reaction of the crowds in Versailles, the deputies
recongregated in an indoor tennis court, some three blocks from their hall.
With hundreds of men and women in attendance outside and with others
seeping inside to mix with the deputies, the Assembly swore an emotional
and almost unanimous oath, its second in three days. Proposed by Mounier
and drawn up by Target, the oath marked yet another revolutionary escala-
tion, affirming that the members would never separate until they had established a constitution, even if they were forced to meet elsewhere in the
kingdom: "The National Assembly exists wherever its members come together."[8]

Yet even after the oath, a consensus seemed to remain that the good king
had been duped and led astray by the majority of his advisers, advisers who
were none other than the great aristocrats and courtiers whom the Third
perceived as their principal enemies. "Has not the best of kings been led
astray," asked Delandine, "by the arrogant aristocrats who surround him?"
Indeed, at the conclusion of the Tennis Court Oath the deputies broke out
in another vigorous cry of "long live the king." "In times of peace and in
times of violence," wrote Dinochau, "we have always adored and given
thanks, with respectful tenderness, for the name and sacred person of the
king."[9] For the next two days the deputies did their best to believe the

---

May 30; Pellerin, entry of June 13. Durand and Turckheim wrote much the same thing:
Durand, entry of June 19; Jean de Turckheim in L'Alsace pendant la Révolution française, ed.
Rodolphe Reuss, 2 vols. (Paris, 1880–94), 2:72 (letter of June 18).

[7] Maurice Hutt, "The Role of the Curés in the Estates General of 1789," Journal of Ecclesiastical History 6 (1955), 190–220; and Ruth F. Necheles, "The Curés in the Estates General
of 1789," JMH 46 (1974), 425–44.

[8] AP, 8:137–38. Also Jean-Sylvain Bailly, Mémoires d'un témoin de la Révolution, 3 vols.
(Paris, 1821–22), 1:181–92 (entry of June 20); Pierre-Paul Nairac, ms. "Journal": A.D. Eure,
5 F 63, entry of June 20; Laurent-François Legendre to electors and municipal officials in
Brest: RF 39 (1900), 525 (letter of June 20); Pierre-François-Balthazar Bouche to municipality of Forcalquier: A.C. Forcalquier, Series D, "Correspondance 1789," letter of June 20;
Jacques-Antoine Creuzé-Latouche, Journal des Etats généraux et du début de l'Assemblée nationale, 18 mai-29 juillet 1789, ed. Jean Marchand (Paris, 1946), 131–34 (entry of June 20).

[9] Antoine-François Delandine, Mémorial historique des Etats généraux, 5 vols. (n.p., 1789),

rumors they heard that Necker was winning out over the reactionary ministers, and that the king's coming address would confirm the actions of the Third Estate.[10] Although in constitutional terms the National Assembly had effectively claimed ultimate sovereignty—through its decrees of June 17 and 20—most deputies preferred not to consider the full implications of their actions as they concerned the monarchy. They shunted from their thoughts the possibility that the king might dissolve the Assembly: "The principal and fundamental question," concluded Bailly, "had not yet been broached." Since king and Assembly were both representatives of the nation, seeking the best interests of the population, they should invariably hold the same fundamental positions and work in collaboration.[11]

⌐ Unity and collaboration appeared far more tenuous, however, after the king directly confronted the Assembly in the "royal session" of June 23. The idea for such a session apparently originated with Necker, who opposed the creation of a "National Assembly," though he urged the king to order the merging of the three estates. But the minister of finance was outmaneuvered by the reactionaries, led by the king's younger brother, the comte d'Artois, and in the end, Louis embraced almost all of the major positions of the conservative Nobles, rejecting the existence of a National Assembly, commanding a vote by order on most questions, and stipulating that the Estates must not touch any of the prerogatives of the nobility except, with their consent, the nobles' tax privileges.[12] In addition, he strongly implied his readiness to dissolve the Assembly if the Third rejected his proposals. ⌐

The commoners arriving at the hall that morning were already in a state of considerable agitation and consternation. They had anticipated bad news since late the previous night when Necker was observed leaving a council meeting with an expression of grim disappointment on his face. Perhaps out of fear, some sixty Third deputies failed to appear at the session.[13] Many who did attend were angered at having to wait hours pressed together in a small anteroom or huddled outside in the rain, while the Nobles and Clergy were comfortably seated ahead of them.[14] When the king at last appeared, the deputies of the first two orders greeted him enthusiastically with "long live the king!" But this time the Third sat silent, "sadness seated on every brow, tears ready to flow for the misfortune of the nation, ... with the

2:142–43; and Jacques Dinochau, *Histoire philosophique et politique de l'Assemblée constituante,* 2 vols. (Paris, 1789), 2:17. Also, Pellerin, entries of June 17 and 20.

[10] Lefebvre, *Recueil, Tome 1,* 2:76, note 172.

[11] Bailly 1:189 (entry of June 20). Also Adrien Duquesnoy, *Journal d'Adrien Duquesnoy,* ed. R. de Crèvecoeur, 2 vols. (Paris, 1894), 1:112–13 (entry of June 21); Nairac, entry of June 15; Gantheret, letter of June 17; Pierre-François Bouche, letter of June 18.

[12] Lefebvre, *Recueil,* 2:6–17.

[13] Nariac, entry of June 22; Michel-René Maupetit, "Lettres (1789–91)," ed. Quéruau-Lamérie, *Bulletin de la Commission historique et archéologique de la Mayenne,* 2e sér., 18 (1902), 323 (letter of June 23). Only 527 deputies would vote that day on the question of parliamentary inviolability: Pellerin, entry of June 23; *AP,* 8:147.

[14] Basquiat and Lamarque, letter of June 23; Bailly, 1:207–8 (entry of June 23).

anguish one feels on seeing the loss of so great and important a trial." Or as the comte de La Gallissonnière described it, with some satisfaction: "It seemed like they were waiting for an execution."[15]

If Louis had pronounced the same speech on May 5, the great majority of the Third Estate would probably have acquiesced. But now everything had changed. After the king had left the hall, the Third deputies and a certain number of the Clergy—following a decision made at the end of the previous evening's session—remained in their seats, rejecting the sovereign's command that they leave the room.[16] There was a series of courageous and eloquent speeches by the assembly's most influential orators—including Mirabeau, Sieyès, Camus, and Barnave—reminding the deputies of their two previous oaths and insisting that their creation of a National Assembly could not be undone by a royal declaration. Then by a massive majority they declared themselves covered by parliamentary immunity. Anyone attempting to disperse or arrest them would be "guilty of a capital offense." It was an extraordinarily audacious act, flaunting the direct orders of the king himself.

But the brave words pronounced collectively concealed the enormous emotional turmoil felt by many deputies, the mixture of fear, anger, and consternation as they attempted to cope with a situation in which the monarch himself, long perceived as the stable core and support of their ambitions for reform, now appeared to have disavowed them. The young Thibaudeau found his father and a group from the Poitou delegation sitting somber and shaken after the royal session: "One could see that they had used up more courage than the amount with which they had been endowed." And Campmas described his feelings after the experience: "That terrible evening when it seemed like everyone was in mourning."[17] In the days that followed there were numerous rumors of the impending arrest of the deputies, rumors that seemed only too plausible given the continued presence of large numbers of troops. Though they were allowed once again to enter their hall, their movements were carefully monitored by soldiers, who permitted the deputies to meet only with their own estates, and barred all spectators from the galleries.[18]

Despite the apparent consensus in the Third's public posture, the deputies' writings reveal enormous variations in individual attitudes toward the king. Some now went further than ever before in their criticisms of Louis. The generally radical Basquiat and Lamarque condemned the royal session

[15] Pellerin, entry of June 23; Delandine, 2:184–85; Augustin-Félix-Elisabeth Barin de La Gallissonnière, ms. journal: Arch. de la Guerre, A4 LVI, entry of June 23.

[16] Pellerin, entry of June 22. The response had also been debated in the "Breton Committee": Henri Grégoire, *Mémoires*, ed. H. Carnot, 2 vols. (Paris, 1837–40), 1:380.

[17] Antoine-Claire Thibaudeau, *Biographie, mémoires, 1765–92* (Paris, 1875), 76–77; Campmas, letter of June 27. Cf. Gaultier de Biauzat, 2:135 (letter of June 23).

[18] E. Leflaive, "Le premier représentant de Beaune au parlement: Claude Gantheret," *Société d'archéologie de Beaune. Histoire, lettres, sciences et arts. Mémoires* 42 (1925–29), 69 (letter of late June); Pellerin, entries of June 25 and 27.

as a "lit de justice"; and the more moderate Pellerin deplored the "absolute will" which the monarch had exercised. Visme was also filled with indignation and proclaimed that the Third must never submit like slaves to such arbitrary authority. He emphasized the sullen silence with which Louis was now treated by the people: "What a lesson for the king!" "It would be impossible to show a more pronounced scorn for royal authority," noted Duquesnoy to the prince de Salm-Salm, "and perhaps never was it more justified. When monarchs forget who they are, . . . they must be taught that there is a force more powerful than all the kings on earth, the force of reason, of justice, and of truth."[19]

Yet a great many others went out of their way to place the king's action in a more positive light. While they might well be infuriated by this "act of despotic power," Legendre, Pellerin, Schwendt, Turckheim, Durand, and Campmas, all continued to subscribe to the pervasive myth of the king misled and "taken by surprise." Meifrund, too, persisted in his conviction that "the truth" had not yet reached the king, though as he phrased it, "we will be faithful to him, in spite of himself, in being faithful to the nation."[20] Like several of the others, Gantheret even began wondering if the Assembly had made a mistake in rejecting Louis's propositions out of hand. Though the deputy had no qualms about attacking the nobles, he had great difficulty confronting the authority of the king. Nevertheless, for the first time, he began seriously pondering the question of whether the monarch had the right to give orders to the "Estates General"—as he continued to call it. Like Gantheret, Gaultier de Biauzat was reconsidering the nature of the king's powers—and to some extent revising his opinions from one letter to the next. While he was certain that Louis was being manipulated, he increasingly worried about "the instability of the king's will"; and he concluded that even if the members of the Assembly "must work in concert with the king . . . they can recognize nothing superior to their own authority."[21]

In the midst of their indecision and uncertainty, however, the commoners found their resolution bolstered by forces from without. As earlier in the month, they continued to receive the strongest possible support from the spectators and the local population, who cheered them on from the streets

[19] Basquiat and Lamarque, letter of June 23; Pellerin, entry of June 23; Laurent de Visme, ms. "Journal des Etats généraux": B.N., N.A.Fr. 12938, entry of June 23; Duquesnoy, 121 (entry of June 24).

[20] Durand, entry June 23; Campmas, letter of June 27. La Salle took a similar position: Nicolas-Théodore-Antoine-Adolphe de La Salle, "Les archives municipales de Sarrelouis," ed. René Herly, *Bulletin de la Société des amis du pays de la Sarre* 4 (1927), 201–2 (letter of June 23); Legendre, 528 (letter of June 23); Etienne-François Schwendt and Turckheim, in *L'Alsace pendant la Révolution française*, ed. Rodolphe Reuss, 2 vols. (Paris, 1880–94), 2:112–13 (letter of June 23); Joseph-Michel Pellerin, *Correspondance, 5 mai 1789–29 mai 1790*, ed. Gustave Bord (Paris 1883), 91 (letter of June 28); Pierre-Joseph Meifrund, ms. journal, copy in l'Institut de la Révolution française, entry of June 23.

[21] Gantheret, letter of June 26; Gaultier, 2:135–36, 145 (letters of June 23, 25, and 29).

outside at every occasion. More important in the immediate political configuration was the backing they received from the liberals in the two privileged orders, now jolted into action by the Third's dramatic resolutions. The majority of the Clergy, who had voted for a common verification of credentials on June 19, had finally succeeded in entering the Assembly three days later, marching in procession and carrying their order's registers into the church of Saint-Louis where the Commons had found temporary refuge. Occurring as Gaultier described it, "in a moment of doubt, fear, and pain," the event had stimulated an emotional outpouring: "We openly wept with indescribable joy, like people whose hearts are so unaccustomed to happiness that they cannot hold up under the emotion caused by such a strange new order of things."[22] Though the ecclesiastics' action was originally only for the verification of credentials, Bailly had cleverly acted as though he "presumed that the joint meeting was permanent and for all questions," and in the enthusiasm of the moment, most of the Clergy quickly accepted the expanded significance of their decision.[23] When the same group of clergymen filed into the National Assembly once again on the day after the king's harangue—avoiding the soldiers' blockade by using an unguarded basement passageway—they enormously reinvigorated the deputies' courage.

Perhaps even more significant for the Assembly's self-confidence was the entry on June 25 of forty-seven nobles. During the first seven weeks of the Estates General, the dynamics within the Second Estate had worked against the liberal position. If a small core of individuals—led by Duport, Lafayette, the Lameth brothers, and the comte de Clermont-Tonnerre—had never wavered in their support for a merger with the Third, many others had become increasingly wary. As late as June 22, the comte de Virieu was still suffering in anguish and indecision over the situation. While he was clearly unhappy with the intransigence of the "aristocrats," he was also irritated and frightened by the Commons and their "violence" in unilaterally creating a National Assembly. The nobles would feel more comfortable, he concluded, if only the Third would give its verbal assurance that noble property and influence would be preserved. But even at that, he mused, "is it words that make reality?" Virieu's "comrade" from Dauphiné, the comte de Lablache, also recounted "the extreme agitation which they had felt for some time," as he and his associates struggled to decide whether to abandon their order.[24] When Virieu polled his friends on June 22, he found only thirty-two prepared to cross over, and of these all but twelve or fourteen

---

[22] Gaultier, 2:134–35 (letter of June 23). See also Jean-Baptiste Poncet-Delpech, "Documents sur les premiers mois de la Révolution," ed. Daniel Ligou, *AHRF* 38 (1966), 434 (letter of June 27).

[23] Bailly, 1:203 (entry of June 22).

[24] François-Henri de Virieu to the marquis de Viennois, letter of June 22; Alexandre-Joseph de Lablache, letter of June 24: both in Archives of the Château d'Avauges, reproduced in A.D. Isère, 1 Mi 461.

were talking of doing so merely to verify credentials.[25] The final decision came after an all-night discussion among the liberals on June 24–25, apparently at the residence of the marquis de Montesquiou. Passing in review all of the events of the previous days—including the king's "act of force," the decision of the majority of the Clergy, and the strong support of the general population—forty-seven gentlemen finally determined to join their commoner and clerical colleagues.[26] Their entry into the hall on the morning of June 25 excited another explosion of emotion. Amidst thunderous applause that lasted well over fifteen minutes, the nobles were introduced one by one—as the secretaries read aloud some of the greatest family names of the kingdom—and the deputies present rushed down from their seats to greet and embrace the new arrivals. Duquesnoy was overcome with joy: "The sight of these brave and virtuous knights, arriving to sit in the midst of a nation accustomed to honoring them, was enormously touching and imposing. . . . The French nobility has covered itself in eternal glory." The very warmth and enthusiasm of the Third's welcome rekindled Lablache's courage and convinced him that he had made the right decision.[27]

At any rate, the full complement of the three orders was finally brought together on the late afternoon of June 27, when the king shifted his position yet again and "invited" the rump of the Clergy and the Nobility to sit with a combined "Estates General." To what extent the king was reacting to the threat of popular uprising and military mutiny, or to what extent he was involved in an elaborate ruse to buy time while a military "coup d'état" was organized, remains uncertain.[28] For a great many Nobles and bishops, it was a deeply humiliating, traumatic experience. Throughout the previous week, Garron de La Bévière had grown increasingly fatalistic about the trend of events. He ultimately concluded that the Nobility "had no choice but to bow to the will of 23 million people, who think they are embracing freedom, but who are actually chaining themselves to an aristocracy of the masses." Yet he was also prepared to fight, if necessary, to defend the monarchy and preserve the Nobles' honor.[29] And even after receiving the king's letter that morning, many of the gentlemen present would have preferred to refuse the "invitation." It took a missive from the comte d'Artois, indicating that the king's life was in danger, to persuade them to cross over to the "National Assembly."[30] When the dissidents entered the hall, they did so

[25] Virieu, letter of June 22.

[26] Virieu, letter of June 25. Also François-Emmanuel Toulongeon, *Histoire de la France depuis la Révolution*, 7 vols. (Paris, 1801), 1:56.

[27] Duquesnoy 1:129, 138 (entries of June 26 and 28); Lablache, letter of June 26. See also Delandine, 2:193–94.

[28] See Pierre Caron, "La tentative de contre-révolution de juin-juillet 1789," *Revue d'histoire moderne* 7 (1906–1907), 5–34, 649–78.

[29] La Bévière, letters of June 23 and 25.

[30] La Gallissonnière, entry of June 27; Jean-Baptiste de Cernon de Pinteville to his brother: A.D. Marne, J 2286, undated letter of ca. June 27; Ambroise-Eulalie de Maurès de Malartic, ms. "Journal de ma députation aux Etats généraux": B.M. La Rochelle, ms. 21, entry of June

with deep and, in some cases, unforgiving bitterness and a sense of dishonor. La Gallissonnière inscribed the scene in his diary: "Thus it was that the representatives of the French nobility, numbering some 210, with tears in their eyes and rage and despair in their hearts," slowly filed into the room. Delaville Le Roulx, one of the few commoners present at the time—the privileged orders having arrived during a prearranged recess—was also impressed by the scene. They entered, he said "some still inflamed with fury, others overwhelmed with sadness and embarrassed even to sit down: . . . an altogether extraordinary sight."[31]

Though the Assembly's reception for these final recruits was cooler than for the earlier crossovers, the "excitement and enthusiasm" were still sufficiently great for Bailly to adjourn the meeting. There were no sessions on June 28 and 29—a Sunday followed by the Monday feast-day of Saint Peter—and the deputies and the population of Versailles and Paris gave themselves over to a general celebration. "These days," as Pellerin described it, "were turned over to joyful festivities, commemorating that moment, forever memorable, when one of the greatest revolutions in the history of the French nation came to pass."[32]

THE MID-JULY CRISIS

When the deputies returned to their benches on June 30, the initial prospects for the newly united National Assembly seemed a good deal short of Pellerin's enthusiastic assessment. Well over a hundred members of the Second Estate and a smaller number of the Clergy began the day with separate meetings of their own and arrived in the Assembly only toward mid-day, ostentatiously entering as a group and sitting separately in the hall. They formally announced that they would not participate in debates—at least not until they received new mandates from their constituencies allowing them to vote by head. They also proclaimed their continued rejection of the National Assembly's decrees of June 17, 20, and 23, and their intention of abiding only by the king's declaration in the royal session. On July 9, they voted in separate session to reject Mirabeau's motion against the military buildup in Paris passed earlier that day, thus maintaining their pretensions of veto power over all legislation.[33] Many of the dissidents—like the baron de Gauville, the comte d'Iversay, the marquis de Montesson, and the mar-

---

27; Raymond-Antoine de Banyuls de Monferré and Michel de Coma Serra to correspondence committee of Perpignan: A.D. Pyrénées-Orientales, C 2119, letter of June 30, 1789; Charles-Elie de Ferrières, *Correspondance inédite*, ed. Henri Carré (Paris, 1932), 77 (letter of June 28).

[31] La Gallissonnière, letter of June 27; Joseph Delaville Le Roulx to the municipality of Lorient: A.C. Lorient, BB 12, letter of June 29.

[32] Bailly, 1:252–53 (entry of June 27); Pellerin, ms., entry of June 27.

[33] Bailly, 1:261–62, 282–84 (entries of June 30 and July 4); Banyuls and Coma Serra, letter of July 4; Malartic, entry of July 9; Durand, letter of June 30; Delaville, letter of July 11.

quis de Laqueuille—left Versailles altogether, some to seek revised mandates, others attempting to resign. Eventually almost all of them returned. Even those who sought to abandon the Assembly were forced back by their constituencies or by a hostile population.[34] Yet a substantial number of noble and clerical deputies—including such intransigent spokesmen as Eprémesnil, Maury, and Cazalès—remained absent from their posts for most of the month.[35] Votes taken during this period suggest that only seven to eight hundred deputies were regularly attending, compared to more than a thousand in August and September.[36]

The absence of the most articulate reactionary leaders during this period undoubtedly helped reduce the confrontational atmosphere within the Assembly. Throughout July and early August many of the deputies from all three estates felt swept up in a new feeling of national unity and brotherhood. The marquis de Sillery had already attempted to set the tone on June 25 in an impassioned plea for reconciliation: "Let us forget the first moments of anxiety that separated us . . . and contemplate the tempest with equanimity, . . . keeping in mind only the happiness of the people entrusted to us; and may this sacred goal bring together our hearts and our minds." Sensing the broad desire for unity and security in the present situation, Sillery drew on the tried and tested image of the paternal monarch: "He calls us his children! Ah! We must all see ourselves as a reunited family, each with a different role in our father's house."[37]

After the two-day break at the end of June, there was a marked transformation in sentiments among many of the previously intransigent deputies. The comte de La Gallissonnière—who had only recently called for exemplary executions of the Third leadership—now found that "the deputies had calmed a bit, their fears were less great, and a new order of things seemed to appear." The baron de Pinteville was moved by the warmth of the Third deputies as they greeted him in the streets of Versailles. He too sensed a sharp reversal in attitudes among individuals who had long held back from a sense of fear and honor, but who were now penetrated with feelings of

---

[34] Louis-Henri-Charles de Gauville, *Journal*, ed. Edouard de Barthélémy (Paris, 1864), 13–14; Maupetit, 18 (1902), 461 (letter of July 11); Francisque Mège, "Notes biographiques sur les députés de la Basse-Auvergne," *Mémoires de l'Académie des sciences, belles-lettres, et arts, Clermont-Ferrand* 7 (1865), 85. Both the abbé de Pradt and the comte de Montrevel fled but were forced back by the threat of popular violence: Michel Leymarie. "Quelques lettres de l'abbé de Pradt, 1789–92," *Revue de la Haute-Auvergne* 34 (1954–55), 89–91; La Bévière, letter of July 22.

[35] Gontier de Biran, letter of July 17; François-Antoine Boissy d'Anglas, "Lettres inédites sur la Révolution française," ed. René Puaux, *Bulletin de la Société de l'histoire du Protestantisme français* 75 (1926), 293, 299 (letters of July 25 and 28); Pierre-Siffren Boulouvard to municipality of Arles: A.C. Arles, AA 23, letter of July 27; La Bévière, letter of July 27.

[36] Among votes in July, the following tallies were recorded: 756 voting on July 4; 728 on July 8; 696 on July 20; 794 on July 24: *AP*, 8:190, 208, 251, 271; Pellerin, entry of July 4. Among later votes: 1003 on August 4; 1009 on Sept. 11; 963 on Sept. 17: *AP*, 8:341, 612; 9:25.

[37] *AP*, 8:154. A better summary is in Delandine, 2:218–22.

patriotism and an impatience to set to work after the long weeks of inactivity. For the marquis de Ferrières the experience was a revelation. Nervous at first, he soon discovered that he was far more at ease with the commoners of the Third Estate than with the great court nobles, whom he had always detested. Though he remained convinced of his order's innate superiority, he believed that the nobility must now reconcile itself to the new social situation and "raise up to its level the wealthy and honest citizens of the bourgeoisie." "I would much prefer," he wrote, "that a bourgeois imagine he's my equal than to see a great aristocrat think I'm his inferior."[38] The marquis de Guilhem-Clermont-Lodève, the chevalier de Boufflers, bishops Talleyrand and La Fare, and archbishop Boisgelin, all made the transition with relative ease. For some it was a question of "bending to circumstances," as Boufflers put it. "There remained only one rational course of action," recalled Talleyrand, "to yield freely before being compelled, and while one could still earn favor from doing so." Others acted with a real measure of idealism and enthusiasm, convinced that "the nobility . . . could also play a useful role in the common hall of the Estates General." "All was forgotten," wrote Pinteville to his brother, "so we could dedicate ourselves to the task at hand."[39]

In any case, by July 11 only eighty nobles were still attending the order's separate sessions, down by half from the week before.[40] Despite their earlier pronouncements, many of the formerly dissident gentlemen and ecclesiastics began openly participating in debates and votes in the general assembly. Duquesnoy took careful note of the July 1 debate on the problem of troop mutinies, the first such discussion in which many of the Third's former adversaries took part. "So the Nobility has now clearly voted by head; if I can believe what I see, a substantial portion of this order fully intends to reconcile itself to public opinion and work for the success of the Estates."[41]

The integration of the Assembly was facilitated by the commoners' self-conscious efforts to help the dissident nobles and clergymen save face and find a meaningful roll in the political process. The recess called on June 27, shortly before the privileged deputies were scheduled to arrive, was conceived to ease the dissidents' embarrassment and prevent their humiliation.[42] Thereafter the patriots frequently ignored the privileged orders' more pro-

---

[38] La Gallissonnière, folio 154; Pinteville, letter of June 27; Ferrières, *Correspondance*, 78–79, 82–83, 120 (letters of July 3 and 10, and Aug. 10).

[39] La Gallissonnière, letter of June 30; Charles-Maurice de Talleyrand, *Mémoires*, ed. Duc de Broglie, 5 vols. (Paris, 1891–92), 1:123–24; Charles-François de Guilhem-Clermont-Lodève to the municipality of Arles: A.C. Arles, AA 23, letter of Aug. 2; Bernard de Brye, *Un évêque d'ancien régime à l'épreuve de la Révolution. Le cardinal A.L.H. de La Fare (1752–1829)* (Paris, 1985), 249–59; Eugène Lavaquery, *Le Cardinal de Boisgelin, 1732–1804*, 2 vols. (Paris, 1920), 2:13–15; Pinteville, letter of June 27.

[40] Bailly, 1:317 (entry of July 11); Gauville, 9.

[41] Duquesnoy, 1:151 (entry of July 2). Cf. Gaultier, 2:153 (letter of July 2); and Pellerin, entry of July 9.

[42] Pellerin, letter of June 27.

vocative comments: "We will have no problem overlooking a few words," wrote Delaville, "as long as the three orders vote together by head."[43] Many commoners self-consciously restricted their own speeches in order to allow the greater participation of nobles and clergymen. The usually irrepressible Gaultier announced he was keeping a low profile in early July, since he and his colleagues "could not ask for more than to see the first two orders take part in the debate." "For the time being," wrote Toulongeon, "the orators of the Third Estate had yielded the rostrum; the nobles, they said, should be allowed to bring out their feelings by speaking their minds."[44]

Throughout this process, the regular discussion meetings of the "bureaus" also played an integrating role—as they had previously helped integrate the differing factions of the Third Estate. Ferrières, who felt unable to talk in the general assemblies for want of lung power, was delighted to discover that he could speak with ease in the smaller discussion groups and that the commoners listened "with a great deal of decency." La Bévière likewise took pleasure that his observations in the bureaus "were appreciated." By the end of the month he was strongly defending the "new system," convinced that the great majority of commoner deputies were "fair" and "reasonable."[45] It was hardly an accident, moreover, that in the first election of bureau presidents, all of those chosen, without exception, were members of the privileged orders.[46] Before stepping down from the presidency at the beginning of July, Bailly urged that future presidents of the full Assembly be chosen by rotation from among the three orders; and for the next two months, this arrangement was carefully followed.[47]

Yet the deference shown by the commoners toward the privileged orders arose not merely from political calculation. Whatever their antagonism toward the "aristocrats," many commoners were still awed by the great nobility and flattered that they might join with them in the same assembly—as long as they felt they were treated as equals. Duquesnoy was effusive with praise for "the finest names in the kingdom" who were now sitting beside them, "the most virtuous men in the kingdom," who gave the Assembly "an air of seriousness" which it had not previously known. Gallot and Gantheret, who normally had little use for "aristocrats," conveyed to their families their obvious pleasure in rubbing shoulders with the Great on the benches of the bureaus or the general sessions. Visme was surprised to find that "there are many talented individuals among the nobles," several of

[43] Delaville, letter of June 26.

[44] Gaultier, 157 (letter of July 3); Toulongeon, 1:111. See also Visme, entry of July 1.

[45] Ferrières, *Correspondance*, 84 (letter of July 10); La Bévière, letters of July 22 and 27. See also Malartic, entry of July 2.

[46] *AP*, 8:185 (July 3).

[47] Bailly, 1:274–75 (entry of July 2); Charles-François Bouche, letter to the "commissaires des communautés de Provence," A.D. Bouches-du-Rhône, C 1046, letter of Aug. 31; La Gallissonnière, folio 153. Thus, in the election of Aug. 29, 802 of the 834 votes cast were for ecclesiastics: A.N., C 83, dos. 818 (1-3).

whom spoke with "remarkable ease." Ménard de La Groye, who had felt almost ashamed of his growing anger toward the Second Estate in early June, again felt comfortable when he dined with them and was elated to observe "so much unity and cordiality among all the members of our Assembly." The astute Ferrières rapidly sized up the situation: "The upper Third will be flattered by the Nobles' consideration toward them; they have no hatred for the Nobles. . . . If the Nobles take one step, the Third will take ten."[48]

In the short term, at least, this sense of unity was fused and tempered in the fires of the great mid-July crisis. Through the first ten days of the month the deputies of the three orders had anxiously followed the growing concentration of troops being assembled in the region of Versailles and Paris, and they were clearly shaken when the king ignored their pleas to have the detachments removed. Tensions were heightened in the face of a growing popular unrest in Paris and an outbreak of military mutinies in Versailles.[49] Yet few could have anticipated the dismissal of Necker on July 12 and the ensuing Parisian insurrection.

Indeed, for most of the representatives, the period from July 12 to 15 was the most harrowing moment in their entire Constituent career. The heavily armed troops positioned in their midst—many of them mercenaries who spoke no French—the full-scale battles in the heart of Paris, the brutal assassination and decapitation of several officials: all left the Assembly confused and terrified. As rumors spread of a popular march on Versailles and of their own impending arrest or execution, the deputies could do little but remain in their hall and hope for the best.[50] In stoic fashion they pursued their debates on the constitution as though nothing were amiss. But Bailly admitted the near impossibility of maintaining composure under such conditions: "The thought of Paris dominated everything else and influenced all our motions."[51] Individuals were constantly pacing in the aisles, stepping outside the hall to look in the direction of Paris, and even putting their ears to the ground to listen for horses or cannon fire. The hundred or so deputies who had been caught by events in the city hurried back to their posts, some by circuitous routes in order to avoid the military blockades. Fearing imminent military action to disband the Assembly, they held permanent sessions on twelve-hour rotating shifts, with some deputies present in the

[48] Duquesnoy, 1:128–31 (entry of June 26); Gallot to his wife, 114 (letter of July 2); Gantheret, letter of July 3; Visme, entry of July 7; François-René-Pierre Ménard de La Groye to his wife: A.D. Sarthe, 10 J 122, letter of July 7; Ferrières, *Correspondance*, 120 (letter of Aug. 10).

[49] The king's reply of July 11 justified the troops by the need to preserve order in the Parisian area: *AP*, 8:219.

[50] Bertrand Barère, *Mémoires*, ed. Hippolyte Carnot, 4 vols. (Paris, 1842–44), 1:257; Delandine, 3:129; Félix Faulcon, *Correspondance. Tome 2: 1789–91*, ed. G. Debien (Poitiers, 1953), 53–56 (entries of July 12–13); and Duquesnoy, 1:184 (entry of July 10); Delaville Le Roulx, July 17.

[51] Bailly, 1:360–61 and 363 (entry of July 14).

hall day and night. The elderly lawyer and historian Thibaudeau returned to his apartment at night, but slept with the door barricaded shut and his son beside him, armed with swords and pistols. Curé Grégoire, anticipating his arrest, hid a portion of the Assembly's archives with Madame Emmery, the wife of his colleague from Lorraine. With the tension almost unbearable, Boissy d'Anglas wrote home to his wife, "I can scarcely describe the frightful state in which I find myself." Gantheret, terrified once again, passed along the rumor that "we were all to be assassinated or, at the very least, to be carried off and arrested."[52]

On July 13, many of the dissident Nobles still present in the Assembly declared their solidarity with the common front, affirming "that the dangers and calamities suffered by the nation no longer permitted them to boycott votes; that from now on they ... promised to share with the rest of the Assembly a common voice and a common heart."[53] Several gave rousing speeches, appealing to Roman examples of courage in the face of crisis and declaring their readiness to die at their posts rather than abandon the task of writing a constitution.[54] They too remained in the hall throughout the night, mixing with the commoners in a spirit of camaraderie. The Poitiers magistrate, Faulcon, described in his diary the scene at three in the morning: "It is here that a merging of ranks begins. These proud nobles, once so favored by the blind chance of birth and by their claims of privilege, sleep now or walk about the hall, mixed together with the commoners."[55]

For the National Assembly, the turning point was not the fall of the Bastille as such. The uncertain stories of armed insurrections and assassinations throughout Paris initially only added to the anxiety, and it was several days later that the capture of the great medieval fortress in the center of Paris became a symbol of victory.[56] The critical event for the deputies was Louis XVI's entry into the Assembly on the morning of July 15. Arriving with only a few minutes advance warning, the king appeared with very little pomp, accompanied only by his two brothers and a handful of soldiers. Badly shaken as much by the threat of a mass military mutiny as by the popular uprisings, he now fully acquiesced to the deputies' declarations of June, accepted the existence of a National Assembly, and vowed to work with the Assembly for the salvation of the Nation.[57] Before the king's appearance, the deputies briefly debated whether they should applaud him in the hall. But once he was in their midst and the essence of his speech became apparent, they lost all sense of decorum and answered his words with thundering and repeated cheers. There was an extraordinary release from

---

[52] Bailly, 1:343, 360–61 (entries of July 13 and 14); Thibaudeau, 82; Grégoire, 1:382–83; Boissy d'Anglas, 286 (letter of July 12); Gantheret, letter of July 15.

[53] Delandine, 3:127.

[54] Bailly, 1:335, 340 (entry of July 13).

[55] Faulcon, 69 (entry of July 15).

[56] E.g., Delandine, 3:166–67.

[57] *AP*, 8:236–37.

the days of pent-up tensions. They stood on their benches, threw their hats in the air, embraced, wept, shouted "long live the king," and clapped again for joy: "as on the first day of a beautiful new century." Several of those present—"so worn out with emotion"—fainted and had to be carried out of the hall (including the stuffy master of ceremonies, the marquis de Brezé, who had tried for weeks to maintain proper order). The distinguished lawyer from Besançon, Jean-Denis Blanc, succumbed to a stroke, literally "dying for joy," as one witness described it.[58] Deputy judges, nobles, and merchants were so moved that they could only recount their experiences in a kind of jumbled kaleidoscope of impressions inscribed in their diaries or written home to colleagues: "I have difficulty controlling my feelings," apologized Delaville, "and I am unable to put any order in my writing."[59] The celebration continued as Louis left the hall and returned on foot to the palace. The weather, wet and stormy since mid-May, had now turned beautiful again, and the king was accompanied by the entire National Assembly, mixed together pell-mell without distinction or order, gathered to protect him from the great surge of people outside.[60] As they reached the palace, the royal band struck up the song by Grétry, "Where are you better than at home with your family."[61] The holiday atmosphere was prolonged over the next three days, as Louis and most of the deputies traveled to Paris and marched in procession through the streets, lined with thousands of citizen soldiers. Here they were welcomed by the deputies Bailly and Lafayette, now appointed mayor and military commander of the city.

On the morning of July 16, almost one month after the creation of the National Assembly, the last of the noble and clerical deputies still boycotting the Assembly formally declared their readiness to participate. In explaining their action, the vicomte de Malartic referred both to "the imperious law of necessity" and to their desire to follow "a king so worthy of leading." The Toul magistrate Claude-Pierre Maillot assessed the situation more succinctly: "Severed heads are a powerful lesson."[62] In the days that followed, numerous nobles commented on the remarkable sense of unity and harmony which they now perceived within the Assembly. Comte de Lablache, so fearful of joining the Third a few weeks before, was now filled with enthusiasm: "All obstacles and difficulties have been overcome. The tide is in and we are ready to sail; no force, no power can halt our advance." "We thought we had found the best road for the good of the country,"

[58] Gaultier, 2:179 (letter of July 16); Faulcon, 74 (entry of July 15); Delaville, letter of July 17. See also, in particular, Bailly, 2:5 (letter of July 15); Jacques Jallet, *Journal inédit*, ed. J.-J. Brethé (Fontenay-le-Comte, 1871), 139 (entry of July 15); Duquesnoy, 1:210 (entry of July 18); Pellerin, entry of July 15; Ferrières, *Mémoires*, 1:139–44.

[59] Delaville, letter of July 17. Also, Maillot, entry of July 18; Lablache, letter of July 16.

[60] E.g., Delandine, 3:144; Pellerin, entry of July 15; Gantheret, letter of July 15.

[61] Poncet, 566 (letter of July 15); Delandine, 3:144; Bailly, 2:9 (entry of July 15).

[62] Malartic, entry of July 16; Maillot, entry of July 18. See also Banyuls and Coma Serra, letter of July 16; and Visme, entry of July 29; Bailly, 2:38–39 (entry of July 16).

mused La Bévière. "We have been shown how to arrive there by another route. . . . That is my manner of seeing things, as a good citizen should. It is time to regenerate the state."[63]

The new feeling of concord was also shared by the commoners. Bouche wrote of the "unity and understanding [which] continue to reign among the three orders"; Maillot of "the strong union" between the privileged and the commoners; Francoville of "a single desire within the Assembly."[64] With the recent turn of events, Lepoutre at last felt secure enough to have his wife send him a few jars of his precious Flemish butter—which he had feared losing in shipment if the Assembly were dissolved. "Peace and unity reign among all members, no matter what their order or profession. . . . It's as if they shared a common will." And he told his wife how he had recently sat in the Assembly next to the duc d'Orléans and the archbishop of Bordeaux, both of whom had conversed with him as with an equal.[65] Indeed, Delandine seemed to envision a complete disappearance of social distinctions: "The union existing among the three orders, held together by a rapprochement of ideas and a unity of desires, . . . will eliminate the arrogant and destructive principles of the aristocracy. . . . Frenchmen of all ranks and all classes, bringing to an end the vain distinctions which have divided them, will unite to build the foundations of their freedom and happiness."[66] This vision of unity and fraternal cooperation between the orders, short lived though it might be, was undoubtedly an element in the extraordinary atmosphere of the night of August 4.

VIOLENCE

Yet there was another critical element in the Assembly's dynamic in the weeks preceding August 4: the fear and apprehension engendered by the explosion of popular violence and the emergence of the lower classes as a political force. Since their arrival in Versailles, many deputies had grown to appreciate the support lent them by the Versailles and Parisian populations.[67] But despite the rhetoric about the public being "their masters," few of the deputies would have defined that "public" to include the lower classes, and few would have envisioned a role for popular violence in the reforming process. For the vast majority of the deputies, collective violence was probably quite foreign to their day-to-day experience. If the eighteenth century

[63] Lablache, letter of July 29; and La Bévière, letter of July 22. See also Delandine, 3:3.

[64] Pierre-François Bouche, letter of Aug. 2; Maillot, entry of Aug. 1; Charles Francoville, "Les rapports du député Charles Francoville au comité de correspondance d'Ardres," in François de Saint-Just, *Chronique intime des Garnier d'Ardres* (Paris, 1973), 118 (letter of Aug. 3).

[65] Pierre-François Lepoutre to his wife: family archives of Adolphe Lepoutre-Dubreuil, Montignac-sur-Vezère, letters of July 16 and 24, and Aug. 4.

[66] Delandine, 4:3.

[67] See above, chap. 3.

had known its occasional grain riots and tax riots—including a spate around Paris in the 1770s and 1780s—the large-scale, provincewide uprisings of the age of Louis XIV had long since disappeared.[68] Those deputies already present in Paris in late April were shocked by the Réveillon riots and by the "wicked madmen," the "pack of scoundrels," who participated in them.[69] They felt scarcely more sympathy for the riots around Versailles in early July.[70] Most would have agreed with Delandine, writing in early July, that the consolidation of the National Assembly must be achieved "through no other force than the force of reason, of justice, and of public opinion."[71]

The deputies were likewise appalled by the violence and killings in Paris following the dismissal of Necker, violence described in graphic, firsthand accounts by delegates who had just returned from the city.[72] Still it could escape no one that the very survival of the Assembly had been threatened. Even during the crisis, some of the deputies were ready to accept the riots as a lesser evil. "No matter how horrible these events may be," wrote Creuzé-Latouche, "we think that the ministers were preparing even more terrible actions." The usually moderate Faulcon noted in his diary, "the behavior of the court and the ministers is so horrible and oppressive, that we must free ourselves from them, no matter what the price."[73] After the fact, once it was clear that the popular uprising and the associated mutinies had been key elements in winning the king's support, nearly all of the patriots tended to justify the violence. By July 16 they had convinced themselves that the murdered officials got what they deserved and that in the current political struggle, "much more was accomplished through fear than through the desire for the good."[74] They persuaded themselves, moreover, that the crowd's actions were specifically conceived to support the objectives of the National Assembly. If "the most faithful and affectionate of people" had acted as they did, concluded Delaville, it was all because of the Nobles' "insistence on voting by order."[75]

This more positive image of the crowds was enhanced by the reception

[68] See Guy Lemarchand, "Troubles populaires au XVIIIe siècle et conscience de classe," *AHRF* 279 (1990), 32–48.

[69] Julien-François Palasne de Champeaux and Jean-François-Pierre Poulain de Corbion to the municipality of Saint-Brieuc, "Correspondance des députés des Côtes-du-Nord aux Etats généraux et à l'Assemblée nationale constituante," ed. D. Tempier, *Bulletins et mémoires de la Société d'émulation des Côtes-du-Nord* 26 (1888), 218 (letter of May 1); Gaultier, 2:16 (letter of April 30).

[70] Durand, entry of July 1; Boullé, 14 (1889), 45 (letter of July 1); Duquesnoy, 1:148–49 (entry of July 2); Ménard, 55–56 (letter of July 3).

[71] Delandine, 3:4.

[72] E.g., Lasalle, 207–8 (letter of July 16); and Pellerin, letter of July 14.

[73] Creuzé, 231, entry of July 14; Faulcon, 65, entry of July 14.

[74] Gaultier, 2:177 (letter of July 16). See also, e.g., Durand, entry of July 16; Visme, entry of July 17; Dinochau, 1: 5–6.

[75] Delaville, letter of July 18. See also the letters of Alquier to the municipality of La Rochelle, dated July 13 and 18: H. Perrin de Boussac, *Un témoin de la Révolution et de l'Empire: Charles-Jean-Marie Alquier* (Paris, 1983), 37–38.

which the deputies received when they traveled to Paris soon after the fall of the Bastille. Almost all commented on the discipline and good order of the citizens' national guard only recently organized by the municipal leaders; on the large numbers of individuals perfectly arrayed along the roads with muskets at their sides.[76] Even more moving was the personal affection, the veritable reverence which the people displayed toward them—a reverence which no one could fail to contrast with the initially cool reception offered to the king. Gallot encountered "the most touching scene imaginable. Men, women, and children held us in their arms, and covered us with tears of joy." "Never has my heart been so moved with feeling," wrote Lofficial to his wife, "a sentiment quite impossible to express." Boissy d'Anglas found it difficult even to slip away for a quiet beer: as soon as people discovered who he was, they rushed up, took off their hats, and began cheering (and anyone who neglected to remove his hat was made to do so by his neighbors).[77]

Yet in most cases the warm affection between the deputies and the masses was of relatively short duration. In the eyes of most legislators the rescue of the National Assembly had been the sole justification for the violence. Yet even after that rescue had been consummated, the unrest in the capital continued and spread rapidly throughout the countryside. Bailly had scarcely taken office in the Paris city hall when he was forced to intervene outside the building to save a woman—found dressed as a man—from being murdered by a crowd.[78] Traveling through the city on July 16, Maillot recoiled in horror before the severed heads paraded on pikes and the lynching of an unknown man which he witnessed inadvertently.[79] Two days later, forty or fifty deputies had to take action in Versailles to prevent a crowd from killing two soldiers, and a smaller detachment from the Assembly rushed to the nearby community of Poissy to rescue a baker, found by the deputies with a noose around his neck about to be hanged. In this case, the baker was saved only after the bishop of Chartres fell to his knees and begged for mercy—a story recounted to the Assembly on July 20 in horrifying detail.[80]

To judge by the deputies' letters and diaries, the single most traumatic event involving collective violence—an event which probably left a far greater impression on the deputies than the attack on the Bastille—was the July 22 lynchings of the royal official Foullon de Doué and his son-in-law, the intendant of Paris, Bertier de Sauvigny—both accused of involvement in grain hoarding schemes. Foulon had been in protective custody in the presence of Bailly and Lafayette when he was dragged out of the city hall

---

[76] E.g., Duquesnoy, 1:210–13 (entry of July 16).

[77] Gallot, 118 (letter of July 20); Lofficial, 91 (letter of July 17); Boissy d'Anglas, 291 (letter of July 17). See also, e.g., Boullé, 14 (1889), 120 (letter of July 21); Durand, entry of July 16; Basquiat and Lamarque, letter of July 17.

[78] Bailly, 2:32 (entry of July 15).

[79] Maillot, entry of July 18.

[80] Delandine, 3:174–75; Pellerin, entries of July 18 and 19; Gaultier, 185–86 (letter of July 18); *AP*, 8:249–51.

council room and hanged from a light post. The man's heart was then cut out and returned to the same council room and presented to the city leaders. "We all looked away," wrote Bailly. Bertier suffered a similar fate after first being presented with his father-in-law's severed head: "It was a day of atrocities and of mourning."[81]

Démeunier's detailed narration of these events to the Assembly sparked a lengthy exchange over what, if anything, should be done to restore law and order to the country.[82] Of the thirty-seven individuals whose contemporary reactions can be ascertained in diaries or letters, only slightly over a fourth—including nine commoners and one curé—were prepared to vindicate the people for the lynchings. For the most part, they followed the logic of Barnave in his oft-cited phrase: "This blood that was shed, was it then so pure?"[83] The two men executed were, after all, "scoundrels"—as Jallet called them—presumed to have participated in plots against Paris and the National Assembly and, perhaps, to have manipulated the food supply. They had been submitted to popular justice and sentenced, as Robespierre wrote, "by the decision of the people."[84] The people had been tricked in the past and understandably mistrusted the Old Regime authorities, fearing that the official tribunals might once again allow the guilty to go free. Significantly, all but one of those sympathetic to the crowds were linked to the most radical faction of the deputies and would soon be associated with the Jacobin Club.[85]

But three-fourths of our witnesses, including moderates, and conservatives alike, condemned such popular violence in strong and uncompromising terms.[86] The large number of judges and legal men were horrified by the way in which the judicial process had been travestied: "No matter how strong the evidence against an individual," wrote the lawyer and legal scholar Gaultier, "can one dispense with the rules of justice which alone can preserve the innocent from the possibility of error?" Delandine had difficulty believing that these were the same people who had stormed the Bastille. If decent citizens were among the crowd, they could only have been

---

[81] Bailly, esp. 2:99 and 123 (entry of July 22).

[82] *AP*, 8:265 (July 23).

[83] Barnave later regretted his words: *Oeuvres de Barnave*, ed. M. Bérenger, 4 vols. (Paris, 1843), 1:107–9.

[84] Maximilien Robespierre to Buissart, *Correspondance de Maximilien Robespierre*, ed. Georges Michon, 2 vols. (Paris, 1926–41), 50 (letter of July 23); Jallet, 155–56 (entries of July 22 and 23).

[85] The ten deputies considered here are Basquiet de Mugriet, Bouchette, Boulouvard, Creuzé-Latouche, Gallot, Jallet, Lepoutre, Ménard de La Groye, Robespierre, and Verdollin. All but Verdollin were associated with the Jacobins.

[86] The 27 deputies considered here are Bailly, Barbotin, Boissy d'Anglas, Boullé, Campmas, Castelanet, Clermont-Tonnerre, Colaud de La Salcette, Delabat, Delandine, Delaville Le Roulx, Durand, Faulcon, Garron de La Bévière, Gaultier de Biauzat, Grellet de Beauregard, Lasalle, Lejean, Mounier, Lofficial, Pellerin, Périsse Du Luc, Rabaut Saint-Etienne, Roussieux, Toulongeon, Turckheim, and Visme.

misled and deceived by "outsiders" or "homeless vagabonds."[87] Indeed, for most of the witnesses the perpetrators of the crimes were scarcely recognizable as the same species of human being. They could only have been "a people of cannibals" (Lofficial); "more barbarous . . . than cannibals, tigers, or lions" (Périsse Du Luc); committing "atrocious and barbarous acts" (Visme).[88] Many of the deputies were so profoundly shaken by the affair, that they would never again view the common people without suspicion and a certain terror. The young Faulcon, who was still only an alternate deputy, made it clear to his friends in Poitou that he was leaving Paris because of his horror over the two killings—killings which he had directly witnessed. "That hideous scene: what unimaginable refinements of cruelty," "Ah! Never will I forget that sight." The Strasbourg deputy Turckheim announced that the violence of July had entirely changed his views on the Revolution. The comte de Clermont-Tonnerre, until that time one of the principal leaders of the liberal nobles, indicated that the two "executions" placed events in an altogether different light: "I feared we might all become barbarous; I thought of the Saint-Bartholomew's Day Massacre . . . and I asked myself, painfully, if we were even worthy of being free."[89]

THE NIGHT OF AUGUST 4

It was a cruel irony that at the very moment when the National Assembly seemed penetrated with a climate of optimism and goodwill, the world outside was aswirl with violence, insurrections, and collective disobedience. Throughout July and early August virtually every session began with a reading of letters sent in from the provinces, appealing for help in the face of threatening "brigands," aristocratic plots, attacks on property, and a general refusal to obey authority—much of it part of the panic upheaval known to historians as the Great Fear. For the first time, representatives began to receive word of violence in their own home towns. But with communications disrupted and the mail even slower than usual, the deputies often waited for days without receiving reliable reports. Curé Barbotin was devastated to hear reports of popular unrest in his province of Hainaut, a region he had imagined to be immune from such troubles: "I am in a state of mortal anxiety. Write to me soon and hide nothing from me. If my house has been struck with misfortune, I will have to know it sooner or later." Misfortune had struck indeed for the comte de Virieu and the marquis de Langon who learned of attacks on their properties in Dauphiné: "Thus, the

---

[87] Gaultier, 2:194 (letter of July 22); Delandine, 3: 229–33.

[88] Lofficial, 96 (letter of July 24); Jean-André Périsse Du Luc to J. B. Willermoz: B.M. Lyon ms. 5430, letter of July 24; Visme, entry of July 22.

[89] Faulcon, 91 and 104 (entry of July 22 and letter of July 28 to Conneau-Desfontaines); Turckheim, 1:255 (report of Nov. 1789); Charles Du Bus, *Stanislas de Clermont-Tonnerre et l'échec de la Révolution monarchique, 1757–92* (Paris, 1931), 123.

honor of being your deputies costs us dearly." The marquis de Ferrières—who had once waxed eloquent on the warm paternal relations
between lords and "vassals"—was overcome with alarm. He wrote to his
wife in Poitou to bury their money in the lower wine cellar, refill the
moat, and flee to Poitiers. (His more sensible wife replied that filling the
moat would only scare the peasants, and that she had to stay home and
bring in the harvest.)[90]

The commoner deputies probably suffered far fewer attacks against their
personal property, but they too remained fearful for the safety of their families, and worried that the chaos would serve as an excuse for foreign intervention, destroying all the gains they had made.[91] No less than the countrypeople, the deputies—both radicals and conservatives—believed in a whole
range of plots perpetrated by a whole range of enemies: "plots hatched in
hell," as Bergasse described them.[92] There appeared to be no other rational
explanation for the apparent simultaneity of the rioting—in what historians
have since determined was a chain reaction panic: "One cannot believe,"
wrote Maupetit, "that warnings were sounded everywhere at the same time
and on the same day." There were rumors of secret conspiracies to destroy
the National Assembly, to starve the people, to sabotage France's credit.
Though the "aristocrats" were considered the most likely agents, there were
also stories of "Guineas from Mr. Pitt" being paid to incite the riots, and of
an impending English strike against the port of Brest.[93] Rumors of this sort
were especially frightening in that executive authority itself was in rapid
decline. The mid-July crisis had been sparked by the dismissal and exile of
Necker, but until that minister could be located and summoned to return—
he had left for Switzerland by a circuitous journey through the Austrian
Lowlands—and until a new cabinet could be formed around him, the royal
government remained in a kind of interregnum.[94] In the provinces, intendants and subdelegates—sobered no doubt by the fate of the intendant of
Paris—had abandoned their posts or gone into hiding, and the vaunted
French bureaucracy was on the verge of collapse. "There is no longer any
governing authority," wrote Périsse Du Luc to his friend in Lyon, "and
Louis XVI is no more king than you are." Dinochau summarized the situation in an essay written several weeks later: "The executive was impotent,
laws had no authority, and the courts had ceased functioning. Tax payments

---

[90] Barbotin, 44–45 and 48–50 (letters of July 28 and 31); Virieu, letter of Aug. 18; Ferrières, *Correspondance*, esp. 94–95, 103, 110–11 (letters of July 21 and 29, and Aug. 7). On
the general situation, see Georges Lefebvre, *The Great Fear* (New York, 1973).

[91] E.g., Maillot, entry of Aug. 1; Gantheret, letter of Aug. 13.

[92] Lamy, 94 (letter to his future wife, July 30).

[93] Maupetit, 19 (1903), 207 and 210 (letters of July 22 and 31). Also, Lepoutre, letter of
July 24; Pellerin, entry of July 28; Campmas, letter of July 25; Gantheret, letter of July 17. On
the obsession with plots, see below, chap. 8.

[94] Necker returned to Versailles on the night of July 28–29, but the new team of ministers
was named only on Aug. 4.

had been almost entirely suspended. . . . Anarchy had emerged from the delirium of freedom."[95]

Despite the obvious gravity of the situation, and despite the high expectations raised by the creation of the National Assembly, the deputies accomplished little in the month that followed the merging of the three estates. In part, it was a question of the deputies' initial reticence to impinge on the prerogatives of "executive authority."[96] In part, there was the need to wait for reports from two critical committees, the Committee on the Constitution and the Committee on Procedures, the latter of particular importance for establishing the rules of order and debate.[97] Frustration rose rapidly as long hours were spent reading letters from constituents, examining deputy credentials, and fruitlessly debating in the bureaus. On the single most pressing item of business, the problem of law and order in the kingdom, the Assembly long seemed paralyzed and unable to reach a decision.[98]

Beginning with a motion by Lally-Tolendal on July 20, most of the debate focused on the possible use of force to overcome anarchy and reassert royal power.[99] At least since early August, some deputies were proposing rapid and far-reaching changes in the seigneurial system, changes designed to match popular expectations as expressed in the cahiers and by the rioters themselves. According to Visme, the idea of dramatically reducing or abolishing seigneurial obligations had been suggested by individual deputies in private meetings for several days prior to August 3.[100] That night two separate though probably overlapping meetings—first in the "Breton Committee" and then in a special assembly set up for the circumstances—developed a plan in which a great noble would make such an appeal the following evening.[101]

We cannot be certain how many deputies were present that Tuesday night, August 4. In later months, the nobles and bishops would earn a reputation for missing the evening sessions. But a total of over a thousand members had been present late that afternoon—perhaps the largest attendance to date—and it seems likely that, in this exceptionally tense and critical moment, a large proportion from all three orders returned after dinner.[102] Fortunately for the patriots, Le Chapelier had just been named to the president's chair—the only Breton Club member to hold the position until well

---

[95] Périsse, letter of July 24, 1789; Dinochau, 1:6.

[96] See below, chap 7.

[97] On the slowness of the committees, see, e.g., Basquiat and Lamarque, letters of July 18 and 21.

[98] Pellerin, esp. letter of July 27; Maupetit, 19 (1903), 210 (letter of July 31).

[99] *AP*, 8:252–55. See also Basquiat and Lamarque, letter of July 20.

[100] Visme, entry of Aug. 3. See also Patrice Kessel, *La nuit du 4 août 1789* (Paris, 1969), 125.

[101] Kessel, 130.

[102] There was a total of 1003: see above, note 36.

into 1790—and the Rennes lawyer undoubtedly helped facilitate the group's plans.[103]

⌐The session began with a reading of the latest version of a proposed decree to impose law and order on the kingdom. But at this point two great nobles, the vicomte de Noailles and the duc d'Aiguillon, successively came forward with dramatic proposals. Though the two speeches differed in details, both called for a law allowing the peasants to obtain their freedom by purchasing the "property" of the seigneurial dues and declaring that taxes would be paid by all citizens in proportion to their incomes.[104] These sensational appeals were followed by three prearranged speeches in support of the proposals, delivered by the commoner patriots Le Grand, Le Guen de Kérangall, and Jean-Denis Lapoule. The wealthy Breton farmer Le Guen, dressed as usual in peasant attire, appealed to the Assembly's emotions. But Lapoule's long analysis of the evils of the seigneurial system in his native Franche-Comté and his rousing injunction to follow the example of "English America" in rejecting all remnants of "feudalism," seems to have made an even greater impact, inspiring the Assembly with a "noble enthusiasm."[105] After a brief note of caution by Dupont de Nemours, the duc Du Châtelet came forward. Courtier and peer of the realm, Châtelet was a former liberal who had embraced the intransigent position of the Noble majority and had fallen under a cloud in popular perceptions as commander of the troops garrisoned in Paris during the mid-July uprising.[106] "Tormented," as Ferrières thought, "with anxiety and wild fears," he not only supported the previous motions, but formally sacrificed and abandoned the seigneurial rights on his own lands, subject to a "just compensation."[107]⌐

⌐From this point in the evening "a kind of magic,"[108] a remarkable and utterly unanticipated spirit of enthusiasm and self-sacrifice seemed to take hold of the Assembly, as numerous deputies came forward to offer up motions, abandoning their own special rights, and calling for the suppression or reform of a whole range of other institutions never envisioned by those who had planned the evening. The rush of motions became so rapid, that no one was altogether certain of the order in which they were made or the individuals who participated.⌐ Numerous great nobles and clergymen—some liberals, others identified with the intransigents—lined up to make their own offerings. The bishop of Nancy moved that seigneurial rights held by the clergy be treated in the same way as those possessed by the nobles. Richier de La Rochelongchamp called for a free court system, curé Thibault

---

[103] On Le Chapelier's election, see below, chap. 6.

[104] Kessel, 137–41. Unless otherwise specified, the account that follows is taken from Kessel and from the *AP*, 8:343–50.

[105] Delandine, 4:83–87.

[106] He had resigned his post on July 16: Kessel, 146–47.

[107] Ferrières, *Mémoires*, 1:187.

[108] Jean-Nicolas-Jacques Parisot: "La nuit du 4 août racontée par le Constituant Parisot," ed. R. Hennequin, *RF* 33 (1927), 20.

for an end to the clergy's pastoral fees, archbishop Boisgelin for sweeping reforms of the indirect salt and excise taxes, the bishop of Chartres—who possessed large personal hunting lands—for the suppression of noble hunting privileges. Châtelet then returned—perhaps out of spite for the bishop's previous motion—with a stunning demand for an end to the tithes, the principal source of clerical income. Some two hours into the meeting, a new tide of renunciations rose from the commoners, anxious to match the generosity of the privileged deputies. The benches were emptied as whole delegations presented themselves at the rostrum, calling for an end to specific provincial and municipal privileges. The extraordinary session ended, now well past midnight, with a series of demands to abolish or transform the annates, the guild system, plurality of benefices, and the general administrative system of the provinces.

At about two in the morning, when there seemed nothing left to abandon, the secretaries attempted to distill the basic principles involved in the myriad of motions, and Le Chapelier read out a summary in sixteen points. Only three motions submitted that evening received a generally negative response from the Assembly and were not retained: Alexandre de Lameth's call for complete religious freedom for Protestants, La Rochefoucauld's demand for the suppression of slavery in the colonies, and the demand by an unknown deputy that the nobility be abolished—all revealing of major points of friction for the future.[109] But otherwise the Assembly voted all sixteen points by acclamation and without discussion. The chevalier de Boufflers summarized the reigning sentiment: "Let us abandon all distinctions; let us only regret that we have nothing else left to sacrifice; let us consider that henceforth the title of "Frenchman" will be distinction enough for every generous soul."[110]

In all, including the complete delegations which came forward to make certain motions, several hundred deputies probably took part in the renunciations. But if we exclude those repudiating local privileges—and who were generally unnamed—we can identify some fifty-five men offering proposals. Of these, over four-fifths were from the privileged orders (60 percent from the nobles, 25 percent from the clergy). Perhaps most remarkable was the extent to which the individuals concerned spread across virtually all political positions in the Constituent Assembly. Though over half could be identified as radicals or liberals in their political orientation during the Constituent Assembly, nearly a fifth would soon be linked to the moderate conservatives and over a quarter to the extreme right.[111] For a few brief mo-

---

[109] Kessel, 148 and 157–58, and the subsequent statement by Foucauld: *AP*, 16:374 (June 19, 1790).

[110] Kessel, 164.

[111] Among the participants in August 4 the following would later be classified as liberals or radicals: Aiguillon, Barère, Beauharnais, Blacons, Brousse, Castillane, Chasset, Cottin, Custine, Duport, Fréteau, Gouy d'Arsy, Grégoire, La Rochefoucauld, La Touche, La Tour-Maubourg, de Lameth, Lapoule, Le Chapelier, Le Guen de Kérangall, Le Grand, Le Peletier de Saint-

ments, the curious combination of idealism, anxiety, and the feelings of fraternity had brought them all together.

To be sure, in the months and years that followed, some of the nobles present claimed that they had opposed the motions of August 4 from the very beginning, and that they had been shouted down and prevented from speaking during the session.[112] In any case, many nobles and bishops—some of whom had been present and others who had only learned of events the next morning—expressed consternation, even outrage in their letters. As we shall discover in the following chapter, noble discontent, combined with clerical unhappiness over the total suppression of the tithes, would help forge the nucleus of a new political faction on the right in late August and September.

For virtually all the commoners, however, and for many of the formerly privileged deputies, the night of August 4 marked a phenomenal and largely unexpected culmination to two months of revolutionary development. Whatever the role of the patriot leadership in initiating the process, the magic of the moment, the volatile psychological blend of social anxiety and the sentiments of brotherhood, went far beyond anyone's expectations. There was no better example of the way in which the inner dynamic of the Assembly and the force of events themselves—most of which were quite beyond the control of the membership—could sweep the deputies forward into more revolutionary positions than they might ever have conceived only a few weeks earlier. In their testimonies of that night, the representatives were distinctly aware of the historical significance of what they had done, but they were stunned and overwhelmed that it had actually come to pass, and quite at a loss to explain it. "Great and memorable night!" exclaimed Duquesnoy. "We wept, we hugged one another. What a nation! What glory! What an honor to be French!" "Posterity will never believe," noted Pellerin late at night in his diary, "what the National Assembly did in the space of five hours." They had "annihilated abuses which had existed for 900 years and against which a century of philosophy had struggled in vain." The Flemish farmer, Lepoutre, instructed his wife to offer an extra pot of beer to their farm hands, "in celebration of the great day of AUGUST FOURTH. . . . You can now think of the French nation as a new nation, a nation free to make a whole set of laws following its own wisdom and for

---

Fargeau, Liancourt, Marguerites, Menou, Montmorency, Noailles, Poix, Régnaud, and Thibault. The following would be associated with the moderate right "Monarchiens": Boisgelin, Boufflers, Estourmel, Juigné, La Fare, Lally-Tolendal, Lubersac, Montrevel, Mortemart, and Virieu. The following would be associated with the extreme right: Béthisy de Mézières, Castries, Châtelet, Cortois de Balore, Desvernay, Digoine, Egmont, Foucauld de Lardimalie, Gauville, Goullard, Malide, Mathias, Richier de La Rochelongchamp, Talaru, and Villequier. In all, 54% were liberal/radical, 18% were moderate/conservative, and 28% were extreme right. On the methods of classifying deputies by political position, see below, chaps. 8 and 9.

[112] Kessel, 150–51, 182–86. There is very little clear evidence of this in contemporary documents.

its greater prosperity." Dinochau described it as totally "unexpected," and he was particularly amazed that they had attacked the "feudal regime," which was the last thing he would have expected to come under fire. "We wept with joy and emotion. Deputies, without distinction, treated one another with fraternal friendship." Gantheret came to much the same conclusion: "In the future, only wealth, talent, and virtue will distinguish one man from another. . . . We are a nation of brothers. The king is our father and France is our mother."[113]

[113] Duquesnoy, 1:267 (entry of Aug. 5); Pellerin, entry of Aug. 4–5; Lepoutre, letter of Aug. 5; Dinochau, 1:20–21, 25, and 42–43; and Gantheret, letters of Aug. 5 and 11.

Factional Formation and the Revolutionary Dynamic

AUGUST TO NOVEMBER

THE NIGHT OF AUGUST 4 was a remarkable moment in the history of the National Assembly and the history of France. Yet the joy and brotherhood, the sense of a unified "French family," which had held sway among the deputies that evening and for much of the previous three or four weeks, was to be short lived. When they returned to their hall late the next morning—after recuperating from the prolonged night session—their enthusiasm persisted, but it was tempered by the challenges and dilemmas which they were compelled to confront. Despite their great act of "generosity," the anarchy in the countryside abated only slowly. On August 7 Necker and the newly appointed deputy-minister, Champion de Cicé, presented the Assembly with an appalling survey of the breakdown of public order and the continuing fiscal crisis: "a frightful picture of disorder and public calamity."[1] Whatever their desire to confine themselves to constitutional reform, the deputies faced the sobering realization that they alone maintained some semblance of authority within the kingdom. They were "the only power actually functioning"; while elsewhere, "the executive authority was impotent, the laws had no force, and the courts had ceased functioning." In the face of the continued popular uprisings churning through the rural areas, the deputies remained tense and uncertain. On two occasions in mid-August rioting even broke out in the streets of Versailles in direct view of the deputies themselves.[2] "As for me," wrote Campmas to his brother, "I am far from sharing the optimism of some of our colleagues. The masses of starving people, the numbers of discontented, the difficulties of every sort imaginable . . . all combine to discourage me." Charles-François Bouche chose an image from his youth in the Alps of Provence: "Have you never found yourself on a high mountain . . . seeing above you a clear and serene sky, but hearing the wind howling through the valleys and caverns below? That is in fact our situation here. While the first sight delights and exalts us, the

---

[1] Malouet, Dufraisse-Duchey, and Tailhardat de La Maisonneuve to the municipality of Riom, letter of Aug. 7, cited in Francisque Mège, ed., *Gaultier de Biauzat, député du Tiers état aux Etats généraux de 1789. Sa vie et sa correspondance*, 2 vols. (Clermont-Ferrand, 1890), 2:232. See also François-Emmanuel Toulongeon, *Histoire de la France depuis la Révolution*, 7 vols. (Paris, 1801), 1:97–99; Alexis Basquiat de Mugriet and Pierre-Joseph Lamarque to the municipality of Bayonne: A.C. Bayonne, AA 51, letter of Aug. 7.

[2] Gaultier, 2:236, 246–47, 250–51 (letters of Aug. 8, 13, and 22); Jacques Dinochau, *Histoire philosophique et politique de l'Assemblée constituante*, 2 vols. (Paris, 1789), 1:6.

second fills us with terror."[3] They were awed and even frightened by the extraordinary task of rebuilding which they now faced. "We find ourselves at present in the midst of a pile of ruins," wrote Bouche's Provençal colleague, Lombard-Taradeau—a phrase echoed by Vernier, Begouën-Demeaux, and Lablache: "It is not enough to destroy; we also have to rebuild, and I confess that the task frightens us."[4] As they attempted to confront the growing array of problems, the deputies' working day grew apace, with sessions frequently lasting ten or twelve hours. Many individuals appeared exhausted and frazzled in the endless rounds of bureaus, committees, and general assemblies unrolling at a rhythm for which most were quite unprepared.[5]

In addition, as they began to consider the implementation of the general principles voted on August 4, and as they set to work defining the Rights of Man and the organizing principals of the new constitution, deep factional divisions rapidly emerged. In part, it was a revival of the old antagonisms between the diverse social, economic, and cultural elements in the Assembly, antagonisms so much in evidence during the Estates General, and epitomized by the conflicts between Nobility and Third Estate. Yet there was also a substantial restructuring and realignment of political affiliations, born of the traumatic experiences of the July crisis and the Great Fear.

During the Estates General and the early weeks of the National Assembly, the master practitioners of the new forms of factional politics had been the Breton deputies and their political allies from a variety of other provinces.[6] Their nightly meetings in a local café to plan strategy and organize disciplined voting, their appeals to the masses and to public opinion, their carefully cultivated links to their constituencies, the inspired leadership of such popular speakers as Mirabeau, Le Chapelier, and Pétion, had all played a significant role in the creation of the National Assembly and the initiation of the Night of August 4. Yet after the heroic days of the early Revolution, the Breton Club's influence went into decline. Whether or not the number of adherents actually diminished, the entry into the Assembly at the end of June of some six hundred deputies from the privileged orders—most of

[3] Jean-François Campmas to his brother, vicaire in Carmaux: B.M. Albi, Ms. 177, letter of Aug. 13; Charles-François Bouche to the *commissaires des communautés de Provence*: A.D. Bouches-du-Rhône, C 1, letter of Aug. 17.

[4] Jacques-Athanase de Lombard-Taradeau, "Lettres (1789–91)," *Le Var historique et géographique*, ed. L. Honoré, 2 (1925–27), 248 (letter of Aug. 13); Théodore Vernier to the municipality of Lons-le-Saunier: A.C. Bletterans (non-classé), "Lettres de Vernier," letter of Aug. 13; Jean-François Begouën-Demeaux to municipal officers of Le Havre: A.C. Le Havre, D(3) 38–39, letter of Aug. 12; Alexandre-Joseph de Lablache to marquis de Viennois: Archives of the Château d'Avauges, reproduced in A.D. Isère, 1 Mi 461, undated but probably early August.

[5] Lombard, 245 (letter of Aug. 11); Campmas, letter of Aug. 13; Vernier, letter of Aug. 30; Guillaume Gontier de Biran to the municipality of Bergerac: A.C. Bergerac, Fonds Faugère, carton 1, letter of Sept. 25.

[6] See above, chap. 4.

whom were clearly conservatives or moderates—invariably decreased the proportionate size of the radical contingent and reduced its hold on the large bloc of moderate patriots within the Third Estate. In the general rejoicing at the merging of the estates, a few of the radicals had sensed the danger to their position. The Breton deputy Delaville Le Roulx despaired that the Assembly would now be "captivated by the seductive manners" of the nobles and bishops; Maillot wondered whether the "flattery and confidence" of the privileged were not more dangerous than their previous "arrogance and pride"; and Creuzé-Latouche feared that the "faint hearted," previously brought into conformity with correct principles by the more "virile minds" among the deputies, would now be won over by moderates and aristocrats.[7]

Indeed, by early September the "Breton Committee" had reverted to an exclusively provincial organization, no longer attended by deputies from other provinces and badly split over several key issues.[8] A radical patriot contingent, with delegations from Brittany, Anjou, Provence, and Franche-Comté at its core, continued to gather on occasion to discuss strategy, but the meetings were largely ad hoc in nature. Lombard-Taradeau portrayed "our party" as an extremely loose factional body improvised on the spot, "each morning, with much discussion in several small groups within the hall before the opening of the session." They had now come to be called, both by themselves and by their opponents, the "Palais Royal of the Assembly"—a reference to their sympathies with the radical journalists and politicians commonly congregating in Paris in the square of the same name. After July 22 seating in the Menus Plaisirs had been rearranged into an oval of tiered bleachers, with the table of the president and the secretaries positioned at one side, and the Palais Royal group rapidly took the habit of sitting together on the president's left.[9] The period also witnessed a new

---

[7] Joseph Delaville Le Roulx to the municipality of Lorient: A.C. Lorient, BB 12, letter of July 29; Claude-Pierre Maillot to an unnamed municipal official of Toul: A.C. Toul, JJ 7, letter of Aug. 1; Jacques-Antoine Creuzé-Latouche, *Journal des Etats généraux et du début de l'Assemblée nationale, 18 mai–29 juillet 1789*, ed. Jean Marchand (Paris, 1946), 166 (entry of June 29).

[8] A. Bouchard, *Le club Breton. Origine, composition, rôle à l'Assemblée constituante* (Paris, 1920), 89–92. Delaville wrote that the Breton delegation had "once again" opened its doors to deputies of other delegations toward mid-Sept. as "before and after June 17," suggesting that the doors had more recently been closed: Delaville, A.C. Lorient, BB 13, letter of Sept. 17. But there is no indication in Delaville's later letters that anything came of this initiative. Neither Gérard Walter, *Histoire des Jacobins* (Paris, 1946) nor Alphonse Aulard, *La société des Jacobins*, 6 vols. (Paris, 1889–97) mentions the Breton Club between Aug. 4 and late Nov. or early Dec. On the internal divisions within the Breton delegation, see Jean-Pierre Boullé, "Ouverture des Etats généraux de 1789," ed. Albert Macé, *Revue de la Révolution. Documents inédits* 15 (1889), 117 (Sept. 8, incorrectly dated in publication); Adrien Duquesnoy, *Journal d'Adrien Duquesnoy*, ed. R. de Crèvecoeur, 2 vols. (Paris, 1894), 1:262–63 (entry of Aug. 3); and Basquiat and Lamarque, letter of Sept. 8.

[9] Lombard, 243 and 274–75 (letters of Aug. 11 and 31). Also Maillot, folio 134 (Sept. 2); Claude-Jean-Baptiste de Garron de La Bévière to his wife: A.D. Ain, 1 Mi 1, letter of Aug. 25; Ambroise-Eulalie de Maurès de Malartic, ms. "Journal de ma députation aux Etats généraux":

infusion of leaders among these patriots on the "left." With only a few exceptions—of which Le Chapelier and Lanjuinais were the most notable—the Breton deputies had always been stronger in sheer enthusiasm and high-decibel interjections than in speaking ability and leadership. After July an exceptionally talented group of younger men, mostly in their twenties and early thirties, emerged as the principal tacticians and orators of the radicals: in particular, Adrien Duport and Charles and Alexandre de Lameth, recently arrived from the liberal wing of the Second Estate, and Antoine Barnave, now breaking away from his more conservative Dauphiné colleagues.

Yet despite their leadership and enthusiasm, the deputies on the left represented only a relatively small minority of the Assembly as a whole. In fact, from mid-August to mid-October, the best organized and most influential faction within the Assembly was not to be found among the radicals at all, but among the conservatives.⫠

THE CONSERVATIVE OFFENSIVE

Throughout the month of July, the organization of the dissident elements of the former First and Second Estates had never entirely dissolved, despite the popular upheavals and the temporary flight of many of the individuals concerned. Even after the original halls of the privileged orders were closed and converted into smaller meeting rooms, a core of the most conservative noblemen and bishops continued to congregate in the dwellings of specific deputies, where, as La Gallissonnière described it, "we debated different questions, we proposed responses, we discussed various plans related to the events of the day."[10] They were clearly acting as a corps on July 16 when they announced they would henceforth join in all Assembly votes and debates. Many observers were convinced that they "are of one mind and are forming a coalition," voting together by prearranged agreement throughout the second half of the month, notably in the debate on July 29 over the new regulations for the organization of the Assembly.[11] This same coalition seems to have coordinated the considerable deputy discipline involved in placing several of its numbers on the new Committee on Research and in the election of Thouret to the presidency at the end of July. Deputies were amazed when numerous nobles and clergymen who had not been seen in

---

B.M. La Rochelle, ms. 21, entries of Sept 1 and 7; deposition of Henri-Jean-Baptiste de Bousmard de Chantraine, *Procédure*, 3:3; and Armand Brette, *Histoire des édifices où ont siégé les assemblées parlementaires de la Révolution* (Paris, 1902), 79–80.

[10] Augustin-Félix-Elisabeth Barin de La Gallissonnière, ms. journal: Arch. de la Guerre, A4 LVI, folio 155, undated.

[11] Delaville, letter of July 29. See also Gontier, letter of Aug. 1; Campmas, letter of Aug. 1; and Lombard, 234 (letter of Aug. 5).

recent weeks suddenly appeared in the electoral meetings of the bureaux and voted as a bloc for the same individuals.[12]

The organizing potential of these groups was strengthened through the gradual return to the Assembly of the most dynamic—and frequently most conservative—of their adherents. The merging of the Estates and the mid-July crisis had sent a substantial number of nobles and upper clergymen scurrying back to the provinces, many vowing never to return. But most were soon persuaded otherwise by a population that looked askance on its deputies deserting their posts. By early August abbé Maury, who had been arrested in Péronne as he attempted to flee, had returned to his bench in Versailles. And on August 10 Duval d'Eprémesnil appeared and delivered a rousing speech announcing that "I return to the bosom of the Assembly, to live or die for the *patrie*."[13]

In the political resurgence of the conservatives, a key event was the disenchantment after the Night of August 4 of a substantial number of the previously patriotic clergymen. While most applauded the renunciations of that evening, they were indignant over the Assembly's subsequent decision to "revise" the decrees and suppress the ecclesiastical tithes outright rather than reimburse them as originally announced. The clergy's fear and anger were accentuated when several of the commoners laced their speeches with anticlerical remarks and when a few deputies—first Buzot and then the nobles La Coste and Alexandre de Lameth—called for the seizure and nationalization of all church land as well.[14] Indeed, the defense of the tithes seems to have unified the clergy more than at any time since the opening of the Estates General, with even Sieyès and the overwhelming majority of the patriot curés joining with the bishops and the other conservative clerics. The ecclesiastical deputies were especially outraged that the Third Estate seemed to be reneging on a promise made only a few weeks earlier—as part of their appeal for clerical support—never to touch ecclesiastical property. In the end, after two days of debate, the clergy agreed as a corps to abandon the tithes—partly out of fear of popular anticlerical attacks, partly in the hope of thus preserving the clerical lands—but the experience left a residue of bitterness. The left-leaning canon from Die, Colaud de La Salcette, was

---

[12] Maillot, letter of Aug. 1; Delaville, letter of Aug. 4; Lombard, 234 (letter of Aug. 5); Boullé, 15 (1889), 101 (letter of Aug. 14); Jacques Jallet, *Journal inédit*, ed. J.-J. Brethé (Fontenay-le-Comte, 1871), 164 (entry of July 28).

[13] *AP*, 8:377 (Aug. 10); J. de Gissac, "Le marquis de Montcalm-Gozon," *Mémoires de la Société des lettres et des arts de l'Aveyron* 2 (1874–78), 45–47; Dominique-Georges-Frédéric Du Four de Pradt, "Quelques lettres de l'Abbé de Pradt, 1789–92," ed. Michel Leymarie, *Revue de la Haute-Auvergne*, 56e année, 34 (1954), 65–95. On the return of the conservative deputies, see also Boissy d'Anglas to Etienne Montgolfier: Archives du Musée de l'air et de l'espace (Le Bourget), Fonds Montgolfier, XVI-14, letter of ca. Aug. 10; Laurent de Visme, ms. "Journal des Etats généraux": B.N., Nouv. Acq. Fr. 12938, entry of Aug. 10; and Jean-Sylvain Bailly, *Mémoires d'un témoin de la Révolution*, ed. Berville and Barrière, 3 vols. (Paris, 1821–22), 2:255–56 (entry of Aug. 11).

[14] *AP*, 8:354 (Buzot, Aug. 6); 8:369–70 (Lacoste and Lameth, Aug. 8).

dumbfounded that the Assembly should abolish the tithes, after its previous promises. "There is general consternation among the clergy," he wrote. "They treat us as though we came from another planet." The once staunchly patriotic curé Pierre-Louis Renaut lamented that "if we resolved to sacrifice our tithes, it was because of the general insurrection in the provinces, the pillage of castles and monasteries, the threat to our rectories, and the fear of the loss of religion." His onetime patriot colleague, Barbotin, reacted even more strongly: the Assembly "seems to have vowed the clergy's ruin, and religion itself will inevitably feel the consequences. And this will not likely be the end of it. They want to put us all on the *portion congrue*."[15] And for this Barbotin never forgave them. Indeed, for many of the lower clergy who had firmly supported the Revolution up until then, the decree on the tithes marked a parting of the ways, pushing them permanently into the camp of the opposition.

The reaction of the nobility to the Night of August 4 was much more complex. There can be no doubt that a number of the nobles, especially those who had not directly experienced the "magic" of August 4, were extremely unhappy with the Assembly's attacks on their seigneurial rights. The noble twosome from Roussillon, Banyuls de Montferré and Coma Serra maintained that they were "coerced and unwilling collaborators, superfluous to everything that is being done." On August 10, the marquis de Thiboutot delivered a long plea for the complete preservation of all feudal rights. And Garron de La Bévière complained to his wife that thousands of gentlemen would now be left without resources and without status and that his own revenues would be greatly reduced: "We are now no more than the first peasants on the land."[16] But the aristocrats soon learned that most of their rights and dues were to be maintained until they could be reimbursed by the peasantry, so that their economic position was far from bleak. A great many eventually accepted the situation with resignation and sometimes even with a measure of enthusiasm. In the days following August 4, the two staunch conservatives, the vicomte de Mirabeau and the marquis de Foucauld de Lardimalie, both continued to support the renunciation of noble privilege. "If such measures are advantageous for the general good," wrote Ferrières to his wife, "I can easily console myself for all that I lose as a

---

[15] Jacques-Bernardin Colaud de La Salcette, "Lettres de Colaud de La Salcette," *Bulletin de la Société départementale d'archéologie et de statistique de la Drôme* 69 (1944), 151 (letter of Aug. 24); Pierre-Louis-Joseph Renaut to abbé Carlier: B.M. Douai, ms. 1035, letter of Aug. 19; Emmanuel Barbotin, *Lettres de l'abbé Barbotin*, ed. A. Aulard (Paris, 1910), 52 (letter of Aug. 23). See also Jean-Joseph Bigot de Vernières to his nephew, *avocat* in Saint-Flour: copies in A.D. Cantal, Fonds Delmas, letter of Aug. 20. All four of these clergymen had previously supported the union of the Clergy with the Third Estate on June 19. The work of Harriet B. Applewhite confirms the Clergy's sharp swing to the right: *Political Alignment in the French National Assembly, 1789–1791* (Baton Rouge, La., 1993), 109.

[16] Raymond-Antoine de Banyuls de Monferré and Michel de Coma Serra to the correspondence committee of Perpignan: A.D. Pyrénées-Orientales, C 2119, letter of Aug. 8; *AP*, 8:379–80; La Bévière: letter of Aug. 6.

noble and a seigneurial lord." Even La Bévière was prepared to accept the inevitable: "If it promotes the general happiness, I have no regrets. We will reduce ourselves to bare essentials, and our children must learn to do likewise. We must yield to necessity."[17]

Of greater importance in the growth of a patriot-conservative rift was the composition of the "Declaration of the Rights of Man and the Citizen." Pursued during the month of August, the debate on the Declaration marked the first broad exploration within the Assembly of an array of Enlightenment themes and their application to the Revolutionary transformation—"a kind of speculative orgy," as one historian has described it.[18] In the beginning, opposition to the general principle of such a declaration was by no means confined to the privileged classes, and was revealing of the deputies' suspicions of the Enlightened ideal of abstract natural rights. With their strong practical and legalistic turn of mind, many of the commoners were initially impatient with the whole project, which they could only view as a waste of time. Whatever the possible intellectual interest of such discussions, the representatives had not come to Versailles to "write philosophical treatises," as Visme put it, nor to pass their sessions debating the "superfluous issues of abstract metaphysics." The patriot magistrates Maillot, Lasalle, and Grellet, and the lawyer Gaultier de Biauzat, all expressed similar disapproving remarks on "metaphysics," a term commonly linked to the proposals of the abbé Sieyès. There was even a risk that such ideas might be misconstrued by the masses, thus undermining social subordination and the respect for property.[19] While they were not necessarily opposed to the principle of a carefully phrased declaration of rights, they preferred to consider it later and publish it as an integral part of the entire Constitution. Other opponents, however, especially among the privileged deputies, rejected the very concept of abstract rights. For the marquis de Ferrières and the comte de Lablache, the so-called "rights of man" could only be equated to the positive law existing within each separate country. The baron de Gauville adopted much the same position, and he took pains to suggest the clauses

[17] *AP*, 8:355, 370–71 (Aug. 6 and 8); Charles-Elie de Ferrières, *Correspondance inédite*, ed. Henri Carré (Paris, 1932), 110 (letter of Aug. 7); La Bévière, letter of Aug. 6.

[18] Roger Barny, "Le conflit idéologique dans la discussion sur les droits de l'homme," in *Les droits de l'homme et la conquête des libertés. Des Lumières aux révolutions de 1848* (Grenoble, 1988), 51. The Declaration is considered here only insofar as it impinged on the Revolutionary dynamic within the National Assembly. See also Marcel Gauchet, *La Révolution des droits de l'homme* (Paris, 1989); Dale Van Kley, ed., *The French Idea of Freedom: The Old Regime and the Declaration of Rights of 1789* (Stanford, 1994); and Philip Dawson, "Le 6e Bureau de l'Assemblée nationale et son projet de Déclaration des droits de l'homme," *AHRF* 50 (1978), 161–79.

[19] Visme, entries of July 9 and 11; Jean-Bernard Grellet de Beauregard, "Lettres de M. Grellet de Beauregard," ed. Abbé Dardy, *Mémoires de la Société des sciences naturelles et archéologiques de la Creuse*, 2e sér., 7 (1899), 71–72 (letter of ca. Aug. 3); Nicolas-Théodore-Antoine-Adolphe de Lasalle, "Les archives municipales de Sarrelouis," ed. René Herly, *Bulletin de la Société des amis du pays de la Sarre* 4 (1927), 214–15 (letter of Aug. 1); Maillot, letter of July 29. Also Gauchet, 60–64; and Dinochau, 1:8–10.

which his own declaration would include: that all men are born dependent, that they are subject to the paternal authority of their superiors, and that throughout their lives they owe homage to God.[20]

[How the balance of opinion came to swing in favor of writing a separate declaration of rights is somewhat unclear and rarely described by our witnesses. It seems likely that the shift emerged from the same volatile psychological state, the combination of fear and generosity, that produced the August 4 Decrees only a few hours later.] Rabaut wrote of the deputies' apprehension that the Revolution might not survive and of their desire to act quickly in order to leave a legacy: "As a father, sick and uncertain of living much longer, turns over to his heirs the title to all his possessions." But Pellerin emphasized the "school of the Revolution," the persuasive eloquence of several of the Assembly's best orators in developing their justifications for a "national catechism." In any case, the critical vote came on the afternoon of August 4, focusing on the amendment of the Jansenist Camus that the declaration must also include a statement of citizens' duties—an amendment rejected by the relatively slim margin of 570 to 433.[21]

According to several witnesses, however, the key issue that united the majority of the clergy and the nobles into a relatively cohesive group was the discussion two weeks later of the specific article of the Rights of Man concerning religious toleration for non-Catholics.[22] Most of the deputies seem to have been ready to accept some measure of civil toleration, along the lines of the edict of November 1787 which had granted a limited legal existence to the former Huguenots. However, the more radical patriots set their sights on complete freedom of religious practice and political and legal equality for French Protestants. In what were widely described as the most tumultuous debates to date, the Palais Royal group seems to have alienated many of their more moderate supporters through their particularly strident anticlerical rhetoric and their impatience and "intolerance" toward their adversaries.[23] As the debate increasingly focused on the issue of the primacy of the Catholic religion in France, sympathy for a conservative position was generated not only among the clerical deputies but also among a large segment of the nobility and a significant portion of the commoners.

For some deputies opposition to toleration was justified by the fear of civil disturbances between rival confessional communities. Others were apprehensive that loosening the hold of Catholic dominance would under-

---

[20] Ferrières, 121 (letter of Aug. 10); Lablache, letter of July 29; Louis-Henri-Charles de Gauville, *Journal*, ed. Edouard de Barthélémy (Paris, 1864), 15.

[21] *AP*, 8:341; Joseph-Michel Pellerin, ms. journal: B.M. Versailles, Ms. 823F, entry of Aug. 4. See also Jean-Paul Rabaut Saint-Etienne, *Précis historique de la Révolution française* (Paris, 1807), 283; and Gauchet, 62–63.

[22] See also the earlier debate on inserting a reference to the Supreme Being in the preamble of the document: *AP*, 8:462–63 (Aug. 20).

[23] See especially Duquesnoy, 1:311–12 (entry of Aug. 23); and Maupetit, 19 (1903), 234–35 (letter of Aug. 24). On the intensity of the debate, see also Boullé, 15 (1889), 104 (letter of Aug. 28); and La Bévière, letter of Aug. 25.

mine the authority of the monarchy, and that the integrity of the Catholic faith might be placed in jeopardy. Indeed, for the first time, the patriots found themselves directly colliding with a religious orthodoxy which, for a great many nobles as well as for the clergy, remained powerful and pervasive.[24] A number of witnesses perceived the debate as a confrontation between religion, on the one hand, and godless philosophy, on the other. The chevalier de La Bévière was convinced that "a few individuals imbued with the principles of philosophy" were attempting to attack the Catholic religion. The comte de Virieu stormed against the "secret and diabolical plans to establish complete freedom for all religions." The Third deputies Gontier de Biran from Bergerac and Pellerin from Nantes seem first to have broken with the radicals over the issue, Gontier concerned with "the threat to religion and the throne" and Pellerin declaring that "our errant brothers [the Protestants] must not ask to practice a religion that would trouble and perturb the Catholics and that would soon resurrect public discord."[25]

The final wording of the article—"No one should be troubled because of their opinions, even religious, provided that the expression of those opinions does not disturb the public order established by law"—was clearly ambiguous, since no one was sure what constituted a disturbance to public order and no one was yet certain what the laws in question would have to say about religion. In this it resembled many of the other articles of the Declaration of the rights of Man, perceived at the time as temporary compromises to be reexamined at a later date.[26] Yet the acceptance of this language was widely considered to be a victory for the conservatives. "Will our posterity ever believe," fumed Lombard-Taradeau, "that the eighteenth century could have produced such a pronouncement? A civil and religious Inquisition has been reestablished." "We fought over fifteen hours," wrote curé Barbotin, "to prevent open religious practice for all faiths."[27] Though not all of the opponents of the Palais Royal group had accepted the article for the same reasons, the debate played a major role in bringing together a wide alliance of clergy and nobles and demonstrating their real prospects for success within the new political process. The baron de Gauville recalled that it was precisely out of this experience that those "attached to their religion and their king" began working together, and that "we began to recognize ourselves." It was also at this time, he added, that they began self-consciously sitting together on the right side of the National Assembly's presi-

[24] See above, chap. 2.
[25] La Bévière, letter of Aug 25; François-Henri de Virieu to the marquis de Viennois: Archives of the Château d'Avauges, reproduced in A.D. Isère, 1 Mi 461, letter of Aug. 25; Gontier, retrospective letter of May 22, 1790; Pellerin, entry of Aug. 23. Also Antoine Durand to Delcamp-Boytré in Gourdan: A.E. Cahors, carton 5–56, letter of Aug. 23.
[26] Pellerin, entry of Aug. 23; AP, 8:480. The vote was decisive enough to preclude a roll call, so the precise vote is unknown. See also Maupetit, 19 (1903), 234 (letter of Aug. 24).
[27] Barbotin, 57 (letter of Aug. 29); and Lombard-Taradeau, 263 (letter of Aug. 23). See also Duquesnoy, 1:309–11 (entry of Aug. 23); and curé Louis Verdet to Guilbert, curé of Saint-Sébastien of Nancy: Arch. Grand Séminaire Nancy, MB 17, folios 1–113, letter of Aug. 28.

dent, directly facing their Palais Royal opponents across the oval of the Menus Plaisirs.[28]

Yet the critical achievement of leadership and organization for the newly emerging right was to be the work of a coalition of more moderate conservatives, known to history as the "Monarchiens."[29] As the Palais Royal faction could trace its lineage to the Breton deputies of the Third Estate, so the core of the Monarchiens revolved around the delegation from Dauphiné, under the undisputed leadership of Mounier.[30] Soon after their arrival in Versailles, Mounier and his associates had linked themselves with several other key deputies—most notably, Malouet from Riom, Bergasse from Lyon, bishop Champion de Cicé from Bordeaux, and the comtes Lally-Tolendal and Clermont-Tonnerre from Paris—all of them enlisting additional colleagues from their respective delegations. The total number of adherents and sympathizers undoubtedly oscillated over time, totalling perhaps two or three hundred individuals at the beginning of September.[31] The central leadership of the group was distinctly elitist in its origins: of the twenty-six adherents identified by Malouet and Reynaud de Montlosier, over half had been members of the two privileged estates; and of the twelve Third Estate deputies, four were actually nobles and seven were magistrates or other high officials.[32] According to Malouet, many within the central leadership were bound by ties of close friendship as well as political ideology: "we were fifteen or twenty deputies," wrote the former naval intendant, "living in close society."[33]

Unlike the extreme right of the recalcitrant nobles and clergy, most of whom sought either a return to the Old Regime or a system of reforms based on the king's declaration of June 23, the Monarchiens affirmed many

[28] Gauville, 19–20. See also, Toulongeon, 1:108.

[29] See especially Jean Egret, *La révolution des notables: Mounier et les Monarchiens* (Paris, 1950) and Robert Griffiths, *Le centre perdu: Malouet et les "Monarchiens" dans la Révolution française* (Grenoble, 1988).

[30] Only one or two deputies from Dauphiné, in particular Barnave, were not initially associated with the Monarchiens: Egret, 127.

[31] The radical Jean-André Périsse Du Luc estimated 150–200: letter to J. B. Willermoz: B.M. Lyon ms. 5430, Sept. 17; Malouet claimed there were more than three hundred: Pierre-Victor Malouet, *Mémoires*, 2 vols., ed. Baron Malouet (Paris, 1868), 1:303–4. See also *Journal des impartiaux*, initial "Exposé," 3; and note 64 below.

[32] The following are described as having been key figures in the Monarchien leadership: Bergasse, Boisgelin (archbishop), Bonnay (marquis), Chabrol (noble), Clermont-Tonnerre (comte), Deschamps (noble), Dufraisse-Duchey (Third noble), Durget, Faydel, Guilhermy (Third noble), Henry de Longuève (Third noble), La Luzerne (bishop), Lachèse, Lally-Tolendal (comte), Lézay-Marnésia (marquis), Madier de Montjau (noble), Malouet, Mathias (curé), Mounier (Third Noble), Paccard, Pradt (vicaire-général), Redon, Reynaud de Montlosier (noble), Sérent (comte), Tailhardat de La Maisonneuve, and Virieu (comte): Malouet, deposition in *Procédure*, 1:168; and *Mémoires*, 1:271–72; François-Dominique de Reynaud de Montlosier, *Mémoires*, 2 vols. (Paris, 1830), 1:277. See also Egret, 126–28. Of the 124 deputies known by name to have supported the Monarchiens in their demand for a two-house legislature, 100 had been members of the Clergy or the Nobility. See below, note 64.

[33] Malouet, deposition in *Procédure*, 1:168.

of the transformations of July and August and had originally perceived themselves as patriots. But they were extremely wary of moving too far and too fast. As Mounier's friend the comte de Virieu put it, "It is important to be sensible, deliberate, moderate, cool"; "otherwise, we will destroy and tear and break everything, and whatever we build will not stand."[34] Most of the group had been terrified by the recent popular uprisings, were obsessively fearful of the specter of anarchy, and vigorously supported the enforcement of law and order.[35] It was in part from the desire for a strong central authority to counter the popular unrest, in part from a deep reverence for tradition that they sought to maintain ultimate sovereignty in the hands of the king. Many of the Monarchiens—like Malouet, Bergasse, and Virieu—were also strongly attached to the traditional values of religion. The basic elements of the Monarchien position had already emerged in speeches delivered to the Assembly in July, and notably in Mounier's debate with Mirabeau on July 16 over the king's right to choose his ministers, but they were perhaps best articulated in Mounier's "manifesto" of mid-August, *Considérations sur les gouvernements*.[36]

It was sometime in late July or early August that the Monarchiens set out self-consciously to beat the radicals at their own game.[37] In relatively short order, the new conservative coalition had surpassed the Palais Royal faction in their level of organization. While the Breton Club had evolved in an essentially democratic fashion, with relatively loose discipline and public debates in a café to which all were invited, and while the Palais Royal group operated with an even looser ad hoc organization, the Monarchiens followed their more authoritarian penchant by establishing a small decision-making "central committee." Convened in private at one of the member's homes—and sometimes in bishop La Luzerne's apartment in the château of Versailles—the committee sent out written directives through a system of subcommittees to all its potential adherents. Thus, in the Assembly elections at the end of August, little slips of paper were distributed to over three hundred deputies, listing the names to be inscribed on ballots for president, secretaries, and members of the influential Committee on Research.[38] On the floor of the National Assembly, Virieu assumed the role of a veritable

---

[34] Virieu, letter of July 21. See also Jean-de-Dieu Boisgelin de Cucé to comtesse de Gramont: A.N., M 788, pièce 109, ca. Aug. 17.

[35] Egret, 92–103, 122–24. See especially the speeches of Virieu and Malouet on Aug. 8: *AP*, 8:372–73; Jean-Joseph Mounier, *Exposé de la conduite de M. Mounier dans l'Assemblée nationale et des motifs de son retour en Dauphiné*, 3 parties (Paris, 1789), esp. 1:23; and Jean de Turckheim, *L'Alsace pendant la Révolution française*, ed. Rodolphe Reuss, 2 vols. (Paris, 1880–94), 1:249–66.

[36] *Considérations sur les gouvernements et principalement sur celui qui convient à la France* (Paris, [Aug.] 1789). On the Mounier-Mirabeau debate, closely followed by many deputies, see Bailly, 2:36–38 (entry for July 16); Ferrières, *Mémoires*, 3 vols. (Paris, 1825), 1:148–49; and Pellerin, entry of July 16.

[37] Walter, 18–19.

[38] Malouet, 1:301–2; Montlosier, 1:277; Gaultier, 2:269–70 (letter of Sept. 1).

party whip. As the young count from Dauphiné described it, "I resolved to place myself at the vanguard of the most difficult and dangerous operations which no one else was ready to do. . . . I devoted myself to inspiring courage in weaker men." The patriot Périsse Du Luc, who had known Virieu as a fellow Mason, was amazed at his activities: "He is to be seen in every corner of the hall, pleading, speaking, shouting, spying to see who is for and against."[39]

Whatever the differences in their ultimate objectives, the Monarchiens and the "aristocrats" of the extreme right seemed to have established a working alliance by late August or early September. Eprémesnil, Maury, and Cazalès were said to be participating in the Monarchien central committee, and though they differed in their views on certain issues, the three frequently spoke in the Assembly in defense of Monarchien positions.[40] On September 17, Périsse wrote that "the alliance of the Clergy, of the near totality of the Nobles, and of a smaller number of the Commons is so strong now that they are never divided on any votes. All, without exception, rise together or remain seated to manifest their opinions."[41] Clearly, many of the "aristocrats" were prepared to follow the rules of the game and work within the newly evolved parliamentary system in tandem with the Monarchiens, convinced of the real possibility of halting and perhaps reversing the Revolution through political organization and majority votes.

The overall strength of these factional groupings is difficult to assess with precision. For a variety of reasons, the Assembly barred the recording of individual deputy options in roll call votes, and usually only the total breakdowns for and against are preserved.[42] One indication of the growing power and discipline of the right is the vote for officers within the Assembly. Every two weeks an election of the president and three of the six secretaries was organized within the Assembly's thirty bureaus.[43] The elections between July 3 and August 3 seem generally to confirm the atmosphere of a united front. Of the fifteen individuals elected during this period, four were linked to the Breton Club, four to the future Monarchien group, and the remainder were essentially nonaligned. Perhaps equally significant, eight of the fifteen were representatives of the former privileged estates.[44] Although the

[39] Virieu, letters of Aug. 25 and Sept. 29; Périsse, letter of Sept. 17.

[40] Montlosier, 1:277; Périsse Du Luc, letter of Sept. 17. See also Philip Kolody, "The right in the French National Assembly, 1789–91," Ph.D. dissertation, Princeton Univ., 1967, 122–34; and Albert Mathiez, "Etude critique sur les Journées des 5 et 6 octobre 1789," *RH* 67 (1898), 266, 273.

[41] Périsse, letter of Sept. 17.

[42] Antoine-François Delandine, *Mémorial historique des Etats généraux*, 5 vols. (n.p., 1789), 2:146–47; Pellerin, entries of June 17 and July 9; and Gaultier, 2:168 (letter of July 9). See also Applewhite, xxii.

[43] Duquesnoy was convinced that the votes for president mirrored his colleagues' political propensities at a given point in time: Duquesnoy, 2:138 (entry of Dec. 6, 1789).

[44] See *AP*, 33:88. Among the fifteen, the duc d'Orléans and Thouret declined their elections. Those probably affiliated to the Breton group were Grégoire, Le Chapelier, Pétion, and Sieyès;

Breton Le Chapelier was named president at the beginning of August, it was only after the winner, the moderate Thouret, had resigned.

But after the middle of August, the Monarchiens not only won four presidential elections in succession but also largely dominated the secretariat's table. On August 31, they engineered a clean sweep of the presidency—La Luzerne, bishop of Langres—and the three new secretaries—Redon, Deschamps, and Henry de Longuève. Indeed, Mounier's coalition was probably the only group systematically organizing for elections during this period. The scraps of voting records remaining reveal that in September the Monarchien candidates alone received significant blocs of votes in every bureau, with the rest of the votes being spread out over an enormous range of individual deputies.[45] The election in mid-September of the Monarchien comte de Clermont-Tonnerre was perhaps even more galling to the left, in that, by the rotation procedure tacitly agreed upon since July, the post should normally have gone to a member of the Third Estate.[46]

The patriots on the left were only too aware of these successes. Durand wrote home of the "alliance formed between the Clergy, the Nobility, and a part of the Commons, which together constitute a new aristocracy"; Lombard complained that "our party is absolutely in the minority"; and Robespierre concluded that "the majority of the National Assembly is the avowed enemy of liberty."[47] The Monarchien Virieu, however, had a strongly different point of view: "For the last three weeks," he wrote, "respectable men, weary of the tyranny of the radicals [enragés] . . . have quietly united and retaken control with a majority of at least two to one. Suddenly the radicals find themselves defeated at every turn. Most recently we have elected the president and all three new secretaries, despite all their opposition."[48]

THE SEPTEMBER DEBATES AND THE LIMITED VICTORY OF THE RIGHT

The growing factional divisions within the Assembly had a powerful effect on the debates during the first weeks of September concerning the fundamental structures of the constitution and the balance of authority within the state.[49] The eight-man Constitutional Committee had worked for weeks to

---

those soon to be attached to the Monarchiens were Clermont-Tonnerre, Lally-Tolendal, abbé de Montesquiou, and Mounier; probably "non-aligned" at this point were Emmery, Fréteau de Saint-Just, Lafayette, Le Franc de Pompignan, Liancourt, d'Orléans, and Thouret.

[45] A.N., C 83, dossier 818 (6–7).

[46] Maillot, letter of Aug. 30; and Charles-François Bouche, letter of Aug. 31.

[47] Durand, letter of Aug. 31; Lombard-Taradeau, 271 (letter of Aug. 30); Maximilien Robespierre, *Correspondance*, ed. Georges Michon, 2 vols. (Paris, 1926–41), 51 (letter of Sept. 5).

[48] Virieu, letter of Sept. 1. See also, Vernier, letter of Aug. 3; Boullé, 15 (1889), 114 (letter of Sept. 8); Maillot, entry of Aug. 30; La Bévière, letter of Aug. 30.

[49] On the September debates, see especially Egret, 136–59; and Keith Michael Baker, *Inventing the French Revolution* (Cambridge, 1990), 271–305; also Ran Halévi, "La république

draw up a basic document for discussion, but it had been deeply divided over the number of houses in the new legislature and the powers of the king in relation to that legislature. The Monarchien majority on the Committee—Mounier, Bergasse, Champion de Cicé, Clermont-Tonnerre, and Lally-Tolendal—found it impossible to reach a consensus with the radicals Sieyès and Le Chapelier.[50] At the core of contention was the issue of royal veto power over legislation, with the Monarchiens demanding an unlimited veto and Sieyès and Le Chapelier pressing for no veto at all. Distressed by the evident split among the former patriot allies, the Paris national guard commander Lafayette, who now rarely attended the Assembly himself, attempted to mediate. The meeting took place on the afternoon and evening of August 26 on the neutral ground of Thomas Jefferson's Paris apartment, and brought together the three Dauphinois, Mounier, the comte d'Agoult, and the chevalier de Blacons, on the one hand, and the radical patriot trio of Duport, Barnave, and Alexandre de Lameth, on the other. Lafayette probably hoped that the friendship between Mounier and Barnave and the absence of the more fiery deputies from the two sides—the Bretons and the comte de Virieu—might facilitate a reconciliation. But if the deputies on the left revealed themselves ready to compromise and accept some form of restrictive or limited veto, Mounier remained steadfastly intransigent: "When I believed that a principle was true," he later wrote, "I was compelled to defend it."[51]

With no compromise in sight, the committee was forced to pass on the question to the full Assembly, which took up the issue of the veto at the very end of August. For both sides, the stakes of the debate seemed extremely high. Many of the radicals were now convinced that they were in the minority in the Assembly and that the Monarchiens and the aristocrats were trying to obtain an unlimited royal veto in order to undo all the previous Revolutionary gains. Such suspicions seemed all the more pertinent in that Louis XVI had still not given his formal ascent to any of the Assembly's major decrees of August. "I have come increasingly to realize," wrote the patriot Vernier, "that our Assembly is divided . . . and that the nobles and the clergy want to make use of the veto to have all of our reforms rejected." In Durand's opinion, most of those backing the veto did so "either for personal advantage or from dishonest intentions"; and Périsse assessed the situation as a battle between despotism, on the one hand, and liberty and patriotism, on the other. Virieu was scarcely less Manichaean in his views, describing the radicals as "scoundrels" and "madmen," "this heinous party

monarchique," in *Le siècle de l'avènement républicain*, ed. François Furet and Mona Ozouf (Paris, 1993), 182–96.

[50] Mounier, *Exposé*, 1:26, 47. Talleyrand, the eighth member of the Committee, seems never to have been in Mounier's camp.

[51] Mounier, *Exposé*, 1:41–44. Also Mathiez, 67 (1898), 266–67; Louis Gottschalk and Margaret Maddox, *Lafayette in the French Revolution through the October Days* (Chicago, 1969), 227–30; and Paul Bastid, *Sieyès et sa pensée* (Paris, 1939), 76–77.

of conspirators" bent on creating a republic in which the whole country would be lost in fire and blood.[52] The Monarchiens were convinced, moreover, that the radical left had directly incited the Parisian riots of August 30–31, in which a list of "bad citizens" in the Assembly was drawn up and an armed march on Versailles planned to force the deputies to reject the veto. Though the attack was easily halted by Lafayette's national guard, many of the conservative and moderate deputies were profoundly upset, outraged by this threat to freedom of opinion. The incident probably helped further consolidate the alliance between the Monarchiens and the extreme right.[53]

By all accounts the debate over the veto, which lasted a full two weeks, was raucous and tumultuous. Both factions realized that the outcome would depend on which side was best able to win over the fluid center of the Assembly, estimated by Périsse to represent about one-third of the deputies. For a time, no one was willing to predict which position would emerge victorious.[54] Speakers were frequently interrupted by hostile comments from opponents, and veritable shouting matches were orchestrated across the hall by "the two parties existing in the Assembly," now openly referred to as such in newspaper accounts.[55] On occasion the Palais Royal group systematically disrupted the proceedings in order to stall for time or force a roll call vote.[56] Yet the speeches themselves were of the highest quality, delivered by the best minds of the Assembly, probing and learned, passing in review much of eighteenth-century thought on the theory and practice of political organization, with frequent references to the English and American examples and the writings of the philosophes. Most of the deputies, particularly those not closely tied to one faction or another, seemed able to push aside the disruption of the parliamentary infighting and to follow the discussions with rapt fascination.

Thus, like the discussions on the Rights of Man, the September debates marked another important step in the Revolutionary education of the deputies. For the first time, some found themselves following the logic of popular sovereignty to its full implications for the limitation of the king's powers. Doctor Campmas admitted to his brother that he had not initially understood the importance of the veto question, imagining it to be only "a minor difficulty"; but that the orators "of superior talent" had convinced him that the relation between the king and the legislature was at the core of

---

[52] Vernier, letter of Aug. 30; Durand, letter of Sept. 4; Périsse, letter of Sept. 2; Virieu, letter of Sept. 29.

[53] See Mathiez, 67 (1898) 267, 273; and *AP*, 8:512–14; Mounier, *Exposé*, 1:42–44; and La Bévière, letter of Aug. 30. Also Begouën, letter of Sept. 2; Maillot, entry for Sept. 2; and Boullé, 15 (1889), 114–15 (letter of Sept. 8).

[54] Périsse, letter of Sept. 2; Durand, letter of Sept. 5; and Vernier, letter of Sept. 8.

[55] See, e.g., *AP*, 8:601 (Sillery's speech of Sept. 7). There were frequent references in the *Moniteur*, on which the *AP* is based, to the turbulence and polarization of the Assembly.

[56] Lombard, 325 (letter of Sept. 13).

the whole constitution. Sallé de Choux was stunned by the extraordinarily rapid evolution in ideas: only a year earlier, they were begging the king to reform a certain number of abuses, and now they were discussing whether the monarch would have any control over new laws. Ménard de La Groye recounted his exuberance in listening to "orators who astonished me by their eloquence, their insights, their wisdom," and described the two week's debates to his wife as "the most wonderful period in my life." Delandine was also thrilled by the experience: "Never have such important subjects been discussed in France, never has a more noble career been opened up to journalists and orators." A staunch royalist in his previous writings, he seemed quite amazed by the audacity of the issues raised about the foundations of the king's authority: "this question so new in France, this question whose solution might be either the seed of slavery or the safeguard of liberty for all our descendants."[57]

Though the polarization of a substantial portion of the Assembly had initially focused the debate on the dichotomous choice between an absolute veto and no veto at all, the deputies soon came to realize the tangle of interrelated issues concerning the basic power balance within the new government. What, after all, was meant by a royal "veto"? Could such a veto be overridden, and if so, in what manner and over what period of time? Would the Assembly maintain a permanent existence, or come into being at specific intervals or only when called into being by the king? Would there be more than one Assembly, and if so would each of them have vetoes over the other's legislative decisions? On several occasions the Assembly had to modify its focus of debate to take into account an expanding understanding of the issues.[58]

By early September increasing numbers of both moderate and radical deputies began leaning toward a third alternative: the so-called "suspensive veto," by which the king might block a new law, unless it was passed again at a later date. It was evident from the speeches, however, that different supporters had very different conceptions of the meaning of the suspension involved. For some of the radicals, the proposal was seen as a *pis aller* compromise: their real preference was for no veto, but they were convinced that there was insufficient support for this option and that a suspensive veto was better than an absolute veto.[59] Others saw it as a positive step in the direction of popular democracy, in which a veto would trigger an *appel au peuple* to determine the "general will," a kind of national referendum on any law

---

[57] Campmas, letter of Sept. 6; *AP*, 9:85; François-René-Pierre Ménard de La Groye, *François Ménard de La Groye, député du Maine aux Etats généraux. Correspondance, 1789–1791*, Florence Mirouse, ed. (Le Mans, 1989), 93, 96 (letters of Sept. 1 and 4); Delandine, 5:6 (entry for Sept. 1).

[58] See, e.g., the debate of Aug. 29: *AP*, 8:509–10.

[59] E.g., Jean-François-Marie Goupilleau to his cousin, sénéchal in Rochefervière: B.M. Nantes, Collection Dugast-Matifeux, no. 98, letter of Oct. 26; Robespierre, printed opinion of early Sept.: *AP*, 9:81.

which the king opposed.[60] Frequently the modalities of such a referendum were left vague, but when the deputies elaborated their ideas, they usually assumed that the *appel* would be organized rapidly: either directly, through votes in local assemblies, or indirectly, through a new general election of deputies during which the issue would be discussed. The veto could then be overridden either a few weeks later by the same legislature repassing the law, or by the following legislature, often assumed to be elected within a year.[61] Other, more moderate proponents, however, saw the suspensive veto less as an exercise in popular democracy than as a means of preserving the prerogatives of the king against the "arbitrary authority of the deputies." They conceived the override process as being far more difficult, made no mention of direct referendums, and would require two or even three successive legislatures—each meeting for one or two years—to pass the same law.[62] In the end, the position in favor of a suspensive veto was almost certainly strengthened when it became generally known that the king himself was ready to accept it—much to the chagrin of the Monarchiens, who argued that "even if the king were to refuse [the absolute veto], the nation should grant it to him."[63]

After more than a week of debates without a conclusion, the Assembly opted to set aside temporarily the question of the veto and consider the number of chambers to be established in the new legislative assembly. This switch in focus may have been a parliamentary maneuver by the radicals, designed to split their opponents on the right. If such was the case, the move succeeded remarkably well. On September 10, by the massive majority of 849 out of 1,060 present, Mounier's proposal for a periodically elected lower house, balanced by an upper senate with lifetime membership, was repudiated in favor of a unicameral legislature. The deputies supporting Mounier consisted of the core of the Monarchien leadership plus an additional diverse contingent of nobles and clergymen.[64] But the overwhelming majority of the commoners and a large contingent of the former privileged deputies rejected it. A few of the "aristocrats" reportedly claimed they were following a *politique du pire*, hoping that a legislature with a single chamber

---

[60] Baker, 289–95.

[61] See, e.g., the speeches by Pétion, Salle, Rabaut, Harmand, Alexandre de Lameth, Dupont de Nemours, Barère, and Gaultier de Biauzat: *AP*, 8:529–34, 551–52, 567–73, 580–84, 9:56–57, 60–62.

[62] This was Thouret's proposal—the proposal, in fact, which ultimately passed: *AP*, 8:580–81; also, Maupetit 19 (1903), 245–46 (letter of Sept. 14).

[63] *AP*, 8:610 (Sept. 11). Though the deputies ultimately refused to allow a reading of the king's statement in the Assembly, the king's opinion was widely known: Vernier, letter of Sept. 8.

[64] A conclusion derived from an analysis of the partial list of adherents printed in *Le secrétaire de l'Assemblée nationale* 9 (Sept. 10, 1789), 4–6. A little over 200 deputies seem to have backed the two-house legislature. This included the 89 voting for the measure; and most of the 122 who abstained on the vote but who were said actually to have supported it, objecting primarily to the measure's wording.

would be all the more unstable and transient.[65] Others of the nobles, however, particularly those from the provinces, feared that an upper house would soon be dominated by the same great aristocrats and courtiers who had lorded over them under the Old Regime. It was a rare incident in which social divisions within the nobility may have had a significant impact on events.[66]

The veto issue itself finally came to a vote the next day, after a session lasting nearly twelve hours without a break. The two successive roll calls revealed that the deputies remained strongly divided over the three possible options, no one of which carried an absolute majority: about 220 for no veto at all, about 450 for a suspensive veto, and 325 for an absolute veto.[67] It was only after those opposed to the veto threw their support to the suspensive veto on the second vote that the latter option handily won, 673 to 325.[68] The partial lists of voters that can be reconstructed suggest that the deputies split sharply by political factions and social origins. The Monarchien position of an "indefinite veto" received a solid backing from a large number of privileged deputies—at least three-fifths of all of the advocates of this option. Among the Palais Royal radicals and their affiliates supporting no veto, by contrast, only about one-eighth were from the privileged orders.[69]

In the immediate aftermath of the vote, after the double defeat of their policies on two successive days, the Monarchiens resigned from the Constitutional Committee. The new committee elected by the Assembly would be distinctly less conservative in its membership, though by no means radical, with Sieyès, Le Chapelier, and Talleyrand now joined by Rabaut Saint-Etienne, Thouret, and the Parisians Target, Tronchet, and Démeunier.[70] Yet

[65] Duquesnoy, 1:327 (enrty of Sept. 10); Toulongeon, 1:113–14; Mounier, *Exposé*, 1:53.

[66] Ferrières, *Correspondance*, 149–50 (letter of Sept. 18); and Gauville, 21. See also the commentaries of Pellerin: entry of Sept. 10; Rabaut, 195–96; Dinochau, 2:42; and La Bévière, letters of Sept. 4 and 10.

[67] This breakdown is extrapolated from the two roll calls. In the first, 733 deputies voted for some form of veto, 143 voted for no veto, and another 76 abstained. Vernier made it clear, however, that it was essentially the Breton and the Comtois deputies (presumably those of the Third Estate and a portion of the clergy) who abstained, because of what they felt was an ambiguity in the specific wording of the motion (the meaning of the word "*sanction*"). But Vernier also made it clear that the deputies from these two provinces opposed any veto: letters of Sept. 12 and 22. In the second roll call, 325 voted for an "indefinite" veto, and 673 for a suspensive veto: *Le secrétaire de l'Assemblée nationale* 10 (Sept. 11, 1789), 6–7.

[68] Maupetit noted that all the Breton deputies voted for the suspensive veto on the final vote: 19 (1903), 245 (letter of Sept. 13).

[69] Votes have been determined for 136 deputies based on the partial list in the *Le secrétaire de l'Assemblée*, cited above; the speeches and printed opinions found in the *AP*, vols. 8 and 9; and opinions expressed in deputy letters and diaries of the period. Of 32 known to have supported the absolute veto, 19 (59%) were nobles (16) or clergy (3); of 38 known to have supported the suspensive veto, 11 (30%) were nobles (10) or clergy (1); of 66 known to have voted for no veto, 8 (12%) were nobles (7) or clergy (1).

[70] See the following chapter.

in many respects, the proud and extremely sensitive Mounier had resigned too soon. The critical vote on the length of the suspensive veto, the time that would elapse before the king's veto could be nullified, was put off for ten days while the Assembly took up other pressing problems and attempted to pressure the king into formally accepting the decrees of August 4. Finally on September 21 Louis announced he would publish the decrees—after the Assembly agreed to take into account the king's "observations" when implementing the general decrees into concrete laws.[71] In the midst of the general elation over this news, the Monarchien president, Clermont-Tonnerre, quickly pushed through a decree that would require three successive legislatures to pass a given law before a royal veto could be rejected.[72] The proposal was massively approved by 728 of the 952 voting, with apparently only the Palais Royal radicals voting in opposition.[73] Since the Assembly had already decided that the legislative sessions would last two years—another defeat for the radicals on the left[74]—the veto would necessarily be prolonged through three legislatures and might easily last four or even six years.

Some historians have interpreted the vote on the veto as a decisive victory for the left.[75] It was clear to the deputies themselves, however, that the suspensive veto would be all but impossible to override and was virtually tantamount to an absolute veto; that the king had in fact been granted enormous potential powers over the legislature; and that in this respect the Monarchiens had won the day. Indeed, the whole idea of the *appel au peuple* was forgotten and would find no mention in the final constitution. "Thus," explained Delandine, who had opposed the two-legislature override, "any minister fearing the effects of a sound law would have up to six years to dissuade public opinion against it." Or in the phrase of Duquesnoy, who supported it, the decree "has all the advantages of an absolute veto without any of the inconveniences."[76]

Vernier, who had tightly embraced the Palais Royal on almost every issue, was sobered by the vote: "Yesterday, through shrewdness, cunning, and cabal, . . . our enemies the royalists won the day." Goupilleau could only lament, "It pains me to see the enemies of the public good assume

[71] *AP*, 9:53.

[72] *AP*, 9:54–55. Clermont-Tonnerre clearly used his powers as president to take advantage of the renewed goodwill toward the king and close the debates before any of the radicals had been allowed to speak.

[73] Vernier noted that the number voting against the two-legislature suspension (224) was almost exactly the same as that supporting no veto on Sept. 11, implying that largely the same groups of deputies had been involved each time: letter of Sept. 22.

[74] *AP*, 8:616–19 (Sept. 12, speeches by Robespierre, Dubois-Crancé, Buzot, and Le Pelletier).

[75] Baker, 301–5; and Halévi, 195–96. Halévi argues that the veto was so powerful that it was impossible to use. It would be used, however, under the Legislative Assembly.

[76] Delandine, 5:197–98 (entry for Sept. 22); Duquesnoy, 1:354 (entry of Sept. 21).

their arrogant airs once again."[77] The Breton deputies were so depressed by the decision that they seriously considered abandoning the Assembly altogether.[78] The vote had only confirmed what many on the left had already perceived, that their group was now clearly in the minority and that most of the unaligned moderates were frequently siding with the Monarchiens and the "aristocrats." It was in this state of mind that the radical Volney proposed organizing new elections as soon as possible in the hope of obtaining an Assembly less influenced by a strong aristocratic presence and more truly reflective of the social composition of the country as a whole.[79]

Volney and his friends could scarcely have been encouraged on September 28 when the Monarchiens once again won the Assembly's internal elections, claiming both the presidency and two of the three secretariats. For the Monarchien leadership it must have seemed a partial vindication that the new president in question was Mounier himself.[80]

THE OCTOBER DAYS: BREAK AND CONTINUITY

In the early days of October, outside events once again burst in upon the deliberations of the deputies, as tens of thousands of Parisian citizens and national guardsmen descended on Versailles, as hundreds funneled into the meeting hall to present their grievances, and as violence and bloodshed swept through the royal palace and the streets and courtyards surrounding it. In part it had the character of a traditional grain riot, with large numbers of women—defenders of the family economy and usually immune from prosecution—leading the way and calling for bread, and with a certain number of men following close behind encouraging them. But both women and men were also aware of the new political realities and were following after their fashion the debates and the factional disputes within the Assembly. The calls for bread were joined with threats against the "aristocratic" deputies on the right—now seemingly in control of the Assembly—and with demands to bring the king to Paris and send away troops recently moved to the capital. When the Parisians succeeded in forcing Louis XVI and his government to move to the city, the Assembly quickly declared itself "inseparable" from the monarchy and made plans to transfer its meetings to Paris.[81]

The extent to which deputies themselves played a role in inciting the

---

[77] Vernier, letter of Sept. 22; Goupilleau, undated letter of ca. Sept. 21; also Boullé, 16 (1889), 24 (letter of Sept. 19–21). Garron de La Bévière, by contrast, considered that the right had claimed a great triumph over "la minorité": letter of Sept. 22.

[78] Delaville, letter of Sept. 22.

[79] *AP*, 9:36 (session of Sept. 18).

[80] Virieu, letter of Sept. 29; Mounier, *Exposé*, 2:4–5.

[81] On the October Days, see esp. Mathiez, "Etude critique"; and Barry Shapiro, *Revolutionary Justice in Paris, 1789–90* (Cambridge, 1993), chap. 4.

uprising may never be answered. The Monarchien leaders had little doubt of the connivance of the elder Mirabeau, and perhaps of the duc d'Orléans, in a move to install the popular patriot duke as a kind of mayor of the palace with ultimate power over the king.[82] Orléans' abrupt departure for England immediately after the riots only added to suspicions; and given what we know of Mirabeau's mind through his correspondence of 1790 and 1791—extraordinarily fertile in scheming and plots—involvement on his part would not seem implausible.[83] Most of the radical deputies were extremely bitter and unhappy with the situation on the eve of the October Days: with the persistent opposition from the right in the Assembly, and the continued failure of the monarchy to promulgate certain decrees. Although Louis and his ministers had seemed ready to cooperate when he promised to publish the decrees of August 4, now they were procrastinating with the promulgation of the Declaration of the Rights of Man and with the initial articles of the constitution. The king's letter to this effect, delivered to the Assembly on October 5—coupled with a perceived insult to the Revolution during a recent royalist reception for the Flanders regiment—triggered an explosion of protest from deputies on the left, with rhetoric angrier and more hostile toward the monarchy than ever before.[84] It appeared to the patriots that the king and the aristocrats—buttressed by a strong political organization in the Assembly itself—were once again attempting to erase many of the previous Revolutionary gains. The moderate comte de Dieusie was mystified by Louis's decisions, which he could only attribute to exceptionally bad counsel from the king's advisers. In an exasperated letter Barnave vented his frustration toward the ministers and the conservatives in the Assembly, who "have never wanted a constitution": "each time they find themselves holding the upper hand, they attempt, with unbelievable bad faith, to reject everything they had previously seemed to accept."[85]

But if many of the radical deputies in question cultivated close ties with certain Parisian leaders, agitators, and journalists, it is difficult to prove any direct links to the insurrection, and it is unlikely, in any case, that individuals in the Assembly would have been able to affect the precise timing of the revolt.[86] Most of the deputies were surprised by the events—more so perhaps than by the insurrection of mid-July. There was no mention in the debates of an impending crisis in Paris before the day of the riot itself.

[82] See the depositions by numerous of the Monarchien leaders, notably that of Bergasse: *Procédure*, 1:20.

[83] See in particular Mirabeau's *mémoires* to the king in *Correspondance avec le comte de la Marck*, 3 vols., Adrien de Bacourt ed. (Paris, 1851). Orléans was virtually forced to leave the country by Lafayette: Shapiro, 95–96.

[84] *AP*, 9:342–45.

[85] Jean-Charles-Antoine Morel de Dieusie, "L'Assemblée provinciale d'Anjou, d'après les archives de Serrant (1787–89)," ed. M. de La Tremoïlle, *Anjou historique* 2 (1901–1902), 55 (letter of Sept. 21); and letter from Barnave to an unknown, cited in Mathiez 68 (1898), 272.

[86] Mathiez, esp. 68 (1898), 272–73, 282–84; and 69 (1899), 50–52.

While the deputies—in their letters and diaries—were aware of the difficulties of Parisian subsistence, and frequently complained of the quality of bread available in Versailles,[87] they were primarily concerned with the state's continuing financial difficulties, so dangerous for the survival of the Revolutionary regime.[88] Boullé found the October Days "perhaps more astonishing than those of last July." Curé Pous spoke of "this revolution which was made in less than twenty-four hours."[89]

In any case, the events of October 5–6 were a jolting experience for the deputies. For most individuals in the Assembly, it was their first face-to-face confrontation with the mobilized Parisian crowds. Initially only a small group of women with their spokesman Maillard appeared on the visitor's platform to make their appeal. But then, tired and impatient after hours outside in the rain, the women began entering the hall in large numbers, muddy and bedraggled, wedging themselves onto the benches between the deputies, shouting for bread when the Assembly tried to conduct business as usual on matters concerning the constitution. Most stayed on even after the Assembly adjourned. Someone broke into the deputies' refreshment stall and the women and a sprinkling of men sat down to a boisterous picnic of wine and meats before the amazed deputies who had remained behind to watch.[90]

More than simply disrupting the meeting, the crowds physically threatened many of the deputies both inside and outside the hall. With an unexpected political savvy, the people seemed to have targeted specific political groups, particularly the Monarchiens. A crowd of men came by Mounier's house at night threatening to cut off his head; Faydel was cornered at his secretary's desk by a crowd of women who pulled at his garments and tried to force him to issue an edict providing more bread; bishop La Luzerne found himself intimidated and insulted; and Malouet was surrounded on the Place des Armes by a dozen men with pikes until Mirabeau rushed over to extricate him—an experience which Malouet still remembered with terror many years later.[91] The clerical deputies also came in for considerable abuse. Threatened by the crowds, abbé Pous returned to his room and locked his door, "plunged in sorrow"; while his colleague, curé Samary, was so ill treated by the rioters that he suffered a complete nervous breakdown and was incapacitated for weeks. Another curé, more robust by nature,

[87] E.g., Campmas, letter of Aug. 8; Bigot de Vernière, letter of Aug. 20; Gontier de Biran, letter of Aug. 21; Claude Gantheret to Pierre Leflaive, his brother-in-law: private collection of Françoise Misserey, letter of Sept. 13; Pierre-François Lepoutre to his wife: familly archives of Adolphe Lepoutre-Dubreuil, Montignac-sur-Vezère, letter of Aug. 29.

[88] E.g., Basquiat and Lamarque, letter of Sept. 29; Pierre-Marie Irland de Bazôges to Henri Filleau, magistrate in Poitiers: A.D. Deux-Sèvres, Fonds Beauchet-Filleau, unclassed register of "lettres politiques, 1788–90," letter of Sept. 25; Verdet, letter of Oct. 1.

[89] Boullé, 16 (1898), 52 (letter of Oct. 6, misdated in printed version); Paul-Augustin Pous, "Correspondance inédite," *Revue de l'Anjou* 22 (1879), 277 (letter of Oct. 6).

[90] See esp. Mounier, *Exposé*, 2:15–16, 20–22. Also, Duquesnoy, 1:401–5 (entry of Oct. 7).

[91] *Procédure*, 1:232 (Faydel); and 1:169 (Malouet); Mounier, *Exposé*, 2:25; Malouet, 2:3.

fought off a crowd with his umbrella and managed to knock down four men before making his escape. Pursued by yet another band of men and women, curé Vallet of Gien and the elderly bishop of Auxerre struggled up four flights of stairs into a nearby building and confessed one another, while waiting for the worst—which fortunately never came.[92] The rioters seemed less discriminating of the political positions of the clergymen, however, than of those of the lay deputies, and even strongly patriotic priests like Thomas Lindet found themselves "exposed to the utmost danger" and to "public loathing" simply "because of the clerical habit they wore."[93]

The fact that none of the deputies was physically injured or killed may tell us something of the continuing aura of respect for the deputies in general. Yet even those deputies—the great majority—who were not personally threatened by the rioters, often witnessed acts of violence which they could not soon forget. Charles-François Lebrun was walking home as the Parisians opened fire on the royal guard, and he was forced to leap over a wall and hide between two wagons. Boullé, standing further away, heard the shots and the drums and saw the great crowds surging through the streets: "Oh my God, how many storms must we pass through before we attain our national regeneration?" The courtier comte de La Chastre watched from his château window on the early morning of the 6th as the crowds broke into the palace grounds and decapitated one of the guards. He then rushed to the aid of the queen and collapsed in despair when he found her room in shambles, empty and stained with blood.[94]

The count soon found the queen and the king safe in the opposite wing of the palace. But the lives of the royal couple and of the Constituent deputies themselves were unalterably changed by the episode. Under popular pressure, the king agreed to move his family and his entire government to Paris, to be followed soon thereafter by the National Assembly. In addition, Louis now accepted the Declaration of the Rights of Man and all of the constitutional articles which he had previously avoided signing. At long last, the king seemed to reconcile himself to sharing power with the Constituent Assembly; and for the next year and a half, he and his ministers would generally cooperate with the deputies. In this sense, the October Days marked a stunning victory for the policies of the patriots and the left.

Not surprisingly, some deputies on the left expressed their general satisfaction with the course of events. Once Boullé had overcome his fright, he concluded that it had all been for the best and that "once again we owe our salvation to the Parisians." Goupilleau was delighted with the outcome of

[92] Pous 22 (1879), 277–78 (letter of Oct. 6); *AP*, 9:405 (deliberation of Oct. 10); Claude-Benjamin Vallet, "Souvenirs de l'abbé Vallet, député de Gien à l'Assemblée constituante," *Nouvelle revue rétrospective* 16 (1902), 325–26.

[93] Thomas Lindet, *Correspondance de Thomas Lindet pendant la Constituante et la Législative (1789–92)*, ed. Amand Montier (Paris, 1899), 5 (letter of Oct. 8).

[94] *Procédure*, 1:2ll-12 (La Chastre); and 1:219 (Lebrun); Boullé, 16 (1889), 54 (letter of Oct. 6).

this "second Revolution" which had "humiliated the aristocracy." "One can hope," noted Gallot in a letter to his wife, "that the aristocracy has been so overwhelmed that it will never rise again."[95] Merle, Dinochau, and Lepoutre all took pains to explain the popular violence in terms of the great suffering of the common people: "it was because of their suffering that this storm was aroused among a people normally so gentle and humane."[96]

But the majority of our witnesses were far less rosy in their descriptions of the events. Moderates like Delandine, Lasalle, and Boissy d'Anglas were shocked and repelled by the violence. Indeed, Delandine's final *Mémorial*, with its account of October, was dramatically different in tone from his earlier writings. The glowing optimism of August was replaced by a deeply pessimistic view of the masses whom he had once idealized: "A virtuous man who supported the cause of the common people has found nothing but ingratitude for his pains." The people's "natural inconstancy, the ease with which they are led to disastrous opinions, the restlessness which causes them continually to change their positions: all lead them imperceptibly to a state of slavery to their passions."[97] As for the Monarchiens, the entire group was devastated and despondent. On the evening of October 6 and on the following morning, the leadership grimly gathered in Bergasse's apartment to evaluate the situation. All were horrified by the actions of the "mobs" for which they experienced deep physical revulsion: "the vilest riffraff of Paris," as Bergasse described them. Mounier and Lally-Tolendal, "in despair," urged the entire right to abandon the National Assembly. Malouet seemed to waiver between retreat and combativeness. In fact, during the following days, Mounier, Lally, La Luzerne, and several other Monarchiens did indeed withdraw from the Assembly; and Bergasse, while never formally resigning, essentially ceased attending.[98]

Nevertheless, the effects of the October Days on the political dynamics and internal alignments of the Assembly were considerably less than is sometimes suggested by historians. Though there were numerous deputy requests for passports, the Assembly moved quickly to limit the number granted, fearing the political effects in the provinces of such departures. In all, only eleven individuals seem to have resigned their posts during Octo-

---

[95] Boullé, 16 (1889), 59 (letter of Oct. 9); Goupilleau, letter of Oct. 9; Jean-Gabriel Gallot, *La vie et les oeuvres du Docteur Jean-Gabriel Gallot*, ed. Louis Merle (Poitiers, 1961), 129 (letter of Oct. 6). Also, François-Joseph Bouchette, *Lettres*, ed. C. Looten (Lille, 1909), 264–66 (letter of Oct. 6).

[96] The quote is from André-Marie Merle to the municipality of Mâcon: A.C. Mâcon, D (2) 13, carton 21 bis, letter of Oct. 13. Also, Dinochau, 2:104; Lepoutre, letter of Oct. 7.

[97] Delandine, 6:3–4; Lasalle, 244 (letter of Oct. 6); Boissy d'Anglas, Archives de l'Air, letter of Oct. 24.

[98] Malouet, 2:4–5; Montlosier, 1:301–2; Bergasse to his brothers in Marseille, cited in Etienne Lamy, *Un défenseur des principes traditionnels sous la Révolution: N. Bergasse* (Paris, 1910), 120 (letter of mid to late Oct.); Mounier, *Exposé*, 2:34–40. See also the *compte-rendu* of Turckheim who resigned at this time: 1:188–89.

ber, with thirty-seven more departing in November and December.[99] Even among those who actually departed, many had already been weary of the Assembly and had been planning such a move well beforehand.[100] After considerable soul searching, most of the Monarchiens opted to remain at their posts and continue the struggle. Despite his initial desperation, the comte de Virieu vowed to fight on: "the sacred fire which burned within me is not yet extinguished"; and he ultimately repudiated Mounier's departure and his efforts to rally the Estates of Dauphiné against the Assembly. His Dauphiné colleague, the comte de Lablache, who had found a niche for himself in the Finance Committee, working long hours with Necker on the budget, also criticized Mounier and announced his intention of remaining as long as he could serve the "public good." The conservative chief magistrate from Bergerac, Gontier de Biran, affirmed his determination to stay on regardless of his anguish and disappointment: "I think that if it were not for the honor and desire of doing our duty, few of us would remain here." And Clermont-Tonnerre, absent for almost a week, returned to his bench and became active once again.[101]

On October 15 right and left alike departed the hall they had known for twenty-four extraordinarily eventful weeks and followed the king to Paris. After the three days which they allotted themselves to find new lodging in the capital, they assembled at their temporary quarters in the ordination hall of the episcopal palace adjoining the cathedral of Notre Dame. By all accounts, the new meeting place was scarcely bearable, so small that many of the delegates had to stand in the back or listen from adjoining rooms, and with a makeshift wooden balcony for spectators which soon collapsed, seriously injuring seven deputies.[102] The representatives were only too happy on November 9 to move into their permanent home in the "Manège" of the Tuileries Palace. The Assembly's architect had done his best to transform this long and narrow indoor riding arena into a viable hall. Tiered benches were constructed on all sides of the rectangle, with special balconies added for spectators and for alternate deputies and lobbyists. But many com-

---

[99] Brette, *Recueil*, vol. 2; A.N., C 32, dossier 266; and a wide variety of biographic sources, including the Fichier Lefebvre and the *DC*. Eleven are estimated to have left in October, 26 in November, 11 in December. Of these, 19 were clergymen, 15 commoners, and 14 nobles. See also, Boullé, 16 (1889), 58–59 (letter of Oct. 9). Cf. Hyppolyte-Adolphe Taine, *Les origines de la France contemporaine. La Révolution* (Paris, 1878), 139; and Eric Thompson, *Popular Sovereignty and the French Constituent Assembly, 1789–91* (Manchester, 1952), 24.

[100] See Garron de La Bévière, letters of Aug. through Oct.; Irland de Bazôges, letter of Sept. 22; Banyuls de Montferrat and Coma Serra, letter of Aug. 30.

[101] Virieu, letters of Oct. 12, 16, and 20; Lablache, letter of Oct. 20; Gontier, letter of Oct. 12; Delaville, letter of Oct. 13. Also, e.g., Boisgelin, letter of Oct. 14; and Paul Messié, "Le comte de Marsane-Fontjuliane, député de Montélimar aux premières assemblées révolutionnaires," *Bulletin de la Société départementale d'archéologie et de statistique de la Drôme* 76 (1964), 85–91.

[102] Brette, *Histoire des édifices*, 101–4; Boullé, 16 (1889), 83 (letter of Oct. 10); La Bévière, letter of Oct. 20; Begouën-Demeaux, letter of Oct. 28; Merle, letter of Oct. 19; Guillaume Bonnemant to municipality of Arles: A.C. Arles, AA 23, letter of Oct. 20; Ferrières, 179 (letter of Oct. 20).

1. Hall of the Menus Plaisirs on the Night of August 4, 1789. After the creation of the National Assembly, the meeting hall in Versailles was rearranged from a rectangular, churchlike nave to an oval amphitheater, in order to facilitate debate. Candle chandeliers were also added to permit evening sessions. Here the deputies line up at the rostrum (*far left*) or appeal to the secretaries and the president, Le Chapelier (*center across oval*), to make their motions dismantling the "feudal system." Despite their ostensible union, the deputies are still sitting largely by estate: the Clergy across the oval to the left; the Nobles across to the right; and the Third, many still in their prescribed black costumes, in the foreground.
(Bibliothèque nationale)

plained of the unbearable heat in the room—"the poor deputies are roasted as if they were in an oven"—and of the limited space for spectators, down from the three thousand places in the Menus Plaisirs to less than three hundred. The rectangle was entirely divided in the middle by the president and the secretaries, on one side, and by the speaker's podium, on the other. Thus, the structure of the hall compelled everyone to sit either on the left or on the right: a physical reality that invariably contributed to the polarization of the Assembly.[103]

Many deputies of all political persuasions were initially distressed by the move to Paris, and many among the clergy and the nobility would never feel comfortable there.[104] Only a few days after their arrival, a baker was lynched under particularly gruesome circumstances, causing considerable

---

[103] Brette, *Histoire des édifices*, 162–70; La Bévière, letter of Nov. 9; Jean-Pierre Boullé to the municipality of Pontivy: A.C. Pontivy, on microfilm in A.D. Morbihan, 1 Mi 140, letter of Nov. 10; Maupetit, 20 (1904), 102 (letter of Nov. 22).

[104] Duquesnoy, 1:421 (entry of Oct. 8); Alexandre de Lameth, *Histoire de l'Assemblée constituante*, 2 vols. (Paris, 1828–29), 1:422. See also below, chap. 8.

2. Hall of the Manège and the "Labor of Target." The former indoor riding stable in Paris became the home of the Constituent on November 9, 1789. In this conservative caricature, the deputy Target, a key member of the Constitutional Committee, is pregnant and about to give birth to the Constitution. The engraving reveals the "bureau" of the president and secretaries (*right*) and the speaker's rostrum (*left*), above the "visitor's stand" (*la barre*) where nondeputies appeared to address the Assembly. Special sections of the balconies were reserved for alternate deputies, lobbyists, and the general public. The view is toward the "right" end of the hall, where the "Capuchins" normally sat.
(Bibliothèque nationale)

emotion among the delegates.[105] But with the vigorous efforts of the Parisian municipal government and a new decree permitting martial law, the rioting was quickly controlled and the capital remained relatively quiet over the next several weeks. Contingents of the cavalry and the national guard were installed to protect the episcopal meeting hall, a task rendered all the more practical by the hall's location on an island in the Seine.[106] Even the conservative deputies had to admit that the atmosphere was remarkably peaceful, "a calm that we could scarcely have hoped for, even in a village."[107] Deputy attendance within the Assembly, exceptionally meager in the week after the insurrection, rose rapidly. By the end of October and early November, close to a thousand delegates were regularly cramming their way into

---

[105] Boullé, 16 (1889), 74–76 (letter of Oct. 23); Boissy d'Anglas, Archives de l'Air, letter of Oct. 24. See also, *AP,* 9:472.
[106] Montlosier, 1:318.
[107] Irland de Bazôges, letter of Oct. 23. See also curé Verdet, letter of Oct. 26.

the hall to attend the debates—virtually the same number as in early August.[108]

With the continued presence of most of the Monarchien contingent, and its continued association with the "aristocratic" deputies, the right remained as a powerful and influential force within the Assembly. On many issues they could count on the support of the moderates, generally shocked by the events of early October, and far less sympathetic with the common people than they had been previously. The moderates Fréteau de Saint-Just, Camus, and Thouret captured the three presidential elections immediately following the riots. And the factional organization of the Monarchiens and their allies, the considerable coordinating capabilities forged in August and September, remained strong enough to elect the Monarchien archbishop Boisgelin to the presidency at the end of November.[109] Candidates of the former Palais Royal faction and their allies on the left, by contrast, were unable to capture a single election, and were usually a distant second or third.[110]

Basking in his recent victory in the presidential election, Boisgelin congratulated himself for having rejected all the predictions of doom by Mounier and Lally and for having stayed on to fight. Where would he be now, he mused, "if I had listened to the advice everyone was giving me."[111] During the same period, Boisgelin's alliance continued to obtain election of its adherents to various committees, culminating in a dramatic vote in late November that gave them control once again of the powerful Committee on Research.[112] The radical printer from Lyon, Périsse Du Luc, complained bitterly of this election which turned over the Committee to "the Revolution's greatest enemies." And in fact, the right immediately used its power to launch an investigation of the left's role in the October Days.[113]

Two debates in the weeks following the October Days, one on the fate of church property and the other on the question of political participation, were revealing of the enduring divisions within the Assembly and the en-

---

[108] Etienne-François Schwendt in Reuss, 1:218–19 (letter of Oct. 20); Boullé, A.D. Morbihan, letter of Nov. 3; Jean-Baptiste Poncet-Delpech, *La première année de la Révolution vue par un témoin*, ed. Daniel Ligou (Paris, 1961), 135–36 (letter of Nov. 14); Duquesnoy, 2:17 (entry of Nov. 4).

[109] *AP*, 33:88–89.

[110] In the Oct. 10 election, when much of the right was still absent, the probable candidate of the left, Emmery, was second with 228 out of 553 votes. On Nov. 10, Emmery came in a distant third. On Nov. 23 the second place candidate of the left, the duc d'Aiguillon, captured only 166 votes out of 680: A.N., C 83, dos. 818 (18–19); Poncet-Delpech, 147, 169n.

[111] Boisgelin, pièce 141, undated letter of ca. late Nov.

[112] *AP*, 10:249. Of the 12 new members, only 2 (Tuault de La Bouvrie and Vieillard) were associated with the left. Eight (the marquis de Foucauld de Lardimalie, bishop Talaru de Chalmazel, Tailhardat de La Maisonneuve, Chabrol, Henry de Longuève, abbé Yvernault, Durget, and the marquis de Monspey) were linked to the Monarchiens or the extreme right.

[113] Périsse, letter of Dec. 27; *Procédure*, 1:245 (deposition of Henry de Longuève); also Rabaut Saint-Etienne, *Précis*, 313–16.

during influence of the conservatives. The advent of the Revolution had temporarily obscured the monarchy's fiscal crisis, yet the deputies had pledged their responsibility for the debts of the Old Regime, and by autumn the financial needs of the state were insistently pressing themselves on the Assembly.[114] The sale of church lands for the benefit of the state had already been proposed on a number of occasions—most recently by Dupont de Nemours in a long speech of September 24—so that the formal motion to this effect by bishop Talleyrand on October 10 could scarcely have been a surprise.[115] Though it is impossible to reconstruct the final breakdown of votes in the roll call of November 2, the deputies' letters and speeches indicate that the measure was generally supported by the leadership of the left, and opposed by leaders on the right and by most members of the former privileged orders.[116] In the long debates—unrolling, ironically, beneath the stained glass windows of the episcopal palace—the left generally avoided the philosophical and anticlerical rhetoric that got them into such trouble on the question of religious toleration, but an important segment of the Assembly remained suspicious of their motives. By the beginning of November the original proposal—that all clerical lands be declared state property—was headed for almost certain defeat, particularly after the powerful speeches delivered by the Monarchien clergymen Montesquiou and Boisgelin.[117] The conservative Irland de Bazôges, the moderate Visme, and the Breton Boullé all agreed in this assessment.[118] The measure finally passed on November 2 only after the original motion was changed to the ambiguous rendering that church lands "be placed at the disposal of the nation," and after it was specified that individual provinces would have the right to control and oversee all final decisions.[119] The latter provision, inserted following the strong opposition from several provincial delegations, seemed potentially to vitiate the enforcement of the entire degree.[120] Indeed, many deputies on both the right and the left were convinced that only a portion of church lands—perhaps those belonging to monks and nonresident clergymen—would ever be seized, and that the vote might be construed as a victory for the conservatives.[121]

[114] Marcel Marion, *Histoire financière de la France depuis 1715. Vol. II. 1789–1792* (Paris, 1919), 39–51. See also below, chap. 8.

[115] *AP*, 9:147–68.

[116] Only 8 (26%) of the 31 known to have supported the motion were members of the former privileged estates. Nineteen (76%) of the 25 known to have opposed the motion were members of the former privileged estates.

[117] Begouën, letter of Oct. 31; Duquesnoy, 2:9 (entry of Oct. 31); Merle, letter of Nov. 2; and Boullé: A.D. Morbihan, letter of Nov. 3.

[118] Boullé, ms., letter of Nov. 3; Visme, entry of Nov. 2; Irland, letter of Nov. 2.

[119] *AP*, 9:649. The measure finally passed by 568 to 346 (with 40 abstentions).

[120] Particular opposition came from delegations from the northern frontier and Languedoc: Boullé, A.D. Morbihan, letter of Nov. 3; Pous, 281 (letter of Nov. 14).

[121] On the right: Boisgelin, letter of Nov. 3; curé Fournetz, in L. Desgraves, "Correspondance des députés de la sénéchaussée d'Agen aux Etats généraux et à l'Assemblée nationale,"

If neither of the major factions could claim a clear victory on the issue of Church land, the radical left was badly defeated on another, the question of eligibility for political participation. The creation of a distinction between active and passive citizens, and the institution of tax qualifications for suffrage and for holding various offices were first discussed on October 20. By all accounts, the debates over the next ten days—alternating with those on church land—were extremely stormy, pitting "the two systems" within the Assembly (as Boullé described them) against one another.[122] The left did everything in its power to block what Robespierre called "the work of the aristocratic party within the Assembly," first in the context of local elections and then in regards to eligibility for the National Assembly. Not only would such measures be violations of the Declaration of the Rights of Man, it was argued, but they would succeed in disenfranchising a substantial proportion of the deputies' own constituencies, who had in fact participated in the elections earlier that spring.[123] But still trembling from their experience with the Parisian constituency earlier that month, the bulk of the moderates joined with the right and passed decrees requiring various levels of tax paying for various levels of political participation, as well as property ownership to serve in the National Assembly.[124] At the beginning of December the left attempted to override the tax and property qualifications by creating loopholes in the system, allowing poorer citizens to qualify for participation under certain conditions. They were defeated once again, though this time by two remarkably close votes of 439 to 428 and 453 to 443.[125] Observers at the time were impressed by the extent to which the Assembly was split in half, almost exactly corresponding to the two sides of the hall, left and right of the president's chair.[126]

Recueil des travaux de la société académique d'Agen. Sciences, lettres, et arts, 3e sér., I (1967), 81 (letter of Dec. 5); curé Renaut, letter of Nov. 30. On the left: Campmas, letter of Dec. 1; Antoine-René-Hyacinthe Thibaudeau, *Correspondance inédite*, ed. H. Carré and Pierre Boissonnade (Paris, 1898), 24 (letter of Nov. 3); Goupilleau, letter of Nov. 2; Vernier, letter of Nov. 3; Merle, letter of Nov. 4. Also, the moderate, Maupetit, 19 (1903), 371 (letter of Nov. 3). Not all deputies shared this opinion, however: e.g., Bouchette, 284–85 (letter of Nov. 4). See also Marion, 50.

[122] Boullé, 16 (1889), 83–84 (letter of Oct. 30). Debates on this question are poorly covered in the official accounts: *AP*, 9:469–70, 478–79, 589–92, 594–600. See also Patrice Gueniffey, *Le nombre et la raison: la Révolution française et les élections* (Paris, 1993), chap. 1.

[123] *AP*, 9:478–79, 598–99; also, Robespierre, 58, (letter to Buissart, undated, ca. Nov. 5); and Jacques-Samuel Dinochau, *Courier de Madon à l'Assemblée nationale permanente*, issue of Nov. 3.

[124] Basquiat and Lamarque, letter of Oct. 24; Maupetit, 19 (1903), 368–69 (letter of Oct. 31). The votes were not recorded, but they apparently so decisive that the left was not even able to force a roll call.

[125] *AP*, 10:359–61 and 414–15. See also Merle, letter of Dec. 8; Duquesnoy, 2:141–42 (entry of Dec. 7); and Basquiat and Lamarque, letter of Dec. 5.

[126] Visme, letter of Dec. 7; Delaville, letter of Dec. 9; Dominique-Joseph Garat, *Journal de Paris* (Paris, 1789–91), 1602–1603 (Dec. 7); Boullé, A.D. Morbihan, letter of Jan. 15, 1790; Dinochau, *Courier de Madon*, issue of Dec. 3.

Indeed, for Jean-François Campmas, reflecting in a letter to his brother on the general political atmosphere of the Assembly at the beginning of December, the factional clashes were even more vigorous now than they had been in Versailles. He considered it ironic that the right continued to complain of being "coerced" by the left and pressured in its votes. In fact, he observed, "the opposition is still so strong, that we must, as it were, force through decrees at the point of a sword."[127] And even then, their side did not always win. Clearly, to the end of 1789, the configuration on the right remained a power to be reckoned with.

THE FORMATION OF THE JACOBINS

It was sometime toward late November or early December that a group of patriot deputies resolved to form a more coherent association to match the organization on the right. Renting a room in the Dominican convent of Saint Jacques, a block or so from the new hall of the Manège, they initially called themselves the "committee of the Revolution," before embracing the more cautious designation of the "Society of the Friends of the Constitution." Already by January they had also adopted the popular name of their monastic meeting hall, the Jacobins. Many of the adherents were veterans of the Breton committee, though the latter "club" had long since ceased to exist as anything more than a provincial caucus.[128] The direct predecessor was rather the loose coalition of the "Palais Royal," including such leaders as Target, Le Chapelier, Mirabeau, and the increasingly inseparable cluster of friends: Duport, Barnave, and the brothers Lameth.[129] Whatever the continuities with the past, the Jacobins rapidly created a new kind of patriot structure, more highly centralized and institutionalized, patterned in many respects after the organization developed by the Monarchiens. Several of the early adherents made it clear that the prime motive for the creation of the club was to counter the offensive of the conservatives. Boullé, who had participated from the very beginning, described its foundation "for the advancement of the spirit of the Revolution, which has recently been opposed by the majority of the Assembly on two occasions." Both Dubois-Crancé and La Revellière-Lépeaux directly associated the creation with the effort to oust the right from positions of leadership within the Assembly. Everyone knew, wrote La Revellière, that "the aristocratic party commonly chose the Assembly officers because it held meetings in which it was decided in advance who was to be elected." It was for this reason that the deputies of the

---

[127] Campmas, letter of Dec. 1.

[128] Bouchard, 94; Edna Hindie Lemay, *La vie quotidienne des députés aux Etats généraux* (Paris, 1987), 216. The Breton caucus continued to meet even after the foundation of the Jacobins: Delaville, letter of Nov. 30.

[129] Lameth, 1:422–23; Walter, 32. Faydel included Mirabeau in the early Jacobins: letter to Jean Filsac, avocat in Cahors: A.N. W 368, no. 822, 4e partie, Jan. 24 and Mar. 21, 1790.

left "decided to hold meetings of their own so that they could ensure the Patriots' control of the bureaus."[130]

This chronology of the creation of the Jacobin Club is significant. It has sometimes been suggested that the left seized control early in the Revolutionary process and thereafter dominated politics in France, at the expense of the monarchy and of the former privileged classes, both of which had essentially capitulated soon after the creation of the National Assembly. By October, as François Furet and Denis Richet have written, "the battlefield had essentially been conquered, the fight was over: the Revolution had been won."[131] Yet the evidence presented here would suggest a far more complex picture. At least through the end of 1789, the newly constituted Jacobins remained a minority within the National Assembly, while both the king— through the potential leverage of the suspensive veto—and the coalition on the right retained real measures of power. The political dynamic of the early Assembly entailed an intense and ongoing political struggle between relatively evenly matched contingents on the right and on the left, a competition in which each side vied for the allegiance of a large nonaligned center, and in which each emulated the other in the developing patterns of factional organization. This dialectic of interaction was to continue with even greater intensity into the winter and spring of 1790.

---

[130] Boullé, A.D. Morbihan, letter of Dec. 18, 1789; Louis-Marie de La Revellière-Lépeaux, *Mémoires*, 3 vols. (Paris, 1895), 1:85; Edme-Louis-Alexis Dubois-Crancé, *Lettre de M. Dubois de Crancé . . . à ses commettants* (Paris, 1790), 10.

[131] *La Révolution française* (Paris, 1973), 99. See also François Furet, *Interpreting the Revolution*, trans. Elborg Forster (Cambridge, 1981), 46.

PART THREE

Politics and Revolution

The Deputies as Lawgivers

THE STRUGGLE FOR SELF-DEFINITION

From its inception the ostensible purpose, the principal raison d'être of the National Assembly was to draw up a constitution. This was the task to which the deputies had solemnly committed themselves in their Tennis Court Oath, an objective that was further underscored on July 9, 1789 when they adopted the designation of "Constituent Assembly." They were, as they phrased it, following in the footsteps of Lycurgus and Solon, of Numa and Penn. Theirs was "a special political calling," to organize France's first "constitutional convention" and establish the basic structures of government for ages to come.[1] Yet in actual practice, by the autumn of that year, the Assembly's objectives and guiding principles were a good deal more ambiguous and uncertain. In their letters and diaries, the delegates frequently struggled for self-definition, for a precise delineation of their mission. The ambiguity of their aims was partly related to the revolutionary circumstances. Unlike Solon or Penn, the men of '89 found themselves in the midst of an unusually fluid situation, in which all traditional political values were being put into question, in which the very boundaries and definitions of sovereignty were continually in flux, in which their own conceptions of themselves could be transformed daily by the "school of the Revolution." What is more, they were compelled to establish a new regime while the old regime was still very much in place. "The deputies," wrote Rabaut Saint-Etienne, "were long frustrated with the terrible handicap of trying to create a monarchy when they already had a monarch." In his more extravagant moments, Duquesnoy even wondered if it would not have been preferable to suspend the king's "executive power" provisionally, while the Assembly set about rebuilding the monarchy, returning his authority later, "more splendid than before."[2]

Yet Duquesnoy knew that such a move would have been politically impossible. For weeks the deputies had been scrupulously careful to separate themselves in their constituent powers from the executive authority of the king. This was a resounding theme in virtually all of their writings in the

[1] Jean-Sylvain Bailly, *Mémoires d'un Témoin de la Révolution*, 3 vols. (Paris, 1821–22), 1:357–58; Alexis Basquiat de Mugriet to the municipality of Bayonne: A.C. Bayonne, AA 51, letter of July 20; and *AP*, 8:562 (speech by Mounier of Sept. 4).

[2] Adrien Duquesnoy, *Journal d'Adrien Duquesnoy*, ed. R. de Crèvecoeur, 2 vols. (Paris, 1894), 2:419 (entry of Feb. 22, 1790); Jean-Paul Rabaut Saint-Etienne, *Précis historique de la Révolution française* (Paris, 1807), 199.

early days of July, when they first came to grips with the problems of civil unrest and military mutiny. "One must never imagine," wrote Dinochau, "that the Assembly could conceive the sacrilegious idea of encroaching on any of the sovereign's prerogatives." "The authority to deal with popular uprisings and military misconduct," argued Boullé, "belongs solely to the executive power."[3] Throughout the summer—and indeed throughout the entire National Assembly—the ideal of the kingship as a source of authority and order in the midst of confusion remained a persistent attraction for a great many individuals.

But despite its well-meaning scruples, the imperious pressure of events soon forced the Assembly to act well beyond the theoretical boundaries of its prerogatives. By the middle of the summer, it was evident to everyone that public confidence in the royal administration was seriously breaking down and that the bureaucracy was in danger of collapse. As administrative links with the countryside dissolved, there was a growing anxiety that the chaos and anarchy of the moment could undermine the whole project, that the new constitution, whatever its virtues, might never be published or implemented. Deputies were equally concerned over the monarchy's inability to resolve the economic and financial crisis. Gilbert Riberolles, the wealthy paper merchant from Rioms, relayed his impressions to his brother: "The situation, it seems to me, makes commercial activity risky for everyone. Anarchy is increasing daily and unless the executive power quickly resumes its functions, the kingdom will be on the edge of collapse."[4] Whatever their respect for the monarchy in general, the repeated inconsistency and unreliability of the specific king with whom they had to deal, forced them to reevaluate their position. By the autumn of 1789 it had become evident to the patriot majority that the Assembly alone was in a position to command obedience, that the responsibility of wielding executive authority had been thrust upon them, like it or not. "In a state where no public authority exists," concluded Boissy d'Anglas, the deputies had no choice for the time being but to take the initiative and place the monarchy somewhat in abey-

[3] Jacques Dinochau, *Histoire philosophique et politique de l'Assemblée constituante*, 2 vols. (Paris, 1789), 2:16–17; Jean-Pierre Boullé, "Ouverture des Etats généraux de 1789," ed. Albert Macé, *Revue de la Révolution. Documents inédits* 14 (1889), 43 (letter of July 1). See also Jean-Bernard Grellet de Beauregard, "Lettres de M. Grellet de Beauregard," ed. Abbé Dardy, *Mémoires de la Société des sciences naturelles et archéologiques de la Creuse*, 2e sér., 7 (1899), 72 (letter of ca. July 3); Joseph Delaville Le Roulx to municipality of Lorient: A.C. Lorient, BB 12 (letter of July 4); Michel-René Maupetit, "Lettres (1789–91)," ed. Quéruau-Lamérie, *Bulletin de la Commission historique et archéologique de la Mayenne*, 2e sér., 19 (1903), 209 (letter of July 29); Antoine-François Delandine, *Mémorial historique des Etats généraux*, 5 vols. (n.p., 1789), 3:268–70 (entry of July 31).

[4] Francisque Mège, *Notes biographiques sur les députés de la Basse-Auvergne* (Paris, 1865), 126–27 (letter of Aug. 24). See also Claude-Pierre Maillot to an unnamed municipal official of Toul: A.C. Toul, JJ 7, fols. 167 and 168v° (letters of Sept. 22 and 25); Dinochau, 2:2; Delandine, *Mémorial historique*; Jean-François Begouën-Demeaux to municipal officers of Le Havre: A.C. Le Havre, D(3) 38–39, letter of July 27, and elsewhere.

ance. Doctor Campmas came to much the same conclusion. After all, as he wrote to his brother, "it is not the Nation who made the Revolution; and if it had still been possible to keep the machine running, we would never have been called."[5] The first year of the Revolution would witness an expansion of the Constituent's control over vast areas of administrative and executive authority, often with the full complicity of the royal ministries themselves, rendered impotent without the legitimizing force of the Assembly.

Similar difficulties, moreover, rendered the fine distinctions between constitutional activities and legislative activities largely untenable. In the opening weeks, the Assembly's objectives had seemed quite straightforward: to set down the basic organizing principles of the state and the government, much as the Americans had done two years earlier in Philadelphia. But the subsequent breakdown in authority in the country, coupled with the sweeping decrees of August 4–5, had quite transformed the deputies' commission. Their labors on the constitution *per se* were continually interrupted by the need to pass laws for raising taxes, reorganizing the regional administration, insuring the food supply, dismantling the seigneurial system, and organizing the military and the national guard. For a time, they strove to differentiate between their various decrees. The king's veto powers were limited, after all, to legislative acts and not to the articles of the constitution itself. But in practice, it often seemed impossible to disentangle one from the other. On December 14, 1789 they haggled for hours over the constitutional status of the new law on municipal organization, before finally deciding that they were too pressed for time to resolve the issue. They soon took the habit of sending all their decrees for the king's signature and of largely ignoring the distinctions.[6] It was only in late 1790 that a special committee was created—the "Committee on Revisions"—to sort through the myriad of decrees and to attempt systematically to determine what was constitutional and what was merely "legislative."

At once a constituent body and a legislature, assuming to some degree all three of the powers of government delineated by Montesquieu, the Assembly was invariably forced to pursue its labors on several fronts at once. Again and again, it found itself distracted from its prime objective of drafting a constitution and compelled to act immediately to fill holes in the dike, to grapple with the new laws and decrees on the specific problems of keeping state and society afloat. For the deputies involved, the situation could be immensely frustrating, and they complained repeatedly of the lack of order

---

[5] François-Antoine Boissy d'Anglas to Etienne Montgolfier: Archives du Musée de l'air et de l'espace (Le Bourget), Fonds Montgolfier, letter of Oct. 24; Jean-François Campmas to his brother, vicaire in Carmaux: B.M. Albi, Ms. 177, letter of Nov. 1. See also Maupetit, 19 (1903), 228 (letter of Aug. 10); Jean-de-Dieu Boisgelin de Cucé to Comtesse de Gramont: A.N., M 788, letter of Oct. 10; and Eric Thompson, *Popular Sovereignty and the French Constituent Assembly, 1789–91* (Manchester, 1952), 72–76.

[6] *AP*, 10:563; Duquesnoy, 2:165–66 (entry of Dec. 14). Cf. Antoine Durand to Delcamp-Boytré in Gourdan: A.E. Cahors, carton 5–56, letter of Sept. 14.

and system in their work and of the imperious press of events driving them forward: "Overwhelmed with responsibilities and distracted by endless contingencies," wrote Lombard-Taradeau, "we must work now on one question, now on another, despite our strong desire to concentrate on one issue at a time."[7] Yet despite the extraordinary difficulties under which they worked, despite their general lack of experience in operations of this kind, their work would in many respects prove remarkably successful. And the process of lawmaking would, in itself, substantially contribute to the Revolutionary growth of the deputies.[8]

ORGANIZING THE ASSEMBLY

In the earliest days of the Third Estate, organization and order were not the preeminent virtues of the Assembly, and both outside observers and the deputies themselves took frequent note of the chaotic character of debate. Imagine, wrote Mirabeau in the second issue of his newspaper, "more than five hundred men thrown together in a room, brought in from different regions, unknown to one another, with no leader, with no hierarchy, all free, all equal, none with the right to give orders and none ready to obey them; and everyone, in the French manner, wishing to speak before they listen."[9] Deputies were continually interrupting one another, shouting at each other at the top of their lungs, climbing on benches or pillar pedestals to make themselves heard, disputing for hours over procedural issues.[10] The former intendant Monneron recorded the scene in May as he sat in the hall with his diary on his knees: "Uproar on one side, protests on the other. 'I demand the floor!'—'No more motions!'—'Calm!'—'Quiet!'—'Return to your benches!'—'Sit down!'—'I demand a vote!' Such is the faithful portrait of our representatives."[11] The confusion was compounded by the frequent presence of outsiders mixed with the deputies themselves. Journalists, sightseers from Paris, visitors from the deputies' hometowns, as well as alternate deputies and members of the other two estates, all managed to slip

[7] Jacques-Athanase de Lombard-Taradeau, "Lettres (1789–91)," *Le Var historique et géographique*, ed. L. Honoré, 2 (1925–27), 330 (letter of Oct. 15, 1789).

[8] On the general process of lawmaking, see especially André Castaldo, *Les méthodes de travail de la Constituante* (Paris, 1989); and Patrick Brasart, *Paroles de la Révolution. Les assemblées parlementaires, 1789–1794* (Paris, 1988).

[9] Honoré-Gabriel Riqueti de Mirabeau, *Lettres à mes commettants*, no. 2 (May 1789).

[10] See, e.g., Jean-François Gaultier de Biauzat, *Gaultier de Biauzat, député du Tiers état aux Etats généraux de 1789. Sa vie et sa correspondance*, ed. Francisque Mège, 2 vols. (Clermont-Ferrand, 1890), 2:31–32, 39, 53–54 (letters of May 6, 8, and 13); Pierre-Paul Nairac, ms. "Journal": A.D. Eure, 5 F 63, entry of May 6; Maupetit, 17 (1901), 444–45, 448 (letters of May 8 and 12).

[11] Emmanuel Nicod, "Monneron aîné, député de la sénéchaussée d'Annonay," *Revue du Vivarais* 4 (1896), 480.

into the hall or descend from the designated spectator areas and take seats in the midst of the representatives.[12]

The Third Estate was initially wary of establishing formal rules and structures of debate which might be construed as the acceptance of their status as a separate order. The deputies' only concession during the first month was to appoint a "dean" to preside over the meetings. But in their choice they followed the procedures used in the electoral assemblies that spring and designated the oldest member present, a seventy-two-year-old merchant from Amiens, Charles-Florimond Le Roux. Unfortunately, Le Roux had neither the leadership qualities nor the physique to take charge of the situation, and at one point in the meetings he was knocked to the floor by a rush of deputies appealing for the right to speak.[13] After several days of general pandemonium, the Assembly quietly established a "provisional leadership" of "assistants"—one elected from each province—to assist the aged Le Roux and bring some semblance of order to the meetings.[14]

The situation was further ameliorated at the beginning of June when the inept dean stepped down and the deputies, opting for talent over seniority, ultimately replaced him with the academician Bailly.[15] Yet even the eminent and diplomatic Bailly encountered great difficulty in maintaining order. He rang the small bell at his disposal until the ringer fell off, and he harangued the members that they should cease applauding for speeches and conduct themselves in a more sober manner—only to be greeted with vigorous and enthusiastic applause. He finally resigned himself to the situation and concluded that in a time of revolution, the deputies probably needed such enthusiasm and spirit to bring them through the difficulties they faced: "The legislators of the Nation were new to the task and, as it were, apprentices in their political careers; and we all were in need of a certain *macte animo*."[16]

While the boisterous character of debates would persist throughout the National Assembly—and throughout all of the French Revolutionary assemblies—slowly, by trial and error, by imitation and improvisation, the deputies developed a structure for ordering their meetings. In fact, whatever Bailly might think, many of the Third Estate deputies were not political novices—at least in the realm of local and corporate politics. A surprising number were familiar with debate procedures in the English Parliament, and in mid-May, Target promised to distribute a translation of the Parlia-

---

[12] Boissy, ms., letter of June 27; Félix Faulcon, *Correspondance. Tome 2: 1789–91*, ed. G. Debien (Poitiers, 1953), 74 (entry of July 15); Jean-Gabriel Gallot, *La vie et les oeuvres du Docteur Jean-Gabriel Gallot*, ed. Louis Merle (Poitiers, 1961), 73 (entry of May 23); Laurent de Visme, Ms. "Journal des Etats généraux": B.N., Nouv. acq. fr. 12938, entry of June 23.

[13] Maupetit, 17 (1901), 451 (May 15); Gaultier, 2:50 and 52 (letters of May 11 and 13).

[14] *AP*, 8:35 (May 12); Boullé, 11 (1888), 118 (letter of June 1); Visme, entry of May 14; Duquesnoy, 15, 17 (entries of May 12 and 13).

[15] Gaultier, 73–74 (letter of May 22); and *AP*, 8:62 and 64. Le Roux was initially replaced by d'Ailly, who resigned after two days.

[16] Bailly, 1:100–102, 176, 247–48 (entries of June 4, 19, 27).

mentary rules for those who were not.[17] By early June observers noted a remarkable penetration of English practices and vocabulary into the Third Estate: "Anglomania is in evidence everywhere," wrote a noble deputy who attended one of their sessions. "You can hear nothing but 'address,' 'amendment,' 'bill,' 'honorable member,' 'commons.'"[18]

Once the National Assembly had been created, the members established a Committee on Rules to draft a permanent policy for parliamentary debate and internal organization. After long delays caused by the press of events, the merging of the three estates, and the mid-July crisis, a relatively brief *règlement* for the Assembly was discussed and accepted on July 29. True to the infatuation with things English, large sections of the new rules were taken directly from the House of Commons.[19] Yet, according to Boullé, there was always a somewhat provisional character to the rules so adopted. Anxious to move on to the constitution itself, and still uncertain as to which procedures were best suited, the deputies pragmatically accepted them, largely as they had been drawn up by the committee: "Since only experience can guide us in questions of this kind, it was preferable to accept the rules as they were, but with the possibility of changing them later as experience might dictate."[20] In fact, the rules were far from covering all the contingencies of debate, so that the Assembly was frequently forced to improvise. Some of the articles were ignored or forgotten: those limiting deputies to a single committee, for example, or stipulating that a motion could not be discussed on the same day it was introduced. There was a creative side to Revolutionary procedures as there was to Revolutionary legislation, and soon the Assembly had evolved a parallel set of customary practices which the deputies tacitly agreed to follow. Though there were several proposals to modify or update the rules, the members were preoccupied with questions which seemed far more important and they preferred to bequeath the task to a later "legislative" assembly.[21]

Nevertheless, the July *règlement* did provide a general framework for constitutional and legislative action over the next two years, and established many of the Assembly's basic institutional structures. Perhaps the single most important element in the document—and the one which did generate a significant debate—was the stipulation that a simple majority from a mini-

[17] Maupetit, 17 (1901), 449 and 18 (1902), 138 (letters of May 12 and 21); Jacques-Antoine Creuzé-Latouche, *Journal des Etats généraux et du début de l'Assemblée nationale, 18 mai–29 juillet 1789*, ed. Jean Marchand (Paris, 1946), 93 (entry of June 10); Joseph-Michel Pellerin, ms. journal: B.M. Versailles, Ms. 823F, entry of July 8.

[18] "Correspondance d'un député de la noblesse avec la Marquise de Créquy," ed. B. d'Agours, *Revue de la Révolution. Documents inédits*, 2 (1883), 33 (letter of June 13). Also Duquesnoy, 1:35 (entry of May 22); and Edna Hindie Lemay, "Les modèles anglais et américains à l'Assemblée constituante," *Transactions of the 5th International Congress on the Enlightenment, Pisa, 1979* (Oxford, 1980), 2:872–84.

[19] Castaldo, 84–99, 308.

[20] Boullé, 15 (1889), 20–21 (letter of Aug. 4).

[21] Castaldo, 296n, 300, 331, 336.

mum quorum of two hundred members would suffice for the passage of all decrees. This critical decision was achieved only after the defeat of proposals by the privileged orders to require a two-thirds or three-fourths vote on all issues.[22] The rule of the majority was never again put into question.

The *règlement* also validated the system of internal officers, the president and the six secretaries, initially developed in June and July out of the earlier arrangement of the dean and his assistants. In reality, the considerable potential powers of the president were substantially reduced by the short, two-week duration of his tenure. While several individuals held the post more than once—including Thouret who held it four times, and André and Bureaux de Pusy who held it three times each—no one after Bailly held it twice in succession.[23] In general, moreover, the presidents were closely scrutinized by the Assembly in all their actions and were vigorously taken to task if they failed to follow the rules or seemed openly to favor one faction over another. They frequently felt compelled to consult the full Assembly whenever important controversies arose: on whether individual deputies should be allowed to speak out of order, for example. Nevertheless, the president remained the ceremonial center of the National Assembly and the chief representative of that body in relations with the king and his ministers. In most day-to-day affairs he exercised considerable control over the speaker's platform and played a central and often dominant role in establishing the subject and sequence of debate and in assuring the order and continuity which the early assemblies had so badly lacked. In practice, moreover, many of the individuals chosen were powerful personalities, skillful in speaking and in asserting leadership. Over half of the presidents were members of the nobility or the upper clergy and, as a group, they spoke over ten times more often than the average deputy.[24] When one factional group succeeded in controlling the presidency through successive tenures—as the Monarchiens had done from mid-August through early October 1789 and as the Society of 1789 would do from May to September 1790—the presidency might attain a substantially greater degree of continuity and power.

The six secretaries also played an important role in the organization of the Assembly. As a group, the individuals holding this office were somewhat less prominent than the corps of presidents: participating in debates only about four times as much as the average deputy and coming in an over-

[22] Duquesnoy, 1:243–44 (entry of July 29); Boullé, 15 (1889), 21–22 (letter of Aug. 4); Guillaume Gontier de Biran to the municipality of Bergerac: A.C. Bergerac, Fonds Faugère, carton 1, letter of Aug. 1.

[23] *AP*, 33:88–91.

[24] The 47 men who held the presidency spoke an average of 181 times each during the life of the assembly (excluding speeches given in their functions as president), compared to an average of 17 times for all of the deputies. See below, note 88, for sources and methods. Of the 47 who held the presidency, 23 (49%) had been elected to the Third Estate; 18 (38%) to the Nobility; and 6 (13%) to the Clergy.

whelming proportion from the Third Estate.[25] Yet named for a month at a time rather than for two weeks (with three secretaries elected every two weeks), they might rival the president in their influence over the everyday affairs of the Assembly. Since much of the work of the secretaries was less immediately visible than that of the presidents, they were often less closely scrutinized by the deputies as a whole and ultimately more independent. Normally only one or two, by rotation, were involved in the actual recording of the minutes of the meetings. The others took turns with such varied functions as writing the final drafts of motions and decrees, maintaining the sign-up lists of those wishing to speak on given questions, distributing work among the various bureaus and committees, arranging the publication of decrees and key speeches, and generally overseeing the membership— including the handling of resignations, replacements, and requests for leaves and passports.[26] Unless major factional barriers existed, the presidents seem to have worked closely with the secretaries in the general direction of the Assembly, and in some cases the secretaries played a dominant role in the adoption of decrees.[27] It is not surprising, then, that the left early concentrated its efforts on seizing control of the secretariat, an objective which it achieved many months before it was able to dominate the presidency.[28]

Over the months, as the Assembly became increasingly established and institutionalized, a variety of other positions and responsibilities were created to facilitate its functioning. By 1790 individual deputies or groups of deputies had been named as archivists, treasurers, and commissioners to oversee the Assembly's printing needs, the creation of the *assignats*, and the organization of building facilities. The various deputy officers were assisted in their tasks by a growing force of hired employees: sergeants at arms to aid in maintaining order in the hall, and clerks to help handle the huge increase in paperwork. Despite the Assembly's efforts to limit expenditures, the total staff increased some eightfold between June 1789 and February 1790.[29] Once the Assembly had moved to Paris, this burgeoning bureaucracy was assisted by a substantial expansion of office facilities. The Manège of the Tuileries left much to be desired as a general assembly hall. But it had the immense advantage of adjoining the two disaffected monasteries of the Capuchins and the Feuillants, where a whole array of offices could be established for the committees, officers, and staffs of the Assembly.[30]

---

[25] The 169 men who were secretaries gave an average of 78 speeches each. A total of 23 secretaries (14%) came from the Clergy; 30 (18%) from the Nobility, and 116 (69%) from the Third Estate.

[26] A.N., C 26–85; Grellet, 82 (letter of May 29, 1790); and Jean-Louis-Claude Emmery, documents from his service as secretary: B.N., Nouv. acquis. Fr., 2633, esp. folio 122.

[27] Jean-Pierre Boullé to the municipality of Pontivy: A.C. Pontivy, on microfilm in A.D. Morbihan, 1 Mi 140A, letter of Nov. 3, 1789.

[28] See below, chap. 8.

[29] There were only eight clerks in June 1789, but 65 on February 4, 1790: Emmery, folios 112 and 152; and *AP*, 11:434–35.

[30] See esp. Armand Brette, *Histoire des édifices où ont siégé les assemblées parlementaires de la Révolution* (Paris, 1902).

BUREAUS AND COMMITTEES

The development of a system of regularly elected officials and accepted rules of debate was of major importance in stabilizing and institutionalizing the Assembly and providing a framework for writing a constitution. But, in many respects, the single most important organizational development was the emergence of the committee system. As many other institutions in the Assembly, however, the use of committees developed only slowly, after an initial period of experimentation.

During the first weeks of the Estates General, the principal organizational subdivision within the Third Estate remained the Old Regime province. The provincial delegations had early begun meeting on their own initiative for the coordination of regional objectives, and on occasion the Assembly made specific use of provincial "governments" for discussions and elections of committees. In the winter of 1789–90 these same regional caucuses met frequently within the National Assembly to hammer out the new territorial divisions of the kingdom.[31] But the majority of the Third soon came to fear that the use of such groupings could reinforce provincial particularism and hinder their efforts to achieve national unity. At the beginning of June the deputies accepted Target's suggestion that they split into twenty randomly selected "bureaus" of thirty deputies each to serve as discussion groups in which all members might have the opportunity of presenting their positions.[32] Individuals were distributed among the bureaus on the basis of an alphabetical list of deputies by electoral district, and the groupings were to be reformed with a different membership once a month. After the two privileged orders joined the Third at the end of June, the system was expanded to thirty bureaus, with forty members each.[33] Although Malouet suggested that individual bureaus be given different areas of focus, the idea of specialization was initially rejected as undemocratic. Rather, all of the groups would meet each evening and deliberate—but not vote—on the same complex agenda of issues. Each would then prepare a report for the general Assembly.[34]

In the early weeks, these bodies were extremely popular with many deputies—particularly with those who felt uncomfortable speaking before hundreds of colleagues in the general sessions—and they probably played an important role in integrating individuals into the National Assembly.[35] Yet

---

[31] See above, chap. 4. The first Third Estate commission of "adjoints" assisting the dean was selected by provincial caucuses, as were all or part of the later National Assembly committees on Finance, Commerce and Agriculture, Royal Domaines, and Feudalism.

[32] Olivier-J. Frederiksen, "The Bureaux of the French Constituent Assembly of 1789," *Political Science Quarterly* 51 (1936), 421–26; Georges Lefebvre, "Les bureaux de l'Assemblée nationale en 1789," *AHRF* 22 (1950), 134–40; Castaldo, 197–99.

[33] Castaldo, 120, 125.

[34] Frederiksen, 421–23; Gaultier, 2:161 (letter of July 6); Lofficial, 81 (letter of July 9).

[35] See above, chap. 4. Also Boullé, 14 (1889), 44 (letter of July 1); and Gallot, 114 (letter of July 2).

not all deputies favored them. Robespierre had vigorously objected to their creation from the beginning, arguing that they were a waste of time, that they would favor intrigues, and that "it is better to allow each deputy to reflect individually in silence."[36] By late summer the existence of the bureaus had become another subject sharply dividing left and right. Monarchiens like Mounier and Clermont-Tonnerre praised them as forums for moderate deliberation free from the pressures of the spectators whose presence encouraged demagoguery and political posturing.[37] But the Palais Royal group saw the bureaus as a ploy of the conservatives for manipulating the deputies outside the public eye. The bureaus, argued Bouche, "were the tomb of patriotic zeal." "They can even become dangerous," wrote Durand, "in that more casual and informal conversations [in the bureaus] might cause individuals to lose their fervor and energy."[38]

Yet the critical factor influencing the majority of the moderate, non-aligned deputies against the use of the bureaus was their inefficiency. Though the institution had been created to facilitate debate, it soon seemed to have quite the opposite effect, slowing deliberation through interminable meetings and endless reports to the Assembly from each of the forty bureaus—"these miserable reports," as Duquesnoy called them. "Since we have been divided into bureaus," wrote Poncet-Delpech, "we scarcely have time to eat and sleep." Even the marquis de Ferrières, who personally enjoyed the experience of small group discussions, ultimately concluded that "they are not very useful."[39] The bureaus met increasingly rarely during the great debates of August and September, ceasing altogether by the end of September, except as organs for vote collection in the election of officers and committee members.[40]

But just as the bureaus were falling into decline, the far more specialized institutions of the committees were taking an increasingly prominent role in the Assembly process.[41] Despite the early prejudice toward the "undemocratic" idea of appointing limited groups of individuals to undertake specific tasks, the exigencies of time and the magnitude of the problems which the deputies were encountering soon led to a change of heart. But the concept of a general "committee system" developed only gradually. The committees

[36] Cited by Creuzé-Latouche, 58 (entry of June 5).

[37] Jean-Joseph Mounier, *Exposé de la conduite de M. Mounier dans l'Assemblée nationale et des motifs de son retour en Dauphiné*, 3 parties (Paris, 1789), 1:13; Jean Egret, *La révolution des notables: Mounier et les monarchiens* (Paris, 1950), 85; Louis-Henri-Charles de Gauville, *Journal*, ed. Edouard de Barthélémy (Paris, 1864), 15–16.

[38] Pellerin, entry of July 30; Durand, entry of July 31. See also Creuzé, 175 (entry of July 1); and Egret, 119–21.

[39] Duquesnoy, 1:164 (entry of July 6); Jean-Baptiste Poncet-Delpech, *La première année de la Révolution vue par un témoin*, ed. Daniel Ligou (Paris, 1961), 38 (letter of June 13); Charles-Elie de Ferrières, *Correspondance inédite*, ed. Henri Carré (Paris, 1932), 98 (letter of July 24).

[40] Frederiksen, 431–37; François-Dominique de Reynaud de Montlosier, *Mémoires*, 2 vols. (Paris, 1830), 1:250; Maupetit, 19 (1903), 245 (letter of Sept. 14).

[41] The best overall study of the National Assembly committees is Castaldo, 204–54.

were initially created in an ad hoc manner, one by one, to confront individual crises as they arose. In this sense, the progressive organization of individual committees testifies to the Assembly's expanding power in relation to the royal government.

The first four committees were all organized on June 19, 1789 in response to the immediate problems facing the newly created National Assembly: the need to check deputy credentials (the Verifications Committee); to draw up key statements articulating its position (Drafting); to set up rules for debate (Rules); and to elaborate a response to the ongoing food crisis (Subsistence). But only the first of these survived for more than a few weeks, with the limited task of certifying the credentials of later replacement deputies.[42] Far more significant was the creation of two committees in mid-July to confront the two most pressing challenges facing the National Assembly: the drafting of a constitution and the resolution of the budgetary crisis. The Constitutional Committee, organized in its definitive form on July 14, was without a doubt the single most powerful body in the Assembly during the first year of the Revolution.[43] It not only took charge of virtually all aspects of establishing the constitution and other associated legislation, but it served as a kind of general steering committee, determining the overall order and pace of debate. It was variously referred to as "a sort of factory for legislation," a "Council of State," or more frequently and simply, "the Committee."[44] After the resignation and replacement of the Monarchien members in mid-September, the committee was comprised of the same eight deputies through the end of the Constituent Assembly—with only a temporary expansion in late 1789 to handle the creation of new territorial divisions. Several of the committee's members had already been closely linked to one another in the last years of the Old Regime and all, except Thouret, either resided in Paris or were frequent visitors there.[45] In any case, the committee rapidly developed a cohesiveness and sense of unity which helped maintain an element of continuity in the Assembly despite the frequent changes in presiding officers.

[42] A list of the committees, with their membership and date of creation, is in *AP*, 32:545–70. The list contains errors, however, and needs to be verified.

[43] See R. Delagrange, *Le premier comité de constitution de la Constituante* (Paris, 1899); and Michael P. Fitzsimmons, "The Committee of the Constitution and the Remaking of France, 1789–1791," *French History* 4 (1990), 23–47. The archives of the committee have been almost entirely lost.

[44] Ernest Lebègue, *La vie et l'oeuvre d'un Constituant: Thouret* (Paris, 1910), 236 and 237; Claude Gantheret to Pierre Leflaive, his brother-in-law: private collection of Françoise Misserey, letter of July 28, 1790.

[45] See above, chap. 6. The eight permanent members were Démeunier, Le Chapelier, Rabaut Saint-Etienne, Sieyès, Talleyrand, Target, Thouret, and Tronchet. Target and Tronchet were colleagues in the Paris bar and had collaborated in the anti-Maupeou struggle. Target also knew Talleyrand, Sieyès, and Le Chapelier through the Committee of Thirty; and Rabaut Saint-Etienne through their common struggle for religious toleration. Démeunier, Talleyrand, Target, Sieyès, and Rabaut had all frequented various of the Old Regime salons in Paris.

Compared to the Constitutional Committee, the Finance Committee was far larger—the largest in the Assembly, with sixty-four members—and substantially less cohesive. It had been created on July 11 and was empowered to investigate and seek solutions for a whole range of issues concerning the current fiscal difficulties, the liquidation of state debts, and the elaboration of a new tax system.[46] Because of its size and the breadth of its objectives, it rapidly divided itself into subcommittees focusing on various aspects of the task, from the general debt to public works, coinage, and the king's household. By far the most powerful of these subcommittees, the so-called "Committee of Twelve" worked closely with Necker on all the day-to-day affairs of the ministry. Nevertheless, the task eventually became so burdensome that three offshoot committees had to be created in January 1790 to help share the load: the Committees on Taxes, on Pensions, and on the Liquidation of the Debt.[47]

The period of anarchy and fear at the end of July gave rise to two new organs of policy and internal inquiry: the Committee on Research, a kind of first-generation committee of public safety mandated to investigate all plots and threats to the Revolution; and the Committee on Reports, created to examine the flood of appeals, complaints, and requests for information arriving from all corners of the kingdom. Since their responsibilities frequently overlapped, the two committees came to work closely together as a kind of general committee on internal affairs.[48] The institutional demolition on the Night of August 4 spawned the creation of three more important and powerful committees to oversee the transformation and suppression of various aspects of the Old Regime: an Ecclesiastical Committee to reorganize the structures of the Church; a Judicial Committee to pursue the liquidation of venal offices; and a Feudal Committee to implement an end to the seigneurial system.[49] Thereafter, as the Assembly spread its purview over the whole range of public affairs, a string of specialized committees was created: on agriculture and commerce, and on criminal legislation in September 1789; on military affairs, naval affairs, and the royal domains in October; on the *lettres de cachet* in November; on poverty in January; on the colonies in March; and on Avignon and diplomatic relations in July.

In all, twenty-five permanent standing committees were brought into being during the first year of the Revolution.[50] Some 535 individuals are

---

[46] See Camille Bloch, *Procès-verbaux du Comité des finances de l'Assemblée constituante*, 2 vols. (Rennes, 1922–23).

[47] Bloch, vii, xviii–xxiv; Charles-François Lebrun, *Opinions, rapports, et choix d'écrits politiques* (Paris, 1829), 59–61.

[48] Initially, both were supposed to have their membership renewed once a month. But membership seems to have been permanent after April 1790 for the Committee on Research, and after June 1790 for the Committee on Reports. See also Pierre Caillet, *Les Français en 1789 d'après les papiers du Comité des recherches* (Paris, 1991).

[49] Some responsibilities of the Ecclesiastical Committee were later given to the Committees on Alienations (created in March 1790) and on the Tithes (April 1790).

[50] The following permanent committees seem to have existed in July of 1790 (excluding

known to have served on at least one such committee—a bit over two-fifths of all members of the Assembly. Of these, an overall preference was given to commoners, who held more than three-fifths of all the committee spots, compared to roughly one-fifth each for the Nobles and the Clergy.[51] Following the tactics first developed by the Monarchiens, the Jacobins soon became particularly adept at packing the committees with their own members. The proportion of all new positions going to Jacobins (or future Jacobins) rose from one-quarter in 1789 to nearly one-half in 1790. During the same period, the proportion controlled by the conservatives declined from about one-fifth to one-tenth.[52] By 1790 some deputies complained of the difficulties of obtaining committee assignments for those who were not members of a club.[53]

Yet the overall figures on committee membership can also be deceptive. The work load entailed in such assignments was often considerable, quite beyond the capacity and the diligence level of many individuals.[54] There were complaints of meager attendance and suggestions that the relatively small number who did attend could effectively control committee activities.[55] In addition, despite the explicit interdiction in the Assembly's rules, many deputies were members of more than one committee. Six such assignments went to Barnave, Tronchet, and the baron de Menou; seven to the duc de La Rochefoucauld, Fréteau de Saint-Just, and Dupont de Nemours; and eight to Alexandre de Lameth and Gaultier de Biauzat.[56] But despite certain protests that multiple assignments were being used by the left to dominate the legislative process, the majority of the deputies acquiesced in this prac-

---

subcommittees or short-lived committees): the Comité d'agriculture et de commerce; d'aliénation; d'Avignon; des colonies; de constitution; des décrets; des dîmes; diplomatique; des domaines de la couronne; ecclésiastique; féodal; des finances; d'imposition; de judicature; de législation criminelle; des lettres de cachet; de liquidation; de la marine; de mendicité; militaire; des pensions; des rapports; des recherches; de rédaction du règlement de police; de vérification.

[51] A total of 535 (41%) of the 1,315 deputies serving during the entire period of the Constituent Assembly sat on at least one committee, including 89 Clergy (17%), 116 Nobles (22%), and 330 Commoners (62%): *AP*, 32:545–70.

[52] During 1789, the Jacobins—or future Jacobins—obtained 160 (25%) and the conservatives 118 (19%) of a total of 636 committee assignments. In 1790 they obtained, respectively, 135 (48%) and 30 (11%) of 283 new assignments. Cf. Duquesnoy, 2:297 (entry of Jan. 21, 1790).

[53] E.g., Faulcon, 236 (letter to Conneau-Desfontaines, May 29, 1790).

[54] In Nov. 1789, for example, the Committee on Reports was following over 1,000 "affairs," an average of more than 30 per member: Jean-Félix Faydel to the municipality of Cahors: A.M. Cahors, unclassed box of letters from Revolutionary deputies, held in B.M. Cahors, letter of Nov. 15, 1789.

[55] Castaldo, 210–11; C. Bloch, xvi; *AP*, 17:341 and 651 (July 25 and Aug. 7, 1790).

[56] Overall, 318 deputies had been assigned to 1 committee; 120 to 2; 42 to 3; 34 to 4; 13 to 5; 3 to 6; 3 to 7; and 2 to 8. See also Alison Patrick, "The Second Estate in the Constituent Assembly, 1789–1791," *JMH* 62 (1990), 233–45.

tice.[57] Both Bureaux de Pusy and Fréteau de Saint-Just attempted to decline such assignments, citing the fact that they already sat on other committees. But in both instances, their resignations were refused by the full Assembly. The moderate patriot Duquesnoy—who sat on only one committee himself—saw a positive value in multiple memberships, since it placed the most energetic and articulate patriots in positions of committee leadership and provided greater continuity within the Assembly: "It is thus natural and necessary that the same individuals sit on all the committees."[58]

Moreover, in electing committee members the Assembly often took into account the deputies' individual talents and interests. All but two of the twelve members on the Naval Committee had careers directly related to the navy or to commercial shipping; all but one on the Military Committee were linked to the army, including several veteran soldiers and the noted military theorist, the comte de Gomer. Two-thirds of the Ecclesiastical Committee were either priests or lawyers with considerable experience in ecclesiastical affairs—and two, Durand de Maillane and Lanjuinais, were nationally known specialists in canon law; and the Feudal Committee was dominated by Merlin de Douai, one of the country's foremost specialists on feudal law.[59] Indeed, there seemed to be a growing identification of committee service with professional proficiency. In December 1789, the vicomte de Beauharnais even proposed that the bureaus be abolished altogether and that all committees be reorganized to take into account individual expertise.[60]

Yet not all of the successful committee members arrived at their task with previous experience in the field. Most of the deputies of the Third Estate were pragmatic men who had busied themselves before the Revolution seeking practical solutions for the problems of their age.[61] When he was first named to the Finance Committee, Theodore Vernier admitted that he knew next to nothing about the royal budget and fiscal system. But with the same kind of diligence and persistence which had ensured his success as a lawyer and magistrate in Lons-le-Saunier, he rapidly mastered the subject, and he even published a book, explaining in layman's terms to the public—and to himself, no doubt—the mysteries of Old Regime finances and the Constituent Assembly's reorganization of the system.[62] Much the same phenomenon

[57] Castaldo, 212–14; *AP*, 10:720, 11:266–67; Duquesnoy, 2:84 (entry of Nov. 25, 1789).
[58] *AP*, 10:618 (Dec. 16, 1789); and 11:186 (Jan 15, 1790); Duquesnoy, 2:299 (entry of Jan. 21, 1790).
[59] Norman Hampson, "The Comité de la marine of the Constituent Assembly," *The Historical Journal* 2 (1959), 132; Bertrand Barère, *Mémoires*, ed. Hippolyte Carnot, 4 vols. (Paris, 1842–44), 1:280–81.
[60] *AP*, 10:346 (Dec. 1, 1789). Beauharnais's motion was rejected since reorganization would mean a considerable loss of time.
[61] See above, chap. 2.
[62] Théodore Vernier, *Les éléments de finances* (Paris, 1789); André Pedoux, *Théodore Vernier* (Besançon, 1895), 7–8; Théodor Vernier to the municipality of Lons-le-Saunier: A.C. Bletterans (non-classé), "Lettres de Vernier," letters of Aug. 13 and 23, and Oct. 20, 1789; and Apr. 21, 1790.

seems to have occurred when the parlementary magistrate Roederer joined and eventually came to dominate the Tax Committee; or when the bailliage judge Barère initiated himself to the perplexities of the royal domains and the laws governing the confiscation of Protestant property.[63] Dinochau, who served on three committees, emphasized the virtues of committee work as a training for public service, as "a school where the more assiduous members are educated to public affairs."[64] In this way, the amateur citizen legislators of the earlier bureau system could be transformed into quasi-professionals through the professionalization of the committee system itself.

By 1790 the committees had become the workshops in which new laws and articles to the constitution were developed and initially debated. Most motions were systematically referred to committees before being considered in the full Assembly, so that their work came to set the rhythms of the constitutional process.[65] To be sure, committee proposals were rarely accepted unchanged and without debate, particularly in the early months of the Assembly's existence. In October 1789, Duquesnoy found that "there is in the Assembly an unfortunate spirit of mistrust toward everything produced by the committees."[66] But as the deputies moved beyond debates on the guiding principles and general division of power within the constitution, and as they concentrated more on the technical details of implementation, it was evident that the committees alone had the expertise necessary for understanding the full ramifications of many laws. "These committees," wrote Dinochau, "regulate the order of debate, classify questions, and maintain a continuity of principles, thus preventing an incoherence which might otherwise have menaced our decrees."[67]

Indeed, the committees became increasingly powerful not only within the National Assembly, but within the royal government as well. Whatever the deputies' early reticence to assume the powers of the "executive," the ministers were soon deferring to the Assembly on all manner of questions, refusing to take responsibility for decisions without the authority of the appropriate committees. Since "executive authority was playing dead"—in Charles de Lameth's phrase—the committees emerged as veritable de facto ministries.[68] Men like Roederer on the Tax Committee, Grégoire and Durand de Maillane on the Ecclesiastical Committee, or Merlin ("the Sorcerer") on the Feudal Committee undoubtedly knew more about their areas of concern and wielded more real power in the implementation of laws than

[63] Kenneth Margerison, *Pierre-Louis Roederer, Political Thought and Practice during the French Revolution* (Philadelphia, 1983), 34–40; Barère, 1:289–91, 317.

[64] Dinochau, 2:183.

[65] Castaldo, 229.

[66] Duquesnoy, 1:445 (entry of Oct. 14, 1789).

[67] Dinochau, 2:182. Also, Castaldo, 326–27.

[68] Alexandre de Lameth, *Histoire de l'Assemblée constituante*, 2 vols. (Paris, 1828–29), 2:51–53. See also Antoine-René-Hyacinthe Thibaudeau, *Correspondance inédite*, ed. H. Carré and Pierre Boissonnade (Paris, 1898), 56–57 (letter of Dec. 22, 1789).

any of the corresponding ministers. Indicative of the committees' growing power was the decree of February 5, 1790 which granted them authority to respond directly to queries from the provinces and to proffer advice on the interpretation of laws without consulting the Assembly or the government. Equally significant was the February 16 decree according them full sub-poena power to obtain documentation from royal and municipal adminis-trations deemed necessary for their work.[69] Scarcely six months after the creation of the National Assembly, the Military Committee had become "a war council, a central administrative office"; the combined Committees on Reports and Research were a veritable ministry of the interior; and the Committee on Decrees had assumed the role of a watchdog closely oversee-ing the activities of the chancellery. When Necker retired in September 1790, the powerful "Committee of Twelve," with which he had worked so closely, seized control of the entire royal treasury in the name of the Na-tional Assembly.[70]

LEADERSHIP AND ORATORY

But if leadership within the nation was clearly passing to the National As-sembly and its committees, leadership within the Assembly itself was often far more difficult to ascertain. Most histories of the Constituent Assembly emphasize the activities of a handful of major "leaders," such as Mounier, Sieyès, Mirabeau, Barnave, and Robespierre. Yet the deputies themselves were frequently wary of the pretensions of individuals to assume prepon-derant roles. In the early weeks of the Revolution, suspicions of this kind aroused considerable hostility toward both Mounier and the Breton group. Mirabeau also provoked such mistrust. No other individual came closer to exercising true charisma within the Assembly, deeply stirring the deputies and sometimes entirely changing their minds on certain fundamental issues through the sheer force of his personality and his rhetoric.[71] Yet he never succeeded in dominating the Constituent process as he probably hoped to do, and he was long excluded from both the presidency and secretariat and from the major committees.[72] In a secret report to the king he revealed an

[69] *AP*, 11:436, 618–19.

[70] Mirabeau, 1:383–84 (letter of Oct. 16, 1789); Charles-Elie de Ferrières, *Mémoires*, 3 vols. (Paris, 1825), 1:166–67; *AP*, 10:159 (creation of the Committee on Decrees, Nov. 21, 1789); J. F. Bosher, *French Finances, 1770–1795: From Business to Bureaucracy* (Cambridge, 1970), 219, 221, 225. On the Diplomatic Committee, see Barry Rothaus, "The Emergence of Legislative Control over Foreign Policy in the Constituent Assembly," Ph.D. Dissertation (Univ. of Wisconsin, 1968), esp. 158–87; and Thompson, 135–57.

[71] No other deputy is mentioned more frequently in the letters and diaries than Mirabeau. See, e.g., Lepoutre, letter of Oct. 28, 1789; Maupetit, 19 (1905), 372 (letter of Nov. 3, 1789); Visme, entry of Nov. 7, 1789; and Campmas, letter of Aug. 24, 1790.

[72] He was never named secretary and became president only in January 1791, shortly before his death. He never sat on the most powerful committees (Constitution, Finances, Research,

element of bitterness at his failure to play a more powerful role. The Assembly, he wrote, "supports men of talent when they serve its purposes; it humiliates them if they oppose it; it thinks itself too powerful to need instruction, too progressive to retreat, too strong to compromise." The vicomte de Toulongeon, who was not a forceful orator, seemed to agree. Those with pretensions for leadership, he wrote, "had little influence on deputy opinions. They themselves realized that they could only lead the Assembly where it wanted to go." "Those men who stood out in the Assembly were of little importance," wrote Boissy. "The Revolution was not made by a few men, but by the whole nation."[73]

Nevertheless, if leadership in the Assembly was never confined to a few dominant individuals, certain segments of the deputies rapidly emerged with greater influence and authority than others. Such influence might originate in an individual's pre-Revolutionary reputation, or in brochures he had written, or in his talents and application in committee work. But to rely on the deputy witnesses, the single most important source of prominence and impact within the Assembly was an individual's success at the speaker's rostrum. Oratory was, after all, a central activity in the political life of the Constituent—particularly as opposed to the Old Regime where state power revolved around the king's will and ministerial decisions. At a time when so many accepted values were regularly put into question, the deputies found themselves constantly groping for new formulations to describe and prescribe the changing political realities. Both within the Assembly and in the society in general, it was an extraordinarily creative period in the history of language. "Everything is new to us," wrote Clermont-Tonnerre. "We are moving towards a regeneration, and we have created new words to express new ideas."[74] Thus, a successful and compelling manipulation of the spoken language became one of the most important—though certainly not the only—sources of power within the Assembly.[75]

In the first months of the Estates General and the National Assembly virtually all of the deputies seemed only too eager to try their hand at this new form of power. Commentaries on the "inexhaustible loquaciousness" of their colleagues were among the most common complaints in the deputies' early letters and diaries. Duquesnoy described the meetings of the Third Estate in his usual acerbic style: "The Assembly is made up of numerous men of law who, having enjoyed a minor reputation at the minor bar of their minor towns, now assumed that they would be noticed and play a

---

etc.), but was named later to the Military and Diplomatic Committees, and the Committees on Avignon and the Colonies—the last three only in 1790.

[73] Mirabeau, 2:420–21 (message to the court, Dec. 23, 1790); Toulongeon, 1:57–58; Boissy, ms., letter of Jan. 14, 1791.

[74] *AP*, 8:603 (Sept. 9, 1789). Also, Ferdinand Brunot, *Histoire de la langue française des origines à nos jours. Tome IX. La Révolution et l'Empire* (Paris, 1967).

[75] Lynn Hunt, *Politics, Culture, and Class in the French Revolution* (Berkeley, 1984), chap. 1; François Furet, *Interpreting the French Revolution* (Cambridge, 1981), esp. 46–61.

considerable role." "We have a maddening desire to speak," bemoaned Maupetit. Even the most insignificant point "will immediately arouse forty would-be orators who may spend three days rendering a question more confusing than before." Palasne de Champeaux was convinced they had all contracted a severe case of "logodiarrhea."[76] There were innumerable criticisms of the bombast, the endless repetition, the insistence on developing each argument entirely from the beginning with all the appropriate, and inappropriate, scholarly flourishes, ignoring the fact that the dozen previous speakers had already developed the same subject. Durand found that the speeches given the first day a topic was raised were often much more interesting than those given in the following sessions, after the members had a night or two to prepare lengthy locutions filled with semi-irrelevant digressions: "essays," as Bouche called them, "written at leisure to be published in the newspapers and then read before the Assembly, as though they had just been improvised."[77] "In general," wrote Creuzé-Latouche, "the urge to speak without having anything new to say is a common disease among members of the Assembly." And like many of his colleagues, he concluded that the proceedings were plagued by the presence of too many lawyers: "We have a multitude of lawyers here. Their habit of continually elaborating, enumerating, demonstrating, refuting, summarizing, and declaiming greatly slows the debates."[78]

In fact, the problem probably arose as much from the deputies' schooling in traditional rhetoric classes as from their training in the law. In any case, there is some evidence that the quality and relevance of the oratory gradually improved. Intensely aware of the newness of the experience and of the need for an initiation to this novel form of politics, Creuzé was nevertheless optimistic about the future: "It is to be hoped that we will mature over time and that the very importance of our task will lead us to speak only when we have something essential to say." Already by late September 1789, the Poitou magistrate Lofficial felt that the excessive oratory of the first weeks had diminished significantly.[79] But perhaps more important, an internal winnowing process was at work within the Assembly. In part, this involved the progressive self-elimination of individuals from the pool of deputies prepared to speak. Once the three orders had joined together, the prospect of addressing an assembly of over a thousand people required a greater measure of courage and self-assurance than many were able to muster. It also

---

[76] Durand, entry of May 16; Duquesnoy, 1:57 (entry of May 30); Maupetit, 19 (1903), 227, 354 (letters of Aug. 10 and Sept. 18); Julien-François Palasne de Champeaux, "Correspondance des députés des Côtes-du-Nord aux Etats généraux et & l'Assemblée nationale constituante," ed. D. Tempier *Bulletin et mémoires de la Société d'émulation des Côtes-du-Nord 26* (1888), 261 (letter of Oct. 14).

[77] Durand, entry of May 15, 1789; and Charles-François Bouche to the *commissaire des communautés de Provence*: A.D. Bouches-du-Rhône, C 1046, letter of Aug. 16, 1789.

[78] Creuzé, 32 (entry of May 29, 1789).

[79] Creuzé, 31–32 (entry of May 29, 1789); Lofficial, 115 (letter of Sept. 25, 1789).

required an exceptional degree of lung power. Both the specially constructed salle des Menus Plaisirs in Versailles and the converted riding stable of the Manège in Paris had notoriously abysmal acoustics. Some of the deputies adapted with ease: Barnave and Mirabeau, naturally gifted with an extraordinary public presence; the abbé Maury, archbishop Boisgelin, and pastor Rabaut, all experienced in sermon oratory; the marquis de Foucauld de Lardimalie and Pierre-Louis Prieur (dubbed "Monsieur Crieur" by Boufflers) with bellowing voices that could dominate even the most clamorous assemblies.[80] Some, like Malouet, with softer voices and softer personalities, were able to master the new situation after a great deal of discipline and practice. But others found the transition far more difficult. Jean-Joseph Mounier, who had won a national reputation through his genius for persuasion and compromise among small groups of notables in Dauphiné, was enormously frustrated by his inability to speak effectively and dominate the Assembly in Versailles. The nationally known legal theorist Durand de Maillane, "having too soft a voice to make himself heard," was forced to abandon the rostrum during one of his first speeches. And much the same problem plagued Faulcon and Creuzé-Latouche. "There are about fifty or sixty individuals," wrote Lofficial, "whose lungs are strong enough to make themselves heard throughout our immense hall."[81]

But the winnowing process also entailed an active and aggressive weeding by the deputies' peers. During the first weeks of meetings, many of the Third Estate delegates carefully observed their colleagues' oratory.[82] Nairac took care to rank them by their "eloquence," their "capacity," and their "energy," as well as their "knowledge."[83] But in addition to jotting comments in their diaries, the deputies openly manifested their assessments to the speakers themselves. They were impatient and pitiless toward mediocrity of oratory or ideas. Anyone who appeared muddled in his reasoning, overly verbose and repetitious, or unable to speak loud enough to make himself heard was immediately treated with satirical comments, hoots and jeers, or sarcastic laughter. The first speech by the lawyer Moreau was "so diluted with useless verbiage that the orator was drowned out by universal murmurs of protest"; and the Bordeaux magistrate Lavenue presented "a commentary so exceptionally silly that he was unanimously hooted down."[84]

A certain number of deputies—Dupont de Nemours and Robespierre, for example—doggedly determined to make their ideas known despite ini-

[80] F. Bussière, "Le Constituant Foucauld de Lardimalie," *RF* 22 (1892), 210; Gustave Laurent, *Notes et souvenirs inédits de Prieur de la Marne*, (Paris, 1912), 62.

[81] Egret, esp. 11–12; Faulcon, 202 (letter of May 4, 1790); Creuzé, 90 (letter of June 10); Louis-Prosper Lofficial, "Lettres de Lofficial," ed. Leroux-Cesbron, *La nouvelle revue rétrospective* 7 (1897), 110–11 (letter of Sept. 14, 1789); Gaultier, 2:220–21 (letter of Aug. 1, 1789).

[82] Gaultier de Biauzat, 2:74 (letter of May 22); Visme, entry of May 9; Maupetit, 17 (1901), 448–49 (letter of May 12); and Duquesnoy, 1:57 (entry of May 30).

[83] Nairac, entries of May 13–19.

[84] Creuzé, 10–11 (entry of May 25, 1789); Duquesnoy, 1:80 (entry of June 9, 1789).

tial bad treatment received from their colleagues, rapidly improved their oratory style and adapted to the new political culture. Others, like the abbé Maury and the two Mirabeau brothers positively delighted in sparring with the Assembly, in returning taunt for taunt. But anyone with thin skin for this kind of treatment soon learned to confine his activities to listening, voting, and participation in bureau and committee work. "With my sensitivity," commented Grellet de Beauregard, "I would have been altogether sick, if I had to face such humiliations." "The Assembly is too severe," concluded Garron de La Bévière: "The majority of those who venture forth to speak, are unable to escape without being interrupted by grumbling or jeers."[85] The intellectuals Bergasse and Volney, both of whom had achieved considerable recognition through their writings and salon presence before the Revolution, reacted with disgust and lassitude to the new forms of politics. Bergasse rapidly abandoned the Assembly altogether, largely out of political opposition, but also delighted with the possibility "to go off and live in peace somewhere and devote myself to my important writings." Though Volney stayed on, a staunch patriot to the end, he soon ceased participating in debate: "I never enter the Assembly hall without a feeling of nervous contraction. These procedures, this turmoil exhaust me. The slightest failure deeply affects me and I fall back into a kind of melancholic indifference."[86]

For many of the privileged deputies, accustomed to positions of leadership and elite status under the Old Regime by virtue of their titles and pedigrees, the encounter with these new political values could be extremely trying. After the forced union, many of the nobles, both lay and ecclesiastic, were disconcerted by the turbulence and lack of respect of the National Assembly. The vicomte de Malartic commented frequently in his diary on the "indecency" and lack of "propriety" in the debates, on the "insulting" scorn shown by the commoners toward other members—and notably toward the nobility. "A gentleman cannot even raise his voice to speak without being hooted down," wrote La Bévière in a bitter letter to his wife: "there is no more respect and deference for the nobility." Jean de Turckheim, a noble who sat with the Third but who closely identified himself with the aristocracy, divulged a near physical revulsion for the aggressive and hostile debating atmosphere of the Assembly. He would never forget his chagrin and humiliation when he first attempted to speak: "I was so badly received, so little listened to, and so brutally interrupted, that I no longer dared to speak." Archbishop Boisgelin's debut was scarcely more auspicious: a long harangue in a lachrymose style, adapted perhaps from the

---

[85] Gérard Walter, *Robespierre* (Paris, 1946), 76–86; Visme, entry of May 18, 1789; Grellet, 82 (letter of May 29, 1790); Claude-Jean-Baptiste de Garron de La Bévière to his wife: A.D. Ain, 1 Mi 1, letter of Sept. 1, 1789.

[86] Etienne Lamy, *Un défenseur des principes traditionnels sous la Révolution: N. Bergasse* (Paris, 1910), 81–82; Jean Gaulmier, *Un grand témoin de la Révolution et de l'Empire: Volney* (Paris, 1959), 88. The abbé Sieyès may have felt similar emotions: Montlosier, 1:255.

funeral oratory with which he had marked his career, "was interrupted several times with stifled laughter." Many years later, the abbé de Pradt still remembered the pain and consternation of the upper clergy as they tried to adapt to the National Assembly: "They were like the knights of old, armed only with lances, when they first encountered guns."[87]

In any case, after the winnowing operation had worked its course, the number of deputies persisting as frequent speakers in the National Assembly was relatively limited. We can examine the oratorical leadership over the entire period of the Assembly through an analysis of the most complete account of Assembly proceedings, the *Archives parlementaires*.[88] In all, only about three-fifths of the deputies are known to have spoken during the entire National Assembly, and a substantial proportion of this group participated only once or twice.[89] Relatively low on the list, well below the overall average of seventeen speeches per deputy, were the magistrates of the lower courts (about thirteen speeches each), the deputy merchants (eight), those involved in agriculture (between two and three), and the deputy curés (about two). On the whole, the clerical deputies participated an average of only about four times each and well over half never opened their mouths during the entire Assembly—a further indication of the limited impact of the First Estate after the early days of the Assembly. By contrast, the nobles seem largely to have held their own, with an average of about twenty-one speeches per deputy, only a fraction below that of the commoner deputies.[90]

[87] Ambroise-Eulalie de Maurès de Malartic, ms. "Journal de ma députation aux Etats généraux": B.M. La Rochelle, ms. 21, entries of June 30 and July 1, 2, and 4; La Bévière, letters of July 10 and 12; Jean de Turckheim, *Compte rendu* to his electors in Strasbourg, in *L'Alsace pendant la Révolution française*, ed. Rodolphe Reuss, 2 vols. (Paris, 1880–94), 1:261; Jacques Jallet, *Journal inédit*, ed. J.-J. Brethé (Fontenay-le-Comte, 1871), 112 (entry of July 2, 1789); Dominique-Georges-Frédéric du Four de Pradt, *Les Quatre Concordats*, 3 vols. (Paris, 1818), 2:53.

[88] I have used vol. 33 of the *AP*, which is the index to vols. 8–32, the proceedings of the Constituent Assembly. Included as a "speech" is any spoken statement by any deputy as recorded in the *AP* index, excluding printed statements never actually pronounced. A sample comparison of the index with the actual pages of the *AP* suggests that about 5 to 10% of deputy speeches in the latter are not included in the former. But usually the missing speeches involved the reading of letters, the formal interjections of presidents and secretaries, or very short—often one-sentence—comments. For the early months of the Revolution, the *AP* is based primarily on the *Moniteur*, which is itself, for the period before Nov. 1789, a reconstruction based on a variety of newspaper accounts. A comparison of certain of the most complete diaries—such as that of Joseph-Michel Pellerin—proves that the *AP* skips some speeches altogether, particularly in the earliest months. It is probably progressively more complete from the fall of 1789: see *AP*, 8:i–ii; and *Moniteur*, 1:1. Cf. Edna Hindie Lemay, "Les révélations d'un dictionnaire: du nouveau sur la composition de l'Assemblée nationale constituante (1789–1791)," *AHRF*, no. 284 (1991), 163–71, who relies on an earlier, impressionistic study of Alphonse Aulard, *Les orateurs de l'Assemblée constituante* (Paris, 1882).

[89] In all, 766 of the total 1,315 deputies (58%) are known to have spoken at least once; 336 (44%) of the 766 speakers spoke only once or twice.

[90] Overall, the deputies averaged 17.4 speeches per individual. Clergymen averaged 4.4; nobles, 21.4; and the commoners, 21.9. Fifty-five percent of the clergy (176 of 322) never participated, compared to 39% of the nobles (129 of 332) and 37% of the Third (244 of 663).

3. Assembly Leaders at the Tennis Court Oath, June 20, 1789. The famous rendering
by Jacques-Louis David was begun over a year after the event, but it admirably conveys
the thrill and exuberance of the moment. It also provides portraits of many of our witnesses
and key participants. Among the more prominent (numbered in circles): 1) Maupetit
(carried in sick with a fever); 2) Le Chapelier (in a solid row with his Breton colleagues);
3) Delaville Le Roulx (the balding Breton merchant); 4) Malouet (the conservative, turning
his back as he swears); 5) Barère (composing his newspaper); 6) Prieur de La Marne
("Monsieur Crieur" leading the cheering with his penetrating voice); 7) Charles-François
Bouche (Provençal lawyer and historian); 8) Dom Gerle (not in fact present on June 20);
9) abbé Grégoire (the liberal young curé, embracing Gerle and Rabaut); 10) Rabaut Saint-
Etienne (Protestant pastor from Nîmes); 11) the president Bailly (scientist and academician,
administering the oath); 12) abbé Sieyès (dressed in layman's clothes, seated and calm
in the midst of the commotion); 13) Pétion de Villeneuve (lawyer and reformer from
Chartres); 14) Robespierre (baring his breast, ready to sacrifice himself); 15) Dubois-Crancé
(newly ennobled, holding the hilt of his sword); 16) the comte de Mirabeau (in a dark,
commoner's coat); 17) Barnave (brilliant speaker from Grenoble, the youngest man
present); 18) Camus (Parisian Jansenist, trying to persuade the lone dissenter); and 19)
Gaultier de Biauzat (lawyer and ex-Jesuit from Auvergne). (Bibliothèque nationale)

After the first few weeks of the Assembly, a relatively small contingent
of deputies played a dominant role at the rostrum. During the full tenure
of the Constituent Assembly, just forty members (3 percent of the total)
accounted for half of all recorded participation; and seventy-one (5 percent of the total) accounted for two-thirds. Examining the roster of the
top forty (Appendix III), one is impressed by the presence of the lesser
known deputies Camus, André, Démeunier, Regnaud, Bouche, Gaultier

de Biauzat, and Goupil, interspersed among such high-profile personalities as Mirabeau, Barnave, Malouet, and Maury. Though the index can
tell us nothing of the quality and impact of such oratory, it would suggest nevertheless that oratorical leadership in the Assembly went well beyond the "great speakers" who figure most prominently in the standard
accounts of the Revolution.[91]

At the top of the participation scale, there was a clear dominance of the
former Third Estate: ten of the top eleven, fourteen of the top seventeen
were representatives of the commoners. Among the Second Estate, it was
the contingent of "liberal" nobles, those who had joined the Third Estate
before June 27 or who in other ways demonstrated their early attachment to
patriot positions who led their order (with an average of forty-three
speeches each).[92] Indeed, the single most loquacious professional group in
the entire Assembly—averaging seventy-two speeches per individual—was
the corps of robe nobles from the Parlements. This group included the
articulate young magistrate from Aix, Antoine-Balthazar André (the number two position on the speaking role) and the two liberal Paris magistrates,
Fréteau de Saint-Just (twelfth) and Adrien Duport (eighteenth).[93] But the
second most talkative segment was the corps of lawyers (averaging forty-five
speeches each), most of whom were commoners. Eight of the Assembly's
top fourteen speakers represented this profession, including the number one
orator, the Parisian canon lawyer and polymath, Armand-Gaston Camus, as
well as Le Chapelier (third), Regnaud (sixth), Bouche (seventh), and
Robespierre (twentieth).[94] Obviously, for both the lawyers and the *parlementaires*, speaking ability had often been integral to a successful career under the Old Regime.

It is not insignificant that the fourth and fifth most active participants in
the National Assembly, the comte de Mirabeau and Nicolas Démeunier,
had been professional men of letters under the Old Regime. Indeed, if Mirabeau had not died six months before the end of the session, he almost
certainly would have led the entire National Assembly.[95] Yet beyond these
two key figures, the number of "philosophes" in the Assembly's leadership
was relatively meager.[96] Another six deputies among the top twenty partici-

[91] Of the 18 "orators of the French Revoluton" included in the collection of speeches edited
by François Furet and Ran Halévi, only 8 were in the top 40: *Orateurs de la Révolution française. I. Les Constituants* (Paris, 1989).

[92] Included here are those listed as such by James Murphy and Patrice Higonnet, "Les députés de la noblesse aux Etats généraux de 1789," *RHMC* 20 (1973), 244–46.

[93] Other parlementaires ranking high were Roederer (23d), Briois de Beaumetz (37th), and
Le Peletier de Saint-Fargeau (50th).

[94] Among those 47 lawyers for whom the distinction can be made, the actively practicing
lawyers averaged 138 speeches each, while those who never practiced averaged 30.

[95] At the time of his death, in early April 1791, Mirabeau had made 439 speeches; Camus,
his closest competitor, had made 389.

[96] The only other professional philosophes—by our definition—in the top 50 was Dupont
de Nemours (number 29).

pants—Camus, Bouche, Lanjuinais, Fréteau, Martineau, and Goupil—can be linked to the Jansenists. The strong Jansenist presence among the leadership of the National Assembly—despite the group's small numbers in the total membership—underscores the significant role played by this sect in the early stages of the Revolution.[97] Yet the great majority of the leading speakers of the Assembly were neither Jansenists nor philosophes, but men trained above all in the legal professions.

Perhaps the most consistent characteristics of the principal orators of the Constituent—both radicals and conservatives—were their relative youth and their tendency to come from the larger towns of the kingdom. In general, those residing in communities of less than eight thousand inhabitants spoke less than the average for all deputies; and the larger the place of residence, the more frequently they spoke, with Parisian members of the Third Estate registering the highest rates of all.[98] As for the age of the deputies, the top twenty speakers—and the top fifty, as well—averaged a full six years younger than the National Assembly as a whole. Among the top twenty, Barnave and Regnaud were in their twenties; and André, Le Chapelier, Démeunier, Lanjuinais, Prieur, Duport, Cazalès, and Robespierre were all in their thirties. In fact, there was a remarkable and consistent correlation between deputy age and the average number of speeches delivered.[99]

CONSTITUENCY RELATIONS

The deputies themselves were well aware of the relative youth of many of their most active leaders and lawmakers.[100] Less commonly emphasized was the importance of deputy interactions with their constituencies. According to certain theoretical positions enunciated by the membership, direct interactions of this kind should not have been significant in the constitutional process. For the abbé Sieyès, in his June 17 declaration, the new constitution should arise entirely out of the National Assembly itself: "The interpretation and presentation of the general will of the nation belongs to it and it alone." Each deputy should consider himself free in his deliberations, the representative of the entire country and not of a specific order or electoral

---

[97] See Dale Van Kley, *The Religious Origins of the French Revolution* (New Haven, 1996), esp. chap. 6.

[98] The average numbers of speeches by the population of the town of residence were as follows: under 2,000: 6.2; 2,000–8,000: 11.9; 8,000–20,000: 18.1; over 20,000 (including Paris): 35.4. For the Third Estate alone: under 2,000: 6.0; 2,000–8,000: 13.7; 8,000–20,000: 22.9; 20,000–100,000: 47.8; Paris: 91.0.

[99] The average numbers of speeches by age cohort were as follows: under 30: 46.1; 30–39: 29.9; 40–49: 16.5; 50–59: 11.8; 60–69: 6.3; over 69: 2.6. The top 50 speakers had an average age of 40.6 years; the top 20 speakers, 40.3; the entire National Assembly had an average age of 46.4.

[100] See above, chap. 1.

district.[101] Such also was the message of the major speech by Talleyrand in early July, which proposed to nullify the "binding mandates" frequently inserted in the deputies' cahiers; and of a series of speeches by Le Chapelier, Pétion, and Mirabeau in the spring of 1790.[102] In their letters and diaries, several of the delegates specifically stressed their independence of action and their determination to rely on their conscience above all else. Cernon de Pinteville threatened to resign if "in order to earn the support of my constituents, I must act against my principles."[103]

But this idealized position of deputy detachment from the opinions of their constituencies was seldom maintained in practice. From their earliest residence in Versailles, virtually all of the Third Estate deputies—and a considerable number of the noble and clerical delegates as well—sent back news and printed materials to individuals and correspondence committees in the towns they represented. During the interregnum between the decline of the royal bureaucracy in the summer and fall of 1789 and the creation of the new system of regional administration in the spring of 1790, this correspondence assumed the character of a veritable institution. Deputies found themselves overwhelmed with letters, as local citizens struggled to make sense of the flood of paper and the lengthy and unfamiliar laws arriving daily from the Assembly.[104] With the lines of power between the Assembly and the royal ministries altogether uncertain, it was only logical for local notables to write to those few individuals in the new power structure with whom they were familiar.[105] Some deputies were compelled to hire secretaries to assist them in the task, while certain delegations picked one of their members—permanently or by rotation—to assume the burdens of correspondence for the whole group. Gaultier de Biauzat even prepared regular printed accounts of debates and new laws which could be distributed to towns and villages throughout his electoral district.[106]

---

[101] *AP*, 8:127.

[102] *AP*, 8:200–203 (July 7, 1789), 13:106–8, 113–15 (Apr. 19, 1790). Also, Lameth, 2:134–38.

[103] Jean-Baptiste de Cernon de Pinteville to his brother: A.D. Marne, J 2286, entry of Dec. 21, 1789. See also Durand, entry for Sept. 4, 1789; and Henri Quatrefages de Laroquete, in François Rouvière, *Quatrefages de Laroquete* (Paris, 1886), 86, 89.

[104] E.g., François-Antoine Boissy d'Anglas, "Lettres inédites sur la Révolution française," ed. René Puaux, *Bulletin de la Société de l'histoire du Protestantisme français* 75 (1926), 429–32 (letter of Aug. 19, 1789); Thomas Lindet, *Correspondance*, ed. Amand Montier (Paris, 1899); Jean-Louis Gouttes to J. B. Cabanès, cadet, "bourgeois": A.C. Argelliers, S 12 A, letter of April 2, 1790; Ferrières, *Correspondance*, 56 (letter of ca. June 5, 1789); Antoine Durand, *Lettres de Versailles sur les Etats généraux*, ed. A. Frugier and J. Maubourguet (Blois, 1933), 33–34. See also Alison Patrick, "Paper, Posters, and People: Official Communication in France, 1789–1794," *Historical Studies* 18 (1978), 1–23.

[105] See, e.g., Boissy d'Anglas, ms., XVI-30, letter of ca. Mar. 1790; Périsse Du Luc, letter of Dec. 27, 1789.

[106] L. Desgraves, "Correspondance des députés de la sénéchaussée d'Agen aux Etats-Généraux et à l'Assemblée nationale," *Recueil des travaux de la société académique d'Agen. Sciences, lettres, et arts*, 3e sér., I (1967), 11–12; A.C. Marseille, BB 360; Jean-Jacques-François Mil-

During the early weeks of the Revolution the representatives were intensely aware that the moral support of the population was the only real force at their command, a predicament that rendered Rousseau's concept of the "general will"—or at least their understanding of that concept—more relevant and meaningful than ever before. There were endless readings of letters of support arriving in the Assembly from around the country. Such letters, as Bailly put it, "established the foundation on which the National Assembly's authority rested, the expression of the general will."[107] But there was also a curious circular process entailed in this relationship. The deputies maintained that they themselves were the voice of the general will, but in order to survive before the forces of counterrevolution, they were obliged to cultivate and, if necessary, incite and engender popular support for that general will. In that critical summer of 1789, certain patriots found themselves striving, as it were, to create a market for the Revolution as they saw it. "Our enemies have been forced to yield," wrote Barnave in mid-July, but "only the power of the general will can discourage them. We must not lose a minute in publicizing sound ideas in every corner of the provinces." "It is through correspondence of this kind, established throughout the country," concurred Maillot, "that public opinion can be educated, and that the Third Estate can be invested with all the strength of the general will."[108]

On occasion, individual deputies might serve as the active tutors in the instruction and conversion of public opinion, aggressively soliciting letters of adherence from their electors for specific decrees. If a town did not respond, the deputy would write back with greater insistence and announce his humiliation that other districts had shown greater patriotism. As a last resort, he would write the town's "spontaneous" adhesion himself and beg the city fathers to append their signatures.[109] Some deputies went even further, involving themselves in the creation of municipal national guards or Revolutionary committees, and even returning home to oversee the situation more closely.[110] Such was the case of François-Nicolas Buzot, who pur-

---

lanois to the municipality of Lyon: B.M. Lyon, mss. 1471–73; Pierre-Siffren Boulouvard to municipality of Arles: A.C. Arles, AA 23, letter of Oct. 8, 1789; Gaultier, 2:266–67 (letter of Aug. 29, 1789).

[107] Bailly, 1:261 (entry of June 30). See also Boullé, 11 (1888), 18 (letter of May 22); Creuzé-Latouche, 60–61 (entry of June 5); Visme, entry of July 1; Périsse du Luc, letter of July 24.

[108] Egret, 91; Maillot, letter of June 3.

[109] E.g., François-Joseph Bouchette, *Lettres*, ed. C. Looten. (Lille, 1909), 239 (letter of Aug. 8, 1789); Gaultier, 2:266, (letter of Aug. 26, 1789); Thibaudeau, 62–63, 85–87 (letters of Dec. 26, 1789 and May 21, 1790); Maximilien Robespierre, *Correspondance*, ed. Georges Michon, 2 vols. (Paris, 1926–41), 47 (letter of July 23, 1789).

[110] Boullé, 15 (1889), 19 (letter of July 28—incorrectly printed July 29); Boissy, "Lettres inédites," 289, 291–92 (letters of July 15 and 18); Bouche, letter of Aug. 8; Lombard-Taradeau, 245–47 (letter of Aug. 13); Jean-François-Pierre Poulain de Corbion in "Correspondance des deputés des Côtes-du-Nord," 245, 251 (letters of July 31 and Aug. 21); Robespierre, 46–47 (letter of July 23).

sued a vigorous campaign to direct his town of Evreux, step by step, along the path of Revolution. Guillaume Bonnemant likewise worked energetically to advance the revolutionary spirit in his native Arles. In the latter case, however, the constituents proved far less tractable, prompting a bitter complaint about their letters: "nothing you say comes up to the standards of our century!"[111]

Yet, to rely on the testimony of our witnesses, the positions taken by Bonnemant and Buzot were not typical. Rather, the great majority—especially among the commoners—actively sought the opinions of their home districts as part of their decision-making process. Whatever their theoretical status as embodiments of an abstract general will, few could detach themselves from the concrete territorial districts which had sent them to Versailles. They were provincial notables, accustomed to elite positions within their local societies, and it was only good policy to cultivate relations with colleagues and neighbors with whom they would have to live. And many undoubtedly harbored ambitions for future positions worthy of their talents and status in the departmental and municipal administrations.

The majority of the deputies conveyed an image of service and responsibility. "I will devote my life to demonstrating my worthiness of your confidence and respect" (Alquier of La Rochelle); "I will submit myself, gentlemen, to your instructions. I ask you to enlighten me with your wisdom. You will find me a docile pupil" (comte de La Roque from Périgueux); "I beg you to support me with your counsel and suggestions, and to assist me in the success I so ardently hope to achieve" (Delaville Le Roulx from Lorient).[112] Several individuals insisted that they would follow the views of their constituencies even when those views were in conflict with their own. After the Night of August 4, Schwendt opposed the preservation of Strasbourg's municipal privileges, yet he promised the city to support them nevertheless. "Wherever the interests of my constituency are concerned," observed Maillot, "I will always set aside my personal opinions."[113]

Constituencies closely followed the actions of their representatives, taking them to task if they strayed from local opinion; and most deputies appeared extremely sensitive to criticisms of this sort. Some were attacked for having signed or for not having signed published petitions and resolutions; or for having signed too far down the list; or for not having spoken frequently enough; or for having taken leave of their posts without the permission of

[111] François-Nicolas-Léon Buzot to the municipality of Evreux: A.C. Evreux, 13a D1, letter of July 21, 1789. Buzot seems to have been present in Evreux on July 21 when the town established its "comité révolutionnaire." Also Guillaume Bonnemant: A.C. Arles, AA 23, letter of Nov. 30, 1789.

[112] H. Perrin de Boussac, Un témoin de la Révolution et de l'Empire: Charles-Jean-Marie Alquier (Paris, 1983), 35; Delaville, letter of May 15, 1789; Jean-François de La Roque to the municipality Périgueux: A.M. Périgueux, AA 26, letter of May 15, 1790.

[113] Schwendt, in Reuss, 1:234–35 (letter of Nov. 1, 1789); Maillot, letter of Sept. 25. Also, Lepoutre, letter of Sept. 27, 1789.

the bailliage notables. Merle was castigated and even threatened with death for words reputedly pronounced in Paris (utter slander, according to him). Goupilleau, criticized for failing to support his district within the Assembly, poured out his chagrin in a three-page letter ("I am so deeply unhappy!").[114]

To judge solely by the correspondence (which was not necessarily disinterested), deputies passed days and even weeks acting on the requests of their fellow citizens, requests which were often only indirectly related to their duties as representatives. Bouchette spent months seeking government assistance for the construction of locks and canals around his town of Bergues. Bonnemant took up the cause of the levees on the Rhône, Grellet de Beauregard the roads in Limousin, Begouën-Demeaux the port and fortifications of Le Havre, and Lepoutre the cultivation of tobacco in Flanders. "As I see it," Gontier de Biran explained, "each deputy will be working for the best interests of his own particular district." Merle, who ceaselessly involved himself in aiding both his town of Mâcon and specific individuals who lived there, was even more frank: "It seems to me altogether reasonable that anyone who is able to profit from his present position, will certainly do so."[115]

The deputies' preoccupation with serving their constituencies reached a pinnacle during the great rush in the winter and spring of 1790 to harvest "the fruits of the Revolution"—as the contemporary phrase put it—to obtain for their cities the local seats of the administrative, judicial, and ecclesiastical units created in the new division of the kingdom.[116] Here at last was one Revolutionary challenge for which both deputies and townsmen were well prepared: trained, as they were, through the endless municipal battles pursued under the Old Regime for the preservation and expansion of local rights and privileges. Even those who had rarely or never previously participated in the debates now threw themselves with relish into the bargaining and horse trading and Machiavellian manipulations which dominated the Assembly for weeks.[117] Indeed, more deputies probably spoke before the general session during this period than at any time since the early weeks of the Assembly.[118]

[114] Jean-François-Marie Goupilleau to his cousin, sénéchal in Rochefervière: B.M. Nantes, Collection Dugast-Matifeux, no. 98, letter of Sept. 24, 1790; André-Marie Merle to the municipality of Mâcon: A.C. Mâcon, D(2) 13, carton 21 bis, Jan. 7, 1790. Also, e.g., Gontier, letter of May 22, 1790; Jacques-Louis Guino, letter to National Assembly, Oct. 23, 1789: A.N., C 32, dos. 265; Pinteville, letter of Sept. 12, 1789.

[115] Bouchette, 402–7 (letter of June 15, 1790); Bonnemant, letters of Dec. 12, 1790 and May 27, 1791; Grellet, 88–89 (letter of June 2, 1790); Begouën, letter of Oct. 9, 1790; Lepoutre, letters of Apr. 22 and 25, and Nov. 23, 1790; Gontier, letter of Jan. 2, 1790; Merle, letter of Nov. 13, 1789.

[116] See Ted Margadant, *Urban Rivalries in the French Revolution* (Princeton, 1992).

[117] E.g., Merle, numerous letters of 1790; Lindet, 27–32 (letters of Dec. 4, 12, 17); Nicolas-Théodore-Antoine-Adolphe de La Salle, "Les archives municipales de Sarrelouis," ed. René Herly, *Bulletin de la Société des amis du pays de la Sarre*, no. 4 (1927), 255–56, 262–68 (letters of Dec. 1, 19, 29); Gontier, numerous letters of 1790.

[118] During the period covered by volume 11 of the *AP* (from Dec. 24, 1789 to Mar. 1,

Nervous over the stakes involved and over the future prosperity of their towns, many city fathers were not content with epistolary pleas to their representatives, but also sent delegations to Paris to present their cases to anyone who would listen. The use of lobbyists by a variety of interest groups had existed since the earliest days of the Assembly. In July 1789 commercial and manufacturing interests from various provincial cities had sent a permanent commission to work with the deputies and the key committees. This commission was particularly successful in organizing a pro-slavery lobby to fend off the abolitionist positions of certain of the more radical deputies.[119] But the great bulk of the "external deputies" or "supplicant deputies," as they were variously called, represented individual towns. By January 1790 curé Lindet estimated that there were perhaps as many as three thousand in Paris, circling about the Assembly and its membership.[120] Certain deputies expressed their irritation with the time and money spent on such men, "who are wasting their own time and are making us waste ours," as Lindet grumbled. But most seemed readily to adapt themselves to this additional aspect of their legislative task. "I am spending most of my days with Muraire," noted Lombard-Taradeau, in reference to the lobbyist from Draguignan. "We work together in all our efforts and busy ourselves ceaselessly with the means of obtaining our goals." Schwendt met daily with de Crolbois from Strasbourg; Gallot and Lofficial regularly dined with Bresson and Godet from Fontenay; Merle worked closely with the two delegates from Mâcon to "unite his efforts with theirs."[121]

The swarms of lobbyists diminished considerably after the summer of 1790, once the division of the kingdom had been substantially completed and the principal Revolutionary "fruits" had been culled. But to the end of the National Assembly, the deputies met and sought to satisfy the occasional visiting dignitaries from their electoral districts, and continued their attempts to integrate local opinions and objectives into the legislative process. If a few aggressively strove to transform public views and to push their constituencies more rapidly in a "radical" direction, the majority took pains to sound out and to represent those constituencies as accurately as they could. Whatever the theories of Sieyès and Talleyrand, whatever the deputies' earlier grand declarations about their own independence and the end of imperative mandates, most of the commoners—and a great many of the noble and clerical delegates as well—had a clear conception of the need for close deputy-constituent relations as part and parcel of the new phenomenon of representative democracy.

1790), 332 different deputies are known to have spoken, more than during any other comparable period in the first year of the Revolution.

[119] See J. Letaconnoux, "Le comité des députés extraordinaires des manufactures et du commerce de France et l'oeuvre économique de l'Assemblée constituante," *AR* 6 (1913), 149–208. Also Delaville, letter of Sept. 11, 1789; and Begouën, letter of Dec. 30, 1789.

[120] Lindet, 57 (letter of Jan. 13). Cf. Faydel, letter of Jan. 2, 1790; and Rabaut, 237.

[121] Lindet, 35 (letter of Dec. 31, 1789); Lombard, 347 (letter of Aug. 17, 1790); Schwendt, in Reuss, 1:220 (letter of Oct. 20, 1789); Gallot, 131, (letter of Jan. 11, 1790); Merle, letter of Dec. 3, 1789.

Jacobins and Capuchins

THE REVOLUTIONARY DYNAMIC THROUGH APRIL 1790

IN MOST general studies of the French Revolution, the history of the Constituent Assembly from the fall of 1789 through the spring of 1791 is conceived as a kind of interlude, a pause in the action, in which the primary focus of analysis switches from the high drama of the initial Revolutionary acts to the humdrum account of constitution making and legislative achievement. Yet to rely on those witnesses who lived through the period, the Revolutionary transformations, the Revolutionary "becoming" did not end with the march on Versailles and the relocation of the king and the Assembly to Paris. In a great many cases the perceptions and psychology of individuals continued to evolve well into 1790 and sometimes beyond. The factors impelling that evolution remained complex, and included the ever-wavering position of the monarch and the actions of the masses in Paris and the provinces. Of particular importance during this period, however, was the interaction between the various factional alignments in the Assembly and between the social groupings and ideological positions which those factions represented.

THE DEPUTY OUTLOOK AFTER OCTOBER

As the days of autumn grew shorter and the Assembly moved from Versailles to Paris, the letters and diaries of our witnesses revealed certain changes in attitude and outlook. In the heady days of the Estates General and the early National Assembly most individuals imagined that the constitution could be achieved in a matter of weeks. In June both Maupetit and Branche had predicted their work would soon be completed. The comte de Crécy and the magistrate Lasalle made much the same prognosis in August and September.[1] But as the end of the year approached, the objective of completion seemed increasingly to recede toward the horizon. Not only was

---

[1] Michel-René Maupetit, "Lettres de Maupetit (1789–91)," ed. Quéruau-Lamérie, *Bulletin de la Commission historique et archéologique de la Mayenne*, 2e sér., 18 (1902), 333 (letter of June 26); Xavier Lochmann, "Maurice Branche de Paulhaguet, député à l'Assemblée constituante," *Almanach de Brioude*, (1990), 217 (letter of June 27); Denis-Ferdinand de Crécy to Hecquet de Bérenger, trésorier de la guerre: A.N., AB XIX 3562(1), letter of Aug. 14; Nicolas-Théodore-Antoine-Adolphe de Lasalle, "Les archives municipales de Sarrelouis," ed. René Herly, *Bulletin de la Société des amis du pays de la Sarre*, no. 4 (1927), 234 (letter of Sept. 23).

the constitution to be far more inclusive and elaborate than anyone had previously imagined, but the deputies' task was greatly complicated by the responsibilities of running a transitional administration and holding the kingdom together until the new government could be implemented. Bouchette's earlier facetious remark that the Assembly might last longer than the Council of Trent now seemed distinctly less amusing. The new time frame often required considerable economic and psychological adjustment, as deputies found themselves increasingly worried about their wives and children, and the status of their personal affairs, neglected now for over half a year.[2]

It was a sign of the evolving mood when representatives began writing home for warmer clothes—having taken only spring and summer apparel for the Estates—and demanding provisions of hometown cheese or wine to bolster their morale during the long months away from their homes.[3] It was about the same period that many—like Lofficial, Couderc, Duquesnoy, and Ferrières—began pressing their wives to join them in Paris. Only a few of the commoners had originally brought their families to the Estates General. The stay in Versailles was expensive enough for the deputies alone, and in any case, their spouses were commonly required at home to look after farms and businesses and care for the children. But by autumn, a substantial number seem to have made new arrangements and set up conjugal relations in Paris.[4]

The move to Paris invariably brought other changes to individuals' lives. As they had done in Versailles, the commoner deputies continued to lodge together in groups, in the same building or apartment, in order to economize on rent. But there were often realignments of roommates as solidarities based on provincial origins gave way to those based more specifically on political philosophy. The tight cohesion and esprit de corps of the Comtois or Provençal or Artesian delegations declined measurably after the

[2] François-Joseph Bouchette, *Lettres*, ed. C. Looten (Lille, 1909), 224 (letter of May 20). See also Jacques-Athanase de Lombard-Taradeau, "Lettres (1789–91)," *Le Var historique et géographique*, ed. L. Honoré, 2 (1925–27), 256 (letter of Aug. 19).

[3] François-René-Pierre Ménard de La Groye, *François Ménard de La Groye, député du Maine aux Etats généraux. Correspondance, 1789–1791*, Florence Mirouse, ed. (Le Mans, 1989), 114 (letter of Oct. 2, 1789); Bouchette, 349 (letter of Feb. 20, 1790); Pierre-François Lepoutre to his wife: family archives of Adolphe Lepoutre-Dubreuil, Montignac-sur-Vezère; Claude Gantheret to Pierre Leflaive, his brother-in-law: private collection of Françoise Misserey, letters of Oct. 11 and 22, 1789.

[4] Louis-Prosper Lofficial, "Lettres de Lofficial," ed. Leroux-Cesbron, *La nouvelle revue rétrospective* 7 (1897), 192 (Oct. 24, 1789); Guillaume-Benoît Couderc, "Lettres de Guillaume-Benoît Couderc (1781–92)," ed. M. O. Monod, *Revue d'histoire de Lyon* 423 (letter of Dec. 28, 1789); Adrien Duquesnoy, *Journal d'Adrien Duquesnoy*, ed. R. de Crèvecoeur, 2 vols. (Paris, 1894), 2:151 (entry of Dec. 10, 1789); Charles-Elie de Ferrières, *Correspondance inédite*, ed. Henri Carré (Paris, 1932), 191 (letter of Nov. 10, 1789). Also François-Henri de Virieu to the marquis de Viennois: Archives of the Château d'Avauges, reproduced in A.D. Isère, 1 Mi 461, wife's letter of Oct. 10, 1789; Claude Fricaud to Jean-Marie Gelin, avocat in Charolles: copies of the originals kindly provided by Doctor Robert Favre, letter of Feb. 3, 1790.

arrival in Paris. Branche, who had previously shared rooms with a curé from his home parish, now took up residence with four other deputies, at least three of whom joined him regularly at the Jacobin Club. So too the radicals Robespierre and Lepoutre abandoned their more moderate Versailles room-mates, Lepoutre to move in with the Jacobin curé Nolf, and Robespierre to lodge separately with a Parisian family.[5] Though they had all lived near one another in Versailles, the deputies found themselves scattered far and wide across the great metropolis. To some extent at least, the relative distance of a deputy's lodgings from the meeting hall was a rough measure of the indi-vidual's involvement and commitment to the Revolution. While many of those most swept up in events sought residences as near to the Manège as possible, the more conservative deputies often preferred a greater distance, far from the noise and bustle of the city center—and from the potential dangers of the politicized crowds.[6] Some of the conservative curés were particularly miserable in the capital, complaining endlessly of their aliena-tion from the urban world in which they were forced to reside, of their anxiety toward popular violence, and of their difficulty in sleeping.[7] The marquis de Ferrières, who took up residence near the Paris Observatory, across town from the Assembly, was obsessively fearful of going out at night, of being robbed or run over by speeding carriages or of disappearing into a quagmire of mud. The pious Garron de La Bévière, who expressed much the same distaste with the city, was also shocked by the immorality of the place, and especially by the large number of prostitutes whom he en-countered almost everywhere.[8]

Others, however, felt anything but isolated in the city and delighted in pursuing an active social life outside the Assembly. For those dwelling near the center, the clubs, the cafés, the bookstores, the newspaper offices, the colonnades of the Palais Royal created an intense intellectual environment, unlike anything they had known in Versailles, an environment that played no small role in their continued revolutionary development. The Constitu-ent period was marked by an Indian summer of the Old Regime salon cul-ture, and substantial numbers of deputies were enthusiastic participants. Ar-thur Young described the regular evening gatherings at the apartment of

[5] Lochmann, 220 (letter of Oct. 22); Lepoutre, letters of Oct. 17 and 22, 1789; Edna Hindie Lemay, "La majorité silencieuse de la Constituante: un micro-groupe, les députés du Tiers etat du Nord et du Pas-de-Calais," *Etudes sur le XVIIIe siècle* 5 (1978), 170.

[6] E.g., Ferrières, *Correspondance* 324 (letter of Nov. 1790); Jean Colson, "Notes d'un curé Saargovien, député aux Etats généraux de 1789," ed. Arthur Benoît, *Revue nouvelle d'Alsace-Lorraine et du Rhin* 8 (1888), 145.

[7] E.g., Emmanuel Barbotin, *Lettres de l'abbé Barbotin*, ed. A. Aulard (Paris, 1910), 72–74, 76 (letters of Oct. 26 and Nov. 6, 1789); Paul-Augustin Pous, "Correspondance inédite," *Revue de l'Anjou* 23 (1897), 201 (letter of Oct. 14, 1790); Jean-Joseph Bigot de Vernières to his nephew, avocat in Saint-Flour: copies in A.D. Cantal, Fonds Delmas, letter of Dec. 5, 1789; Colson, 139–40.

[8] Ferrières, *Correspondance*, 178, 180 (letters of Oct. 20 and 21); Claude-Jean-Baptiste de Garron de La Bévière to his wife: A.D. Ain, 1 Mi 1, letter of Oct. 29, 1789.

the duc de Liancourt in the Tuileries Palace where deputies of all three orders mixed freely over dinner. There were also the Sunday afternoon salons with Madame de Genlis where similar groups of deputies—generally more politically advanced—debated the issues of the day. Other popular gathering places included the salons of Madame Bailly, Madame Necker, and Madame de Beauharnais, or—for the conservatives among them—the home of Duval d'Eprémesnil.[9] "One can truthfully say," wrote Madame de Staël, who was always present in her mother's salon, "that Parisian society was never more brilliant and never more serious than during the first three or four years of the Revolution, from 1788 through 1791. . . . All the strength of Revolutionary liberty and all the gracious manners of the Old Regime were combined in the same individuals."[10] The new cultural synthesis among the patriot deputies was also reflected in the rapidly evolving mode in clothing. In their last meeting at Versailles the deputies had formally abolished the costume distinctions for the three orders originally prescribed by the king—costumes already abandoned in practice except for certain ceremonies. Observers took note thereafter of the evolution in fashion toward a more casual attire, particularly prominent among the younger and more progressive deputies. In early 1790 Young was nonplussed by the number of deputies he encountered attired "au polisson," in dress coats, without powdered wigs, and with long boots replacing the more traditional knee breeches and buckled shoes. The clothing style of the later Revolution, with all it symbolized of a transformation in values, was already taking shape in early 1790.[11]

Nevertheless, the principal impression conveyed by the witnesses during the fall and winter was not that of a vibrant social life but of endless meetings and grinding toil. After the transfer to Paris, Assembly meetings commonly occurred seven days a week, from nine in the morning until ten or eleven at night, with only a short break in the late afternoon for dinner. On occasion, the Assembly even dispensed with the afternoon recess in order to resolve particularly pressing issues before adjourning, and it was not unknown for the evening session to be prolonged until midnight or one in the morning.[12] Somehow, the representatives had also to find time to prepare

[9] Arthur Young, Travels in France during the years 1787, 1788 and 1789 (Gloucester, Mass., 1976), 226, 231, 234–35 (entries of Jan. 12, 15, and 18, 1790); Bertrand Barère, Mémoires, ed. Hippolyte Carnot, 4 vols. (Paris, 1842–44), 1:294–95; Dominique de Reynaud de Montlosier, Mémoires 2 vols. (Paris, 1830), 2:328, 334; Augustin Challamel, Les clubs contre-révolutionnaires (Paris, 1895), esp. 553–61.

[10] Anne-Louise-Germaine de Staël, Considérations sur les principaux événements de la Révolution française, 3 vols. (London, 1818), 1:383.

[11] Young, 227 (entry of Jan. 12, 1790); Gauville, 41 (entry of Feb. 4, 1790); La Bévière, letter of Nov. 4, 1789; Antoine-René-Hyacinthe Thibaudeau in Félix Faulcon, Correspondance. Tome 2: 1789–91, ed. G. Debien (Poitiers, 1953), 141 (letter of early Jan. 1790); Jean-François Campmas to his brother, vicaire in Carmaux: B.M. Albi, ms. 177, letter of Apr. 10, 1790.

[12] André Castaldo, Les méthodes de travail de la Constituante (Paris, 1989), 290–91; Campmas, letter of Mar. 7, 1790. See also Duquesnoy, 2:335 (entry of Jan. 30, 1790).

for such meetings, studying proposed laws and reading the endless brochures written by colleagues and distributed to the deputies as they entered the hall. Campmas concluded that it was quite impossible to read everything, and Périsse complained that his eyes were rapidly wearing out: "So many great questions, arriving concurrently, on which we must form opinions! So many issues clustered together which have to be studied!" The situation was especially daunting for many of the clerical and military deputies who found themselves altogether unprepared and overwhelmed by such discussions. "Indeed, it's enough to drive someone like me to despair," wrote curé Rousselot. "I can find only tedium in operations beyond my grasp and for which I have no vocation." "Ah!" sighed the comte de La Roque, after several months of sessions, "I can only say, with a noble self-confidence, that I am one of the least enlightened members of the Assembly."[13] But even those lawyers and judges and doctors who considered themselves "enlightened," found that the burdens of their responsibilities could take a toll on their health. An avid and committed patriot in every respect, Claude Fricaud longed, nevertheless, to get away for a few weeks to his home in Charolles "to restore my moral strength before being swallowed up again in this place." Durand suffered from "fatigue and lassitude, the result of continual tension." After a period of three months without a single day off, Campmas found that "half of the deputies are under great pressure." "Our every moment is taken up," he wrote, "and I think we will die here from mental exhaustion, from weariness, and from lack of exercise."[14] One should not underestimate the effects of sheer overwork, fatigue, and tension in exacerbating the political infighting and factional strife so characteristic of the Assembly during this period.

Perhaps the exhaustion and overwrought anxiety experienced by the deputies also influenced another characteristic feature of deputy psychology at this time: a widespread preoccupation with the threat of counterrevolutionary plots. The idea of an "aristocratic plot" had been present in both popular and elite reflection since the earliest days of the Revolution—notably, during the July crisis and the Great Fear. But never did concerns for such plots seem more pervasive in the letters and speeches of the deputies than in the weeks and months following the October uprising.[15] Increasingly, for a great many representatives, all public disturbances, all recalcitrance to authority, virtually any occurrence with potentially negative consequences for

---

[13] Campmas, letter of Mar. 8, 1790; Jean-André Périsse Du Luc to J. B. Willermoz: B.M. Lyon, ms. F.G. 5430, letter of Dec. 27, 1789; Claude-Germain Rousselot to his nephew, Joseph Rousselot: Fonds Girardot, A.D. Haute-Saône, letter of Jan. 1, 1790; Jean-François de La Roque to the municipality of Périgueux: A.M. Périgueux, AA 26, letter of Aug. 9, 1790.

[14] Fricaud, letters of Feb. 3, 1790; Antoine Durand to his cousin, A.M. Cahors, unclassed box of letters from Revolutionary deputies, letter of May 23, 1790. Campmas, letters of Feb. 7 and May 23, 1790.

[15] See Haim Burstin, "Riflessioni sul tema del complotto in Francia tra Ancien régime e Rivoluzione," in *Storia e paine*, eds. L. Guidi et al. (Milan, 1992), 203–18.

the patriot cause were construed as part and parcel of a generalized conspiracy. Arthur Young was struck in January by the rumors among his deputy friends of impending invasions, of designs on their lives, of threats to kidnap the king. The generally cynical and level-headed Duquesnoy clearly felt the Assembly to be beleaguered and under siege: "attacked from all sides by opposition, threatened from every direction by insurrections and factions, instigated by the remnants of the aristocracy." All the riots and lynchings in Paris had been fomented by secret opponents seeking to create anarchy (Pierre-François Bouche); the challenge of the Parlement of Metz to the Assembly's authority was but "a single part of a general plan undertaken to destroy the Revolution" (Barnave); the rise in grain prices in the late spring of 1790 "was too sudden, too unexpected, too uniform throughout the kingdom not to have been the fruit of a secret maneuver" (Fricaud). There were even theories that the collapse of the spectators' balcony in the hall of the *archevêché* was part of a hidden plot to assassinate the deputies.[16] Not everyone was convinced by such accusations. The conservative marquis de Ferrières and the Monarchien Faydel claimed to give them no credence, and were certain that they had been manufactured by "our demagogues" to suit their own purposes.[17] Yet the obsession with conspiracies was not solely confined to the left of the Assembly—as has sometimes been suggested.[18] The Monarchiens themselves—including Faydel—could easily slip into the same mode of explanation, with the machinations of the patriot "demagogues" replacing those of the aristocrats as the source of all their troubles. On the eve of the October Days, for example, many of the participants in the Monarchien alignment—Bergasse, Mounier, Turckheim, and others— were convinced that the growing unrest in Paris was part of a general plot on the part of the left to attack their position and overthrow the king. And similar convictions were expressed during the winter and spring of 1790 by the Monarchiens' successors, the "Impartials."[19]

In fact, plot theories in general were a cultural constant under the Old

[16] Young, 222–23 (entries of Jan. 10 and 11, 1790); Duquesnoy, 2:272 (entry of Jan. 12, 1790); Pierre-François-Balthazar Bouche to the municipality of Forcalquier: A.C. Forcalquier, Series D, "Correspondance 1789," letter of Feb. 2, 1790; *AP*, 10:84 (speech by Barnave, Nov. 17, 1789); Fricaud, letter of May 31, 1790; Jean-Pierre Boullé, "Ouverture des Etats généraux de 1789," ed. Albert Macé, *Revue de la Révolution. Documents inédits* 16 (1889), 80 (letter of Oct. 26, 1789).

[17] Ferrières, *Correspondance*, 224 (letter of June 29, 1790); Jean-Félix Faydel to the municipality of Cahors: A.M. Cahors, unclassed box of letters from Revolutionary deputies, held in B.M. Cahors, letter of Jan. 2, 1790.

[18] Norman Hampson, *Prelude to Terror: The Constituent Assembly and the Failure of Consensus* (Oxford, 1988), 61–62; François Furet, *Interpreting the French Revolution*, trans. Elborg Forster (Cambridge, 1981), 55, 62–63.

[19] See the depositions of the Monarchiens in *Procédure*. Also, Virieu, letter of Jan. 28, 1790; Louis Verdet to Guilbert, curé of Saint-Sébastien of Nancy: Arch. du Grand Séminaire de Nancy, MB 17, folios 1–113, letter of Feb. 6, 1790; Jean-Félix Faydel to Jean Filsac, avocat in Cahors: A.N., W 368, no. 822, 43e partie, letter of Mar. 21, 1790; and A.M. Cahors, letter of Jan. 9.

Regime at every level of society, a common mode of explanation for all manner of social and economic phenomena which otherwise seemed quite incomprehensible: thus the famous "famine plot persuasion" so widely held in the eighteenth century.[20] Such explanations seemed all the more credible given what was known of the Machiavellian intrigues by which Old Regime court nobles had vied for power and influence. Yet the obsession with plots at this particular period in the Revolution is also revealing of the profound insecurity felt by a great many of the Constituents. Tensions were high as the Assembly struggled to construct a new Revolutionary administration to provide institutional links with the countryside. Until the new municipal and departmental governments could be created and set in motion, the deputies were forced to confront the kingdomwide anarchy with little real power beyond their abstract claims to sovereignty and the goodwill of the enthusiastic but undisciplined urban patriots and national guardsmen. Despite an outward pose of swaggering self-confidence, many deputies felt deeply troubled and uncertain about the future, about their ability to resolve the immense problems of reorganizing the kingdom, and about the assumption of responsibility for the fate of France. In a society long accustomed to noble domination and deference for superiors, it was easy to imagine that the "aristocrats" maintained far more power and organizational capabilities than they possessed in reality. "Such are the anxieties of a nascent liberty," wrote Antoine Durand in a moment of lucidity, "that one conceives enemies everywhere plotting against it, that one gives oneself over to imagination, whether to gratify one's hopes or feed one's fears."[21]

Moreover, one should not overlook the very real conspiracies against the Revolution uncovered by various of the National Assembly and Parisian surveillance committees in the winter of 1789–90. Boullé, Vernier, Duquesnoy, Dusers, and Merle, all wrote with evident anguish about the widely publicized plots of the marquis de Favras, as well as the January uprisings of popular classes in central Paris and of national guardsmen on the Champs-Elysées.[22] Lafayette himself had warned the deputies to be prepared for the church bells or drum rolls that would indicate an impending attack. "So I was right in warning you," wrote Merle, "that the obsessions of the aristocracy have not yet disappeared, and that you should continue to

---

[20] Steven L. Kaplan, *The Famine Plot Persuasion in Eighteenth-Century France* (Philadelphia, 1982). Cf. Georges Lefebvre, *The Great Fear* (New York, 1973), esp. part II; and Arlette Farge and Jacques Revel, *The Vanishing Children of Paris* (Cambridge, Mass., 1991), esp. chap. 4.

[21] Durand, letter to his cousin, May 23, 1790.

[22] Jean-Pierre Boullé to the municipality of Pontivy: A.C. Pontivy, on microfilm in A.D. Morbihan, 1 Mi 140, letter of Jan 12, 1790; Théodore Vernier to the municipality of Lons-le-Saunier: A.C. Bletterans (non-classé), "Lettres de Vernier," letter of Jan. 12, 1790; Duquesnoy, 2:276–77 (entry of Jan. 12, 1790); Charles-Guillaume Dusers to the municipality of Vannes: A.D. Morbihan, 262 E(s), letter of Dec. 29, 1789; André-Marie Merle to the municipality of Mâcon: A.C. Mâcon, D (2) 13, carton 21 bis, letter of Dec. 28, 1789. Also Barry Shapiro, *Revolutionary Justice in Paris, 1789–90* (Cambridge, 1993), chap. 6.

be watchful."[23] Patriot fears were rendered all the more real and palpable by the scarcely concealed counterrevolutionary threats of dissident conservative deputies within the National Assembly itself.

POLITICAL ALIGNMENTS AT THE BEGINNING OF 1790

Throughout the first year of the Revolution, the majority of the deputies probably avoided permanent affiliations with specific political groupings. Yet those "clubs" that did exist continued to exercise considerable influence on the Assembly. Moreover, the final weeks of 1789 and the beginning of 1790 were marked by a growing polarization of the Constituent's political life.

The once powerful alignment of the "Monarchiens" had never entirely dissolved after the October Days, despite the departure of several of its key leaders. In late December and early January the faction was formally resurrected under the strong tutelage of two of Mounier's former allies, the ex-intendant Malouet and the comte de Clermont-Tonnerre. Reacting to the recent creation of the Jacobin Club, they hoped to engineer a new alignment of "moderate patriots" and "sensible men." Malouet had initially attempted to reach an understanding with Lafayette and the group of moderate patriot nobles in his entourage, all of them disturbed by the threats of popular unrest and the drift toward radical democracy. In the end, however, the two groups were unable to achieve a compromise and Malouet and his associates resolved to act on their own.[24]

In early January the deputy from Riom drew up a list of "Principles" and "Rules of Order" for the new club of the "Impartials," as they called themselves.[25] As the Monarchiens before them, the Impartials placed great stress on the vigorous executive authority of the king and the need to maintain strong law and civil control. While they acknowledged the gains won from the mid-July uprisings in Paris, now that "the Revolution is over," they argued, such popular disturbances must be rigorously repressed. In addition—and this was a major bone of contention with the Fayettistes—Malouet and most of his friends strongly identified with the Catholic church, asserting that Catholicism must be confirmed as the state religion and that only a portion of church land should be sold. The principal objective, in Malouet's view, was to halt the anarchy and consolidate the gains already won under a reinvigorated constitutional monarchy.[26] In their private correspondence, however, other adherents to the group divulged an agenda that

[23] Merle, ibid.

[24] Pierre-Victor Malouet, *Mémoires*, 2 vols., ed. Baron Malouet (Paris, 1868), 2:45–48, 96–97; Louis Gottschalk and Margaret Maddox, *Lafayette in the French Revolution: From the October Days through the Federation* (Chicago, 1973), 140–42, 147–48; *Journal des Impartiaux*, "Exposé," 4–7, 10–11.

[25] Both printed in the *Journal des Impartiaux*, no. 1.

[26] *Journal des Impartiaux*, no. 1, p. 11; Malouet, 2:96–97.

appeared distinctly more conservative. The comte de Virieu, for example, announced that his own aim was to peacefully "overturn" the existing Revolutionary regime. The people must be shown that it was in their own best interest to reject the "tyranny of the bourgeoisie."[27]

In the beginning, the Impartials dreamed of creating a broad coalition which could take control of the Assembly, and Clermont-Tonnerre promised to bring over some two hundred Jacobins and a large contingent of moderates of various stripes. In fact, the group fell far short of such ambitious objectives. Malouet admitted that only about forty deputies came together at their first meeting, and the club had grown to only seventy-two in early February, including a certain number of non-deputies like the journalist Mallet Du Pan.[28] Of these, only about twenty can be identified with any certainty, but this partial list suggests a strong continuity with the former Monarchiens and a clear predominance of the former privileged orders.[29] Following the techniques pioneered by the Monarchiens and subsequently copied by the Jacobins, the Impartials set up a highly organized club structure: regular club meetings in the evenings and on Sunday mornings, a central steering committee, and a correspondence committee which attempted, with only limited success, to stimulate the creation of similar clubs in the provinces.[30] The real strength and potential influence of the group, however, came from its rapid rapprochement with the much more numerous extreme right of the Assembly. Despite the club's name and despite Malouet's efforts to distance himself from the "aristocrats," there could be little doubt where the members' sympathies lay on most issues. Faydel, the club's first vice-president, not only hated the Jacobins with a passion but also expressed great admiration for the extreme right orator Cazalès and for the conservative publication *Les actes des apôtres*. Indeed, the group often seemed to construct their entire policy as a reaction to the positions of the Jacobins and the "deplorable democracy" which that group represented. Most contemporaries—including the Jacobin Rabaut Saint-Etienne, the moderate Lafayette, the Impartial Puisaye, and the "aristocrat" baron de Gauville—

---

[27] Virieu, letter of Jan. 28, 1790. Also Verdet, letter of Feb. 6, 1790; and Faydel, A.N., letter of May 8, 1790, and B.M. Cahors, letter of Jan. 9, 1790.

[28] Malouet, 2:28; Pierre-Marie Irland de Bazôges to Henri Filleau, magistrate in Poitiers: A.D. Deux-Sèvres, Fonds Beauchet-Filleau, unclassed register of "lettres politiques, 1788–90," letter of Jan. 29, 1790; Verdet, letter of Feb. 6, 1790.

[29] From a wide variety of sources, the following have been identified as members of the Impartials: Béthisy de Mézières (bishop), Boisgelin (bishop), Bonnay (marquis), Boufflers (chevalier), Du Châtelet (duc), Clermont-Tonnerre (comte), Fontanges (archbishop), Faydel (lawyer), Gontier de Biran (chief magistrate/noble), Hutteau (lawyer), Henry de Longuève (magistrate/noble), Lachèse (chief magistrate), La Fare (bishop), Lannoy (comte), Malouet (naval intendant), Montesquiou (former agent-general of the Clergy), Puisaye (comte), Redon (lawyer), Verdet (curé), and Virieu (comte). Of the 20, 13 were from the former privileged orders and 14 were noble.

[30] Challamel, 100–102; Faydel, A.N., letters of Jan. 24 and Feb. 14.

clearly associated the group with the privileged orders on the right. Despite his smug condescension toward those "tainted with impartiality," Gauville appreciated that Malouet and his friends were usually dependable allies. "Only a few shades of difference," wrote Puisaye, "distinguished the Impartials from those we called the 'right.'"[31] Indeed, both in numbers and in oratorical presence, the Impartials rapidly emerged as the junior partners in a coalition with the extreme right.

Unfortunately, we know much less about the organization and objectives of the far right than about the moderate right. Unlike the Impartials, who went out of their way to print manifestos and publicly announce their activities and positions, the "aristocrats" seemed to prefer secrecy, and their existence is known only indirectly through contemporary hearsay and later memoirs. According to the Poitevin deputy Thibaudeau, they consisted of a core group of about two hundred deputies—substantially more than the Impartials—around the leadership of the abbé Maury, the vicomte de Mirabeau, the marquis de Foucauld de Lardimalie, and the chevalier de Cazalès. Other key figures commonly mentioned included Duval d'Eprémesnil and Reynaud de Montlosier. Malouet had also been invited to participate in the group, but he claimed to have appeared only briefly in order to report on the formation of the Impartials.[32] Heir to the alignment of dissident nobles and clerics who had continued meeting separately after the merging of the three estates, the group consisted almost entirely of deputies from the former privileged orders. The large contingent of clergy within the faction probably explains the nickname of "the blacks" which they rapidly acquired.[33] It may also explain the choice of their first meeting house, the convent of the Grands Augustins on the *quai* of the same name across the river from the National Assembly. For generations, this convent had housed the regular meetings of the General Assembly of the Clergy, and many of the former episcopal delegates to that institution now sat as deputies to the National Assembly. By early 1790, they were commonly referred to as the "Augustinian Club" and invariably contrasted in the mind of contemporaries with the "Jacobin Club." A publishing house and bookstore just next door served as the informal meeting spot where members came to talk and read the latest conservative tracts.[34]

Though we know next to nothing of the group's organization, they apparently maintained a central committee of "commissioners" and, like the

[31] Jean-Paul Rabaut Saint-Etienne, *Précis historique de la Révolution française* (Paris, 1807), 313; Gottschalk and Maddox, 151–52; Joseph-Geneviève de Puisaye, *Mémoires du comte de Puisaye . . . qui pourront servir à l'histoire du parti royaliste français durant la dernière Révolution*, 6 vols. (London and Paris, 1803–25), 2:339–40; Gauville, 59. Also, Faydel, A.N., letters of Mar. 28 and May 8, 1790.

[32] Thibaudeau in Faulcon, 141 (letter of early Jan.); Duquesnoy, 2:229–30 (entry of Dec. 30, 1789); *Journal des Impartiaux*, "Exposé," 6–7.

[33] On the group's membership, see below and chap. 9.

[34] Simon-Edme Monnel, *Mémoires d'un prêtre régicide*, ed. Denis-Alexandre Martin, 2 vols. (Paris, 1829), 1:109–10.

Jacobins and the Impartials, they used their meetings to plan parliamentary strategy.[35] "All these individuals," wrote Thibaudeau, "begin by preparing in their committees the insidious proposals which they hope to pass in the Assembly." Campmas too was impressed by their organization, "entirely systematic" in all the debates, "no matter what the subject."[36] But the association of clerics and gentlemen found little favor among the highly politicized population living near the Augustinians, and they were harassed until they were forced to move, first to the cloister of Saint-Honoré on the right Bank, and eventually to the apartments of individual deputies.[37]

Boisgelin's portrait of the extreme right deputies was scarcely flattering: "You cannot imagine the harm which this group has done and continues to do. . . . Nothing could be more stupid. They understand neither circumstances nor human nature." For Madame de Staël, their policies entailed little more than a *politique du pire*: "The aristocrats directed endless insults at the patriot party. Refusing all compromise with circumstances, they imagined they could help their cause by worsening it. Determined to maintain their reputation as prophets, they ardently promoted their own misfortune, for the pleasure of seeing their prophecies fulfilled."[38]

But if the "aristocrats" as a group could scarcely display the same political finesse and organizational skills as the patriots, or even the Impartials, few were so utterly intransigent and devoid of logic as Madame de Staël would lead us to believe. Reynaud de Montlosier—who was not, to be sure, the most conservative of the group, but who may have been relatively representative—made it clear that he never wished to turn back the clock altogether: "Obviously, I had no desire for the exaggerated liberty and Revolutionary equality, as they were conceived by [the left]; but neither did I wish to return to the despotism of the Old Regime"; he sought rather "the suppression of past abuses, while respecting the principal foundations of the previous system."[39] The letters of the Poitevin noble and magistrate Irland de Bazôges reveal a highly intelligent but deeply conservative individual who had prided himself all his life on "my attachment to rules and discipline"; and who was now shocked and profoundly upset by the Assembly's attacks on noble and church property: "All traditional ideas have been overturned." But even at that, he persisted in his hope that "in the new order of things, after all is said and done, I may still be called to participate in political life."[40]

[35] *Journal des Impartiaux*, "Exposé," 6–7.

[36] Thibaudeau in Faulcon, 141; Campmas, letter of Dec. 24, 1789. Also Verdet, letter of Feb. 6, 1790.

[37] Duquesnoy, 2:229–30 (entry of Dec. 30, 1789); Montlosier, 2:309–11.

[38] Jean-de-Dieu Boisgelin de Cucé to Comtesse de Gramont: A.N., M 788, letter of Oct. 10, 1789; Staël, 1:298–99.

[39] Montlosier 1:186, 196–97.

[40] Irland, letters of Jan. 8 and 18, and Apr. 10, 1790.

Perhaps the most reactionary of all, the extreme right orator Duval d'Eprémesnil sought the return of most of the Old Regime institutions, including all church land, seigneurial dues, the Parlements, and the basic elements of the tax system. Yet even Eprémesnil was prepared to accept certain changes as *faits accomplis*, notably the suppression of a number of the more inequitable taxes and the remnants of personal servitude. He also seemed to assume the continued existence of a National Assembly, though he demanded a much greater role for the nobility in a revised scheme of things.[41]

At times, at least, the extreme right seemed ready to play by the rules of the new system. Visme was impressed by the assiduousness of Maury and Cazalès in the Finance Committee, even though they commonly opposed the majority's decisions. Vernier commented on the right's efforts to use perfectly legitimate parliamentary procedures to manipulate the Assembly toward its own ends: "In this way they build confidence in procedures which they once seemed to scorn."[42] For the time being, the great danger was not that they might seek a direct overthrow of the Revolution, but that they might attempt to pervert the system from within. Indeed, throughout the fall and winter of 1789–90, the principal leaders of the extreme right coalition were taking an increasingly active role in National Assembly debates. The number of speeches delivered by deputies of the moderate right—the Monarchiens and the Impartials—dropped from September to March, continuing downward even after the departure of four of the major Monarchien leaders in October. During the same period, the most notable speakers of the extreme right were participating ever more frequently. From late 1789 to the end of the Constituent the "aristocrats" were clearly the principal spokesmen for the conservatives in the Assembly (see chart 1).[43]

The third major factional group in the Assembly, the Jacobin Club, is only slightly better known during its early existence than the extreme right. Initially the club produced neither minutes of its meetings nor an official newspaper nor a published membership list, and formal rules and a manifesto for the society appeared only in February.[44] From the small core which

[41] *AP*, 19:311 (speech of Sept. 29, 1790).

[42] Laurent de Visme, ms. "Journal des Etats généraux": B.N., Nouv. acq. fr. 12938, entry of Dec. 17, 1789; Vernier, letter of Jan. 5, 1790.

[43] See above, chap. 7, for an explanation of sources and method. Included in the count of the "Augustinians/Capuchins" are all those signing the April 19 protest—attacking the National Assembly for its refusal to accept the dom Gerle motion of April 12 (see below)—who were not known members of the Impartials. Included in the count of the "Monarchiens/Impartials" are all the known adherents as listed above, n. 29, and in chap. 6. Though the lists are incomplete, they probably include most of the members who actually spoke in the Assembly.

[44] See, in general, F.-A. Aulard, *La Société des Jacobins*, 6 vols. (Paris, 1889–97), vol. 1; Gérard Walter, *Histoire des Jacobins* (Paris, 1946); A. Bouchard, *Le club breton. Origine, composition, rôle à l'Assemblée constituante* (Paris, 1920). Also Boullé, A.D. Morbihan, letter of Jan. 6, 1790.

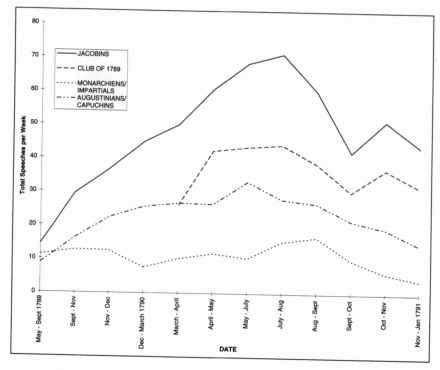

Chart 1: Deputy Participation in Debates by Factional Alignments.

first began meeting in late November, it seems to have grown rapidly. Du-quesnoy estimated a membership of about 180 deputies toward the end of December, and Gallot suggested some 200 to 300 in mid-January. But for a time, in late winter, the number of deputy sympathizers and associates was certainly even greater than that, perhaps as high as the 400 proposed by Lameth.[45] Estimates for this period are difficult however, since in the first months of 1790 the Jacobins—like the coalition on the right—represented a kind of blanket confederation united against the perceived common en-emy. It included deputies of such widely varying tendencies as the moderate nobles Lafayette, Liancourt, and La Rochefoucauld—who had seriously en-tertained an alliance with Malouet—the unpredictable comte de Mirabeau, and the "enragé" democrats Barnave, Pétion, Robespierre, and the Lameth brothers. After the first great split in the left in the spring of 1790, the number of militant Jacobins seems to have stabilized at about 200 deputies.[46]

[45] Duquesnoy, 2:229 (entry of Dec. 30, 1789); Jean-Gabriel Gallot, *La vie et les oeuvres du Docteur Jean-Gabriel Gallot*, ed. Louis Merle (Poitiers, 1961), 132 (letter of Jan. 12); Walter, 35; Alexandre de Lameth, *Histoire de l'Assemblée constituante*, 2 vols. (Paris, 1828–29), 1:423.
[46] Thus, in the vote for the Committee on Research in April 1790, the nine Jacobin deputies elected received almost exactly the same number of votes, varying between 196 and 206: A.N., C 38 (dossier 334). In December 1790, 205 deputies are thought to have

But during the winter, the total number of adherents was probably close to that of the coalition on the right.

Like the Impartials and the "Augustinian Club," the Jacobins met regularly in the evenings whenever the Assembly itself was not in session—three times a week in January 1790.[47] As their numbers expanded, the group moved from the Dominican refectory to the order's more spacious library. Here the room was arranged much like a miniature Manège, with rows of benches facing each other along the two long walls, and the president's table at the center of one side, facing the speaker's rostrum. The room was adorned, somewhat incongruously, with shelves of theological texts and portraits of religious leaders. The night meetings were usually poorly lit, to save on expenses, and visitors commented on the curiously somber, almost mystical setting for the great debates unrolling there.[48]

As the arrangement of the Jacobins' hall was closely modeled on that of the National Assembly, so too were the internal organization and the rules for debate. The official regulations drawn up by Barnave in early February specified that discussions would be governed by the procedures of the Constituent. Unlike the relatively informal Breton Club, however, the patriots had now devised a system of committees, including a central steering committee for the general direction of the society. The first such central committee seems to have consisted of Mirabeau, Barnave, Alexandre de Lameth, Duport, and Robespierre—so that the leadership of the Jacobins was distinctly radical from the very beginning, more so perhaps than the political orientation of the membership as a whole. Perhaps equally important was the club's correspondence committee. According to Boullé, the society initially had no procedures for establishing affiliated societies in the provinces, and created such arrangements only in response to requests from throughout the kingdom.[49] But rapidly thereafter, the members began vigorously encouraging the creation of a national network. The Jacobins' "formidable colonies," as Mirabeau called them, soon became one of the greatest sources of the society's strength and the principal justification for its claim to represent the will of the nation.[50]

Unlike Malouet's manifesto for the Impartials, the Jacobin rules were noticeably vague on the policy orientations of the club—presumably since a certain imprecision was essential for holding together individuals of such diverse political positions.[51] Ultimately, Barnave specified only three broad tenets. First—and fundamental, given the society's official name—members

---

adhered to the group: Aulard, 1:xxxiv–lxxvi, complemented by the general index in vol. 6. Also below, chap. 9.

[47] Lepoutre, letter of Jan. 29, 1790.

[48] Walter, 35.

[49] Boullé, A.D. Morbihan, letter of Jan. 6, 1790.

[50] Honoré-Gabriel de Riquetti, comte de Mirabeau, *Correspondance avec le comte de La Marck*, 3 vols., Adrien de Bacourt ed. (Paris, 1851), 2:453 (letter of ca. Dec. 23, 1790).

[51] 'Règlements" in Aulard, 1:xxviii–xxxiii.

must dedicate themselves to upholding the new constitution. Second, they would support political equality for the common man—underscoring the club's systematic, if largely unsuccessful, opposition to the creation of a two-tiered system of "active" and "passive" citizens. Third, the society would dedicate itself to combating plots and counterrevolutionary activity. Most of the Jacobins were convinced that "the party opposed to national regeneration" was linked to the Favras conspiracy, participated regularly in the "Austrian committee" led by the queen, and was doing everything in its power to trick the people and create a civil war. For this reason, as Rabaut conceived it, "the deputies of the patriot party deployed as much energy unraveling plots as their adversaries used in forming them."[52]

Yet the more radical members of the club specified that their goal was not simply to uncover plots and defend the gains already won, but to push the Revolution forward, to root out and reform abuses wherever they were found and to entirely transform the country. "Their sole objective," wrote Rabaut, "was to reform prior injustice. But since the whole regime was a tissue of injustice, everything had to be transformed." Robespierre concurred: "In their audacious attempt to clean the Augean stables, the patriots of the National Assembly have undertaken a task that is almost beyond human strength."[53] Indeed, sometime during that fall and winter a new idealism and intensity began to appear in the letters written home by some, though not all, of the Jacobin deputies—a strikingly new vocabulary that was not generally present in their early correspondence from Versailles, but which seems to have emerged in the course of the Revolutionary experience itself. It was an idealism which laid great stress on the full development of democracy and the glorification of the common people: a vision clearly influenced by the writings of Rousseau, but also by the events through which the deputies had passed and the part played by the crowds in successively rescuing the Revolution. Many of the deputy witnesses involved represented precisely that minority who had exonerated the violence of the crowds in July, August, and October.[54] But it was often the end of 1789 or the first months of 1790 before the new vocabulary and rhetorical style began to appear. One could see the transition in Dinochau's newspaper, the *Courier de Madon*, as the humorous, sarcastic, Voltairian tone of the first issues in early November gave way to an intensely patriotic, almost utopian rhetoric with a strong Rousseauist flavor and a continual emphasis on "the good people."[55] The wealthy magistrate Ménard de La Groye experienced a similar metamorphosis. Once so close to the aristocracy in Le Mans and Versailles, he now rapidly distanced himself from "this vain and arrogant nobility" and fully embraced the cause of the common people, especially the

[52] Rabaut, *Précis*, 256–58.

[53] Ibid., 295; Maximilien Robespierre, *Correspondance*, ed. Georges Michon, 2 vols. (Paris, 1926–41), 66 (letter to Buissart, Mar. 4, 1790).

[54] See above, chaps. 5 and 6.

[55] *Courier de Madon*, Nov. 1789 through May 1790.

Parisians: "Ah, the good people, the good French people," he wrote to his wife. "How slandered they have been by those who have said that liberty would never suit them."[56] It was a new style of language echoed by several of our Jacobin witnesses—Buzot, Merle, Fricaud, Gallot, and Lepoutre, for example—a similarity of phrasing and of sentiment, the sketch of a veritable ideology that undoubtedly reflected the impact of the Jacobin meetings themselves.[57]

Foiled in many of their early impatient attempts to effect rapid equality and democracy, the Jacobins increasingly viewed their task as one of educating and manipulating their more benighted colleagues, whose votes were necessary if they were to obtain a majority. "Since the opinion of many representatives was not always as advanced as our own," wrote curé Grégoire, he and his Jacobin associates were compelled to use a variety of political tactics and maneuvers. Périsse Du Luc dwelled at length on the painstaking work involved: "You could not believe the factions we had to assemble, the art of tactics we had to deploy. . . . How many exaggerated proposals we had to make in order to obtain lesser ones; how many step-by-step gradations we planned in advance to bring deputies along, slowly and progressively, from one decree to the next!" To believe the vicomte de Toulongeon—who soon placed himself in the more moderate wing of the patriots—elite leadership, the status of vanguard, became almost a mystique in itself for the Jacobins: "Affecting always to lead, they were often assumed to be at the forefront; and this very appearance established a habit that became in the end a reality."[58]

By the end of 1789, in the eyes of many witnesses, the factional struggle between the two major coalitions increasingly dominated the entire Assembly. The patriotic newspaper L'observateur expressed the generally held view in early January: "For the last month, two associations have existed in Paris composed of members of the National Assembly. The first meets in the Jacobins of the rue Saint-Honoré, the second in the Grands Augustins. Both have a numerous membership, and both are a source of uneasiness for Parisians from the influence they can have over the Assembly."[59] The image of two armed camps preparing for battle appeared again and again in the deputies' descriptions. For Boullé, the Assembly, "appears split, in a most remarkable manner, into two nearly equal parties, so that one could imagine two armies facing one another." Barbotin evoked "two armies ready to do

---

[56] Ménard, 124, 246 (letters of Oct. 13, 1789 and July 20, 1790).

[57] Gallot, 130 (letter of Jan. 9, 1790); Lepoutre, letters of Jan. 1 and Mar. 17, 1790; Merle, letters of Nov. 2 and Dec. 10, 1789; Feb. 22 and Apr. 26, 1790; François-Nicolas-Léon Buzot to the municipality of Evreux: A.C. Evreux, 13a D1, letter of Feb. 18, 1790; Fricaud, letter of May 3, 1790.

[58] Henri Grégoire, Mémoires, ed. H. Carnot, 2 vols. (Paris, 1837–40), 1:387; Périsse, letter of Dec. 27, 1789; François-Emmanuel Toulongeon, Histoire de la France depuis la Révolution, 7 vols. (Paris, 1801), 1:108.

[59] Quoted in Walter, 93–94.

battle"; Lindet, "an arena of gladiators." "The parties in the Assembly stand out each day more clearly," wrote Duquesnoy. "They are becoming more intense, more opposed to one another, more obstinately attached to their own views; insults and abuse are more common, and mutual scorn is more apparent."[60]

Indeed, the passions aroused by these political confrontations were soon exerting a major impact on relationships among the deputies, forging friendships and creating antagonisms of extraordinary intensity. By the spring of that year, former friends and colleagues who sat at opposite ends of the hall were no longer on speaking terms and felt nervous even to be seen with one another. As much as he detested the "aristocrats" in general, Périsse was deeply saddened by the irreparable barrier that now seemed to divide him from many of his former Masonic brothers—and particularly from his friend, the comte de Virieu: "The division within the Assembly is so extreme, that I would be suspected by the Friends of the Constitution if I were seen having relations with any of them."[61] Doctor Gallot, on the other hand, described the bonds of fraternity which joined the Jacobins inseparably to their fellow deputies on the left "who espouse correct ideas": "There are two or three hundred of us here," he wrote in mid-January, "bound together forever. Without even knowing one another's names, we are such good friends and so strongly linked, that hereafter, it will be impossible to travel in the kingdom, without encountering colleagues and friends."[62] Factional passions of this kind cannot explain everything about the Revolutionary process in the National Assembly during the winter and spring of 1790. But neither can they be ignored.

THE ADVANCE OF THE LEFT THROUGH FEBRUARY 1790

In the weeks after October, the tempo of activity picked up perceptibly, as the Assembly began the immense task of dismantling and reconstructing the institutional structures of the Old Regime. The deputies themselves were often amazed by the pace and scope of the operations: "Since we have come to reside in Paris," wrote Lepoutre to his wife, "we are moving ahead with giant steps, and our descendants will find it difficult to believe . . . that the French Nation could make a revolution in so little time."[63] The first priority was to establish a new system of local administration at the town and regional levels. The importance of this undertaking was evident if the Assem-

---

[60] Boullé, A.D. Morbihan, letter of Dec. 15, 1789; Barbotin, 82 (letter of Jan. 6, 1790); Thomas Lindet, *Correspondance de Thomas Lindet pendant la Constituante et la Législative (1789–92)*, ed. Amand Montier (Paris, 1899), 156 (letter of May 8, 1790); Duquesnoy, 2:142 (entry of Dec. 7, 1789).

[61] Périsse, letter of May 12, 1790.

[62] Gallot, 132 (letter of Jan. 12, 1790).

[63] Lepoutre, letter of Nov. 17, 1789.

THE CAPUCHINS

4. (*Left*) Curé Emmanuel Barbotin. From a small parish in northern France, where he collected a modest revenue, he had arrived in Versailles a fervent patriot, bitterly opposed to the "mercenary" bishops. He was terrified by the popular violence of July and early August, but it was the "rape" of the tithes and the anticlerical rhetoric of mid-August that pushed him definitively into the camp of the conservatives, where he voted solidly with the Augustinians and Capuchins. His parishioners elected him mayor of the village in 1790, but he was forced to abandon his post in 1791 after he refused the ecclesiastical oath of allegiance to the constitution. (Bibliothèque nationale)

5. (*Right*) Comte François-Henri de Virieu. Raised at Versailles and trained as a soldier, he was active in the Freemasons and a passionate reader of Rousseau, as well as a devout Catholic. He was one of the leaders of the liberal nobles in Dauphiné, but after joining the National Assembly in June 1789, he was appalled by the popular anarchy (his own château was burned) and angered by the antireligious policies of the patriots. Leader and "whip" of the Monarchien/Impartial coalition, he became more closely linked to the Capuchins after the dom Gerle affair. In 1791, he joined the emigrant armies and was killed in the siege of Lyon in 1793. (Bibliothèque nationale)

bly were to implement throughout the country the decrees it was voting in Paris. "In general," explained Antoine Durand, "we have come to believe that as soon as we establish the regional administrations, our constitution will be consolidated and protected from all threats of its enemies."[64] The task of drawing up the new divisions of the kingdom was immense and monopolized Assembly sessions for days on end from December through

[64] Durand, letter to his cousin, May 23, 1790. Cf. Alexis Basquiat de Mugriet and Pierre Joseph de Lamarque to the municipality of Bayonne: A.C. Bayonne, AA 51, letter of Oct. 16, 1789; Merle, letter of Dec. 16, 1789; and Lepoutre, letter of Jan. 16, 1790.

THE MODERATES

6. (*Left*) Jean-François Campmas. An obscure physician from a village in the Massif Central near Albi, he arrived in Versailles with a deep love for the king and a Christian belief that emphasized the religion of Jesus and the equality of men. He was horrified by the popular violence and feared democracy. At times the debates overwhelmed and exhausted him, and he was wholly lost in the budgetary discussions. Yet he maintained strong sympathies with the patriots, and as he listened to speeches in the Assembly, he was slowly won over to more radical positions. (Bibliothèque nationale)

7. (*Right*) Claude Gantheret. A Burgundy wine and grain merchant who had briefly studied medicine and who had been chosen deputy almost by accident in the horse trading of the Dijon electoral assembly. He was initially frightened by events and terrified by the boldness of the Breton Club proposals. But he was converted to the new patriot vision in June 1789, partly through his satisfaction at seeing the nobles "humiliated." During the Assembly he spent as much time scheming to profit from grain shortages as he did at his legislative tasks. (Bibliothèque nationale)

February. But beyond the creation of the new departments and municipalities, the deputies took up a vast array of constitutional and legislative
reforms, reforms that ranged from taxes, the penal code, and the armed
forces to the judiciary, the ecclesiastical structures, and the seigneurial system. There will be no attempt here to follow all of these manifold operations through the spring and early summer of 1790, operations which have
already been explored in detail by institutional historians.[65] We will focus

[65] See, e.g., Philippe Sagnac, *La législation civile de la Révolution* (Paris, 1898); Jacques Go-
dechot, *Les institutions de la France sous la Révolution et l'Empire* (Paris, 1968); Marie-Vic
Ozouf-Marignier, *La formation des départements: la représentation du territoire français à la fin du*

THE JACOBINS

8. (*Left*) Jean-André Périsse Du Luc. A wealthy book publisher from Lyon, who was active in the leadership of various Masonic, mystical illuminist, and spiritist movements before the Revolution, and who had played an important role in municipal politics and the Intermediary Commission during the Pre-Revolution. His earlier belief in the Enlightened merger of commoners and nobles was shattered on the eve of the Revolution by the "arrogance" and "racism" of many of the aristocrats whom he had once considered his "brothers." Initially skeptical of the Breton Club proposals, he rapidly gravitated toward the left in June 1789 and by the end of the year was a strong supporter of the Jacobins. (Bibliothèque nationale)

9. (*Right*) François-Joseph Bouchette. A rich landowner and lawyer from Bergues in Flanders. Though Flemish was his native tongue, he prided himself in his French culture and had acquired an impressive library of Enlightened French writings. But aside from an inveterate anticlericalism, there was little evidence of Enlightenment thought in his long correspondence with his closest friend. He was passionately involved in municipal politics and had struggled for years with the noble subdelegate. His conversion to the left in June 1789 seemed closely linked to his hometown feuds with the privileged hierarchy and his abiding hatred of nobles. (Bibliothèque nationale)

rather on those developments of particular importance in the changing revolutionary—or counterrevolutionary—psychology, and which most stood out in the minds of the deputies as indicated by their testimonies.

The single most decisive debate during December turned once again on the question of church land. At the root of the problem was the continuing

---

XVIIIe siècle (Paris, 1989); Ted Margadant, *Urban Rivalries in the French Revolution* (Princeton, 1992).

THE JACOBINS

10. (*Left*) Théodore Vernier. He had briefly attended a Catholic seminary before joining the army and then returning home to Lons-le-Saunier, to become a respected and prosperous lawyer. Fifty-eight years old in 1789, cautious by nature, and a fervent monarchist, he seemed a very unlikely radical. But his antinoble sentiments were inflamed by an unusually bitter fight in Franche-Comté between nobles and Third Estate, and his entire Comtois delegation early linked itself to the Breton Club and later to the Jacobins. Still, by his own account, it was only after the Revolution had begun that he came to realize the extent of inefficiency in the regime and the need for a total transformation of institutions. Later he would be one of the rare Girondin leaders to survive the Terror, returning from exile to serve several subsequent regimes. (Bibliothèque nationale)

11. (*Right*) François-René-Pierre Ménard de La Groye. Born to a wealthy family of judges and barristers, who had "lived nobly" in Le Mans for generations, he had been frustrated in his courtship of a young noble woman because of his caste status. He became deeply involved in Pre-Revolutionary politics and was exiled by *lettre de cachet* in 1788 for opposing the May Edicts. In Versailles and Paris he moved slowly but steadily to the left, influenced first by the intransigence of the privileged orders and then by the "school" of Revolutionary debate. By late 1789 he had fully adopted the new Jacobin rhetoric, imbued with Enlightenment phrases and generally glorifying the common people, and he had cut all ties with the aristocrats he once seemed to admire. He served as Jacobin mayor of Le Mans during the Terror. (Bibliothèque nationale)

state financial crisis which cast its shadow over the entire first year of the Assembly. "The need for money," observed the marquis de Ferrières, "has halted our progress. We are like the man whose brilliant plans for the day are disrupted in the morning by the inopportune appearance of his creditors."[66] In truth, many of the deputies had great difficulty understanding the arcane and extraordinarily complex subject of Old Regime finance. "Four-fifths of the members understand nothing at all," wrote Doctor Campmas, who felt reduced to the level of "counting on his fingers like a fishwife."[67] Yet they soon understood only too well the fundamental conclusion that the fiscal and financial crisis which had brought down the Old Regime could now undermine the Revolutionary regime itself.[68] This general anxiety had been a key factor in the vote of November 2 placing church land "at the disposal of the nation." The November decree, however, had left considerable ambiguity as to the Assembly's true intentions and had done little to resolve the crisis.

Only two weeks later Necker shocked the deputies with the announcement that the wolf was at the door and that the Assembly had no choice but to come up with 170 million *livres* by January 1 in order to meet its obligations to the state's creditors.[69] After long and complex discussions on the various options available, the patriots turned once again to the sale of land, and above all to the property of the church. The debates on these proposals between December 18 and 21 were exceptionally heated and rancorous and drew an attendance estimated at 1,100 representatives, virtually the whole body of deputies present in Paris at the time. "Never," Visme felt, "has the Assembly been so well attended."[70] The push for the complete seizure of church property was spearheaded once again by a "phalanx" of radicals, mobilized by the nascent Jacobin group. For a Jacobin like Boullé, the issue represented not only a financial imperative but also the opportunity to recoup the left's perceived defeat on the previous decree: "[the opposition] continues to take advantage of the wording of the November 2 decree, limiting the nation's rights over ecclesiastical property to a simple right of inspection."[71] Opposing such a law was the alignment of the "Augustinians," led in the debates by the indomitable abbé Maury who, according to Merle, "threw himself into a kind of convulsion," and threatened to have

[66] Ferrières, *Correspondance*, 195 (letter of ca. late Apr. 1790).

[67] Campmas, letters of Aug. 29 and Sept. 12, 1790. Also, e.g., Dominique-Joseph Garat, *Journal de Paris*, 1545 (Nov. 27, 1789); and Vernier, letter of Apr. 6, 1790.

[68] On the general question, see Marcel Marion, *Histoire financière de la France depuis 1715. Vol. II. 1789–1792* (Paris, 1919), esp. 7–38; John Bosher, *French Finances, 1770–1795: From Business to Bureaucracy* (Cambridge, 1970), 219; and Florin Aftalion, *The French Revolution, an Economic Interpretation* (Cambridge, 1990), 56.

[69] *AP*, 10:56–65 (Nov. 14).

[70] Visme, entry of Dec. 19.

[71] Boullé, A.D. Morbihan, letter of Dec. 22.

"his party" boycott the Assembly altogether if the measure passed.[72] In the end however, under the imperious pressures of financial necessity, the majority of the Assembly was convinced to put aside its earlier religious scruples and authorize the sale of 400 million *livres* of both church and royal land and the printing of promissory certificates to pay off the creditors—the first *assignats*. The law, which passed by a substantial majority, represented a major defeat for the right.[73]

The rapid evolution of deputy opinion was further illustrated by the vote a few days later in favor of political rights for non-Catholics. Only four months earlier, in the debates on the Rights of Man and the Citizen, the patriots had found it impossible to achieve such a measure. During the intervening months, however, both the patriots and their clerical opponents sensed a rapid shift in the views of the delegates, a shift attributed by Rabaut to the presence of the small but visible contingent of Protestant deputies who were demonstrating to all present their sense of civic responsibility and devotion to the nation.[74] It was once again the Jacobins who took the lead in pushing through a new edict of toleration. In their night meeting of December 22 they elaborated a motion that would grant religious and political freedom to both Protestants and Jews. Ultimately, after the vigorous opposition of the right and especially the clergy, the left was forced to "postpone" the decision on the Jews, but the Christmas Eve vote in favor of the Protestants was apparently massive.[75] The joy among the patriots was unbounded: "Today," wrote Boullé, "the nation itself recalls to its bosom those unfortunate children cast aside by fanaticism and intolerance. . . . God alone has the right to judge men's conscience, and a simple error cannot be the basis for excluding someone from the constitution."[76]

These two key votes in the second half of December were substantial indications of the movement of the moderate deputies in the direction of the left. At almost the same moment, the patriot coalition contrived a dramatic turnabout in the composition of the Committee on Research, replacing the conservatives with a majority of known liberals, at least eight of whom were Jacobins.[77] By early January, numerous deputy witnesses were commenting in their letters on the evident erosion of the right within the Assembly. Guillaume-Benoît Couderc, the Protestant banker from Lyon, was convinced that "aristocratic influence is declining perceptibly from day to day." Curé Lindet concurred: "The party of the opposition is decreasing in numbers. . . . Though it wins small victories, it is losing the decisive is-

[72] Merle, undated letter of ca. Dec. 19.

[73] Visme, entry of Dec. 19; Garat, 1668 (issue of Dec. 19).

[74] Jean-Paul Rabaut Saint-Etienne, "Rabaut Saint-Etienne, sa correspondance pendant la Révolution (1789–93)," ed. Armand Lods, *RF* 35 (1898), 162 (letter of Nov. 4, 1789).

[75] Boullé, A.D. Morbihan, letter of Dec. 25; Garat, 1691 (issue of Dec. 26); Dinochau, issues of Dec. 21–24. The Jews were not fully emancipated until Sept. 1991.

[76] Boullé, A.D. Morbihan, letter of Dec. 25.

[77] *AP*, 11:2. Of the new twelve-man committee, eleven were clearly on the left.

sues." The Breton merchant Delaville Le Roulx, so pessimistic the previous autumn, now suggested, for the first time, that the members of his "party" had gained "the upper hand."[78]

Much of the credit for the creation of a patriot majority belonged no doubt to the newly created Jacobins and their leadership in organizing the left coalition and successfully courting the moderates. But the obstructionist tactics pursued by the "Augustinians" and several particularly outrageous tirades by abbé Maury—for one of which he was formally censored by the Assembly—also contributed to the flight from the right: "One is embarrassed to sit near a bishop of Perpignan or a vicomte de Mirabeau or an Eprémesnil, men whose principles are so much opposed to both public welfare and common sense."[79] Such developments were compounded, moreover, by the geography of the deputies' new hall—divided starkly in half by the president's table and the speaker's platform. Each deputy was forced to make a daily symbolic affirmation as to which side he was on. "Those who know anything of the Assembly," commented Duquesnoy, "cannot help but notice the curious and progressive desertion and depopulation of that part of the hall where abbé Maury sits; and that there is no longer a sufficient number of seats on the other side of the hall." By mid-January, the Assembly staff had to install more benches on the left to accommodate all the new arrivals.[80] The new trend culminated in the middle of January with the election to the presidency of the celebrated Parisian lawyer Target, one of the founding members of the Jacobin Club, and the first radical patriot so elected since the beginning of August.[81]

THE RELIGIOUS QUESTION AND THE
ABORTIVE RESURGENCE OF THE RIGHT

By the early weeks of 1790, the coalition of the Augustinians and the Impartials had clearly become a minority faction within the Assembly. It persisted nevertheless as a powerful and relatively cohesive bloc of deputies capable of attracting enough uncommitted votes to defeat the left on certain issues. Thus, the debate on February 20–22 over peasant uprisings in southwestern France led to a decree considerably tougher and more supportive of "law and order" than the conciliatory position urged by the Jacobins—to the extent that the "aristocrat" baron de Gauville claimed a victory

[78] Couderc, 420 (letter of Dec. 28); Lindet, 38 (letter of Jan. 5); Joseph Delaville Le Roulx to the municipality of Lorient: A.C. Lorient, BB 13, letter of Jan. 18. See also Ménard, 166 (letter of Jan. 1); and Jean-François-Marie Goupilleau to his cousin, sénéchal in Rochefervière: B.M. Nantes, Collection Dugast-Matifeux, no. 98, letter of Jan. 11.

[79] Duquesnoy, 2:269 (entry of Jan. 9). See also Boullé, A.D. Morbihan, letters of Jan. 6, 24, and 30, 1790; and Garat, 86–87 (Jan. 22).

[80] Duquesnoy, 2:196–97, 269 (entries of Dec. 21, 1789 and Jan. 11, 1790); Thibaudeau in Faulcon, 141 (letter of Jan. 31).

[81] Target was elected on Jan. 18. See also Young, 234 (entry of Jan. 18).

for his side.[82] Between February and April, the alliance on the right remained sufficiently strong and well organized to elect the president of the National Assembly on three separate occasions: the abbé de Montesquiou on February 28, the marquis de Bonnay on April 12, and the comte de Virieu on April 27. For a few months, at least, the alternation of the presidency between candidates on the left and on the right gave political activities in the Assembly almost the character of a two-party system.

Without a doubt, it was the issue of religion which gave the conservatives the best prospects for reviving their position within the Assembly. We have already noted the importance of religious and ecclesiastical questions—at the end of August, in early November, and in the middle of December—in bringing together a coalition on the right and forging some sense of common purpose among elements as diverse as great nobles, humble clergymen, and a scattering of commoners.[83] To be sure, some of the nobles in question undoubtedly viewed religion with a cynical eye, hoping to use it as a convenient lever for reversing their Revolutionary losses. Others supported the orthodox faith primarily as a buttress to traditional monarchy and the general principle of hierarchical authority. But there were also perceptible differences in religious sensibilities among the deputies, differences which paralleled in some instances the divisions between orders.[84] Many individuals—clergy, nobles, or commoners—who supported the right in the winter and spring of 1790, were mobilized by their religious convictions and their belief that deist or atheist patriots were plotting an attack on the Catholic faith. While few of the patriots actually envisioned such an attack, a significant segment of the left was motivated by a veritable ideology of anticlericalism, a deep revulsion for what they conceived as a superstitious reverence for clerically dominated religion. Though the left had succeeded for a time in muting these convictions, their successes in December on the issues of church land and Protestant toleration had given them a new sense of confidence. The intensification of anticlerical rhetoric would substantially inflame the partisan passions between left and right.

A major skirmish occurred in the middle of February over the disposition of the regular clergy. The admission of new recruits into religious houses had been suspended the previous November, but now a proposal for the complete suppression of all religious orders was introduced by the Ecclesiastical Committee and strongly supported by the Jacobins.[85] The monks and nuns found support not only from the upper clergy, but also from a substantial number of nobles and from a scattering of commoners.[86] The

---

[82] Gauville, 45 (entry for Feb. 22). Cf. Maupetit, 20 (1904), 201 (letter of Feb. 24); and Vernier, letter of Feb. 23.

[83] See above, chap. 6.

[84] See above, chap. 2.

[85] *AP*, 11:543–46, 574–92 (debates of Feb. 11 to 13).

[86] Duquesnoy, 2:384 (entry of Feb. 13); Guillaume Gontier de Biran to the municipality of Bergerac: A.C. Bergerac, Fonds Faugère, carton 1, letter of Mar. 13; Bouchette, 344–45 (letter of Feb. 14).

debates grew particularly impassioned as the clergy accused one patriot orator of blasphemy and then demanded that the Assembly remove all doubt by declaring Catholicism to be the official state religion.[87] But the regulars had long been the least popular element within the clergy, and the radicals succeeded in winning over a sufficient number of the uncommitted to pass the decree on February 13. Laurent Visme was amazed, nevertheless, by the transformation of deputy attitudes: "The evolution of opinion is remarkable to watch. The suppression of the regulars, once perceived as a major problem, has now come to be seen, even by the most moderate deputies, as a just and natural procedure."[88]

Far more tempestuous was the complex battle joined in early April over a range of measures affecting the church and the clergy. Once again, the central bone of contention was the question of ecclesiastical property. Like the decree of November 2, the laws passed in mid-December had remained vague on the amount of church land to be sold—indicating only an unspecified combination of church and royal property worth 400 million *livres*—and had failed to include instructions for implementing the decree. Well into 1790, many deputies—encouraged by reports from the ecclesiastical committee—assumed that only a portion of church lands would actually be sold and that the sale would be largely confined to monastic property. Indeed, this was one of the considerations which had swayed opinion toward the suppression of the regulars.[89] Yet deputy anxiety over the financial stability of the Revolutionary state continued to grow, incited by another pessimistic report from Necker on March 6.[90] In their letters and speeches not only the Jacobins, but many of the more moderate representatives as well seemed obsessed by the threat of bankruptcy. With only the most tenuous grasp of the complex forces influencing state finances, many came to associate the crisis with a general counterrevolutionary plot. They were convinced that insidious forces were creating anarchy in the countryside to undermine taxpaying, "telling the people," as Fricaud described it, "that they would do best to hold on to their money, and that their contributions would be useless, since everything would soon fall apart and bankruptcy was inevitable." "The rumor of a bankruptcy is steadily gaining ground," noted Riffard de Saint-Martin, and if such an event did transpire, "the anti-revolutionaries will have achieved one of their most fervent hopes."[91] Fears such as these measurably affected the views of deputies who might otherwise have objected to the massive sale of ecclesiastical lands.

[87] *AP*, 11:589–90.

[88] Visme, entry of Feb. 13. Also Ménard, 191 (letter of Feb. 12).

[89] Dusers, letter of Jan. 26, 1790; Duquesnoy, 2:352–53 (entry of Feb. 5, 1790); *AP*, 11:438 (Treilhard report).

[90] *AP*, 12:46–57.

[91] Fricaud, letter of Mar. 31; François-Jérôme Riffard de Saint-Martin, "La Révolution vue de Paris et d'Annonay," *La revue universelle* 142 (1988), 57 (letter of Feb. 16). See Vernier, letters of Jan. 3, Feb. 27, and Mar. 7; Merle, letter of Mar. 14; Campmas, letter of Mar. 8; Gantheret, letters of Mar. 12 and 29; and Faydel, B.M. Cahors, letters of Feb. 20 and Mar. 6.

The critical debate on the question—and one of the key debates in the entire first half of 1790—began on April 9. Two successive committee reports—one from the Finance Committee, one from the Tithe Committee—brought together an array of measures concerning the clergy and national finance.[92] It was no longer a question of placing ecclesiastical holdings "at the disposal of the nation" or of targeting a few selected parcels for sale, but of the state's taking control of all such land. At the same time, the previously created *assignats*, backed by the future sale of church property, would be converted into legal tender for general circulation throughout the land. In presenting the proposed decree, the Jacobin Charles-Antoine Chasset, spokesman for the Tithe Committee, made no effort to appease clerical sensibilities. Beyond the problem of the financial crisis, he emphasized the need to strip the church of its land once and for all, both to end its status as a separate order and to halt the ambitions of the enemies of the Revolution who were looking to a landholding clergy as "a fulcrum of support." Then, in order to estimate the cost of state support necessary for the disenfranchised clergy, he took the highly unusual step of announcing a proposed massive reduction of the clerical corps still only in the planning stage in the Ecclesiastical Committee. Thus, the Assembly also found itself in a preliminary confrontation over the impending Civil Constitution of the Clergy.[93] "We are approaching the critical moment," wrote Campmas to his brother, "and if we come out on top, the Revolution will be won."[94]

In their speeches and in their letters and diaries, the deputies bore witness to the range of institutional and ideological issues at stake. Roederer developed a full spectrum of anticlerical arguments, striking out at the "hypocrisy" of the upper clergy who were living off the sweat of the poor.[95] Others attempted to emphasize the positive purification of religion that could transpire if the church were freed from its concerns for material wealth—thus anticipating one of the most common defenses of the Civil Constitution.[96] Still others preferred to restrict themselves to the basic economic arguments, to the necessity of rapidly mobilizing revenues to guarantee the confidence of state creditors. The Arles deputy Bonnemant suggested in his letters what many others were perhaps thinking, that the sale of church land would create a whole class of citizens bound by vested interests to the survival of the Revolution.[97]

The opponents of the decrees also argued from a number of positions.

[92] *AP*, 12:679 and 693 (debates of Apr. 12).

[93] *AP*, 12:611–19.

[94] Campmas, letter of Apr. 10, 1790.

[95] *AP*, 12:685 (speech of Apr. 12). Cf. Dinochau, issue of Apr. 12; and Edme-Louis-Alexis Dubois-Crancé, *Lettre de M. Dubois de Crancé . . . à ses commettants* (Paris, Aug. 1790), 14–16.

[96] *AP*, 12:675–78 (speech of Treilhard, Apr. 11, 1790); Maupetit, 20 (1904), 372–73 (letter of Apr. 12, 1790).

[97] Jean-Joseph Lucas de Bourgerel to municipal officials in Vannes: A.D Morbihan, 262 E(s), letter of May 22, 1790; Guillaume Bonnemant to the municipality of Arles: A.C. Arles, AA 23, letter of Apr. 16.

The conservative noble Irland de Bazôges construed the proposal as an outrage to the sacred rights of property; Faydel maintained that it would not fail to raise taxes; and the marquis de Bouthillier contended that it would have an adverse effect on clerical recruitment and thus, indirectly, on religion itself.[98] But the most vigorous opposition came from the clerical deputies, who divulged in their speeches the extraordinary bitterness and sense of betrayal felt by the majority of their order. The compromise which they had long hoped for and had even come to assume, entailing the partial sale of selected properties, now seemed brutally torn asunder. Boisgelin, "with vigor and energy of expression," entered into a long litany of the Assembly's "broken promises" to the clergy—beginning with the Third Estate's early declaration that it would never touch church property, and continuing with the November 2 decree which, in his view, had been entirely travestied. In the end, "one might ask which of your decrees will actually be regarded as laws?"[99] The bishop of Nancy also argued that the Assembly had reneged on its promises. The seizure of church property to appease a few "capitalists" was "revolting"; and he accused the deputies of utterly ignoring the church's commitment to social and humanitarian services. He also announced that the minority could never accept such a decree, essentially repudiating the idea of majority rule on an issue involving religion.[100]

It was in the midst of a bitter exchange between bishop La Fare and the Jacobin Voidel that an altogether unexpected event occurred, greatly transforming the character of the debate. Long pained by insinuations that the seizure of church property was a veiled attack on religion, the pious Carthusian monk and Jacobin, dom Christophe-Antoine Gerle, abruptly moved that Catholicism be declared the state religion. The motion was intended to disarm the right, and calm the doubts of moderate Catholics, and initially, according to Poncet-Delpech, the majority had been strongly supportive: "As proof that this truth was engraved in every heart, most of the Assembly instinctively stood up ready to profess it."[101] But the left leadership, sensing that it was losing control of the situation, had quickly regrouped and counterattacked, and passions exploded at both ends of the hall, an explosion that Ménard compared to the eruption of Mount Vesuvius.[102] On the left, it was the occasion for an outpouring of fury against a clerical minority perceived to be doing all in its power to frustrate the development of a new constitution. In their letters and diaries, the radical deputies pictured the conservative ecclesiastics and their aristocratic allies as perfect hypocrites, interested solely in preserving their wealth and privileges. Lucas described

[98] Irland, letter of Apr. 10; Faydel, B.M. Cahors, letter of Apr. 17; *AP*, 12:686–89 (speech of Apr. 12).

[99] *AP*, 691–98 (Apr. 12); Faulcon, 2:177 (letter to Barbier, April 13).

[100] *AP*, 12:678–83 (Apr. 11).

[101] Jean-Baptiste Poncet-Delpech, *La première année de la Révolution vue par un témoin*, ed. Daniel Ligou (Paris, 1961), 275 (letter of Apr. 12).

[102] Ménard, 201 (letter of Apr. 16).

them all unequivocally as "the enemies of the Revolution." Lindet spoke sarcastically of "the litany of our 304 saints"—the number supposedly embracing the dom Gerle motion—"ready to die for executive authority and live for their clerical lands and their pensions from the royal treasury." The right had no other end in mind than to "light the torches of fanaticism" (Boullé), and "incite a civil war" (Merle).[103]

The deputies on the right, by contrast, stressed their religious motives for supporting dom Gerle. Many seemed genuinely convinced that the patriots were hostile to Catholicism, and were favoring the Protestants, if not the atheists. They pointed to the recent Jacobin selection of the Protestant pastor, Rabaut Saint-Etienne, as president of the National Assembly. Irland de Bâzoges felt that the financial needs of the state were a pretense "enabling them to destroy first the clergy and then religion." The conservative lawyer from Burgundy, Antoine-Marie Paccard, recalled the first article of his cahier which specified that "the Catholic, apostolic, and Roman religion be the sole dominant religion in the kingdom." Gontier de Biran supported dom Gerle because "I owe this expression of faith to my religion"—though he also took care to link that religion to "the legitimate authority of the king": "I pride myself in my inviolable attachment to religion, the fatherland, and the king."[104]

After an uproarious session, as tumultuous as any to date, the left finally engineered an adjournment until the next day. A lengthy discussion ensued that night in the Jacobin Club, and the entire membership, including dom Gerle, agreed on the motion's potential for engendering Protestant-Catholic hostilities. The next day, April 13, both factions arrived in force at 9 A.M., with the "blacks" bedecked in their finest ceremonial dress and cassocks, many, as Dinochau thought, "with a warlike bearing, seeming to call their champions to combat."[105] Eventually, the motion by the Jacobin baron de Menou—with important amendments from the duc de La Rochefoucauld—carried the day. The motion asserted that so majestic a matter as religious belief could never be the subject of legislation and issued a declaration recalling that the Catholic religion alone had been promised financial support by the National Assembly—implicitly granting it a favored status.[106] While no vote count was ever recorded, the victory of the left seems to have been relatively slim. Shortly before the final decision was taken, a motion by the right to reopen debate was defeated by the margin of 495 to 400. When the conservatives ultimately lost their case, they rose with their hands to-

[103] Lucas, letter of Apr. 16; Lindet, 145–46 (letter of May 4); Boullé, A.D. Morbihan, letter of May 5; Merle, letter of Apr. 14.

[104] Irland, letter of Apr. 16; Paul Montarlot, *Les députés de Sâone-et-Loire aux assemblées de la Révolution, 1789–99* (Autun, 1905), 180–81; Gontier, letter of May 22, 1790. Also Claude-Benjamin Vallet, "Souvenirs de l'abbé Vallet, député de Gien à l'Assemblée constituante," *Nouvelle revue rétrospective* 16 (1902), 385–86.

[105] *Courier de Madon*, issue of Apr. 13.

[106] *AP*, 12:716 (Apr. 13); also Delaville, letter of Apr. 14; Lameth, 2:91–93.

ward heaven and began an oath: "We swear, in the name of God and of religion, that we profess . . ."—but the end was drowned out by the shouts of the spectators.[107] It was a dramatic gesture, conceived no doubt in part for effect. Yet it also conveyed the deep sense of anger and indignation experienced by a significant number of the deputies.

Encouraged no doubt by the closeness of the vote, and still hopeful of overturning it, the opposition leadership set about organizing a protest. On April 14 the bishop of Clermont announced he would boycott all future discussions of clerical property and "a large number of clerics and some members of the nobility rose and adhered to this declaration."[108] The same day six conservative members of the Ecclesiastical Committee resigned in protest.[109] During the following evenings, the conservatives and many of their sympathizers met in the chapel of the Capuchins, adjoining the hall of the National Assembly. On April 19 they drew up a formal protest against the declaration of the Assembly majority, soliciting signatures of adhesion from as many deputies as possible, and making arrangements to have the document published and distributed throughout the country.[110]

Of approximately 400 deputies who had supported dom Gerle's motion on April 13, only 292 actually signed the protest. In all likelihood, the great majority of these individuals had previously adhered to the "Augustinians." Indeed, curé Colson, who was present, saw a direct continuity between the earlier alignment and the "Capuchin Club," as the group rapidly came to be called. But the Capuchins also included a substantial number—probably well over half—of the Impartials, a faction which badly split over the issue.[111] As a group, the adherents were overwhelmingly dominated by the former privileged orders and were strongly aristocratic in character. Nine out of ten were representatives of either the clergy or the nobility. Indeed, among the handful of twenty-three commoners adhering, a third were actually nobles or clergymen who had been elected by the Third Estate.[112] The single largest contingent (56 percent) consisted of ecclesiastics, including almost all of the bishops and about half of the curés.[113] Yet if we consider the social origins of the Capuchins rather than the estate they represented, nearly three-fifths are found to belong to the nobility, and of these, two-thirds were true

---

[107] *AP*, 12:716, 719. According to Bouchette, the vote to reopen debate was supported by the "parti noir": 384 (letter of Apr. 14).

[108] Lindet, 133 (letter of Apr. 14); Faydel, B.M. Cahors, letter of Apr. 17.

[109] A.N., C 40, dos. 355, fol. 4.

[110] *Déclaration d'une partie de l'Assemblée nationale sur le décret rendu le 13 avril 1790 concernant la religion* (Paris, April 19, 1790). Also, e.g., Lucas, letter of May 4; Lindet, 136–39, 162 (letters of Apr. 14 and 18, and May 16); Lameth, 2:148–49.

[111] Colson, 145. Eleven of the 20 Impartials listed above in note 29 adhered to the Capuchin protest.

[112] Eight nobles and one canon.

[113] Of the 292, 164 were clergy, including 101 curés, 50 bishops and other upper clergy, and 13 in a variety of other categories. In all, 49.5% of the total 204 curés sitting in the Assembly at the time were Capuchins.

"aristocrats" who could trace back their lineage to the sixteenth century or earlier.[114] The aristocrats also dominated among the Capuchin leadership. Over three-fourths of the speeches delivered by Capuchins were made by members of the nobility and two-thirds of these were by individuals with lineages dating to the pre-1600 period.[115] It is also noteworthy that a substantial proportion came from the south of the kingdom, and particularly from the Massif Central and the interior Midi—regions that were among the most isolated and economically backward in the kingdom.[116]

Of those deputies who voted for dom Gerle's motion but refused to adhere to the Capuchin protest, many were moderate patriots who felt deeply torn between their Catholic persuasion and their loyalty to the Revolution. In a long letter to his friend the marquis de La Celle, Grellet de Beauregard explained why he had ultimately refused to sign the petition. Though he firmly believed that Catholicism should be the state religion, he also felt strongly committed to the idea of majority rule, and he feared that the National Assembly could not survive if individuals refused to abide by that rule. In addition, he was only too aware of the political ramifications to any such protest. He knew that those leading the Capuchin group were identified with many other positions which he could not accept, and that signing such a protest might make him politically suspect to his colleagues and thus less able to serve the interests of his constituency.[117] Maupetit wrote much the same analysis to his colleague in Mayenne: "As an individual, I could easily sign the same declaration. It would be a personal testimony that I profess the Catholic religion." But in his role as a deputy he would never participate, since it was essential to take into account the motives of "the opposition party" who had actually drafted the April 19 protest.[118] Other wavering deputies—like Charles-Guillaume Dusers—were reassured by the Assembly's April 13 declaration implying that "only the Catholic, apostolic, and Roman religion would have its expenses assumed by the nation: which is tantamount to recognizing the faith of our fathers as the national religion."[119]

With much of the opposition now boycotting the debates, all of the decrees on church lands and the *assignats* easily passed between April 14 and

[114] Of the 292 "Capuchins," 166 (57%) were nobles; 111 of these 166 (67%) were from families ennobled before the seventeenth century.

[115] Of the 890 speeches made by Capuchins—or future Capuchins—during the first year of the Revolution, 693 (78%) were by nobles of any estate; 457 (66%) of the 693 speeches were by nobles of ancient lineage.

[116] One hundred fifty-eight (54%) came from south of the line La Rochelle-Geneva. Cf. the 30% of all deputies who represented southern France: Edna Lemay, "La composition de l'Assemblée constituante: les hommes de la continuité?" *RHMC* 24 (1977), 349.

[117] Jean-Bernard Grellet de Beauregard, "Lettres de M. Grellet de Beauregard," ed. Abbé Dardy, *Mémoires de la Société des sciences naturelles et archéologiques de la Creuse*, 2e sér., 7 (1899), 80–83 (letter of May 29, 1790).

[118] Maupetit, 20 (1904), 454–55 (letter of May 5).

[119] Dusers, letter of Apr. 20. Cf. Campmas, letter of Apr. 16.

20.[120] In the meantime, the Parisian crowds, tipped off by men working next door in the Assembly's print shop, had invaded the Capuchin chapel and forced the group to abandon their meetings there. Compelled to leave their original hall, the Capuchins continued to meet regularly, first on the neighboring rue Royale or in the Sorbonne, and eventually in deputy homes.[121] The group's continuing strength was revealed by the April 27 victory of their presidential candidate, the comte de Virieu, in an extremely tight race with the Jacobin nominee, the duc d'Aiguillon.[122] By early May, the Capuchin coalition had arranged the publication of some forty thousand copies of their April 19 declaration and had begun circulating the document throughout the kingdom—a document conceived as an appeal to the people, sent over the heads of the Assembly majority.[123] Shaken in their confidence, several of the patriot deputies shared their anxiety with their provincial correspondents, preparing their constituents for a possible popular reaction against the Assembly. "Everywhere there are attempts to seduce the people," wrote Vernier, "novena prayers, sermons, false insinuations. The cause of religion is equated to the existence of clerical lands." Thibaudeau likewise complained of the numerous copies of the minority declaration distributed in his province of Poitou. Campmas feared an impending "religious war" in Languedoc and "an increase in the sparks of fanaticism." The whole affair was particularly disquieting in that it occurred on the eve of the departmental elections, and there were rumors of conservative plots to influence the outcome.[124]

In retrospect, we know that the minority protest did play a significant role in creating popular dissatisfaction with the Assembly, and that in certain rural sectors of the kingdom it served as a dress rehearsal for the later crisis of the clerical oath to the Civil Constitution of the Clergy in the winter and spring of 1791.[125] But the countrypeople did not frequently divulge their views directly to the Assembly and the deputies had very little knowledge of rural opinion. By contrast, a great outpouring of letters soon began arriving from the towns and cities of the nation. And much to the

[120] Marion, 114, 117–18, 120.

[121] Dinochau, issue of May 13; Lucas, letter of May 4; Lameth, 2:148; Challamel, 134–36; Gottschalk and Maddox, 345–46.

[122] Virieu won only on the third round of balloting, by a vote of 393 to 371: *AP*, 15:296. Virieu resigned two days later and was replaced by the nonaligned patriot abbé Goutte.

[123] Boullé, A.D. Morbihan, letter of May 5; Maupetit, 20 (1904), 454 (letter of May 5); Lindet, 139 (letter of Apr. 18).

[124] Vernier, letters of May 4 and June 15; Antoine-René-Hyacinthe Thibaudeau, *Correspondance inédite*, ed. H. Carré and Pierre Boissonnade (Paris, 1898), 82 (letter of May 10); Campmas, letter of May 16. Also Joseph-Bernard de Lélia de Crose to the municipality of Nantua: B.M. Lyon, ms. 2191, letter of Apr. 17; Maupetit, 447, 450 (letters of Apr. 24 and 25); Lindet, 146–47 (letter of May 5); Faulcon, 2:172, 178, 206–7 (letters of Apr. 11 and 13, and May 5); and Dinochau, issue of Apr. 22.

[125] Timothy Tackett, *Religion, Revolution, and Regional Culture in Eighteenth-Century France: The Ecclesiastical Oath of 1791* (Princeton, 1986), 19–20, 210–18.

delight—and perhaps amazement—of the patriots, the response seemed overwhelmingly in favor of the majority and opposed to the Capuchins. Within a few weeks at least ninety collective statements had been received in Paris, adhering to the decree of April 13 and/or castigating the protest declaration of the right—compared to a tiny handful supporting the Capuchins.[126]

To what extent this enthusiastic endorsement had been orchestrated by the deputies themselves is difficult to say. While the Jacobins did circulate a pamphlet on the question to their "formidable colonies," all evidence suggests strong grassroots support for the Assembly's position from the urban patriots.[127] But whatever the origins of the letters, this vigorous adherence had an enormous impact. The deputies on the right were sobered and disconcerted, as their pretensions of representing a silent majority seemed undermined. The conservative marquis de Ferrières was convinced that the Capuchin declaration had been a fiasco: "You have seen," he wrote to his friend de Chacé, "the obstinacy with which the whole of France rejected this declaration." The Impartial Gontier de Biran, admitted the barrage of angry letters arriving from all over his bailliage after he signed the protest.[128] Among the patriots, however, the response from the provincial towns brought a new sense of confidence. Whether from personal scruples or from a fear of constituency reactions, the deputies found the reform of the church among the most difficult of all Revolutionary transformations to accept. But as more adhesions to the majority were read daily in the Assembly—to the cheers of the deputies and the crowds in the galleries—the majority who had supported the decrees could only feel exhilarated. Maupetit and Lucas described their enormous relief and a new thrill of self-confidence as the results of this quasi-referendum became known. Campmas was ecstatic over the flood of positive letters, "conveying an expression of the general will and a complete adhesion to all the Assembly's decrees."[129] Thus, the dom Gerle affair and the great debates of April 1790 played a critical role in the evolving psychology of the Assembly and helped lay the groundwork for a sweeping reorganization of the French church that would have been quite inconceivable for the great majority of the deputies only a few months earlier.

[126] Timothy Tackett, *La religion, l'église, la France* (Paris, 1986), 235–39 (data updated and corrected from the English version).

[127] Michael L. Kennedy, *The Jacobin Clubs in the French Revolution. The First Years* (Princeton, 1982), 153.

[128] Ferrières, *Correspondance*, 208 (letter of June 20); Gontier, letter of May 22.

[129] Lucas, letters of May 28 and June 12; Maupetit, 20 (1904), 460–61 (letter of May 12); Campmas, letter of June 26.

To End a Revolution

As THE DEPUTIES passed the first anniversary of their convocation in Versailles, the political dynamic within the Assembly had perceptibly modified. The failure of the Capuchin coalition to arouse any evident national support had been a major setback for the representatives on the right. The patriot groups, by contrast, felt buoyed and reassured, not only by the apparent acceptance of their position in the dom Gerle affair, but by the generally favorable reception of the *assignats* and a widespread enthusiasm for the sale of church lands. As summer approached, they could also count on the establishment of the new departmental and district administrations. After long months with only improvised and tenuous links between the Revolutionary legislature and the French population, the deputies looked hopefully to the creation of permanent institutional structures binding Paris and the provinces. The optimistic mood was strengthened on May 29 by Jacques Necker's favorable report on the financial situation.[1] While new sources of disquiet continued to arise—like the Protestant-Catholic conflicts in Montauban and Nîmes and the brief threat of a war with England—the letters and diaries of the spring and early summer were no longer as obsessed with conspiracies and counterrevolution and many seemed distinctly more positive. Dinochau concurred with Lafayette's speech of May 12 that counterrevolution was now impossible in the kingdom. Even the inveterate pessimist Théodore Vernier appeared more sanguine. "Everything is going well," he wrote in early May. "The cries of rage from our ennemies are only the final convulsions of despair." Most members of the opposition now "affirm that they must follow the old adage and yield to necessity and to the exigencies of events."[2]

In the short term, however, the decline of the conservative bloc was less a victory for the Jacobin left than for a new coalition of the patriot center. The spring and summer of 1790 marked the rise to prominence of the Society of 1789, whose principal objective was to work with the monarchy and bring the Revolution to a close.

---

[1] François-René-Pierre Ménard de La Groye, *François Ménard de La Groye, député du Maine aux Etats généraux. Correspondance, 1789–1791*, Florence Mirouse, ed. (Le Mans, 1989), 222 (letter of June 1); and *AP*, 15:712–20.

[2] Jacques Dinochau, *Courier de Madon*, issue of May 13; Théodore Vernier to the municipality of Lons-le-Saunier: A.C. Bletterans (non-classé), "Lettres de Vernier," letters of May 4 and 18. Cf. Jean-François Campmas to his brother, vicaire in Carmaux: B.M. Albi, Ms. 177, letter of May 9.

THE KING'S NEW DIRECTION

The real attitudes of Louis XVI through the winter and spring may never be known for certain. The king's long periods of dogged, inarticulate silence were broken only occasionally by public statements that may have been written by others. In a letter of October 12 to his cousin the king of Spain, Louis conveyed bitterness over his forced residence in Paris and maintained that his acceptance of Assembly decrees had been coerced.[3] If we can believe his most conservative minister, Guignard de Saint-Priest, the king cooperated with the Revolutionaries only through a kind of *politique du pire*: "He had convinced himself that the Assembly would be discredited through its own errors. The king's weakness led him to take hold of this idea, thus relieving him of the need for a permanent opposition, too difficult for his character."[4] Yet throughout this period he continued to vacillate depending on events and on the latest advice from councilors or family, torn between his aspiration to serve the people and his desire to please his courtiers and maintain the authoritarian traditions of his royal predecessors.

However this may be, in the eyes of the patriot deputies, the position of the king was clearly evolving for the better. The more moderate ministers— Necker, the foreign affairs minister Montmorin, and the keeper of the seals Champion de Cicé—had taken the initiative in cooperating with the Assembly in the monarch's name.[5] A dramatic instance of this had come in early November after the king chastised the Parlement of Rouen for its failure to cooperate with the Constituent. After the Parlement backed down, the king asked the deputies to drop the whole matter, and "the overwhelming majority of the National Assembly rose to their feet in a transport of affection," ratifying the monarch's request.[6] It was in this spirit of cooperation that the Assembly had given the king a blank check in January 1790 to establish his household budget. Louis responded that he would not even consider such a question until the state's budget crisis was resolved, and the hall resounded with choruses of "long live the king!" The old enthusiasm and devotion for the monarch seemed to return in the descriptions of many deputies, both moderate and radical alike. "It is impossible to observe the goodness of this king, the father of his people, without a feeling of great emotion," wrote Vernier. "Heaven seems to have chosen him to be the leader of our restoration." Duquesnoy summed up what he thought were the views of many of

---

[3] John Hardman, *Louis XVI* (New Haven, Conn., 1993), 174.

[4] François-Emmanuel Guignard de Saint-Priest, *Mémoires, règnes de Louis XV et de Louis XVI*, 2 vols, ed. baron de Barante (Paris, 1929), 2:24–25.

[5] Jean-Pierre Boullé to the municipality of Pontivy: A.C. Pontivy, on microfilm in A.D. Morbihan, 1 Mi 140, letter of Nov. 10, 1789; Claude-Germain Rousselot to his nephew, Joseph Rousselot: Fonds Girardot, A.D. Haute-Saône, letter of Jan. 1, 1790.

[6] Dominique-Joseph Garat, *Journal de Paris* (Paris, 1789–91), 1472 (issue of Nov. 13, 1789); also Adrien Duquesnoy, *Journal d'Adrien Duquesnoy*, ed. R. de Crèvecoeur, 2 vols. (Paris, 1894), 2:29 (letter of Nov. 9, 1789).

his colleagues: "Though the king does not possess a broad intelligence nor a profound mind, though he has certain difficulties in expressing himself, he reveals nevertheless generally clear ideas, a spirit of justice, and above all, a heart that is good, sensible, infinitely honest, and filled with an ardent desire to do good."[7]

The rapprochement between the king and the deputies had attained an impressive climax at the beginning of February when the monarch appeared in person before the Assembly. For some weeks prior to that date both Lafayette and the liberal ministers had argued that the best means of preserving royal authority and stabilizing the government was to embrace the National Assembly and publicly repudiate all counterrevolutionary movements. Though Louis was probably not initially enthusiastic about the idea, he seems to have been persuaded by the influential courtier comte de Ségur and perhaps by the queen, who hoped that such a move might split the patriots.[8]

During the last weeks of January the deputies had heard frequent rumors of an impending royal visit, so that they were scarcely surprised on the morning of February 4 to find their hall rearranged and adorned with special decorations.[9] When the king actually appeared toward midday, the symbolism surrounding the visit was carefully conceived to please the deputies. Like the "citizen king" they so ardently hoped him to be, he wore simple dress and was accompanied only by his ministers—in stark contrast to the regal apparel of May 5 and June 23. He rejected the throne prepared for him, but remained standing while he addressed the deputies, side by side with the Assembly president Bureaux de Pusy, who also remained standing.[10] Most of the speech was probably written by Necker and was tailor-made to appeal to the moderates in the hall.[11] The ostensible purpose of the visit was a plea for unity in the face of a new wave of peasant uprisings sweeping across provinces of southwestern France. The king specifically affirmed the Assembly's new administrative divisions of the kingdom and the general proposition of positions open to talent. At the same time he encouraged the strengthening of "executive authority" and urged the protection of religion, property, and the titles of the "honored race" of the nobility. The most

[7] Vernier, letter of Jan. 5, 1790; Duquesnoy, 2:247, 254 (letters of Jan. 4 and 5). Also, Garat, 19 and 22 (entries of Jan. 4 and 5); Dinochau, issue of Jan. 5; and Alexandre de Lameth, *Histoire de l'Assemblée constituante*, 2 vols. (Paris, 1828–29), 2:350–51.

[8] Jean Egret, *Necker, ministre de Louis XVI* (Paris, 1975), 390–95; Louis Gottschalk and Margaret Maddox, *Lafayette in the French Revolution: From the October Days through the Federation* (Chicago, 1973), 114, 205–6; Lameth, 2:329; Saint-Priest, 2:26–27.

[9] Vernier, letters of Jan. 26 and 28; Michel-René Maupetit, "Lettres de Maupetit (1789–91)," ed. E. Quéruau-Lamérie, *Bulletin de la Commission historique et archéologique de la Mayenne*, 2e sér., 20 (1904), 188–89 (letter of Feb. 2).

[10] Antoine-René-Hyacinthe Thibaudeau, *Correspondance inédite*, ed. H. Carré and Pierre Boissonnade (Paris, 1898), 69 (letter of Feb. 5); Garat, 141–44 (issue of Feb. 4); Duquesnoy, 2:349 (entry of Feb. 4).

[11] Egret, *Necker*, 390; *AP*, 11:429–31.

dramatic moment in the speech came when he promised to educate the dauphin with full respect for the new constitutional principals. After the king retired from the hall, he was escorted by a delegation of deputies back to the Tuileries Palace. There the party was met by the queen who also affirmed that the young heir to the throne—who stood by her side—would be raised in a manner befitting the transformed status of the monarchy.[12]

Almost all of the deputy-witnesses reporting on the event were enormously moved and exhilarated. The Impartials, who were convinced that the monarch must have read their manifesto before writing his speech, were ecstatic. "We are amazed," wrote curé Verdet to a colleague in Lorraine, "that this speech so closely conforms to our 'Impartial' principles. It is tempting to think that this action ultimately originated with us."[13] The Jacobins, too, felt that their policies and leadership had been vindicated. Many hoped that royal support for the Revolution would remove the threat of plots and counterrevolution which had so long weighed upon them. "I wept several times," confided Vernier, "and I am not alone in having done so. Thus, the sovereign himself, at one with his people, has determined the outcome of the Revolution." Dusers also wept with joy over the words of "our citizen monarque": "What relief it brought to our hearts! How soothing it was, in the midst of the cruel anguish and troubles of every sort which have so long beset us!" Lepoutre described it as "one of the most wonderful moments of my life," and he instructed his wife to read the king's speech to the workers on their farm in northern France and to give them all an extra stein of beer to toast the king's health. Merle admitted he had long hoped to see the king "in our midst, taking part in our work, and with this sign of approval, lending it the force it so badly needed"; while Fricaud felt certain that this "moving speech" would mark "a total victory over the aristocracy."[14]

In fact, it was the "aristocrats" of the Assembly, the conservatives of the far right, who displayed the least enthusiasm for the king's visit. Maury, Eprémesnil, the vicomte de Mirabeau, the marquis de Laqueuille and a whole segment of deputies on their side of the hall had ostentatiously rejected the president's proposal for the ceremony to be used in welcoming the king: an action interpreted by those present as a condemnation of the whole event. "I admit," wrote the baron de Gauville, "that I was unable to take part in the applause and the cries of 'vive le Roi' which arose from the

---

[12] Jean-Joseph Lucas de Bourgerel to municipal officials in Vannes: A.D Morbihan, 262 E(s), letter of Feb. 5; Thibaudeau, 71 (letter of Feb. 5).

[13] Louis Verdet to Guilbert, curé of Saint-Sébastien of Nancy: Arch. Grand Séminaire Nancy, MB 17, folios 1–113, letter of Feb. 6.

[14] Vernier, letter of Feb. 4; Charles-Guillaume Dusers to the municipality of Vannes: A.D. Morbihan, 262 E(s), letter of Feb. 9; Pierre-François Lepoutre to his wife: family archives of Adolphe Lepoutre-Dubreuil, Montignac-sur-Vezère, letter of Feb. 5; André-Marie Merle to the municipality of Mâcon: A.C. Mâcon, D (2) 13, carton 21 bis, letter of Feb. 5; Claude Fricaud to Jean-Marie Gelin, avocat in Charolles: copies of the originals kindly provided by Doctor Robert Favre, letter of Feb. 4.

left side of the hall. I could only see the debasement of the majesty of the throne."[15]

It was partly in reaction to these recalcitrants, "more royalist than the king," and partly in response to Louis's appeal for unity, that the Constituents decided to swear a new oath of allegiance. The president read the oath formula: "I swear to be faithful to the nation, to the law, and to the king, and to maintain with all my strength the Constitution decreed by the National Assembly and accepted by the king," and the deputies came forward, one by one, to pronounce the phrase "I do so swear." In the end, even the extreme right "Augustinians" grudgingly took part. When the deputies had finished, the alternate deputies insisted that they too be allowed to take part, followed by the diverse lobbyists in residence, the Assembly police and secretarial staff, and all the spectators present in the galleries.[16] That evening more came forward—judges from the Châtelet, representatives from Parisian secondary schools, and many others. In the following days citizens throughout the city and the kingdom took similar oaths in their districts and parishes. A great series of celebrations ensued, culminating in a magnificent thanksgiving *Te deum* at the cathedral of Notre-Dame.[17]

In the short term, the "new direction" taken by Louis XVI—as Lameth called it—had far less effect on the Assembly than the royal ministers had hoped.[18] The period of concord and good feelings created by the king's speech and the oath lasted scarcely more than a few days.[19] The Impartials and the Augustinians, temporarily divided over the king's visit, were soon cooperating once again, the intense interfactional rivalries persisted almost unabated, and the various Constituent committees continued to chip away at executive prerogatives. Yet during the following weeks, the new mood of collaboration between king and Assembly undoubtedly helped reinforce a spirit of moderation among an important segment of the deputies. It also helped pry open a growing division among the representatives on the left.

DIVISION OF THE LEFT AND THE TRIUMPH OF '89

Even as the perceived threat of counterrevolution subsided, the original coalition of the Friends of the Constitution—held together, in part, by fear of

---

[15] Louis-Henri-Charles de Gauville, *Journal*, ed. Edouard de Barthélémy (Paris, 1864), 41 (entry for Feb. 4); Duquesnoy, 2:347–48 (entry of Feb. 4).

[16] *AP*, 11:432–35.

[17] Thibaudeau, 72–73 (letter of Feb. 5); Garat, 143–44 (issue of Feb. 4); Alexandre-Joseph de Lablache to the marquis de Viennois: Archives of the Château d'Avauges, reproduced in A.D. Isère, 1 Mi 461A, letter of Feb. 5; Dusers, letter of Feb. 9; Maupetit, 20 (1904), 198 (letter of Feb. 14).

[18] Lameth, 2:329.

[19] Thibaudeau, 68, 73 (letter of Feb. 5); Maupetit, 20 (1904), 192 (letter of Feb. 5); Lablache (letter of Feb. 5).

the common danger—seemed to lose much of its cohesion. "While dangers were imminent," wrote Alexandre de Lameth with a note of bitterness, "the Assembly remained together, and the contestants closed ranks beside one another, as on a field of battle. . . . Among those adhering to the same cause, there reigned a unity of will and action which gave them strength and assured their success. But once that success had been attained, an imprudent self-confidence took hold of many deputies . . . destroying the very unity to which they owed their triumph."[20] The precise nature of the fissures within the left coalition are often obscure. In part, it was a question of personal rivalries between several of the principal Jacobin leaders, particularly among the liberal nobles. By the spring the marquis de Lafayette became convinced that Charles de Lameth, his former comrade in arms, was threatening his control of the Paris national guard. A similar rivalry between Lafayette and Mirabeau had all the characteristics of an Old Regime court intrigue, especially after April when both began vying for influence with the king.[21] In part, it was a question of a growing impatience with the style and general atmosphere, the obstreperous and unruly democratic politics which reigned among the Jacobins—especially as more and more non-deputies began attending the club. Sieyès railed against this "band of rowdies," "malicious, always in turmoil, shouting, intriguing, acting unpredictably and without moderation." The marquis de Paroy was "exhausted with the boisterous character of their meetings, with the ravings of the speakers, with the necessity of winning the favor of the crowds." Other deputies complained that they were unable to speak or even find seats because of the press of "outsiders" in the meetings.[22]

But there were also divisions on the left over political philosophy. The first Jacobin association had always represented an uneasy alliance. Malouet had sensed the potential fissures scarcely a month after the club had formed, when he had nearly succeeded in luring away a contingent of the more moderate nobles. The moderates in question were especially nervous over the radicals' glorification of the common people and their push for greater political democracy. "Sometimes," wrote Schwendt, "our democratic orators altogether miss the mark. A democracy is inappropriate for us and would only bring anarchy."[23] The deputies were sensitized to the issue through the continuing popular actions in Paris. By spring, enormous crowds often gathered in and around the Assembly hall to manifest their support for specific issues—during the dom Gerle debate, for example, or

---

[20] Lameth, 2:5.

[21] Gottschalk and Maddox, 316–17, 343–44.

[22] Paul Bastid, *Sieyès et sa pensée* (Paris, 1939), 100; Guy Le Gentil de Paroy, *Mémoires. Souvenirs d'un défenseur de la famille royale pendant la Révolution (1789–1797)*, ed. J. de Paroy (Paris, 1895), 147.

[23] Etienne-François Schwendt, "L'Alsace pendant la Révolution française. Correspondance adressées à Frédéric de Dietrich," ed. Rodolphe Reuss, *Revue d'Alsace* 78 (1931), 106 (letter of May 24).

during the May debates over the king's powers in war and peace. Deputies were also angered and frightened by the continuing violence of the Parisians, such as the lynchings, in late May of four reputed thieves freed by the Châtelet court—an incident leading to the first full alert of the national guard in several months.[24] In their desire for the enforcement of law and order, many representatives were reevaluating the position of the monarchy and strongly encouraging a rapprochement with Louis XVI as a counterweight to popular unrest. It was in this context that Lafayette began pursuing secret negotiations with Louis, negotiations in which he specified the substantial powers which he hoped to see reserved for the king.[25]

Already in January a variety of subgroups of deputies associated with the Jacobins had begun meeting in parallel "committees," separate from the larger club. Such was the group congregating for dinner parties at the residence of the duc de Liancourt, a group whose participants would largely abandon the Jacobins only three months later.[26] Equally important was the loose affiliation of deputies and nondeputies first organized by the abbé Sieyès and the marquis de Condorcet in late 1789, and calling themselves the "Society of 1789." Conceived as an intellectual gathering with no specific political mission, the group included such notable figures as Bailly, Lafayette, and the lawyer-publisher Jacques Brissot.[27]

The first overt political split on the left occurred toward the middle of March, when the liberal comte de Crillon openly seceded from the Jacobins with a contingent of other deputies and began holding separate meetings in his Parisian *hôtel*. Crillon and his followers had apparently clashed with the Jacobin leadership over the permission given to nondeputies to vote in the club, and attempts to preserve the coalition had only superficial success. "The crack within the Jacobins," wrote Virieu on March 19, "remains visible, despite an effort at replastering. Its offshoot, the Crillon Club, continues to meet."[28] While the size and membership of the Crillon faction is not known, it apparently included the duc de La Rochefoucauld and the influential commoners Thouret, Démeunier, Lapoule, and Le Chapelier.

---

[24] François-Antoine Boissy d'Anglas, "Correspondance de Boissy d'Anglas avec le marquis de Satillieu au début de la Révolution," ed. H. Hillaire, *Revue du Vivarais* 48 (1942) and 49 (1943), letter of May 27; Félix Faulcon, *Correspondance. Tome 2: 1789–91*, ed. G. Debien (Poitiers, 1953), 2:233 (letter of May 24); Schwendt, *Revue d'Alsace*, 106 (letter of May 24); Gottschalk and Maddox, 384–85.

[25] Gottschalk and Maddox, 326–36.

[26] Arthur Young, *Travels in France during the years 1787, 1788 and 1789* (Gloucester, Mass., 1976), 220, 226, 234 (entries of Jan. 5, 12, and 18, 1790). See above, chap. 8.

[27] Mark Olsen, "A Failure of Enlightened Politics in the French Revolution: The Société de 1789," *French History* 6 (1992), 303–34; Keith Michael Baker, "Politics and Social Science in Eighteenth-Century France: the *Société de 1789*," in *French Government and Society, 1500–1850* (London, 1973), 208–50; Augustin Challamel, *Les clubs contre-révolutionnaires* (Paris, 1895), 425–28; and Claude Perroud, "Quelques notes sur le Club de 1789," *RF* 39 (1900), 253–62.

[28] François-Henri de Virieu to the marquis de Viennois: Archives du Château d'Avauges, reproduced in A.D. Isère, 1 Mi 461, letter of Mar. 19; Duquesnoy, 2:467–69, 480 (entries of Mar. 16 and 21).

The defection of Le Chapelier, leader of the radical patriots in the early months of the Revolution and founding member of both the Breton club and the Jacobins, was particularly striking. The fact that he was joined by Thouret and Démeunier suggests that the Constitutional Committee, of which all three were members, was increasingly distancing itself from the Friends of the Constitution.[29] Equally dramatic, however, was the departure from the Jacobins of Lafayette and several of his deputy friends. Like the members of the Crillon group, the commander of the Paris national guard claimed to be disconcerted by the large number of non-deputy radicals permitted to attend and by the election of the "enragé" Robespierre to the club's presidency.[30]

The withdrawal of Lafayette from the Jacobins coincided with a growing politicization of the Society of 1789, to which the general also belonged. According to Condorcet, the association's principal objective remained "much more philosophical than political," the gathering together of an Enlightened "company of the friends of mankind" to explore "social verities." Yet by the middle of April, the society had clearly transformed itself into a veritable "party," with dues and membership rolls, a series of committees, a projected newspaper, and elegant dinner meetings on the rue Saint-Honoré—all in accordance with a plan for a "club of 1789" drawn up by abbé Sieyès at the end of March.[31] At about the same time, the group also established a "correspondence committee," indicating its intention of inaugurating a network of provincial affiliates, in competition with those established by the Jacobins.[32] Whatever the club's official pronouncements, some of the discussions went beyond abstract intellectual debates to treat the specific policies and legislation of the Assembly.[33] At the end of April, both the duc de Liancourt and the comte de Crillon and their respective coteries seem to have merged with the new society. The group could claim a substantial contingent of the most distinguished liberal nobles in the Assembly—including Mirabeau and Talleyrand—as well as such noted commoners as Bailly, Le Chapelier, Barère, Rabaut Saint-Etienne, Garat, Thouret, and Roederer.[34]

Officially, no strictures were taken against members of the Club of '89 who wished to maintain their ties with the Jacobins; and at first some deputies—like Mirabeau and Barère—seemed to have attended both.[35] But many

[29] Gérard Walter, *Histoire des Jacobins* (Paris, 1946), 53–54; Duquesnoy, 2:468–69, 507 (entries of Mar. 16 and Apr. 3); Jean-de-Dieu Boisgelin de Cucé to comtesse de Gramont: A.N., M 788, letter of Mar. 17.

[30] Gottschalk and Maddox, 317–19; Walter, 54–55.

[31] *Journal de la Société de 1789*, no. 1 (June 5), 3; Challamel, 425–28; Baker, 210–11; Olsen, 307–10; Boisgelin, undated letter (pièce 140).

[32] *Journal de la Société de 1789*, no. 3 (June 19), 34–35.

[33] Olsen, 307.

[34] Challamel, 400–417; Faulcon, 2:223 (letter of May 15); and Gottschalk and Maddox, 354.

[35] Challamel, 416–17; *Journal de la Société de 1789*, no. 1 (June 5), 3; Baker, 213.

of the "Eighty-niners" were clearly unhappy with the evolution of the Jacobins. Though they continued to sit on the left side of the hall, they came to view themselves as a party of moderation, eschewing popular violence and threats to property and seeking to stabilize the new regime and terminate the Revolution.[36] Duquesnoy described them as the true "popular party," following not the whims of the crowds, but "the most sacred of all the legislator's duties, the protection of property." They sought to develop a tight working relationship with the king, who, it was hoped, had now fully embraced the concept of a constitutional monarchy. In some respects, such positions were not far removed from those of the Impartials. The '89 deputies differed from Malouet's group, however, in their strong opposition to the church and in their acceptance of proposals for sweeping transformations in ecclesiastical structures.[37] Indeed, only three of the clerical deputies—including the freethinkers Sieyès and Talleyrand—chose to affiliate with the new club. On the other hand, the group rapidly aligned itself with the royal ministry—especially with the foreign minister Montmorin—and with the powerful Constitutional Committee, of which at least six of eight members were adherents. By the late spring the deputies of '89 were sometimes referred to as "the Constitutionals," in part because of their close ties with "the Committee."[38]

Already at the end of the winter there had been indications in Assembly debates of the growing division between the radical Jacobins, on the one hand, and those drifting toward moderation, on the other. In the February discussions on peasant uprisings in the provinces, Le Chapelier and Barnave had taken distinctly differing positions, with the Breton leader, speaking for the Constitutional Committee, now affirming the necessity of repressing popular violence. It was a clash that had been rehearsed earlier in the Jacobin Club itself and that perhaps marked Le Chapelier's break with his former political associates.[39] But the critical development occurred during two major debates in the month of May: on the organization of the judicial branch and on the right to declare war and negotiate peace.

Long postponed in favor of more pressing matters, sustained consideration of the new court system began only at the end of April.[40] At this time a crisis arose in the Jacobin Club when the radicals failed to hold the disci-

---

[36] Honoré-Gabriel Riqueti de Mirabeau, *Correspondance avec le comte de la Marck*, 3 vols., Adrien de Bacourt ed. (Paris, 1851), 3:48–50 (letter dated Feb. 9, 1991).

[37] Adrien-Cyprien Duquesnoy, *Lettre d'Adrien Duquesnoy sur la prétendue division du parti populaire de l'Assemblée nationale* (n.p., Aug. 17, 1790), 3; and *Journal de la Société de 1789* 2 (June 12), 1–12.

[38] Baker, 214; Paroy, 146–47; Jean Girardot, "Jean-Xavier Bureaux de Pusy," *Bulletin de la Société d'agriculture, lettres, et arts de la Haute-Saône*, n. sér., no. 21 (1788–89), 69. Within the Constitutional Committee, Sieyès, Le Chapelier, Rabaut Saint-Etienne, Talleyrand, Démeunier, and Thouret were all members. On Tronchet's independence, see Lameth, 2:237.

[39] *AP*, 11:652–53 (Feb. 20); Duquesnoy, *Journal* 2:406 (entry of Feb. 20).

[40] See Eric Thompson, *Popular Sovereignty and the French Constituent Assembly, 1789–91* (Manchester, 1952), 86–98.

pline of the full membership on the use of juries in civil suits—a measure introduced and strongly backed by the Jacobin leader Duport, and a centerpiece in his plan for a democratized judicial system. If we can believe Dusers, who now broke with the club he had backed since its creation, only "about a hundred enthusiastic philosophers, with 'professor' Duport at their head," supported the measure which was voted down on April 30 by "a majority of four-fifths of all the votes." That night, as Alexandre de Lameth described it, the radicals were forced to admit that all their plans "were now overturned" by the decision, and that the question had "created an unfortunate split in the party."[41]

On the far more dramatic and stormy debate over the king's right to confirm the electorate's choice of judges—a debate lasting almost a week and closely followed by all the deputies—the coalition on the left ultimately held together in sufficient numbers to reject a royal veto. Yet the majority was meager—with an apparent margin of only about fifty votes out of nearly a thousand.[42] The principal proponent of royal authority was clearly the "Capuchin" coalition of the moderate and extreme right—with strong speeches in favor of the king made by Cazalès, Maury, Irland de Bazôges, and Clermont-Tonnerre.[43] Yet observers were surprised to see a significant number of nobles previously associated with the patriot party now deliberating in favor of greater royal power. "Several great nobles linked to the court who until then had constantly voted with the patriot party," wrote Campmas, "now revealed their true colors."[44] Though no specific names were given, the "great lords" in question almost certainly included the patriot nobles attached to Lafayette, Crillon, and La Rochefoucauld and now associated with the Society of 1789. Significantly, the Constitutional Committee likewise announced its support for the king.[45]

Even more divisive for the left, however, was the lengthy deliberation between May 15 and 22 on the constitutional rights of initiating war and

[41] Dusers, letter of May 4; André Fribourg, *Le club des Jacobins en 1790 d'après de nouveaux documents* (Paris, 1910), 30; Lameth, 2:261.

[42] The vote itself is not recorded. Nevertheless, in a vote immediately afterward on whether the king would be presented with one or several candidates—where a vote for "several" would have given the king a choice after all—the tally was 503 for a single candidate, 450 for several: *AP*, 15:420–21 (May 6). See also Vernier, letter of May 7; Lucas, letter of May 8; Dusers, letter of May 11.

[43] *AP*, 15:390, 392–99, 417 (May 5 and 7). Also Jean-Félix Faydel to Jean Filsac, avocat in Cahors: A.N., W 368, no. 822, 4e partie, letter of May 8; François-Joseph Bouchette, *Lettres de François-Joseph Bouchette (1735–1810)*, ed. Camille Looten (Lille, 1909), 389 (letter of May 8).

[44] Campmas, letter of May 9. See also Thomas Lindet, *Correspondance de Thomas Lindet pendant la Constituante et la Législative (1789–92)*, ed. Amand Montier (Paris, 1899), 152 (letter of May 7); and Maupetit, 20 (1904), 456–59 (letter of May 8).

[45] On May 5, Cazalès asked to know the opinion of the Constitutional Committee. Despite the efforts of the Jacobins Alexandre and Charles de Lameth to block this inquiry, Démeunier came forward and announced that the "la majorité du comité" supported the king's right to "institute"—and thus to veto, if he wished—the judicial candidates elected by the people: *AP*, 15:399–400.

peace. For many observers, the debate was one of the most important of the entire first year of the Revolution and was compared to the September debates on the king's veto.[46] The issue emerged unexpectedly when the foreign minister abruptly announced that Spain and England were on the verge of war over an obscure territorial dispute in North America. If war actually broke out there would be immediate pressure to reactivate the alliance between Spain and France, and so the king had ordered the precautionary arming of several French warships. The question was politicized when the minister Montmorin and his deputy friends in the Society of 1789 attempted to rush through a ratification of the king's actions without a serious discussion.[47] The radical Jacobins, in particular, feared that the monarch might use the threat of war to solidify his control over the army and pervert the constitution. "In fact," wrote Basquiat, "[this question] encompasses in itself the whole of the constitution. For the peace of the state and the happiness of the French people are dependent on the wise use of the armed forces."[48]

The debate also marked another important step in the Revolutionary education of the deputies. For many, it brought a first realization that popular sovereignty might be expanded to questions of international relations; and that the right to make war, the profession par excellence of the Bourbon kings, must be entirely reexamined. "Never," wrote Dusers, "has a greater question been debated in any political assembly, nor examined by any legislature."[49] Soon the more radical speakers were proposing that offensive wars be outlawed altogether and that the other European powers be urged to do likewise. "For the first time," argued Volney, the Assembly "has cast its watchful regard beyond the frontiers of the French state," in order to conceive "the universality of humankind, as though it formed but a single society."[50] The drama of the debates was closely followed by European ambassadors and the Parisian population in general. On the last day crowds estimated at between twenty-five and fifty thousand people were said to have waited on the terrace outside the Assembly and in the neighboring Tuileries Gardens.[51]

[46] E.g., Faulcon, 2:222 (letter of May 15); Lepoutre, letter of May 19; Claude Gantheret to Pierre Leflaive, his brother-in-law: private collection of Françoise Misserey, letter of May 24. Also Norman Hampson, *Prelude to Terror: The Constituent Assembly and the Failure of Consensus* (Oxford, 1988), 130–34.

[47] See *AP*, 15:510–11, 516–17 (May 14 and 15).

[48] Alexis Basquiat de Mugriet to the municipality of Saint-Sever: A.C. Saint-Sever, II D 31, letter of May 22. Also Boullé, letter of May 15; and Pierre-Marc-Gaston, duc de Lévis, "Lettres du duc de Lévis, 1784–1795," ed. duc de Lévis-Mirepoix, *La Revue de France* 4 (1929), 442 (letter of May 16).

[49] Dusers, letter of May 25.

[50] *AP*, 15:576. See also the speeches by Pétion and Barnave: 536–44, 641–44.

[51] Lepoutre, letter of May 23; Maupetit, 20 (1904), 469–70 (letter of May 23); Lameth, 2:312–13; Henri Quatrefages de Laroquete, in François Rouvière, *Quatrefages de Laroquete* (Paris, 1886), 32; Schwendt, *Revue d'Alsace*, 105 (letter of May 24).

As might have been expected, the radical Jacobin orators—Pétion, Robespierre, and the baron de Menou—generally supported the control of the National Assembly over both war and peace, though the king was to be given some initiative for negotiating peace treaties.[52] By contrast, the extreme right demanded that virtually all such authority be maintained by the monarch. If such powers were withdrawn from the king, announced Cazalès, "we would have to reveal a great secret to the people: henceforth, they would no longer have a king."[53] It is unclear whether the Club of 1789 had defined a collective position at the beginning of the debates, but on the third day of discussions the comte de Crillon proposed a compromise in which the king and the legislature would share authority over war and peace. This position, with certain modifications, was the stance adopted in the Society's newspaper.[54]

A pivotal moment in the long debate came with a speech on May 20 by Mirabeau. In desperate need of funds, the comte-philosophe had recently become the secret adviser of the king, and had initiated a rapprochement with Lafayette, as part of a grand strategy to reinforce monarchical authority. Now he broke decisively with the Jacobins and supported a compromise similar to that of Crillon in which the king and the Assembly would collaborate in the war and peace process.[55] The radicals Gaultier de Biauzat and Barnave attempted to attack Mirabeau and defend their position, with Barnave elaborating a lengthy address he had presented to the Jacobins the previous night.[56] But two days later Le Chapelier took the floor and reiterated Mirabeau's proposal with a few amendments of his own. After he had finished speaking, as one newspaper described it, there was a long moment of silence, followed by a scattering of protest, soon drowned out by "near universal applause."[57]

It was another defeat for the radical Jacobins and a dramatic victory for the Society of 1789 which had taken the offensive in the name of moderation and the support of the monarchy. "The Jacobins have lost many of their partisans," wrote Fricaud at the end of May, "through a division between the party of the Lameth brothers and the party of the comte de Mirabeau."[58] With tensions between the two factions riding high, a public split occurred on June 4, over the Jacobins' nomination for the presidency of the Assembly. Mirabeau, along with the other members of the Club of

[52] *AP*, 15:536–44, 559, 611.

[53] *AP*, 15:641. See also the speeches of Virieu, Montlosier, and Maury: ibid., 530, 544–47, 564–75.

[54] *Journal de la Société de 1789*, no. 1 (June 5), 26–51; and no. 2 (June 12), 12–32. Also *AP*, 15:564. The duc de Biron and the comte de Custine, two leading members of the Society initially argued that all such powers should be given to the king: *AP*, 15:515–16, 528–29.

[55] *AP*, 15:618–26. See also Vernier, letter of May 20.

[56] *AP*, 15:638–39, 641–44; Bouchette, 394 (letter of May 22); Faulcon, 2:229, 231 (letters of May 20 and 22). Also Lameth, 2:280–82, and 314–15.

[57] *AP*, 15:653–54.

[58] Fricaud, letter of May 31.

'89 still attending the Jacobins, vigorously supported the abbé Sieyès as the most appropriate president for the first anniversary of the National Assembly. But the majority of the Jacobins opted rather for Le Peletier de Saint-Fargeau. Thereafter, Mirabeau, accompanied by Le Chapelier, Talleyrand, and a large contingent of the Breton deputies, ostentatiously walked out of the club and announced they would henceforth sit exclusively with the Society of 1789.[59] The fact that Sieyès was actually elected president on June 8 gave clear evidence of the Society's growing influence in the Assembly.[60]

At approximately the same time, the Society also took steps to greatly expand its membership within the Assembly, offering free "associate" status to any deputy who did not normally reside in Paris and who could not afford the club's costly dues. By the middle of June, "more than a hundred associate members" had been admitted in this manner, and perhaps 160 deputies altogether were attending the meetings, a number only slightly smaller than the rump of deputies who had remained faithful to the Jacobins.[61] Among those deputies with full membership in the Society of 1789, slightly over half were from the Third Estate, including a substantial number of lawyers, magistrates, and merchants or bankers, and a single individual from the agricultural classes.[62] Excluding the three clerics, the remainder of the club consisted of representatives from the nobility. Even more than in the Capuchin group, the "Eighty-niner" nobles were aristocrats, with three-fourths from families who could trace their lineage to the sixteenth century or earlier.[63] They also originated predominantly from Paris (three-fifths of the total) and represented a distinctly different generation, averaging nine full years younger than the nobles of the far right.[64] Indeed, virtually all of the nobles in question were younger Parisian aristocrats who had long associated with one another and who had supported liberal reforms since the Pre-Revolutionary period.[65] It was precisely this group which formed the most active leadership within the club: two-thirds of all speeches by mem-

[59] Walter, 68–69; Alphonse Aulard, *La société des Jacobins*, 6 vols. (Paris, 1889–97), 1:138–41.

[60] *AP*, 16:138. Also the *Journal de la Société de 1789*, no. 4 (June 26), 34–40.

[61] Challamel, 400–417—complemented with additional indications from a wide variety of biographic sources. Some 59 deputies were full members of the Society of 1789 in the spring of 1790. To these must be added the estimated 100 associate members: *Journal de la Société de 1789*, no. 3 (June 19), 34; also Baker, 214.

[62] Of the known members of the Society of 1789 in our sample, 32 (54%) were members of the Third Estate, including 8 lawyers, 9 magistrates, and 4 merchants or bankers.

[63] Of the 31 who were nobles (in any Estate), 23 (74%) could trace their families to the sixteenth century or earlier.

[64] Of the 55 for whom the residence is known, 33 (60%) resided in Paris; and 45 (82%) resided in towns over 20,000. Overall, only 14 (25%) came from south of the La Rochelle-Geneva line. The nobles in the Society of '89 averaged 37.5 years old in 1789; those in the Capuchin coalition averaged 46.6 years.

[65] Of the 25 noble members who had been elected by the Second Estate, 22 were classified by Murphy and Higonnet as "liberals" in the summer of 1789; of these, 19 resided in Paris: Jean-Marie Murphy and Patrice Higonnet, "Les députés de la noblesse aux Etats Généraux," *RHMC* 20 (1973), 244–46.

bers of the Society were made by nobles, and about half of these were made by aristocrats of ancient lineage.[66] Moreover, some 44 percent were affiliated with the Freemasons, three and a half times the proportion of Capuchins. Over a third of the membership had published during the Old Regime or was linked to scientific, literary, or agricultural associations.[67] To a far greater extent than any of the other factions, the Society of 1789 was integrated into the Enlightenment culture of the late eighteenth century.

The radicals who remained faithful to the Jacobins were strikingly different in their social and cultural backgrounds. In an overwhelming proportion—over 80 percent—they were representatives of the Third Estate.[68] Among the small contingent of noble Jacobins, moreover, well over half came from families ennobled since the sixteenth century.[69] Though nobles were more active in the club's leadership than their numbers might suggest, they still accounted for only about one-fourth of all speeches given by the membership during the first year of the Revolution. The eight most frequent Jacobin speakers were all commoners.[70] Compared to the large contingent of Parisians in the Society of '89, only about 6 percent of the Friends of the Constitution originated in the capital. Indeed, three-fifths came from towns with under eight thousand inhabitants and nearly two-fifths lived in communities of less than two thousand. It was one of the curious ironies of the period that those who most fervently supported the Parisian lower classes came overwhelmingly from small towns and rural regions.[71]

Though it is difficult to assess the deputies' financial positions, the majority of the Jacobins—provincial lawyers and small-town officeholders for the most part—were decidedly less wealthy than the great aristocrats, bankers, and merchants who dominated the Club of 1789, and many were among the more humble members of the Third Estate.[72] The Jacobins themselves were intensely self-conscious of the differences in lifestyle. The Club stal-

[66] Of a total of 5,238 speeches by members of the Society, 3,279 (63%) were by nobles of any order; 1,516 (46%) of the 3,279 were by nobles of ancient lineage.

[67] Twenty-six (44%) were masons; and 22 (37%) were involved in the other specified activities.

[68] The earliest list of the Jacobins, dating from late 1790, is apparently incomplete: see Aulard, 1:xxxiv–lxxvi. Supplementing this list by indications in Aulard's index at the end of volume 6 and by a variety of individual biographies, we find a total of 205 deputy members. Twenty of these 205, however, sat with the Club of 1789 in June 1790 and have not been included here. One hundred fifty-three (83%) of the 185 had been elected to the Third Estate.

[69] Fourteen (56%) of the 25 Jacobin nobles (elected from any of the three estates) for which the lineage is known were from families ennobled after the sixteenth century.

[70] The eight Jacobin deputies delivering the most speeches during the period from May 1789 to July 1790 were Charles-François Bouche, Barnave, Goupil de Préfelne, Reubell, Robespierre, Pétion, Lanjuinais, and Grégoire.

[71] Of the 185 Jacobins, 113 (61%) lived in communities of under 8,000 inhabitants; 67 (36%) lived in communities under 2,000; and 11 (6%) came from Paris. Fifty-nine (32%) came from south of the line La Rochelle-Geneva.

[72] See above, chap. 1.

wart Dubois Crancé delighted in stressing the aristocratic character of the Eighty-niners' meetings on the rue Saint-Honoré: "The sumptuous meeting room, the elegant and refined company, the magnificent but extremely costly dinners; while the Jacobins, seated soberly on their wooden benches, ponder the public welfare in the glow of their oil lamps."[73] The Jacobins differed likewise in their cultural backgrounds. Overall, only one in ten had been members of the Masons—less than a fourth as many as from the Club of '89—and one in seven had published or been associated with academies or other learned societies.[74] Not a single member of this, the most radical segment of the Constituent deputies in the spring of 1790, would have qualified as a professional "philosophe" before the Revolution.[75] Almost without exception, the most distinguished Jacobins in terms of Old Regime intellectual careers had been legal specialists—men like Bouche, Creuzé-Latouche, Durand de Maillane, Lanjuinais, Robespierre, Gaultier de Biauzat, Merlin de Douai, Pétion de Villeneuve, or Baudouin de Maisonblanche. Nine of the eleven most active Jacobin orators were legal men by profession.[76] In the National Assembly, as in the kingdom generally, it was often the men of law who represented the most important bastion of radicalism.

But for the time being, on the first anniversary of the Assembly and for several months thereafter, it was the Parisian intellectuals and liberal aristocrats of the Club of '89 who wielded the greatest influence in the Constituent. To be sure, the Jacobins had not retreated from the fight, and they continued to dominate many of the important committees and to give more total speeches in the Assembly than any of the rival factions.[77] Yet the new alignment not only dominated the powerful Constitutional Committee, but revealed the potential for creating a solid bloc of support, rallying to its cause a broad segment of the "sensible men" ("les hommes sages") of the center, many of whom had not previously participated in factional politics. Dubois-Crancé deplored the number of "honest deputies, upright but weak men" who had been seduced by "various personalities, distinquished until now by their professed patriotism." To believe the *Chronique de Paris*, the Société "becomes larger and more brilliant every day."[78] Particularly revealing was the Club's domination of the presidency. Between the middle of May and the end of September 1790, nine of the eleven presidents of the

---

[73] Dubois-Crancé, 22.

[74] Respectively, 19 (10%) and 25 (14%) of the total sample of 185.

[75] See above, chap. 2.

[76] Of the top eleven, only Grégoire and Charles de Lameth were not trained in the law. Forty-seven of the Jacobins were lawyers, 33 were magistrates, 18 were other kinds of officeholders, 3 were law professors, and 6 held other miscellaneous professions probably entailing a law degree: a total of 107 of the 185 (58%).

[77] See graph, chap. 8.

[78] *Chronique de Paris*, issue of June 15, 1790, cited in Olsen, 304. Also Olsen, 327; and Dubois, 22.

National Assembly came from the Society of 1789—"the friends of order and liberty"—as Madame de Staël called them.[79]

The rise of the Club of '89 closely coincided, moreover, with a new offensive by the king to win favor with the Assembly. On May 29 Louis announced to the deputies a "proclamation" which strongly endorsed "the important work in which the National Assembly is engaged" and urged all French citizens "to rally around the law with courage, and support with all their strength the creation of the constitution." It even seemed directly to castigate the Capuchin group, attacking those who would incite "empty fears and false interpretations of the National Assembly's decrees . . . , concealing self-interest or personal passions under the sacred veil of religion." The announcement raised an outpouring of enthusiasm: "The hall resounded with applause from the Assembly, mixed with expressions of joy from the spectators and repeated cries of 'vive le roi.'"[80] At the end of the first year of Revolution, with the fear of impending counterrevolution greatly abated and with the king now apparently solidly behind them, a majority of the deputies seemed ready to follow the Society of 1789.

THE CIVIL CONSTITUTION OF THE CLERGY AND
THE SUPPRESSION OF THE NOBILITY

While the rapprochement with the king provided an enormous boost to the moderate patriots, it was a cruel blow to the aspirations of the Capuchins. Still reeling from their apparent defeat in the dom Gerle "referendum," they now had to face what seemed for all the world like a direct rebuke from the monarch himself, a rebuke which in Fricaud's opinion "fully drove them to despair."[81] Yet two major constitutional laws voted in the course of June 1790 left the nobles and ecclesiastics on the right even more frustrated and prepared, in many cases, to abandon the whole experiment with parliamentary government: first, the reorganization of the French clergy and, second, the suppression of the hereditary nobility.

The Ecclesiastical Committee's printed proposal for a "Civil Constitution of the Clergy" had already been presented to the deputies in the middle of

---

[79] Anne-Louise-Germaine de Staël, *Considérations sur les principaux événements de la Révolution française*, 3 vols. (London, 1818), 1:399. During this period, only Le Peletier (the Jacobin candidate elected June 21) and the Capuchin marquis de Bonnay were not members of the Society.

[80] *AP*, 15:737–38; Dusers, letter of June 1; Boullé, letter of June 2; Vernier, letter of May 30; Lepoutre, letter of May 30; Etienne-François Schwendt, in *L'Alsace pendant la Révolution française*, ed. Rodolphe Reuss, 2 vols. (Paris, 1880–94), 2:55 (letter of June 3); Faulcon, 2:237–39 (letter of May 30). The deputies confirmed their confidence in the monarch by accepting his plan to move out of Paris for the summer and voting by acclamation his *liste civile*, which had been pending since January: *AP*, 16:93, 158–59 (June 4 and 9).

[81] Fricaud, letter of May 31. See also Bouchette, 397 (letter of May 31); and Schwendt, *Revue d'Alsace*, 219 (letter of May 30).

April, but it was another month and a half before the project could be considered in systematic fashion.[82] When the debate finally opened on May 29, the mood of the patriots, both Eighty-niners and Jacobins alike, was scarcely conducive to a sympathetic treatment of the clergy. For Grellet de Beauregard, the antipathy toward the clerical corps could be attributed in part to an ideological position: "Much of what is happening today has been influenced by the old quarrels between the sect of philosophers and the clergy." But whatever the anticlerical bias which many patriots brought with them to Versailles, it was the experience of the Assembly—and Grellet recognized this as well—which had heated their passions to the boiling point.[83] For months, the majority of the clerical deputies had worked tooth and nail to thwart almost every substantial reform which the patriots sought to institute. Both the Society of 1789 and the Friends of the Constitution were angered by the clergy's publicity campaign to undermine the Assembly's decrees and put into question its support of Catholicism. The generally moderate bailliage judge from Nantua, Lilia de Crose, raged against the clerics and accused them of fomenting a whole series of plots against the Revolution. "Ah, calotins!" he wrote, using the harsh epithet for the clergy, "even in the throes of death, you are remarkably spiteful and malicious."[84] Most patriots were convinced that the bishops had no other motive for their actions than the preservation of their immense wealth. Was it not significant, they asked, that the bishop's propaganda barrage began immediately after the Assembly had nationalized church property? "The clergy," wrote Maupetit, "never wants to separate its temporal self-interest from religion itself"; while Faulcon seethed against "all these Tartuffe-like bishops who preach piety only to perpetuate the abuses of the Old Regime." Indeed, a measure of vindictiveness seemed to slip into the testimonies of many of our witnesses. "They are out to get the clergy," judged the marquis de Ferrières, who sat on the right, but who had no particular fondness for priests.[85]

The reform package which the Ecclesiastical Committee presented—a complex mixture of Jansenist, Gallican, and physiocratic proposals—was remarkably radical, and included the complete reorganization of the dioceses, the lay election of bishops and curés, the suppression of all clerical positions without cure of souls, and a sweeping reduction of clerical salaries. The Assembly's consideration of the package spread out over more than three

[82] *AP*, 13:163, 166–75 (report by Martineau, Apr. 21).

[83] Jean-Bernard Grellet de Beauregard, "Lettres de M. Grellet de Beauregard," ed. Abbé Dardy, *Mémoires de la Société des sciences naturelles et archéologiques de la Creuse*, 2e sér., 7 (1899), 83 (letter of May 29).

[84] Joseph-Bernard de Lilia de Crose to the municipality of Nantua: B.M. Lyon, ms. 2191, letter of May 26.

[85] Maupetit, 21 (1905) (letter of June 2), 101–2; Faulcon, 2:181 (letter of Apr. 14); Charles-Elie de Ferrières, *Correspondance inédite*, ed. Henri Carré (Paris, 1932), 203 (letter of June 14).

weeks, from May 29 to June 22.[86] But the only substantial collision between left and right occurred during the first three days, when the deputies considered the general principles of the proposed legislation and the Assembly's authority to involve itself in such questions.

It was Boisgelin who served once again as the spokesman for the bishops. In a long and learned speech, he admitted the need for extensive reforms, but he entirely rejected the competence of the Constituents to undertake such measures, and he called for a series of national and regional church councils as the only legitimate means of initiating them. Significantly, in the light of later developments, little was said of the authority of the pope. Boisgelin made it clear, however, that a national council would not automatically approve the Assembly's proposals, and he rejected in advance the lay election of bishops and curés and the suppression of cathedral chapters. Other Capuchin participants in the debate went further than the archbishop of Aix, proclaiming that the Civil Constitution was schismatic or heretical and that it was inspired by Protestantism.[87] The clerical speakers were countered point for point by members of the Ecclesiastical Committee and other deputies versed in canon law. With equally learned arguments, they called on several centuries of conciliar, Gallican, and Jansenist theory—all buttressed with quotations in Latin and references to scripture and the teachings of the church fathers.[88]

Once a strong majority of the deputies had affirmed the Assembly's competence to reform the clergy, most of the right ostentatiously washed their hands of the debates and withdrew from further participation. A handful of conservative curés continued to enter the fray, and a few lay leaders like Foucauld de Lardimalie and Eprémesnil contributed occasional bursts of invective. But in general "once the Assembly had taken up the Civil Constitution of the Clergy, the right side of the hall condemned itself to total inaction," and frequently their benches were all but empty.[89]

Even at the left end of the hall, however, only a tiny proportion of the deputies took a significant role in the discussions. The major contributions to the debate were dominated by a small group of patriot curés and lay specialists in theology and canon law, many of them Jansenists: above all, Camus, Treilhard, Grégoire, Fréteau, Goutte, Goupil, and Lanjuinais. It was orchestrated throughout by the Parisian lawyer and devout Jansenist, Martineau, speaker for the Committee, who took on all comers with his overpowering erudition and withering sarcasm.[90] Several of the Assembly's

---

[86] *AP*, 15:712–51 and 16:2–616.

[87] *AP*, 15:724–31 and 16:10–16, 44–46.

[88] See especially the speeches of Treilhard, Camus, and Gouttes: *AP*, 15:744–51; and 16:3–10, 17–18.

[89] Dinochau, issues of June 8 and 15; Boullé, letters of June 5 and 9; Maupetit, 21 (1905), 108 (letter of June 9). Deputies on the right contributed only 44 (17%) of the 261 speeches on the Civil Constitution, most of these made during the first three days of debates.

[90] The eight men mentioned, by themselves, accounted for 95 (36%) of the 261 speeches— many of which were exceptionally long and developed.

most prominent orators—Mirabeau, Barnave, Alexandre de Lameth, Démeunier, Malouet, and Maury—remained mute or intervened only on peripheral questions or procedural issues.[91] Among our deputy witnesses, a few of the more religiously concerned were genuinely enthused by the debates and attracted to the ideal of returning the church to its primitive purity.[92] But a great many others scarcely mentioned the issue at all, or found it wearisome and time-consuming. Boullé was irritated that it forced the Assembly to postpone the completion of legislation on the judiciary. Dinochau appeared overcome with ennui at the "antiquated foolishness" which the debaters insisted on elucidating: their citations from the Bible, their references to sundry saints or to "lambs" and "sheep," or their tired allusions to Jansenism and Molenism. By his account, the left frequently "allowed itself to burst out with laughter." Even many years later, Lameth maintained a certain condescension toward the affair, implying that Enlightened people generally avoided such questions. He acknowledged, nevertheless, that by abandoning the debate to "the Jansenist contingent" the patriot leadership had abdicated their responsibility and committed a major error with grave consequences for the later Revolution.[93]

The passage of the final version of the Civil Constitution on July 12 marked a harsh turn of events for the conservative clergy and especially for the bishops. Despite the cynicism of the patriots, much of the clergy in the "Capuchin" coalition probably opposed the new provisions for religious reasons. Increasingly convinced that their opponents were godless philosophers out to destroy Catholicism, they had done everything in their power, working within the system, to defeat the successive waves of Church related decrees. But they had ultimately failed on every score. Now their dejection and bitterness were visible to all. Ménard found his own bishop of Le Mans deeply depressed, viewing everything "from a grim perspective." "Our poor bishops," wrote the marquis de Ferrières at the end of June, "have long faces indeed." Archbishop Boisgelin, who did grieve for his lost benefices as much as for religion, poured out his ire to his onetime mistress: "At last we approach the final decision. . . . All the Assembly's supposedly sympathetic inclinations towards the clergy are beginning to vanish. All is lost. I will have 30,000 *livres* a year, and nothing more. Nothing for all my abbeys, nothing unless I reside in my diocese, nothing but dependency on the municipal government."[94] Increasingly the bishops ceased attending or abandoned the Assembly. The bishop of Nancy, author of the opening sermon

---

[91] Barnave spoke briefly only two times; the other six never spoke at all.

[92] Campmas, letter of May 23; Dusers, letter of June 18.

[93] Boullé, letter of June 2; Dinochau, issue of June 2 and 15; Lameth, 2:363–64, 369, 391. Bouchette and Merle never mentioned the debate; Faulcon mentioned it only once: 2:243–44 (letter of June 9). On the Jansenists and the Civil Constitution, see Yann Fauchois, "Les Jansénistes et la Constitution civile du clergé," in *Jansénisme et Révolution* (Paris, 1990), ed. Catherine Maire, 195–209; and Dale Van Kley, *The Religious Origins of the French Revolution* (New Haven, Conn., 1996), chap. 6.

[94] Ménard, 221 (letter of May 28); Ferrières, 225 (letter of June 29); Boisgelin, undated letter of late June 1790 (pièce 114).

in the Estates General, left in July to take the waters and was never seen again. Over the next twelve months, at least fourteen others seem also to have departed.[95] Boisgelin himself, the humanist academician who had once fancied himself a moderate, but who had been driven by events into a position of intransigence, now essentially withdrew from the Assembly. Like the majority of the episcopal deputies, he retained his membership in the Constituent but no longer actually appeared there.[96] From July 1790 through the end of the year the bishops' participation in Assembly debates dropped to less than one-fourth its previous level.[97]

It was in the midst of the debates on the Civil Constitution, during the night session of June 19, that the Assembly voted to suppress the hereditary nobility and all the symbolic accoutrements pertaining to the Old Regime caste structure. Compared by contemporaries to the Night of August 4, this new series of Revolutionary suppressions was probably less spontaneous than the first.[98] In recent weeks similar measures had been frequently proposed by the radical press and openly discussed by both Jacobins and members of the Society of 1789. The Jacobin Goupil de Préfelne had prepared an elaborate motion to this effect which he had apparently planned to present in another session, perhaps the following day on the anniversary of the Tennis Court Oath.[99]

In fact, only a small number of conservative deputies were present on the night of June 19.[100] By general agreement, evening sessions were supposed to be confined to questions involving specific groups or localities, and the meeting began as anticipated, with the presentation of visiting delegations from the Victors of the Bastille and the national guard units of Chartres and Tours. But then the evening was transformed by the appearance of an amazing collection of some thirty "foreigners"—from throughout Europe and the Near East—modestly describing themselves as "representatives of the human race."[101] Speaking with heavy accents and dressed in the costumes of their native countries—rumored to have been provided by the Paris opera—they praised the Revolution and asked permission to attend the up-

---

[95] Based on Brette, *Recueil*, vol. 2, and a wide variety of other biographic sources. Also, Augustin Sicard, *Le clergé de France pendant la Révolution*, 3 vols. (Paris, 1912–27), 2:110–13; and Bernard de Brye, *Un évêque d'Ancien régime à l'épreuve de la Révolution. Le cardinal A.L.H. de La Fare (1752–1829)* (Paris, 1985), 269–74.

[96] Sicard, 2:462, 466, 474–75; and Bouchette, 484 (letter of Jan. 10, 1791).

[97] The bishops averaged about 2.7 speeches per week between May and July 1790, but 0.6 by October and November.

[98] Boullé: letter of June 23; Gilbert Riberolles in Francisque Mège, "Notes biographiques sur les députés de la Basse-Auvergne," *Mémoires de l'Académie des sciences, belles-lettres, et arts, Clermont-Ferrand* 12 (1870), 129 (letter of June 22); and Gantheret, letter of June 21.

[99] Mirabeau, 2:34 (letter of June 4); Ferrières, 214 (letter of June 22); Faulcon, 2:255 (letter of June 20); Gottschalk and Maddox, 409 and 421; and Lameth, 2:445.

[100] Ferrières, 214 (letter of June 22).

[101] *AP*, 16:373.

coming Festival of Federation.[102] This theatrical spectacle was the signal for a stunning departure from the announced agenda. Alexandre de Lameth came forward to demand the removal of the figures of the four "conquered provinces" under the feet of Louis XIV's statue on the Place des Victoires in Paris—figures deemed symbolically unworthy of a free people about to celebrate its first anniversary. It is likely that those who had orchestrated the evening intended to stop at this point. But then an obscure deputy from Rouergue, Joseph-Marie Lambel, who was a member of no clubs and who had spoken only two times previously, stepped to the rostrum and demanded that all hereditary titles be abolished. Though the left was probably unprepared for such a motion that evening, a crowd of young liberal nobles reacted quickly and rushed forward to offer their own sacrifices. In rapid succession, coats of arms, noble liveries, noble rites of the church, names taken from feudal property, and hereditary nobility in general were all abandoned.

Unlike the Night of August 4, however, all those who demanded suppressions sat on the left and a vigorous movement of opposition arose immediately among the conservative nobles present. They were indignant that a constitutional decision of this kind should be initiated in a night session when so much of the right was absent. Foucauld also protested the injustice to families honored for past services to the kingdom. Baron Landenberg-Wagenbourg proclaimed in sorrowful tones that the Constituent had no authority in questions of his "race," and that all nobles "are born with the blood of their fathers and nothing can prevent them from living and dying as nobles." Pandemonium swept through the Manège as the marquis d'Ambly, the marquis de Digoine, the président de Grosbois, and the comte d'Egmont surged to the rostrum to profess their outrage, only to be drowned out by the cheers and screams of the spectators and the deputies on the left. The comte de Lévis shouted out his resignation on the spot. Tumult broke out in the stands as well, and several women were said to have fainted. But with the right utterly outnumbered, all of the motions were voted into law.[103]

For most of the commoner deputies present that night, it was another sublime moment of triumph and exhilaration. From the earliest days of the Estates General, they had reproached the nobles for their insolence and arrogance, their refusal to treat them as equals. Their feelings of aversion had only been sharpened by the long months in which the majority of the aristocrats combined with the conservative clergy in opposing reforms every step of the way. In this sense, "this wonderful night," this new step toward a democracy of status as well as of legal and political rights, brought sentiments of sweet satisfaction. "So we have revenge at last for all the humilia-

---

[102] Ferrières, 209–10 (letter of June 22).

[103] *AP*, 16:374–79; Dinochau, issue of June 19; Riberolles, 129 (letter of June 22); Ferrières, 205–7 and 214–15 (letters of June 20 and 22).

tions we had to endure from these arrogant little counts" (Gantheret); "their pride and vanity are cut down" (Lilia); "it's the final humiliating blow against the nobility" (Lepoutre). It was the end of "this vain and deplorable prejudice," as Ménard now saw it, "which attributed distinction to the blind chance of birth and flattered the vanity of a few by humiliating the great majority."[104] Many of the commoners who owned seigneurial lands recognized that they too would be affected by the new decrees, yet they enthusiastically took steps to comply. Ménard, formerly "de La Groye," gave careful instructions to his wife to drop the particled portion of their name, both for themselves and for their young sons who were still in school. Fricaud and Riberolle did likewise, excising forever "these miserable remnants of arrogance," as Riberolle called them. Within a few days, the deputies found a whole new set of names, many of them quite unrecognizable, inscribed in the membership rolls—like Monsieur Du Motier (Lafayette) or Gabriel Riquet (Mirabeau).[105]

The conservative nobles, however, were beside themselves with indignation. Within days a whole series of written protests were submitted to the Assembly, many of them professions of faith in a hereditary, "racial" nobility.[106] Two major themes predominated in almost all the protests: the Assembly's incompetence to vote such a decree and the decree's affront to their honor as gentlemen. While there was some disagreement as to the true source of nobility—whether it stemmed from the monarchy or God or their biological makeup—all agreed that the Constituent had no authority in the question and that its actions were consequently null and void. In this, they followed a logic surprisingly similar to that of the clergy in their opposition to the Civil Constitution. Indeed, one of the protesters specifically linked the present protest to his opposition toward the new ecclesiastical decrees.[107] As the baron de Gauville put it, "A piece of oak cannot be transformed into a piece of pine by one of your decrees." "The advantages which nature has granted me," wrote the duc d'Havré et Croÿ, "are outside the sphere that is touched by human law."[108] Even more infuriating, the new decree added insult to injury. All nobles were prepared to die for the nation, declared Foucauld, and they had already agreed to cede their feudal rights. But they could never abandon their honor, "the most sacred property which a gentleman can possess." Even Ferrières, who generally urged moderation on his colleagues for pragmatic reasons, was despondent about the future: "The lowliest peasant will imagine himself the equal of a noble and will think he

[104] Gantheret, letter of June 21; Lilia, letter of June 20; Lepoutre, letter of June 22; Ménard, 234 (letter of June 22). See also Dusers, letter of June 25.

[105] Ménard, 247 (letter of July 20); Fricaud, letter of June 28; Riberolles, 129–30 (letter of June 22). Also Maupetit, 21 (1905), 121 (letter of June 30); Rousselot, letter of June 28; Lindet, 193 (letter of June 27).

[106] *AP*, 16:379–89.

[107] *AP*, 16:379 (comte d'Alençon).

[108] Gauville, 46; *AP*, 16:381.

no longer owes either consideration or deference." Some presented brief chronicles of their families, vowing that they could never abandon the honor they owed both to their ancestors and their posterity. It was on the question of symbols and honorific rights, those symbols "which most recall the feudal system and the spirit of chivalry," that the nobility would draw the line against cooperation with the Revolutionary regime. To lose their honor would be to lose their very identity.[109]

A few of the more astute patriot deputies soon realized the extent to which June 19 had revolted and infuriated the former second estate. It "has heated the bile of the nobles," wrote Campmas. "I acknowledge that it was useless, and I fear it may be dangerous. . . . I myself am indulgent, and I would not be scandalized if our local lady continued to call herself 'countess,' as long as her rights were limited to words and not to things." Maupetit, who had long served as agent for a noble family in Maine, concluded that "we have been most impolitic. We might have left to time the slow destruction of an ancient tree whose roots had already been largely cut away." The suppression "may revolt many individuals who remain attached to such prejudices." Looking back on the event a year and a half later, Rabaut concluded that the decree "aroused the fury of the privileged classes more than any other which had been passed to date." It was from that day on, he believed, that "the majority of the nobles of the kingdom became the irreconcilable enemies of the Constitution," and that large numbers both inside and outside the Assembly began disavowing the whole Revolutionary experience "rather than renouncing their honor."[110]

For the conservative noble deputies, as for the bishops and the Capuchin clergy, June 1790 marked a major parting of the ways. Over the next fifteen months, to the end of the Constituent, almost one-fifth of the nobles—including such leaders as Cazalès and Mirabeau the younger—would abandon the Assembly and leave to join the emigrant armies vowing to overthrow the Revolution.[111] Though their participation in debates would not drop as precipitously as that of their clerical allies, it declined steadily in the months after June to a near record low by the end of the year. In November and December 1790 the conservative nobles delivered less than two-fifths as many speeches as during April and May.[112] Never again after July 1790

---

[109] *AP*, 16:379–80, 382, 386 (Foucauld, Burignot de Varenne, Mirabeau, and Montboissier); Ferrières, 220–21 (letter of June 26)

[110] Campmas, letter of June 26; Maupetit, 21 (1905), 119–20 (letters of June 21 and 25); Jean-Paul Rabaut Saint-Etienne, *Précis historique de la Révolution française* (Paris, 1807), 265–67.

[111] Thirty-two (19%) of the 168 nobles on the right present in the Assembly in June 1790.

[112] Twenty-six conservative nobles participated in debates in the 39 days covered by volume 16 (May 31 to July 8, 1790) of the *AP*; but only 10 (38%) so participated during the 38 days covered by volume 21 (Nov. 26, 1790 to Jan. 2, 1791). Conservatives are defined here as those mentioned in the *Liste par lettres alphabétiques des députés du côté droit aux Etats-Généraux au mois de septembre 1791* (Paris, 1791).

would a conservative be elevated to the presidency of the Assembly.[113] The conservative coalition of the moderate and extreme right, which the previous autumn had been a serious contender for control of the Assembly, would cease to exist as a major political power within the Assembly.

COMMEMORATING THE REVOLUTION: THE FEDERATION OF 1790

Through the first year of the Revolution, the eminently rational and practical minded deputies had shown little affinity for prearranged ceremonies. The opening rituals of the Estates General had not been of their making, and the great oaths of June 17, June 20, and February 4 had been largely spontaneous. But throughout much of the month of June, ceremony increasingly became the order of the day. After the enormous popular enthusiasm for the Assembly and the king generated by the Corpus Christi procession of June 3, 1790, the deputies were out in force one week later to march with the monarch on the Octave of Corpus Christi. Just one year earlier it had been almost impossible to find even twenty deputies willing to participate in the same processions.[114] The new interest in symbolic representations was also evident in the costumed appearance of the "delegates of the human race" on June 19; in the decision to install busts of Franklin, Washington, and Rousseau in the hall on June 22; and in the removal of the "captive provinces" from the statue of Louis XIV at the beginning of July. "We have taken a liking for ceremonies," wrote the no-nonsense lawyer Bouchette, somewhat nonplussed by all that was happening.[115] In many respects, this taste for ceremony was indicative of the growing hope that the Revolution could be ended, that it was time to cease making a Revolution and to begin celebrating and commemorating one instead.

The idea of commemorating the fall of the Bastille did not originate in the Constituent Assembly but in the Parisian districts. The spring of 1790 had seen a wave of "federation" ceremonies in the provinces, in which local national guard units came together to profess their mutual solidarity. Not to be outdone, the Parisians sought to organize a "general federative pact" of their own, conceived to take place on July 14 and to assemble representatives of national guard units from throughout the kingdom. While Lafayette and Bailly were initially hesitant, preferring to wait until the constitution was completed, they eventually agreed to bring the proposal before the king and the Assembly.[116] Thereafter, the Society of 1789, of which both the

---

[113] There would be 31 elections from July 1790 to the end of the Assembly. During the same period, no conservatives would sit at the secretariat's desk. See *AP*, 33:88–91.

[114] See above, chap. 2.

[115] Dinochau, issue of June 22; Dusers, letter of July 2; Bouchette, 402 (letter of June 9).

[116] Gottschalk and Maddox, 434–42; and Henri Leclercq, *La Fédération* (Paris, 1929), 292–338.

mayor and the commander were leading members, seems to have strongly supported the idea as a means of rallying the country toward the consolidation of the Revolution under a strengthened constitutional monarchy. Plans were drawn up by the Society-dominated Constitutional Committee and presented to the full Assembly on June 7, to be discussed off and on over the next month. As it was ultimately conceived, the "Festival of Federation" was fundamentally conservative in character. Delegations from the national guards and from all branches of the armed services would come before the king and the nation and swear to preserve property, pay their taxes, and maintain the freedom of the grain trade, as well as to maintain their loyalty to the National Assembly and the monarch.[117] The Federation, as Boullé put it, "will consolidate the unity which must exist among all citizens" and "disconcert once and for all the enemies of the country." Indeed, the memory of the Bastille itself and of the popular uprising of the previous July was largely set aside.[118]

To be sure, not all of the deputies were equally enthralled by the idea. The far right was scarcely enthusiastic about an event that would underscore the alliance of the king with the patriot Revolutionaries. The conservative clergy, sullen and resentful after their recent defeat on the Civil Constitution, announced that their July 14 oath would be restrictive and would not apply to "spiritual matters."[119] Yet the strongest note of suspicion arose from the left. Rumors spread widely of a coup planned by royalist forces or by Lafayette. Both Barnave and Alexandre de Lameth feared that national guard units might try to coerce the National Assembly during the Federation parade, forcing it to strengthen the power of the king or even "destroying the Assembly and blocking the fulfillment of the Revolution." On July 4, Barnave pushed through a motion that the Assembly would receive no petitions and could make no decrees outside the Manège itself.[120]

In the meantime, Louis XVI was quickly warming to the idea of a great patriotic celebration in which he was to take a central part, and he "did everything he could to facilitate the organization of the Federation."[121] On occasion he even summoned up a measure of enthusiasm and leadership that surprised almost everyone. At the height of the festivities he went out daily to greet new arrivals or review the troops or inspect the preparations of the parade grounds, frequently stopping to chat with soldiers or by-

---

[117] *AP*, 16:117–19, 136–37; 696.

[118] Boullé, letter of June 9. Also, Mona Ozouf, *Festivals and the French Revolution* (Cambridge, Mass., 1988), esp. 33, 43–44.

[119] *AP*, 17:17 (speech by bishop de Bonnal, adhered to by the conservative clergy); Dusers, letter of June 8.

[120] Lameth, 2:454–55, 461–62; *AP*, 16:696. See also Vernier, letter of July 18; and Gottschalk and Maddox, 515.

[121] François-Emmanuel Toulongeon, *Histoire de la France depuis la Révolution*, 7 vols. (Paris, 1801), 1:214.

standers. The night before the Federation ceremony, he welcomed Lafayette and a delegation of guardsmen into the Tuileries Palace with a simple but moving speech, assuring them that "the king was their father, their brother, their friend; and that he could not be happy without their happiness, great without their glory, powerful without their liberty, rich without their prosperity." He also announced that he hoped soon to visit his entire kingdom and to see the guardsmen in their hometowns. While we do not know if he composed the speech himself, those present that evening were convinced that he was sincere. For a time at least, Louis seemed ready and willing to assume the role of patriot king which the deputies had so long hoped he would assume. From their point of view, it was perhaps his finest hour.[122]

As the Assembly settled on the final details of the ceremony, debating at length the wording of the oaths and the seating arrangements of the participants, the Federation—like the Revolution itself—was taking on a life of its own. The central procession of the Festival was to converge on the drill fields of the Ecole militaire west of Paris. The construction of earthenwork stands for the spectators, required digging out and lowering the entire immense parade area by several feet. It was a monumental task, and when word went out that the paid workmen would never be able to finish in time, Parisians of every walk of life began streaming out to lend a hand: young and old, men and women, rich and poor, soldier and civilian. Working well into the night, the volunteers were accompanied by music, dancing, and singing. Witnesses even noted several of the Constituents—Le Chapelier, Gérard, dom Gerle, and Lafayette himself—wielding a shovel or pushing a wheelbarrow. Virtually all of the deputy witnesses walked out to watch the spectacle, and few episodes left them more uniformly impressed.[123] All commented on the goodwill and good humor of those involved, on the spirit of equality and mutual assistance, on the lack of envy or fights or squabbles of any kind. "It is impossible to express the enthusiasm which reigns in Paris at this moment" (Lepoutre); "it is a magnificent sight and a crushing blow against the aristocracy" (Lilia); "there is no parallel in all of history, and it is unlikely that there will ever be one" (Boullé).[124] The Federation preparation became a kind of metaphor for the Revolution and the people's triumph over the obstacles to liberty.

By the second week of July, national guardsmen from all over the kingdom began arriving in the city. For a period of ten days, the Assembly's spectator galleries were exclusively reserved for the visitors, with each deputy allotted a certain number of tickets for their constituencies. Deputies

[122] *AP*, 17:83; Toulongeon, 1:219–20; Gottschalk and Maddox, 531–32.

[123] E.g., Vernier, letters of July 9 and 13; Jean-François Gaultier de Biauzat, *Gaultier de Biauzat, député du Tiers état aux Etats généraux de 1789. Sa vie et sa correspondance*, ed. Francisque Mège, 2 vols. (Clermont-Ferrand, 1890), 2:324 (letter of July 8); Maupetit, 21 (1905), 206 (letter of July 10); Lameth, 2:451–54; Rabaut, 270–73; Toulongeon, 1:215–16; Gottschalk and Madox, 509–11.

[124] Lepoutre, letter of July 10; Lilia, letter of July 9; Boullé, letter of July 13.

found themselves spending much of their time greeting and entertaining the recent arrivals. Gaultier went out to Villejuif for the formal entrance ceremonies of those from his home province of Auvergne, meeting them with a detachment of Paris guardsmen and then marching around Paris to all of the principal political centers. He made arrangements for everyone to meet each evening in a café at a corner of the Palais Royal to recount the day's events. Boullé did much the same with the Bretons, especially his friends and neighbors from Pontivy, helping them find lodging with the Parisians. Lafayette invited over a hundred guardsmen to his house for dinner, setting up a tent for that purpose in the garden.[125]

Unfortunately, Federation Day itself was not well served by the weather.[126] As the deputies left their hall about 10 A.M. to join the general procession, they were met by a driving downpour, with strong winds that rendered their umbrellas useless. Successive waves of rain continued throughout the day, leaving everyone muddy and soaked to the skin. Yet the mood remained upbeat, and as they left the Tuileries Gardens and began their march, they were met with enormous enthusiasm from the huge crowds of spectators lining the route and cheering from sidewalks, windows, and trees.[127] With Lafayette and a first detachment of the Paris national guard in the lead, they proceeded in two columns of two deputies each across the Place royale, down the right bank of the Seine, and over a specially constructed pontoon bridge at Chaillot into the Champ-de-Mars on the left bank. As they entered through the newly built triumphal arch, the view from the floor of the stadium left an unforgettable impression. They were at the end of a huge arena, more than three-quarters of a kilometer in length, "transformed as if by magic," with three or four hundred thousand people cheering, while bands played and cannons fired. The first units of the national guard had already taken their places, with their brilliant, multicolored uniforms and a myriad of flags and banners. At the center of the field stood a great round pedestal, with stairs leading up from all sides to the altar of the nation, "designed in the new style," "with a simple and classical form," where some two hundred priests wearing tricolor sashes prepared to officiate.[128] The two columns of deputies split as they walked around the altar and proceeded to their seats at the far end of the arena, in a specially constructed pavilion just outside the Ecole militaire. Then they waited and watched for three hours as the remaining guardsmen of the eighty-three departments and the military men of the various services entered and took their places. At last, Louis entered, bedecked in his finest royal robes. He was seated on

[125] *AP*, 16:153; Gaultier, 2:326–29 (letter of July 13); Boullé (letter of July 13); Gottschalk and Maddox, 520–21.

[126] The following description is based on a compilation of various of the deputy accounts. See also Gottschalk and Maddox, 535–48; and Leclercq, *La Fédération*, 339–59.

[127] Gaultier, 2:330–31 (letter of July 15); Ménard, 244 (letter of July 15); Schwendt, *Revue d'Alsace* 78 (1931), 228 (letter of July 14).

[128] Lameth, 2:463; Gaultier, 2:330 (letter of July 15).

a relatively simple royal throne, next to a chair for the National Assembly president, and surrounded by the deputies themselves. The royal family, the court, and the ministers were relegated to another section of the pavilion, away from the center of power. No one could miss the symbolism of the seating arrangements, and the striking transformation since the ceremony of May 5, 1789 in the hall of the Menus Plaisirs.

After bishop Talleyrand and his two hundred assistants had celebrated the mass, the oath ceremony itself began. Lepoutre noted with satisfaction that just at this moment the rains abated and a few rays of sun emerged—though he could not decide if it was the result of divine intervention, or of the dissipating effects of the Revolutionaries' cannon fire.[129] Lafayette read out the oath for the armed forces, which the forty thousand men present immediately affirmed. Then the deputies stood at their seats and repeated the more simple oath which they had already taken the previous February. Finally, the monarch stood, raised his right hand, and in a loud and firm voice pronounced his own oath: "I, king of the French, do swear to use all powers delegated to me by the constitutional laws of the state to maintain the constitution decreed by the National Assembly and accepted by me, and to assure the execution of the laws." In these solemn words, sworn before an altar by a man who took religion seriously, Louis seemed once again fully to accept his role as constitutional monarch. Although the king's pronouncement did not carry well throughout the immense stadium, word of his oath passed from person to person through the crowd, and a great roar of approval spread like a wave to the far end of the stadium, some eight hundred meters away, followed by long and repeated shouts of "vive le roi."[130] After the final *Te Deum* offering thanks to God and the blessing of the flags of the armed contingents, the deputies returned to their hall by the same route, tired, muddy, and hungry—but thrilled at the day's proceedings and greatly relieved that all had passed peacefully.[131]

The festival continued another week after the oathtaking ceremony, always in the same spirit of peace, brotherhood, and unity. The king went out on at least three more occasions to review troops, on the Champ de Mars or along the Champs-Elysées. There were boating jousts on the Seine, and balloon ascensions, and endless feasts and dances to which the deputies were invariably invited. There was also a formal consecration of the "oriflamme," a re-creation of the sacred banner of the medieval kings, long housed in the church of Saint-Denis but lost to the English during the Hundred Years' War. Modified to include the words "Fédération" and "Constitution"—hardly medieval in conception—it was now presented to the Assembly rather than to the king, and suspended from the ceiling vault

[129] Lepoutre, letter of July 16.

[130] *AP* 17:85; and, e.g., Lameth, 2:464–65; Gaultier, 2:330–31 (letter of July 15); Ferrières, 240–41 (letter of July 18); Ménard, 244 (letter of July 15).

[131] Pierre Ludière to the municipality of Tulle: A.D. Corrèze, 1 E Dep. 272–199, letter of July 18; Campmas, letter of July 17–18; Lindet, 207 (letter of July 16).

above the deputies' heads.[132] Perhaps most memorable of all were the nightly "illuminations." In a world without electric lighting, the appearance of thousands of colored Persian lanterns throughout the city produced a stunning effect. The deputies were particularly impressed by the lamps suspended from the ruins of the Bastille, as the Parisians sang and danced, and from trees and ropes along the Champs-Elysées, where orchestras played and families of all classes picnicked on the grass during the long summer twilight. For Toulongeon, it was a time which "can only be described by those who experienced it. The emotions aroused by such scenes will long remain in the memories of those who took part." "There was a general feeling of exhileration and joy," wrote Maupetit. "Everyone," concluded Ménard, "now formed but a single people of brothers. One might have thought that all individuals were moved by a single soul."[133]

It was indeed an extraordinary moment. After a remarkable fourteen months, in which exuberance and terror, optimism and trauma had been constantly interwoven, events seemed at last to have fallen into place. The king, the deputies, and the whole population seemed joined together in order and harmony. Louis XVI was now at one with the Assembly, having fully accepted his status as limited king-executive. By all appearances, the moderates had triumphed in the Assembly, led by some of the finest thinkers of the Constituent, and by a general who might easily have used his popularity to seize power, but who had not done so, and who, in the estimate of the marquis de Ferrières, "had won the hearts of all the deputies."[134] If the Assembly had not yet finished its work, many of the most intractable problems had been tackled and hopefully resolved, and the deputies talked of going home by All Saints' Day. By all appearances, the Revolution was over.

[132] *AP*, 17:90 (July 15); Toulongeon, 1:224–25; Dusers, letter of July 16.

[133] Toulongeon, 1:227; Maupetit, 21 (1905), 210–11 (letter of July 19); Ménard, 244 (letter of July 15). See also Boullé, letter of July 24; Lindet, 210 (letter of July 20); Vernier, letter of July 18; Lucas-Bougeral, letter of July 20; Faulcon, 2:270–71 (letter of July 21).

[134] Ferrières, 237 (letter of July 13).

THE Revolution, of course, was not over. It was only just beginning. Yet for the deputies of the Constituent Assembly, the decrees of June 1790—the suppression of the hereditary nobility and the initial passage of the Civil Constitution of the Clergy—were perhaps the last great Revolutionary acts. Though much remained to be accomplished, and though the Assembly would prolong its existence for well over a year, the fundamental constitutional decisions had largely been made, and most of the final months would be devoted to consolidation and cleanup. It is significant that the single most powerful committee during this period, the Committee on Revisions, primarily concerned itself with the review and systematization of decrees already passed. In several instances that Committee, and the Constituent as a whole, even retreated from the spirit of the original decisions. The vanguard of Revolutionary leadership now passed outside the Assembly: to the Parisian sections, to the publishing offices of radical journalism, to a variety of clubs and national guard units in Paris and the provinces.

And nevertheless, the first year of their tenure in Versailles and Paris had been a remarkable period in the lives of the deputies, a period in which a great many had experienced a lasting transformation in their conceptions of themselves, of society, and of the nature of the body politic. Based on a close examination of the deputies' careers before and after the convocation of the Estates General and on the testimonies of over a hundred deputy-witnesses, the present study has attempted to chart this transformation in collective psychology and to evaluate certain hypotheses which scholars have proposed to explain the Revolutionary phenomenon.

One of the principal difficulties in formulating such explanations is that the Revolution was not a homogeneous and unilinear process. It developed rather in fits and starts, in a series of successive stages, each of which entailed a distinct alignment of forces, a distinct configuration of cause and consequence. For the period that concerns us, from the Pre-Revolution through the summer of 1790, our inquiry confirms the oft-cited observation of Daniel Mornet that "the origins of the Revolution is one story, the history of the Revolution another."[1] The conclusion here is that for the deputies in Versailles and Paris a pivotal moment, dividing a first phase of "origins" from a second phase of "history," occurred in the early summer of 1789.

For the first phase, our study reinforces one of the central tenets of much "revisionist" history, that a severe fiscal and political crisis of the royal government was a *sine qua non* to the outbreak of revolution. The story of this crisis has often been recounted. In part, it involved a long-term structural

[1] Daniel Mornet, *Les origines intellectuelles de la Révolution française* (Paris, 1933), 471.

problem: the need for ever greater state revenues to compete in the struggle for European supremacy, combined with an inequitable tax base and an antiquated tax assessment and collection system. In part, it entailed the effective opposition to fiscal reforms of certain powerful corporate bodies, of which the parlements were undoubtedly the most important. The monarchy's difficulties were augmented, however, by a severe failure of leadership. The inconsistency and vacillation of the last two Bourbon kings, their continual change of ministers, and their inability to sustain support for any given solution, made it impossible for the government to effect fundamental reforms, even though the need for such reforms was well understood by the ministers. Contradictions of policy left the monarchy all the more open to charges of despotism and arbitrary authority. Target had sized up the problems of Louis XVI in his private diary of 1787: "instability, increasing from day to day, in the exercise of power."[2] Indeed, at the time Target wrote, an impending bankruptcy had brought the government to a near standstill. For the overwhelming majority of the population, for whom state finance remained utterly mysterious, this crisis was altogether unanticipated. "The French people," reflected Pétion in early 1789, "are quite astonished by the present situation; they have arrived at this point without having anticipated it." "It is not the Nation who made the Revolution," Doctor Campmas would write in November 1789. "If it had still been possible to keep the machine running, we would never have been called."[3]

Yet the problems of the monarchy alone cannot explain the behavior of the representatives in Versailles after they were convened. In the long history of France, there were other instances of monetary crises and disastrous leadership and other meetings of the Estates General, but none had produced reactions with the scope and radical character of 1789. To understand the actions of the deputies after they were brought together, it has been necessary to study their political culture and state of mind on the eve of the Revolution. In this perspective, we have focused on three areas of deputy experience: the intellectual, the political, and the social.

Of these three areas, the deputies' intellectual experience probably had the least direct impact on their options during the initial phase of the Revolution. All of the representatives from all three orders had come into contact with elements of Enlightenment thought and language. Yet individuals might receive and adapt the diverse and often contradictory ideas of the age—or reject them altogether—in sharply differing manners. That a few of the future deputies, such as Sieyès and Volney, were strongly influenced by the more radical political thought of the Enlightenment, cannot be denied. But it is a mistake to generalize from the writings of a few intellectuals to

[2] Target's diary, printed as a supplement to Paul-Louis Target, *Un avocat du XVIIIe siècle* (Paris, 1893), 47.

[3] Jérôme Pétion de Villeneuve, *Avis aux Français sur le salut de la patrie* (n.p., 1789), 226; Jean-François Campmas to his brother, vicaire in Carmaux: B.M. Albi, Ms. 177, letter of Nov. 1.

the attitudes of the representatives as a whole. Especially in the provinces, where most of those representatives resided, the impact of the radical Enlightenment on the working assumptions of the future deputies, on their day-to-day modes of analysis, seems to have been practically nil. The small group of self-proclaimed disciples of Rousseau probably preferred the *Confessions* and the *Nouvelle Héloïse* to the *Social Contract*. Once the Revolution had begun, this group would evolve toward every conceivable point on the political spectrum, from radical Jacobinism, to moderate monarchism, to reactionary counterrevolution. The evidence explored here does not support the contention of many revisionists that Rousseau's ideas were fundamental to the deputies' political culture on the eve of the Revolution.

The Pre-Revolutionary writings of the deputies are revealing of men prepared for political reform and impatient with arbitrary authority. But they also evince a deep affection for the monarchy, an emotional attachment for which the "father king" was more than a convenient metaphor, and for which the image of the sanctified kingship was often still in vogue—even for a deist radical like Dinochau.[4] Whatever the multisecular trends in the image of the king—from the late Middle Ages through the end of the Old Regime—there is little evidence among the individuals examined here of the distinctive eighteenth-century "desacralization of the monarchy" stipulated by some historians.[5] If there was one domain in which Enlightenment ideas did penetrate the political thinking of many Third Estate deputies— and strongly affect their subsequent decisions—it was in their views on the wealth and power of the clergy. A profound anticlericalism, coexisting with a continued faith in a Christian or deist God, exercised a pervasive influence on a great number of the commoner representatives and on a scattering of the nobles as well. Indeed, for most of the men of 1789 a Voltairian passion to *"écraser l'infâme"* was far more influential than a Rousseauist obsession with the "general will."

In general, however, the deputies' writings reveal a cultural imprint much broader than that of the Enlightenment of the *philosophes*, including an interest in scholarly research of all kinds, in the classical literary genres, in science, and in the law. It was probably in the latter domain that members of the Third Estate had achieved their most eminent renown before 1789. A juridical vocabulary and mode of thought, a jurist's conception of justice and equity had an enormous impact on a whole segment of the commoner deputies. Though such a tradition was not necessarily in opposition to the Enlightenment, Bailly was convinced that the men of law and the men of letters were more often rivals than allies. The jurist authors of radical *mémoires judiciaires*—described by Sarah Maza and David Bell—were little

---

[4] In Sept. 1789, Dinochau could still speak of "adoring the sacred name and giving thanks for the person of the king": Jacques-Samuel Dinochau, *Histoire philosophique et politique de l'Assemblée constituante*, 2 vols. (Paris, 1789), 2:17–18.

[5] E.g., Jeffrey Merrick, *The Desacralization of the French Monarchy in the Eighteenth Century* (Baton Rouge, La., 1990).

present among the generally cautious lawyers and magistrates who sat in the Estates General.[6] The impatience of many of the men of law with "philosophical treatises" and "abstract metaphysics"—frequently associated by them with the writings of Sieyès—was very much in evidence during the discussions of the Rights of Man in August 1789. "Nothing is more dangerous in politics," the Breton magistrate Boullé had written, "than an abstract theory. . . . In all likelihood, it is experience alone that can teach us if a specific solution is workable or not."[7] In any case, on the eve of the Revolution, the deputies' pamphlets remained vague on the objectives of the Estates General and on the justification for change—with individual authors appealing as much to precedent, custom, history, and tradition, as to reason or natural rights.

For the most part, the deputies' political culture before the Revolution was shaped less by books and essays than by their concrete political and social experience under the Old Regime. A substantial number of the Third deputies had already gained practice in collective political processes through their participation in municipal government and local professional organizations. At least a fifth of the Third Estate deputies—and probably many more—had been mayors or other town administrators. The activities of the anti-Maupeou forces in the 1770s, and the struggles between Jansenists and Jesuits, between parlement and king, had also familiarized them with political protest at the national level. Moreover, the actions of the royal government itself, during its intermittent periods of vigor, had profound effects on the politicization of the future representatives. Many of the basic reforms which the Third Estate would soon espouse—a written constitution, fiscal equality, the opening of positions to talent—were first proposed by the government in various of its decrees. Even before the monarchy had launched the electoral process for the Estates General, it had conceived and implemented the provincial assemblies in which many of the deputies had sat. And through Brienne's decree of July 1788 and Necker's policies thereafter, it had instigated the municipal mobilization of 1788, a movement of critical importance in the political apprenticeship of the future deputies. But in addition, the actions of the government helped incite the first coherent conservative reaction, the systematic organization by late 1788 of groups dedicated to the preservation of existing social and political structures. In short, on the eve of the Revolution, the Third Estate deputies were arguably more familiar with the forms of Revolutionary politics than with the content of future Revolutionary thought. The depiction—by historians from Alexis de Tocqueville to François Furet—of the representatives of

---

[6] Sarah Maza, *Private Lives and Public Affairs: The Causes Célèbres of Prerevolutionary France* (Berkeley, 1993); David A. Bell, *Lawyers and Citizens: The Making of a Political Elite in Old Regime France* (Oxford, 1994).

[7] See above, chap. 6; also Jean-Pierre Boullé, "Ouverture des Etats-généraux de 1789," ed. Albert Macé, *Revue de la Révolution. Documents inédits* 15 (1889), 117 (letter of Sept. 8, 1789, misdated in printed version); and 16 (1889), 25 (letter of Sept. 19, 1789).

1789 as political novices, whose knowledge of public affairs was limited to the writings of Enlightenment thinkers, cannot be sustained.

As for the social experience of the deputies, the present inquiry has demonstrated the sharp difference in backgrounds and careers between members of the three orders, and above all, between Nobles and Commoners. A generation of "revisionist" scholarship has persuasively challenged the class analysis of the split between Nobility and Third Estate, and revealed that the two frequently shared a similar relationship to the dominant mode of production. But to challenge a class explanation of the Revolution, is not to put into question all social explanation—as the revisionists would seem to suggest. In fact, the divisions between the deputies of the two estates were more encompassing than those of class, and included significant differences in wealth, education, and status. From the perspective of the present inquiry, the more multivariate model of social interaction proposed by Max Weber is probably more useful than that of Marx and Engels. A large percentage of the Noble deputies were extremely wealthy aristocrats of military training and comparatively limited secondary education, for whom the ideals of hierarchy, honor, and in many cases, orthodox Catholicism were still very much alive. Indeed, a more traditional hierarchical and religious worldview could persist even among nobles, like Garron de La Bévière, who pursued a rational, "capitalist" exploitation of their seigneurial lands.

By contrast, the great majority of the Third deputies were substantially less wealthy (though frequently at the pinnacle of the local commoners), decidedly not aristocratic (though sometimes at the fringes of the legal nobility), and had passed long years at school, including extensive training in the law. There were, to be sure, numerous exceptions in both the Second and Third Estates, and a certain degree of overlap. We must not lose sight of that small minority of young liberal aristocrats sitting in the Second Estate, many of whom would play leadership roles in the course of the Constituent. Yet the great majority of the deputies of the two orders resided in two very different social and cultural universes.

To what extent such differences in social experience had engendered a self-conscious sense of conflict and injustice on the part of the future Third Estate representatives is difficult to ascertain. Most of the latter were successful men from families who had prospered over several generations, men who had necessarily to follow the dictates of the Old Regime value system, and for whom open expressions of resentment could have been self-defeating and dangerous. A minority of intellectuals—like Périsse Du Luc or Delandine—may have thought of themselves, and dreamed of being accepted, as members of a common Enlightened elite, a "nobility of talent." But a great many others could not have been impervious to the gap between rhetoric and reality. The explosion of antinoble sentiments in 1788–89 was suggestive of a long festering anger on the part of many future Third deputies—witness the testimony of Gaultier de Biauzat on his previously repressed hatred of the aristocrats. Attacks leveled against the nobility, for their status pretensions and privileges as much as for their specific policies, were among the most pervasive unifying elements in the Third's brochure literature in the months preceding the opening of the Estates General. The equally vigorous defense of privilege and noble superiority which burst forth from the Second Estate at almost the same time, was indicative of the Nobility's sensitivity and fear of Third resentment.

But whatever the social tensions experienced by the deputies before May 1789, whatever their desires for reform, whatever the extent of their political apprenticeship, few of the future Constituents had anticipated the transformations that were about to take place. For the great majority, it was only after May 5, in the extraordinarily creative process of the Assembly itself, that a "Revolution of the Mind" came about. Once again, a failure of leadership on the part of the monarchy played a role in the developing collective psychology. If the king had immediately presented the Estates General with a program, the majority of the Third would very likely have followed. But in fact, no such program was announced, and many commoners soon became convinced that the "good monarch" had now decided to place the fate of the nation in their hands. Without intending it, the king, by his very inaction, contributed in conveying the idea of self-determination, and in strengthening the Third Estates' sense of power and self-confidence. The emergence of a Revolutionary psychology also involved an element of group interaction. The assemblage of so many highly motivated and talented men, a number of whom were articulate orators, generated a dynamic of mutual encouragement, emulation, and instruction, a collective "therapy" that rapidly took on a life of its own. The dynamic was amplified through the intensity and emotion of the experience, through the weeks of alternating frustration and exhilaration, which all witnesses described as the most momentous period of their lives. It was strengthened, in addition, by the great crowds of people who followed and cheered the efforts of the Third from the streets and from the galleries. By their continued presence and active expression of support, the crowds and spectators instilled in the deputies a new meaning for the phrase "public opinion," very different from the abstract, literary conception of the Old Regime. With the soaring rhetoric, the support of the crowds, the perceived support of the king, and their successive triumphs over apparently insurmountable obstacles, the commoners developed a sense of optimism, a feeling that they were on the wings of destiny.

Assembly meetings also entailed an intense pedagogical experience, as many of the finest minds of the country shared their diverse perspectives—some long contemplated, others improvised for the moment—listened to one another, reacted to one another, evolving new ideas as they went, or picking and selecting from the vast corpus of eighteenth-century thought. Frequently the "school of the Revolution" held session in a series of great debates: those of May 13–18 on the strategy to be used with the Nobility; of June 15–17 on the rights of the Assembly and the seat of sovereignty; of

July 7–8 on the nature of deputy mandates. Though the more radical alignment of the Breton delegation—fresh from its bitter confrontation with the provincial nobility—played a significant role in these debates, it by no means dominated them. Indeed, the Bretons' proposals were initially repudiated and rejected by the majority.

The Assembly process also served to crystallize and intensify social antagonisms, making many deputies far more self-conscious of those antagonisms than ever before. Throughout May and June a group dynamic, parallel to that developing within the Third Estate, was also operative among the Nobles and the Clergy, a dynamic that pushed the majority of the privileged in quite the opposite direction, toward ever more conservative and intransigent positions. Despite the efforts of the small liberal minority, the preponderance of the Nobles took the lead in rejecting any form of compromise and in extolling the virtues of caste privilege. The Third deputies reacted strongly to this intransigence, but perhaps even more strongly to the Nobles' social attitudes toward them. The commoner witnesses, even many who had not previously expressed social hostilities, commented on the intolerable haughtiness and arrogance of their opponents. It was in the face of this experience that the arguments of the Breton group had their greatest impact and that the club, for a time, was able to organize debate in the Third Estate. More than an intellectual position, the Third's attitude toward the Nobles appeared as an instinctive and visceral antipathy. Indeed, we should not underestimate the extent to which the commoners' actions were energized by a revolt against scorn and condescension. Social animosity, born of a status struggle more than of a class struggle, was perhaps the single most potent ingredient in the origins of a Revolutionary psychology in June 1789.

For some individuals, the conviction that a new political order and a new system of social values could actually be realized, swept over them suddenly, with all the force of a conversion experience. For others, the change would develop more gradually and with much hesitation in the course of the following weeks and months. But in most cases, it was only after the Revolutionary dynamic had been set in motion that the deputies began to "understand" the more radical political proposals of the Enlightenment thinkers and of the Breton group and its following. It was in early June that Maupetit attained a new understanding of the abbé Sieyès's brochure which he had first read the previous February. It was only after the fact, that many deputies began to evolve a coherent ideology—or rather several different ideologies—to explain and justify their actions, ideologies in which diverse elements of eighteenth-century thought were brought together and synthesized. Specific references in deputy testimonies to the ideas of the Enlightenment, largely absent in May and early June, became more common in the summer and fall of 1789. The letters and diaries of our witnesses confirm the suggestions of Roger Chartier that a cohesive concept of the "Enlightenment" was as much a product of the Revolution as the Revolution was a product of the Enlightenment.[8]

The initial phase of the Revolution also witnessed a reevaluation of royal authority, as the deputies began issuing decrees implicitly asserting their sovereignty for writing a constitution and levying taxes. Yet even after the creation of the National Assembly, many deputies avoided drawing the logical conclusions of their actions, hoping—if they actually articulated their feelings—that the will of the king and the will of the nation would remain inseparable. Most Third deputies were prepared to question the political and social power of the nobility well before they questioned the powers of the monarchy. Even among many of the radicals, the kingship long retained a fascination, an almost emotional attraction. These resilient bonds of affection help explain the Assembly's extraordinarily emotional reception of Louis XVI on July 15 and again on February 4.

After the first phase of the Revolution, the period from late June to early August appears as a transitional interlude. For a time numerous conservative and aristocratic elements of the two privileged orders—outraged by their forced merger with the National Assembly and terrified by the mid-July crisis—fled or returned home to seek new instructions from their electorates. The rump remaining, predominantly liberal or moderate in its opinions, experienced a period of relative internal harmony and good feelings, a sentiment of camaraderie that was reinforced by the dramatic common experiences of July. Such sentiments of brotherhood were a significant factor in creating the atmosphere of the Night of August 4. Yet for some deputies of all three orders it was also a period of great volatility and uncertainty, leading to a substantial reevaluation and recrystallization of political alliances, a process that was accelerated following the return in August of the errant aristocratic conservatives. In the weeks and months that followed, during what we have termed the "second phase" of the Revolution, a new constellation of cause and effect came into play in the collective psychology of the deputies, a constellation in which contingent circumstances, constituency pressures, and factional politics were of particular importance.

The Revolutionary consciousness was affected, in part, by a series of outside events impinging on the decisions and perceptions of the deputies. It was the Great Fear, the deterioration of the royal bureaucracy, and the general breakdown in civil obedience through the autumn of 1789 which compelled the deputies to encroach on an "executive authority" once deemed untouchable, and to improvise responses for all manner of questions which they had never previously considered. It was the impending state bankruptcy which forced them to reevaluate their initial opposition to the seizure of church land and the reorganization of the French clergy. It was the

[8] Roger Chartier, *The Cultural Origins of the French Revolution* (Durham, N.C., 1991), 5, 87–89.

threat of war in the spring of 1790 which led many individuals to an expanded vision of a Revolution that would transform international relations.
Elected to advise the king on a constitution, the representatives rapidly became involved in sweeping reforms of laws and institutions, so that the
"Constituent" became a de facto "legislative" assembly as well. The members found themselves compelled to create an increasing number of committees to confront and adapt solutions to a whole array of new and unanticipated problems. The school of the Revolution continued to convene in
periodic major debates to grapple with such problems: in August and September on the relations of the king and the legislature; in October–November, mid-December, and again in April 1790 on the disposition of church
property; and in May 1790 on control over the judiciary and over military
and foreign policy.

The period after June 1789 also witnessed a growing influence on the
Assembly of deputy constituencies. While a few of the members sought to
impose their own vision of the Revolution on the voters they represented,
most professed a heavy sense of responsibility toward the views of those
voters and a willingness to present their views within the Assembly. Initially
tenuous and haphazard, correspondence between deputies and a variety of
municipal or regional committees soon developed into a veritable institution—especially in the months before the new administrative system could
be organized. But not all members had the same conception of those to be
included within their "constituencies." Most of the Third Estate deputies
identified with the relatively small milieu of urban notables from which the
deputies themselves had originated and with whom they were most closely
in contact. Very few would have incorporated the peasantry into their
working definition of representation. However, a small but influential minority—essentially those associated with the more radical members of the
Jacobin club—came to see the lower classes and especially the Parisian population as an essential element in their constituency. Very early, this minority began pushing a far more democratic vision of representation in which
popular sovereignty meant the sovereignty of the entire male population,
and in which the voice of the masses, even when expressed in actions of
violence, was endowed with a certain mystique.[9] A tolerance of individual
deputies toward collective violence in July and August was one of the best
predictors of later political radicalism. The majority of the deputies, however, after a brief flirtation with the urban masses in June and early July
1789, became frightened and repelled by popular uprisings and by the very
idea of universal democracy.

Finally, from the summer of 1789 the Revolutionary activities of the deputies were increasingly influenced by political factionalism. To be sure, em-
bryonic factions had existed since the Pre-Revolutionary period. By late

[9] Cf. Jack Richard Censer, *Prelude to Power. The Parisian Radical Press, 1789–1791* (Baltimore, 1976), esp. chap 3.

1788 a "patriot party" originating in the provinces and municipalities—and supported subsequently by the more recently formed Committee of Thirty—was confronting a rival conservative, "aristocratic party," inspired by Eprémesnil's "committee of one hundred" in Paris and by various grassroots reactions in the provinces. Once in Versailles, the organized activities of the Dauphiné delegation and the Breton club were countered from the earliest days by conservative "clubs" formed among both the Nobility and the Clergy. Following the brief popular front of July and August, the new conservative alignment of the Monarchiens, in alliance with the extreme right, appeared for a time as the best organized faction in the Constituent. But the most intense polarization of the Assembly occurred after the October Days. The popular violence in the midst of Versailles and the forced return of the king to Paris had a powerful effect in hardening positions and in creating the inveterate opposition of the right and the right's suspicion of the entire Patriot agenda. Still, the events of October did not bring the immediate triumph of the patriots. The Friends of the Constitution—created in late November on the model of the Monarchiens—directly inspired the organization of the conservative Impartials and Capuchins. While most of these groups were umbrella coalitions, uniting a range of positions, the radical Jacobins—those remaining after the formation of the Society of 1789 as a political coalition—rapidly acquired the characteristics of a modern political party, with a central committee, a national organization, a platform, and tight voting discipline. By means of such "parties" it was possible for relatively small groups of effective speakers and organizers, well placed in the clubs' governing committees, to control and concentrate leadership to a far greater degree than during the first phase of the Revolution. Yet even in 1790 no one individual, nor even small groups of individuals, were able to exercise effective domination of the Assembly—as Mirabeau himself would ruefully attest.

The political dialectic of action and reaction between factions, between Monarchiens and Patriots, and later between Capuchins and Jacobins, increasingly dominated the life of the Assembly and added a whole new character to Revolutionary psychology.[10] The rivalries were all the more intense in that there was a clear social character to many of the alignments. The conservative groups were overwhelmingly dominated by the privileged orders, especially wealthy aristocratic soldiers and various elements of the clergy. The radical Jacobins, by contrast, consisted primarily of men of law and lesser officials, often relatively modest in their fortunes and careers, and commonly residing in small towns or in rural areas. In this sense, sociocultural divisions among the deputies persisted as a powerful force in shaping perceptions and politics within the Assembly.

---

[10] Cf. the thesis of D.M.G. Sutherland, *France, 1789–1815: Revolution and Counterrevolution* (Oxford, 1985), who sees a similar dialectical interaction operative at the national level between "revolutionary" and "counterrevolutionary" impulses.

But the radical Jacobins were never able to dominate the proceedings during the first year of the Revolution. Indeed, by the spring of 1790, a synthesis seemed to have emerged in the political dialectic through the rise to prominence of the Society of 1789. Led by some of the most eminent thinkers and liberal nobles of the Assembly, the new coalition was especially successful in attracting a following among the majority of deputies who had previously refused adherence to any party, but who were now prepared to support a rapprochement with the king in order to bring the Revolution to a close.

An analysis of the breakdown of that political synthesis after the summer of 1790 and the Assembly's failure to end the Revolution would carry us well beyond the purview of the present study. It would necessitate a consideration of both the final fifteen months of the Constituent Assembly and the period of the Legislative Assembly that followed. In retrospect, the triumph of the Society of 1789 appears as only a brief hiatus in a moving reality, an alignment soon swept away, almost out of memory, by the evolving events. By the second half of 1790, the alliance on the right was rapidly dissolving through the lassitude and departures of its adherents, disillusioned by their failure to achieve their objectives through parliamentary methods. Thereafter, the Eighty-niners, already beset by internal rivalries, would find that the center position they had sought to occupy was progressively isolated and perceived as a de facto right. By the autumn, a revitalized Jacobin contingent would take definitive control of the elections of Assembly officers, both the presidents and secretaries.

But the Assembly would also find itself increasingly isolated from substantial elements of the French population. Some of the Constituents' later difficulties were of their own making. The exclusion of a segment of the population from political participation and the decision to abolish seigneurial dues only after the lords had been reimbursed for their "property" were contributing factors in the origins of future insurrections. The Civil Constitution of the Clergy and the later requirement of a religious oath from all parish clergymen provoked enormous opposition and untold complications in the provinces. A substantial segment of the clergy throughout the kingdom would be thrown into the hands of the "counterrevolution"— along with large elements of the lay population who supported that clergy. In no area of its law making was the Constituent so moved by ideological considerations as in its policies on the clergy and religion.

Yet for the most part, the Assembly's actions were not ideologically driven. We have seen that the most important contingent of leadership during the first year of the Revolution came not from the philosophers and the men of letters, but from the lawyers and jurists; and that a juridical culture, a juridical mode of thought continued as a prominent element in much of the Constituent's activities. Most of these deputies revealed themselves to be practical men, intense and passionate, yet pragmatic and capable of compromise. Indeed, a case can be made that under normal conditions, the Constitution which they completed in September 1791 might well have been viable. The history of democracy since the eighteenth century has demonstrated the potential for success of a wide array of specific institutional arrangements. But the one crisis which the Revolutionaries were never able to overcome was the renunciation of the very idea of constitutional monarchy by a substantial segment of the aristocratic elite and by the reigning monarch himself. Though for a time the conservative aristocracy in the Assembly had been willing to play by the rules of the new political system, by the summer of 1790—with the passage of the Civil Constitution and the suppression of the nobility—a large number had ceased participating and had abandoned the experiment altogether. By the beginning of 1792, half of the former Second Estate deputies had left France, many of them to enter into armed rebellion against the very regime which their Assembly had just created. And even before the end of the session, on June 21, 1791, Louis XVI would attempt to flee his kingdom, denouncing the Constituent deputies as "rebels," indicating his rejection of the bulk of the Assembly's decrees, and leaving open the possibility of repressing the new Revolutionary government by force with the aid of foreign powers. The Flight to Varennes, in particular, the capture of Louis and his family, and the deputies' actions in forcing the king to rule under a constitution he had openly rejected—and through which he retained, nevertheless, a suspensive veto—was to leave a tragic flaw at the core of the first Revolutionary settlement. It was a tragedy which the first French constitution and the government it established would never succeed in overcoming.

Marriage Dowries of Deputies in *Livres*

THIRD ESTATE DEPUTIES

Name	Occupation	Residence	Date	Bride's Dowry	Dowry Value in 1787[1]
Alquier[2]	Advoc.Gen.	La Rochelle	1781	50,000	52,000
Audier-Massillon[3]	Bail.Judge	Aix	1779	60,000	62,400
Begouën-Demeaux[4]	Wholesaler	Le Havre	1776	640,000	627,200
Bévière[5]	Notary	Paris	1758	60,000	73,800
Boulouvard[6]	Wholesaler	Arles	1764	22,000	32,120
Bourdon[7]	Procureur	Dieppe	1774	18,000	16,200
Buzot[8]	Lawyer	Evreux	1784	14,000	11,060
Camus[9]	Lawyer	Paris	1766	40,000	42,400
Chavoix[10]	Proc./Law.	Brive	1768	12,250	9,065
Chasset[11]	Lawyer	Villefranche	1776	16,500	16,170
Chenon de Beaumont[12]	Tax Judge	Le Mans	1772	15,000	12,450
Cigongne[13]	Wholesaler	Saumur	1761	9,000*	11,700

*One-half of common dowry; individual portions unknown.

[1]To take into account fluctuations in French currency, sums have been transformed into their value in the *livre* of 1787, based on data for trends in the price of grain: Ernest Labrousse, *La crise de l'économie française à la fin de l'Ancien régime et au début de la Révolution* (Paris, 1944), 625.
[2]H. Perrin de Boussac, *Un témoin de la Révolution et de l'Empire: Charles-Jean-Marie Alquier* (Paris, 1983), 18–19.
[3]*DC.*
[4]A.D. Seine-Maritime, 2 C 1826 (July 2, 1776).
[5]*DC.*
[6]*DC.*
[7]A.D. Seine-Maritime, 2 C 592 (May 7, 1774).
[8]Jacques Hérissay, *Un Girondin, François Buzot* (Paris, 1907), 22.
[9]Albert Mathiez, "La fortune de Camus," *AR* 15 (1923), 334–37.
[10]A.D. Gironde, 3 E 13 159 (Feb. 6, 1768), copy kindly provided by Jean Boutier.
[11]A.D. Rhône, 10 C 2151 (Jan. 8, 1776).
[12]A.D. Sarthe, II C 2566 (Oct. 5, 1772).
[13]A.D. Maine-et-Loire, C 3135 (Apr. 20, 1761).

APPENDIX I *cont'd.*

Name	Occupation	Residence	Date	Bride's Dowry	Dowry Value in 1787
Cochon[14]	Bail.Judge	Fontenay/Comte	1774	20,000	18,000
Cottin[15]	Land Owner	Nantes	1783	38,000	39,900
Delandine[16]	Librarian	Lyon	1779	51,500	53,560
Desmazières[17]	Bail.Judge	Angers	1772	16,000	13,280
Drevon[18]	Lawyer	Langres	1772	16,000	13,280
Dubois[19]	Procureur	Châtellerault	1770	20,000	14,800
Dubois-Crancé[20]	Ex-Soldier	Vitry/François	1772	50,000	41,500
Filleau[21]	Bail.Judge	Niort	1772	10,000	8,300
Fontenay[22]	Manufacturer	Rouen	1770	50,000*	37,000
Guinebaud[23]	Wholesaler	Nantes	1777	30,000	30,000
Lebrun[24]	Land Owner	Dourdan	1777	256,000	256,000
Le Couteulx[25]	Banker	Rouen	1775	646,983	504,646
Lepoutre[26]	Farmer	Linselles	1772	11,500	9,545
Ménard de La Groye[27]	Bail.Judge	Le Mans	1772	60,000	49,800
Merle[28]	Lawyer	Mâcon	1779	25,000	26,000
Meynier[29]	Wholesaler	Nîmes	1753	60,000	73,800

*One-half of common dowry; individual portions unknown.

[14]Philip Dawson, *Provincial Magistrates and Revolutionary Politics in France, 1789–1795* (Cambridge, Mass., 1972), 89–90.

[15]*DC.*

[16]A.D. Rhône, 3 E 17419 (May 5, 1779).

[17]A.D. Maine-et-Loire, C 555 (Apr. 24, 1772).

[18]A.D. Haute-Marne, 2 C 27/476–79 (Aug. 4, 1772).

[19]P. Dubois-Destrizais, "Nouvelles recherches sur Jean-Claude Dubois, constituant, maire de Châtellerault," *Bulletin de la Société des antiquaires de l'Ouest*, 4e série, 9 (1967), 193–218.

[20]A.N., C 353.

[21]A.D. Deux-Sèvres, 3 Q 18/715 (Apr. 22, 1772).

[22]A.D. Seine-Maritime, 2 C 1804 (Nov. 7, 1770).

[23]A.D. Loire-Atlantique, II C 3002 (Apr. 22, 1777).

[24]*DC.* This is Charles-François Lebrun.

[25]A.D. Seine-Maritime, 2 C 1822 (June 17, 1775).

[26]*DC.* Date of marriage estimated. He received 6,260 florins at a time when there were approximately 1.84 florins to the *livre.*

[27]Pierre Ballu, *François Ménard de La Groye (1742–1815). Magistrat manceau* (Le Mans, 1962), 10.

[28]A.D. Saône-et-Loire, C 3113 (July, 31, 1779).

[29]*DC.*

APPENDIX I *cont'd.*

Name	Occupation	Residence	Date	Bride's Dowry	Dowry Value in 1787
Milscent[30]	Bail.Judge	Angers	1780	40,000	43,200
Mougins[31]	Lawyer	Grasse	1777	43,000	43,000
Mounier[32]	City Judge	Grenoble	1782	10,000	10,700
Paccard[33]	Lawyer	Chalon	1778	10,000	10,100
Pellerin[34]	Lawyer	Nantes	1780	12,000	12,960
Repoux[35]	Lawyer	Autun	1774	18,000**	16,200
Ricard[36]	Bail.Judge	Nîmes	1777	20,000	20,000
Roederer[37]	Parl.Judge	Metz	1777	24,000	24,000
Roussier[38]	Wholesaler	Marseille	1774	40,000	36,000
Sallé de Choux[39]	Law Prof.	Bourges	1777	20,000	20,000
Sancy[40]	Chât.Judge	Chalon	1756	14,500	17,835
Sollier[41]	Lawyer	Marseille	1774	15,300	13,770
Thévenot[42]	Lieut.de Pol.	Langres	1773	7,950	6,519
Thoret[43]	Doctor	Bourges	1777	8,000	8,000
Verdollin[44]	Lawyer	Annot	1770	13,000	9,620

**Groom's dowry; bride's dowry unknown.

[30]A.D. Maine-et-Loire, C 574 (Apr. 9, 1780).
[31]Mougins de Roquefort family archives, Château de Roquefort, livre de raison.
[32]*DC.*
[33]A.D. Saône-et-Loire, C 1604 (Sept. 7, 1778).
[34]A.D. Loire-Atlantique, II C 3017 (Apr. 23, 1780).
[35]A.D. Saône-et-Loire, C 1039 (Jan. 9, 1774).
[36]*DC.*
[37]Kenneth Margerison. *Pierre-Louis Roederer, Political Thought and Practice during the French Revolution* (Philadelphia, 1983), 6.
[38]A.D. Bouches-du-Rhône, 2 C 1529 (Jan. 27, 1774).
[39]*DC.*
[40]A.D. Saône-et-Loire, C 1666 (Mar. 6, 1756).
[41]A.D. Bouches-du-Rhône, 2 C 1602 (June 12, 1774).
[42]A.D. Haute-Marne, 4 E 44/577 (Apr. 27, 1773).
[43]*DC.*
[44]Fichier Lefebvre.

NOBLE DEPUTIES

Name	Occupation	Residence	Date	Bride's Dowry	Dowry Value in 1787
Ballidart[45]	Prés.Judge	Vitry	1772	20,000	16,600
Bureaux de Pusy[46]	Soldier	Besançon	1792	100,000	100,000
Burignot[47]	Bail.Judge	Chalon	1786	125,000**	135,000
Cipières, Mq.[48]	Soldier	Marseille	1764	130,000	189,800
Guilhem, Mq.[49]	Naval Off.	Arles	1774	50,000	45,000
La Bévière[50]	Ex-Soldier	Longes	1770	84,000	62,160
Lameth, Ct.[51]	Sold/Court	Paris	1784	822,500 +	649,775 +
Le Carpentier[52]	Parl.Judge	Rouen	1775	140,000	109,200
Le Peletier[53]	Parl.Judge	Paris	1786	298,916	322,829
Luxembourg, Dc.[54]	Ex-Soldier	Paris	1771	400,000	288,000
Marsanne, Ct.[55]	Ex-Soldier	Montélimar	1773	120,000	98,400
Perrigny, Mq.[56]	Ex-soldier	Le Mans	1760	60,000	73,800
Poix, Pr.[57]	Sold/Court	Paris	1767	1,131,833	1,029,968
Vincent[58]	Ex-Soldier	Trévoux	1764	86,000	125,560

**Groom's dowry; bride's dowry unknown.

[45]A.D. Aube, 2 C 197 (May 31, 1772).
[46]Jean Girardot, "Un ami de Lafayette," *Bulletin de la Société d'agriculture, lettres, sciences et arts de la Haute-Saône* (1957), 14.
[47]A.D. Saône-et-Loire, C 1668 (Oct. 22, 1786).
[48]A.D. Bouches-du-Rhône, 2 C 1509 (Aug. 28, 1764).
[49]A.D. Bouches-du-Rhône, 2 C 367 (Feb. 21, 1774).
[50]A.D. Rhône, 10 C 1096–97 (Nov. 27, 1770).
[51]A.D. Val-d'Oise, E 1677, Apr. 6, 1784. The value of declared items in the dowry was 822,500 *livres*. But this did not include two plantations in Saint-Domingue, whose value was not declared.
[52]A.D. Seine-Maritime, 2 C 1821 (May 9, 1775).
[53]A.N., 90 AP 50 (1) (May 4–6, 1786).
[54]Paul Filleul, *Le duc de Montmorency-Luxembourg* (Paris, 1939), 27–29.
[55]Paul Messié. "Le comte de Marsane-Fontjuliane, député de Montélimar aux premières assemblées révolutionnaires," *Bulletin de la Société départementale d'archéologie et de statistique de la Drôme* 76 (1964), 75.
[56]*DC.*
[57]A.N., Minutier central, Etude LXXXVIII, t. 711 (Sept. 1767).
[58]A.D. Rhône, 10 C 1062–63 (May 23, 1764).

Estimated Deputy Fortunes and Incomes in *Livres* at the End of the Old Regime

THIRD ESTATE DEPUTIES

Name	Occupation	Residence	Total Fortune	Estimated Income[1]
Anson[2]	Royal Admn.	Paris		40,000
Boulouvard[3]	Wholesaler	Arles		4,000
Camus[4]	Lawyer	Paris		23,000
Delaville[5]	Wholesaler	Lorient		12,600
Durand de Maillane[6]	Lawyer	St.-Rémy	100,000	[20,000]
Faulcon[7]	Bail.Judge	Poitiers		7,200
François[8]	Farmer	Marsac	70,000	[3,500]
Gérard[9]	Planter	St.-Domingue	1,400,000	[70,000]
Lepoutre[10]	Farmer	Linselles		2,000
Maupetit[11]	Seign.Admn.	Mayenne		75,000

[1]Figures in brackets are estimated all or in part from the individual's total fortune, where income is assumed to be one-twentieth of the fortune, a quotient for estimations widely used in the eighteenth century.

[2]*AP*, 9:407 (Oct. 10, 1789). He offered 12,000 *livres* as a gift to the nation, declaring this to be somewhat more than a fourth of his revenues.

[3]Pierre-Siffren Boulouvard to the municipality of Arles: A.C. Arles, AA 23, letter of Oct. 9, 1789.

[4]Fichier Lefebvre.

[5]Joseph Delaville Le Roulx to the municipality of Lorient: A.C. Lorient, BB 13, letter of Nov. 7, 1789.

[6]Albert Mathiez, "La fortune du conventionnel Durand de Maillane," *AHRF* 3 (1926), 281–82. From his declaration of the Year IV.

[7]G. Debien, ed., "Introduction" to *Correspondance de Félix Faulcon, Tome 1: 1770–89* (Poitiers, 1939).

[8]G. de Lagrange-Ferrègues, "Jean François, député de l'Assemblée nationale de 1789," *Revue de l'Agenais* 83 (1957), 229–33.

[9]Fichier Lefebvre. This is Jean-Baptiste Gérard.

[10]*DC*.

[11]*DC*. Income from his position as financial administrator for the duchess of Mayenne in 1779.

APPENDIX II *cont'd.*

Name	Occupation	Residence	Total Fortune	Estimated Income
Pellissier[12]	Doctor	St.-Rémy		5,000
Prieur[13]	Lawyer	Châlons		1,700
Richond[14]	Lawyer	Le Puy	96,900	[4,845]
Thibaudeau[15]	Lawyer	Poitiers		6,000
Thouret[16]	Lawyer	Rouen		[13,000]

NOBLE DEPUTIES

Name	Occupation	Residence	Total Fortune	Estimated Income
Aiguillon, Dc.[17]	Court/Sold.	Paris		500,000
Antraigues, Ct.[18]	Writer	Paris		38,000
Biencourt, Mq.[19]	Soldier	Paris		50,000
Boufflers, Chev.[20]	Writer/Sold.	Paris		55,000
Châtelet, Dc.[21]	Soldier	Paris		400,000
Cocherel, Mq.[22]	Planter	St.-Domingue	1,200,000	[60,000]
Coiffier[23]	Naval Capt.	Moulins	229,000	[11,450]
Destutt de Tracy[24]	Soldier	Paris		29,000
Failly, Ct.[25]	Ex-Soldier	Vitry/François	1,550,000	[77,500]
Foucauld, Mq.[26]	Ex-Soldier	Lardimalie	600,000	[30,000]

[12]A.N., C 353, declaration of the Year IV. Estimated income from lands, excludes income from medical practice.

[13]Gustave Laurent, *Notes et souvenirs inédits de Prieur de la Marne* (Paris, 1912), 46–48.

[14]*DC.* Declaration of wealth at time of death (Oct. 1791).

[15]Antoine-Claude Thibaudeau, *Biographie, Mémoires, 1765–92* (Paris, 1875), 63.

[16]Ernest Lebègue, *La vie et l'oeuvre d'un Constituant: Thouret* (Paris, 1910), 30. In 1787 he was said to have received 7,000 *livres* in *rentes* plus the income from 120,000 *livres* in commercial investment (est. 6,000 *livres*).

[17]Daniel L. Wick, *A Conspiracy of Well-Intentioned Men: The Society of Thirty and the French Revolution* (New York, 1987), 110.

[18]L. Pingaud, *Un agent secret sous la Révolution et l'Empire* (Paris, 1893), 44.

[19]*DC.*

[20]*DC.*

[21]*DC.*

[22]*DC.*

[23]*DC.* From sale of property after emigration.

[24]*DC.* Revenues inherited in 1779.

[25]*DC.*

[26]F. Bussière, "Le constituant Foucauld de Lardimalie," *RF* 22 (1892), 214.

APPENDIX II *cont'd.*

Name	Occupation	Residence	Total Fortune	Estimated Income
La Bévière[27]	Ex-Soldier	Longes		16,000
La Chastre, Vc.[28]	Soldier	Mont		47,457
Lafayette, Mq.[29]	Court/Sold.	Paris		108,000
La Tour du Pin, Ct.[30]	Ex-Soldier	Paris		80,000
Le Peletier[31]	Parl.Judge	Paris		117,000
Liancourt, Dc.[32]	Court/Sold.	Versailles		446,000
Mercey, Bn.[33]	Ex-Soldier	Mercey		10,000
Murat, Mq.[34]	Ex-Soldier	Montfort	1,200,000	[60,000]
Orléans, Dc.[35]	Court	Paris		6,800,000
Robecq, Pr.[36]	Ex-Soldier	Paris		200,000
Satillieu, Mq.[37]	Army Engin.	Satillieu		19,000
Sillery, Mq.[38]	Ex-Soldier	Paris	2,000,000	[100,000]
St.-Simon, Mq.[39]	Ex-Soldier	Paris		100,000
Vassé, Mq.[40]	Soldier	Le Mans		90,800

[27]Claude-Jean-Baptiste de Garron de La Bévière to his wife: A.D. Ain, 1 Mi 1, letter of Aug. 6.

[28]*DC.*

[29]Louis Gottschalk and Margaret Maddox, *Lafayette in the French Revolution through the October Days* (Chicago, 1969), 19.

[30]*DC.*

[31]A.N., 90 AP 50 (2). Extrapolated from the account of his revenues of 177,623 *livres* over 18 months.

[32]*DC.*

[33]F. Grandgérard, *Le bon vieux temps. Histoire d'un village franc-comtois* (Mercey-sur-Sâone, 1911), 262–83.

[34]*DC.*

[35]*DC.*

[36]*DC.*

[37]H. Hillaire, "Journal des recettes du marquis de Satillieu," *Revue du Vivarais* 44 (1937), 86.

[38]*DC.*

[39]*DC.*

[40]Charles Girault, "La propriété foncière de la noblesse sarthoise au XVIIIe siècle," *Provence de Maine*, 2e sér., 35 (1955), 202.

Leading Deputy Speakers during the National Assembly

Name	Bailliage	Estate	Occupation	Age in 1789	Speeches
1. Camus	Paris	T	Lawyer	49	605
2. André	Aix	N	Parl.Judge	30	497
3. Le Chapelier	Rennes	T	Lawyer	35	447
4. Mirabeau, Ct.	Aix	T	Letters	40	439
5. Démeunier	Paris	T	Letters	38	435
6. Regnaud	St.-Jean-d'Angély	T	Lawyer	27	420
7. Bouche, Ch.-Fr.	Aix	T	Lawyer	52	395
8. Malouet	Riom	T	Intendant	49	354
9. Lanjuinais	Rennes	T	Law Prof.	36	353
10. Martineau	Paris	T	Lawyer	56	353
11. Barnave	Dauphiné	T	Lawyer	28	350
12. Fréteau de Saint-Just	Melun	N	Parl.Judge	44	338
13. Prieur	Châlons/Marne	T	Lawyer	33	331
14. Gaultier de Biauzat	Clermont-Ferrand	T	Lawyer	50	326
15. Maury	Péronne	C	Abbot	43	314
16. Goupil de Préfelne	Alençon	T	Bail.Judge	62	305
17. Reubell	Colmar	T	Lawyer	42	296
18. Duport	Paris	N	Parle.Judge	30	284
19. Cazalès	Rivière-Verdun	N	Caval.Offic.	31	282
20. Robespierre	Arras	T	Lawyer	31	276
21. Defermon des Chapelières	Rennes	T	Procureur	37	270
22. Folleville	Péronne	N	Milt.Offic.	40	263
23. Roederer	Metz	T	Parl.Judge	35	259
24. Chabroud	Dauphiné	T	Lawyer	39	228

Continued on next page

APPENDIX III *cont'd.*

Name	Bailliage	Estate	Occupation	Age in 1789	Speeches
25. Lameth, Ch. Ct.	Arras	N	Caval.Offic.	32	225
26. Thouret	Rouen	T	Lawyer	43	225
27. Foucauld, Mq.	Périgueux	N	Ex-Offic.	34	224
28. Pétion	Chartres	T	Subdel.Law	33	216
29. Dupont de Nemours	Nemours	T	Cons.d'Etat	50	215
30. Merlin	Douai	T	Lawyer	35	215
31. Garat, aîné	Ustaritz	T	Lawyer	54	204
32. La Rochefoucauld, Dc.	Paris	N	Letters	46	196
33. Tronchet	Paris	T	Lawyer	63	196
34. Noailles, Vc.	Nemours	N	Soldier	33	186
35. Target	Paris-hors-Murs	T	Lawyer	56	183
36. Lameth, Alex.	Péronne	N	Caval.Offic.	29	169
37. Briois de Beaumetz	Arras	N	Parle.Judge	30	167
38. Reynaud de Montlosier	Riom	N	Letters	34	165
39. Vernier	Lons-le-Saunier	T	Lawyer	58	165
40. Gouttes	Béziers	C	Curé	50	164

CONTENTS

PUBLICATION LIMITATIONS preclude the presentation of a separate bibliography. The reader is referred to the notes in the text and to the bibliographical references for individual deputies in the *DC* of Edna Lemay. The following is a selection of the principal archival and printed sources used.

ARCHIVES OF THE NATIONAL ASSEMBLY

Although the Constituent Assembly officially established its archives in the early weeks of its sessions—and named Armand-Gaston Camus its first archivist—a great many documents were subsequently lost. I have consulted primarily series C and D in the Archives nationales. Series C (nos. 14–133) includes a wide variety of materials from the Assembly's secretariat or *bureau*, including the original minutes of the Assembly, records of internal elections, resignations and requests for leaves of absence, and a considerable collection of letters and petitions received from around the kingdom. Series D (with over 40 subseries) contains the records of the Assembly committees, although many of these collections are extremely fragmentary. The loss of almost all materials from the Constitutional Committee is particularly regrettable.

GENERAL PRINTED SOURCES

Almanach royal. Paris, 1789.

Almanach de Paris. Première partie, contenant les noms et qualités des personnes de condition pour l'année 1789. Paris, 1789.

Archives parlementaires de 1787 à 1860, recueil complet des débats législatifs et politiques des chambres françaises. Première série (1787–1799), 82 vols., eds. Jérôme Mavidal, Emile Laurent, et al. Paris, 1867–1913.

Aulard, F. A. *La société des Jacobins. Recueil de documents pour l'histoire du club des Jacobins de Paris*, 6 vols. Paris, 1889–97.

Brette, Armand. *Recueil de documents relatifs à la convocation des Etats généraux de 1789*, 4 vols. Paris, 1894–1915.

Dugour, ed. *Ecole de politique, ou collection, par ordre de matières, des discours, des opinions, des déclarations de la minorité de l'Assemblée nationale*. Paris, n.d. [ca. 1791].

Ilovaïsky, Olga, ed. *Recueil de documents relatifs aux séances des Etats généraux. Tome II. Les séances de la Noblesse, 6 mai–16 juillet 1789. I. 6–27 mai.* Paris, 1974.

Journal de la Société de 1789. Paris, 5 June through 15 Sept. 1790.

Lefebvre, Georges, and Anne Terroine, eds. *Recueil de documents relatifs aux séances des Etats généraux. Tome premier. I. Les préliminaires. La séance du 5 mai.* Paris, 1953.

Lefebvre, Georges, ed. *Recueil de documents relatifs aux séances des Etats généraux. Tome premier. II. La séance du 23 juin.* Paris, 1962.

Liste par lettres alphabétiques des députés du côté droit aux Etats généraux au mois de septembre 1791. Paris, 1791.

Liste par ordre alphabétique de bailliages et sénéchaussées de MM. les députés de la majorité de l'Assemblée nationale, vulgairement appelés le côté gauche ou les enragés se disant patriotes. Paris, ca. April 1791.

Procédure criminelle instruite au Châtelet de Paris, sur la dénonciation des faits arrivés à Versailles dans la journée du 6 octobre 1789, 3 vols. Paris, 1790.

DEPUTY LETTERS, DIARIES, MEMOIRS, AND NEWSPAPERS

A central source for the present study consists of the series of correspondence, memoirs, diaries, and newspaper accounts, written by the deputies of the Estates General and the National Assembly. Manuscript and printed materials have been grouped together here, listed by individual or delegation, for easier reference. The order with which each deputy sat is indicated in parentheses: C for Clergy; N for Nobility; T for Third Estate.

Collective Testimonies

Correspondance de Bretagne, 4 vols. Rennes, 1789–90.

Correspondance de MM. les députés des communes de la province d'Anjou avec leurs commettants, relativement aux Etats généraux tenant à Versailles en 1789, 2 vols. Angers, 1789. (27 April through 15 October 1789. Said to have been written by Pilastre and Leclerc.)

"Correspondance des députés de la sénéchaussée d'Agen aux Etats généraux et à l'Assemblée nationale," ed. L. Desgraves, *Recueil des travaux de la société académique d'Agen. Sciences, lettres, et arts,* 3e sér., 1 (1967), 9–191.

Delegation of deputies from Béarn. 14 ms. letters, 30 June through 13 October 1789, signed by Mourot, Pémartin, Noussitou, Darnaudat, and the alternates, Noé and Esquille: A.D. Pyrénées-Atlantiques, C 1377.

Delegation of deputies from Besançon. 29 ms. letters, 18 Aug. 1790 through 18 July 1791, signed by Martin and Lapoule (occasionally also by Demandre): A.D. Doubs, L 167.

Delegation of deputies from Bourg-en-Bresse. 93 ms. letters, 27 Apr. 1789 through 26 Sept. 1791, signed by Populus, Bouveiron, Picquet, and/or Gautier des Orcières (occasionally also by Gueidan and Bottex): A.D. Ain, L (non-classée).

Delegation of deputies from Lyon. Ms. register of letters, 27 June 1789 through 5 Oct. 1791, signed by several deputies, but mostly written by Millanois, secretary of the Lyon delegation: B.M. Lyon, mss. 1471–73.

Delegation of deputies from Marseille. Ms. letters, May 1789 through Oct. 1791, written by the "semainier," rotating weekly among deputies of the 3 orders: Sinéty, Cipières, Villeneuve-Bargemon, Davin, Delabat, Lejeans, Castelanet, Peloux, and Roussier: A.C. Marseille, BB 358–61 and 4 D 43.

Delegation of deputies from Périgueux. 17 ms. letters, 9 Aug. 1789 through 7 Nov. 1790, signed by Loys, Fournier de La Charmie, and La Roque: A.C. Périgueux, AA 26.

Delegation of deputies from Vesoul. 5 ms. letters, 10 May through 14 June 1789, signed by Esclans and Bureaux de Pusy: A.D. Haute-Saône, E 618 and E 758.

Individual Testimonies

Note: The deputies described here as "principal witnesses" are indicated with an asterisk.

Agoult*, Jean-Antoine, comte d' (N). 11 ms. letters, 16 June through 27 Oct. 1789, to the marquis de Viennois: A.D. Isère, 1 Mi 461.

Alquier, Charles-Jean-Marie (T). 9 ms. letters, 20 June through 8 Aug. 1789, to the municipality of La Rochelle: A.M. La Rochelle. (Extracts published in H. Perrin de Boussac, *Un témoin de la Révolution et de l'Empire: Charles-Jean-Marie Alquier* [Paris, 1983].)

André*, Antoine-Balthazar-Joseph d' (N). 23 ms. letters, 1789 through 1790, to the *commissaires des communautés de Provence*: A.D. Bouches-du-Rhône, C 999.

Anonymous (N). "Correspondance d'un député de la noblesse avec la marquise de Créquy," ed. B. d'Agours, *Revue de la Révolution. Documents inédits* 2 (1883), 1–8, 33–41, 65–74, 97–104, 139–43. (13 May through 8 Aug. 1789. Deputy has not been identified.)

Antraigues, Emmanuel-Henri-Louis-Alexandre, comte d' (N). "Correspondance du marquis de Satillieu au début de la Révolution. Lettres du comte d'Antraigues," *Revue du Vivarais* 60 (1956), 69–74, 94–107. (19 letters, 5 Dec. 1788 through 18 Feb. 1789.)

Bailly*, Jean-Sylvain (T). "Correspondance de Bailly avec Necker," ed. Paul Robiquet, *RF* 19 (1890), 256–79. (4 Aug. 1789 through 7 Mar. 1791. Almost all are related to the administration of Paris.)

———. *Mémoires d'un témoin de la Révolution*, ed. Berville and Barrière, 3 vols. Paris, 1821–22. (21 Apr. through 21 Nov. 1789; little on Constituent Assembly after 15 July.)

Banyuls de Montferré*, Raymond-Antoine de (N). 24 ms. letters written with Coma-Serra, 16 May through 7 Sept. 1789, to the correspondence committee in Perpignan: A.D. Pyrénées-Orientales, C 2119. (Excerpts published in Jean Capeille, *Histoire de la maison des chevaliers de Banyuls de Montferré* [Céret, 1923], 450–60.)

Barbotin*, Emmanuel (C). *Lettres de l'abbé Barbotin*, ed. A. Aulard. Paris, 1910. (31 letters, 13 Apr. 1789 through 27 Jan. 1790, mostly to his replacement, abbé Englebert Baratte.)

Barère*, Bertrand (T). *Mémoires*, ed. Hippolyte Carnot, 4 vols. Paris, 1842–44.

———. *Le point du jour*. Paris, 19 June 1789 through 1 Oct. 1791.

Barnave*, Antoine-Pierre-Joseph-Marie (T). Ms. drafts of letters, 1789 through 1791, to diverse: A.N., W 12. (Most are undated. Some are reproduced in "Lettres inédites de Barnave," ed. M. J. de Beylié, *Bulletin de l'Académie delphinale*, 4e sér., 19 [1905], 279–305.)

Barnave*, Antoine-Pierre-Joseph-Marie (T). *Introduction à la Révolution française*, in *Oeuvres de Barnave. Vol I*, ed. Bérenger de la Drôme. Paris, 1843.

Basquiat de Mugriet*, Alexis (T). 122 ms. letters (many written jointly with Lamarque): 1) 70 copies, May through Dec. 1789, to the municipality of Bayonne: A.C. Bayonne, AA 51; and 2) 52 originals, 22 May 1789 through 17 Sept. 1791, to the municipality of Saint-Sever: A.C. St. Sever, II D 31.

Baudouin de Maisonblanche*, Jean-Marie (T). "Correspondance des députés des Côtes-du-Nord à l'Assemblée constituante," ed. D. Tempier, *Bulletin et mémoires de la Société d'émulation des Côtes-du-Nord* 27 (1889), 21–63. (25 letters, 13 Aug. 1790 through 17 Sept. 1791, written with Couppé to the municipality of Lannion.)

Begouën-Demeaux*, Jean-François (T). 162 ms. letters, 24 June 1789 through 26 Sept. 1791, sent to the municipal officers of Le Havre: A.C. Le Havre, D(3) 38–39.

Bigot de Vernières*, Jean-Joseph (C). Copies of 25 ms. letters, 9 May 1789 through 27 Aug. 1791 (6 undated), to his nephew, Bigot de Vernières, lawyer in Saint-Flour: A.D. Cantal, Fonds Delmas 176, pièces 56–156.

Biron*, Armand-Louis de Gontaud, duc de (N). *Lettres sur les Etats généraux*, ed. R. de La Lande. Paris, 1865. (Cursory, diarylike entries, 10 May through 14 Nov. 1789, sent to the chevalier de Roger in an unspecified number of letters.)

Blacons, Henri-François-Lucrétius, de (N). 3 ms. letters, 5 July through 10 Nov. 1789, to the marquis de Viennois: A.D. Isère, 1 Mi 461.

Boisgelin de Cucé*, Jean-de-Dieu-Raymond de (C). "Lettres de M. de Boisgelin, archevêque d'Aix, à la comtesse de Gramont (1776–1789)," ed. A. Cans, *RH* 79 (1902), 316–23; 80 (1902), 65–77, 301–17.

———. 24 ms. letters, summer 1789 to spring 1790 (most without dates), to the comtesse de Gramont: A.N., M 788.

Boissy d'Anglas*, François-Antoine (T). 23 ms. letters, 27 June 1789 through 6 July 1791, to Etienne Montgolfier: Archives du Musée de l'air, XVI 11–38. (Many are undated, or were misdated at a later time; they are not always in chronological order and approximate dates must be determined by internal evidence.)

———. "Lettres inédites sur la Révolution française," ed. René Puaux, *Bulletin de la Société de l'histoire du Protestantisme français* 75 (1926), 282–99, 425–35. (13 letters, July through Sept. 1789, to the *lieutenant-général* of Annonay.)

———. "Correspondance de Boissy d'Anglas avec le marquis de Satillieu au début de la Révolution," ed. H. Hillaire, *Revue du Vivarais* 48 (1942), 209–16; 49 (1943), 53–59, 135–49. (24 letters, all but 2 from before the Revolution.)

———. "La Révolution vue de Paris et d'Annonay," *La revue universelle*, no. 139 (1988), 47–57; no. 141 (1988), 50–59; no. 142 (1988), 54–63; no. 143 (1988), 53–62; no. 145 (1989), 53–62. (7 letters, 2 Dec. 1789 through 7 Oct. 1790, mostly to Louis-Théodore Chomel, avocat du roi in Annonay.)

Bonnemant*, Guillaume (T). Copies of 69 ms. letters (some written jointly with Boulouvard and/or Guilhem), 21 Aug. 1789 through 1 Oct. 1791, to the municipality of Arles: A.C. Arles, AA 23.

Bouche*, Charles-François (T). 36 ms. letters, 12 May through 17 Sept. 1789, to the *commissaire des communautés de Provence*: A.D. Bouches-du-Rhône, C 1046. (Selections published in Octave Teissier, *Biographie des députés de Provence à l'Assemblée nationale de 1789* [Marseille, 1897], 2–9.)

Bouche*, Pierre-François-Balthazar (T). 55 ms. letters, 10 May 1789 through 17

Sept. 1791, to the municipality of Forcalquier: A.C. Forcalquier, Series D, "Correspondance de 1789."

Bouchette*, François-Joseph (T). *Lettres de François-Joseph Bouchette (1735–1810)*, ed. Camille Looten. Lille, 1909. (247 letters, 27 Apr. 1789 through 3 Oct. 1791, mostly to a friend, Winoc-Antoine Moutton.)

Boullé*, Jean-Pierre (T). 86 ms. letters, 1 May 1789 through 3 Nov. 1790 (missing Feb. to Apr. 1790), to the municipality of Pontivy: A.C. Pontivy, on microfilm in A.D. Morbihan, 1 Mi 140. (The letters through 30 Oct. 1789 [including that of 11 Aug. 1789, lost at the time the microfilm was made] are reproduced in "Ouverture des Etats généraux de 1789," ed. Albert Macé, *Revue de la Révolution. Documents inédits* 10 [1887], 161–71; 11 [1888], 11–20, 45–53, 113–20; 12 [1888], 7–14, 35–42, 49–58, 109–12; 13 [1888], 11–17, 65–79; 14 [1889], 26–32, 42–51, 82–92, 114–23; 15 [1889], 13–28, 99–120; 16 [1889], 15–29, 45–84.)

Boulouvard*, Pierre-Siffren (T). Copies of 43 ms. letters (plus 33 letters written jointly with Bonnemant and/or Guilhem), 12 June 1789 through 24 June 1791, to the municipality of Arles: A.C. Arles, AA 23.

Branche, Maurice (T). 8 ms. letters, May through Nov. 1789, to his constituency: B.M. Clermont-Ferrand, Fonds Paul Le Blanc, ms. 1329 (7 letters); and A.D. Puy-de-Dôme, F 133 (copy of 1 letter). (Excerpts published in Xavier Lochmann, "Maurice Branche de Paulhaguet, député à l'Assemblée constituante," *Almanach de Brioude* [1990], 199–238.)

Brulart de Sillery*, Charles-Alexis, marquis de (N). Ms. "Journal des Etats généraux," 2 April 1789 through 4 June 1790, used as the basis for letters to the correspondence committee of the "nobility of Champagne": A.N., KK 641–43.

Buschey des Noës, Adrien-Georges (T). "Les débuts de la Révolution de 1789 racontés par Adrien-Georges Buschey," ed. Veuclin, *Comité des travaux historiques et scientifiques. Bulletin historique et philologique* (1900), 274–77. (Report of 6 Oct. 1791.)

Buzot*, François-Nicolas-Léon (T). Ms. copies of 10 letters, 5 Aug. 1789 through 30 Aug. 1790, to the municipality of Evreux: A.C. Evreux, 13a D1 (Registre de correspondance administrative).

———. *Mémoires sur la Révolution française*, ed. Guadet. Paris, 1823.

Campmas*, Jean-François (T). 73 letters, 30 May 1789 through 8 Oct. 1790, to his brother, vicaire in Carmaux: B.M. Albi, ms. 177.

Camusat de Belombre*, Nicolas-Jean (T). Ms. notes for letters, 6 May through 8 Aug. 1789, to an unknown party in Troyes: A.N., W 306, no. 377. (Selections published in Henri Diné, "Le journal de Camusat de Belombre, député du Tiers de la ville de Troyes," *AHRF* 37 [1965], 257–69.)

Castellane*, Boniface-Louis-André, comte de (N). Ms. notes, 4 May 1789 through 17 Apr. 1790: B.N., Nouv. acq. fr., 4121. (Attributed to Castellane in the B.N. inventory.)

Chastenay-Lanty, Erard-Louis-Guy, comte de (N). Ms. notes and correspondence: A.D. Côte-d'Or, 4 F 2–4.

Chatrian, Laurent (C). Ms. "Anecdotes ecclésiastiques de l'Assemblée nationale," 1789 through 1791: Archives du Grand Séminaire de Nancy, MC 81–84: "Journal ecclésiastique du diocèse de Nancy," vols. 11:289–384; 12:305–68; 13:205–312; 14, 1e partie:117–72; and 14, 2e partie:105–14.

Chatrian, Laurent (C). Ms. "Galerie des Etats généraux": Archives du Grand Séminaire de Nancy, MC 35. (Written in 1799 with later annotations.)

Coiffier*, Henri (N). 26 ms. letters, 8 May through 12 June 1789, to the prince de Condé: A.D. Oise, J 138 (27 bis).

Colaud de La Salcette*, Jacques-Bernardin (C). "Lettres de Colaud de La Salcette," *Bulletin de la Société départementale d'archéologie et de statistique de la Drôme* 69 (1944), 137–56. (13 letters, 1 June 1789 through 27 Jan. 1790, to chanoine Agnès in Die.)

Colson*, Jean (C). "Notes d'un curé Saargovien, député aux Etats généraux de 1789," ed. Arthur Benoît, *Revue nouvelle d'Alsace-Lorraine et du Rhin* 8 (1888), 41–50, 93–111, 132–46. (Written sometime after the September Massacres.)

Coma-Serra*, Michel de (N). 24 ms. letters written with Banyuls de Montferré, 16 May through 7 Sept. 1789, to the correspondence committee of Perpignan: A.D. Pyrénées-Orientales, C 2119.

Coster*, Sigisbert-Etienne (C). "Récit des séances du clergé," in *Les séances des députés du Clergé aux Etats généraux de 1789*, ed. Albert Houtin. Paris, 1917, pp. 81–143. (6 May through 27 June 1789.)

Couderc, Guillaume-Benoît (T). "Lettres de Guillaume-Benoît Couderc (1781–92)," ed. M. O. Monod, *Revue d'histoire de Lyon* 5 (1906), 405–25; 6 (1907), 53–71. (7 letters, 12 Feb. 1789 through 24 Jan. 1791, to his uncle in Geneva.)

Couppé*, Gabriel-Hyacinthe (T). "Correspondance des députés des Côtes-du-Nord à l'Assemblée constituante," ed. D. Tempier, *Bulletin et mémoires de la Société d'émulation des Côtes-du-Nord* 27 (1889), 21–63. (18 letters, 4 Sept. 1790 through 19 June 1791, written with Baudouin to the municipality of Lannion.)

Crécy, Denis-Ferdinand, comte de (N). 5 ms. letters, 21 May through 24 Oct. 1789, to Hecquet de Bérenger, *trésorier de la guerre*: A.N., AB XIX 3562 (1).

Creuzé-Latouche*, Jacques-Antoine (T). *Journal des Etats généraux et du début de l'Assemblée nationale, 18 mai–29 juillet 1789*, ed. Jean Marchand. Paris, 1946.

Delandine*, Antoine-François (T). *Mémorial historique des Etats généraux*, 5 vols. N.p., 1789. (A kind of analytical diary of events, published monthly, May through Oct. 1789.)

Delaville Le Roulx*, Joseph (T). Ms. copies of 189 letters, 30 Apr. 1789 through 21 Aug. 1790, to the municipality of Lorient: A.C. Lorient, BB 12–13. (Selections published by Louis Chaumeil in *Les journées de 89, d'après Delavilleleroulx* [Lorient, 1940].)

Dieusie, Jean-Charles-Antoine Morel, comte de (N). "L'Assemblée provinciale d'Anjou, d'après les archives de Serrant (1787–89)," ed. M. de La Trémoïlle, *Anjou historique* 2 (1901–1902), 44–70. (7 letters, 21 Sept. to 15 Dec. 1789, to the comte de Walsh-Serrant.)

Dinochau*, Jacques-Samuel (T). *Histoire philosophique et politique de l'Assemblée constituante*, 2 vols. Paris, 1789. (Vol. 1 covers Aug. 1789; vol. 2, Sept. through ca. 10 Oct.)

———. *Courier* [sic] *de Madon à l'Assemblée nationale permanente*, 25 tomes. Paris, 2 Nov. 1789 through 30 May 1791. (Probably continued after May, but not preserved in the B.N.)

Dolomieu*, Charles-Emmanuel de Gratet de (C). "Journal abrégé des séances des Etats généraux tenues à Versailles en 1789," ed. G. Letonnelier, *Bulletin de l'Académie delphinale*, 6e sér., 15–17 (1944–46), 249–78. (4 May through 15 June 1789.)

Dubois-Crancé*, Edmond-Louis-Alexis (T). *Analyse de la Révolution française depuis l'ouverture des Etats généraux jusqu'au 6 Brumaire an IV de la République*, ed. Thomas Jung. Paris, 1885.

Duquesnoy*, Adrien-Cyprien (T). *Journal d'Adrien Duquesnoy*, ed. R. de Crèvecoeur, 2 vols. Paris, 1894. (May 1789 through Apr. 1790.)

Durand de Maillane, Pierre-Toussaint (T). Ms. notes of meetings, 16 May through 12 Aug. 1789, to electors of the sénéchaussée of Arles: A.D. Bouches-du-Rhône, 110 E BB 33. (Incomplete copy sent from Arles to Eyragues.)

———. *Histoire apologétique du Comité ecclésiastique de l'Assemblée nationale*. Paris, 1791.

Durand*, Antoine (T). *Lettres de Versailles sur les Etats généraux*, ed. A. Frugier and J. Maubourguet. Blois, 1933. (4 letters written to two men in Domme, Périgord.)

———. Ms. journal, 2 May through 6 Oct. 1789, written as first drafts of letters sent to Delcamp-Boytré in Gourdan: A.E. Cahors, carton 5–56.

———. 53 ms. letters, 3 Jan. 1790 through 25 Sept. 1791, to the municipality of Cahors: A.M. Cahors, unclassed box of letters from Revolutionary deputies, held in B.M. Cahors.

Dusers*, Charles-Guillaume (T). 82 ms. letters, 29 Dec. 1789 through 20 Sept. 1791, to the municipality of Vannes: A.D. Morbihan, 262 E(s).

Duval de Grandpré*, Charles-François (T). "Correspondance de Duval de Grandpré, député de la sénéchaussée de Ponthieu," ed. J. Vacandard, *Bulletin de la Société des études locales dans l'enseignement public. Groupe de la Seine-Inférieure*, no. 21 (1929), xii–xxxv; no. 22 (1930), xiii–xxxi. (12 letters, 6 May 1789 through 3 Feb. 1790, to Guignon de Cambard, mayor of Eu.)

Emmery, Jean-Louis-Claude (T). Ms. "Journal," 5 May to 10 June 1789: A.N., Nouv. acq. fr. 2633, ff. 33–81. (According to his own notes, much of this has been copied from newspapers or from the diary of his colleague, François Mathieu de Rondeville.)

Faulcon*, Félix (T). *Correspondance. Tome 1: 1770–89*, ed. G. Debien. Poitiers, 1939 (in *Archives historiques du Poitou*, tome 51); and *Correspondance. Tome 2: 1789–91*, ed. G. Debien. Poitiers, 1953 (in *Archives historiques du Poitou*, tome 55). (110 letters for the Revolutionary period, 12 June 1789 through 20 July 1791, to numerous individuals; and personal journal, 1 May 1789 through 19 Sept. 1791.)

Faydel*, Jean-Félix (T). 31 ms. letters, 24 Sept. 1789 through 25 July 1790, to the municipality of Cahors: A.M. Cahors, unclassed box of letters from Revolutionary deputies, held in B.M. Cahors.

———. 27 ms. letters, 2 Jan. through 20 Nov. 1790, to Jean Filsac, avocat in Cahors: A.N. W 368, no. 822, 4e partie (43–68). (Excerpts published in Pierre de Vaissière, *Lettres d'aristocrates. La Révolution racontée par des correspondances privées* [Paris, 1907], 183–94.)

Ferrières-Marçay*, Charles-Elie, marquis de (N). *Correspondance inédite*, ed. Henri Carré. Paris, 1932. (172 letters, 20 Apr. 1789 through 1 Nov. 1791, almost all written to his wife.)

———. *Mémoires*, 3 vols. Paris, 1825.

François*, Jean (T). "Jean François, député de l'Assemblée nationale de 1789," ed. G. de Lagrange-Ferrègues, *Revue de l'Agenais* 83 (1957), 229–52. (Contains excerpts of 32 letters to his daughter and wife, 19 June 1789 through 3 Sept. 1791, preserved in a private collection.)

Francoville, Charles-Bruno (T). "Les rapports du député Charles Francoville au comité de correspondance d'Ardres," in François de Saint-Just, *Chronique intime des Garnier d'Ardres*. Paris, 1973, pp. 111–22. (Excerpts of 7 letters, 28 Apr. through 8 Aug. 1789, to correspondence committee of Ardres.)

Fricaud*, Claude (T). 21 ms. letters, 19 Jan. 1790 through 24 June 1791, to Jean-Marie Gelin, notary and vice-president of the district in Charolles: copies of the originals kindly provided by Doctor Robert Favre.

Gagon du Chenay*, Marie-Toussaint (T). 15 ms. letters, 31 July 1790 through 5 Oct. 1791, to the district of Dinan: A.D. Côtes-du-Nord, 3 L 23.

Gallot*, Jean-Gabriel (T). *La vie et les oeuvres du Docteur Jean-Gabriel Gallot*, ed. Louis Merle. Poitiers, 1961. (18 letters, 21 May 1789 through 24 Jan. 1790, to his wife; personal journal, 21 Apr. through 31 July 1789.)

Gantheret*, Claude (T). 112 ms. letters, 13 May 1789 through 20 Sept. 1791, to Pierre Leflaive, his brother-in-law, négociant in Le Poil: private collection of Françoise Misserey, Dijon. (Excerpts published in E. Leflaive, "Le premier représentant de Beaune au parlement: Claude Gantheret," *Société d'archéologie de Beaune. Histoire, lettres, sciences et arts. Mémoires* 42 (1925–29), 57–128; and Françoise Misserey, "Un Constituant à Paris: les soucis et les craintes de Claude Gantheret," *Annales de Bourgogne* 60 [1988], 5–19.)

Garat, Dominique-Joseph (T). *Mémoires sur la Révolution*, ed. E. Miron. Paris, 1862. (Nothing prior to 1792.)

———. *Journal de Paris*. Paris, 1789–91. (Garat provided the regular analysis of events in the National Assembly from late June 1789 through Sept. 1791. The paper itself began long before and ended long after the Revolution.)

Gaultier de Biauzat*, Jean-François (T). *Gaultier de Biauzat, député du Tiers état aux Etats généraux de 1789. Sa vie et sa correspondance*, ed. Francisque Mège, 2 vols. Clermont-Ferrand, 1890. (110 letters, 23 Apr. through 29 Aug. 1789 and selections through 22 Oct. 1791, to the correspondence committee of Clermont-Ferrand. Originals are in B.M. Clermont-Ferrand and A.D. Puy-de-Dôme, F 140–41.)

———. *Journal des débats et des décrets*. Paris, 29 Aug. 1789 through 1 Oct. 1791. (His colleagues, the deputies Jean-Antoine Huguet and Jean-Baptiste Grenier, also contributed. The newspaper continued long after the end of the Constituent.)

Gauville*, Louis-Henri-Charles, baron de (N). *Journal du Baron de Gauville*, ed. Edouard de Barthélemy. Paris, 1864. (May 1789 to July 1790.)

Geoffroy*, Claude-Jean-Baptiste (T). 28 ms. letters, 25 June 1789 through 31 July 1791, to Jean-Marie Gelin, notary and vice-président of the district in Charolles: Private collection of Doctor Robert Favre.

Gontier de Biran*, Guillaume (T). 63 ms. letters, 26 June 1789 through 25 May 1790, to the municipality of Bergerac: A.C. Bergerac, Fonds Faugère, carton 1. (Excerpts in *Les Jurades de la ville de Bergerac. Tome XIII, 1774–1789* [Bergerac, 1904], 359–75.)

Goupilleau*, Jean-François-Marie (T). 21 ms. letters, 11 May 1789 through 4 Dec. 1790, to his cousin, *sénéchal* in Rochefervière: B.M. Nantes, Collection Dugast-Matifeux, no. 98.

Gouttes*, Jean-Louis (C). 12 ms. letters, 14 Mar. 1790 through 26 May 1791, to J. B. Cabanès, cadet, "bourgeois": A.C. Argelliers, S 12 A.

Grégoire*, Henri (C). *Mémoires*, ed. H. Carrot, 2 vols. Paris, 1837–40.

Grellet de Beauregard*, Jean-Bernard (T). "Lettres de M. Grellet de Beauregard," ed. Abbé Dardy, *Mémoires de la Société des sciences naturelles et archéologiques de la Creuse*, 2e sér., 7 (1899), 53–117. (21 letters, 12 June through 14 Sept. 1789 and 29 May 1790 through 19 Apr. 1791, to the marquis de La Celle.)

Guilhem-Clermont-Lodève*, Charles-François, marquis de (N). Ms. copies of 9 letters, 21 May 1789 through 7 Apr. 1790 (plus 3 others signed jointly with other deputies), to the municipality of Arles: A.C. Arles, AA 23.

Guilhermy, Jean-François-César de (T). *Papiers d'un émigré, 1789–1829*, ed. Colonel G. de Guilhermy. Paris, 1886.

Irland de Bazôges*, Pierre-Marie (N). 90 ms. letters, 4 Sept. 1789 through 25 July 1791, to Henri Filleau, magistrate in Poitiers: A.D. Deux-Sèvres, Fonds Beauchet-Filleau, unclassed register of "lettres politiques, 1788–90."

Jallet*, Jacques (C). "Trois lettres de l'abbé Jallet," ed. D. Marié, *AHRF* 22 (1950), 326–49. (3 letters, 18 and 22 May, and 4 Sept. 1789, to Guyot, *receveur des décimes* in Poitiers.)

———. *Journal inédit*, ed. J.-J. Brethé. Fontenay-le-Comte, 1871. (27 April through 31 July 1789.)

Labeste*, François-Victor (T). 18 ms. letters, 29 July 1789 through 21 May 1792, to the municipality of Cunières: A.D. Marne, E Suppl. 2534.

La Bévière*, Claude-Jean-Baptiste de Garron de (N). 97 ms. letters, 24 Apr. through 15 Dec. 1789, to his wife: A.D. Ain, 1 Mi 1.

Lablache*, Alexandre-Joseph, comte de (N). 31 ms. letters, 2 May 1789 through 10 Apr. 1790, to the marquis de Viennois: A.D. Isère, 1 Mi 461.

Lacharmie, Jean-François (T). 4 ms. letters, 9 Aug. 1789 through 7 Nov. 1790, to the municipality of Périgueux: A.M. Périgueux, AA 26.

Lafayette*, Marie-Joseph-Paul-Yves-Roch-Gilbert du Motier, marquis de (N). *Mémoires, correspondance et manuscrits*, 6 vols. Paris, 1837–38. (Vols. 2–4 contain notes, memoirs, and letters or parts of letters, covering the entire Constituent period [often undated], to diverse.)

La Gallissonnière*, Augustin-Félix-Elisabeth Barin, comte de (N). Ms. journal, 2 May through 27 June 1789 (with an "avant-propos historique" and some additional comments on the weeks after 27 June) : Arch. de la Guerre, A4 LVI.

La Marck*, Auguste-Marie-Raymond, comte de (N). *Correspondance entre le comte de Mirabeau et le comte de La Marck*, 3 vols., ed. Bacourd. Paris, 1851. (85 letters, 11 Oct. 1789 through 25 Mar. 1791, to the comte de Mirabeau and others.)

Lamarque*, Pierre-Joseph de (T). 13 ms. letters, 12 Oct. 1790 through 30 Sept. 1791, to the municipality of Saint-Sever: A.C. St. Sever, II D 34. (See also Basquiat de Mugriet.)

Lameth*, Alexandre-Théodore-Victor, comte de (N). *Histoire de l'Assemblée constituante*, 2 vols. Paris, 1828–29. (Ends in July 1790.)

Langon, Nicolas-François, marquis de (N). 8 ms. letters, 2 July 1789 through 20 Feb. 1790, to the marquis de Viennois: A.D. Isère, 1 Mi 461.

La Revellière-Lépeaux*, Louis-Marie de (T). *Mémoires*, 3 vols. Paris, 1895.

La Roque, Jean-François, comte de (N). 8 ms. letters, 6 May through 22 Oct. 1790, to the municipality of Périgueux: A.M. Périgueux, AA 26.

La Salle*, Nicolas-Théodore-Antoine-Adolphe de (T). "Les archives municipales de Sarrelouis," ed. René Herly, *Bulletin de la Société des amis du pays de la Sarre*, no. 4 (1927), 191–323. (110 letters, 9 June 1789 through 5 Aug. 1791, to the municipal officials in Sarrelouis.)

Laurence*, Louis-Jean-Jacques (T). "Journal," ed. comte Charles de Beaumont,

Le Carnet historique et littéraire 12 (1902), 60–86. (23 Apr. through 14 June 1789.)

Lebrun, Charles-François (T). *Opinions, rapports, et choix d'écrits politiques.* Paris, 1829. (An introductory "Notice biographique" contains extensive memoirs of his career before 1789 and a few pages on the Constituent Assembly.)

Le Carlier, Marie-Jean-François (T). Ms. letters, 20 June through 29 Dec. 1789, to the municipal officials in Laon: A.M. Laon, AA 38. (Apparently destroyed during World War II.)

Le Clerc de Lassigny de Juigné*, Louis-Jean-Baptiste de (N). 45 ms. letters, 14 Apr. 1789 through 24 Aug. 1791, written to his wife and mother: Archives of the Château de Saint-Martin, Taradeau (Var), kindly shown to me by the comtesse de Gasquet.

Legendre*, Laurent-François (T). 395 ms. letters, 1789 through 1791, to the electors and municipal officials in Brest: A.M. Brest. (Excerpts, primarily on the major journées, are in *RF* 39 [1900], 515–58; and 40 [1901], 46–78.)

Lepoutre*, Pierre-François (T). 238 ms. letters, 8 May 1789 through 3 Sept. 1791, to his wife Marie-Angélique Delputte: family archives of Adolphe Lepoutre-Dubreuil, Montignac-sur-Vezère.

Lévis*, Pierre-Marc-Gaston, duc de (N). "Lettres du duc de Lévis, 1784–1795," ed. duc de Lévis-Mirepoix, *La Revue de France* 4 (1929), 227–74, 425–44; 5 (1929), 258–95, 418–42, 614–49. (For the Constituent period, 20 letters, 20 May 1789 through 22 Sept. 1791 [16 of which are from 1791], to his wife Pauline.)

——. *Souvenirs et portraits.* Paris, 1813.

Lézay-Marnésia, Claude-François-Adrien, marquis de (N). 9 ms. letters, 9 Nov. 1789 through 28 Mar. 1790, to his wife: private archives. (Excerpts published in Elisabeth Bourget-Besnier, *Une famille française sous la Révolution et l'Empire: la famille de Lézay-Marnésia* [Paris, 1985], pp. 23–38.)

Lilia de Crose*, Joseph-Bernard de (T). 64 ms. letters, 7 Nov. 1789 through 2 Apr. 1791, to the municipality of Nantua: B.M. Lyon, ms. 2191. (Excerpts published in Blanche Dominjon-Bombard, "Joseph-Bernard de Lilia de Crose, député de Nantua à la Constituante (1789–91)," *Bugey*, année 73, vol. 16 [1981], 81–107.)

Lindet*, Thomas (C). *Correspondance de Thomas Lindet pendant la Constituante et la Législative (1789–92)*, ed. Amand Montier. Paris, 1899. (98 letters from the Constituent period [some in résumé only], 19 Aug. 1789 through 30 Sept. 1791, to the municipal government and to his brother in Bernay.)

Lofficial*, Louis-Prosper (T). "Lettres de Lofficial," ed. Leroux-Cesbron, *La nouvelle revue rétrospective* 7 (1897), 73–120, 169–92. (22 letters, 18 May through 24 Oct. 1789, to his wife.)

Lombard-Taradeau*, Jacques-Athanase de (T). "Lettres (1789–91)," *Le Var historique et géographique*, ed. L. Honoré, 2 (1925–27), 230–48, 255–78, 322–42, 347–67. (33 letters, 5 Aug. 1789 to 19 Sept. 1791, to the municipal officials of Draguignan.)

Lucas de Bourgerel*, Jean-Joseph (T). 71 ms. letters, 4 June 1789 and 26 Jan. 1790 through 24 Sept. 1791, to the municipal officials in Vannes: A.D Morbihan, 262 E(s).

Ludière*, Pierre (T). 46 ms. letters (5 written jointly with Melon), 5 Sept. 1789 through 31 Oct. 1790, to the municipality of Tulle: A.D. Corrèze, 1 E Dep. 272/199.

Maillot*, Claude-Pierre (T). Ms. register of 16 letters, 5 May through 3 Oct. 1789, addressed to an unnamed municipal official of Toul: A.C. Toul, JJ 7. (Substantial excerpts published in Albert Denis, "La Révolution à Toul en 1789," *Annales de l'Est* 5 [1891], 544–68.)

———. *Huit lettres de C.-P. Maillot, membre de l'Assemblée constituante au maire de Villey-Saint-Etienne (1790–91)*, ed. Léon Manet. N.p., 1936.

Malartic*, Ambroise-Eulalie de Maurès, vicomte de (N). Ms. "Journal de ma députation aux Etats généraux," 14 Apr. through 3 Oct. 1789: B.M. La Rochelle, ms. 21.

Malouet*, Pierre-Victor (T). *Correspondance de Malouet avec les officiers municipaux de la ville de Riom, 1788–1789*, ed. F. Boyer. Riom, n.d. (Includes 10 letters, 5 Aug. through 16 Nov. 1789, to the municipality of Riom [some signed by other deputies].)

———. *Mémoires*, 2 vols., ed. Baron Malouet. Paris, 1868.

Maupetit*, Michel René (T). "Lettres (1789–91)," ed. Quéruau-Lamérie, *Bulletin de la Commission historique et archéologique de la Mayenne*, 2ème sér., 17 (1901), 302–27, 439–54; 18 (1902), 133–63, 321–33, 447–75; 19 (1903), 205–50, 348–78; 20 (1904), 88–125, 176–203, 358–77, 446–72; 21 (1905), 93–124, 204–23, 325–63, 365–88; 22 (1906), 67–95, 213–39, 349–84, 454–93; 23 (1907), 87–115. (253 letters, 25 Apr. 1789 through 27 Sept. 1791, to Dupont-Grandjardin, magistrate and mayor in Mayenne.)

Meifrund*, Pierre-Joseph (T). Ms. letters, 7 May 1789 through 21 Sept. 1791: A.C. Toulon L 104 (D4 1). (Apparently lost by the archives. The Institut de la Révolution française possesses a copy of 14 letters through 3 July 1789.)

Melon*, Antoine (T). 25 ms. letters (5 written jointly with Ludière), 19 Sept. 1789 through 15 Aug. 1790 (1 undated), to the municipality of Tulle: A.D. Corrèze, 1 E Dep. 272/199.

Ménard de La Groye*, François-René-Pierre (T). *Correspondance (1789–1791)*, ed. Florence Mirouse. Le Mans, 1989. (246 letters, 12 Apr. 1789 through 16 Oct. 1791, to his wife.)

Menu de Chomorceau*, Jean-Etienne (T). "Un Constituant au travail: Jean-Etienne Menu de Chomorceau, lettres et discours," ed. Jean-Luc Dauphin, *Etudes villeneuviennes*, no. 14 (1990), 41–59. (17 letters, Feb. 1789 through Mar. 1791, to diverse.)

Merle*, André-Marie (T). 126 ms. letters, 13 Oct. 1789 through 15 Sept. 1791, written to the municipality of Mâcon: A.C. Mâcon, D (2) 13, carton 21 bis.

Mirabeau*, Honoré-Gabriel de Riquetti, comte de (T). *Lettres*, ed. Lescure. Paris, 1866.

———. *Lettres du comte de Mirabeau à ses commettants*. Paris, 10 May through 24 July 1789.

———. *Correspondance entre le comte de Mirabeau et le comte de La Marck*, 3 vols., Adrien de Bacourt, ed. Paris, 1851. (132 letters, 24 Apr. 1789 through 21 Mar. 1791, to the comte de La Marck; also various notes and letters to diverse, and 50 notes to the court, 1 June 1790 to 3 Feb. 1791.)

Missy, Samuel-Pierre-David-Joseph de (T). *Lettres inédites d'un armateur rochelais*, ed. de Richemond. La Rochelle, 1889. (10 letters, 13 Nov. through 29 Dec. 1789, to his cousin, de Richemond, while Missy was still a substitute deputy.)

Monnel*, Simon-Edme (C). *Mémoires d'un prêtre régicide*, 2 vols., ed. Denis-Alexandre Martin. Paris, 1829.

Monneron*, Charles-Claude-Ange (T). Ms. journal, 2 May through 12 Sept. 1789: in the private collection of Jules Rousset in 1896. (Excerpts in Emmanuel Nicod, "Monneron aîné, député de la sénéchaussée d'Annonay," *Revue du Vivarais* 4 (1896), 479–86.

Montjallard, Jean-Joseph-André (C). "Lettres de l'abbé Montjallard, curé de Barjols," ed. Edmond Poupé, *Bulletin de la Société d'études scientifiques et archéologiques de Draguignan* 30 (1914–15), xci–ciii. (3 letters, 1 and 20 Sept., and 5 Nov. 1789, to the mayor of Barjols.)

Morges, Pierre-François-de-Sales, comte de (N). 10 ms. letters, 12 July through 14 Oct. 1789 (2 undated), to the marquis de Viennois: A.D. Isère, 1 Mi 461.

Mounier, Jean-Joseph (T). *Exposé de la conduite de M. Mounier dans l'Assemblée nationale et des motifs de son retour en Dauphiné*, 3 parties. Paris, 1789.

Nairac*, Pierre-Paul (T). Ms. "Journal," 27 Apr. through 2 July 1789: A.D. Eure, 5 F 63.

Nompère de Champagny*, Jean-Baptiste, comte de (N). *Souvenirs de M. de Champagny, duc de Cadore.* Paris, 1846. (Written between 1822 and 1828.)

Palasne de Champeaux*, Julien-François (T). "Correspondance des députés des Côtes-du-Nord aux Etats généraux et à l'Assemblée nationale constituante," ed. D. Tempier, *Bulletin et mémoires de la Société d'émulation des Côtes-du-Nord* 26 (1888), 210–63. (33 letters, usually written jointly with Poulain de Corbion, 28 Apr. through 16 Oct. 1789, to the correspondence committee of Saint-Brieuc.)

Paroy, Guy Le Gentil, marquis de (N). *Mémoires. Souvenirs d'un défenseur de la famille royale pendant la Révolution (1789–1797)*, ed. J. de Paroy. Paris, 1895.

Pellerin*, Joseph-Michel (T). Ms. journal, 1 Apr. through 15 Oct. 1789: B.M. Versailles, ms. 823F.

———. *Correspondance, 5 mai 1789–29 mai 1790*, ed. Gustave Bord. Paris 1883. (To the municipality of Guerande.)

Périsse Du Luc*, Jean-André (T). 47 ms. letters, 8 Apr. 1789 through 31 Dec. 1791, to J. B. Willermoz: B.M. Lyon, ms. F.G. 5430. (Excerpts in Alice Joly, *Un mystique lyonnais et les secrets de la franc-maçonnerie, 1730–1824* [Mâcon, 1938], 270–306.)

Pinteville*, Jean-Baptiste de, baron de Cernon (N). 20 ms. letters, 24 Apr. 1789 through 18 Nov. 1790, to his brother: A.D. Marne, J 2286. (Excerpts published in "Extraits de la correspondance de Jean-Baptiste de Pinteville, baron de Cernon, député de la noblesse de la Constituante," ed. R. Popelin, *Mémoires de la Société d'agriculture, commerce, sciences et arts du département de la Marne*, 2e sér., 26 [1936–46], 7–25.)

Poncet-Delpech*, Jean-Baptiste (T). *La première année de la Révolution vue par un témoin (1789–90)*, ed. Daniel Ligou. Paris, 1961. (40 "bulletins," Apr. 1789 through May 1790, to the municipality of Montauban.)

———. "Documents sur les premiers mois de la Révolution," ed. Daniel Ligou, *AHRF* 38 (1966), 426–46, 561–76. (9 additional "bulletins," May through July 1789, and diverse other letters.)

Poulain de Corbion*, Jean-François-Pierre (T). "Correspondance des députés des Côtes-du-Nord aux Etats généraux et à l'Assemblée nationale constituante," ed. D. Tempier, *Bulletin et mémoires de la Société d'émulation des Côtes-du-Nord* 26 (1888), 210–63. (33 letters, usually written jointly with Palasne de Champeaux, 28 Apr. through 16 Oct. 1789, to the correspondence committee of Saint-Brieuc.)

Pous*, Paul-Augustin (C). "Correspondance inédite d'un membre de l'Assemblée constituante," *Revue de l'Anjou* 21 (1878), 286–307; 22 (1879), 268–89; 23 (1879), 84–100, 189–212; 24 (1880), 11–34, 137–52. (88 letters or excerpts, 3 July 1789 through 21 Sept. 1791, to Fons-Lacaussade, curé of Saint-Germain and Landes-Roqueplane, avocat in Pous's parish of Mazamet.)

Pradt*, Dominique-Georges-Frédéric Du Four de (C). "Quelques lettres de l'abbé Du Pradt, 1789–92," ed. Leymarie, Michel, *Revue de la Haute-Auvergne* 34 (1954), 65–95. (17 letters, Aug. 1789 through Sept. 1792, to diverse members of his family in Allande.)

———. *Les quatre Concordats*, 3 vols. Paris, 1818.

Prieur, Pierre-Louis (T). *Notes et souvenirs inédits de Prieur de la Marne*, ed. Gustave Laurent. Paris, 1912.

Puisaye*, Joseph-Geneviève, comte de (N). *Mémoires du comte de Puisaye . . . qui pourront servir à l'histoire du parti royaliste français durant la dernière Révolution*, 6 vols. London and Paris, 1803–1808. (Vol. 1 covers the period through ca. Feb. 1790, when he apparently ceased attending.)

Quatrefage de Laroquete*, Henri (T). Excerpts in François Rouvière, *Quatrefages de Laroquete*. Paris, 1886. (Excerpts from ca. 50 letters, ca. 25 Aug. 1789 through 7 Sept. 1791, written to general d'Albignac.)

Rabaut Saint-Etienne*, Jean-Paul (T). "Rabaut Saint-Etienne, sa correspondance pendant la Révolution (1789–93)," ed. Armand Lods, *RF* 35 (1898), 78–89, 157–77, 259–77. (22 letters, 30 Mar. 1789 through 27 Aug. 1791, to diverse.)

———. *Précis historique de la Révolution française*. Paris, 1807.

Rangeard*, Jacques (C). *Procès-verbal historique des actes du clergé, député à l'assemblée des Etats généraux des années 1789 et 1790*. Paris, 1791.

Regnaud, Michel-Louis-Etienne [de Saint-Jean-d'Angély] (T). *Journal de Versailles*. Paris, 1789–1790. (Regnaud seems to have been the principal author between Sept. 1789 and Dec. 1790.)

Renaut*, Pierre-Louis-Joseph (C). 30 ms. letters, 27 June 1789 through 30 Sept. 1791 (1 undated), to abbé Carlier, curé of Bavay: B.M. Douai, ms. 1035.

Reynaud de Montlosier*, François-Dominique de (N). *Mémoires*, 2 vols. Paris, 1830.

Ricard de Séalt*, Gabriel-Joseph-Xavier (T). 11 ms. letters, 10 May through 13 July 1789, to La Tour, intendant of Aix: A.N., AB XIX 3359 (4).

Robespierre*, Maximilien (T). *Correspondance*, ed. Georges Michon, 2 vols. Paris, 1926–41. (39 letters, 23 May 1789 through 10 Aug. 1791, to diverse.)

Roederer, Pierre-Louis (T). *Esprit de la Révolution*. Paris, 1831.

Roger*, Jean-Pierre (T). "Lettres du constituant Roger," ed. R. Rumeau, *RF* 43 (1902), 68–82. (10 letters, 5 Oct. 1790 and June through Oct. 1791.)

Roulhac, Guillaume-Grégoire de (T). "Lettres de Grégoire de Roulhac, député aux Etats généraux (mai–août 1789)," ed. Paul d'Hollander, *Bulletin de la Société archéologique et historique du Limousin* 119 (1991), 144–67. (13 letters, 25 May through 24 Aug. 1789, to the municipality of Limoges.)

Rouph de Varicourt*, Pierre-Marin (C). Ms. journal, 26 Apr. through 29 Sept. 1789: Archives of the Schloss Moestroff, Luxembourg; microfilm copy in Brotherton Library, University of Leeds.

———. "Mémoires de M. de Varicourt, ancien curé de Gex," ed. Abbé P. Boulot, *Bulletin de la Société Gorini* (1911), 113–24, 271–84, 369–77; (1912), 182–92, 299–308, 372–83; (1913), 67–77, 158–66, 312–19.

Rousselot*, Claude-Germain (C). 36 ms. letters, 21 May 1789 through 27 Sept. 1791, mostly to his nephew, Joseph Rousselot: copies of originals (now lost) held by Jean Girardot, to be donated to A.D. Haute-Saône. (Published by Anne-Marie Malingrey, *Correspondance de l'Abbé Rousselot, Constituant, 1789–1795* [Paris, 1992].)

Saint-Martin*, François-Jérôme Riffard de (T). "La Révolution vue de Paris et d'Annonay," *La revue universelle*, no. 139 (1988), 47–57; no. 141 (1988), 50–59; no. 142 (1988), 54–63; no. 143 (1988), 53–62; no. 145 (1989), 53–62. (18 letters, 5 Jan. 1790 through 15 Mar. 1791, mostly to Louis-Théodore Chomel, *avocat du roi* in Annonay.)

Schwendt*, Etienne-François (T). *L'Alsace pendant la Révolution française*, ed. Rodolphe Reuss, 2 vols. Paris, 1880–94. (Contains 52 letters, 1 June 1789 through 8 Oct. 1791, to the municipality of Strasbourg, including 21 signed jointly with Turckheim.)

———. "L'Alsace pendant la Révolution française. Correspondance adressée à Frédéric de Dietrich," ed. Rodolphe Reuss, *Revue d'Alsace* 69–78 (1921–31). (Contains 55 letters, 29 Oct. 1789 through 31 Dec. 1790, and 15 July 1791, to Frédéric de Dietrich.)

Sieyès, Emmanuel-Joseph (T). Personal papers and notes written during the Constituent: A.N., series 284 AP.

Talleyrand, Charles-Maurice de (C). *Mémoires du prince de Talleyrand*, ed. duc de Broglie, 5 vols. Paris, 1891–92.

Thibaudeau*, Antoine-René-Hyacinthe (T). *Correspondance inédite*, ed. H. Carré and Pierre Boissonnade. Paris, 1898. (81 letters, 1 May 1789 through 9 Sept. 1791, mostly to the municipality of Poitiers.)

———. *Mes souvenirs sur les principaux événements de la Révolution.* Paris, 1895.

Thibault*, Anne-Alexandre-Marie (C). "Journal des séances du Clergé," in *Les séances des députés du Clergé aux Etats généraux de 1789*, ed. Albert Houtin. Paris, 1917, pp. 1–55. (From 6 May through 24 June 1789.)

Toulongeon*, François-Emmanuel, vicomte de (N). *Histoire de la France depuis la Révolution*, 7 vols. Paris, 1801. (Vols. 1 and 2, pp. 1–88, cover the Constituent period.)

Turckheim*, Jean de (T). *L'Alsace pendant la Révolution française*, ed. Rodolphe Reuss, 2 vols. Paris, 1880–94. (Contains 26 letters, 28 May through 9 Oct. 1789, to the municipality of Strasbourg, including 21 signed jointly with Schwendt.)

Vallet*, Claude-Benjamin (C). "Souvenirs de l'abbé Vallet, député de Gien à l'Assemblée constituante," *Nouvelle revue rétrospective* 16 (1902), 219–40, 313–36, 385–408; 17 (1902), 25–37.

———. *Récit des principaux faits qui se sont passés dans la salle de l'ordre du Clergé.* Paris, 1790.

Verdet*, Louis (C). 56 ms. letters, 27 Apr. 1789 through 1 Oct. 1791, to Guilbert, curé of Saint-Sébastien in Nancy: Archives du Grand Séminaire de Nancy, MB 17, folios 1–113.

Verdollin d'Annot*, Jacques (T). 22 ms. letters, 23 May 1789 through 27 May 1790, to the *commissaire des communautés de Provence*: A.D. Bouches-du-Rhône, C 1337.

Vernier*, Théodore (T). 263 ms. letters, 7 July 1789 through 19 Sept. 1791, to the municipality of Lons-le-Saunier: copies in A.C. Bletterans (non-classé), dossier "Lettres de Vernier."

Villemort*, Marie-Mesmin Du Bouex, marquis de (N). "Lettres du marquis de Villemort au comte François d'Escars (1790–1791)," ed. Henri Calvet, *Archives historiques du Poitou* 52 (1942), 5–167. (80 letters, 7 Aug. 1790 through 29 Sept. 1791.)

Virieu*, François-Henri, comte de (N). 28 ms. letters, 22 June 1789 through 3 Apr. 1790, to the marquis de Viennois: A.D. Isère, 1 Mi 461.

Visme*, Laurent de (T). Ms. "Journal des Etats généraux," 5 May 1789 through 18 Feb. 1790: B.N., Nouv. acq. fr. 12938. (Document unsigned, but internal evidence strongly suggests Visme's authorship.)

All deputies to the National Assembly are followed by a letter in parentheses: C = Clergy, N = Nobility, T = Third Estate, Cn = Colonies, A = alternate.